A UNIVERSE OF STAR WARS. COLLECTIBLES

Identification and Price Guide
2nd Edition

Stuart W. Wells III

Written, photographed, and designed by Stuart W. Wells III

Published by

krause publications
700 East State Street • Iola, WI 54990-0001
715/445-2214 • FAX: 715/445-4087   www.krause.com

Please call or write for our free catalog of publications. Our toll-free number to place an order or obtain a free catalog is (800) 258-0929.

ISBN: 0-87349-415-6
Library of Congress Card Catalog Number: 2001099541

Front cover:
Boba Fett 12" (Kenner 1979).
Star Wars lunchbox and thermos (King Seeley-Thermos 1977).
Star Wars Micro Collection, Bespin World (Kenner 1982).
Darth Maul head container (Applause 1999).

Back cover:
Darth Vader removable helmet, New Power of the Force (Kenner 1998)

Spine:
R2-D2 with booster rockets (Hasbro 1999)

ACKNOWLEDGMENTS

A number of avid Star Wars collectors were kind enough to let me photograph their collections. Thanks especially to: Rob Rintoul, Rob Johnson, Wats Wacker, Morgan McClain, Harry Rinker Jr. and Marc Patten.

Many manufacturers of Star Wars items supplied information, catalogs or photographs. Thanks to: Don Post Studios, Alan Payne at Icons, Don Schmidt at Tiger Electronics, Tracy at Illusive Originals, Chaz Fitzhugh at Applause, Jim Schneider at Star Jars, Joshua Izzo at Topps, and Matt Mariani at Decipher, Inc. Thanks also to Kenner, Galoob, JusToys for all the trips through their showrooms during Toyfair for many years.

There are many excellent Web sites which post pictures of new and classic Star Wars toys. These are helpful in obtaining the correct name of figures and vehicles not otherwise seen and, in some cases, the UPC code.

The Empire Strikes Back *Series figure:* Greedo *and* Return of the Jedi *Series figure: Bib Fortuna (Kenner 1981–83)*

CONTENTS

Action Figures: Alphabetical

Books

Ceramics

Clothing and Accessories

Coins and Premiums

Comics 136

Craft and Activity Toys 161

Die Cast.................164

Dolls and Figures

Electronic and Computer....................180

Food Collectibles

Games and Puzzles

Household

Masks, Helmets and Costumes

Micro Figures and Vehicles

Model Kits

Paper Collectibles

Recordings and Stills

Role Play Toys.....................................243

School and Office Supplies

Statues 250

Trading Cards 253

Vehicles and Accessories

Wall Art

Index 282-288

THIS BOOK COVERS

Star Wars Collectibles

Made Between 1976 and 2002

This book covers Star Wars collectibles from the beginning, through the first quarter of 2002, with additional information on forthcoming items for *Attack of the Clones*. This is from the very beginning of the first or classic age of Star Wars through the end of the second age of Star Wars collectibles, perhaps destined to be known someday as the "Silver Age," based on the Star Wars Trilogy Special Edition, and well into the third age based on Episode I, *The Phantom Menace*, now II, *Attack of the Clones* and eventually III.

From the collecting point of view, these ages were also known as famine, feast, famine, feast, and finally innundation.

Distribution in the United States

This book covers Star Wars collectibles distributed in the United States. While just about every foreign item makes its way to a few collectors in the United States, the only items listed here are ones which were distributed in enough quantity to be generally available. The most significant of these are the "Tri-Logo" action figures. These figures came on header cards with logos for "Return of the Jedi" in three languages (thus the name) and were intended for foreign markets. However, they were widely distributed in the United States as the Star Wars phenomenon was winding down in 1984–86. A few foreign figures, such as the Power of the Force Yak Face, are listed for completeness. Although never distributed in the United States, it is a necessary and expensive figure for collectors who want to complete their collections. Other figures on foreign header cards are worth less than their U. S. counterparts and are more likely to be bought by a collector as a temporary measure, until the more desirable American figure can be acquired. A more recent example is the Pizza Hut PVC figures which came out as in-store premiums in 1995 in Australia, but were distributed in quantity to comic shops in the United States in 1997, in sets of four.

Categories

The book is divided into sections based on the categories which collectors most frequently use in organizing their collections. The amount of coverage given to any category depends on its popularity. Action figures are the most popular Star Wars collectible and so they are given the most coverage — 85 pages, with additional sections on the vehicles, accessories and the 12 inch dolls. Actually, many of the less popular categories could just as well have been grouped in a section called "Other Stuff" because that is how most collectors view the items. However, this would have made it hard to use the book.

Grading

Most Star Wars items are graded on a 10-point scale from C-10 (the best) down to C-1. Hardly anything old qualifies as a C-10 and nobody admits that anything they are trying to sell is a C-1, so the actual number of categories is probably less than 10. Prices in this book are for items in their original packaging in "near mint" condition, which corresponds to about C-9 or C-9.5. The occasional extraordinary item that is actually "mint" (i.e. C-10) commands a slightly higher price. How much higher depends on how much better than an ordinary near mint copy it actually is. Mint means the same thing, regardless of age and type of product. It is not the same thing as "new." Many, probably most, new action figure header cards are not mint. They have been handled when they were put in the shipping box, taken out of the box and hung on a rack, maybe dropped on the floor, handled by the checkout clerk, etc. This leaves an item which is a defect-free collectible, acceptable anywhere at the near-mint price. The figure inside is most likely mint, but rarely the package. "Near mint" does vary somewhat with the type of product. Some kinds of things are simply more durable than others and do not normally show any wear from normal handling. For those things, there is very little difference between the ordinary, (i.e. near mint) and the extraordinary, (i.e. mint) and probably very little difference in price.

Prices

A single price is given for each listed item. This represents the full retail price or asking price. Prices vary from one dealer to another and from one location to another so prices actually fall into a range. But even though no single price can be perfect for all situations, a price range of, for example, $40 to $100 is no more meaningful than a single price, and even less satisfying. The single price given in this book should be used as a guideline or baseline. If you can find the item that you want to buy for 10% to 25% less than this price you are getting a good deal. If you are paying more, but you really want the item, that's okay too. Just shop around a little first to see if you can do better.

This book is based on the author's research. The author is not a dealer in Star Wars collectibles and not associated with any dealer or manufacturer nor with Lucasfilm Ltd. or any of its licensees.

INTRODUCTION

The Star Wars Phenomenon

The Star Wars phenomenon started in 1977, and, after a little slump in the late 1980s, it is still going strong. Collectibles from the classic movie were available beginning in late 1976—first a poster and a book, then the comics in early 1977 and finally, after the movie opened, a few games and puzzles. The real flood didn't start until 1978 when the action figures actually arrived.

In *Star Wars* collecting, Kenner (now Hasbro) is King. Almost anything made by Kenner/Hasbro, and a lot of things they never quite made, is collected more intensely than anything, however attractive, made by anyone else. Was this inevitable? It didn't seem to be so at the time.

The first *Star Wars* collectible available to the general public was the original paperback book. I call it "*Star Wars* collectible #1." There was also a teaser poster, which was given out at the San Diego Comics Convention, held earlier that fall, but it was available only at the convention. If you are a computer person, you can call this "collectible #0" if you like. Anyway, the book appeared in November 1976, a full 7 months before the movie opened, and it was available at bookstores everywhere. Later book editions had a different cover and can easily be distinguished by the date on the copyright page. Unlike some of the most valuable action figures, the original paperback cannot be faked. Nevertheless, this paperback is not as valuable as any of the early action figures. A hardcover version of the book which came out in the fall is worth a lot more, but still not as much as the action figures.

Star Wars collectible #2 is the first issue of the comic book series from Marvel. It's worth a lot more than the paperback book and the 35¢ test issue of this comic is more valuable than many of the early action figures. A couple of issues of the comic came out before the movie opened. Other pre-opening collectibles include articles in movie magazines about the forthcoming movie and *Time* magazine which ran a two-page spread calling *Star Wars* the best movie of the year.

Many of today's *Star Wars* collectors were kids filled with wonder when they first saw the movie. They saw the movie 10 times in the theater and now they are

Advertisement for early Star Wars action figures and vehicles (Kenner 1978–79)

Advertisement for early Star Wars figures (Kenner 1980–81)

grown up, have some money and want to collect the neat toys that they played with in their youth. Even these fans might have collected the comic books and the earliest toys, by Kenner and others, who hastily scrambled to get licenses. Many of these items came out before the first action figures, which did not appear until 1978. Nevertheless, it's the first action figures that everyone collects, and that have the highest prices. Don't you wish you bought all the figures offered in the advertisements pictured in this section—at their original prices!

Alright, you can't do that, but you can buy the current figures. There have been a lot of *Star Wars* red tag specials for the last two years. This was because of the vast amount of merchandise Hasbro made for *Episode I The Phantom Menace* and in the year before. Most toy stores wanted lots of action figures, vehicles and everything else from the new movie on their shelves, starting in early 1999. This meant that a lot of 1997 and 1998 merchandise was available at bargain prices starting after Christmas 1998 and for some years after that. The new movie was a big a hit, but not as big as the previous movies. It's harder to impress 8 year-olds today, and the movie was aimed more at 6-year-olds anyway. The real problem was that nothing could possibly have lived up to

the hype and anticipation that the movie generated. Lots of merchandise was sold, but way more of it was ordered than could be sold and new toys filled the action figure aisles. Pretty soon both Power of the Force and Episode I toys were in the bargain bins.

The red tag specials for the 1997 to 1998 toys from the classic movies and for the overstocked toys from *The Phantom Menace* started in late 2000 and lasted for a full year. Some action figures can still be found for $1.97. Locally, Toys "R" Us stores got lots of Freeze Frame figures originally sold in early 1998 many of which were the Collection 1 ".00" figures with "Saelt-Marae" misspelled "Sealt-Marie." All 13 of the figures with this error were available and a card back with the error is pictured on page 21. Kay-Bee stores didn't get any of them, but they got some of the R2-D2 figure with the slide reading "Shutting down the Imperial trash compactor" instead of "Shutting down the Death Star trash compactor." This previously scarce variation had been selling for $200.00, but the price quickly dropped to $50.00

As if that wasn't enough, the big sell-off also featured such previously scarce, and valuable, items as Mynock Hunt "cinema scene" packs, Darth Vader Gunner Station figures, AT-ATs for $10 to $20 each, etc. etc. These bargains were not to be missed and I saw a lot of collectors in the stores who weren't missing them.

Today, there is often a substantial price difference between a figure on an [.0000] revision card and on an [.0100] or [.0200] card. I wonder whether this will continue. Some of the changes are fairly trivial. With a number of Episode I figures, the only difference is the inclusion of the Innovision logo on the back of the newer card.

Slide for R2-D2 figure with "Imperial" error (Kenner 1998)

Episode I Battle Droid without and with Innovision Logo (.0100 and .0200 header cards) (Hasbro 1999)

Boba Fett figures got a new revision number for the change of a "," to a "." There were similar minor changes in cards in the classic series, but only major changes have much of an effect on price now. I expect that the price difference between many of these header cards will decrease with time. In addition, new stock of the scarce, earlier version may yet appear—it's happened before. Try to keep these factors in mind while you consider paying big bucks for tiny differences on the back of a header card.

There will be other price convergence as well. Some of the exotic variations, such as red carded action figures with short lightsabers in a long slot, have held up well so far, but, in the final analysis, the only difference between these figures and the normal short lightsaber versions is the crease in the clear plastic figure holder inside the bubble. At least with some other variations, such as Jedi Knight Luke Skywalker, brown vest vs. black vest, there is a real difference in the figures. With the pictured figures, current prices make sense. The brown vest sells for $75, a lot more than the black vest, while the short lightsaber in the long slot is $20.00, a little less than the original long lightsaber version. However, with the Ben (Obi-Wan) Kenobi, the short lightsaber in long tray version sells for over $1,000 – way over. It's your money, but if you pay $100 (or $1,000) today, will somebody pay you $200 (or $2,000) a few years from now? And, no, I don't have a picture to show you—I take my own advice.

The best lesson to draw from this is not to pay $50 or $100 or $200, or whatever, for a recent figure. No matter how scarce the variation seems to be, you can't really know for sure until all the warehouses are empty and the guys who bought all 25 of them at some local store finally sell off their stock. By then, most collectors will be looking for some new, seemingly scarce item, and the price will probably be more reasonable anyway.

What should a savvy collector like you do, to build a prime collection? Look for those bargains! Go to a lot of stores until you find the items you are missing. Use your feet (to go to a lot of places) and your eyes (to look through all the racks) and don't pay through the nose unless you have to.

Savvy collectors will be looking in the bargain bins for vehicles and ships, both common and deluxe action figures, carry cases, and role play weapons. Deluxe creatures, 12" dolls, and store exclusives shouldn't last long enough to get there, but you never know. *Attack of the Clones* figures will take their turn in the bargain bins eventually. Retailers will be smarter this time, and won't order quite so much stock, so the sales won't last as long.

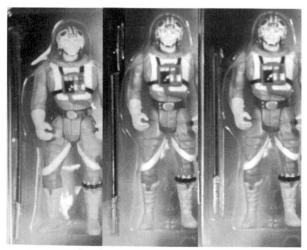

Luke Skywalker, X-wing pilot with long lightsaber, with short lightsaber in long slot, and with short lightsaber (close-ups) (Kenner 1995–96)

Jedi Knight Luke Skywalker in brown vest and in black vest (Kenner 1995–96)

Early Bird Certificate Package, back (Kenner 1977)

STAR WARS: CLASSIC FIGURES

STAR WARS
Kenner (1977–1986)

Time magazine picked *Star Wars* as the best picture of the year in a two-page feature when it opened in early summer 1977 (*Time*, May 30, 1977). It played to packed houses for about a year, but it has been off the big screen since 1980. The special edition, with added scenes and improved special effects, opened on January 31, 1997. For both releases, there were sequels—and action figures.

The very first *Star Wars* action figures arrived in 1978, in the mail. Of course, they only did so if you bought the famous Early Bird Package. The figures came in a white plastic tray in a white mailer box. There were four figures—R2-D2, Luke Skywalker, Princess Leia and Chewbacca—all individually bagged, along with a bag of plastic pegs for the display stand which was included in the Early Bird Package. Already there were variations. In the very earliest packages, Chewbacca has a dark green plastic rifle instead of the later black plastic and Luke has a telescoping lightsaber. Some people call it a double telescoping lightsaber as it not only extends out of his arm, it also telescopes out of the middle of the blade and almost reaches the floor. This version lightsaber can occasionally be found on carded Luke Skywalker and sometimes even on Darth Vader and Ben (Obi-Wan) Kenobi figures. It adds about $1,000 to the value of the Luke Skywalker figure and $2,000 to the value of the other two! It also increases the value of the loose figure, but it can be faked, even on a carded figure. For that kind of money, anything can be faked.

Early Bird "Figures" (Early 1978)
Early Bird figures R2-D2, Luke Skywalker (telescoping lightsaber, Princess Leia, and Chewbacca (green blaster rifle), in tray and box $450.00
See under Carry Cases and Display Stands for listing of the Early Bird Package.

Packaging Variations—Header Cards

Star Wars action figures are heavily collected, both on their original header cards and loose. Every tiny variation in the figure or the packaging makes a difference in the price and *Star Wars* figures have many of both kinds of variations. The chief variation comes about because Kenner continued to produce the original figures for many years, but changed the movie logo to *The Empire Strikes Back* and then to *Return of the Jedi* as each of those new movies premiered. After the

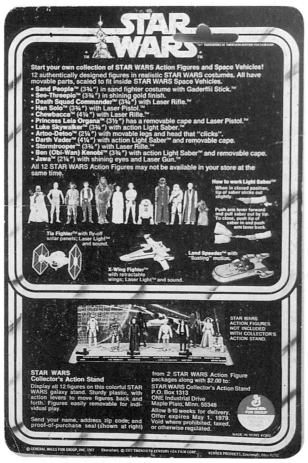

12-Back header card (Kenner 1978)

movies, figures were issued on *Power of the Force* header cards with a collectible coin as a premium.

In addition, most of the figures were available in the United States on foreign "Tri-Logo" header cards which had *Return of the Jedi* movie logos in three languages. There are variations among Tri-Logo header cards as well, but all are lumped together for pricing purposes. This means that there are four or five different packages for most figures, before you even consider the normal variations that occur in any action figure line, such as hair color or other changes to the figure and photo or text changes to the card.

Packaging Variations—Card Backs

The most significant of the header card changes involves the first group of figures to be produced, which includes all of the major characters. The cards for these figures have a picture and list on the back which shows just the original 12 figures. Consequently, these figures are called 12-backs and command the highest prices, as befits the earliest figures. Nine of the figures were released in the initial assortment and the other three—Death Squad Commander, Jawa and Sand People—were added fairly quickly. All these figures appeared on 12-back cards. Original figures on 12-back cards are scarce and desirable, so they are worth a lot more money—$75.00 to $100.00 more at current prices.

The second figure release added eight new figures and the card back was changed to reflect this, becoming 20-backs. The original 12 figures also appeared on these cards. After all, Kenner wanted you to buy all 20! The earliest of these cards are lacking the Boba Fett mail-in offer, while later issues contain the offer.

The 21st figure was the regular Boba-Fett figure and it had a 21-back card. Most collectors treat 20 and 21-back figures as part of the same series, without distinction or price difference. They are listed as 20/21-backs in this book.

The first of *The Empire Strikes Back* figures appeared on 31-back cards, but the earlier 21 figures were re-released on 21-back cards with *The Empire Strikes Back* logo. There are also figures on so-called 32-backs which are 12-back cards with a sticker listing the other 20 figures. When 10 more figures were added in the second release, the cards were changed to 41-backs.

Six more figures were added in the third *The Empire Strikes Back* release, but R2-D2 with Sensorscope and C-3PO with removable limbs replace the earlier versions of these figures and consequently all of them were released on 45-backs. 47-back cards came later, when two of the final figures (TIE Fighter Pilot and Zuckuss) of the third release were added. The very last figure was 4-LOM, making 48-back cards. Zuckuss actually appeared on this card, and not on the 47-back card which first listed him.

The pattern continued with the *Return of the Jedi*. The first use of this logo was on 48-backs, but prior to that, some 48-back cards contained a *Revenge of the Jedi* offer. These later cards command a premium, as does anything that mentions this title.

New *Return of the Jedi* figures appeared first on 65-back cards. With the second figure release came 77-backs and finally, with the addition of Lumat and Paploo, 79-backs.

Power of the Force figures only come on 92-back cards, but they do come with coins. *Droids* and *Ewoks* figures had their own cards, one per series and only the A-Wing pilot and Boba Fett figure crossed over. Otherwise they have their own group of cartooney looking figures.

Collectors, however, had Tri-Logo cards to worry about. There are a lot of variations in these cards; so many that collectors just ignore them. All tri-logo cards for a given figure

Package Backs: 21-Back; 48-Back with Revenge of the Jedi *figure offer; 92 back with coin offer (Kenner 1979–85)*

Star Wars Series Figures: Ben (Obi-Wan) Kenobi (white hair) and Hammerhead (Kenner 1978)

sell for the same price, subject, of course, to condition.

Within each group of 12-backs, 20-backs, etc., there are variations. There are two slightly different 12-backs, eight different 20-backs, and two or more versions of most of the others, for a total of 45 different U.S. header cards.

Figure Variations

The most significant of the figure variations was with the Jawa, where the original version had a vinyl cape. This was quickly changed to cloth, which was used for all the rest of the figures. The few vinyl-caped Jawas are the most valuable of all the *Star Wars* figures and currently sell in the $3,500.00 range, with loose figures going for $250.00 to $300.00. Care in buying is essential, because a loose Jawa in cloth cape is only worth $15.00 and a fake vinyl cape is not hard to make.

All *Star Wars* action figure prices are volatile and generally increasing. This will almost certainly continue with the forthcoming release of another movie in the series.

All of the figures are listed below in the chronological order in which the various batches or groups were released. This is a shortened list, with variations only briefly noted. A much more detailed list of the figures, in alphabetical order, and with all variations described, is given in the next section of this book. Prices in each section are the same. The purpose of this chronological list is to allow you to compare the value of a given figure with the values of all the others that

appeared in the same series. The alphabetical list lets you compare a figures value with all other versions of the same figure.

STAR WARS SERIES
Kenner (1978–79)

First series, 12-back cards (1978)

Artoo-Detoo (R2-D2) (#38200)	$350.00
Ben (Obi-Wan) Kenobi (#38250) **gray hair**	700.00
Ben (Obi-Wan) Kenobi (#38250) **white hair**	800.00
Chewbacca (#38210) **black blaster rifle**	300.00
Chewbacca (#38210) **green blaster rifle**	325.00
Darth Vader (#38230)	600.00
Death Squad Commander (#38290)	350.00
Han Solo (#38260) **large head**, dark brown hair	950.00
Han Solo (#38260) **small head**, brown hair	850.00
Jawa (#38270) **vinyl cape**	3,500.00
Jawa (#38270) **cloth cape**	275.00
Luke Skywalker (#38180) **blond hair**	750.00
Princess Leia Organa (#38190)	750.00
Sand People (#38280)	400.00
See-Threepio (C-3PO) (#38220)	300.00
Stormtrooper (#38240)	400.00

Second Series, New Figures on 20/21-back cards

Boba Fett (#39250)	1,500.00
Death Star Droid (#39080)	200.00
Greedo (#39020)	300.00
Hammerhead (#39030)	225.00
Luke Skywalker X-Wing Pilot (#39060)	300.00

Power Droid (#39090) 175.00
R5-D4 (#39070) 300.00
Snaggletooth (#39040) **red** 175.00
Walrus Man (#39050) 275.00
Reissue Figures on 20/21-back cards
Artoo-Detoo (R2-D2) (#38200) 200.00
Ben (Obi-Wan) Kenobi (#38250) **gray hair** 175.00
Ben (Obi-Wan) Kenobi (#38250) **white hair** 175.00
Chewbacca (#38210) 225.00
Darth Vader (#38230) 300.00
Death Squad Commander (#38290) 150.00
Han Solo (#38260) **large head**, dark brown hair 650.00
Han Solo (#38260) **small head**, brown hair 550.00
Jawa (#38270) **cloth cape** 200.00
Luke Skywalker (#38180) **blond hair** 250.00
Princess Leia Organa (#38190) 275.00
Sand People (#38280) 150.00
See-Threepio (C-3PO) (#38220) 100.00
Stormtrooper (#38240) 150.00

THE EMPIRE STRIKES BACK

In the second movie of the series we learn the secret of Luke's parentage and meet Yoda, played by a puppet, and Lando Calrissian played by Billy Dee Williams. There are lots of new figures. Luke looses his hand, C-3PO gets chopped into pieces, Han Solo gets to cool off on the way to Jabba's palace, and Lando gets his ship and favorite Wookiee back. Not to worry, though, because before the movie is over Luke gets a new hand, C-3PO gets put back together and Lando turns out to be a good guy and not a traitor.

Lots of neat figures and vehicles were produced. They are cheap by the standards of the first series, but valuable by any other standard.

THE EMPIRE STRIKES BACK SERIES
Kenner (1980–82)

Third Series, New Figures (1980)
Bespin Security Guard (#39810) **white** $75.00
Bossk (Bounty Hunter) (#39760) 125.00
FX-7 (Medical Droid) (#39730) 75.00
Han Solo (Hoth Outfit) (#39790) 100.00
IG-88 (Bounty Hunter) (#39770) 150.00
Imperial Stormtrooper (Hoth Battle Gear) (#39740) . . 100.00
Lando Calrissian (#39800) **no teeth** 75.00
Lando Calrissian (#39800) **white teeth** 75.00
Leia Organa (Bespin Gown) (#39720) **crew neck** . . . 200.00
Leia Organa (Bespin Gown) (#39720) **crew neck,
    new package** 175.00
Leia Organa (Bespin Gown) (#39720) **turtle neck** . . . 200.00
Leia Organa (Bespin Gown) (#39720) **turtle neck,
    new package** 175.00
Luke Skywalker (Bespin Fatigues) (#39780) 250.00
Luke Skywalker (Bespin) (#39780) new package 150.00
Rebel Soldier (Hoth Battle Gear) (#39750) 75.00

Fourth Series, New Figures (1981)
AT-AT Driver (#39379) 90.00
Dengar (#39329) 100.00
Han Solo (Bespin Outfit) (#39339) 175.00
Imperial Commander (#39389) 75.00
Leia Organa (Hoth Outfit) (#39359) 175.00

The Empire Strikes Back Series Figures: IG-88 and AT-AT Commander (Kenner 1980)

Lobot (#39349) 70.00
Rebel Commander (#39369) 150.00
2-1B (#39399) 100.00
Ugnaught (#39319) blue smock 80.00
Yoda (#38310) **brown snake** 300.00
Yoda (#38310) **orange snake** 225.00

Fifth Series, New Figures (1982)
Artoo-Detoo (R2-D2) (with Sensorscope) (#69590) . . 75.00
AT-AT Commander (#69620) 80.00
Bespin Security Guard (#69640) **black** 65.00
Cloud Car Pilot (Twin Pod) (#69630) 125.00
C-3PO (Removable Limbs) (#69600) 90.00
4-LOM (#70010) 300.00
Imperial TIE Fighter Pilot (#70030) 125.00
Luke Skywalker (Hoth Battle Gear) (#69610) 125.00
Zuckuss (#70020) 125.00

Reissue Figures on The Empire Strikes Back header cards
Artoo-Detoo (R2-D2) (#38200) 150.00
Ben (Obi-Wan) Kenobi (#38250) **gray hair** 125.00
Ben (Obi-Wan) Kenobi (#38250) **white hair** 125.00
Boba Fett (#39250) 400.00
Chewbacca (#38210) 125.00
Darth Vader (#38230) 125.00
Death Star Droid (#39080) 150.00
Greedo (#39020) 125.00
Hammerhead (#39030) 125.00
Han Solo (#38260) **large head**, dark brown hair 250.00
Han Solo (#38260) **small head**, brown hair 325.00
Jawa (#38270) **cloth cape** 125.00
Luke Skywalker (#38180) **blond hair** 275.00

Luke Skywalker (#38180) **brown hair** 325.00
Luke Skywalker (X-Wing Pilot) (#39060) 125.00
Power Droid (#39090) 125.00
Princess Leia Organa (#38190) 325.00
R5-D4 (#39070) 140.00
Sandpeople (#38280) 125.00
See-Threepio (C-3PO) (#38220) 150.00
Snaggletooth (#39040) **red** 150.00
Star Destroyer Commander (#38290) 125.00
Stormtrooper (#38240) 125.00
Walrus Man (#39050) 125.00

RETURN OF THE JEDI

The third movie in the series had the distinct advantage of being able to tie up all the loose ends and have the Rebels win. Solo is rescued, Jabba gets his just deserts, the new, improved, and even bigger Death Star is blown up, and the Ewoks steal the show. Everybody went home happy.

Collectors were happy too, with plenty of figures and vehicles to collect. They were even happier a couple of years later when the series had finally run its course with kids and the figures finally became red tag specials. Super Powers figures were red tag specials around the same time. You just couldn't go wrong, no matter what you bought.

There were a lot of *Return of the Jedi* figures produced and a number of them, particularly figures from the sixth series, were still available wholesale to comic shops and similar outlets in the early 1990s.

The Empire Strikes Back *Series figure: Greedo and* Return of the Jedi *Series figure: Bib Fortuna (Kenner 1981–83)*

Return of the Jedi *Series Figure: Han Solo (Trench Coat) and Boba Fett (Kenner 1984)*

RETURN OF THE JEDI SERIES
Kenner (1983–84)

Sixth Series, New Figures (1983)
Admiral Ackbar (#70310) $30.00
Bib Fortuna (#70790) 30.00
Biker Scout (#70820) 35.00
Chief Chirpa (#70690) 30.00
Emperor's Royal Guard (#70680) 40.00
Gamorrean Guard (#70670) 25.00
General Madine (#70780) 30.00
Klaatu (#70730) **tan arms** or **gray arms** 30.00
Lando Calrissian (Skiff Guard) (#70830) 45.00
Logray (Ewok Medicine Man) (#70710) 30.00
Luke Skywalker (Jedi Knight) (#70650) with **green**
    lightsaber 100.00
Luke Skywalker (Jedi Knight) (#70650) with **blue**
    lightsaber 175.00
Nien Nunb (#70840) 35.00
Princess Leia Organa (Boushh Disguise) (#70660) . . . 55.00
Rebel Commando (#70740) 30.00
Ree-Yees (#70800) 30.00
Squid Head (#70770) 30.00
Weequay (#70760) 35.00

Seventh Series, New Figures (1984)
AT-ST Driver (#71330) 30.00
B-Wing Pilot (#71280) 30.00
8D8 (#71210) 30.00
The Emperor (#71240) 35.00
Han Solo (Trench Coat) (#71300) 50.00

Klaatu (Skiff Guard) (#71290) 30.00
Lumat (#93670) 45.00
Nikto (#71190) 30.00
Paploo (#93680) 45.00
Princess Leia Organa (Combat Poncho) (#71220) . . . 60.00
Prune Face (#71320) 30.00
Rancor Keeper (#71350) 30.00
Teebo (#71310) 45.00
Wicket W. Warrick (#71230) 50.00

Reissue Figures on Return of the Jedi header cards
Artoo-Detoo (R2-D2) (with Sensorscope) (#69420) . . . 40.00
AT-AT Commander (#69620) 45.00
AT-AT Driver (#39379) 40.00
Ben (Obi-Wan) Kenobi (#38250) **gray hair** 50.00
Ben (Obi-Wan) Kenobi (#38250) **gray hair** new
    package 50.00
Ben (Obi-Wan) Kenobi (#38250) **white hair** 50.00
Bespin Security Guard (#39810) **white** 35.00
Bespin Security Guard (#69640) **black** 55.00
Boba Fett (#39250) 325.00
Boba Fett (#39250) new package 350.00
Bossk (Bounty Hunter) (#39760) 75.00
Chewbacca (#38210) 50.00
Chewbacca (#38210) new package 45.00
Cloud Car Pilot (Twin Pod) (#69630) 45.00
Darth Vader (#38230) 50.00
Darth Vader (#38230) new package 45.00
Death Squad Commander (Star Destroyer Com-
    mander) (#38290) 75.00
Death Star Droid (#39080) 75.00

Dengar (#39329) 35.00
4-LOM (#70010) 50.00
FX-7 (Medical Droid) (#39730) 75.00
Greedo (#39020) 75.00
Hammerhead (#39030) 75.00
Han Solo (#38260) **large head**, dark brown hair,
   new package 185.00
Han Solo (#38260) **large head**, brown hair 175.00
Han Solo (#38260) **small head**, brown hair new
   package 200.00
Han Solo (Bespin Outfit) (#39339) 85.00
Han Solo (Hoth Battle Gear) (#39790) 75.00
IG-88 (Bounty Hunter) (#39770) 75.00
Imperial Commander (#39389) 40.00
Imperial Stormtrooper (Hoth Battle Gear) (#39740) . . . 50.00
Imperial TIE Fighter Pilot (#70030) 60.00
Jawa (#38270) **cloth cape** 45.00
Lando Calrissian (#39800) **white teeth** 45.00
Leia Organa (Bespin Gown) (#39720) **turtle neck** . . . 150.00
Leia Organa (Bespin Gown) (#39720) **crew neck** . . . 125.00
Lobot (#39349) 35.00
Luke Skywalker (#38180) **blond hair** 225.00
Luke Skywalker (#38180) **blond hair** new package . . 175.00
Luke Skywalker (#38180) **brown hair** 300.00
Luke Skywalker (#38180) **brown hair** new package . 175.00
Luke Skywalker (Bespin Fatigues) (#39780) new
   package, **yellow hair** 140.00
Luke Skywalker (Bespin Fatigues) (#39780) new
   package, **brown hair** 100.00
Luke Skywalker (Hoth Battle Gear) (#69610) 40.00
Luke Skywalker (X-Wing Fighter Pilot) (#39060) 50.00
Power Droid (#39090) 55.00
Princess Leia Organa (#38190) 450.00
Princess Leia Organa (Hoth Outfit) (#39359) 100.00
Princess Leia Organa (Hoth Outfit) (#39359) new
   package 75.00
R5-D4 (Arfive-Defour) (#39070) 65.00
Rebel Commander (#39369) 40.00
Rebel Soldier (Hoth Battle Gear) (#39750) 35.00
See-Threepio (C-3PO) (Removable Limbs) (#69430) . 35.00
Snaggletooth (#39040) **red** 55.00
Stormtrooper (#38240) 50.00
Too-Onebee (2-1B) (#71600) 50.00
Tusken Raider (Sand People) (#38280) 75.00
Ugnaught (#39319) 35.00
Walrus Man (#39050) 60.00
Yoda (#38310) **brown snake** 100.00
Yoda **The Jedi Master**, (#38310) **brown snake** 100.00
Zuckuss (#70020) 50.00

THE POWER OF THE FORCE

The Power of the Force figures were produced after all three movies had come and gone. Kenner wanted to keep the figure series alive and so they changed the name of the series and added silver colored aluminum coins as an in-package premium.

Without a new movie to pump-up sales, less of these figures were ordered and many that were scheduled were never made. As sales slowed, collector interest waned and the figures became red tag specials. When the collectors finally realized that they didn't have these figures, it was too late and so now they are among the most valuable of *Star Wars* figures. Several were released only overseas.

There were 15 new figures and 22 figures which were

reissued in this series. All of them came with coins, making a total of 37 figures that came with coins. However, two of the foreign release figures (AT-AT Driver and Nikto) came with coins from other figures, so only 35 different coins came with these 37 figures. Two other foreign Power of the Force figures (Imperial TIE Fighter Pilot and FX-7) are claimed to exist in some publications and denied in others.

However, coins were also available as a mail-in premium with a proof of purchase from some prior *The Empire Strikes Back* and *Return of the Jedi* figures and so there are actually 62 coins in the series to collect. See the COINS section of this book.

THE POWER OF THE FORCE SERIES
Kenner (1985)

Eighth Series, New Figures (1985) with silver coin
A-Wing Pilot (#93830) $100.00
Amanaman (#93740) 275.00
Anakin Skywalker (#93790) foreign release 2,250.00
Artoo-Detoo (R2-D2) Pop-up Lightsaber (#93720) . . . 175.00
Barada (#93750) 100.00
EV-9D9 (#93800) 150.00
Han Solo (Carbonite Chamber) (#93770) 250.00
Imperial Dignitary (#93850) 75.00
Imperial Gunner (#93760) 150.00
Lando Calrissian (General Pilot) (#93820) 110.00
Luke Skywalker (Battle Poncho) (#93710) 125.00
Luke Skywalker, Stormtrooper Outfit (#93780) 450.00

Power of the Force Figure: Yak Face (Kenner 1985)

*Power of the Force Figure: Luke Skywalker
(X-Wing Fighter Pilot) (Kenner 1985)*

Romba (#93730) 50.00
Warok (#93810) 75.00
Yak Face (#93840) foreign release 1,900.00

Reissue Figures on Power of the Force header cards
AT-AT Driver (#39379) foreign release only 550.00
AT-ST Driver (#71330) 60.00
B-Wing Pilot (#71280) 30.00
Ben (Obi-Wan) Kenobi (#38250) **white hair** 125.00
Ben (Obi-Wan) Kenobi (#38250) **gray hair** 125.00
Biker Scout (#70820) 80.00
Chewbacca (#38210) 100.00
Darth Vader (#38230) 100.00
The Emperor (#71240) 75.00
Gamorrean Guard (#70670) foreign release only. . . . 250.00
Han Solo (Trench Coat) (#71300) 550.00
Imperial Stormtrooper (#38240) 275.00
Jawa (#38270) **cloth cape** 100.00
Luke Skywalker (Jedi Knight) (#70650) with **green
    lightsaber** 275.00
Luke Skywalker (X-Wing Fighter Pilot) (#39060) 100.00
Lumat (#93670) 50.00
Nikto (#71190) foreign release only. 600.00
Paploo (#93680). 45.00
Princess Leia Organa (Combat Poncho) (#71220) . . 100.00
See-Threepio (C-3PO) Removable Limbs (#69430) . . 80.00
Teebo (#71310) 210.00
Wicket W. Warrick (#71230) 210.00
Yoda (with **brown snake**) (#38310). 500.00

TRI-LOGO (RETURN OF THE JEDI)

There is no series of figures which has the words "Tri-Logo" on it. Tri-Logo is just the universally used collector's shorthand name for figures on header cards with *Return of the Jedi* logos in three languages. It is not even really a single series, as there are differences among Tri-Logo header cards depending on the countries that were the intended market for these figures. Collectors generally ignore such differences and all such cards for a given figure have the same value. Generally, a figure on a Tri-Logo card has a lower value than the same figure on any other type of card from the 1970s and 1980s.

There are foreign versions of *Star Wars* figures from many countries and some of them always end up in the United States, in the hands of some collectors. What makes Tri-Logo carded figures into a "domestic series" in the eyes of collectors and dealers, even though they were manufactured for foreign markets, is that they were distributed in quantity in this country at many stores. As the least desirable version of *Star Wars* figures and the last ones distributed, they often spent the longest time at toy stores. They were knocked onto the floor by collectors looking for scarce figures and plastered with red tag stickers. Consequently, Tri-Logo figures are often in lesser condition than those from other series, which further reduces their value. Figures on beat-up cards are often worth little more than the corresponding loose figure.

TRI-LOGO "SERIES"
Kenner (1984–86)

Reissue Figures on Tri-Logo header card
Admiral Ackbar (#70310) $25.00
Amanaman (#93740) 150.00
Anakin Skywalker (#93790) foreign release. 125.00
Artoo-Detoo (R2-D2) (#38200) 35.00
Artoo-Detoo (R2-D2) (Sensorscope) (#69590) 28.00
Artoo-Detoo (R2-D2) (Pop-up Lightsaber) (#93720) . 150.00
AT-AT Commander (#69620). 35.00
AT-AT Driver (#39379). 90.00
AT-ST Driver (#71330) 30.00
A-Wing Pilot (#93830) 75.00
B-Wing Pilot (#71280) 30.00
Barada (#93750) 60.00
Ben (Obi-Wan) Kenobi (#38250) **gray hair** 75.00
Ben (Obi-Wan) Kenobi (#38250) **white hair** 75.00
Bespin Security Guard (#39810) **white** 25.00
Bespin Security Guard (#69640) **black** 25.00
Bib Fortuna (#70790) 25.00
Biker Scout (#70820) 25.00
Boba Fett (#39250). 700.00
Bossk (Bounty Hunter) (#39760). 55.00
C-3PO (Removable Limbs) (#69600) 25.00
Chewbacca (#38210) 60.00
Chief Chirpa (#70690) 25.00
Cloud Car Pilot (Twin Pod) (#69630) 30.00
Darth Vader (#38230) 45.00
Death Squad Commander (#38290) 75.00
Death Star Droid (#39080) 125.00
Dengar (#39329) 50.00
8D8 (#71210) 100.00
Emperor (#71240) 35.00
Emperor's Royal Guard (#70680) 75.00
EV-9D9 (#93800) 125.00

Tri-Logo Series Figures: The Emperor, R2-D2 (Sensorscope), and Rancor Keeper (Kenner 1985)

4-LOM (#70010)	28.00
FX-7 (Medical Droid) (#39730)	60.00
Gamorrean Guard (#70670)	25.00
General Madine (#70780)	25.00
Greedo (#39020)	75.00
Hammerhead (#39030)	75.00
Han Solo (#38260) **large head**, dark brown hair	175.00
Han Solo (#38260) **small head**, brown hair	175.00
Han Solo (Bespin Outfit) (#39339)	50.00
Han Solo (Hoth Outfit) (#39790)	40.00
Han Solo (in Carbonite Chamber) (#93770)	225.00
Han Solo (in Trench Coat) (#71300)	35.00
IG-88	175.00
Imperial Commander (#39389)	40.00
Imperial Dignitary (#93850)	50.00
Imperial Gunner (#93760)	135.00
Imperial Stormtrooper (Hoth Battle Gear) (#39740)	50.00
Imperial Stormtrooper (#38240) new package	65.00
Imperial TIE Fighter Pilot (#70030)	90.00
Jawa (#38270) **cloth cape**	75.00
Klaatu (#70730) with **tan arms** or **gray arms**	20.00
Klaatu (in Skiff Guard Outfit) (#71290)	35.00
Lando Calrissian (#39800)	75.00
Lando Calrissian (General Pilot) (#93820)	75.00
Lando Calrissian (Skiff Guard Disguise) (#70830)	25.00
Leia Organa (Bespin Gown) (#39720)	115.00
Leia Organa (Hoth Outfit) (#39359)	100.00
Lobot (#39349)	90.00
Lograj (Ewok Medicine Man) (#70710)	25.00
Luke Skywalker (#38180) **blond hair**	225.00
Luke Skywalker (#38180) **brown hair**	260.00
Luke Skywalker (Bespin) (#39780) yellow hair	125.00
Luke Skywalker (Bespin) (#39780) brown hair	125.00
Luke Skywalker (Hoth Battle Gear) (#69610)	35.00
Luke Skywalker (in Battle Poncho) (#93710)	100.00
Luke Skywalker (Jedi Knight) (#70650) **blue lightsaber** (#70650)	200.00
Luke Skywalker (Jedi Knight) (#70650) **green lightsaber**	125.00
Luke Skywalker (X-Wing Fighter Pilot) (#39060)	100.00

Luke Skywalker (Stormtrooper Outfit) (#93780)	250.00
Lumat (#93670)	30.00
Nien Nunb (#70840)	60.00
Nikto (#71190)	35.00
Paploo (#93680)	65.00
Power Droid (#39090)	75.00
Princess Leia Organa (#38190)	150.00
Princess Leia Organa (Boushh Disguise) (#70660)	150.00
Princess Leia Organa (Combat Poncho) (#71220)	35.00
Prune Face (#71320)	35.00
R5-D4 (#39070)	75.00
Rancor Keeper (#71350)	60.00
Rebel Commander (#39369)	40.00
Rebel Commando (#70740)	20.00
Rebel Soldier (Hoth Battle Gear) (#39750)	25.00
Ree-Yees (#70800)	25.00
Romba (#93730)	35.00
See-Threepio (C-3PO) (#38220)	45.00
Snaggletooth (**red**) (#39040)	75.00
Squid Head (#70770)	25.00
Teebo (#71310)	35.00
Tusken Raider (Sand People) (#38280)	75.00
2-1B (#39399)	75.00
Ugnaught (#39319)	45.00
Walrus Man (#39050)	100.00
Warok (#93810)	60.00
Weequay (#70760)	25.00
Wicket W. Warrick (#71230)	35.00
Yak Face (#93840) foreign release	400.00
Yoda (with **brown snake**) (#38310)	110.00
Zuckuss (#70020)	28.00

(THE TV ANIMATED SERIES) DROIDS
"The Adventures of R2-D2 and C-3PO"
Kenner (1985)

The real movies were gone from the theaters, but there was still money to be made, so a couple of Ewok movies (*The*

Ewok Adventure and *Ewoks: The Battle For Endor*) were produced, along with both an Ewoks and a Droids animated ABC television series. I didn't see any of them when they came out and they put me to sleep when I try to watch them on television now. My grandson liked them when he was four years old, but now that he is five he has outgrown them. They must do the same to just about everybody, because the figures didn't attain much of a collector following. In fact, the greatest interest in the Droids and Ewoks figures for the first ten years or so was in the coins rather than the figures. Although the coins are not part of the 62-coin regular set, they do form their own sets and sell for between $10.00 and $15.00 each. This was undeserved, because, judged on their own, the figures are not too bad. Recently, however, the figures have drawn more collector interest and now command prices in the same range as Tri-Logo figures.

One Droids figure—Boba Fett—has always been the exception; but only because he is a very popular figure from the previous lines and his Droids figure is very scarce. Collectors also want Vlix, a Droids figure produced only in Brazil, and not distributed in the United States. For the $5,000 or so he sells for, collectors would be better off flying to Brazil and looking for him there.

Another area of interest in these figures centers on the unproduced 1986 figures. There were six new Ewoks and eight new Droids advertised in Kenner's 1986 catalog, but they never appeared. Collectors are looking for prototypes, packaging proofs, and similar items for these unreleased figures. The catalog itself is also highly collectible.

3¾" Figures (1985) with copper or gold colored coin

A-Wing Pilot (#93830) reissue	$175.00
Artoo-Detoo R2-D2 (#71780) with pop-up lightsaber	100.00
Boba Fett (#39260)	1,100.00
Jann Tosh (#71840)	40.00
Jord Dusat (#71810)	40.00
Kea Moll (#71800)	40.00
Kez-Iban (#71850)	40.00
See-Threepio C-3PO (#71770)	125.00
Sise Fromm (#71820)	100.00
Thall Joben (#71790)	30.00
Tig Fromm (#71830)	125.00
Uncle Gundy (#71880)	40.00

EWOKS
Kenner (1985)

3¾" Figures (1985) with copper or gold colored coin

Dulok Shaman (#71150)	$35.00
Dulok Scout (#71160)	35.00
Urgah Lady Gorneesh (#71170)	35.00
King Gorneesh (#71180)	35.00
Wicket W. Warrick (#71250)	35.00
Logray (Ewok medicine man) (#71260)	35.00

LOOSE FIGURES

A lot of *Star Wars* figures are collected as loose figures.

Droids Figure: Artoo-Detoo (R2-D2) (Kenner 1985)

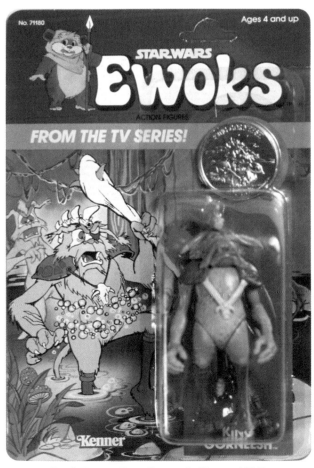

Ewok Figure: King Gorneesh (Kenner 1985)

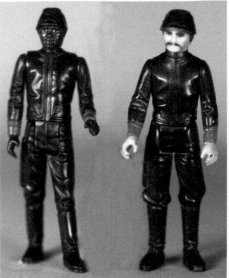

Loose Figures: Amanaman, Bespin Security Guards Black and White, Luke Skywalker Imperial Stormtrooper (Kenner 1980–85)

This is a popular type of collecting for persons whose mothers did not throw away all their *Star Wars* figures when they left home. There's nothing like finding half the figures for your collection in a box in your own attic. The condition of the figure and finding the correct weapons and accessories is usually the challenge. The prices below are for near mint figures complete with original weapons and accessories. The list of recently available replacement weapons given at the end is to remind collectors that not all available weapons are "originals."

Loose figures

Admiral Ackbar, with staff	$10.00
Amanaman, with skull staff	125.00
Anakin Skywalker, no accessories, foreign release	30.00
Artoo-Detoo (R2-D2) no accessories	15.00
Artoo-Detoo (R2-D2) (with Sensorscope)	12.50
Artoo-Detoo (R2-D2) with Pop-up Lightsaber	100.00
Artoo-Detoo (R2-D2) (Droids)	50.00
AT-AT Commander, with pistol	10.00
AT-AT Driver, with rifle	10.00

AT-ST Driver, with pistol	10.00
A-Wing Pilot, with pistol	50.00
Barada, with staff	40.00
Ben (Obi-Wan) Kenobi **gray hair**, with lightsaber	15.00
Ben (Obi-Wan) Kenobi **white hair**, with lightsaber	15.00
Bespin Security Guard **black**, with pistol	10.00
Bespin Security Guard **white**, with pistol	10.00
Bib Fortuna, with brown cloak and staff	10.00
Biker Scout, with pistol	15.00
Boba Fett, with pistol	45.00
Bossk (Bounty Hunter) with rifle	15.00
B-Wing Pilot, with pistol	10.00
Chewbacca, with black rifle	15.00
Chewbacca, with green rifle, (Early Bird Figure)	35.00
Chief Chirpa, with long club	10.00
Cloud Car Pilot (Twin Pod) with pistol and light	20.00
Darth Vader, with lightsaber	12.00
Death Squad Commander, with pistol	15.00
Death Star Droid, no accessories	10.00
Dengar, with rifle	10.00
Dulok Shaman	10.00
Dulok Scout	10.00

Loose Figures: Cloud Car Pilot, Sise Fromm, Lady Gorneesh, and Anakin Skywalker (Kenner 1978–85)

Loose Figures: Rebel Soldier Hoth Gear, Lando Calrissian General Pilot, and Yak Face (Kenner 1980–85)

8D8, no accessories. 10.00
Emperor, with cane. 10.00
Emperor's Royal Guard, with staff. 10.00
EV-9D9, no accessories 85.00
4-LOM, with weapon. 15.00
FX-7 (Medical Droid) no accessories 10.00
Gamorrean Guard, with axe 10.00
General Madine, with staff 10.00
Greedo, with pistol 10.00
Hammerhead, with pistol 12.50
Han Solo with **large head**, with pistol 25.00
Han Solo with **small head**, with pistol. 35.00
Han Solo (Bespin Outfit) with pistol. 15.00
Han Solo (Carbonite Chamber) with carbonite sheet . 110.00
Han Solo (Hoth Outfit) with pistol 15.00
Han Solo (in Trench Coat) with pistol 15.00
IG-88 (Bounty Hunter) with rifle and pistol. 15.00
Imperial Commander, with pistol. 10.00
Imperial Dignitary, no accessories. 35.00
Imperial Gunner, with pistol. 100.00
Imperial Stormtrooper, with weapon 15.00
Imperial Stormtrooper (Hoth Gear) with rifle 10.00
Imperial TIE Fighter Pilot, with pistol. 15.00
Jann Tosh. 10.00
Jawa **vinyl cape**, with weapon 275.00
Jawa **cloth cape**, with weapon 13.00
Jord Dusat 15.00
Kea Moll. 15.00
Kez-Iban. 15.00
King Gorneesh. 10.00
Klaatu, with **tan arms** or **gray arms**, with apron and
    spear. 10.00
Klaatu (in Skiff Guard Outfit) with weapon. 10.00
Lando Calrissian **no teeth** version, with pistol. 15.00
Lando Calrissian **white teeth** version, with pistol . . . 15.00
Lando Calrissian (Skiff Guard Disguise) with spear. . . 15.00
Lando Calrissian (General Pilot) with cape and pistol . 65.00
Leia Organa (Bespin Gown) **crew neck**, in cloak
    with pistol 20.00
Leia Organa (Bespin Gown) **turtle neck**, in cloak
    with pistol 20.00
Leia Organa (Hoth Outfit) with pistol 25.00
Lobot, with pistol 8.00

Logray (Ewok Medicine Man) with mask, staff and
    pouch 10.00
Logray (Ewoks) 10.00
Luke Skywalker **blond hair**, with lightsaber. 35.00
Luke Skywalker **brown hair**, with lightsaber 75.00
Luke Skywalker (in Battle Poncho) with poncho and
    pistol. 75.00
Luke Skywalker (Bespin Fatigues) **brown hair**, with
    pistol and lightsaber. 20.00
Luke Skywalker (Bespin Fatigues) **yellow hair**,
    with pistol and lightsaber 20.00
Luke Skywalker (Hoth Gear) with rifle 10.00
Luke Skywalker, Imperial Stormtrooper Outfit, with
    removable helmet and pistol 175.00
Luke Skywalker (Jedi Knight) with **green light-
saber**, cloak and pistol 50.00
Luke Skywalker (Jedi Knight) with **blue light-
saber**, cloak and pistol 60.00
Luke Skywalker (X-Wing Pilot) with pistol 15.00
Lumat, with bow 17.00
Nien Nunb, with pistol. 10.00
Nikto, with staff. 10.00
Paploo, with staff 18.00
Power Droid, no accessories 10.00
Princess Leia Organa, with pistol 45.00
Princess Leia Organa (Boushh Disguise) with
    helmet and weapon 15.00
Princess Leia Organa (Combat Poncho) with pistol. . . 20.00
Prune Face, with cloak and rifle 10.00
R5-D4, no accessories 10.00
Rancor Keeper, with prod 10.00
Rebel Commander, with rifle. 10.00
Rebel Commando, with rifle 10.00
Rebel Soldier (Hoth Gear) with pistol 10.00
Ree-Yees, with weapon 10.00
Romba, with spear 25.00
See-Threepio (C-3PO) no accessories 15.00
C-3PO (Removable Limbs) with back pack 10.00
See-Threepio (C-3PO) (Droids) 50.00
Sise Fromm 50.00
Snaggletooth (**blue**) from Cantina Adventure Set . . . 350.00
Snaggletooth (**red**) with pistol. 10.00
Squid Head, with pistol and cloak 10.00

Mail-In Boba Fett figure (Kenner 1980)

Teebo, with club, mask and pouch.	15.00
Thall Joben.	15.00
Tig Fromm	50.00
Tusken Raider (Sand People) with cloak and weapon.	15.00
2-1B, with weapon	10.00
Ugnaught, in blue smock with case	10.00
Ugnaught, in lavender smock with case.	12.50
Uncle Gundy.	15.00
Urgah Lady Gorneesh	10.00
Walrus Man, with pistol.	12.50
Warok, with bow and pouch	25.00
Weequay, with spear.	20.00
Wicket W. Warrick, with spear	15.00
Wicket W. Warrick (Ewoks)	12.00
Yak Face, with staff, foreign release	275.00
Yoda, with **brown snake** and stick	25.00
Yoda, with **orange snake** and stick.	20.00
Zuckuss, with rifle.	10.00

Replica Equipment (1997)

Set #1: 25 different weapons.	$19.00
Set #2: 16 different weapons.	12.00
Replica Stormtrooper helmet	5.00

These are **not** by Kenner. They are advertised in such places as *Previews* magazine for sale in comic shops. They include lightsabers of various colors, telescoping and regular, and just about anything else needed to complete your loose figure, if you don't have the authentic weapon. Of course, it makes it easy to fool the unsuspecting, as well. Be careful so that you do not fall into this category yourself!

MAIL-INS

Mail-Ins

Boba Fett with Rocket Launcher (mail-in offer) unpainted blue/gray with red missile, with mailer box and letter.	$200.00
Bossk, Boba Fett, Darth Vader, IG-88, in plastic bags with Kenner logo, plus white mailer box listing the figures (#38871, 1980)	200.00
Bossk (1980)	25.00
4-LOM (1982).	25.00
Admiral Ackbar (1983)	20.00
Nien Nunb (1983).	20.00
The Emperor (1984)	20.00
Anakin Skywalker (1985)	40.00

Sy Snootles and the Rebo Band (Kenner 1985)

CLASSIC SERIES—MULTI-PACKS

Only one multi-pack of new figures was produced as part of the classic series—Sy Snootles and the Rebo Band. These exotic musicians came on a header card as part of the Return of the Jedi series. If it had been the '90s they would have been put out in a window box instead.

SY SNOOTLES AND THE REBO BAND

Sy Snootles and the Rebo Band (#71360, 1984)	
Original *Return of the Jedi* header card	$150.00
Reissue on Tri-Logo header card	100.00
Loose: Sy Snootles, Droopy McCool or Max Rebo, each	15.00

RE-ISSUE SETS

While no other new figures came out in multi-packs, Kenner did produced "Action Figure Sets" of three re-issue (i.e. left over) figures for each of the three movies. They were subtitled "Hero Set," "Villain Set," "Rebel Set," etc. They are quite scarce and there is some uncertainty as to their value.

Two six-pack sets of figures were issued for *The Empire Strikes Back* movie. These are not as valuable as the three packs. Last, and least, *Return of the Jedi* two-packs were issued with leftover figures. They are worth the price of the two loose figures contained in the pack (if they have their weapons) and maybe an additional dollar or two for oddity.

Star Wars Action Figure Sets—Three-Packs
Villain Set: Darth Vader, Stormtrooper and Death

Two-Pack: Snowtrooper and Han Solo Trenchcoat (Kenner 1984)

Squad Commander (#38650) $1,000.00
Hero Set: Han Solo, Princess Leia Organa and Ben
  (Obi-Wan) Kenobi (#38660) 1,000.00
Android Set: C-3PO, R2-D2 & Chewbacca (#38640) 1,000.00

Star Wars Three Packs with backdrops
Hero Set: Luke X-Wing Pilot, Ben Kenobi & Han
  Solo (#39450) 1,250.00
Droid Set: R5-D4, Death Star Droid, Power Droid
  (#39460) 1,250.00
Villain Set: Sand People, Boba Fett, Snaggletooth
  (#39470) 1,250.00
Creature Set: Hammerhead, Walrus Man, Greedo
  (#39480) 1,250.00

The Empire Strikes Back—Three Packs
Rebel Set: 2-1B, Princess Leia Organa (Hoth
  Outfit), and Rebel Commander (#69650) 900.00
Bespin Set: Han Solo (Bespin Outfit) Ugnaught, and
  Lobot (#69660) 900.00
Imperial Set: Imperial Commander, Dengar, and
  AT-AT Driver (#69670) 900.00
Rebel Set: Princess Leia Organa (Hoth Outfit),
  Artoo-Detoo (R2-D2) with sensorscope, and
  Luke Skywalker (Hoth Battle Gear) (#70040) . . . 900.00
Bespin Set: See-Threepio (C-3PO) with Removable
  Limbs, Ugnaught, and Cloud Car Pilot (#70070) . . 900.00
Imperial Set: Zuckuss, AT-AT Driver, and Imperial
  TIE Fighter Pilot (#70080) 900.00

Hoth Rebels: Han (Hoth), Rebel Soldier, (FX-7) 900.00
Bespin Alliance: Bespin Security Guard (white),
  Lando, Luke (Bespin) 900.00
Imperial Forces: Bossk, Imperial Stormtrooper
  (Hoth Battle Gear), IG-88 . . . . 900.00

The Empire Strikes Back—Six-Packs
Rebel Soldier, C-3PO, R2-D2, Han Solo (Hoth),
  Darth Vader and Stormtrooper (Hoth) (#39320) . 750.00
Darth Vader, Stormtrooper (Hoth Battle Gear), AT-AT
  Driver, Rebel Soldier, IG-88 & Yoda (#93390) . . . 750.00

Return of the Jedi—Three Packs
Admiral Ackbar, General Madine, and Rebel
  Commando (#93550) 750.00
Gamorrean Guard, Squid Head, and Bib Fortuna
  (#93570) 750.00
Rebel Set: Admiral Ackbar, Leia (Boushh), Chief
  Chirpa 750.00
Imperial Set: Biker Scout, Emperor's Royal Guard,
  Bib Fortuna 750.00

STAR WARS: NEW FIGURES

THE POWER OF THE FORCE (NEW)
Kenner (1995–98)

Kenner reintroduced the *Star Wars* action figures starting in 1995—almost two years before the release of the Star Wars Trilogy, Special Edition. Better early than late! The first item to appear was the Classic Edition 4-Pack and, in some ways, it is the functional equivalent of the Early Bird Figures from the original series—an initial four figures which are not on their own header cards.

The Classic Edition 4-Pack caused quite a bit of controversy when it first appeared because the figures were very close to being identical to the original Luke Skywalker, Han Solo, Darth Vader and Chewbacca from 1978. These original loose figures sell for over $25.00 each and there was some fear that collectors could be duped. Just enough difference between new and old was discovered so that these fears proved groundless. Now the 4-pack has risen considerably in value, so it is even less likely that someone will open one and try to pass off the new figures as the old ones.

If you find one of these 4-packs in below average condition and buy it to obtain the loose figures, don't ignore the trading cards. The cards form a distinct group of promo cards for the *Star Wars* Widevision trading cards series and are worth about $8.00 each or about $25.00 for the set.

Star Wars Power of the Force Classic Edition
  4-Pack, including Luke Skywalker, Han Solo,
  Darth Vader, and Chewbacca with 4 Topps
  "Star Wars Widevision" special promo cards
  K01–K04 (#69595, July 1995) $60.00

The reintroduction of *Star Wars* action figures was a resounding success and hooked many collectors who had played with *Star Wars* figures as kids when they first came out. Collector interest in the original figures—always strong got even stronger.

Classic Edition 4-Pack (Kenner 1995)

Packaging Variations

The most significant packaging changes in the new series is in the color of the header card. The 1995 and 1996 header cards have a red or orange laser blast running diagonally across them, while the 1997 cards have a green laser blast. Shadows of the Empire figures, from late 1996, are on purple laser blast cards. In 1998, the cards remained green, but all figures have a "Freeze Frame Action Slide." Most 1997 green cards have a holographic picture sticker, but limited quantities of many of the figures were issued without this sticker. All green cards, and late 1996 red cards for some figures, have collection numbers at the top. In 1998, the collection numbers are at the bottom and the cards are color coded by collection. Hopefully, the following information will help you sort all of these changes out.

Package Printing Numbers

All of Kenner's 1995–98 action figures have a small printed number on the back, at the bottom, which can be used to distinguish earlier packages from later ones. The first six digits of the number are unique to the particular figure and do not change even if the UPC code or the figure's name are changed. It's no doubt used at the factory to see that the figures are matched up with the correct header cards. However, it's the two digits after the "decimal point" that collectors look at. These are package revision numbers and their function is similar to the "extension" part of a computer file name. The first version of each package is numbered ".00" and each time there is a printing change this number is increased, so that if there have been three changes, the number will read ".03" and so on. Many of the figures have had printing changes on their header cards. These range from name changes for the figure or his weapons, "Collection number" changes, and photo changes, down to correction of tiny typographical errors. All of these changes affect the value of the figure, and the earlier version is almost always the more valuable. If you are at a store or a show, and can't remember whether the "Han Solo in Carbonite Freezing Chamber" or "Han Solo in Carbonite Block" is the scarce figure, or whether the "Collection 2" or the "Collection 3" Grand Moff Tarkin figure is the first version, just look at this code. The one you want is the one with the lower revision code, usually ".00". However, this number only works for *printing*

Ben (Obi-Wan) Kenobi
Long Lightsaber (Kenner 1996)

changes, not for variations in the figure itself.

Throughout this book, these numbers are reported in [brackets] so as to distinguish them from UPC codes, which are listed in (parentheses).

POWER OF THE FORCE (NEW)

Princess Leia was the hot early figure. She did not appear on the back of the header cards and many collectors thought she had not been released. Actually, she had been part of the original shipments and the only reason she was scarce was that every collector bought her as soon as she was spotted. Then she was not shipped for a while and prices increased still further. In the fall of 1996 she appeared again, along with Lando Calrissian from the second batch, who had also been scarce, and prices fell. Some collectors must have taken this personally, because we have seen these figures in stores with their header cards broken intentionally.

The last two figures, Jedi Knight Luke and Han Solo in Carbonite, shipped with the Shadows of the Empire figures. A wording variation was detected on the Han Solo in Carbonite package, providing some collector interest.

Figure Variations

In addition to the packaging variations, there are several important variations in the figures. The one that affects the most figures is the change from the ridiculously long early lightsabers to shorter lightsabers. This yielded variations for Darth Vader, Luke Skywalker, and Ben (Obi-Wan) Kenobi. The later figure also had a packaging change with his original head photo being replaced by a full-figure photo. If short lightsabers were not enough, some figures were found with short lightsabers in the plastic slots designed for long sabers. Luke Skywalker (Jedi Knight) originally came with a brown vest, but this was switched to black, matching the rest of his costume. Boba Fett was issued with a black circle on the back of each hand. Originally he had a bar across this circle, forming two "half-circles." A very few have even been found with a black circle on only one hand and they are very scarce, and valuable.

Except for these few popular variations, all of the figures were shipped (and purchased) in enormous quantity, keeping the price for most figures at or near the retail level.

RED CARD SERIES
Kenner (1995–96)

3¾" Figures (Asst. #69570, 1995)

Ben (Obi-Wan) Kenobi (#69576) head photo,
    long lightsaber [.00] $50.00
    Reissue, full-figure photo, long lightsaber [.01] . . . 50.00
    Reissue, full-figure photo, short lightsaber 15.00
    Variation: short lightsaber in long tray, scarce . . 1,500.00
Chewbacca (#69578) [.00] 15.00
C-3PO (#69573) [.00] 10.00
Darth Vader (#69572) with long lightsaber [.00] 25.00
    Reissue, short lightsaber 15.00
    Variation: short lightsaber, long slot 45.00
Han Solo (#69577) [.00] 15.00
Luke Skywalker (#69571) long lightsaber [.00] 40.00

Reissue, short lightsaber, long slot 700.00
    Reissue, short lightsaber 15.00
Princess Leia Organa (#69579) 3 bands on belt 20.00
    Variation: 2 bands on belt [.00] 15.00
R2-D2 (#69574) [.00] 15.00
Stormtrooper (#69575) [.00] 12.00
Second Batch (Asst. #69570, March 1996)
Boba Fett (#69582) half circles on hand [.00] 50.00
    Variation: half circle one hand, full circle on
    other hand, scarce 350.00
    Reissue, with full circle on both hands [.01] 15.00
Han Solo in Hoth Gear (#69587) open hand [.00] 25.00
    Variation, closed hand 15.00
Lando Calrissian (#69583) [.00] 10.00
Luke Skywalker in Dagobah Fatigues (#69588)
    long lightsaber [.00] 30.00
    Reissue, short lightsaber [.01] 20.00
    Variation: short lightsaber in long slot 25.00
Luke Skywalker in X-Wing Fighter Pilot Gear
    (#69581) long lightsaber [.00] 25.00
    Reissue, short lightsaber 15.00
    Variation: short lightsaber in long slot 20.00
TIE Fighter Pilot (#69584) warning on sticker [.00] . . . 25.00
    Reissue, warning on card [.01] 12.00
TIE Fighter Pilot (#69673) [.02] 6.00
Yoda (#69586) [.00] 12.00
Yoda (#69672) [.01] with hologram 35.00
Third Batch (Sept. 1996 with Shadows of the Empire figures)
Han Solo in "Carbonite Freezing Chamber"
    (#69613) [.00] 18.00
    Reissue: in "Carbonite Block" (#69613) [.01] 12.00
Jedi Knight Luke Skywalker (#69596) brown vest [.00] . . 75.00
    Variation: black vest [.00] 12.00

SHADOWS OF THE EMPIRE

Shadows of the Empire figures appeared in September 1996 and were very popular. All the collectors bought them and then looked at every minute detail in an effort to spot some valuable variation. Unfortunately, none were found and

Red Card Figures: C-3PO, 1st Batch; Han Solo (Hoth Gear), 2nd Batch; and Luke Skywalker (Jedi Knight) 3rd Batch (Kenner 1995–96)

*Princess Leia (Boushh Disguise)
Shadows of the Empire card (Kenner 1996)*

*Tatooine Stormtrooper, Collection 1
red transition card (Kenner 1996)*

none of the figures seemed to be scarce. They are based on the book series, not any of the movies.

All of the Shadows of the Empire figures were available at a few Kay-Bee stores in Dec. 1997. There were only a handful of each figure, but they stayed on the racks for several weeks. This indicated that most collectors were already well supplied and that price increases would be modest, at best. With no one looking for these figures, everyone was surprised when, in early 1998, it was reported that Princess Leia in Boushh Disguise had been reissued on a purple header card that said "Collection 1." This packaging variation has proven to be extremely scarce.

PURPLE CARD SERIES
Kenner (1996)

3¾" Figures (Sept. 1996)
Chewbacca (Bounty Hunter) (#69562) [.00] $12.00
Dash Rendar (#69561) [.00] 20.00
Luke Skywalker (Imperial Guard) (#69566) [.00] 20.00
Prince Xizor (#69594) [.00] 12.00
Princess Leia (Boushh Disguise) (#69602) [.00] 12.00
    Reissue, Princess Leia (Boushh) **Collection 1**
    (#69818) [.01] 300.00
Two-Packs: *See Multi-Figures, infra*

POWER OF THE FORCE 1996

The fourth batch of Power of the Force figures appeared

in December 1996 with the captions "Collection 1" or "Collection 2" at the top. Nobody knew what that was supposed to mean. The two collections appeared at the same time, and the earliest versions came on a header card with a red laser blast, the same color used on the other new "Power of the Force" figures from 1995–96.

These proved to be quite scarce, as the header cards were all quickly changed to a green laser blast design. Just as collectors were digesting these changes, holographic sticker pictures were added to the cards.

The Tatooine Stormtrooper (red-carded) and the Sandtrooper (green-carded) are identical—only the name had been changed to confuse the weary collector. That figure, and most of the other initial figures in Collections 1 and 2, also had changes in the name of their weapon. R5-D4 has no weapons, but a small parts warning was added and the latch was changed from straight to hooked by the time the green cards appeared.

TRANSITION—RED "COLLECTION" CARDS
Kenner (1996)

Fourth Batch (Dec. 1996)
Collection 1 Figures (Asst. #69570, Dec. 1996)
Death Star Gunner (#69608) [.00] $25.00
Greedo (#69606) [.00]. 25.00
Tatooine Stormtrooper (#69601) [.00] 25.00

Tusken Raider, Collection 2 red transition card (Kenner 1996)

Collection 2 Figures (Asst. #69605, Dec. 1996)
Jawas (#69607) 25.00
Luke Skywalker in "Stormtrooper Disguise"
    (#69604) [.00] 35.00
Momaw Nadon "Hammerhead" (#69629) [.00]. 35.00
R5-D4 (#69598) no small parts warning and
    straight latch [.00] 25.00
R5-D4 (#69598) with small parts warning and
    straight latch 20.00
Tusken Raider (#69603) closed hand [.00] 25.00
    Variation: open hand. 75.00

POWER OF THE FORCE 1997

As 1997 began, the three Collection 1 and and five Collection 2 figures were appearing on green header cards with holo pictures. All of the early interest focused on the year's most popular figure, Princess Leia as Jabba's Prisoner. This scantily-clad number initially sold for $15.00 to $20.00 as all of the early ones were grabbed by eager collectors or dealers. However, more appeared and the price started to fall. As still more arrived and the figure became common, the price fell to be the same as the other figures.

Many new figures appeared in both Collection 1 and Collection 2, and figures for Collection 3 started to arrive. Some of these early 1997 figures were shipped in staggering quantities and figures such as Bib Fortuna, Emperor Palpatine, Lando Calrissian Skiff Guard, Bossk, 2-1B,

Admiral Ackbar, 4-LOM, and Grand Moff Tarkin were mind-numbingly common.

Collection Numbers

The idea of the "collection number" was to sort the action figures into groups so that "Collection 1" would be the Rebel Alliance, "Collection 3" would be the Galactic Empire and "Collection 2" would be the various non-aligned aliens. The point of all this, and the real idea, was that the boxes shipped to the stores would indicate which collection was in the box and so the store would have to devote space for all three collections and there would always be a wide variety for sale—plenty of Rebels, plenty of Aliens and plenty of Imperial forces.

Unfortunately, there weren't equal numbers of each type, and new figures were not added at uniform rates in each group, but almost all boxes have to contain 16 figures. Except for the occasional "Block Case" of all one figure, Kenner doesn't ship more than three of any one figure in any assortment, and usually it's no more than two.

The result was that a lot of figures came out in the "wrong" collection and later in the "right" collection. The seven most important (i.e. valuable) collection "errors" are Grand Moff Tarkin, Luke Skywalker Jedi Knight, Luke Skywalker in Ceremonial outfit Ponda Baba, Rebel Fleet Trooper, Weequay Skiff Guard, and Yoda, all of whom came out first in Collection 2, but were soon switched to other collections (Luke in Ceremonial, Luke Jedi Knight, Yoda, and Rebel Fleet Trooper, Collection 1; other three to Collection 3). All of these are quite difficult to find in the error collection and are worth about three to four times as much as they are with the correct number.

The next most valuable error is Boba Fett from Collection 1, which sell for about 50% more than the correct Collection 3 version. The other collection errors: Hoth Rebel Soldier, AT-ST driver, Han Solo Carbonite, Luke in Hoth Gear, TIE-Fighter Pilot, and Yoda, all from Collection 2 together with Emperor Palpatine, Darth Vader, and Bib Fortuna from Collection 1 have proven to be fairly easy to find and command only a small premium. Overall, that's 17 collection error figures to look for.

Peg Holes and Stand-Up Bubbles

There are two other packaging variations that you can see on the 1995–97 figure line by looking at the peg holes used for hanging the figures and at the plastic bubbles on the card.

Around June 1997, or so, figures started showing up with a slightly wider hook-shaped hanging slot cut out at the top of the package. This lets that scarce figure at the back of the store's hanging peg easily fall off right into your hands (and the figures next to it fall off onto the floor). The easiest place to notice this difference is to look at the horizontal length of the slot, and particularly at the downward hanging part of the header card that remains. It's about 25% wider than the original.

Around the same time, figures appeared with an altered

Sandtrooper, Collection 1, green card, plain picture (Kenner 1997)

Package revision numbers ".00" and ".01" (Kenner 1996–97)

plastic bubble. The original plastic bubble is a simple rectangular box with slightly tapered sides so that the box is slightly smaller at the top, than at the base. The new plastic bubble has a more pronounced slant at the top, but the big change is at the bottom. An outward slanting secondary bubble has been added to the shape, so that the carded figure will stand up if placed on a flat surface.

Holo Stickers or Plain Picture

A holo sticker picture was added to the header cards about the time that they switched from red/orange to green. The very earliest green cards were for the three "Collection 1" and five "Collection 2" figures that appeared briefly on red header cards. The first boxes of these green-carded figures had plain pictures of the characters on the front, similar to the ones used on all the red cards. Soon, these green-carded figures and all the subsequent ones had holographic picture stickers over the plain picture. Initially the holographic stickers could be removed (carefully) to reveal the plain picture underneath. No one noticed that the holo stickers had different glue starting in about July 1997 and could no longer be removed without leaving a residue and making a few bubbles in the cardboard underneath. Figures would occassionally show up without the holo sticker and in early 1998, when the green cards were about to be phased out in favor of the Freeze Frame cards, a large number of tail-end green cards showed up without holo pictures. Probably Kenner ran out of the holo

pictures and didn't want to print more.

The differences in peg holes, bubbles, and presence or absence of a holo sticker are all legitimate packaging variations and not errors. Initially there were even price differences, but today there are none. There is a lesson here. The lesson is "Don't pay too much for that supposedly scarce variation, it may not matter much in the end." Go look for it in the stores, where you won't pay a premium if you find it.

As the packaging changes occurred, collectors started to notice changes in the eight-digit number codes on the package back. The code for the first issue of any figure ended in ".00" and as the package changed, the code changed to ".01" and ".02" while the first six digits stayed the same, even when the figure got a new UPC code. Actually these codes appeared on the packages from 1995 on, but collectors had not payed any attention to them until 1997 when the large number of packaging changes made their function, and usefulness, clear. These printing/packaging codes are noted in this book in [brackets] to distinguish them from UPC codes, which are noted in (parentheses).

Figure Variations

Boba Fett occassionally comes with the same "black circle on one hand" or other scarce variations that occurred in the red cards, while Ponda Baba has been found with a grey beard instead of the normal black bird. These and a few other variations have had the most significant effect on price. However, Han Solo in Endor Gear changed his pants color from Navy blue (almost black) to brown, but this has not affected its value. These variations are covered more thoroughly in the Action Figur—Alphabetical section.

Summary

With so many variations, what do you look for? Start with the three figures on Collection 1 and five figures on Collection 2 transition red cards, and the scarce figures on cards with the "wrong" collection numbers. Basically, you can never go wrong with a package having printing number ".00." Pay no attention to changes in the peg hooks and bubbles and to any card variation after ".01." Many of the card printing changes from the original ".00" card to the corrected ".01" are quite trivial and where both cards are generally available, there is little difference in price. This variation

Bib Fortuna, Collection 1, Luke Skywalker in Hoth Gear, Collection 2 and Ponda Baba, Collection 3 (Kenner 1997)

seems most likely to mirror the variation between 20-back to 21-back cards from the original series.

Enough plain picture figures were issued so that there is no difference in value between the plain and holo picture versions. If you are like me, you think that the plain picture is more attractive, so you look for it anyway.

GREEN CARD SERIES
Kenner (1997)

Reissues of Transition Figures (Early 1997)
Death Star Gunner (#69608) Col. 1 [.01] $12.00
Greedo (#69606) Col. 1 [.01]. 12.00
Jawas (#69607) Col. 2 [.01] 15.00
Luke Skywalker (Stormtrooper Disguise) (#69819)
   Col. 2 [.01]. 12.00
Momaw Nadon "Hammerhead" (#69629) Col. 2 [.01]. . 12.00
R5-D4 (#69598) Col. 2 [.01] with warning 20.00
Sandtrooper (prev. Tatooine Stormtrooper) Col. 1
   (#69601) [.01] 15.00
Tusken Raider (#69603) Col. 2, closed hand 45.00
Tusken Raider (#69603) Col. 2 [.01] open hand. 12.00

Reissues of Red Cards (April–Aug. 1997)
Ben (Obi-Wan) Kenobi (#69576) Col. 1 [.02] 6.00
Boba Fett (#69582) Col. 1 [.02]. 30.00
Chewbacca (#69578) Col. 1 [.01] 6.00
C-3PO (#69573) Col. 1 [.01] 10.00
Han Solo (#69577) Col. 1 [.01] 10.00
Jedi Knight Luke Skywalker (#69816) Col. 1 [.02] 10.00
Luke Skywalker (Stormtrooper Disguise) (#69819)
   Col. 1 [.02]. 12.00
Luke Skywalker (X-Wing Fighter Pilot) (#69581)
   Col. 1 [.02]. 15.00
Princess Leia Organa (#69579) Col. 1 [.01] 12.00
Princess Leia (Boushh Disguise) (#69818) Col. 1
   [.01 & .02]] 18.00
R2-D2 (#69574) Col. 1 [.01] 15.00

Yoda (#69586) Col. 1 [.03] 12.00

Second Batches: (March–Aug. 1997)
AT-ST Driver (#69623) Col. 2 [.00]. 12.00
Bespin Han Solo (#69719) Col. 1 [.00] 6.00
Bib Fortuna (#69812) Col. 2 [.01] 10.00
Bib Fortuna (#69634) Col. 1 [.00] 12.00
Bossk (#69617) Col. 2 [.00 & .01] 12.00
Darth Vader (#69572) Col. 1 [.01] 15.00
Darth Vader (#69802) Col. 3 [.02] 6.00
Death Star Gunner (#69809) Col. 3 .02] 10.00
Emperor Palpatine (#69633) Col. 1 [.00] 12.00
Emperor Palpatine (#69811) Col. 3 [.01] 6.00
Han Solo in Endor Gear (#69621) Col. 1 [.00]
   blue pants 12.00
Hoth Rebel Soldier (#69631) Col. 2 [.00] 12.00
Hoth Rebel Soldier (#69821) Col. 1 [.01] 10.00
Jedi Knight Luke Skywalker (#69816) Col. 2 [.01] 25.00
Lando Calrissian as Skiff Guard (#69622) Col. 1 [.00] . 10.00
Luke Skywalker in Hoth Gear (#69619) Col. 2 [.00] . . . 12.00
Luke Skywalker (Hoth Gear) (#69822) Col. 1 [.01] 10.00
Ponda Baba (#69708) Col. 2 [.00]. 40.00
Ponda Baba (#69708) Col. 3 [.01] 6.00
Rebel Fleet Trooper (#69696) Col. 2 [.00] 30.00
Rebel Fleet Trooper (#69696) Col. 1 [.01] 10.00
Sandtrooper (#69808) Col. 3 [.02] 6.00
Stormtrooper (#69803) Col. 3 [.01] 10.00
TIE Fighter Pilot (#69806) Col. 3 [.04] 12.00
TIE Fighter Pilot (#69673) Col. 2 [.03] 12.00
2-1B Medic Droid (#69618) Col. 2 [.00] 10.00
Weequay Skiff Guard (#69707) Col. 2 [.00] 30.00
Weequay Skiff Guard (#69707) Col. 3 [.01] 6.00
Yoda (#69672) Col. 2 [.02] 10.00

Third Batches (Sept.–Nov. 1997)
Admiral Ackbar (#69686) Col. 2 [.00] 10.00
ASP-7 Droid (#69704) Col. 2 [.00] 10.00
AT-ST Driver (#69823) Col. 3 [.02] 6.00
Boba Fett (#69804) Col. 3 [.03] 20.00
Dengar (#69687) Col. 2 [.00]. 12.00

Han Solo in Endor Gear, green card Collection 1 (brown pants) (Kenner 1997); Back of card with "Sealt-Marie" error (Kenner 1998)

Emperor's Royal Guard (#69717) Col. 3 [.00] 10.00
EV-9D9 (#69722) Col. 2 [.00] 12.00
4-Lom (#69688) Col. 2 [.00] 12.00
Gamorrean Guard (#69693) Col. 2 [.00] 10.00
Garindan (Long Snout) (#69706) Col. 3 [.00]. 6.00
Grand Moff Tarkin (#69702) Col. 3 [.01]. 6.00
Grand Moff Tarkin (#69702) Col. 2 [.00]. 40.00
Han Solo (Endor Gear) (#69621) Col. 1
   brown pants 15.00
Han Solo in Carbonite (#69613) Col. 1 [.03] 8.00
Han Solo in Carbonite (#69613) Col. 2 [.02] 8.00
Luke Skywalker (Ceremonial Outfit) (#69691)
   Col. 1 [.01]. 8.00
Luke Skywalker (Ceremonial Outfit) (#69691)
   Col. 2 [.00]. 40.00
Malakili (Rancor Keeper) (#69723) Col. 2 [.00] 10.00
Nien Nunb (#69694) Col. 2 [.00] 10.00
Princess Leia Organa (Jabba's Prisoner) (#69683)
   Col. 1 [.00]. 6.00
Saelt-Marae (Yak Face) (#69721) Col. 2 [.00] 12.00
Snowtrooper (#69632) Col. 3 [.00]. 8.00

Special
Four figure set of Han Solo in Endor Gear, Lando
   Calrissian as Skiff Guard, AT-ST driver, and
   Darth Vader (J.C. Penney catalog 1997) 25.00

POWER OF THE FORCE 1998

The new header card packaging for 1998 added a 35mm Freeze Frame Action Slide as an in-package premium and color codes the "Collection Number" (Red for Collection 1, Yellow for Collection 2 and Blue for Collection 3) on a strip at the bottom of the package. The color code stripes were a great help in separating new packages from old ones in the early days. Loose figures do **not** include the 35mm slide. In-package premiums are a separate collectible once they are removed from the package.

Just about every beast, accessory, and vehicle issued in 1998 came with an exclusive figure.

The high points of the 1998 figures included the first Biggs Darklighter figure, Darth Vader in removable helmet, with his finely sculpted head revealed, Captain Piett, Ishi Tib, Mon Mothma, and the Expanded Universe figures.

The first batch of Freeze Frame Action Slide Collection 1 figures arrived on schedule in February 1998. Happily or unhappily, they all had a printing error and so corrected versions, with new printing numbers arrived quickly as well. The error is on the back of the header card, under the picture of Jabba and Han, where weary collectors are advised to "Collect all these *Star Wars* Action Figures." In the list that follows, "Saelt-Marae" is misspelled as "Sealt-Marie"—two errors in just 10 letters. The error is the same on all packages and the corrected version has the higher printing number: ".01" versus ".00" for the new figures and other numbers on the reissues.

This series of figures has been very popular with collectors. Distribution was spotty and some reissue figures were very hard to track down. Prices are generally higher than prices for the 1997 figures. However, a large supply of many of the figures appeared at local stores in March and April 2000. Prices fell as all of the Collection 1 figures with the "Sealt Marie" printing error were available, along with such scarce figures as the new R2-D2 with the "Imperial trash compactor" slide.

GREEN CARD—
FREEZE FRAME SERIES
Kenner (1998)

3¾" Figures (1998) with Freeze Frame Action Slides
8D8 (#69834) Col. 2 [.00] $10.00
Admiral Ackbar (#69686) Col. 2 [.01]. 12.00
AT-AT Driver *see Fan Club Exclusives below*

Han Solo in Carbonite, Collection 1, Gamorrean Guard, Collection 2, and Emperor Palpatine, Collection 3 (Kenner 1998)

AT-ST Driver (#69623) Col. 3 [.03] scarce 75.00
Ben (Obi-Wan) Kenobi *renamed Obi-Wan (Ben) Kenobi.* 10.00
Biggs Darklighter (#69758) Col. 2 [.00] 20.00
Boba Fett (#69804) Col. 3 [.04] 50.00
 Variations, **Black circle** on one hand or **no circle**
 or **no emblem** on chest, or **no skull** on shoulder . 500.00
C-3PO (Pull-Apart Feature) (#69832) Col. 1 [.00] 15.00
Captain Piett (#69757) Col. 3 [.00] nameplate error . . . 30.00
 Reissue with "Blaster Pistol and Baton" [.00] 100.00
Chewbacca as Boushh's Bounty (#69882) Col. 1 [.00] . 15.00
Darth Vader (Removable Cape) (#69802) Col. 3 [.03] . . 20.00
Darth Vader (Removable Helmet, Detachable
 Hand) (#69836) Col. 3 [.00] 40.00
Death Star Droid *see Fan Club Exclusives below*
Death Star Trooper (#69838) Col. 3 [.00] 25.00
Emperor Palpatine (#69811) Col. 3 [.02] 10.00
Emperor's Royal Guard (#69717) Col. 3 [.01] 25.00
Endor Rebel Soldier (#69716) Col. 1 [.00] error 20.00
 Reissue, "Saelt-Marae" corrected [.01] 10.00
EV-9D9 (#69722) Col. 2 [.01] 15.00
Ewoks: Wicket & Logray (#69711) Col. 2 [.00] 18.00
Gamorrean Guard (#69693) Col. 2 [.01] 15.00
Garindan (#69706) Col. 3 [.01] 40.00
Grand Moff Tarkin (#69702) Col. 3 [.02] 12.00
Han Solo (#69577) Col. 1 [.02] 18.00
Han Solo in Carbonite (#69817) Col. 1 [.04]
 misspelling 20.00
 Reissue, "Saelt-Marae" corrected [.05] 10.00
Bespin Han Solo with (#69719) Col. 1 [.01] misspelling. 20.00
 Reissue, "Saelt-Marae" corrected [.02] 10.00
 Reissue, "Unbeknownst" corrected [.03] 15.00
Han Solo in Endor Gear (#69621) Col. 1 [.01]
 misspelling 20.00
 Reissue, "Saelt-Marae" corrected [.02] 12.00
Hoth Rebel Soldier (#69821) Col. 1 [.02] misspelling. . . 20.00
 Reissue, "Saelt-Marae" corrected [.03] 10.00
Ishi Tib (#69754) Col. 3 [.00] 20.00
Lak Sivrak (#69753) Col. 2 [.00] 20.00
Lando Calrissian as Skiff Guard (#69622) Col. 1
 [.01] misspelling 20.00
 Reissue, "Saelt-Marae" corrected [.02] 10.00

Lando Calrissian in General's Gear (#69756) Col. 1
 [.00] misspelling 20.00
 Reissue, "Saelt-Marae" corrected [.01] 10.00
Lobot (#69856) Col. 1 [.00] 15.00
Bespin Luke Skywalker with "Detachable Hand" and
 with "Lightsaber and Blaster Pistol" (#69713)
 Col. 1 [.00] with misspelling 30.00
 Reissue, "Saelt-Marae" corrected [.01] 10.00
Luke Skywalker in Ceremonial Outfit (#69691) Col. 1
 [.01 sic] 12.00
Luke Skywalker in Stormtrooper Disguise (#69819)
 Col. 1 [.03] misspelling 25.00
 Reissue, "Saelt-Marae" corrected [.04] 12.00
Luke Skywalker (New Likeness, Blast Shield
 Helmet) (#69691) Col. 1 [.00] 15.00
Malakili (Rancor Keeper) (#69723) Col. 2 [.01] 15.00
Mon Mothma (#69859) Col. 1 [.00] 20.00
Nien Nunb (#69694) Col. 2 [.01] 20.00
Obi-Wan (Ben) Kenobi (#69576) Col. 1 [.03]
 misspelling 25.00
 Reissue, "Saelt-Marae" corrected [.04] 20.00
Orrimaarko (Prune Face) (#69858) Col. 1 [.00] 15.00
Pote Snitkin *see Fan Club Exclusives below*
Princess Leia Organa (New Likeness) (#69824)
 Col. 1 [.00] 10.00
Princess Leia Organa in Ewok Celebration Outfit
 (#69714) Col. 1 [.00] misspelling 20.00
 Reissue, "Saelt-Marae" corrected [.01] 10.00
Princess Leia Organa as Jabba's Prisoner (#69683)
 Col. 1 [.01] misspelling 15.00
 Reissue, "Saelt-Marae" corrected [.02] 10.00
Princess Leia in Hoth Gear *see Fan Club Exclusives below*
Rebel Fleet Trooper (#69696) Col. 1 [.01] misspelling . . 25.00
 Reissue (#69696) Col. 1 [.01 sticker] 20.00
 Reissue, "Saelt-Marae" corrected [.02] 18.00
Ree-Yees (#69839) Col.3 [.00] 25.00
R2-D2 with (Pop-Up Scanner) (# 69831) Col. 1 [.00]. . . 15.00
 Variation, "Imperial trash compactor" on slide 50.00
Saelt-Marae (Yak Face) (#69721) Col. 2 [.01] 15.00
Sandtrooper (#69808) Col. 3 [.03] scarce 125.00
Snowtrooper (#69632) Col. 3 [.02] 20.00

Princess Leia, Expanded Universe; Ben (Obi-Wan) Kenobi, Flashback Photo; and Han Solo, CommTech (Kenner 1998–99)

Stormtrooper (#69803) Col. 3 [.02] 15.00
TIE Fighter Pilot (#69806) Col. 3 [.05] 50.00
Ugnaught (#69837) Col. 2 [.00] 12.00
Weequay Skiff Guard (#69707) Col. 3 [.02] scarce . . . 350.00
Zuckuss (#69747) Col. 3 [.00] 30.00

Fan Club exclusives (early 1999) sold in sets of two
AT-AT Driver (#69864) Col. 3 [.0000] 25.00
Death Star Droid (#69862) Col. 3 [.00} 25.00
Pote Snitkin with (#69863) Col. 3 [.00} 25.00
Princess Leia Organa in Hoth Gear (#84143) Col. 3
    [.0000] 25.00

3-D PLAYSCENE
(Expanded Universe)
Kenner (1998)

These figures are from the comics, video games, and novels figures, and not from the movies. They were released in November 1998, and include Mara Jade and Grand Admiral Thrawn, from *Heir to the Empire*, and Kyle Katarn, from *Dark Forces*. They are very popular with collectors. No one has reported finding figures with ".00" revision numbers, and the numbers lised are the earliest known.

Expanded Universe, 3-D PlayScene figures
Dark Empire comics
Clone Emperor Palpatine (#69886) [.02] $20.00
Imperial Sentinel (#69887) [.01] 20.00
Luke Skywalker (in Black Cloak) (#69883) [.01]. 20.00
Princess Leia (in Black Cloak) (#69884) [.03] 20.00

Heir to the Empire novels
Grand Admiral Thrawn (#69888) [.02] 25.00
Mara Jade (#69891) [.03] 25.00
Spacetrooper (#69892) [.03] 25.00

Dark Forces video game
Dark Trooper (#69894) [.01] 30.00

Kyle Katarn (#69893) [.02] 30.00

FLASHBACK PHOTO
Kenner (1998–99)

Flashback Photo figures came with a detachable pull-down photo which showed the figure from the original movies, and, when pulled down, showed the same or a related figure from the (then) forthcoming Episode I movie. These revealed some essential plot points for that movie, such as that Queen Amidala is Luke and Leia's mother.

The first wave of eight figures appeared in November 1998, and a second wave of three new figures came out in June 1999. They have four digit revision numbers, as do their Flashback Photos. Even the Flashback Photos have variations. The earlier ones have a down-arrow on the front and back of the pull-tab, while later ones have an up-arrow and a down-arrow on the front and no arrow on the back.

3¾" Figures (1998–99) with Flashback Photos
Anakin Skywalker (#84047) [.0000] $12.00
Aunt Beru (#84049) [.0000] 15.00
Ben (Obi-Wan) Kenobi (#84037) [.00] 10.00
C-3PO (#84041) [.0000] 10.00
Darth Vader (#84046) [.00] 10.00
Emperor Palpatine (#84042) [.00] 15.00
Hoth Chewbacca (#84051) [.00] 10.00
Luke Skywalker (#84036) [.00] 10.00
Princess Leia in Ceremonial Dress (#84038) [.01]
    with Celebration Gown photo (incorrect) 10.00
    with Freedom Fighter outfit (correct) 10.00
R2-D2 (#84043) [.01]
    Lightsaber packed left side 10.00
    Lightsaber packed right side 100.00
Yoda (#84039) [.00] 15.00

COMMTECH CHIP
Hasbro (1999)

CommTech Chip Figures appeared with a new batch of Star Wars figures in 1999. These are the same types of chips used on the *Episode I* figures listed below. Hasbro has not given up on selling the classic characters just because it has a whole new movie to work with. The chips had either a chrome or a white background.

The R2-D2 figure with holographic Princess Leia was supposed to have been omitted briefly because of production problems. Between hoarding and "briefly," most collectors can't find it at all. Princess Leia was designated as "Princess Leia Hood Up" on Hasbro's Web site, but not on the figure. Wuher was originally a *Star Wars Insider* magazine exclusive, but was later available in stores.

3¾" Figures (Hasbro 1999) with COMMTech Chips
Admiral Motti (#84366) [.00] $30.00
Darth Vader (#84203) [.00] 20.00
Greedo (#84201) [.0000] 8.00
Han Solo (#84202) [.0000] 8.00
Jawa with Gonk Droid (#84198) [.0000]
   with two foot holes 8.00
   with no foot holes 50.00
   with one foot hole 60.00
Luke Skywalker with "T-16 Skyhopper Model"
   (#84211) [.0000] 8.00
Princess Leia (#84361) [.0000] 25.00
R2-D2 with "Holographic" Princess Leia (#84199)
   [.0000] 45.00
   with foot peg on side of foot 300.00
Stormtrooper with "Battle Damage" (#84209) [.0000] . . 20.00
Wuher (#84389) [.0100] 15.00

STAR WARS:
EPISODE I FIGURES

STAR WARS EPISODE I— THE PHANTOM MENACE
Hasbro (1999–2000)

"A generation before Star Wars: A New Hope …. In a galaxy far, far away, an evil force is gaining strength and threatens an entire civilization. Two courageous Jedi, a young queen, a Gungan outcast, and a slave boy named Anakin, band together to save a planet under attack as the fate of the galaxy hangs in the balance."

The long, long awaited movie starred Jake Lloyd as young Anakin Skywalker, Ewan McGregor as a younger Obi-Wan Kenobi, Liam Neeson as Qui-Gon Jinn, and Natalie Portman as the teenage Queen Amidala. Anthony Daniels and Kenny Baker came back as C-3PO and R2-D2. Jar Jar Binks was voiced by Ahmed Best, but was completely computer generated. Supporting characters included Samuel L. Jackson as Mace Windu, Terence Stamp as Supreme Chancellor Valorum, and Brian Blessed as Boss Nass.

The Phantom Menace toy avalanche began on May 3, 1999 and most stores opened just after midnight to lines of eager collectors. Stock was adequate and most of the figures

Mace Windu, Episode I *Sneak Preview Mail-in Figure (Kenner 1999)*

were still available the following morning and for a few days. The figures sold well and many Toys "R" Us stores pulled their few remaining figures and had none for about a week to preserve stock for a previously scheduled pre-Memorial Day sale. Many secondary outlets such as drug stores and even grocery stores carried figures and they just kept coming.

Initial figures were shipped to toy stores in three "collections." Collections two and three came in boxes containing 16 figures, with five different figures in each box. Collection one came in a double length box of 32 figures with eight different. However, the Battle Droids came in four different design patterns and collectors naturally wanted one of each color. This turned out to be a good move as packaging changes made the earliest versions of the figures, with revision numbers ending in ".00", fairly scarce. Many stores only got "Collection 1" figures such as Battle Droids with revision numbers ending in ".0100". Even these proved to be worthwhile investments as package revision ".0200" was on the shelves within a month.

There were 16 additional figures added to the mix over the next year or so. None of these had package revisions, but there were some very scarce variations to look for. Common versions of all these figures were produced in huge quantities and remained on retailers' racks for years. Many can still be found for under $2.00.

This glut of unsold figures greatly reduced the production and distribution of the final 13 figures and they remain quite scarce. This fact is well known by toy store employees,

Obi-Wan Kenobi (Jedi Duel) Episode I *(Kenner 1999)*

Darth Maul (Jedi Duel) Episode I *(Kenner 1999)*

so they buy up any final figures as soon as they hit the racks and sell them to dealers or at shows.

Sneak Previews (1998–99) boxed
Stap and Battle Droid with "Firing Laser Missiles"
  (#84069) $35.00
Mace Windu (#84138) mail order 30.00

3¾" Figures (Hasbro 1999) with CommTech Chips
Early Figures: (May 1999)
Anakin Skywalker (Tatooine) (#84074) Col. 1 [.00]. . . $12.00
  Reissue [.0100] 7.00
Battle Droid (#84092) Col. 1
  Brown [.00]. 25.00
  Reissue Brown [.0100]. 18.00
  Reissue Brown [.0200]. 7.00
  Tan [.00] 25.00
  Reissue Tan [.0100] 18.00
  Reissue Tan [.0200] 7.00
  Lightsaber slashed [.00] 25.00
  Reissue Lightsaber slashed [.0100]. 18.00
  Reissue Lightsaber slashed [.0200] 7.00
  Blaster Battle scars [.00] 25.00
  Reissue Blaster Battle scars [.0100] 18.00
  Reissue Blaster Battle scars [.0200]. 7.00
Boss Nass (#84119) Col.3. [.0000] 8.00
  Reissue [.0100]. 7.00
C-3PO (#84106) Col. 2 [.00] 10.00
  Reissue [.0100]. 7.00

Chancellor Valorum (#84132) Col.3. [.0000]
  small parts warning 12.00
  Variation: [.0000] black sticker over warning. 10.00
  Reissue [.0100]. 7.00
Darth Maul (Jedi Duel) (#84088) Col. 1 [.00] 18.00
  Reissue [.0000]. 20.00
  Reissue [.0100] 7.00
  Variation: [.00] or [.0100] with Black Vest, scarce . 500.00
Darth Sideous (#84087) Col. 2 [.00] 12.00
  [.0100]. 7.00
Gasgano with Pit Droid (#84116) [.0000] 10.00
  Reissue Col.3. [.0100]. 7.00
  Reissue [.0200] 6.00
Jar Jar Binks (#84077) Col. 1 [.00] 20.00
  Reissue [.0100] 12.00
  Reissue [.0200] 6.00
Ki-Adi-Mundi (#84123) Col.3. [.0000]. 10.00
  Reissue [.0100] 6.00
Mace Windu (#84084) Col.3. [.0000] 12.00
  Reissue [.0100] 6.00
Obi-Wan Kenobi (Jedi Duel) (#84073) Col. 1 [.00] 10.00
  Reissue [.0100] 6.00
Padmé Naberrie (#84076) Col. 1 [.00]. 12.00
  Reissue [.0100] 6.00
Queen Amidala (Naboo) (#84078) Col. 1 [.00]. 12.00
  Reissue [.0100] 6.00
Qui-Gon Jinn (Jedi Duel) (#84072) Col. 1 [.00] 10.00
  Reissue [.0100] 6.00
Ric Olie (#84109) Col. 2 [.00] 8.00

 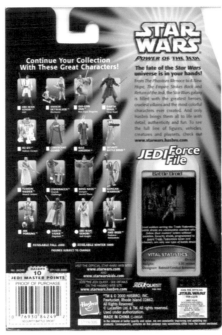 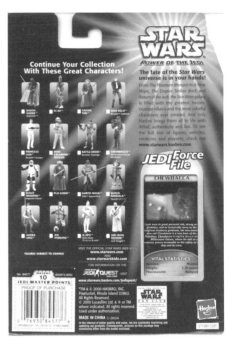

Anakin Skywalker (Naboo Pilot) Episode I; and Power of the Jedi ".0000" and ".0300"card backs (Kenner 2000–01)

Reissue [.0100] 6.00
Senator Palpatine (#84082) Col. 2 [.00]. 12.00
Reissue [.0100] 6.00
Watto (#84093) Col. 2 [.00] 10.00
Reissue [.0100] 6.00

Later Figures
Adi Gallia (#84124) Col. 3 [.0000] $12.00
Anakin Skywalker (Naboo) (#84112) Col. 1 [.0100] 7.00
Captain Panaka (#84108) Col. 2 [.0000] 12.00
Captain Tarpals (#84121) Col. 3 [.0000] 12.00
Darth Maul (Tatooine) (#84134) Col. 1 [.0000]. 7.00
Variation: [.0000] with Black Vest 500.00
Destroyer Droid (#84181) Col. 2 [.0000] 7.00
Naboo Royal Security (#84079) Col. 2 [.0000] 7.00
Nute Gunray (#84089) Col. 2 [.0000]. 6.00
Obi-Wan Kenobi (Naboo) (#84114) Col. 1 [.0100] 7.00
Ody Mandrell (#84117) Col. 3 [.0100] 7.00
OOM-9 (#84127) Col. 3 [.0000]
Binoculars packed upper left 30.00
Col. 3 [.0000] Binoculars packed over left hand 7.00
Queen Amidala (Coruscant) (#84111) Col. 1 [.0100] . . 15.00
Qui-Gon Jinn (Naboo) (#84113) Col. 1 [.0100] 7.00
R2-D2 (#84104) Col. 2 [.0000] 7.00
Variation: . . . .
Rune Haako (#84091) Col. 2 [.0000] 6.00
Yoda (#84086) Col. 2 [.0000] 7.00
Without "Episode 1" on card 30.00

Final Figures (2000)
Anakin Skywalker (Naboo Pilot) (#84246) Col. 1
[.0000]. $15.00
Darth Maul (Sith Lord) (#84247) Col. 1 [.0000] 15.00
Darth Sidious (Holograph) (#84081) Col. 2 [.0000] . . . 30.00
Destroyer Droid (Battle Damaged) (#84126) Col. 1
[.0000] 20.00
Jar Jar Binks (Naboo Swamp) (#84252) Col. 1 [.0000] . 30.00
Naboo Royal Guard (#84083) Col. 2 [.0000] 20.00
Obi-Wan Kenobi (Jedi Knight) (#84244) Col. 1 [.0000]. 20.00
Pit Droids (2-pack) (#84129) Col. 2 [.0000] 25.00
Queen Amidala (Battle) (#84273) Col. 2 [.0100] 30.00

Qui-Gon Jinn (Jedi Master) (#84107) Col. 1 [.0000]. . . 20.00
R2-B1 Astromech Droid (#84128) Col.3. [.0000] 25.00
Sio Bibble (#84257) Col. 2 [.0000] 45.00
TC-14 Protocol Droid (#84276) Col.3. [.0000] 35.00

POWER OF THE JEDI
Hasbro (2000–2002)

Power of the Jedi figures include characters from all four movies. They come with a "Jedi Force File" which is an eight page fold-out The header card is generic and does not contain anything that identifies the figure—the character's name is only printed on the front of the Jedi Force File and the UPC bar code is on a sticker on the back. The card revision number is still present, but the only revisions are to the names and photos of the other available figures which are listed on the back. Most of the figures are available on two or more different header cards, but they are not necessarily in sequence. A given figure may well appear on an ".0100" and on a ".0400" card but not on a ".0200" or ".0300" card.

3¾" Figures (Hasbro 2000–01) with Jedi Force File
Anakin Skywalker, Mechanic (#84254) Col. 1 [.0000]. $12.00
Reissue [.0100] 8.00
Aurra Sing, Bounty Hunter (#84584) Col. 1 [.0300] . . . 15.00
Reissue [.0400] 8.00
Battle Droid, Boomer Damage (#84563) Col. 1 [.0100] 12.00
Reissue [.0300] 10.00
Reissue [.0400] 8.00
Battle Droid, Security (#84249) Col. 2 [.0000] 12.00
Reissue [.0100] 8.00
Ben (Obi-Wan) Kenobi, Jedi Knight (#84362) Col. 1
[.0100]. 12.00
Bespin Guard, Cloud City Security (#84638) Col. 2
[.0400]. 10.00
Boss Nass, Gungan Sacred Place (#84473) Col. 2
[.0000]. 12.00
Reissue [.0100] 10.00
Chewbacca, Dejarik Champion (#84363) Col. 2 [.0000] 15.00
Reissue [.0001] 8.00

Chewbacca, Millennium Falcon Mechanic (#84577)
Col. 1 [.0300] 12.00
Reissue [.0400] 8.00
Coruscant Guard (#84277) Col. 2 [.0000] 15.00
Reissue [.0100] 12.00
Reissue [.0300] 12.00
Reissue [.0400] 8.00
Darth Maul, Final Duel (#84506) Col. 1 with
break-apart battle damage [.0000 with sticker] . . . 15.00
Reissue [.0100] without sticker. 8.00
Darth Maul, Sith Apprentice (#84561) Col. 1 [.0300] . . 15.00
Reissue [.0400] 10.00
Darth Vader, Emperor's Wrath (#84637) Col. 1 [.0400]. 10.00
Darth Vader, Dagobah (#84472) Col. 1 [.0100] 15.00
Reissue [.0400] 8.00
Ellorrs Madak, Duros (#84647) Col. 2 (Fan Choice
Figure #1 [.0400] 8.00
Fode and Beed, Pod race Announcer (#84474) Col. 2
[.0100]. 15.00
Gungan Warrior (#84274) Col. 2 [.0000] 20.00
Reissue [.0100] 15.00
Reissue [.0400] 10.00
Han Solo, Bespin Capture (#84564) Col. 1 [.0100] . . . 20.00
Reissue [.0300] 15.00
Reissue [.0400] 10.00
Han Solo, Death Star Escape (#84626) Col. 1 [.0400]. 10.00
IG-88, Bounty Hunter (#84587) Col. 2 [.0100] 15.00
Reissue [.0300] 10.00
Jar Jar Binks, Tatooine (#84267) Col. 2 [.0300] 13.00
Reissue [.0400] 10.00
Jek Porkins, X-Wing Pilot (#84457) Col. 2 [.0000] 15.00
Reissue [.0100] 12.00
Reissue [.0300] 10.00
K-3PO, Echo Base Protocol Droid (#84643) Col. 2
[.0100]. 15.00
Reissue [.0400] 10.00
Ketwol (#84634) Col. 2 [.0400] 10.00
Lando Calrissian, Bespin Escape (#84589) Col. 2
[.0300]. 15.00
Reissue [.0400] 8.00

Leia Organa, General (#84642) Col.1 [.0000] 12.00
Reissue [.0100] 8.00
Leia Organa, Bespin Escape (#84588) Col. 1 [.0300] . 12.00
Reissue [.0100] 8.00
Luke Skywalker X-Wing Pilot (#84571) Col. 1 [.0400] . . 8.00
Mas Amedda (#84136) Col. 2 [.0000] 15.00
Reissue [.0100] 12.00
Reissue [.0300] 12.00
Reissue [.0400] 8.00
Mon Calamari Officer (#84644) Col. 2 [.0100] 12.00
Reissue [.0300] 12.00
Reissue [.0400] 8.00
Obi-Wan Kenobi, Jedi (#84251) Col. 1 [.0000]. 12.00
Reissue [.0100] 8.00
Obi-Wan Kenobi, Cold Weather Gear (#84573)
Col. 1 [.0300]. 15.00
Reissue [.0400] 12.00
Obi-Wan Kenobi, Jedi Training Gear (#84651) Col. 2
[.0300]. 15.00
Reissue [.0400] 8.00
Plo Koon, Jedi Master (#84568) Col. 2 [.0100] 15.00
Reissue [.0300] 12.00
Reissue [.0400] 8.00
Queen Amidala, Theed Invasion (#84567) Col. 2
[.0100]. 15.00
Reissue [.0300] 15.00
Reissue [.0400] 8.00
Qui-Gon Jinn, Mos Espa Disguise (#84253) Col. 1
[.0000]. 12.00
Reissue [.0100] 8.00
Qui-Gon Jinn, Jedi Training Gear (#84559) Col. 1
[.0400]. 12.00
R2-D2, Naboo Escape (#84259) Col. 1 [.0000] 12.00
Reissue [.0100] 8.00
R2-Q5, Imperial Astromech Droid (#84629) [.0400]. . . 12.00
Sabe, Queen's Decoy (#84137) Col. 2 [.0400] 12.00
Saesee Tiin (#84569) Col. 2 [.0300] 12.00
Reissue [.0400] 8.00
Sandtrooper, Tatooine Patrol (#84579) Col. 1 [.0400]. . . 8.00
Scout Trooper Imperial Pilot (white) (#84586) Col. 1

Leia Organa, Bespin Escape; Boss Nass, Gungan Sacred Place; and R2-D2, Power of the Jedi (Kenner 2000–01)

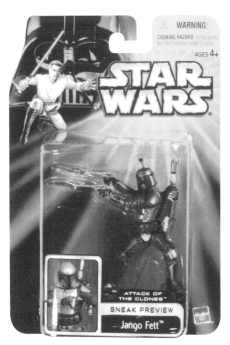

Battle Droid, Boomer Damage; FX-7 Medical Droid, Power of the Jedi; and Jango Fett, Sneak Preview (Hasbro 1999–2002)

[.0100]. 12.00
   Reissue [.0300] 10.00
Scout Trooper Imperial Pilot (dirty) (#84586) [.0400] . . 10.00
Sebulba, Bonta Eve Challenge (#84266) Col. 2
   [.0100]. 12.00
Shmi Skywalker (#84271) Col. 2 [.0400] 8.00
Tessek (#84639) Col. 2 [.0300] 12.00
   Reissue [.0400] 8.00
Tusken Raider, Desert Sniper (#84248) Col. 2 [.0000]. 15.00
   Reissue [.0100] 15.00
   Reissue [.0300] 12.00
   Reissue [.0400] 8.00

POWER OF THE JEDI (TRANSITION)

Starting in 2002, Hasbro dropped the "Jedi Force File" fold-out from the Power of the Jedi header card design and printed the character's name on the front. The back was changed to contain the character biographical information. For lack of a better name, these are called "Transition" header cards. Since the cards are no longer generic, the package revision number no longer works the same as on earlier figures in the Power of the Jedi line-up. The decimal point has been dropped and the last four digits now seem to represent distinct character numbers. The first ones seen include figures with numbers "0000" thru "0500" respectively.

3¾" Figures (Hasbro Asst #84555, 2002) Transition
BoShek (846640) [0700] $10.00
Eeth Koth, Jedi Master (#84662) Col. 2 [0500] 8.00
FX-7, Medical Droid (#84656) Col. 2 [0000] 8.00
Imperial Officer (#84659) Col.2 [0300] 8.00
Queen Amidala, Royal Decoy (#84657) Col. 2 [0100]. . . 8.00
R4-M9 . . . . 10.00
Rebel Trooper, *Tantive IV* Defender (#84658) Col. 2
   [0200]. 8.00
Teebo 10.00
Zutton, Snaggletooth (#84661) Col. 2 [0400] 8.00

ATTACK OF THE CLONES

These figures were not released at press time. The following list includes the expected early figures.

Sneak Preview Figures, Green Card
Clone Trooper 7.00
Jango Fett. 7.00
R3-T7 . . . . 7.00
Zam Wesell 7.00

3¾" Figures (Hasbro 2002) blue card
#01 Anakin Skywalker, Outland Peasant Disguise, (#84852).
   . . . . 7.00
#02 Padmé Amidala, Arena Escape (#84855) 7.00
#03 Obi-Wan Kenobi, Coruscant Chase (#84854) 7.00
#04 C-3PO, Protocol Droid, (#84856) 7.00
#05 Kit Fisto, Jedi Master (#84858) 7.00
#06 Super Battle Droid (#84853) 7.00
#07 Boba Fett, Kamino Escape (#84863) 7.00
#08 Tusken Raider Female with Child (#84864) 7.00
#09 Captain Typho (#84862) 7.00
#10 Shaak Ti, Jedi Master (#84872) 7.00
#11 Battle Droid, Arena Battle (#84865) 7.00
#12 Plo Koon, Arena Battle (#84868) 7.00
#13 Jango Fett, Kamino Escape (#84857) 7.00
#14 R2-D2, Coruscant Sentry (#84645) 7.00
#15 Geonosian Warrior, (#84867) 7.00
#16 Dexter Jettster, Coruscant Informant (#84866) 7.00
#17 Clone Trooper, (#84635) 7.00
#18 Zam Wesell, Bounty Hunter, (#84655). 7.00
#19 Royal Guard, Coruscant Security, (#84831). 7.00
#20 Saesee Tiin, Jedi Master, (#84832) 7.00
#21 Nikto, Jedi Knight, (#84823) 7.00
#22 Anakin Skywalker, Hanger Duel, (#84605) 7.00
#23 Yoda, Jedi Maser, (#84615). 7.00
#24 Jar Jar Binks, Gungan Senator, (#84821) 7.00
#25 Taun We, Kamino Cloner (#84822) 7.00
#26 Luminara Unduli, Jedi Master, (#84833) 7.00
#27 Count Dooku, Dark Lord, ... 7.00
#28 Mace Windu, Geonosian Rescue, ... 7.00

LOOSE FIGURES

Only a few exotic variations and some scarce recent figures, have attained any collector value as "loose figures." Exotic variations are so rare that no accepted market price is known. The merely "scarce" figures are listed below. All the other common figures are worth about $3.00. The only reason that they cost that much is that a dealer has to transport them to the show or advertise, take your order, and ship them to you, and needs some compensation for his time. If you are trying to sell your loose common figures you better not expect to get much for them. All loose figure prices include the weapons and accessories which came with the figure.

LOOSE FIGURES FROM CARDS
Kenner (1995–2002)

Loose New Power of the Force Figures, scarce
Admiral Motti	$15.00
AT-AT Driver	12.50
Aunt Beru	5.00
Ben (Obi-Wan) Kenobi, with long lightsaber	12.50
Biggs Darklighter	5.00
Boba Fett, with half circle on hand	10.00
Captain Piett	10.00
Clone Emperor Palpatine	10.00
Dark Trooper	10.00
Darth Vader, with long lightsaber	12.50
Darth Vader, removeable helmet	15.00
Death Star Droid, with mouse droid	12.50
Death Star Trooper	12.50
Ewoks: Wicket and Logray, each	5.00
Grand Admiral Thrawn	10.00
Han Solo in Hoth Gear, with open hand	10.00
Imperial Sentinel	10.00
Jedi Knight Luke Skywalker, with brown vest	30.00
Kyle Katarn	10.00
Luke Skywalker, with long lightsaber	17.50
Luke Skywalker in Dagobah Fatigues, with long lightsaber	17.50
Luke Skywalker (in Black Cloak) Expanded Universe	10.00
Luke Skywalker in X-Wing Fighter Pilot Gear, with long lightsaber	12.50
Mara Jade	10.00
Mon Mothma	7.00
Ponda Baba, grey beard	20.00
Pote Snitkin	12.50
Princess Leia in Hoth Gear	12.50
Princess Leia (in Black Cloak) Expanded Universe	10.00
Ree-Yees	12.50
R2-D2 with holographic Princess Leia	15.00
Spacetrooper	10.00
Wuher	5.00

Loose *Episode I* figures, scarce
Captain Panaka	5.00
Captain Tarpals	5.00
Darth Sidious (Holographic)	9.00
Destroyer Droid (Battle Damaged)	8.00
Jar Jar Binks (Naboo Swamp)	10.00
Queen Amidala (Battle)	15.00
R2-B1 Astromech Droid	10.00
Sio Bibble	15.00
TC-14	15.00

LOOSE FIGURES FROM VEHICLES, CREATURES & PLAYSETS

Many of the new Power of the Force vehicles came with exclusive figures. Starting in 1998, it was hard to find a vehicle without one. The most interesting of these exclusives is the Wedge Antilles error figure. The first batches of the *Millennium Falcon* carry case came with a Wedge Antilles with a white stripe down each arm. This was clearly visible as the figure can be seen in the gun turret of the ship. Later batches of these carry cases corrected the figure.

Exclusive figures from vehicles, creatures and playsets

Ewoks: Wicket and Logray; and Biggs Darklighter
(Kenner 1998)

AT-AT Driver and AT-AT Commander from AT-AT vehicles
(Kenner 1997)

Sebulba and Anakin Skywalker from Episode I *Podracer vehicles (Kenner 1999–2000)*

are rather scarce, in loose condition, since relatively few were issued compared with regular carded figures. However, many of the vehicles, creatures, playsets, games, etc. were themselves discounted substantially, making the figures available at a good price. Loose figures from multi-figure packs are listed with the packs and would be worth a lot less individually than in their original group.

Loose Figures from new Power of the Force vehicles
Airspeeder Pilot from Airspeeder vehicle $5.00
AT-AT Commander, from Electronic Imperial AT-AT
    Walker vehicle 5.00
AT-AT Driver, from Electronic Imperial AT-AT
    Walker vehicle 5.00
A-Wing Pilot, from A-Wing Fighter vehicle 5.00
Biker Scout Stormtrooper, from Imperial Speeder
    Bike vehicle 5.00
Cloud Car Pilot from Cloud Car vehicle 5.00
Destroyer Droid (Rolling) from R2-D2 Carryall Playset . 5.00
Han Solo from Jabba the Hutt creature 5.00
Han Solo from Tauntaun creature 5.00
Han Solo in Carbonite, from Boba Fett's *Slave I*
    vehicle 5.00
Han Solo in Carbonite from Jabba's Palace display
    stand 5.00
Imperial Scanning Crew figure from *Millennium Falcon* carry
    case (reissue) 5.00
Jawa from Ronto figure 5.00
Luke Skywalker in Endor Gear, from Speeder Bike
    vehicle 5.00
Luke Skywalker (in Hoth Gear) from Tauntaun creature . 5.00
Luke Skywalker (in Hoth Gear) from Wampa creature . . 5.00
Luke Skywalker (Jedi) from Rancor creature 5.00
Princess Leia Organa in Endor Gear, from Speeder
    Bike vehicle 5.00
Rebel Speeder Bike Pilot from Speeder Bike vehicle . . . 5.00
Sandtrooper from Dewback creature 5.00
Sandtrooper and Patrol Droid from Cantina at Mos
    Eisley display stand 5.00
Scout Trooper from Power Racing Speeder Bike 5.00
Swoop Trooper, from Swoop vehicle 5.00
Tusken Raider from Bantha creature 5.00
Wedge Antilles, from *Millennium Falcon* carry case,
    with white stripes down arms, error figure 10.00

Correct figure, no white stripes 8.00

Loose Figures from *Episode I* vehicles
Anakin Skywalker from Anakin Skywalker's Pod
    Racer vehicle 5.00
Battle Droid from Stap vehicle 5.00
Battle Droid from Armored Scout Tank vehicle 5.00
Battle Droid (Break Apart) from Theed Generator
    Complex playset 5.00
Darth Maul from Sith Speeder vehicle 5.00
Gungan Warrior from Femba creature/vehicle 10.00
Jar Jar Binks from Gungan Assault Cannon 5.00
Jar Jar Binks from Kaadu creature 5.00
Qui-Gon Jinn (Swimming) from Opee creature 5.00
Qui-Gon Jinn from Eopie creature 20.00
R2 Unit (Red) from Electronic Naboo Royal Star-
    ship vehicle 10.00
Sebulba from Sebulba's Pod Racer vehicle 5.00

Loose Figures from Power of the Jedi vehicles
Bespin Security Guard from Carbon-Freezing
    Chamber playset 5.00
Paploo from Imperial AT-ST and Speederbike
    vehicles 5.00
Imperial Pilot from TIE Interceptor vehicle 5.00
Sullustan Pilot from B-Wing Fighter vehicle 5.00

Loose Figures from Games
Han Solo from *Millennium Falcon* CD-Rom Game 5.00
Han Solo, Stormtrooper from Escape the Death
    Star board game 5.00
Darth Vader from Escape the Death Star board
    game 5.00
Rorworr, Wookie Scout from Invasion of Theed
    RPG Game 8.00
    on mini-card, as issued 15.00

Oola and Salacious Crumb, Fan Club Exclusive (Kenner 1998)

MAIL-IN EXCLUSIVE FIGURES

There have been quite a few mail-in exclusive figures in the new series. The first to be offered was the Froot Loops mail-in Han Solo in Stormtrooper disguise. Both the cereal box and the figure are collectible. Since this offer was not tied to any *Star Wars* event or product, many collectors missed it. By contrast, the Spirit of Obi-Wan Kenobi mail-in from Frito Lay was tied to the theater release of the Special Editions of the movies in early 1997. Hardly anyone was unaware of it. The figure can not truly be said to be an action figure as it is not articulated, but Kenner treats it as one on its Web site and collectors have generally considered it so, as well.

The theater edition Jedi Knight Luke Skywalker is the most valuable of the exclusive figures. It was given away during the first showing of the Special Edition of *Star Wars, A New Hope* on January 31, 1997. There was no prior announcement, not all theaters got the figure and there was no sign of any such figure when I saw the picture at 7:00 p.m. that day. A number of alert movie theater ushers and ticket takers did quite well for themselves by taking home a supply. The figure is identical to the common version sold in stores —only the header card is different.

Mail-in Figures
Mail-in Han Solo in Stormtrooper disguise, in plastic bag, (Froot Loops offer) with mailer box $35.00
Spirit of Obi-Wan Kenobi, with box (Frito Lay offer, 1997) 15.00
Cantina Band Member, Official Star Wars Fan Club exclusive, in plastic bag, with five musical instruments (#69734, 1997) in white mailer box . . 15.00
Cantina Band Set, five figures: (All five figures are the same as above. Only the instruments are different.) Official Star Wars Fan Club 50.00
 Loose: Doikk N'ats with Fizzz Instrument 10.00
 Loose: Figrin D'an with Kloo Horn Instrument. . . . 10.00
 Loose: Ickabel with Fanfars Instrument. 10.00
 Loose: Nalan with Bandfill Instrument 10.00
 Loose: Techn with Omnibox Instrument 10.00
B'Omarr Monk, Hasbro Internet Web site offer, in plastic bag, with instruction sheet (#69718, 1997–98) in white mailer box 15.00
Oola and Salacious Crumb, Official Star Wars Fan Club exclusive (#69871, May 1998) in window box 20.00
Kabe and Muftak, Internet exclusive (#84071) in window box. 20.00

Give-away figure
Jedi Knight Luke Skywalker, Exclusive Star Wars Trilogy Edition, carded, movie theater give-away (1997). 75.00

Specials
Four figure set of Han Solo in Endor Gear, Lando Calrissian as Skiff Guard, AT-ST driver and Darth Vader (JC Penney catalog 1997) 20.00

MILLENNIUM MINTED COIN COLLECTION
Kenner (1998)

The original Power of the Force coins are a popular collectible and Kenner is bringing them back in 1998 in the

Bespin Han Solo, Millennium Minted Coin (Kenner 1998)

Millennium Minted Coin Collection series. Each figure in the series comes with a gold-colored coin mounted on a display pedestal. Figures and coins are packaged in a window box which has a back window so you can see the back of the coin. The back of the coin is different from the back of the original coins, so even someone who doesn't notice that the original coins are silver-colored should still be able to tell them apart. The initial boxes appeared in early April and included just three different figures. The combination costs about $10.00, which is about $3.00 to $4.00 more than the figure alone. This seems about right, but a lot of collectors are reluctant to buy still another version of a character that they already own.

4" Figures with Gold Coin (Asst. #69675, April 1998)
in window box (Toys "R" Us exclusive)
Bespin Han Solo (#84022) [551371.00] with text. . . . $25.00
 [.01] no text 10.00
 with variant coin 30.00
Chewbacca (#84023) [551375.00] with text. 25.00
 [.01] no text 10.00
C-3PO (#84024) [.00] 10.00
Luke Skywalker in Endor Gear (#84026) [.00] with text 25.00
 [.01] no text 10.00
Princess Leia in Endor Gear (#84027) [.00] with text. . 25.00
 [.01] no text 10.00
Snowtrooper (#84028) [551379.00] with text 25.00
 [.01] no text 10.00
Emperor Palpatine (#84029 [.00] 10.00

EPISODE I LIGHT-UP FIGURES
Hasbro (2000)

These figures are designed to portray the holographic communications seen in *Episode I* by having a clear plastic figure with a base that projects a light through them. They are WalMart stores exclusives.

Deluxe Luke Skywalker's Desert Sport Skiff (Kenner 1996)

Deluxe Boba Fett (Kenner 1997)

Episode I Light-Up figures (WalMart exclusives)
Light-up Darth Maul figure as holograph (#84372) 15.00
Light-up Qui-Gon Jinn figure as holograph (#84371) . . 15.00

DELUXE FIGURES

Deluxe figures have met with a decidedly mixed review among collectors and in collector publications. None of the weapons/accessories in these packages appeared in the movie. When the first deluxe figure featured a "Capture Claw," many purists feared that Kenner would start issuing figures with every manner of absurd gear, as they have done with Batman. Fortunately, no Deluxe Ninja Luke Skywalker was planned. Only a few of the deluxe figures have been created, and they follow the basic concept behind the Mini-Rigs from the original series which was to sell weapons and accessories that fit in with the ones featured in the film and could be envisioned as "just off camera."

The next three deluxe figures featured popular characters with somewhat unmovie-like devices, but the last three (Probe Droid, Snowtrooper, and Hoth Rebel Soldier) came much closer to the basic concept and were much more popular with collectors. Other one- and two-man weapons, radar and communication stations, loading dock, cargo handling, refueling and repair droids, and equipment would also fit the concept and these could have included soldiers for each side as well. However, the kids probably prefer weapons and accessories associated with the major characters. Anyway, the deluxe figures have turned out to be among the few *Star Wars* items that I have seen discounted, so both Kenner and collectors may be lucky that only seven different ones were made.

For 1998, Kenner added to, or replaced this line-up with Gunner Station figures. The first two were Han and Luke plus the guns from the *Millennium Falcon* which they used in the first movie. These were eventually given something to shoot at with

the addition of Darth Vader and his TIE Fighter. They must have been good shots, because Darth Vader was very hard to find, although he did turn up briefly at red tag time.

Episode I deluxe figures came with a handle which allowed you to swing their lightsabers around. They were among the first figures to be discounted and you can still find some of them around almost three years later.

Power of the Jedi deluxe figures have more promise. They come with accessories which are actually seen in the movies such as a Bacta Tank (with Luke) and a Sail Barge Cannon (with Leia). Neither of these have previously appeared in the action figure line. The packages for the figures do not say "Deluxe" anywhere, but they follow the same concept of a figure plus a large accessory.

DELUXE FIGURES
Kenner (1995–2002)

First Wave (Asst. #69610, 1996)
Deluxe Crowd Control Stormtrooper with "Flight-Action Thruster Pack and Capture Claw" (#69609,1996) on red *Power of the Force* header card, with 2 warning stickers [533029.00] . . $35.00
   Variation, with 1 warning sticker 15.00
   Reissue, printed warnings [.01] 7.00
   Loose, with complete Thruster Pack 4.00
Deluxe Luke Skywalker's Desert Sport Skiff with "Blasting Rocket Launcher and Rapid-Deploy Wings" (#69611, 1996) on red *Power of the Force* header card [533032.00] 10.00
   Loose, with complete Sport Skiff 4.00
Deluxe Han Solo with Smuggler Flight Pack plus "Battle-Pivoting Blaster Cannons and Cargo Claw" (#69612, 1996) on red *Power of the Force* header card [533035.00] 10.00
   Loose, with complete Flight Pack 4.00

Second Wave
Deluxe Boba Fett with "Wing-Blast Rocketpack and Overhead Cannon" (#69638, 1997) on green *Power of the Force* header card [536817.00] card says "Weaponry: Photon Torpedo" 15.00
    Variation [.01] says "Weaponry: Proton Torpedo" 12.00
    Loose, with complete Rocketpack 4.00
Note: Scarce variations: Circle on one hand, or no emblem on chest, or no skull on shoulder, each . 500.00
Deluxe Probe Droid with "Proton Torpedo and Self-Destruct Exploding Head" (#69677, 1997) on green *Power of the Force* header card [536814.00] with red color scheme back picturing Shadows of the Empire figures. 25.00
    Variation [.01] 10.00
    Variation [.02] green color scheme. 8.00
    Loose, complete 4.00

Third Wave
Deluxe Hoth Rebel Soldier with "Anti-Vehicle Laser Cannon" (#69744, 1997) on green *Power of the Force* header card [540061.00] 10.00
    Loose, with complete Laser Cannon 4.00
Deluxe Snowtrooper with "E-Web Heavy Repeating Blaster" (#69724, 1997) on green *Power of the Force* header card [540058.00] 10.00
    Loose, with complete Blaster. 4.00

GUNNER STATIONS

Gunner Stations (Asst. #69655, May 1998)
Millennium Falcon with Luke Skywalker (#69848) on green *Power of the Force* header card [551811.00] with warning sticker $12.00
    with printed warning [.01] 10.00
Millennium Falcon with Han Solo (#69766) on green *Power of the Force* header card [551809.00] with warning sticker 12.00
    With printed warning [.01]. 10.00
TIE Fighter with Darth Vader (#69847) on green *Power of the Force* header card

[551811.00] with warning sticker 30.00

EPISODE I

***Episode I* Deluxe** (Asst. #84045, May 1999) with Lightsaber Handle which Triggers Battle Swing
Deluxe Darth Maul (#84144) [560012.0000] $7.00
Deluxe Obi-Wan Kenobi (#84152) [560021.0000]. 7.00
Deluxe Qui-Gon Jinn (#84148) [560017.0000] 7.00

Trophy Assortment (Asst. #84275)
Darth Maul with Sith Infiltrator (#84409) [567698.0000] 10.00

POWER OF THE JEDI

Power of the Jedi Deluxe (Asst. #84475, Dec. 2001)
Darth Maul with Sith Attack Droid (#84654) $10.00
Luke Skywalker in Echo Base Bacta Tank (#84652) . . . 10.00
Princess Leia with Sail Barge Cannon (#84653). 10.00

Boba Fett special "300th Figure" (#84566) [.0100] 25.00
    Reissue: [.0200] 15.00

ELECTRONIC FIGURES

With electronic figures you can add "bells and whistles" to your action figure – litterally. The only one that actually does this is the Electronic Power F/X R2-D2 figure. It's one of my favorite loose figures. The others all just add lights.

ELECTRONIC POWER F/X
Kenner (1997)

There are five Electronic Power F/X figures and all of them, except R2-D2, come with a light-up feature and an action feature controlled by hidden buttons and levers. The packages have diorama scenes which can be cut out and the first two figures, Ben and Darth, interconnect to allow a simulated duel. Luke can also connect with Darth for a duel, but not with the Emperor, who is facing the wrong way. The first version of the Emperor's package pictures his energy bolts

TIE Fighter with Darth Vader, Gunner Station; Luke Skywalker in Echo Base Bacta Tank, Power of the Jedi; Electronic Power F/X R2-D2 (Kenner/Hasbro 1998, 2001, 1997)

shooting up, but the corrected version pictures them shooting down. In the movie scene, Luke was taking his punishment lying on the deck, not flying around the room like Peter Pan.

Electronic Power F/X (Asst. #69615) green header cards
Ben (Obi-Wan) Kenobi with "Glowing Lightsaber
    and Remote Dueling Action" (#69643, 1997) on
    green *Power of the Force* header card [536820.00] $10.00
    Loose on stand, with backdrop cut-out 4.00
Darth Vader with "Glowing Lightsaber and Remote
    Dueling Action" (#69644, 1997) on green
    Power of the Force header card [536823.00] 10.00
    Loose on stand, with backdrop cut-out 4.00
Luke Skywalker with "Glowing Lightsaber and
    Remote Dueling Action" (#69746, 1997) on
    green *Power of the Force* header card [541867.00]. . 10.00
    Loose on stand, with backdrop cut-out 4.00
R2-D2 (Artoo-Detoo) with "Light-Up Radar Eye,
    Authentic Sounds and Remote Action"
    (#69646, 1997) on green *Power of the Force*
    header card [536826.00] 10.00
    Variation [.01] blue UPC code bars 8.00
    Variation [.02] black UPC code bars 7.00
    Loose on stand, with backdrop cut-out 4.00
Emperor Palpatine with "Dark Side Energy Bolts
    and Remote Action" (#69726, 1997) on green
    Power of the Force header card [541864.00]
    energy bolts pictured pointing up 12.00
    Variation [.01] energy bolts pointing down 10.00
    Loose on stand, with backdrop cut-out 4.00

LARGER FIGURES

EPIC FORCE

Bespin Luke Skywalker,
Epic Force (Kenner 1998)

These 5" figures were introduced at the 1998 Toy Fair. Other than the size, the gimmick is the rotating base, which lets the collector see all sides of the figure without removing it from the package. Three figures appeared at first, and Boba Fett is the most desirable figure of the three, but it is not scarce. C-3PO arrived in late May. Each package back pictures three figures—C-3PO plus the other two from the initial batch of three. However, there were five figures announced for the initial batch and there is no sign of Han Solo Stormtrooper which was supposed to be the fifth figure. Instead we got an ordinary Stormtrooper.

5" Epic Force Figures with in-package rotating base.
Darth Vader (#69761) [548761.00] $10.00

Obi-Wan Kenobi, Mega Action (Hasbro 2001)

Bespin Luke Skywalker (#69762) [548763.00] 10.00
Boba Fett (#69763) [548765.00] 10.00
C-3PO (#69764) [548767.00] 10.00
Princess Leia Organa (#69843) [.00]. 10.00
Stormtrooper (#69842) [.00] 10.00

Epic Force Three-pack, boxed (FAO Schwarz)
Three-pack of Chewbacca, Han Solo, and Obi-Wan
    Kenobi (#84281) 65.00

Episode I **5" Epic Force Figures** (1999)
Darth Maul (#84156) [.0000]. 15.00
Obi-Wan Kenobi (#84157) [.0000]. 15.00
Qui-Gon Jinn (#84179) [.0000] 15.00

MEGA ACTION

Hasbro produced these 6" figures in 2000. They have levers and other devices so that you can activate their action moves by hand. The Destroyer Droid is the best of the lot.

Power of the Jedi 6" Mega Action Figures (Asst. #84355)
Obi-Wan Kenobi Mega Action Figure with "Light-
    saber Battle Moves" (#84528) [569876.0000]. . . . $13.00
Darth Maul Mega Action Figure with "Lightsaber
    Attack Moves" (#84529) [.0000]. 13.00
Destroyer Droid Mega Action Figure "Converts to
    Attack Mode" (#84538) [570772.0000]. 15.00

MULTI-PACKS

There are two different ways to create a Multi-Packs. The first is to put two or more figures in the same package, and the second is to put two or three regular carded figures in an outer package. Kenner/Hasbro has tried both methods, with mixed results. The most popular to date are the "Cinema Scenes" three-packs.

One thing they should have tried, but did not, was to package a squad of Stormtroopers or Battle Droids so that loose figure collectors could complete their armies at a reasonable price. Why not a squad of three plus an exclusive officer figure, for the "Cinema Scenes" line – four figures for the price of three?

"CINEMA SCENES" THREE-PACKS
Kenner (1997–2000)

The "Cinema Scenes" three-packs first appeared in June 1997 with the Death Star Escape group. Although Kenner calls them "Cinema Scenes" packs, this phrase doesn't appear anywhere on the package, but the back of the package contains a scene from the movie, with sprocket holes down each side to look like a piece of 70mm film. They are collected, in part, because each one contains at least one figure that is not otherwise available.

The Death Star Escape was a Toys "R" Us exclusive and included a Han Solo Stormtrooper figure which had only been released as the Froot Loops mail-in. The Cantina Showdown was a WalMart exclusive, at least at first, and included the never-before released Dr. Evazan. The third group featured the first-ever versions of Jabba's Dancers. Later packages had not one, but all three exclusive figures. The Mynock Hunt is notoriously scarce, although it was available at Kay-Bee stores in quantity for a while.

Three-packs are produced in much smaller quantities than carded figures, contain from one to three exclusive figures, and retail for the same price as three separate figures, making them a pretty good deal.

Cinema Scenes Three-Packs in green *New Power of the Force* window boxes
Death Star Escape with Chewbacca captured
    flanked by Han Solo and Luke Skywalker
    dressed as Stormtroopers, with removable
    helmets (#69737) [542704.00] or [.01] $45.00
    Loose, 3 figures with backdrop. 18.00
Cantina Showdown with Dr. Evazan, Ponda Baba,
    and Obi-Wan Kenobi (#69738, 1997)
    [544550.00]. 20.00
    Variation [.01] box lists assortment #69650 . . . . . 18.00
    Variation, with Dr. Evazan hair black 25.00
    Loose, 3 figures with backdrop. 12.00

Second Batch (Kenner Asst. #69650, 1998)
Final Jedi Duel with Emperor Palpatine, Darth Vader,
    and Luke Skywalker (#69783) [548078.00] or [.01] 28.00
    Loose, 3 figures with backdrop. 12.00
Jabba The Hutt's Dancers with Rustall, Greeta, and
    Lyn Me (#69849) [553300.00] 15.00
    Loose, 3 figures with backdrop. 10.00
Mynock Hunt with Princess Leia in Hoth Gear, Han
    Solo in Bespin Gear, and Chewbacca, all with
    respirators (#69868, 1998) [554609.00] 50.00
    Loose, 3 figures with backdrop. 25.00
Purchase of the Droids with Uncle Owen Lars,

Mynock Hunt, Cinema Scenes Three-pack (Kenner 1998)

    C-3PO, and Luke Skywalker (#69778, 1998)
    [549672.00] 20.00
    Variation [.01] box 15.00
    Loose, 3 figures with backdrop. 9.00

Later Batches (Hasbro Asst. #84035, 1999) in revised green *New Power of the Force* window boxes
Jedi Spirits with deceased Anakin Skywalker, Yoda,
    and Obi-Wan Kenobi (#84058) clear figures 18.00
    Loose, 3 figures with backdrop. 9.00
Cantina Aliens with Labria, Takeel and Nabrun
    Leeds (#84059) 18.00
    Loose, 3 figures with backdrop. 9.00
Jabba's Skiff Guards with Klaatu Barada and Nikto
    (#84061) 15.00
    Loose, 3 figures with backdrop. 9.00
Rebel Pilots with Ten Numb, Wedge Antilles, and
    Arvel Crynyd (#84057) 15.00
    Loose, 3 figures with backdrop. 9.00

EPISODE I CINEMA SCENES

Episode I (Asst #84115, 1999–2000) with CommTech chip
Mos Espa Encounter with Sebulba, Jar Jar Binks,
    and Anakin Skywalker (#84161) [.0000] $20.00
    Loose, 3 figures with backdrop. 10.00
Watto's Box with Watto, Graxol Kelvyyn, and Shakka
    (#84159) [564836.0000] 30.00
    Loose, 3 figures with backdrop. 10.00
Tatooine Showdown with Qui-Gon Jinn, Darth Maul,
    and Anakin Skywalker (#84158) 20.00
    Loose, 3 figures with backdrop. 10.00

TWO-PACKS

SHADOWS OF THE EMPIRE
Kenner (1996)

One package variation showed up in the Shadows of the Empire two-packs. Boba Fett vs. IG-88 packages with printing code ".01" stated on the back that Boba Fett's "Vehicle of Choice:" was the *Slave I*. This was the final line in his description, after "Weapon of Choice" Earlier packages, with printing code ".00" omitted the phrase "Vehicle of Choice:"

Princess Leia and Han Solo, Princess Leia Collection; and Han Solo and Chewbacca, Silver Anniversary (Kenner 1998; Hasbro 2002)

but did include the words "*Slave I.*"

Two-Packs, on purple header card with special comic book
Darth Vader vs. Prince Xizor (#69567, 1996) $25.00
Boba Fett vs. IG-88 (#69568, Sept. 1996) [532459.00]
    without "Vehicle of Choice" on data card. 30.00
    with "Vehicle of Choice: *Slave I*" [.01]. 25.00

PRINCESS LEIA COLLECTION
Kenner (1998)

With four new outfits and four new hairstyles, the Princess could launch her own signature clothing collection for women who are well proportioned, but a little shorter than the average super-model. The white outfit she is wearing with R2-D2 is a little austere, but the same material looks quite handsome in the low-cut version with see-through cape shown with Luke Skywalker and it is nicely accessorized with belt and silver necklace. Her hair includes a single braid that hangs down a little below her derriere. The Endor outfit, shown with Wicket, is a casual number, with designer tears up the front which show a little thigh in combat. She also sports two long, below-waist length braids (on her head) and long hair from the Ewok Celebration Outfit figure. With Han Solo she is wearing a maroon dress, with a floor-length lace top attached to white shoulder pads which extend all the way up to her chin. The only difference between the ".00" and ".01" package backs is the color of the names on the file card – black on the ".00" and red on the ".01" figures.

Princess Leia Collection (Asst. #66935, Feb. 1998)
    on green header card
Princess Leia and R2-D2 (#66936) [549367.00] $25.00

Princess Leia and R2-D2 [.01]. 10.00
Princess Leia (Medal Ceremony) and Luke
    Skywalker (#66937, 1998) [549370.00]. 25.00
    Princess Leia and Luke Skywalker [.01]. 10.00
Princess Leia (Bespin) and Han Solo (#66938)
    [549373.00] 25.00
    Princess Leia and Han Solo [.01] 10.00
Princess Leia (Endor Celebration) and Wicket
    the Ewok (#66939) [549376.00] 30.00
    Princess Leia and Wicket the Ewok [.01] 10.00

MAX REBO BAND
Kenner (1998)

Max Rebo Band Pairs (WalMart) (Asst #69670, 1998)
Joh Yowza and Sy Snootles (#84018) [555086.00] . . $35.00
Barquin D'an with "Kloo Horn" and Droopy McCool
    with "Chidin Kalu" (#84019) [553419.01]. 35.00
    Card back variation. 35.00
Max Rebo with "Red Ball Organ" and Doda Bodona-
    wieedo with "Slither Horn" (#84021) [556354.00] . 38.00

OTHER TWO-PACKS

***Episode I* Two-pack**
The Final Lightsaber Duel, Darth Maul vs. Obi-Wan
    Kenobi, with Break-apart Darth Maul (#84322) . . $15.00
Power of the Jedi Two-pack
Darth Maul & Darth Vader, Masters of the Dark Side
    (#84557). 18.00

SILVER ANNIVERSARY
Hasbro (2002)

Celebrating the 25th anniversary of the original Star Wars film, Hasbro released two-pack figures from the movie in early 2002.

Silver Anniversary Two-packs (Asst. #84485, 2002)
Han Solo and Chewbacca Death Star Escape
  (#84669) [6124500100] $16.00
Luke Skywalker & Princess Leia Organa Swing to
  Freedom (#84668) [6124500000] 16.00
Obi-Wan Kenobi and Darth Vader Final Duel
  (#84671) [6124500200] 16.00

WHOLESALE CLUB PACKS

These are three figures, in original packages, with an outer corrugated cardboard package with holes so the the original packages show through. They are sold to various "wholesale club" stores, where they generally sell to members (customers) at a small discount from the prevailing toy store price for three figures. So far there have been two groups of three sets of these three-packs. There does not seem to be a lot of collector interest in them to date, with one exception, probably because the included figures are all common and the packs appeared much later than the original release of the figures. The one exception is the group two pack which contains a reissue Lando Calrissian on a green header card. This scarce version was never sold separately.

Wholesale Club Three-Packs
Group One (1996) all figures are on red header cards
Set One: Han Solo, Chewbacca, and Lando Calrissian . $40.00
Set Two: R2-D2, Stormtrooper, and C-3PO 35.00
Set Three: Luke Skywalker, Obi-Wan Kenobi, and
  Darth Vader 40.00

Group Two (1997) all figures are on green header cards
Star Wars: Luke Skywalker in Stormtrooper
  Disguise, Tusken Raider, and Obi-Wan
  Kenobi [547448.00] (#69851) 30.00
The Empire Strikes Back: Lando Calrissian, Luke
  Skywalker in Dagobah Fatigues, and TIE
  Fighter Pilot [547449.00] (69852) 75.00
Return of the Jedi: Jedi Knight Luke Skywalker,
  AT-ST Driver, and Princess Leia in Boushh
  Disguise [547450.00] (69853) 30.00

Wholesale Club *Episode I* Two-Packs (1999)
CommTech 2-pack with Electronic CommTech Reader, and
  Anakin Skywalker (Tatooine) 20.00
  Darth Maul Jedi Duel (#84379) 20.00

Obi-Wan Kenobi Jedi Duel (#84374) 20.00
Qui-Gon Jinn Jedi Duel (#84373) 20.00
Jar Jar Binks (#84378) 20.00

Padme Naberrie and Obi-Wan Kenobi (Jedi Duel)
  (#84286). 20.00
Anakin Skywalker (Naboo) and Obi-Wan Kenobi
  (Naboo) 20.00
Darth Maul (Jedi Duel) and Anakin Skywalker
  (Tatooine) (#84392). 25.00
Jar Jar Binks and Qui-Gon Jinn (Naboo) 20.00
Queen Amidala (Naboo) and Qui-Gon Jinn (Jedi
  Duel) (#84391) 20.00

CARRY CASES
AND DISPLAY STANDS

The first display stand for Kenner's *Star Wars* action figures was available well before the first figures appeared. It was the one included in the Early Bird Certificate Package. Actually, the package only held the backdrop. The pegs to hold the figures came in the package with the Early Bird figures.

The *Star Wars* Action Display Stand was the first of many mail-away premiums. It was offered on *Star Wars* action figure cardbacks for two proofs of purchase plus $2.00. The stand has a plastic base and a cardboard backdrop, plus levers that rotate groups of figures. It originally came in a plain mailer box. Later the stand was offered in *Star Wars* packaging, and finally, in *The Empire Strikes Back* packaging, with six figures, as the Special Action Display Stand.

The *Star Wars* Display Arena also a mail-away premium and consisted of four L-shaped plastic stands and four reversible cardboard backdrops, with pegs for display of up to 14 action figures.

DISPLAY STANDS
Kenner (1977–83)

Early Bird Package, 19" x 9½" flat envelope with
  certificate to purchase soon-to-be released
  figures and cardboard backdrop (#38140)
  Star Wars logo $300.00
See under Action Figures for listing of the Early Bird Figures.

Jabba's Palace 3-D Diorama, and close-up of unique Han Solo in Carbonite figure (Kenner 1998)

Action Display Stand for Star Wars Figures, gray
plastic first offered as a mail-in premium, and
later in stores
    Loose, with original plain box 50.00
    Original *Star Wars* box (#38990) 350.00
    Reissue as Special Action Display Stand in
        The Empire Strikes Back box, with six figures. . 550.00
    Loose, no box 40.00
Display Arena, mail-order premium (1981)
    Original *The Empire Strikes Back* box 40.00
    Reissue in *Return of the Jedi* box 35.00
    Loose 15.00

DISPLAY STANDS
Kenner (1998)

Display 3-D Diorama (Kenner 1998)
Cantina at Mos Eisley with Sandtrooper and Patrol
    Droid (#84063) 18.00
    Fan Club exclusive 18.00
Jabba's Palace with Han Solo in Carbonite (#84068). . 18.00
    Variation: Different Bio card. 10.00

COLLECTOR CASES

Vinyl Collector's Cases were offered in packaging for
each of the movies in turn. The cases each have two storage
trays designed to hold 12 figures each. The backsides had
foot pegs and could be used to display your figures. There
were stickers for the figures so each one would know where
it lived. Later, the Darth Vader and C-3PO head-shaped cases
along with the Laser Rifle carry case and even the Chewbacca
Bandolier Strap proved to be more popular designs, making
the rather plain Collector's Case much more common in *Star
Wars* packaging than in packaging for the later two films.

CARRY CASES
Kenner (1979–84)

Carry Cases
Collector's Case, black vinyl with illustrated cover,
    holds 24 figures (1979–83)
    Star Wars package $30.00
    The Empire Strikes Back package, *Star Wars*
        Pictures (#39190, 1980) 50.00
    Variation, with *The Empire Strikes Back* pictures . 50.00
    Variation, with logo centered 50.00
    Return of the Jedi package 100.00
Darth Vader Collector's Case, black plastic bust of
    Darth Vader, holds 31 figures (#93630, 1980)

illustrated wrapper around base
    Original *The Empire Strikes Back* package,
        no figures 40.00
    With **IG-88**, **Bossk** and **Boba Fett** figures in
        original *The Empire Strikes Back* package
        (#39330) 500.00
    Loose, without figures 15.00
See-Threepio Collector's Case, gold plastic bust of
    C-3PO, hold 40 figures (#70440, 1983)
    illustrated wrapper around base
    Original *Return of the Jedi* package 30.00
    Loose, without figures 15.00
Chewbacca Bandolier Strap, holds 10 figures and
    has two containers for accessories (#70480,
    1983) in 16¼" x 9¼ x 1½" box
    Original *Return of the Jedi* box 8.00
    Loose, without figures 4.00
Laser Rifle Case, rifle-shaped, holds 19 figures
    (#71530, 1984) cardboard base with color
    illustrations
    Original *Return of the Jedi* box. 30.00
    Loose, without figures 20.00

New carry cases appeared along with the return of the
figures in 1995. Generally they have a gimmick. The
Millennium Falcon-shaped carry case came with a Wedge
Antilles figure which was visible in the gun turret. At first the
figure had white arm decorations, which did not match the
uniform in the movie. Collectors and Kenner seemed to have
noticed this about the same time and when later shipments
corrected the error, collectors searched for the original figures. However, a lot of the originals are in circulation, which
has moderated the dealer price.

CARRY CASES
Kenner (1995–2000)

Carry Cases (1995–99)
Electronic Talking C-3PO Carry Case, head and
    shoulders (#27609, Oct. 1996) $20.00
Millennium Falcon Carry Case with exclusive
    Wedge Antilles figure (#27728, Sept. 1997)
        with white arm stripes (error) 50.00
    Reissue, figure with no stripe on arm (1998) 25.00
    Reissue with **Imperial Scanning Crew** figure 60.00
Darth Vader "Official Collector Case" box shaped
    carry case 20.00
R2-D2 Carryall Playset with exclusive **Destroyer
    Droid** (#26226). 20.00

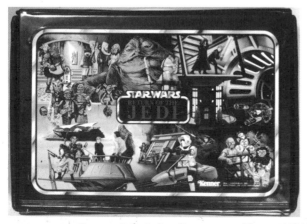 

Return of the Jedi *collector case (Kenner 1983) and* Millennium Falcon *Carry Case (Kenner 1998)*

Star Wars Episode II: Attack of the Clones

 Tusken Raider Female with Tusken child

 Clone Trooper

 Super Battle Droid

 Padmé Amidala Arena Escape

 C-3PO Protocol Droid

 R2-D2 Coruscant Sentry

Obi-Wan Kenobi
Coruscant Chase

Anakin Skywalker
Outland Peasant
Disguise

Kit Fisto Jedi
Master

Zam Wesell Bounty
Hunter

Saesee Tiin Jedi
Master

Captain Typho
Padmé's Head of
Security

Boba Fett Kamino Escape

Jango Fett Kamino Escape

Taun We Kamino Cloner

Dexter Jettster Coruscant Informant

Shaak Ti Jedi Master

Nikto Jedi Knight

 Geonosian
Warrior

 Luminara
Unduli Jedi
Master

 Royal Guard
Coruscant
Security

 Battle Droid
Arena Battle

 Jar Jar Binks
Gungan Senator

 Anakin
Skywalker
Hangar Duel

 Yoda Jedi
Master

 Plo Koon Arena
Battle

Deluxe Obi-Wan Kenobi

Deluxe Mace Windu

Deluxe Jango Fett

Deluxe Darth Tyranus

Obi-Wan Kenobi's
Jedi Starfighter

12" Anakin Skywalker

12" Clone Trooper

12" Obi-Wan Kenobi

Anakin Skywalker's Speeder

Jango Fett's *Slave I*

Zam Wesell's Speeder

ACTION FIGURES: ALPHABETICAL

Kenner/Hasbro (1978–2002)

This section lists every *Star Wars* action figure which has appeared on a header card from 1978 through the first quarter of 2002. The listing is alphabetical by the characters current name and all versions of the same character are listed together. This means that characters which appeared in the original series under names such as "Yak Face" and "Hammerhead" are now listed under their new names, "Saelt-Marae" and "Momaw Nadon" and that "Jedi Knight Luke Skywalker" is listed under "Luke Skywalker." There are three versions of Anakin Skywalker, called "Old" for the one revealed in Return of the Jedi, "Child" for the one played by Jake Lloyd in *Episode I*, and "Young Adult" for the one from *Attack of the Clones*. Darth Vader is treated as a separate character. There is one exception: Ben (Obi-Wan) Kenobi is used for the old character played by Alec Guiness in the classic trilogy, while Obi-Wan Kenobi is used for the younger character played by Ewan McGregor in *Episodes I* and *II*. Cross references are given under the original names. There are many versions of the major characters and Kenner/Harbro has not always been consistent in naming them. This, and collector short-hand, has led to popular names such as Leia "Slave Girl" which are used in advertisement from dealers, but do not appear on the figures. The listings below are organized by true name, but the popular name is given in the descriptions.

Figure and packaging variations which are specific to a given figure are described below, under that figure's listing. Major packaging changes and packaging variations which are common to many figures in a given series were described above in the chronological listings section.

ADI GALLIA

Jedi Knight and one of 12 members of the Jedi Council who votes on whether to train Anakin Skywalker as a Jedi.

Episode I:
Adi Gallia with "Lightsaber" (#84124) Col. 3
   [562934.0000] $12.00
   Loose, with red lightsaber 3.00

ADMIRAL ACKBAR

Admiral Ackbar of the Rebel Alliance Fleet is a Mon Calamari and stands 1.88 meters tall. He was captured when the Empire invaded his home planet and served as a slave to Grand Moff Tarkin. He escaped during a Rebel attack and joined the Rebel Alliance, where he was instrumental in the design of the B-Wing Fighter. Promoted to Admiral, he first appears in *Return of the Jedi* as a senior Rebel Alliance adviser. He commands the attack on the second Death Star during the Battle of Endor.

His figure carried a staff in the classic series and was initially available as a mail-in. The new figure carries a wrist blaster.

Adi Gallia (Hasbro 1999) and Admiral Ackbar (Kenner 1984)

Admiral Ackbar (Kenner 1997 and 1998)

Classic:
Admiral Ackbar (#70310, 1983)
    Original *Return of the Jedi* header card $30.00
    Reissue on Tri-Logo header card 25.00
    Loose, with staff. 10.00

New Power of the Force:
Admiral Ackbar with "Comlink Wrist Blaster" on
    green holo header card (Collection 2, #69686,
    July 1997) [542901.00] with 2nd hook, in
    stand-up bubble. 10.00
    Variation, without holo sticker 10.00
    Reissue, with "Wrist Blaster" on a Freeze
       Frame header card (#69696) [.01] 12.00
    Loose, with black wrist blaster 3.00

ADMIRAL MOTTI

"The senior Imperial Commander in charge of operations on the original Death Star, Admiral Motti often disagreed with the decisions of Darth Vader. His outspokenness almost cost him his life when Vader used the Force to strangle the Admiral into silence." You would have thought that he'd already have figured this out before he made Admiral.

New Power of the Force:
Admiral Motti with "Imperial Blaster" on green
    CommTech header card (#84366, 2000) [.00] . . . $30.00
    Loose, with Imperial Blaster 15.00

AMANAMAN

This yellow and green reptile carries a skull staff where it keeps the skulls of fugitives it hunts down. He was originally available in the Jabba the Hutt Dungeon playset from Sears. The head hunter was a popular collectible, and appeared as Fans' Choice Figure #2 in the Power of the Jedi line. It was issued on a special deluxe figure sized header card without a Jedi Force File fold-out.

Classic:
Amanaman (#93740, 1985) 5"
    Original *Power of the Force* header card. $275.00
    Reissue on Tri-Logo header card 150.00
    Loose, with skull staff. 125.00

Power of the Jedi:
Amanaman, with Salacious Crumb, deluxe figure
    (#84674) [6080250300] 12.00
    Loose, with skull staff, partial human skeleton
      and Salacious Crumb 5.00

ANAKIN SKYWALKER (OLD)

The Anakin Skywalker figure has the gray and tan robes and benevolent face from the days before he was seduced by the dark side of the Force. His character reverted to this form after his death in *Return of the Jedi*. He is treated as a separate character from Darth Vader. Loose figures were available as a mail-in, but packaged figures are all foreign, which accounts for the large disparity in price. He's a lot cheaper in the newer version.

Classic:
Anakin Skywalker (#93790, 1985) foreign release
    Original *Power of the Force* header card $2,250.00
    Reissue on Tri-Logo header card 125.00
    Loose, no accessories 30.00

New Power of the Force:
Anakin Skywalker with "Lightsaber" on Flashback
    Photo header card (#84047) [560226.0000] 12.00
    Loose, with lightsaber 5.00

ANAKIN SKYWALKER (CHILD)

Anakin is strong in the force, and only nine-years old when we first meet him on Tatooine. Too bad we know what happens to him later on.

Episode I:
Anakin Skywalker (Tatooine) with "Backpack and
    Grease Gun" (#84074) Col. 1 [557437.00] $12.00
    Reissue [.0100] 7.00
    Loose, with backpack and grease gun. 3.00
Anakin Skywalker (Naboo) with "Comlink Unit"
    (#84112) Col. 1 [562045.0100] 7.00
    Loose, with comlink unit and cloak with hood 3.00
Anakin Skywalker (Naboo Pilot) with "Flight
    Simulator" (#84246) Col. 1 [563961.0000]. 15.00
    Loose, with flight simulator and helmet 3.00

Amanaman and Anukin Skywalker (Kenner 1985 and 1998)

Anakin Skywalker (Hasbro 1999 and 2000)

Power of the Jedi:
Anakin Skywalker, Mechanic (#84254) Col. 1 on
 Jedi Force File header card [571090.0000] 12.00
 Reissue [.0100]. 8.00
 Loose, with wrench and droid 3.00

ANAKIN SKYWALKER (YOUNG ADULT)

This is the character from *Attack of the Clones* who has grown up as Obi-Wan's apprentice and becomes romantically involved with Queen Amidala. So what if she's an older woman – romance is romance.

Attack of the Clones:
Anakin Skywalker, Outland Peasant Disguise, Col. 1. . . . N/A
Anakin Skywalker, Hangar Duel, Col. 1 . . . . N/A

ASP-7

The ASP-7 droid is a domestic and industrial laborer. It is 1.6 meters tall. The figure comes with a small bundle of supply rods. This droid is from the new Special Edition footage and was not produced in the original figure line.

New Power of the Force:
ASP-7 Droid with "Spaceport Supply Rods" "Newly-
 Created Footage" sticker, on green holo
 header card (Collection 2, #69704, July 1997)
 [540899.00] with 2nd hook, in stand-up bubble. . $10.00
 Loose, with olive drab supply rod bundle 3.00

AT-AT COMMANDER

The AT-AT (All Terrain Armored Transport) Walker is both a weapons platform and a troop transport. Each takes two pilots. The Commander acts as navigator and gunner.

In the new series, an exclusive AT-AT Commander and AT-AT Driver are included with the Electronic AT-AT vehicle, and a 12" doll was released in 1997.

Classic:
AT-AT Commander (#69620, 1982)
 Original *The Empire Strikes Back* header card. . . $80.00
 Reissue on *Return of the Jedi* header card 45.00
 Reissue on Tri-Logo header card 35.00
 Loose, with pistol. 10.00

New: See AT-AT Walker vehicle

AT-AT DRIVER

The AT-AT (All Terrain Armored Transport) Walker takes two pilots. The second acts as navigator and gunner.

The AT-AT driver from the classic series was also included with the MTV-7 vehicle. In the new series, an exclusive AT-AT Commander and AT-AT Driver are included with the Electronic AT-AT vehicle, and a 12" doll was released in 1997.

Classic:
AT-AT Driver (#39379, 1981)
 Original *The Empire Strikes Back* header card. . . $90.00
 Reissue on *Return of the Jedi* header card 40.00
 Reissue on *Power of the Force* header card,
  foreign release only 550.00
 Reissue on Tri-Logo header card 90.00
 Loose, with rifle 10.00

New Power of the Force:
AT-AT Driver with "Imperial Issue Blaster" on green
 Freeze Frame header card (Collection 3,
 #69864) [554796.0000] 25.00
 Loose, with blaster 12.50

AT-ST DRIVER

The AT-ST (All Terrain Scout Transport) Driver is a human Imperial Ground-Assault pilot. He averages 1.8 meters tall.

The first AT-ST Driver issued in the new series came on a Collection 2 header card. This was corrected to Collection 3. There is only a slight premium for the original header card.

Classic:
AT-ST Driver (#71330, 1984)
 Original *Return of the Jedi* header card $30.00
 Reissue on *Power of the Force* header card. 60.00
 Reissue on Tri-Logo header card 30.00
 Loose, with pistol. 10.00

New Power of the Force:
AT-ST Driver with "Blaster Rifle and Pistol" on
 green holo header card (**Collection 2**, #69623,

ASP-7 Droid and AT-AT Commander (Kenner 1997 and 1983)

AT-AT Driver and AT-ST Driver (Kenner 1981 and 1997)

Feb. 1997) [538001.00] with 1st hook, in orig-
inal bubble 12.00
Variation, without holo sticker 12.00
Reissue, [.01] with 2nd hook, in stand-up
bubble 7.00
Reissue, (Collection 3, #69823) [.02] with 2nd
hook, in stand-up bubble 6.00
Reissue on green CommTech header card
(Collection 3, #69623) [.03] scarce 75.00
Loose, with black blaster pistol and rifle 3.00

AUNT BERU

Aunt Beru and Uncle Owen have a moisture farm on Tatooine where Luke is stuck, doing chores, while dreaming of going to the Academy with Biggs and becomming a big-shot pilot. Both get killed when the Stormtroopers raid their farm looking for R2-D2 and the Death Star plans.

Beru got her own figure, while Owen was included in the Purchase of the Droids Cinema Scenes three-pack.

New Power of the Force:
Aunt Beru with "Service Droid" on Flashback Photo
header card (#84049) [560232.0000] $15.00
Loose, with droid 5.00

AURRA SING

Originally a Jedi apprentice trained by the Jedi Master known as the Dark Woman. Aurra Sing left the Jedi and became a bounty hunter and Jedi hater.

Power of the Jedi:
Aurra Sing, Bounty Hunter (#84584) Col. 1 on Jedi
Force File header card [571090.0300] $15.00
Reissue [.0400] 8.00
Loose, with rifle and pistol 3.00

A-WING PILOT

When the A-Wing Pilot figure was reissued in the Droids series, there were no changes in the figure and the only change in the coin was in the color. Both versions are scarce and valuable.

Classic:
A-Wing Pilot (#93830, 1985)
Original *Power of the Force* header card $100.00
Reissue on *DROIDS* header card 175.00
Reissue on Tri-Logo header card 75.00
Loose, with pistol 50.00

New: See A-Wing Fighter vehicle

BARADA

Barada was a Klatoonian slave of Jabba the Hutt. He was the first one killed in the battle at the Sarlacc's pit.

Barada also came with the Jabba the Hutt Dungeon playset from Sears. He has not yet appeared in the new series of figures, except as one of Jabba's Skiff Guards in the Cinema Scenes three-pack.

Classic:
Barada (#93750, 1985)
Original *Power of the Force* header card $100.00
Reissue on Tri-Logo header card 60.00
Loose, with staff. 40.00

New: See Jabba's Skiff Guards, Cinema Scenes

BATTLE DROID

Manufactured by Bactoid Combat Automation for the Trade Federation, they are no match for Jedi, but kick Gungan butt until their Control Ship is destroyed.

It's a good thing that so many *Episode I* figures were available at discount, becaue the Battle Droids' heads come off easily and tend to get lost. This does leaves a large supply of battle damaged Battle Droids available, but if this isn't enough, Hasbro has now released one that shows the type of damage caused by the Gungan army at the battle of Naboo.

Episode I
Battle Droid with "Blaster Rifle" (#84092)
Brown Col. 1 [558449.00] $25.00
Reissue Brown [.0100]. 18.00
Reissue Brown [.0200]. 7.00
Tan Col. 1 [558449.00]. 25.00
Reissue Tan [.0100] 18.00

Aunt Beru (Kenner 1998) and Aurra Sing (Hasbro 2001)

A-Wing Pilot (Kenner 1985) Battle Droid (brown) (Hasbro 1999)

Battle Droid (tan) and Battle Droid Security
(Hasbro 1999 and 2001)

Reissue Tan [.0200] 7.00
Lightsaber slashed Col. 1 [558449.00] 25.00
Reissue Lightsaber slashed [.0100]. 18.00
Reissue Lightsaber slashed [.0200] 7.00
Blaster Battle scars Col. 1 [558449.00] 25.00
Reissue Blaster Battle scars [.0100] 18.00
Reissue Blaster Battle scars [.0200]. 7.00
Loose, any style, with black blaster rifle. 3.00

Power of the Jedi:
Battle Droid, Boomer Damage (#84563) Col. 1 on
    Jedi Force File header card [571090.0100] 12.00
    Reissue [.0300]. 10.00
    Reissue [.0400]. 8.00
    Loose, ... 3.00

BATTLE DROID (SECURITY)

These droids serve as guards at Trade Federation bases and take charge of prisoners. They aren't much of a match for Jedi.

Power of the Jedi:
Battle Droid, Security (#84249) Col. 2 on Jedi Force
    File header card [571100.0000]. $12.00
    Reissue [.0100]. 8.00
    Loose, ... 4.00

BEN (OBI-WAN) KENOBI (OLD)

Two versions of Obi-Wan's head were made in the classic figure series, one with gray hair and one with white hair. They are about equally scarce (or equally common) and there is little or no difference in price between the two versions.

The really scarce figure variation is the telescoping lightsaber which came with just a few of the earliest versions of Luke Skywalker, Darth Vader and this figure . It adds about $2,000 to Obi-Wan's value, but beware of fakes, even on carded figures.

The header card photo was changed during the *Return of the Jedi* figure series. The original photo shows a bare-headed Obi-Wan facing left and holding a yellow lightsaber, which is pointing to the upper left. The new photo shows a

Ben (Obi-Wan) Kenobi, original package (Kenner 1983) and
Ben (Obi-Wan) Kenobi (Kenner 1997)

hooded Obi-Wan facing forward and holding a blue lightsaber which is pointing to the upper right.

In the new figure series, Obi-Wan's photo on the back of the header card ".00" was changed from from a head and shoulders photo to a full figure photo on the ".01" card. In addition, a spelling error was corrected when "an" was changed to "and". More significantly, his lightsaber was shortened, along with Luke's and Darth's, resulting in two different versions of his figure.

Classic:
Ben (Obi-Wan) Kenobi (#38250, 1978) **white** or **gray hair**
    Original *Star Wars* "12 back" header card, **gray** $700.00
    Original *Star Wars* "12 back" header card, **white** . 800.00
    Variation, with telescoping lightsaber, scarce . . 2,500.00
    Loose, with telescoping lightsaber 500.00
    Reissue on *Star Wars* "20/21 back" header card. . 175.00
    Reissue on *The Empire Strikes Back* header card . 125.00
    Reissue on *Return of the Jedi* header card 50.00
    Reissue on *Return of the Jedi* header card new
        package, hooded, holding lightsaber in front . . 50.00
    Reissue on *Power of the Force* header card. . . . 125.00
    Reissue on Tri-Logo header card 75.00
    Loose, with lightsaber 15.00

New Power of the Force:
Ben (Obi-Wan) Kenobi with "Lightsaber and
    Removable Cloak" on red header card
    (#69576, July 1995) bust photo, long light-
    saber [521791.00] 50.00
    Full-figure photo on package back, long
        lightsaber [.01]. 50.00
    Loose, with long lightsaber. 12.50
    Variation, short lightsaber in long tray, scarce . . 1,500.00
    Full-figure photo, short lightsaber [.01] 15.00
    Reissue, with holo sticker. 10.00
    Reissue on green holo header card
        (Collection 1, #69576) [.02] with 2nd hook,
        in stand-up bubble. 6.00
    Reissue, without holo sticker 6.00
    Reissue, as Obi-Wan (Ben) Kenobi with "Light-
        saber" on Freeze Frame header card [.03] 25.00
    Reissue, Saelt Marae spelling corrected [.04] 20.00
    Loose, with blue lightsaber with silver handle 3.00

Ben (Obi-Wan) bust photo (Kenner 1995) and
Bespin Guard (Hasbro 2001)

Bib Fortuna and Biggs Darklighter (Kenner 1983 and 1998)

Ben (Obi-Wan) Kenobi with "Lightsaber" on Flashback Photo header card (#84037) [557526.00]. . . 10.00
Loose, with lightsaber 3.00

Power of the Jedi:
Ben (Obi-Wan) Kenobi, Jedi Knight (#84362) Col. 1
on Jedi Force File header card [571090.0100]. . . . 12.00
Loose, with blue lightsaber 3.00

Bespin Han Solo: See Han Solo (Bespin Outfit)

BESPIN SECURITY GUARD

The 1980 version of the Bespin Security Guard had
white skin and the 1982 version (same name, different UPC
code) had black skin. They are meant to be different figures
and the packages have different photos, but neither package
uses the words "black" or "white." These names have been
added by collectors and dealers to distinguish between the
figures. The white figure can also be found with slightly yel-
lowish skin and a slightly longer, but not quite Fu Manchu-
style mustache. The price is the same in either case. The white
Bespin Security Guard also came with the Cloud Car vehicle.

Classic: white
Bespin Security Guard (#39810, 1980) **white**
Original *The Empire Strikes Back* header card. . . $75.00
Reissue on *Return of the Jedi* header card 35.00
Reissue on Tri-Logo header card 25.00
Loose, with pistol 10.00

Classic: black
Bespin Security Guard (#69640, 1982) **black**
Original *The Empire Strikes Back* header card. . . . 65.00
Reissue on *Return of the Jedi* header card 55.00
Reissue on Tri-Logo header card 25.00
Loose, with pistol 10.00

Power of the Jedi:
Bespin Guard, Cloud City Security (#84638) Col. 2
on Jedi Force File header card [571100.0400]. . . . 10.00
Loose, ... 3.00

BIB FORTUNA

Bib Fortuna is a Twi'lek from the planet Ryloth and
serves as Jabba the Hutt's majordomo.

He first appears in the new series of figures on a
Collection 1 header card, but this was changed to Collection
2. The original Collection 1 card is not especially scarce and
carries only a slight premium over the more common
Collection 2.

Classic:
Bib Fortuna (#70790, 1983)
Original *Return of the Jedi* header card $30.00
Reissue on Tri-Logo header card 25.00
Loose, with brown cloak and staff. 10.00

New Power of the Force:
Bib Fortuna with "Hold-Out Blaster" on green holo
header card (**Collection 1**, #69634, April 1997)
[538955.00] with 1st hook, in original bubble 12.00
Reissue (Collection 2, #69812) [.01] with
2nd hook, in original or stand-up bubble. 10.00
Variation, without holo sticker. 10.00
Loose, with black hold-out blaster 3.00

BIGGS DARKLIGHTER

Biggs Darklighter is a Tatooine native and childhood
friend of Luke. He is the famous missing character of the
original *Star Wars* movie because his scenes with Luke at the
beginning of the movie were cut and all you saw was his
death at the hands of Darth Vader. The Special Edition
restored a brief reunion scene with Luke, just before they both
took off in their X-Wing fighters to attack the Death Star.

He did not appear among the classic figures, but he was
a popular character with figure customizers.

New Power of the Force:
Biggs Darklighter with "Blaster Pistol" on green
Freeze Frame header card (Collection 2,
#69758, 1998) [550387.00] $20.00
Loose, with black blaster pistol and rifle 5.00

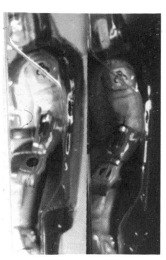

Biker Scout (Kenner 1983 and 1985)

Boba Fett (Kenner 1996) and close-up showing hand detail

BIKER SCOUT (TROOPER)

One of several types of Imperial pilots which appeared in the classic series, but has only been sold with a vehicle in the new series. He is not a highly sought figure in either of these series. In the Power of the Jedi series the name was changed to "Scout Trooper" but just about everybody uses the old name. A variant version of the recent figure shows dirt on the armor to represent battle damage.

Classic:
Biker Scout (#70820, 1983)
    Original *Return of the Jedi* header card $35.00
    Reissue on *Power of the Force* header card. 80.00
    Reissue on Tri-Logo header card 25.00
    Loose, with pistol 15.00

New: See Imperial Speeder Bike vehicle

Power of the Jedi:
Scout Trooper, Imperial Patrol (**white**) (#84586, 2000) Col. 1 on Jedi Force File header card
    [571090.0100] $12.00
    Reissue [.0300]. 10.00
    Loose, with Blaster and Ankle Holster 3.00
Scout Trooper, Imperial Patrol (**dirty**) (#84586, 2001) Col. 1 on Jedi Force File header card
    [.0400] 10.00
    Loose, with Blaster and Ankle Holster 3.00

BOBA FETT

Boba Fett is a notorious bounty hunter. Darth Vader hired him to track down Han Solo's ship in order to lure Luke Skywalker out into the open. Han Solo was his reward and Jabba the Hutt paid handsomely for Solo.

In the original series, Boba Fett also came as an early mail-in figure. It was advertised with a spring-loaded rocket back pack missile, but this was a child safety hazard and was never shipped. A few prototypes exist and are extremely valuable. See "Mail-Ins" in the previous section for a listing of this, and other classic mail-in figures.

The front header card photo was changed during the *Return of the Jedi* figure series. The original photo shows

your favorite bounty hunter facing forward in front of a starry background. The new photo shows him facing to the left, armed to the teeth in front of a blue sky.

The Tri-Logo version of Boba Fett is somewhat different from the versions on other header cards. The plastic is lighter in weight, the comb below the right knee is unpainted and the rocket is shorter and in a matte finish. In the domestic version of Boba Fett he is heavier, has the comb on his right knee painted the same color as the knee band and has a rocket with a glossy finish. Also, the Tri-Logo figures chest plate is a darker green and the shoulder and knee highlights are darker brown than those on the domestic figure.

In the new series of figures, Boba Fett initially came with a black disk painted on the back of each hand that was bisected by a bar that is the same color as the rest of the hand. This appears as two half-moons or half-circles. Later versions of the figure have a complete black disk or full-circle. The half-circle version is scarce and valuable. A comma after the word "Empire" on the ".00" header card was corrected to a period on the ".01" header card. It returned to a comma on the ".02" and ".03" cards.

Classic:
Boba Fett (#39250, 1978–79)
    Original *Star Wars* header card $1,500.00
    Reissue on *The Empire Strikes Back* header card . 400.00
    Reissue on *Return of the Jedi* header card. 325.00
    Reissue on *Return of the Jedi* header card
      new package. 350.00
    Loose, with pistol 60.00
    Reissue on Tri-Logo header card 700.00
    Loose, Tri-Logo version, with pistol. 45.00
Boba Fett (#39260, 1985)
    On *Droids* header card. 250.00
    Loose, cartoon version. 50.00

New Power of the Force:
Boba Fett with "Sawed-Off Blaster Rifle and Jet
    Pack" on red header card (#69582, Feb. 1996)
    with half circles on back of hands [526520.00] "**,**" . 50.00
    Variation [.01] "**.**" half circles 45.00
    Reissue: [.01] full circles on hands 15.00
    Variation, one half circle and one full circle. 350.00
    Loose, with half circles on hand 10.00

With full circles on hand [.01] 10.00
Reissue on green holo header card
(**Collection 1**, #69582) [.02] with 2nd hook,
in original bubble 30.00
Reissue (Collection 3, #69804) [.03] with 2nd
hook, in stand-up bubble 20.00
Reissue, on Freeze Frame header card
(Collection 3, #69804) [.04] 50.00
Variations, **Black circle** on one hand, or **no
circle**, or **no emblem** on chest, or **no skull**
on shoulder 500.00
Loose, with black sawed-off blaster and
beat-up jet pack 3.00

Special Edition:
Boba Fett with "Rocket-Firing Backpack" in Special
Edition 300th Figure box (#84566) [571274.0100] . 25.00
Reissue: [.0200] 15.00
Loose, ... 10.00

Attack of the Clones:
Boba Fett, Kamino Escape, Col. 2 . . . . N/A

BOSSK

Bossk is a freelance Trandoshan bounty hunter. His specialty is catching Wookiees and he first appears in *The Empire Strikes Back*.

His was the famous "secret figure" offered as a mail-in at the end of the original *Star Wars* figure series.

Classic:
Bossk (Bounty Hunter) (#39760, 1980)
Original *The Empire Strikes Back* header card . . $125.00
Reissue on *Return of the Jedi* header card 75.00
Reissue on Tri-Logo header card 55.00
Loose, with rifle 15.00

New Power of the Force:
Bossk with "Blaster Rifle and Pistol" on   green
header card (Collection 2, #69617, Feb. 1997)
[537991.00] with 1st hook and original bubble . . . 12.00
Variation, without holo sticker 12.00
With holo picture [.01] and 2nd hook, with
stand-up bubble 12.00
Loose, with light gray rifle and pistol 3.00

BOSS NASS

As Ruler of the Gungans, he alone can summon the Grand Army to battle, which he does to help rid Naboo of the Trade Federation army. Why he appoints Jar Jar Binks a general is another matter.

Episode I:
Boss Nass with "Gungan Staff" (#84119) Col. 3
[558996.0000] $8.00
Reissue [.0100] 7.00
Loose, with staff 3.00

Power of the Jedi:
Boss Nass, Gungan Sacred Place (#84473) Col. 2
on Jedi Force File header card [571101.0000]. . . . 12.00
Reissue [.0100] 10.00
Loose, without equipment 3.00

B-WING PILOT

This has never been a highly sought figure. He comes in a nifty red jumpsuit.

Classic:
B-Wing Pilot (#71280, 1984)
Original *Return of the Jedi* header card $30.00
Reissue on *Power of the Force* header card 30.00
Reissue on Tri-Logo header card 30.00
Loose, with pistol 10.00

New: See B-Wing vehicle

CAPTAIN PANAKA

Head of Royal Security for Queen Amidala. The trouble is, it's mostly a volunteer force, with no real chance to defend Naboo against the Trade Federation droid army.

Episode I:
Captain Panaka with "Blaster Rifle and Pistol"
(#84108) Col. 2 [562928.0000] $12.00
Loose, with rifle and pistol 5.00

CAPTAIN PIETT

Captain Piett was promoted to Admiral during the assault on Hoth and commanded Darth Vader's ship *Executor*

Boba Fett 300th Figure (Hasbro 2000) and Bossk (Kenner 1983)

Boss Nass (Hasbro 1999) and B-Wing Pilot (Kenner 1985)

Captain Panaka and Captain Tarpals (Hasbro 1999)

Chancellor Valorum (Hasbro 1999) and Chewbacca (Kenner 1978)

until its destruction during the Battle of Endor. The figure essentially replaces the Imperial Commander figure from the classic series.

New Power of the Force:
Captain Piett with "Blaster Rifle and Pistol" on
    Freeze Frame header card (Collection 3,
    #69757, 1998) [550624.00] $30.00
    Reissue: with "Blaster Pistol and Baton" [.00]. . . . 100.00
    Loose, with black pistol and baton 10.00

CAPTAIN TARPALS

Commander of the Gungan army in the battle against the Trade Federation droid army. Unfortunately, they are no match for the droids. As a career military man, think how it must have galled him to see a perpetual screw-up like Jar Jar Binks appointed a general! He probably leads a military coup within months of the end of *Episode I*, with the usual purges, show trials, concentration camps, and executions. If I were Boss Nass, I'd watch my back.

Episode I:
Captain Tarpals with "Electropole" (#84121) Col. 3
    [561426.0000] $12.00
    Loose, with electropole 5.00

CHANCELLOR VALORUM

Chancellor of the Galactic Senate on Coruscant. Not much of a politician, since he fails to see that his one-time ally Senator Palpatine is out to get his job.

Episode I:
Chancellor Valorum with "Ceremonial Staff"
    (#84132) Col. 3 [559003.0000] small parts
    warning $12.00
    Variation: [.0000] black sticker over warning. 10.00
    Reissue [.0100]. 7.00
    Loose, with staff 3.00

CHEWBACCA

Chewbacca is from the planet Kashyyyk and owes a life debt to Han Solo for releasing him from an Empire prison. As Han's partner, he seems to be the brains of the outfit. He was

the one who made the initial deal to transport Obi-Wan and Luke away from Tatooine.

The original figure was included in the Early Bird Package and many of these had a green blaster rifle. All other original series versions of the figure had a black blaster rifle. The front photo was changed during the *Return of the Jedi* series. The original photo shows Chewbacca with slicked-back hair and carrying his weapon. In the new photo Chewie has frizzy hair and no visible weapon.

Classic:
Chewbacca (#38210, 1978) 4¼" figure
    Original *Star Wars* "12 back" header card with
      green blaster rifle $325.00
    Original *Star Wars* "12 back" header card with
      black blaster rifle 300.00
    Reissue on *Star Wars* "20/21 back" header
      card. 225.00
    Reissue on *The Empire Strikes Back* header card . 125.00
    Reissue on *Return of the Jedi* header card 50.00
    Reissue on *Return of the Jedi* header card
      with new frizzy head and shoulders photo 45.00
    Reissue on *Power of the Force* header card 100.00
    Reissue on Tri-Logo header card 60.00
    Loose, with black blaster rifle 15.00
    Loose, with green blaster rifle. 35.00

New Power of the Force:
Chewbacca with "Bowcaster and Heavy Blaster
    Rifle" 4¼" on red header card (#69578,
    July 1995) [521795.00]. 15.00
    Reissue on green holo header card (Collection
      1, #69578) [.01] with 2nd hook, in stand-up
      bubble. 6.00
    Variation, without holo sticker. 6.00
    Loose, with dark gray bowcaster and heavy
      blaster rifle. 3.00

Chewbacca Bounty Hunter Disguise

The Shadows of the Empire storyline takes place between *The Empire Strikes Back* and before *Return of the Jedi*. Chewbacca and Leia go to Coruscant to try to find out who has been attempting to assassinate Luke. Chewbacca disguises himself as Snoova, a Wookiee bounty hunter. Leia is captured by Prince Xizor and Chewbacca contacts Luke

Hoth Chewbacca (Kenner 1998) and
Chewbacca, Dejarik Champion (Hasbro 2001)

Chief Chirpa and Clone Emperor Palpatine, Expanded Universe
(Kenner 1983 and 1998)

and Lando. The three of them and Dash Rendar proceed to rescue the princess.

New: Shadows of the Empire
Chewbacca in Bounty Hunter Disguise, with "Vibro
   Axe and Heavy Blaster Rifle" on a purple
   Shadows of the Empire card (#69562,
   June 1996) [531618.00] $12.00
Loose, with black axe and heavy blaster rifle 3.00

Chewbacca as Boushh's Bounty

"Chewbacca, acting as a prisoner, and Princess Leia, disguised as the bounty hunter Boussh, infiltrate Jabba's Palace. There they hope to rescue the carbonite-encased Han Solo."

New Power of the Force:
Chewbacca as Boushh's Bounty, with "Bowcaster"
   on Freeze Frame header card (Collection
   1, #69882) [553656.00] $15.00
Loose, chain around neck, with bowcaster 5.00

Chewbacca (Dejarik Champion)

Don't forget the cardinal rule of Dejarik: recite after me, "Let the Wookiee Win!" That's probably why the Jedi Force File says he's "Dejarik Champion" while the UPC sticker and Hasbro's Web site say "Dejarik Challenge."

Power of the Jedi:
Chewbacca, Dejarik Champion (#84363) Col. 2 on
   Jedi Force File header card [571100.0000] $15.00
   Reissue [.0001] 8.00
   Loose, with Dejarik table and playing pieces 3.00

Hoth Chewbacca

Coming from a jungle planet, Hoth must have seemed very chilly, even for a well-furred Wookiee.

New Power of the Force:
Hoth Chewbacca with "Bowcaster Rifle" on Flash-
   back Photo header card (#84051) [557536.00] . . $10.00
   Loose, with bowcaster. 3.00

Chewbacca (*Millennium Falcon* Mechanic)

It's a good thing Chewbacca is technically savvy, because Han needs someone to keep his ship in good repair.

Power of the Jedi:
Chewbacca, *Millennium Falcon* Mechanic (#84577)
   Col. 1 on Jedi Force File header card
   [571090.0300] $12.00
   Reissue [.0400] 8.00
   Loose, with welding goggles and torch 3.00

CHIEF CHIRPA

Chief Chirpa is an Ewok, one of eight issued in the *Return of the Jedi* series. He had not been issued in any new series at press time.

Classic:
Chief Chirpa (#70690, 1983)
   Original *Return of the Jedi* header card $30.00
   Reissue on Tri-Logo header card 25.00
   Loose, with long club 10.00

CLONE EMPEROR PALPATINE

"Six years after the destruction of the second Death Star, the galaxy is thrust into turmoil. A reborn evil threatens to enslave the galaxy, and the Republic's closest friend – Luke Skywalker – may become their greatest enemy. With the power to transfer his consciousness to genetic clones, a younger, stronger Emperor Palpatine is perilously close to gaining total control of the galaxy forever." From the Dark Empire comic book series.

New: Expanded Universe
Clone Emperor Palpatine on a 3-D PlayScene
   header card (#69886) Collection 2 [554781.02] . $20.00
   Loose, ... 10.00

CLOUD CAR PILOT

This figure has not been heavily collected, and like several similar figures from the classic series, it will only be issued with a vehicle in the new series.

Classic:
Cloud Car Pilot (Twin Pod) (#69630, 1982)
   Original *The Empire Strikes Back* header card . . $125.00
   Reissue on *Return of the Jedi* header card 45.00
   Reissue on Tri-Logo header card 30.00

Cloud Car Pilot (Kenner 1980) and Coruscant Guard (Hasbro 2000)

Loose, with pistol and light 20.00

New Power of the Force:
None, but look for Cloud Car vehicle

CORUSCANT GUARD

Coruscant guards protect the Galactic Senate and the Chancellor. They have neat blue outfits which look like they might get in the way in battle.

Power of the Jedi:
Coruscant Guard (#84277) Col. 2 on Jedi Force
File header card [571101.0000] $15.00
Reissue [.0100] 12.00
Reissue [.0300] 12.00
Reissue [.0400] 8.00
Loose, ... 3.00

C-3PO (SEE-THREEPIO)

C-3PO is a Cybot Galactica 3PO Human Cyborg Relations Droid and needs no introduction, but he could use a few more buyers. He generally ranks about last in his class in price. In the movies he usually takes a beating and looses verious body parts.

Classic:
See-Threepio (C-3PO) (#38220, 1978)
Original *Star Wars* "12 back" header card $300.00
Reissue on *Star Wars* "20/21 back" header
card 100.00
Reissue on *The Empire Strikes Back* header card . 150.00
Reissue on Tri-Logo header card 45.00
Loose, no accessories 15.00

New Power of the Force:
C-3PO with "Realistic Metalized Body" on red
header card (#69573, July 1995) [521785.00]. . . . 10.00
Reissue on green holo header card
(Collection 1, #69573) [.01] with 2nd hook,
in original or stand-up bubble. 10.00
Loose, without accessories 3.00

C-3PO (Removable Limbs)

The removable limbs version of C-3PO is based on his

C-3PO (Kenner 1983 and Hasbro 1999)

dismemberment and subsequent rescue in the second movie. The Flashback version was described as "Shopworn" on Hasbro's Web site. C-3PO has not been a popular character with collectors.

Classic:
C-3PO (Removable Limbs) (#69600, 1982)
Original *The Empire Strikes Back* header card . . . $90.00
Reissue on *Return of the Jedi* header card as
See-Threepio (C-3PO) (#69430) "now
with removable arms, legs and back pack". . . . 35.00
Reissue on *Power of the Force* header card
as **See-Threepio (C-3PO)** with removable
limbs (#69430) 80.00
Reissue on Tri-Logo header card 25.00
Loose, with back pack and limbs 10.00

New Power of the Force:
C-3PO with "Realistic Metalized Body and Cargo
Net" and sticker saying "New Pull-Apart
Feature" on green Freeze Frame header card
(Collection 1, #69832) [551743.00] 15.00
Loose, with Cargo Net and all limbs 3.00

C-3PO with "Removable Arm" on Flashback Photo
header card (#84041) [560229.0000] 10.00
Loose, with arm 3.00

C-3PO (Naked)

In *Episode I* we learned that young Anakin Skywalker made C-3PO and that he lacked his final gold-colored metal skin. Collectors, and C-3PO himself, regard this version as "Naked."

Episode I:
C-3PO (#84106) Col. 2 [558550.00] $10.00
Reissue [.0100]. 7.00
Loose, no accessories 3.00

DARK TROOPER

"Discovering that Imperial forces have begun developing a new type of Stormtrooper, the Rebels call on Kyle Katarn. His mission: Seek out and destroy the secret Imperial project called Dark Trooper. Known as phase III, this most powerful of the Dark Troopers is actually a figure known as

Dark Trooper (Kenner 1998) and Darth Maul (Hasbro 1999)

Darth Maul and Darth Sidious (Hasbro 2001 and 1999)

General Mohc. Practically unstoppable, he represents the greatest threat to the success of the Rebel Alliance." From the Dark Forces Video game.

New: Expanded Universe
Dark Trooper on a 3-D PlayScene header card
    (#69894) Collection 2 [556418.01] $30.00
    Loose, ... 10.00

DARTH MAUL

Sith apprentice to Darth Sidious with a neat red and black face which makes a great Halloween mask. "Always two there are – a master and an apprentice." Kills Qui-Gon and is cut in half by Obi-Wan. You can buy the cut-in-half version and reinact the scene. No blood, but there wasn't any in the movie either. Lightsabers must cauterize as they slice.

Episode I:
Darth Maul (Jedi Duel) with "Double-Bladed Light-
    saber" (#84088) Col. 1 [558452.00] $18.00
    Reissue [.0000]. 20.00
    Reissue [.0100] 7.00
    Variation: [.00] or [.0100] with Black Vest, scarce . 500.00
    Loose, with lightsaber 3.00
    Loose, (black vest). . . . .

Darth Maul (Tatooine) with "Cloak and Lightsaber"
    (#84134) Col. 1 [562054.0000]. 7.00
    Variation: [.0000] with Black Vest 500.00
    Reissue [0100] . . . .
    Loose, with cloak and lightsaber 3.00
    Loose (black vest) . . . .

Darth Maul (Sith Lord) with "Lightsaber with Re-
    movable Blade" (#84247) Col. 1 [563964.0000] . . 15.00
    Loose, with lightsaber and blade 3.00

Power of the Jedi:
Darth Maul, Final Duel (#84506) Col. 1 with "Break-
    Apart Battle Damage", on Jedi Force File
    header card [571091.0000 with sticker] 15.00
    Reissue [.0100] without sticker. 8.00
    Loose, ... 3.00

Darth Maul, Sith Apprentice (#84561) Col. 1 on Jedi
    Force File header card [571091.0300] 15.00

Reissue [.0400] 10.00
Loose, ... 3.00

DARTH SIDIOUS

Darth Maul's master, seen only as a holographic transmission in *Episode I*. He gives orders to the Trade Federation, which, too late, learns to regret the deal they made with him.

Episode I:
Darth Sidious (#84087) Col. 2 [558544.00] $12.00
    [.0100]. 7.00
    Loose, no accessories 3.00

Darth Sidious (Holograph) (#84081, 2000) Col. 2
    [563967.0000] 30.00
    Loose, no accessories 9.00

DARTH VADER

The front photo was changed during the *Return of the Jedi* series. The original photo shows Darth holding his lightsaber. The new photo is more of a close-up and no lightsaber is visible.

The telescoping lightsaber is a really scarce variation which came with just a few of the earliest versions of Obi-Wan Kenobi, Luke Skywalker and Darth Vader. It adds about $2,000 to its value, but beware of fakes.

In the new series, his lightsaber was shortened, along with Luke's and Obi-Wan's, resulting in two different versions of his figure and the packaging variation of a short lightsaber in a long lightsaber clear plastic tray.

Classic:
Darth Vader (#38230, 1978) 4¼" figure
    Original *Star Wars* "12 back" header card $600.00
    Variation, with telescoping lightsaber, scarce . . 2,250.00
    Loose, with telescoping lightsaber 400.00
    Reissue on *Star Wars* "20/21 back" header card. . 300.00
    Reissue on *The Empire Strikes Back* header card . 125.00
    Reissue on *Return of the Jedi* header card 50.00
    Reissue on *Return of the Jedi* header card,
        new package. 45.00
    Reissue on *Power of the Force* header card. . . . 100.00
    Reissue on Tri-Logo header card 45.00

Darth Vader, new package (Kenner 1983) and
Darth Vader, Emperor's Wrath (Hasbro 2000)

Loose, with lightsaber 12.00

New Power of the Force:
Darth Vader with "Lightsaber and Removable
Cape" 4¼" on red header card (#69572, July
1995) with long lightsaber [521783.00] 25.00
Loose, with long red lightsaber 12.50
Short lightsaber in long package slot 45.00
Short lightsaber version 15.00
Reissue on green holo header card
(**Collection 1**, #69572) [.01] with 2nd hook,
in original bubble 15.00
   Reissue (Collection 3, #69802) [.02] with
   2nd hook, in original or stand-up bubble 5.00
Retooled, *Shadows of the Empire* two-pack
style figure [.02] 20.00
Reissue, on Freeze Frame header card [.03] 6.50
Loose, with red lightsaber with black handle 3.00

Darth Vader with "Lightsaber" on Flashback Photo
header card (#84046) [557538.00] 10.00
Loose, ... 3.00

Darth Vader with "Imperial Interrogation Droid" on
CommTech Chip header card (#84203) [.00] 20.00
Loose, with droid 5.00

Power of the Jedi:
Darth Vader, Emperor's Wrath (#84637) Col. 1 on
Jedi Force File header card [571091.0400] 10.00
Loose, ... 7.00

Darth Vader, Dagobah (#84472) Col. 1 on Jedi
Force File header card [571090.0100] 15.00
Reissue [.0400] 8.00
Loose, ... 3.00

Darth Vader (Removable Helmet)

With his helmet off, Darth reveals what's left of his
original face. There is no equivalent figure from the classic
series. The Anakin Skywalker figure, listed previously, is the
ghostly version seen only at the end of the third movie.

New Power of the Force:
Darth Vader with "Removable Helmet and Light-
saber" and with "Detachable Hand" on Freeze
Frame header card (Collection 3, #69836,

Dash Rendar and Death Squad Commander
(Kenner 1996 and 1978)

1998) [550630.00] $40.00
Loose 15.00

DASH RENDAR

The *Shadows of the Empire* storyline takes place
between *The Empire Strikes Back* and before *Return of the
Jedi*. Dash Rendar, an exceptional pilot, is a former Imperial
Officer cadet and former smuggler, who fought for the Rebel
Alliance in the Battle of Hoth. Leia hired him to help protect
Luke from bounty hunters employed by Prince Xizor. When
Leia is captured by Prince Xizor, he teams up with Luke,
Lando and Chewbacca to rescue the princess. He shoots down
many of Xizor's Black Sun starships with his *Outrider*
starfighter.

New: *Shadows of the Empire*
Dash Rendar, with "Heavy Weapons Pack" on a
purple *Shadows of the Empire* card (#69561,
June 1996) [531616.00] $20.00
Loose, with grey double-barreled pistol and
rifle and shoulder mount backpack 3.00

DEATH SQUAD COMMANDER

The Death Squad Commander's name was changed to
Star Destroyer Commander when he was reissued on *The
Empire Strikes Back* header cards.

Classic:
Death Squad Commander (#38290, 1978)
  Original *Star Wars* "12 back" header card $350.00
  Reissue on *Star Wars* "20/21 back" header
   card 150.00
  Reissue on *The Empire Strikes Back* header
   card as **Star Destroyer Commander** 125.00
  Reissue on *Return of the Jedi* header card 75.00
  Reissue on Tri-Logo header card 75.00
  Loose, with pistol 15.00

DEATH STAR DROID

While not exactly a famous character from the movie,
the classic Death Star Droid has attracted collector interest
and it will be issued late in 1998 in the new series.

Death Star Droid and Death Star Gunner
(Kenner 1979 and 1997)

Classic:
Death Star Droid (#39080, 1978–79)
    Original *Star Wars* header card $200.00
    Reissue on *The Empire Strikes Back* header card . 150.00
    Reissue on *Return of the Jedi* header card 75.00
    Reissue on Tri-Logo header card 125.00
    Loose, no accessories 10.00

New Power of the Force:
Death Star Droid with "Mouse Droid" on green
    Freeze Frame header card (Collection 3,
    #69862) [.00] 25.00
    Loose, with mouse droid 12.50

DEATH STAR GUNNER

The Death Star Gunner is a heavy weapons gunner who operates the Death Star superlaser. Operating big guns must make one grow taller because between Collection 1 and Collection 3 their average height, as listed on the header card, increased from 1.8 meters to 1.83 meters.

New Power of the Force:
Death Star Gunner with "Radiation Suit and Blaster
    Pistol" (#69608, Oct. 1996) on red header
    card (Collection 1) [535194.00]. $25.00
    Reissue, now with "Imperial Blaster and
        Assault Rifle" on green header card [.01] 12.00
    Reissue with holographic picture on green
        header card [.01] with 1st hook, in original
        bubble 10.00
    Reissue on green holo header card
        (Collection 3, #69809) [.02] with 2nd hook,
        in original bubble 10.00
    Loose, with black assault rifle and blaster pistol . . . 3.00

DEATH STAR TROOPER

The Death Star Troopers were elite soldiers who manned the Death Star's Gun towers during the Battle of Yavin. Most were killed in the battle, making the action figure scarce.

New Power of the Force:
Death Star Trooper with "Blaster Rifle" on Freeze
    Frame header card (Collection 3, #69838)

Dengar (Kenner 1997) and
Destroyer Droid (Battle Damaged) (Hasbro 1999)

[551755.00] $25.00
Loose, with black blaster rifle 12.50

DENGAR

Dengar is a freelance human bounty hunter. He stands 1.8 meters tall and first appeared in *The Empire Strikes Back*. Darth Vader employs him to find Han Solo.

Classic:
Dengar (#39329, 1981)
    Original *The Empire Strikes Back* header card . . $100.00
    Reissue on *Return of the Jedi* header card 35.00
    Reissue on Tri-Logo header card 50.00
    Loose, with rifle 10.00

New Power of the Force:
Dengar with "Blaster Rifle" on green holo header
    card (Collection 2, #69687, July 1997)
    [542903.00] with 2nd hook, in stand-up bubble. . . 12.00
    Variation, without holo sticker 12.00
    Loose, with black pistol and blaster rifle 3.00

DESTROYER DROID

One of the really cool aspects of *Episode I* was the Destroyer Droids rolling into battle and then unfolding to shoot. They have a forcefield which protects them from attack, but the field works both ways, so they must stick the nose of their weapons through the field to fire.

Episode I:
Destroyer Droid (#84181) Col. 2 [560435.0000] $7.00
    Loose, no accessories 3.00

Destroyer Droid (Battle Damaged) (#84126) Col. 1
    [566976.0000] 20.00
    Loose, ... 8.00

DROIDS FIGURES

Figures from the *Droids* cartoon series are listed only in the Action Figures—Chronological Section.

8D8

8D8 was designed to work in smelting factories. In the movies he works under EV-9D9 in Jabba's droid operations center. This droid was also available in the Jabba the Hutt Dungeon playset from Sears.

Classic:
8D8 (#71210, 1984)
 Original *Return of the Jedi* header card $30.00
 Reissue on Tri-Logo header card 100.00
 Loose, no accessories 10.00

New Power of the Force:
8D8 with "Droid Branding Device" on Freeze
 Frame header card (Collection 2, #69834)
 [551749.00] 10.00
 Loose, ... 3.00

EETH KOTH

"Eeth Koth is a Jedi Master and Council member known for his highly developed willpower and ability to withstand intense pain. He is an Iridonian Zabrak from Nar Shaddaa, a harsh "smuggler's moon" that forced him to learn fortitude at an early age."

Power of the Jedi:
Eeth Koth, Jedi Master (#84662, 2002) Col. 2 on
 "Transition" header card [6098590500] $8.00
 Loose, ... 3.00

ELLORRS MADAK

Ellorrs Madak is a Duros and earns a living as a free-lance flight instructor and occasional smuggler.

Power of the Jedi:
Ellorrs Madak, Duros (#84647) Col. 2 (Fan Choice
 Figure #1) on Jedi Force File header card
 [571100.0400] $8.00
 Loose, ... 3.00

EMPEROR PALPATINE

Emperor Palpatine is the human dictator of the Galactic Empire. He stands 1.73 meters tall, but mostly he is stooped over. The figure comes with a walking stick in both the original and new versions. He was initially available loose as a mail-in.

In the new series, the figure initially came on a Collection 1 header card. This was quickly corrected to Collection 3, making the original ".00" version somewhat scarce. It commands only a slight premium over the more common corrected version.

Classic:
The Emperor (#71240, 1984)
 Original *Return of the Jedi* header card $40.00
 Reissue on *Power of the Force* header card 75.00
 Reissue on Tri-Logo header card 35.00
 Loose, with cane 10.00

New Power of the Force:
Emperor Palpatine with "Walking Stick" on green
 holo header card (**Collection 1**, #69633,
 April 1997) [538959.00] with 1st hook, in
 original bubble 12.00
 Reissue (Collection 3, #69811, 1997) [.01]
  with 2nd hook, in original or stand-up bubble . . . 6.00
 Reissue, on Freeze Frame header card [.02] 10.00
 Loose, with a black walking stick 3.00

Emperor Palpatine with "Force Lightning" on Flashback Photo header card (#84042) [557532.00] . . . 15.00
 Loose, ... 3.00

EMPEROR'S ROYAL GUARD

The Emperor's guards are human "Sovereign Protectors of the Emperor." They average 1.83 meters tall, about 0.1 meters taller than their Emperor. The figure comes with a force pike and sports a neat red outfit and mask.

Classic:
Emperor's Royal Guard (#70680, 1983)
 Original *Return of the Jedi* header card $40.00
 Reissue on Tri-Logo header card 75.00
 Loose, with pike 10.00

New Power of the Force:
Emperor's Royal Guard with "Force Pike" on green

8D8 (Kenner 1998) and Ellorrs Madak (Hasbro 2001) *The Emperor (Kenner 1985) and Emperor Palpatine (Kenner 1998)*

Emperor's Royal Guard and EV-9D9 (Kenner 1998)

Ewoks: Wicket & Logray (Kenner 1998) and 4-Lom (Palitoy 1983, British Manufacturer)

holo header card (Collection 3, #69717, Sept. 1997) [542911.00] with 2nd hook, in stand-up bubble 10.00
Reissue, on Freeze Frame header card [.01] 25.00
Loose, with light gray pike 3.00

Endor Rebel Soldier: See Rebel Soldier (Endor Gear)

EV-9D9

The EV-9D9 is a Merendata EV Supervisor Droid owned by Jabba the Hutt. It runs Jabba's Droid Operations center. It is 1.6 meters tall. The figure comes with a data entry terminal on a stand. The figure is 4¾" tall, taller than the average human figure which is not to scale with the 1.6 meter given height.

The classic series figure was also available in the Jabba the Hutt Dungeon playset from Sears.

Classic:
EV-9D9 (#93800, 1985)
  Original *Power of the Force* header card. $150.00
  Reissue on Tri-Logo header card 125.00
  Loose, no accessories 85.00

New Power of the Force:
EV-9D9 with "Datapad" 4¾" on green holo header card (Collection 2, #69722, Oct. 1997) [542919.00] with 2nd hook, in stand-up bubble. . . 12.00
  Variation, without holo sticker. 12.00
  Reissue, on Freeze Frame header card [.01] 15.00
  Loose, with black data terminal on stand 3.00

EWOKS FIGURES

Figures from the *Ewoks* cartoon series are listed only in the Action Figures—Chronological Section.

EWOKS: WICKET & LOGRAY

These two characters were previously issued separately in the *Return of the Jedi* figure line and are listed later.

Classic: See Logray, and see Wicket W. Warrick

New Power of the Force:
Ewoks: Wicket & Logray with "Staff, Medicine Pouch and Spear" on green Freeze Frame header card (Collection 2, #69711) [550383.00] $15.00
  Loose Wicket, with hood and spear 5.00
  Loose Logray, with mask, medicine pouch and staff 5.00

4-LOM (Classic)

Kenner reversed the names of 4-LOM and Zuckuss in the original figure line-up and corrected it in the new figures. The original figure was available as a mail-in.

Classic:
4-LOM (#70010, 1982)
  Original *The Empire Strikes Back* header card . . $300.00
  Reissue on *Return of the Jedi* header card 50.00
  Reissue on Tri-Logo header card 28.00
  Loose, with weapon 15.00

New: See Zuckuss

4-LOM (formerly Zuckuss)

The real 4-LOM is a an industrial protocol droid working as a freelance bounty hunter. He makes his first appearance in *The Empire Strikes Back* and somewhat resembles another protocol droid—C-3PO. His programming was altered and he became a thief and eventually a bounty hunter, working with Zuckuss for Jabba the Hutt.

Classic: See Zuckuss
New Power of the Force:
4-LOM with "Blaster Pistol and Blaster Rifle" on green holo header card (Collection 2, #69688, July 1997) [542905.00] with 2nd hook, in stand-up bubble. $12.00
  Variation, without holo sticker. 12.00
  Loose, with black pistol and blaster rifle 3.00

FODE and BEED

As a two-headed announcer, Fode and Beed provide play-by-play and color commentary for the Pod Race. Do they get two pay-checks or one?

4-LOM (Kenner 1997) and Fode and Beed (Hasbro 2001)

Gamorrean Guard and Garindan (Kenner 1983 and 1997)

Power of the Jedi:
Fode and Beed, Pod race Announcers (#84474,
   2001) Col. 2 on Jedi Force File header card
   [571100.0100] $15.00
   Loose, ... 3.00

FX-7

   "The multi-armed medical droid FX-7 was stationed at Echo Base on Hoth, serving as an assistant to the medial droid 2-1B." The two droids treated Luke Skywalker after the Wampa attack and a cold and smelly night in the belly of a Tauntaun. You probably think the Bacta Tank contained some kind of healing liquid, but my guess is cleaning fluid. FX-7 has not been a popular figure with collectors.

Classic:
FX-7 (Medical Droid) (#39730, 1980)
   Original *The Empire Strikes Back* header card . . . $75.00
   Reissue on *Return of the Jedi* header card 75.00
   Reissue on Tri-Logo header card 60.00
   Loose, no accessories 10.00

Power of the Jedi:
FX-7, Medical Droid (#84656, 2002) Col. 2 on
   "Transition" header card [6098590000] 8.00
   Loose, ... 3.00

GAMORREAN GUARD

   The Gamorrean guards work as palace guards for Jabba the Hutt. They are 1.8 meters tall and only slightly less in girth. If they have keen minds and pleasant dispositions, they keep them well hidden beneath their horns, snout, and tusks.

Classic:
Gamorrean Guard (#70670, 1983)
   Original *Return of the Jedi* header card $25.00
   Reissue on *Power of the Force* header card,
      foreign release only 250.00
   Reissue on Tri-Logo header card 25.00
   Loose, with axe 10.00

New Power of the Force:
Gamorrean Guard with "Vibro Ax" on green holo
   header card (Collection 2, #69693, Oct. 1997)
[542909.00] with 2nd hook, in original bubble . . . 10.00
Reissue, on Freeze Frame header card [.01] 15.00
Loose, with black vibro ax with bone handle. 3.00

GARINDAN

   Garindan is a Kubaz spy who sells his services to the highest bidder, like all good spys. He is seen in the Mos Eisley spaceport in the original movie, but he had to wait until the new figures to appear in plastic.

New Power of the Force:
Garindan (Long Snout) with "Hold-Out Pistol" on
   green holo header card (Collection 3, #69706,
   July 1997) [542907.00] with 2nd hook, in
   stand-up bubble. $6.00
Reissue, on Freeze Frame header card
   (#69706) [.01] 40.00
Loose, with black hold-out pistol. 3.00

GASGANO

   Pod race pilot, his many arms and pit droid crew do not prevent him from being one of the many losers.

Episode I:
Gasgano with Pit Droid (#84116) [558993.0000] $10.00
   Reissue Col.3. [.0100]. 7.00
   Reissue [.0200]. 6.00
   Loose, with pit droid 3.00

GENERAL MADINE

   General Madine is from the planet Corellia. He was an Imperial officer, but now fights for the Rebel Alliance. He helped to devise the plan to attack the second Death Star.

Classic:
General Madine (#70780, 1983)
   Original *Return of the Jedi* header card $30.00
   Reissue on Tri-Logo header card 25.00
   Loose, with staff. 10.00

GRAND ADMIRAL THRAWN

   "Five years after the Battle of Endor, the Rebel Alliance has driven the evil Empire into a distant corner of the galaxy.

General Madine and Grand Admiral Thrawn
(Kenner 1983 and 1998)

Grand Moff Tarkin and Greedo (Kenner 1997 and 1998)

But a new danger has arisen: the last of the Emperor's warlords has devised a battle plan that could destroy the Republic. A tactical and military genius, Grand Admiral Thrawn rallied the remnants of the Imperial fleet and set in motion a plan to destroy the New Republic. Using Force-inhibiting ysalamiri, he came vitally close to achieving his evil plans." From the *Heir to the Empire* novels.

New: Expanded Universe
Grand Admiral Thrawn on a 3-D PlayScene header
    card (#69888) Collection 2 [554775.02] $25.00
    Loose, ... 10.00

GRAND MOFF TARKIN

Grand Moff Tarkin is the human commander of the Death Star. He is 1.8 meters tall.

The figure is supposed to come with a blaster rifle and pistol, but actually it just has a large and a small pistol. His figure appeared briefly on a Collection 2 header card before being changed to Collection 3. The original version is quite scarce, accounting for its value.

New Power of the Force:
Grand Moff Tarkin with "Imperial Issue Blaster Rifle
    and Pistol" and sticker on plastic bubble
    which says "Never Before Offered in any
    Kenner Collection" on green holo header
    card (**Collection 2**, #69702, 1997) [540897.00]
    with 2nd hook, in stand-up bubble $40.00
    Reissue (Collection 3, #69702, July 1997) [.01]
       with 2nd hook, in stand-up bubble 6.00
    Variation, without holo sticker 6.00
    Reissue, on Freeze Frame header card [.02] 12.00
    Loose, with large and small black blaster
       pistols 3.00

GREEDO

Greedo is a freelance Rodian bounty hunter. He stands 1.65 meters tall in his green skin, not counting his antenna. He died early in the Cantina scene in the first movie. He should have checked under the table for Han Solo's gun.

Despite this brief movie appearance, he has been a popular figure and appeared fairly early in both the new and the original figure lines. The CommTech chip version was described as being an "All New Sculpt" on Hasbro's Web site.

Classic:
Greedo (#39020, 1978–79)
    Original *Star Wars* header card $300.00
    Reissue on *The Empire Strikes Back* header card . 125.00
    Reissue on *Return of the Jedi* header card 75.00
    Reissue on Tri-Logo header card 75.00
    Loose, with blaster pistol 10.00

New Power of the Force:
Greedo, with "Rodian Blaster Pistol" (#69606, Oct.
    1996) on red header card (Collection 1)
    [535190.00] 25.00
    Reissue, now with "Blaster Pistol" on green
       header card [.01] 12.00
    Reissue with holographic picture on green
       header card [.01] 12.00
    Loose, with black Rodian blaster rifle and pistol . . . 3.00

Greedo with "Blaster" on CommTech Chip header
    card (#84201) [.0000] 8.00
    Loose, with blaster 3.00

GUNGAN WARRIOR

The Gungan are proud warriors, but are overmatched by the Battle Droid army until the Trade Federation control ship is knocked out. They put on a fine parade to celebrate their part in the battle.

Power of the Jedi:
Gungan Warrior (#84274) Col. 2 on Jedi Force
    File header card [571100.0000] $20.00
    Reissue [.0100] 15.00
    Reissue [.0400] 10.00
    Loose, ... 3.00

Hammerhead: See Momaw Nadon

HAN SOLO

In the original series, Luke Skywalker had two hair colors, but Han Solo changed his whole head. He may have gotten the large head in the movies when Leia kissed him, but on the figures it actually is larger. The small head is more common on the earlier cards, but was phased out. The large head is more common on later cards and loose figures. The front picture of Han was changed during the *Return of the Jedi* series. His original picture shows him with his pistol held in his right hand, pointing up. The new picture shows him with his gun pointing directly at you, held in both hands.

This version is the Han Solo we meet in the Mos Eisley Cantina, smuggler, rogue, and the heart-throb of millions of princesses, who, for better (here) or worse (usually), like their men to be a little dangerous.

Classic:
Han Solo with **large head** (#38260, 1978) dark brown hair
    Original *Star Wars* "12 back" header card $950.00
    Reissue on *Star Wars* "20/21 back" header
        card. 650.00
    Reissue on *The Empire Strikes Back* header card . 250.00
    Reissue on *Return of the Jedi* header card,
        new photo 175.00
    Reissue on Tri-Logo header card 175.00
    Loose, with pistol 25.00
Han Solo with **small head** (#38260) brown hair
    Original *Star Wars* "12 back" header card 850.00
    Reissue on *Star Wars* "20/21 back" header
        card. 550.00
    Reissue on *The Empire Strikes Back* header card . 325.00
    Reissue on *Return of the Jedi* header card 200.00
    Reissue on *Return of the Jedi* header card,
        new photo 200.00
    Reissue on Tri-Logo header card 175.00
    Loose, with pistol 35.00

New Power of the Force:
Han Solo with "Heavy Assault Rifle and Blaster" on
    red header card (#69577, July 1995) [521793.00]. 15.00
    Reissue on green holo header card
        (Collection 1, #69577) [.01] with 2nd hook,
        in original or stand-up bubble. 10.00
    Variation, without holo sticker 10.00
    Loose, with black blaster pistol and rifle 3.00

Han Solo with "Blaster Pistol" on Freeze Frame
    header card (Collection 1, #69577) [.02]. 18.00

Loose, with pistol 5.00

Han Solo with "Blaster Pistol & Holster" on Comm-
    Tech Chip header card (#84202) [.0000] 8.00
    Loose, ... 3.00

Han Solo (Bespin Outfit)

On the back of header card version ".01" for the new Freeze Frame issue of this figure "Saelt-Marae" is misspelled as "Sealt-Marie"—two errors in just 10 letters. Version ".02" corrects this error.

Classic:
Han Solo (Bespin Outfit) (#39339, 1981)
    Original *The Empire Strikes Back* header card . . $175.00
    Reissue on *Return of the Jedi* header card 85.00
    Reissue on Tri-Logo header card 50.00
    Loose, with pistol 15.00

New Power of the Force:
Bespin Han Solo with "Heavy Assault Rifle and
    Blaster" on green holo header card (Collection
    1, #69719, Sept. 1997) [542913.00] with 2nd
    hook, in stand-up bubble 6.00
    Reissue, on Freeze Frame header card [.01] 20.00
    Reissue [.02] corrected spelling 10.00
    Reissue, "Unbeknownst" corrected [.03] 15.00
    Loose, with black blaster pistol and rifle 3.00

Power of the Jedi:
Han Solo, Bespin Capture (#84564) Col. 1 on Jedi
    Force File header card [571090.0100] 20.00
    Reissue [.0300] 15.00
    Reissue [.0400] 10.00
    Loose, ... 3.00

Han Solo (Carbonite)

Han Solo was flash frozen in a carbonite chamber and turned over to Boba Fett who delivered him to Jabba the Hutt where he became Jabba's favorite wall decoration. All this was just a test run. Darth Vader's plan was to freeze Luke and turn him over to the Emperor. Kenner keeps changing its mind, from Carbonite Chamber, to Carbonite Freezing Chamber to Carbonite Block, but you get the block and the figure for the price of the figure.

Gungan Warrior (Hasbro 2000) and Han Solo (Kenner 1978)

Han Solo (Kenner 1998) and
Han Solo, Bespin Capture (Hasbro 2001)

Han Solo in Carbonite (Kenner 1996) and
Han Solo, Death Star Escape (Hasbro 2001)

Han Solo (Trench Coat, plain collar) (Kenner 1983)
Han Solo, Endor Gear (Kenner 1998)

On the back of header card version ".04" for the new Freeze Frame issue of this figure "Saelt-Marae" is misspelled as "Sealt-Marie"—two errors in just 10 letters. Version ".05" corrects this error.

Classic:

Han Solo (in Carbonite Chamber) (#93770, 1985)
　　Original *Power of the Force* header card $250.00
　　Reissue on Tri-Logo header card, figure on top . 225.00
　　Loose, with carbonite sheet 110.00

New Power of the Force:

Han Solo in Carbonite with "Carbonite Freezing
　　Chamber" on red header card (#69613, June
　　1996) [532826.00] 18.00
　　Reissue with "Carbonite Block" [.01] 12.00
Han Solo in Carbonite with "Carbonite Block" on
　　green holo header card (Collection 2, #69613,
　　1997) [.02] with 2nd hook, in original or stand-
　　up bubble 8.00
　　Reissue, Collection 1 (#69613, 1997 [.03]
　　　　with 2nd hook, in stand-up bubble 8.00
　　Reissue, on Freeze Frame header card
　　　　(#69817, 1998) [.04] 20.00
　　Reissue, [.05] corrected spelling. 10.00
　　Loose, with carbonite block and black blaster
　　　　pistol 3.00

Han Solo (Death Star)

"Han Solo's reputation as a notorious smuggler and pirate also makes him a target for bounty hunters. After his ship is impounded by the Empire, Han helps Obi-Wan and Luke rescue Princess Leia from the Death Star. A courageous and daring pilot, Solo eventually realizes his personal stake in the Rebels' fight for freedom." Yeah, money, amnesty for his crimes, and the most powerful woman in the galaxy as his lady friend—that's a world-class "personal stake." And now he has to deal with real scum and villany—politicians.

Power of the Jedi:

Han Solo, Death Star Escape (#84626) Col. 1 on
　　Jedi Force File header card [571090.0400]. $10.00
　　Loose, with Imperial blaster. 3.00

Han Solo (Endor Gear/Trench Coat)

In early 1998, Han changed from Navy blue pants to tan or brown pants. These figures have only appeared on plain picture header cards, although these two changes should be independent of each other and brown pants on a holo card is possible. Since there are no text or graphics changes on the printed card, the new version is still numbered version ".00." All of the figures are now being issued on "Freeze Frame" cards, so this particular version should remain quite scarce.

The initial Freeze Frame version misspelled "Saelt-Marae" and this makes it worth somewhat more than the corrected version. Both versions come with brown pants, so the loose brown pants figure is not scarce.

Classic:

Han Solo (in Trench Coat) (#71300, 1984)
　　Original *Return of the Jedi* header card $50.00
　　Reissue on *Power of the Force* header card 550.00
　　Reissue on Tri-Logo header card 35.00
　　Loose, with camo coat and pistol 15.00

New Power of the Force:

Han Solo in Endor Gear with "Blaster Pistol" on
　　green holo header card (Collection 1, #69621,
　　April 1997) [538957.00] with 1st hook, in origin-
　　al bubble or with 2nd hook, in stand-up bubble,
　　navy blue pants 12.00
　　Loose, blue pants, with black blaster pistol 3.00
　　Reissue, brown pants, plain picture 15.00
　　Reissue, on Freeze Frame header card
　　　　(#69621, 1998) [.01] brown pants 20.00
　　Reissue, [.02] corrected spelling. 12.00
　　Loose, brown pants, with black blaster pistol 3.00

Han Solo (Hoth Outfit)

The new Han Solo in Hoth Gear originally came with an open hand, which was too open to hold his blaster pistol. The hand was changed for later versions of the figure. It's called a "closed hand," or a "gripping hand" but there is still an opening between the thumb and fingers.

Classic:

Han Solo (Hoth Outfit) (#39790, 1980)

Han Solo, Hoth Outfit (Kenner 1983) and IG-88 (Hasbro 2001)

Imperial Dignitary and Imperial Gunner (Kenner 1985)

Original *The Empire Strikes Back* header card . . $100.00
Reissue as "Han Solo (Hoth Battle Gear)" on
   Return of the Jedi header card 75.00
Reissue on Tri-Logo header card 40.00
Loose, with pistol 15.00

New Power of the Force:
Han Solo in Hoth Gear with "Blaster Pistol and
   Assault Rifle" on red header card (#69587,
   March 1996) [.00] with open hand 25.00
   Loose, with open hand. 10.00
   Variation, with closed hand. 15.00
   Loose, with closed hand, black blaster pistol
     and assault rifle 3.00

Hoth Rebel Soldier: *See Rebel Soldier (Hoth Gear)*

IG-88

IG-88 is a freelance assassin droid created by Holowan scientists at Darth Vader's request to work as a bounty hunter. Because of its programming, it values Imperial credits much more than organic life, making it a "devastatingly efficient hunting machine." *See also: Two-packs*

Classic:
IG-88 (Bounty Hunter) (#39770, 1980) 4fi" figure
   Original *The Empire Strikes Back* header card . . $150.00
   Reissue on *Return of the Jedi* header card 75.00
   Reissue on Tri-Logo header card 175.00
   Loose, with rifle and pistol 15.00

New: See Shadows of the Empire two-packs.

Power of the Jedi:
IG-88, Bounty Hunter (#84587) Col. 2 on Jedi
   Force File header card [571100.0100] 15.00
   Reissue [.0300] 10.00
   Loose, ... 3.00

IMPERIAL COMMANDER

The Imperial Commander figure has not been issued in an of the new series. His place has been taken by Captain Piett.

Classic:
Imperial Commander (#39389, 1980)
   Original *The Empire Strikes Back* header card . . . $75.00
   Reissue on *Return of the Jedi* header card 40.00
   Reissue on Tri-Logo header card 40.00
   Loose, with pistol 10.00

IMPERIAL DIGNITARY

The tall, skinny and effeminate Imperial Dignitary first appeared in the Power of the Force series and has not been issued in the new series.

Classic:
Imperial Dignitary (#93850, 1985)
   Original *Power of the Force* header card $75.00
   Reissue on Tri-Logo header card 50.00
   Loose, no accessories 35.00

IMPERIAL GUNNER

The Imperial Gunner was originally available in the Power of the Force series and has not been issued in the new series. The closest equivalent is the Death Star Gunner.

Classic:
Imperial Gunner (#93760, 1985)
   Original *Power of the Force* header card. $150.00
   Reissue on Tri-Logo header card 135.00
   Loose, with pistol 100.00

IMPERIAL OFFICER

"Imperial Officers are cunning, calculating and ruthless. They survived a grueling training program to earn their rank.... Failure means death, as many found out in the service of Darth Vader."

Power of the Jedi:
Imperial Officer (#84659, 2001) Col. 2 on "Trans-
   ition" header card [6098590300] $8.00
   Loose, with blaster. 3.00

IMPERIAL SENTINEL

"Six years after the destruction of the second Death Sar, the galaxy is thrust into turmoil. A reborn evil threatens to enslave the galaxy, and the Republic's closest friend – Luke Skywalker– may become their greatest enemy... At the doors of the evil Emperor's palace, giant Imperial Sentinels, twice the size and power of other Imperial guards, await their prisoner – the Jedi Master, Luke Skywalker." From the *Dark Empire* comic book series.

New: Expanded Universe
Imperial Sentinel on 3-D PlayScene header card
    (#69887) Collection 2 [554772.01] $20.00
    Loose, ... 10.00

Imperial Stormtrooper: See Stormtrooper

Imperial Stormtrooper (Hoth Gear): See Snowtrooper

Imperial TIE Fighter Pilot: See TIE Fighter Pilot

ISHI TIB

Ishi Tib comes from Planet Tibrin, where everyone lives in cities build on coral reefs. He, and others from his planet, joined the Rebel Alliance because they are ardent freedom lovers.

New Power of the Force:
Ishi Tib with "Blaster Rifle" on green Freeze Frame
    header card (Collection 3, #69754, March
    1998) [550621.00] $20.00
    Loose, with all equipment. 5.00

JANGO FETT

Attack of the Clones
Jango Fett, Kamino Escape . . . . N/A

JAR JAR BINKS

Originally banished from Otoh Gunga, Jar Jar Binks redeems himself and becomes an unlikely general of the Gungan forces in their battle against the Battle Droid army of the Trade Federation.

Episode I:
Jar Jar Binks with "Gungan Battle Staff" (#84077)
    Col. 1 [558443.00] $20.00
    Reissue [.0100]. 12.00
    Reissue [.0200] 6.00

    Loose, with staff 3.00

Jar Jar Binks (Naboo Swamp) with "Fish" (#84252)
    Col. 1 [556979.0000] 30.00
    Loose, with fish 10.00

Power of the Jedi:
Jar Jar Binks, Tatooine (#84267) Col. 2 on Jedi
    Force file header card [571100.0300] 13.00
    Reissue [.0400] 10.00
    Loose, with long tongue. 3.00

JAWAS

The Jawas are hardware traders and scavengers on Tatooine. They average just 1 meter in height, but drive a big sandcrawler. The original Jawa came with a vinyl cape, but this was quickly changed to cloth. The few vinyl-caped Jawas are the most valuable of all the *Star Wars* figures. Care in buying is essential, because a fake vinyl cape is not hard to make and a loose Jawa in cloth cape is cheap. Even carded figures can be altered with skillful re-gluing of the bubble.

Classic:
Jawa (#38270, 1978) **vinyl cape**, 2¼" figure
    Original *Star Wars* "12 back" header card . . . $3,500.00
    Loose, with weapon and vinyl cape 275.00
Jawa (#38270) **cloth cape**
    Original *Star Wars* "12 back" header card 275.00
    Reissue on *Star Wars* "20/21 back" header
      card. 200.00
    Reissue on *The Empire Strikes Back* header card . 125.00
    Reissue on *Return of the Jedi* header card 45.00
    Reissue on *Power of the Force* header card. . . . 100.00
    Reissue on Tri-Logo header card 75.00
    Loose, with weapon and cloth cape 13.00

New Power of the Force:
Jawas with "Glowing Eyes and Ionization Blasters"
    2½" and 2¼" (Collection 2, #69607, Nov.
    1996) on red header card [535183.00] 25.00
    Reissue, now with "Glowing Eyes and Blaster
      Pistols" on green header card [.01] 15.00
    Reissue with holographic picture on green
      header card [.02] with 2nd hook, in
      stand-up box 6.00

Imperial Sentinel and Ishi Tib (Kenner 1998)

Jar Jar Binks (Hasbro 2001) and Jawas (Kenner 1996)

Jek Porkins and Ketwol (Hasbro 2001)

Loose, two figures with small pistol and large
ionization blaster 3.00

Jawa with Gonk Droid on CommTech Chip header
card (#84198) [.0000] with two foot holes 8.00
with no foot holes. 50.00
with one foot hole. 60.00
Loose, two foot holes. 3.00

Jedi Knight Luke Skywalker: *See Luke Skywalker
(Jedi Knight Outfit)*

JEK PORKINS

Jek Porkins is from Bestine IV. After his homeworld is
conquered by the Empire, he becomes a Rebel Alliance pilot.
In the attack on the Death Star his unit designation was Red
Six.

Power of the Jedi:
Jek Porkins, X-Wing Pilot (#84457) Col. 2 on Jedi
Force File header card [571100.0000] $15.00
Reissue [.0100] 12.00
Reissue [.0300] 10.00
Loose, ... 3.00

KETWOL

Ketwol is an asteroid prospector and part-time scout. He
has secretly provided the Rebel Alliance with materials and
information.

Power of the Jedi:
Ketwol (#84634) Col. 2 on Jedi Force File header
card [571101.0400] $10.00
Loose, ... 3.00

KI-ADI-MUNDI

Jedi Knight and member of the Jedi Council.

Episode I:
Ki-Adi-Mundi with "Lightsaber" (#84123) Col. 3.
[558999.0000] $10.00
Reissue [.0100] 6.00
Loose, with lightsaber 3.00

*Ki-Adi-Mundi (Hasbro 1999) and
Klaatu (Skiff Guard) (Kenner 1983)*

KLAATU

Klaatu can be found with either tan limbs or gray limbs
in the classic figures, and sometimes with some of each. The
price is the same in all cases, but a difference might start to
show up if the figures become more valuable.

If you don't know where this character's name comes
from then you don't know your classic science fiction movies
very well. "Klaatu Barada Nikto" was the phrase which
Patricia Neal said to the robot in *The Day the Earth Stood Still*
to stop it from destroying the world after Michael Rennie
(Klaatu) was shot. You can find it on a lot of T-shirts at
science fiction conventions.

Classic:
Klaatu (#70730, 1983) with **tan arms** or **gray arms**
Original *Return of the Jedi* header card $30.00
Reissue on Tri-Logo header card 20.00
Loose, with apron and spear 10.00

Klaatu in Skiff Guard Outfit

Klaatu is one of Jabba the Hutt's skiff guards, along
with Barada and Nikto. The original figure was also available
in the Jabba the Hutt Dungeon playset from Sears. There is no
new version of the figure, except as one of Jabba's Skiff
Guards in the Cinema Scenes three-pack.

Classic:
Klaatu (in Skiff Guard Outfit) (#71290, 1984)
Original *Return of the Jedi* header card $30.00
Reissue on Tri-Logo header card 35.00
Loose, with weapon 10.00

New: See Jabba's Skiff Guards, Cinema Scenes

K-3PO

K-3PO is a rebel protocol droid and is charge of the
droid pool at Echo Base on Hoth. It helps to coordinate the
evacuation of the base during the Empire's attack.

Power of the Jedi:
K-3PO, Echo Base Protocol Droid (#84643, 2000)
Col. 2 on Jedi Force File header card
[571100.0100] $15.00

Kyle Katarn and Lak Sivrak (Kenner 1998)

Reissue [.0400] 10.00
Loose, with Stentronic Sensor Pack 3.00

KYLE KATARN

"Discovering that Imperial forces have begun developing a new type of stormtrooper, the Rebels call on Kyle Katarn. His mission: Seek out and destroy the secret Imperial project called Dark Trooper. A rogue mercenary loyal to no one, Kyle Katarn has accepted a near-impossible mission to destroy the Empire's ability to develop an army of unstoppable Stormtroopers known as Dark Troopers." From the Dark Forces Video game

New: Expanded Universe
Kyle Katarn on a 3-D PlayScene header card
(#69893) Collection 2 [554787.02] $30.00
Loose, ... 10.00

LAK SIVRAK

Lak Sivrak is a "Shistavanen Wolfman, expert hunter, tracker and Imperial world scout." He fought for the Rebels at the Battle of Hoth and dies in the Battle of Endor.

New Power of the Force:
Lak Sivrak with "Blaster Pistol and Vibro-Blade" on
green Freeze Frame header card (Collection 2,
#69753) [550380.00] $20.00
Loose, with black blaster pistol and rifle 3.00

LANDO CALRISSIAN

Lando is the former captain of the *Millennium Falcon*. He lost the ship in a high-stakes game of sabacc to you know who, but eventually became Baron Administrator of the Cloud City mining and gambling establishment. He gets it back, and is promoted to the rank of General.

There are two versions of the classic character. In one, there is some white showing in his mouth and the figure is described as having "teeth." The other version has the mouth closed and no white teeth or smile is visible.

Classic:
Lando Calrissian (#39800, 1980) **no teeth** version

Lando Calrissian (Kenner 1980 and Hasbro 2001)

Original *The Empire Strikes Back* header card . . . $75.00
Loose, with pistol 15.00

Lando Calrissian (#39800, 1980) **white teeth** version
Original *The Empire Strikes Back* header card 75.00
Reissue on *Return of the Jedi* header card 45.00
Reissue on Tri-Logo header card 75.00
Loose, with pistol 15.00

New Power of the Force:
Lando Calrissian with "Heavy Rifle and Blaster
Pistol" on red header card (#69583, Feb. 1996)
[526523.00] with 1st hook, in original bubble 10.00
Reissue on green header card, Collection 1
(#69583) [.01] (in Wholesale Club three
figure packages only) with 2nd hook and
stand-up bubble. 25.00
Loose, with heavy pistol and light hold-out
pistol, plus blue and black cape 3.00

Lando Calrissian (Bespin)

After originally cooperating with Darth Vader in the capture of Han Solo, and attempted capture of Luke Skywalker, Lando changes sides and has to escape with our heroes.

Power of the Jedi:
Lando Calrissian, Bespin Escape (#84589) Col. 2
on Jedi Force File header card [571100.0300] . . . $15.00
Reissue [.0400] 8.00
Loose, ... 3.00

Lando Calrissian (General)

Lando is promoted to General and leads the attack on the second Death Star, with Nien Numb as his co-pilot. His leadership abilities make him a good choice. However, since it's a suicide mission if our heroes don't knock out the protective force field, maybe he was the only one the Rebel Alliance could get.

On the back of header card version ".00" for the new issue of this figure "Saelt-Marae" is misspelled as "Sealt-Marie"—two errors in just 10 letters. Version ".01" corrects this error. The error version is scarce.

Lando Calrissian: General and Skiff Guard (Kenner 1998 and 1997)

Lobot and Logray (Kenner 1998 and 1983)

Classic:
Lando Calrissian (General Pilot) (#93820, 1985)
  Original *Power of the Force* header card. $110.00
  Reissue on Tri-Logo header card 75.00
  Loose, with cape and pistol 65.00

New Power of the Force:
Lando Calrissian in General's Gear with "Blaster
  Pistol" on green Freeze Frame header card
  (Collection 1, #69756) [547101.00] 20.00
  Reissue, Saelt Marae spelling corrected [.01]. . . . 10.00
  Loose, with black blaster pistol and tan cape 3.00

Lando Calrissian (Skiff Guard)

Lando wears his skiff guard outfit when he works with Leia, Chewbacca, Luke, and R2-D2 to rescue Han from Jabba the Hutt.

On the back of header card version ".01" for the new Freeze Frame issue of this figure "Saelt-Marae" is misspelled as "Sealt-Marie"—two errors in just 10 letters. Version ".02" corrects this error.

Classic:
Lando Calrissian (Skiff Guard Disguise) (#70830, 1983)
  Original *Return of the Jedi* header card $45.00
  Reissue on Tri-Logo header card 25.00
  Loose, with spear. 15.00

New Power of the Force:
Lando Calrissian as Skiff Guard with "Skiff Guard
  Force Pike" on green holo header card
  (Collection 1, #69622, April 1997) [538961.00]
  2nd hook, gold circles 10.00
  Variation, without holo sticker. 10.00
  Reissue, on Freeze Frame header card [.01] 20.00
  Reissue, [.02] corrected version 10.00
  Loose, with gray force pike and helmet. 3.00

Leia Organa, *see Princess Leia Organa*

LOBOT

Lobot is the chief aid to Lando Calrissian in the administration of Cloud City. He is a human/cyborg originally from Bespin.

Classic:
Lobot (#39349, 1981)
  Original *The Empire Strikes Back* header card. . . $70.00
  Reissue on *Return of the Jedi* header card 35.00
  Reissue on Tri-Logo header card 90.00
  Loose, with pistol. 8.00

New Power of the Force:
Lobot with "Blaster Pistol and Transmitter" on green
  Freeze Frame header card, Collection 1,
  (#69856) [553852.00] 15.00
  Loose, ... 7.00

LOGRAY

Logray is an Ewok Medicine Man. He was issued with Wicket, as part of the Ewok pack in the New Power of the Force line-up.

Classic:
Logray (Ewok Medicine Man) (#70710, 1983)
  Original *Return of the Jedi* header card $30.00
  Reissue on Tri-Logo header card 25.00
  Loose, with mask, staff and pouch 10.00

New: See Ewoks: Wicket & Logray, two-pack

See also: EWOKS series

LUKE SKYWALKER

Luke Skywalker was included in the Early Bird Package and many of these figures, plus a few of the original carded figures have a telescoping lightsaber. A genuine telescoping lightsaber adds about $1,000 to the figure's value, but many fakes are believed to exist. Both blond-haired and brown-haired Lukes were made throughout the original series. Blondes may or may not have more fun, but blond Lukes came in both tan pants and lighter colored pants. Brown Lukes only had tan pants. The header card picture was changed during the *Return of the Jedi* series from the original contemplative Tatooine picture to an action gunner picture. Both cards are common and there is little or no difference in price, although the new photo should be slightly preferable to collectors who have earlier versions of the original photo.

Luke Skywalker (Kenner 1978 and 1995)

In the new series, his lightsaber was shortened, along with Darth's and Obi-Wan's, resulting in two different versions of his figure and the packaging variation of a short lightsaber in a long lightsaber clear plastic tray.

Classic:
Luke Skywalker (#38180, 1978) **blond hair**
    Original *Star Wars* "12 back" header card..... $750.00
    Reissue on *Star Wars* "20/21 back" header
        card................................. 250.00
    Reissue on *The Empire Strikes Back* header card . 275.00
    Reissue on *Return of the Jedi* header card..... 225.00
    Reissue, gunner picture, on *Return of the Jedi*
        header card.......................... 175.00
    Reissue on Tri-Logo header card 225.00
    Loose, with lightsaber 35.00
Luke Skywalker (#38180) **brown hair**
    Reissue on *The Empire Strikes Back* header card . 325.00
    Reissue on *Return of the Jedi* header card..... 300.00
    Reissue, gunner picture, on *Return of the Jedi*
        header card.......................... 175.00
    Reissue on Tri-Logo header card 260.00
    Loose, with lightsaber 75.00
    Variation, carded, with telescoping lightsaber,
        blond or brown hair, scarce 2,000.00
    Loose, with telescoping lightsaber 300.00

New Power of the Force:
Luke Skywalker with "Grappling-Hook Blaster and
    Lightsaber" on red header card (#69571, July
    1995) [521781.00] with long lightsaber........ 40.00
    Loose, with long lightsaber and blaster........ 17.50
    Short lightsaber in long slot version, scarce 700.00
    Short lightsaber version.................... 15.00
    Loose, with short lightsaber and blaster........ 4.00

Luke Skywalker (Battle Poncho)

Luke Skywalker in Battle Poncho was issued in the original Power of the Force series, but he has not been issued in the new series. The closest equivalent is the Luke Skywalker in Endor Gear which came with the Speeder Bike vehicle.

Classic:
Luke Skywalker (in Battle Poncho) (#93710, 1985)
    Original *Power of the Force* header card...... $125.00
    Reissue on Tri-Logo header card 100.00

Luke Skywalker, Battle Poncho (Kenner 1985)

Loose, with poncho and pistol 75.00

New: See Speeder Bike vehicle

Luke Skywalker (Bespin)

Luke senses that his friends are in trouble and leaves Yoda and Dagobah for Cloud City. It's a trap of course and Luke loses his innocence—not to mention his hand—but he gets a new outfit.

The front photo was changed during *The Empire Strikes Back* series. The original photo shows Luke standing in front of a white background, preparing to draw his gun. The new photo shows him facing forward with gun drawn in front of a blue background.

On the back of header card version ".00" for the Freeze Frame issue of this figure "Saelt-Marae" is misspelled as "Sealt-Marie." Version ".01" corrects this error. The error version is scarce, and expensive.

Classic:
Luke Skywalker (Bespin Fatigues) (#39780, 1980)
    Original *The Empire Strikes Back* header card .. $250.00
    Reissue on *The Empire Strikes Back* header
        card, new package 150.00
    Reissue on *Return of the Jedi* header card,
        yellow hair.......................... 140.00
    Reissue on Tri-Logo header card 125.00
    Loose, with pistol and lightsaber 20.00
    Reissue on *Return of the Jedi* header card,
        brown hair.......................... 100.00
    Reissue on Tri-Logo header card 125.00
    Loose, with pistol and lightsaber 20.00

New Power of the Force:
Bespin Luke Skywalker with "Detachable Hand"
    and with "Lightsaber and Blaster Pistol" on
    green Freeze Frame header card (Collection 1,
    #69713) [547092.00] 30.00
    Reissue, [.01] "Saelt-Marae" spelling corrected... 10.00
    Loose, with all equipment.................. 3.00

Luke Skywalker (Ceremonial Outfit)

Luke wears this outfit when he receives a medal (along with Han and Chewbacca) after destroying the first Death

Star. The ceremony takes place in the throne room of the Massassi temple and is attended by just about everybody. Most of them attended several times because they were all duplicated in the movie-making process to make the throng seem bigger. Luke must be proud, because (if you believe the figures) he grows from his original 1.72 meters to 1.75 meters. He stays that height while on Hoth, but shrinks back to 1.72 meters after he becomes a Jedi and feels the weight of the universe on his shoulders.

The figure originally appeared on a Collection 2 green card, but this error was soon corrected and the Collection 1 version is the more common. There is only a slight premium for the error card.

New Power of the Force:
Luke Skywalker in Ceremonial Outfit with "Medal of Valor and Blaster Pistol" and "All New Like-ness of Luke" on sticker on green holo header card (**Collection 2**, #69691, Nov. 1997) [540895.00] with 1st hook, in stand-up bubble .. $40.00
Reissue (Collection 1, #69691) [.01] with 2nd hook, in stand-up bubble 8.00
Variation, without holo sticker. 8.00
Reissue on Freeze Frame header card [.01] sic. . . 12.00
Loose, with black blaster pistol and gold medal on brown strap. 3.00

Luke Skywalker (Dagobah)

This figure is based on the period in *The Empire Strikes Back* when Luke is in Jedi training on Dagobah. He is pictured on the header card with Yoda on his back and Yoda figure from the same series comes with a backpack which would allow you to recreate this.

New Power of the Force:
Luke Skywalker in Dagobah Fatigues with "Light-saber and Blaster Pistol" on red header card (#69588, March 1996) with long lightsaber [527601.00] $30.00
Loose, with long lightsaber. 17.50
Short lightsaber in long package slot [.01] 25.00
Short lightsaber [.01] 20.00
Loose, with short lightsaber and black blaster pistol 3.00

Luke Skywalker (Expanded Universe)

"Six years after the destruction of the second Death Sar, the galaxy is thrust into turmoil. A reborn evil threatens to enslave the galaxy, and the Republic's closest friend – Luke Skywalker– may become their greatest enemy... Freed from their detention cell, a group of Rebels begin their escape from the Imperial planet Byss. But the sudden appearance of Luke Skywalker, Jedi Master, could mean unfortunate news for the Rebels. Has Luke fallen under the spell of the dark side?" From the *Dark Empire* comic book series

New: Expanded Universe
Luke Skywalker (in Black Cloak) on a 3-D Play-Scene header card (#69883) Collection 2 [554769.01] $20.00
Loose, ... 10.00

Luke Skywalker (Hoth Gear)

In the new series, the figure initially came on a Collection 2 header card. This was quickly corrected to Collection 1, making the original ".00" version somewhat scarce.

Classic:
Luke Skywalker (Hoth Battle Gear) (#69610, 1982)
Original *The Empire Strikes Back* header card . . $125.00
Reissue on *Return of the Jedi* header card 40.00
Reissue on Tri-Logo header card 35.00
Loose, with rifle 10.00

New Power of the Force:
Luke Skywalker in Hoth Gear with "Blaster Pistol and Lightsaber" on green holo header card (**Collection 2**, #69619, Feb. 1997) [537997.00] 1st hook, in original bubble 12.00
Variation, without holo sticker. 12.00
Reissue (Collection 1, #69822) [.01] with 2nd hook, in original or stand-up bubble 10.00
Variation, without holo sticker. 10.00
Loose, with black blaster pistol and blue lightsaber with silver handle 3.00

Luke Skywalker (Imperial Guard Disguise)

The Shadows of the Empire storyline takes place

Bespin Luke Skywalker and Luke Skywalker, Ceremonial Outfit (Kenner 1998)

Luke Skywalker, Dagobah and Luke Skywalker, Expanded Universe (Kenner 1996 and 1998)

Luke Skywalker, Imperial Guard and Luke Skywalker, Jedi Knight (Kenner 1997 and 1983)

Luke Skywalker, Jedi Knight Special and Luke Skywalker, New Likeness (Kenner 1997 and 1998)

between *The Empire Strikes Back* and before *Return of the Jedi.* Luke and Lando go to the Imperial Center of Coruscant where Leia is held prisoner by Prince Xizor. They steal Imperial Guard uniforms and team up with Dash Rendar and Chewbacca to rescue the princess.

New: Shadows of the Empire
Luke Skywalker in Imperial Guard Disguise, with "Taser Staff Weapon" on a purple *Shadows of the Empire* card (#69566, June 1996) [531622.00] $20.00
    Loose, with dark red helmet and gray staff 5.00

Luke Skywalker (Jedi Knight)

By the time *Return of the Jedi* comes out, Luke is a Jedi Knight and sports a neat black outfit.

Both the original and the new figures had variations. In the original series, the figure came most frequently with a green lightsaber, but some figures had a blue lightsaber instead. In the new series, the first figures to appear had a brown tunic or vest, but most of the figures have a black tunic that is the same color as the rest of the figure. In both series, the variation is an important factor in value. A Jedi Knight Luke Skywalker, in common black vest, was also used as a give-away at the *Star Wars Special Edition* premiere in early 1997. This figure came on a special header card and is listed in the previous section of this book under Mail-In and Exclusive figures.

Classic:
Luke Skywalker (Jedi Knight Outfit) with **green lightsaber** (#70650, 1983)
    Original *Return of the Jedi* header card $100.00
    Reissue on *Power of the Force* header card 275.00
    Reissue on Tri-Logo header card 125.00
    Loose, with cloak, pistol and green lightsaber 50.00
With **blue lightsaber**, scarce
    Original *Return of the Jedi* header card 175.00
    Reissue on Tri-Logo header card 200.00
    Loose, with cloak, pistol and blue lightsaber 60.00

New Power of the Force:
Jedi Knight Luke Skywalker with "Lightsaber and Removable Cloak" on red header card

(#69596, June 1996) [532822.00] with **brown tunic** 75.00
Loose, brown tunic, with cloak and green lightsaber. 30.00
With **black tunic** [.00] 12.00
Loose, black tunic, with cloak and green lightsaber. 3.00
Reissue on green holo header card (**Collection 2**, #69816, 1997) [.01] with 2nd hook, in original bubble 25.00
Variation, without holo sticker 25.00
Reissue (Collection 1, #69816, 1997) [.02] with 2nd hook, in stand-up bubble 10.00
Loose, with silver-handled green lightsaber and black cloak 3.00

Luke Skywalker (New Likeness)

"Aboard the Milllennium Falcon, Luke Skywalker is instructed by Jedi Obi-Wan Kenobi in the art of lightsaber battle and the ways of the Force."

New Power of the Force:
Luke Skywalker with "Blast Shield Helmet and Lightsaber" (New Likeness) on Frame green header card (Collection 1, #69691) [551746.00] . $15.00
    Loose, with lightsaber and helmet 5.00

Luke Skywalker (Stormtrooper)

On the back of header card version ".03" for the new Freeze Frame issue of this figure "Saelt-Marae" is misspelled as "Sealt-Marie"—two errors in just 10 letters. Version ".04" corrects this error.

Classic:
Luke Skywalker, Imperial Stormtrooper Outfit (#93780, 1985)
    Original *Power of the Force* header card. $450.00
    Reissue on Tri-Logo header card 250.00
    Loose, with removable helmet and pistol 175.00

New Power of the Force:
Luke Skywalker in "Stormtrooper Disguise with Imperial Issue Blaster" (#69604, Nov. 1996) on red header card (Collection 2) [535181.00] . . . 35.00
Reissue on green header card [.01] with 1st hook, in original bubble 12.00

Luke Skywalker, Stormtrooper (Kenner 1996 and 1998)

Luke Skywalker, X-Wing Pilot and Lumat (Kenner 1997 and 1985)

Reissue, with holographic picture on green
    header card [.01]. 12.00
Reissue on green holo header card
    (Collection 1, #69819) [.02] with 2nd
    hook, in original bubble 12.00
Variation, without holo sticker. 12.00
Reissue, on Freeze Frame header card [.03] 25.00
Reissue, [.04] spelling corrected. 12.00
Loose, with white helmet and black blaster
    pistol 3.00

Luke Skywalker (Tatooine)

This version of Luke is the first one we meet in the movies. The Flashback version was called "Luke Skywalker Tatooine with Floppy Hat" on Hasbro's Web site, but not on the figure. The CommTech version also seems to be from Tatooine, so I have grouped them here.

Luke Skywalker with "Blaster Rifle and Electro-
    binoculars" on Flashback Photo header card
    (#84036) [557524.00]. $10.00
Loose, with rifle and binoculars 3.00

Luke Skywalker with T-16 Skyhopper Model on
    CommTech Chip header card (#84211) [.0000] . . . 8.00
Loose, with model. 3.00

Luke Skywalker (X-Wing Pilot)

One of Luke's best outfits is his X-Wing Pilot gear, which he first wears in the attack on the Death Star at the battle of Yavin. It's also the one chosen for the 100th collector series doll.

Between header cards ".00" and ".01" in the new series the word "Fighter" was changed to "fighter" in three places.

Classic:
Luke Skywalker: X-Wing Pilot (#39060, 1978–79)
    Original *Star Wars* header card $300.00
    Reissue on *The Empire Strikes Back* header
        card as **Luke Skywalker (X-Wing Pilot)** 125.00
    Reissue on *Return of the Jedi* header card as
        Luke Skywalker (X-Wing Fighter Pilot) 50.00
    Reissue on *Power of the Force* header card. . . . 100.00
    Reissue on Tri-Logo header card 100.00
    Loose, with pistol. 15.00

New Power of the Force:
Luke Skywalker in X-Wing Fighter Pilot Gear with
    "Lightsaber and Blaster Pistol" on red header
    card (#69581, Feb. 1996) with long light-
    saber [526517.00] "Fighter" and [.01] "fighter". . . . 25.00
Loose, with long blue lightsaber 12.50
Short lightsaber in long package slot 20.00
Short lightsaber 15.00
Reissue on green holo header card
    (Collection 1, #69581) [.02] with
    2nd hook, in original bubble. 15.00
Reissue (Collection 1, #69581) [.02] with
    2nd hook, in stand-up bubble. 15.00
Loose, with black pistol and blue lightsaber
    (short) with silver handle 3.00

Power of the Jedi:
Luke Skywalker, X-Wing Pilot (#84571) Col. 1 on
    Jedi Force File header card [571090.0400] 8.00
    Loose, with removeable helmet 3.00

LUMAT

Lumat is an Ewok, one of eight issued in the *Return of the Jedi* series. He had not been issued in any new series at press time.

Classic:
Lumat (#93670, 1984)
    Original *Return of the Jedi* header card $45.00
    Reissue on *Power of the Force* header card. 50.00
    Reissue on Tri-Logo header card 30.00
    Loose, with bow. 17.00

MACE WINDU

Jedi master and senior member of the Jedi Council. He appears again in *Attack of the Clones*.

Episode I:
Mace Windu (#84138) mail order, sneak preview
    figure, boxed $30.00
Mace Windu with "Lightsaber and Jedi Cloak"
    (#84084) Col. 3 [558990.0000]. 12.00
    Reissue [.0100]. 6.00
    Loose, with blue lightsaber and cloak 3.00

Mace Windu and Rancor Keeper (Malakili)
(Hasbro 1999 and Kenner 1985)

MALAKILI (RANCOR KEEPER)

Malakili is Jabba the Hutt's Rancor wrangler. He is a portly human and shows an unnaturally close emotional attachment to his Rancor after Luke kills it.

Classic:
Rancor Keeper (#71350, 1984)
    Original *Return of the Jedi* header card $30.00
    Reissue on Tri-Logo header card 60.00
    Loose, with prod 10.00

New Power of the Force:
Malakili (Rancor Keeper) with "Long-Handled Vibro-Blade" on green holo header card (Collection 2, #69723, Oct. 1997) [542921.00] with 2nd hook, in stand-up bubble 10.00
    Reissue, on Freeze Frame header card [.01] 15.00
    Loose, with a brown-handled silver vibro-blade . . . 3.00

MARA JADE

"Five years after the Battle of Endor, the Rebel Alliance has driven the evil Empire into a distant corner of the galaxy. But a new danger has arisen: The last of the Emperor's warlords has devised a battle plan that could destroy the Republic. Before the death of Palpatine, Mara Jade was the Emperor's right-hand assassin. Five years later and now a successful smuggler, the last thing Mara expected was to stumble upon her former arch-enemy—Luke Skywalker." From the *Heir to the Empire* novels. It gets even weirder when she marries Luke in the comic books.

New: Expanded Universe
Mara Jade on a 3-D PlayScene header card
    (#69891) Collection 2 [554784.03] $25.00
    Loose, ... 10.00

MAS AMEDDA

Mas Amedda is Chagrian Vice Chair of the Galactic Senate. He takes over, temporarily, for the vote of no confidence in Chancellor Valorum.

Power of the Jedi:
Mas Amedda (#84136) Col. 2 on Jedi Force File

Mara Jace and Mas Amedda (Kenner 1998 and Hasbro 2001)

    header card [571101.0000] $15.00
    Reissue [.0100] 12.00
    Reissue [.0300] 12.00
    Reissue [.0400] 8.00
    Loose, ... 3.00

MOMAW NADON (HAMMERHEAD)

The Momaw Nadon, the hammerhead, is an Ithorian scout affiliated with the Rebel Alliance. He is 1.95 meters tall and is first seen in the Mos Eisley Cantina.

His original figure carried a pistol. Now he carries a blaster rifle (called a "Laser Canon" on the first 1996 card).

Classic:
Hammerhead (#39030, 1978–79) 4" figure
    Original *Star Wars* header card $225.00
    Reissue on *The Empire Strikes Back* header card . 125.00
    Reissue on *Return of the Jedi* header card 75.00
    Reissue on Tri-Logo header card 75.00
    Loose with Imperial blaster pistol 12.50

New Power of the Force:
Momaw Nadon "Hammerhead" with "Double-Barreled Laser Canon" (Collection 2, #69629, Nov. 1996) on red header card [535187.00] warning on sticker. 35.00
    Reissue, now with "Double-Barreled Blaster Rifle" on green header card [.01] printed warning. 12.00
    Reissue, with holographic picture on green header card [.01] with 1st hook, in original bubble, with printed warning 12.00
    Loose, with double-barreled blaster rifle 5.00

MON CALIMARI OFFICER

"A peaceful race of amphibians, the Mon Calamari species have adopted the name of their watery homeworld. Unfortunately, they were a target for Imperial enslavement. After striking back and regaining their freedom, the Mon Calamari joined the Alliance and focused their energies on defeating the Empire."

Power of the Jedi
Mon Calamari Officer (#84644) Col. 2 on Jedi Force

File header card [.0100] $12.00
Reissue [571100.0300] 12.00
Reissue [571100.0400] 8.00
Loose, with helmet and blaster pistol 3.00

MON MOTHMA

Mon Mothma is "the senior senator of the Old Republic who went underground to form the Rebel Alliance following the rise of the evil Empire." From the Republic's point of view, she is someone like Thomas Jefferson; from the Empire's, more like Fidel Castro.

New Power of the Force:
Mon Mothma with "Baton" on green Freeze Frame
　　header card (Collection 1, #69859) [553853.00] . $20.00
　　Loose, with white baton 7.00

NABOO ROYAL GUARD

Guards for Queen Amidala, they went underground when the Trade Federation Army attacked (and the queen escaped). They were ready to retake Theed when she returned.

Episode I:
Naboo Royal Guard with "Blaster Pistol and Helmet"
　　(#84083) Col. 2 [563970.0000] $20.00
　　Loose, with black and silver pistol, and helmet 7.00

NABOO ROYAL SECURITY

"Their freedom threatened by the fully-automated, invading Trade Federation army, Naboo Security Forces must battle terrible odds in order to save their homeworld." Actually, they lost, but the Gungans, the queen, Anakin, and a handful of pilots saved the day.

Episode I:
Naboo Royal Security with "Blaster Pistol and Rifle"
　　(#84079) Col. 2 [562931.0000] $7.00
　　Loose, with black and silver pistol, and rifle 3.00

NIEN NUNB

Nien Nunb is a Sullustan, who acts as a rebel pilot and

navigator. He is listed as 1.6 meters tall. In the *Return of the Jedi* movie, he is Lando's co-pilot during the Battle of Endor. The figure was initially available loose as a mail-in.

Classic:
Nien Nunb (#70840, 1983)
　　Original *Return of the Jedi* header card $35.00
　　Reissue on Tri-Logo header card 60.00
　　Loose, with pistol 10.00

New Power of the Force:
Nien Nunb with "Blaster Pistol and Blaster Rifle" on
　　green holo header card (Collection 2, #69694,
　　Oct. 1997) [542917.00] with 2nd hook, in stand-
　　up bubble. 10.00
　　Reissue, on Freeze Frame header card [.01] 20.00
　　Loose, with black blaster pistol and blaster rifle . . . 3.00

NIKTO

Nikto is one of Jabba's guards. The classic figure was also available in the Jabba the Hutt Dungeon playset from Sears. His only new version is as one of Jabba's Skiff Guard in the Cinema Scenes three-pack.

Classic:
Nikto (#71190, 1984)
　　Original *Return of the Jedi* header card $30.00
　　Reissue on *Power of the Force* header card,
　　　　foreign release only 600.00
　　Reissue on Tri-Logo header card 35.00
　　Loose, with staff. 10.00

New: See Jabba's Skiff Guards, Cinema Scenes set.

NUTE GUNRAY

Viceroy of the Neimoidian Trade Federation. Makes a deal with Darth Sidious and lives to regret it, before he dies regretting it even more.

Episode I:
Nute Gunray (#84089) Col. 2 [560438.0000] $6.00
　　Loose, no accessories 3.00

Mon Calimari Officer and Mon Mothma
(Hasbro 2001 and Kenner 1998)

Naboo Royal Guard and Nien Nunb
(Hasbro 1999 and Kenner 1997)

OBI-WAN KENOBI (YOUNG JEDI)

Obi-Wan was an apprentice Jedi at the beginning of *Episode I*. After killing Darth Maul, he takes Anakin as his apprentice, in what (as we all know) will turn out to be fateful decision. There are six different action figures of the young Obi-Wan in just the three years since *Episode I* came out, and there are sure to be many more from *Attack of the Clones*, especially since he can't be killed, either in that movie, or the next! Enough already with the robes—I hope he gets a few new outfits.

Episode I:
Obi-Wan Kenobi (Jedi Duel) with "Lightsaber"
  (#84073) Col. 1 [558434.00]. $10.00
  Reissue [.0100] 6.00
  Loose, with blue lightsaber. 3.00

Obi-Wan Kenobi (Naboo) with "Lightsaber and
  Handle" (#84114) Col. 1 [562051.0100] 7.00
  Loose, with lightsaber and handle. 3.00

Obi-Wan Kenobi (Jedi Knight) with "Lightsaber and
  ComLink" (#84244) Col. 1 [563958.0000] 20.00
  Loose, with lightsaber and comlink 5.00

Power of the Jedi:
Obi-Wan Kenobi, Jedi (#84251) Col. 1 on Jedi
  Force File header card [571091.0000] 12.00
  Reissue [.0100] 8.00
  Loose, ... 3.00

Obi-Wan Kenobi, Cold Weather Gear (#84573) Col.
  1 on Jedi Force File header card [571090.0300]. . 15.00
  Reissue [.0400]. 12.00
  Loose, ... 3.00

Obi-Wan Kenobi, Jedi Training Gear (#84651) Col.
  2 on Jedi Force File header card [571100.0300]. . 15.00
  Reissue [.0400] 8.00
  Loose, ... 3.00

See **Ben (Obi-Wan) Kenobi** for classic (old) character

ODY MANDRELL

Pod race pilot. One of several who wipe-out in the great race scene of *The Phantom Menace*.

Episode I:
Ody Mandrell with "OTOGA 222 Pit Droid" (#84117)
  Col. 3 [561423.0100. $7.00
  Loose, with pit droid 3.00

OOM-9

OOM-9 is the Ground Commander of the Neimoidian Trade Federation droid army.

Episode I:
OOM-9 with "Blaster and Binoculars" (#84127) Col.
  3 [561429.0000] Binoculars packed upper left . . $30.00
  Col. 3 [.0000] Binoculars packed over left hand 7.00
  Loose, with blaster and binoculars 3.00

ORRIMAARKO (PRUNE FACE)

Orrimaarko reappear in 1998. As with Momaw Nadon (Hammerhead) and Saelt Marae (Yak Face) he now bears his real name instead of Prune Face.

Classic:
Prune Face (#71320, 1984)
  Original *Return of the Jedi* header card $30.00
  Reissue on Tri-Logo header card 35.00
  Loose, with cloak and rifle 10.00

New Power of the Force:
Orrimaarko (Prune Face) with "Blaster Rifle" on
  green Freeze Frame header card (Collection 1,
  #69858) [553850.00] 15.00
  Loose, ... 5.00

PADMÉ NABERRIE

Supposedly handmaiden to Queen Amidala, but really her alter ego when she wants to let her hair down (figuratively and literally). Who can blame her, with some of her costumes of state. In Attack of the Clones her name is more accurately given as "Padmé Amidala."

Obi-Wan Kenobi, Jedi and Obi-Wan Kenobi, Cold Weather (Hasbro 2001)

Ody Mandrell and OOM-9 (binoculars upper left) (Hasbro 1999)

Episode I:
Padmé Naberrie with "Pod Race View Screen"
   (#84076) Col. 1 [558440.00]. $12.00
   Reissue [.0100] 6.00
   Loose, with view screen 3.00

Attack of the Clones
Padmé Amidala, Arena Escape, Col. 1 . . . . N/A

PAPLOO

Paploo is an Ewok, one of eight issued in the *Return of the Jedi* series. He had not been issued in any new series at press time.

Classic:
Paploo (#93680, 1984)
   Original *Return of the Jedi* header card $45.00
   Reissue on *Power of the Force* header card. 45.00
   Reissue on Tri-Logo header card 65.00
   Loose, with staff. 18.00

PIT DROIDS

Pit Droids repair podracers and sometimes get sucked through the intake manifold.

Episode I:
Pit Droids (2-pack) (#84129) Col. 2 [567747.0000] . . $25.00
   Loose, both droids 10.00

PLO KOON

Plo Koon is a member of the Jedi Council, seen briefly in *The Phantom Menace.*

Power of the Jedi:
Plo Koon, Jedi Master (#84568) Col. 2 on Jedi
   Force File header card [571101.0100] $15.00
   Reissue [.0300] 12.00
   Reissue [.0400] 8.00
   Loose, with yellow-bladed lightsaber 3.00

PONDA BABA (WALRUS MAN)

Ponda Baba is an Aqualish smuggler and pirate. He is the partner of Dr. Evazan. He strongly resembles the Walrus Man from the original figures, but is dressed differently.

Perhaps this is to hide his replacement arm. Ben Kenobi sliced off the original in the Mos Eisley Cantina.

In the new series, Ponda Baba initially came on a Collection 2 header card. This was quickly corrected to Collection 3, making the original ".00" version scarce.

Classic:
Walrus Man (#39050, 1978–79)
   Original *Star Wars* header card $275.00
   Reissue on *The Empire Strikes Back* header card . 125.00
   Reissue on *Return of the Jedi* header card 60.00
   Reissue on Tri-Logo header card 100.00
   Loose, with Stormtrooper blaster 12.50

New Power of the Force:
Ponda Baba with "Blaster Pistol and Rifle" on green
   holo header card (**Collection 2**, #69708, July
   1997) [540903.00] with 1st hook, in stand-up
   bubble 40.00
   Reissue (Collection 3, #69708 July 1997)
     [.01] with 2nd hook, in stand-up bubble 6.00
   Loose, with black blaster pistol and rifle 3.00
   Variation, grey beard, loose. 20.00

POTE SNITKIN

"Pote Snitkin worked as a helmsman for Jabba the Hutt. The Skrilling piloted one of Jabba's desert skiffs before foolishly battling Jedi Luke Skywalker over the Great Pit of Carkoon." The figure was a Star Wars Fan Club exclusive.

New Power of the Force:
Pote Snitkin with "Force Pike and Blaster Pistol" on
   green Freeze Frame header card (Collection 3,
   #69863, 1999) [.00] fan club exclusive $25.00
   Loose, with black force pike and blaster pistol . . . 12.50

POWER DROID

The Power Droid figure is box shaped and gets around on two mechanical feet. It closely resembles the robots Hewie, Dewie, and Louie from the movie *Silent Running* starring Bruce Dern. The only new version of this figure is included with a Jawa in the CommTech series and called a "Gonk" droid. It has not been issued separately.

Padmé Naberrie and Pit Droids (Hasbro 1999)

Plo Koon and Walrus Man (Ponda Baba)
(Hasbro 2001 and Kenner 1983)

Power Droid and Prince Xizor (Kenner 1978 and 1976)

Classic:
Power Droid (#39090, 1978–79) 2¼" figure
    Original *Star Wars* header card $175.00
    Reissue on *The Empire Strikes Back* header card . 125.00
    Reissue on *Return of the Jedi* header card 55.00
    Reissue on Tri-Logo header card 75.00
    Loose, no accessories 10.00

New: *See Jawa figure*

PRINCE XIZOR

The *Shadows of the Empire* storyline takes place between *The Empire Strikes Back* and before *Return of the Jedi*. Prince Xizor runs the Black Sun criminal organization and wants to ruin Darth Vader and take over his position as the second most powerful figure in the empire. He tries to eliminate Luke Skywalker before Lord Vader can fulfill his promise to deliver Luke alive to the Emperor. He captures Leia, but Luke, Lando, Chewbacca, and Dash Rendar rescue her and get away.

New: Shadows of the Empire
Prince Xizor, with "Energy Blade Shields" on a
    purple *Shadows of the Empire* card (#69594,
    June 1996) [531620.00] $12.00
    Loose with blue energy blade shields with
        black base 3.00

PRINCESS LEIA ORGANA

Luke changes his hair color and pants and Han Solo gets a big head, but Princess Leia's basic figure stays the same throughout the original series. Of course she does get other outfits, but they are different figures. This one wears white. The CommTech version of the figure has the hood up on her head and was called "Princess Leia Hood Up" on Hasbro's Web site, but not on the figure.

Classic:
Princess Leia Organa (#38190, 1978) 3½" figure
    Original *Star Wars* "12 back" header card $750.00
    Reissue on *Star Wars* "20/21 back" header
    card 275.00
    Reissue on *The Empire Strikes Back* header card . 325.00
    Reissue on *Return of the Jedi* header card. 450.00

Princess Leia and Leia Organa, Bespin Gown
(Kenner 1997 and 1980)

    Reissue on Tri-Logo header card 150.00
    Loose, with pistol 45.00

New Power of the Force:
Princess Leia Organa with "'Laser' Pistol and
    Assault Rifle" on red header card (#69579,
    July 1995) [523211.00] 3 band belt 20.00
    Variation, 2 band belt (Nov. 1996). 15.00
    Variation, with holo sticker 15.00
    Reissue on green holo header card
        (Collection 1, #69579) [.01] with 2nd hook,
        in original bubble 12.00
    Variation, without holo sticker 12.00
    Loose with black laser pistol and short rifle 4.00
Princess Leia Organa with "Blaster Rifle and Long-
    Barreled Pistol" and with sticker saying "All
    New Likeness" on green Freeze Frame header
    card (Collection 1, #69824) [551737.00] 10.00
    Loose, with all equipment. 3.00

Princess Leia with "Sporting Blaster" on CommTech
    Chip header card (#84361) [.0000]. 25.00
    Loose, ... 7.00

Princess Leia (Bespin Gown)

There are two versions of this figure. In one the neck is flesh colored (crew neck) and in the other the neck is the same color as the rest of the costume or outfit (turtle neck). Both versions come with the same distinctive cloak. The front photo on the header card was changed during *The Empire Strikes Back* figure series. The original photo shows Leia turned to the left, looking back at the camera. The new photo shows her directly facing the camera.

Classic:
Leia Organa (Bespin Gown) (#39720, 1980)
    Original *The Empire Strikes Back* header
        card, **turtle neck** version $200.00
    Original *The Empire Strikes Back* header
        card, turtle neck, new package 175.00
    Reissue on *Return of the Jedi* header card. 150.00
    Reissue on Tri-Logo header card 115.00
    Loose, in cloak with pistol 20.00
Leia Organa (Bespin Gown) (#39720, 1980)
    Original *The Empire Strikes Back* header

card, **crew neck** version. 200.00
Original *The Empire Strikes Back* header
card, crew neck, new package 175.00
Reissue on *Return of the Jedi* header card. 125.00
Loose, in cloak with pistol 20.00

Power of the Jedi:
Leia Organa, Bespin Escape (#84588) Col. 1 on
Jedi Force File header card [571090.0300]. 12.00
Reissue [.0100] 8.00
Loose, ... 3.00

Princess Leia (Boushh Disguise)

The Shadows of the Empire storyline takes place between *The Empire Strikes Back* and before *Return of the Jedi*. Leia and Chewbacca go to Coruscant to try to find out who has been attempting to assassinate Luke. Leia disguised herself as the Ubesian bounty hunter, Boushh. Leia is captured by Prince Xizor and rescued by Chewbacca, Luke, Lando, and Dash Rendar. Leia keeps the disguise and uses it again attempting to rescue Han Solo from Jabba the Hutt.

Classic:
Princess Leia Organa (Boushh Disguise) (#70660, 1983)
Original *Return of the Jedi* header card $55.00
Reissue on Tri-Logo header card 150.00
Loose, with helmet and weapon. 15.00

New: Shadows of the Empire
Leia in Boushh Disguise, with "Blaster Rifle and
Bounty Hunter Helmet" on a purple *Shadows of the Empire* card (#69602, June 1996)
[532824.00] 12.00
Reissue on a *Shadows of the Empire*
purple holo header card (**Collection 1**,
#69818, 1997) [.01] with 2nd hook. 300.00
Loose, ... 3.00

New Power of the Force:
Leia in Boushh Disguise, with "Blaster Rifle and
Bounty Hunter Helmet" on green holo header
card (Collection 1, #69818, 1997) [.02] with
2nd hook, in original or stand-up bubble. 18.00
Variation, without holo sticker. 7.00
Loose, with grey and brown helmet and long
black blaster rifle 3.00

Princess Leia (Ceremonial)

This outfit is the white number worn when she awards Luke, Han, and Chewbacca the Galactic Medal of Honor.

New Power of the Force:
Princess Leia in Ceremonial Dress with "Medal of
Honor" on Flashback Photo header card
(#84038) [557528.01] $10.00
with Celebration Gown photo (incorrect). 10.00
with Freedom Fighter outfit (correct). 10.00
Loose, ... 3.00

Princess Leia (Combat Poncho)

Princess Leia Combat Poncho was issued in the *Return of the Jedi* series, but she has not been issued in the new series. The closest equivalent is the Princess Leia in Endor Gear which came with the Speeder Bike vehicle.

Classic:
Princess Leia Organa (in Combat Poncho) (#71220, 1984)
Original *Return of the Jedi* header card $60.00
Reissue on *Power of the Force* header card. . . . 100.00
Reissue on Tri-Logo header card 35.00
Loose in poncho with pistol 20.00

New: See Speeder Bikes listed in **Vehicles** Section.

Princess Leia (Ewok Celebration Outfit)

This is a new outfit for the Princess, and a new waist-length hair style, too. The Princess Leia collection figures, with four other outfits and hair styles, came out at about the same time. On the back of header card version ".00" for the new issue of this figure "Saelt-Marae" is misspelled as "Sealt-Marie"—two errors in just 10 letters. Version ".01" corrects this error. The error version is scarce.

New Power of the Force:
Princess Leia Organa in Ewok Celebration Outfit,
on green Freeze Frame header card (Col-
lection 1, #69714, Feb. 1998) [547095.00] $20.00
Variation [.01] "Saelt-Marae" spelling corrected. . . 10.00
Loose, with black pistol 3.00

Princess Leia (Expanded Universe)

"Six years after the destruction of the second Death Star,

Princess Leia Boushh Disguise (Kenner 1983 and 1997)

*Princess Leia, Ceremonial and Princess Leia, Combat Poncho
(Kenner 1998 and 1983)*

Princess Leia, Ewok Celebration and Leia Organa, General (Kenner 1998 and Hasbro 2001)

Princess Leia, Jabba's Prisoner (Kenner 1997 and 1998)

the galaxy is thrust into turmoil. A reborn evil threatens to enslave the galaxy, and the Republic's closest friend – Luke Skywalker – may become their greatest enemy... Hoping to free her brother Luke from the evil of the dark side, Jedi Leia prepares to match her power against that of the reborn Emperor. Boarding his colossal warship, Leia is overwhelmed by the oppression of the dark side." From the *Dark Empire* comic book series.

New: Expanded Universe
Princess Leia (in Black Cloak) on a 3-D Play-
    Scene header card (#69884) Collection 2
    [554778.03] $20.00
    Loose, ... 10.00

Leia Organa (General)

If she is a general, how come she is fighting in a small ground unit on Endor's moon? She's bossy enough to be a general.

Power of the Jedi:
Leia Organa, General (#84642) Col.1 on Jedi Force
    File header card [571090.0000] $12.00
    Reissuc [.0100] 8.00
    Loose, ... 3.00

Princess Leia (Hoth Outfit)

Princess Leia has appeared in a lot of new outfits in the new series, but this classic figure has not appeared. It's probably just as well. There were so many figures in Hoth outfits in the classic series that it was hard to tell them apart.

Classic:
Leia Organa (Hoth Outfit) (#39359, 1981)
    Original *The Empire Strikes Back* header card . . $175.00
    Reissue on *Return of the Jedi* header card. 100.00
    Reissue on *Return of the Jedi* header card,
        new package. 75.00
    Reissue on Tri-Logo header card 100.00
    Loose, with pistol. 25.00

New Power of the Force:
Princess Leia Organa in Hoth Gear with "Blaster
    Pistol" on green Freeze Frame header card
    (Collection 3, #84143) [554892.0000] fan club

exclusive 25.00
Loose, ... 12.50

Princess Leia (Jabba's Prisoner)

Princess Leia appeared in a very skimpy and unprincess-like outfit after she was captured by Jabba the Hutt at the beginning of *Return of the Jedi*. She uses her slave chain to strangle the ugly slug before she escapes.

This figure never appeared with the Classic offerings and so Princess Leia as Jabba's Prisoner, or Princess Leia "Slave Girl" as she is sometimes called, was heavily collected when she first appeared. This pushed her price up to $15.00, but the price fell as more and more supply appeared and now she is no more valuable than other figures. Near the end of 1997 she was available without holo sticker, and this more attractive version is still available in some stores.

On the back of header card version ".01" for the new Freeze Frame issue of this figure "Saelt-Marae" is misspelled as "Sealt-Marie"—two errors in just 10 letters. Version ".02" corrects this error.

The most recent version of this popular figure is as a deluxe figure packaged with Jabba's Sail Barge Cannon.

New Power of the Force:
Princess Leia Organa as Jabba's Prisoner, on
    green holo header card (Collection 1, #69683,
    Sept. 1997) [542899.00] with 2nd hook, in
    stand-up bubble. $6.00
    Variation, without holo sticker. 6.00
    Reissue on Freeze Frame header card [.01]. . . . 15.00
    Reissue [.02] spelling corrected 10.00
    Loose, with gray chain and collar 3.00

PRINCESS LEIA COLLECTION

Figures from the Princess Leia Collection are listed under Two-Packs.

QUEEN AMIDALA

Young elected leader of the Naboo, she does a good job

Queen Amidala, Naboo and Coruscant (Hasbro 1999)

against overwhelming odds. Tough job, but it comes with an impressive wardrobe. Later, she becomes Luke and Leia's mother.

Episode I:
Queen Amidala (Naboo) with "Blaster Pistols"
  (#84078) Col. 1 [558446.00] $12.00
  Reissue [.0100] 6.00
  Loose, with two pistols 3.00

Queen Amidala (Coruscant) (#84111) Col. 1
  [562042.0100] 15.00
  Loose, no accessories 3.00

Queen Amidala (Battle) with "Ascension Gun"
  (#84273) Col. 2 [587763.0100] 30.00
  Loose, with ascension gun 15.00

Power of the Jedi:
Queen Amidala, Theed Invasion (#84567) Col. 2 on
  Jedi Force File header card [571101.0100] $15.00
  Reissue [.0300] 15.00
  Reissue [.0400] 8.00
  Loose, ... 3.00

QUEEN AMIDALA (ROYAL DECOY)

"As the Trade Federation plan to invade peaceful Naboo unfolds, Queen Amidala must appeal to the Senate for help. In times of danger, the handmaidens serve as secret body-guards by posing as the Queen, such as on her way to the Galactic Senate on Coruscant, in which Sabe served as the dependable and nonchalant decoy for the Queen." This outfit might qualify as a "basic black dress," at least for queens.

Power of the Jedi:
Queen Amidala, Royal Decoy (#84657) Col. 2
  on "Transition" header card [6098590100] $8.00
  Loose, ... 3.00

QUI-GON JINN

Jedi Master and member of the Jedi Council. Obi-Wan is his apprentice. Qui-Gon is killed by Darth Maul at the Theed Generator complex.

Episode I:
Qui-Gon Jinn (Jedi Duel) with "Lightsaber" (#84072)

*Qui-Gon Jinn, Jedi Training Gear and Rebel Commando
(Hasbro 2001 and Kenner 1983)*

  Col. 1 [558431.00] $10.00
  Reissue [.0100] 6.00
  Loose, with green lightsaber 3.00

Qui-Gon Jinn (Naboo) with "Lightsaber and Handle"
  (#84113) Col. 1 [562048.0100] 7.00
  Loose, with green lightsaber and extra handle 3.00

Qui-Gon Jinn (Jedi Master) with "Lightsaber and
  ComLink" (#84107) Col. 1 [566973.0000] 20.00
  Loose, with green lightsaber and comlink 3.00

Power of the Jedi
Qui-Gon Jinn, Mos Espa Disguise (#84253) Col. 1
  on Jedi Force File header card [571091.0000] . . . 12.00
  Reissue [.0100] 8.00
  Loose, ... 3.00

Qui-Gon Jinn, Jedi Training Gear (#84559) Col. 1
  on Jedi Force File header card [571091.0400] . . . 12.00
  Loose, ... 3.00

Rancor Keeper: See Malakili

REBEL COMMANDER

The figure was also available loose with the MLC-3 vehicle.

Classic:
Rebel Commander (#39369, 1981)
  Original *The Empire Strikes Back* header card . . $150.00
  Reissue on *Return of the Jedi* header card 40.00
  Reissue on Tri-Logo header card 40.00
  Loose, with rifle 10.00

REBEL COMMANDO

The Rebel Commando is based on the Rebel troops who fought in the Battle of Endor. There is no equivalent figure in the New Power of the Force line-up, but the Endor Rebel Soldier is similar.

Classic:
Rebel Commando (#70740, 1983)
  Original *Return of the Jedi* header card $30.00

Rebel Fleet Trooper and Endor Rebel Soldier
(Kenner 1997 and 1998)

Hoth Rebel Solder and Ree-Yees (Kenner 1997 and 1983)

Reissue on Tri-Logo header card, new package . . 20.00
Loose, with rifle 10.00

REBEL (FLEET) TROOPER

Initially the Rebel Fleet Trooper came on a Collection 2 header card. This was quickly corrected to Collection 1, making the original ".00" version scarce.

This figure was reissued as "Rebel Trooper, *Tantive IV* Defender" in the Power of the Jedi series. "The heroic Rebel troopers were the last line of defense as the ship (Rebel Blockade Runner *Tantive IV*) was boarded by Darth Vader and a platoon of Stormtroopers."

New Power of the Force:
Rebel Fleet Trooper with "Blaster Pistol and Rifle"
   on green holo header card (**Collection 2**,
   #69696, May 1997) [540905.00] with 1st hook,
   in stand-up bubble $30.00
   Reissue (Collection 1, #69696, July 1997) [.01]
      with 2nd hook, in stand-up bubble 10.00
   Reissue, on Freeze Frame header card [.01]
      misspelling] 25.00
   Reissue, on Freeze Frame header card [.01]
      sticker] 20.00
   Reissue, "Saelt-Marae" spelling corrected [.02] . . . 18.00
   Loose, with 3.00

Power of the Jedi:
Rebel Trooper, *Tantive IV* Defender (#84658, 2002)
   Col. 2 on "Transition" header card [6098590200] . . . 8.00
   Loose, with blaster and helmet 3.00

REBEL SOLDIER (ENDOR)

The Endor Rebel Soldier was not included in the classic figure line-up, but the Rebel Commando is similar, and fought in the same battle.

On the back of header card version ".00" for the Freeze Frame issue of this figure "Saelt-Marae" is misspelled as "Sealt-Marie." Version ".01" corrects this error. The original error version is scarce and this is the initial appearance of the figure, which accounts for the price.

New Power of the Force:
Endor Rebel Soldier with "Survival Backpack and
   Blaster Rifle" on green Freeze Frame header
   card (Collection 1, #69716, 1998) [547098.00] . . $20.00
   Reissue, [.01] "Saelt-Marae" spelling corrected. . . 10.00
   Loose, with all gear 3.00

REBEL SOLDIER (HOTH GEAR)

These are rebel soldiers in their ice planet Hoth uniforms. The figure was also available loose with the Snowspeeder vehicle.

In the new series, the Hoth Rebel Soldier initially came on a Collection 2 header card. This was soon corrected to Collection 1, but there is little difference in price between the two versions.

On the back of header card version ".02" for the new Freeze Frame issue of this figure "Saelt-Marae" is misspelled as "Sealt-Marie"— two errors in just 10 letters. Version ".03" corrects this error.

Classic:
Rebel Soldier (Hoth Battle Gear) (#39750, 1980)
   Original *The Empire Strikes Back* header card. . . $75.00
   Reissue on *Return of the Jedi* header card 35.00
   Reissue on Tri-Logo header card 25.00
   Loose, with pistol. 10.00

New Power of the Force:
Hoth Rebel Soldier with "Survival Backpack and
   Blaster Rifle" on green holo header card
   (**Collection 2**, #69631, Feb. 1997)
   [538004.00] with 1st hook and original bubble . . . 12.00
   Variation, without holo sticker. 12.00
   Reissue (Collection 1, #69821, 1997) [.01]
      with 2nd hook and stand-up bubble 10.00
   Reissue, on Freeze Frame header card [.02] 20.00
   Reissue, [.03] "Saelt-Marae" spelling corrected. . . 10.00
   Loose, with white backpack and black blaster rifle . 3.00

REE-YEES

Ree-Yees is a Gran for Kinyen and is last seen on Jabba's sail barge when it is blown to bits. He reappeared in

Ric Olie and Romba (Hasbro 1999 and Kenner 1985)

R2-B1 and R2-D2, Sensorscope (Hasbro 1999 and Kenner 1998)

1998 but it must have been hard for Kenner to put him back together because he is incredibly scarce.

Classic:
Ree-Yees (#70800, 1983)
 Original *Return of the Jedi* header card $30.00
 Reissue on Tri-Logo header card 25.00
 Loose, with weapon 12.50

New Power of the Force:
Ree-Yees with "Blaster Pistols" on green Freeze
 Frame header card (Collection 3, #69839)
 [.00] scarce 25.00
 Loose, with pistols 10.00

RIC OLIÉ

Queen Amidala's pilot aboard her royal starship.

Episode I:
Ric Olié with "Helmet and Naboo Blaster" (#84109)
 Col. 2 [558538.00]........................ $8.00
 Reissue [.0100] 6.00
 Loose, with blaster and helmet 3.00

ROMBA

Romba is an Ewok, one of eight issued in the *Return of the Jedi* series. He had not been issued in any new series at press time.

Classic:
Romba (#93730, 1985)
 Original *Power of the Force* header card $50.00
 Reissue on Tri-Logo header card 35.00
 Loose, with spear......................... 25.00

Sandpeople: See Tusken Raider

R2-B1

Blue astromech droid which attemps repairs to the Naboo Royal Starship under fire. Several are lost in the attempt, which may explain why the figure is so scarce.

Episode I:
R2-B1 Astromech Droid with "Power Harness"
 (#84128) Col. 3. [566157.0000] $25.00

Loose, with power harness 10.00

R2-D2

R2 units are tripodal computer repair and information retrieval robots, or astromech droids. They act as navigators and in-flight repair droids on Rebel X-Wing fighters. R2-D2 is 0.96 meters tall, a little taller then Yoda. In *The Phantom Menace* we learned that it originally belonged to Queen Amidala. We first meet R2 as it repairs her Royal Starship to aid in the escape from Naboo.

Like C-3PO, R2-D2 has not been particularly popular with collectors, even though many versions have been issued. The only really cool one is the Electronic Power/FX figure which makes authentic movie sounds. Of course, it only does that if you remove it from the package. It's only listed in the chronological section.

Classic:
Artoo-Detoo (R2-D2) (#38200, 1978) 2¼" figure
 Original *Star Wars* "12 back" header card $350.00
 Reissue on *Star Wars* "20/21 back" header
  card................................. 200.00
 Reissue on *The Empire Strikes Back* header card . 150.00
 Reissue on Tri-Logo header card 35.00
 Loose, no accessories 15.00

New Power of the Force:
R2-D2 with "Light Pipe Eye Port and Retractable
 Leg" 2½" on red header card (#69574, July
 1995) [521787.00] 15.00
 Reissue on green holo header card (Collection
  1, #69574) [.01] with 2nd hook, in original or
  stand-up bubble........................ 15.00
 Loose, without accessories 3.00

R2-D2 (Booster Rockets)

R2-D2 is an astromech droid on Queen Amidala's Royal Starship. He repairs the ship so it can make good its escape from Naboo.

Episode I:
R2-D2 with "Booster Rockets" (#84104) Col. 2
 [560441.0000] $7.00
 Loose, no accessories 3.00

R2-D2, Sensorscope and R2-D2, Pop-Up Lightsaber
(Kenner 1983 and 1985)

R2-D2 (Holographic Princess Leia)

While young Luke repairs his new droid (actually his mother's old droid, but that's another story) a holographic princess appears and says "Help me Obi-Wan Kenobi, you're my only hope." Knowing that his sister likes to dress as a princess, and sick of helping her every time she gets in trouble, Luke tells the droid to "get out and stay out!" But Uncle Owen makes him go find the droid anyway. No, that's not quite right...Something like that anyway.

New Power of the Force:
R2-D2 with "Holographic" Princess Leia on Comm-
Tech Chip header card (#84199) [.0000]. $45.00
   Variation: foot peg on side of foot 300.00
   Loose, ... 15.00

R2-D2 (Naboo)

Power of the Jedi:
R2-D2, Naboo Escape (#84259) Col. 1 on Jedi
Force File header card [571091.0000] $12.00
   Reissue [.1000] 8.00
   Loose, ... 3.00

R2-D2 (Pop-up Lightsaber)

R2-D2 is serving drinks on Jabba's sail barge, but just as Luke is about to be thrown in the Sarlac pit, R2 sends over his lightsaber and the tables are turned.

Classic:
Artoo-Detoo (R2-D2) with Pop-up Lightsaber (#93720, 1985)
   Original *Power of the Force* header card. $150.00
   Reissue on Tri-Logo header card 175.00
   Loose, with lightsaber 100.00
Artoo-Detoo R2-D2 (#71780) Droids 1985 with pop-
   up lightsaber 100.00
   Loose 50.00

New Power of the Force:
R2-D2 with "Launching Lightsaber" on Flashback
   Photo header card (#84043) [557534.01] with
   Lightsaber packed left side. 10.00
   Variation, Lightsaber packed right side 100.00
   Loose, with lightsaber 3.00

R2-Q5 and R5-D4 (Hasbro 2001 and Kenner 1997)

R2-D2 (Sensorscope)

Like C-3PO, R2-D2 is a popular character, but not always a popular action figure collectible. This figure has never drawn much interest from collectors.

Classic:
Artoo-Detoo (R2-D2) (with Sensorscope) (#69590, 1982)
   Original *The Empire Strikes Back* header card . . . $75.00
   Reissue on *Return of the Jedi* header card
    (#69420) 40.00
   Reissue on Tri-Logo header card 28.00
   Loose, with scope 12.50

New Power of the Force:
R2-D2 with "Spring-Loaded, Pop-Up Scanner,
   Remote Action Retractable Scomp Link,
   Grasper Arm and Circular Saw" on green
   Freeze Frame header card (Collection 1,
   #69831) [551740.00] 15.00
   Variation: "Imperial trash compactor" on slide 50.00
   Loose, ... 3.00

R2-Q5

R2-Q5 units service Imperial TIE fighters and bombers as well as maintaining the weapons and security systems on the second Death Star.

Power of the Jedi:
R2-Q5, Imperial Astromech Droid (#84629) Col. 2
   on Jedi Force File header card [571101.0400] . . $12.00
   Loose, ... 3.00

R5-D4

The R5-D4 is a Modified Astromech Droid used in combat by the Rebel Alliance. It is 1 meter tall. The 1996 figure comes with a yellow projectile and has a concealed launcher which is revealed when the droid is opened at the top. The word "Photon" was dropped from the description of the missile launcher, undoubtedly because it sounded more like *Star Trek* than *Star Wars*.

Classic:
R5-D4 (#39070, 1978–79) 2½" figure
   Original *Star Wars* header card $300.00

Rune Haako and Sabé, Queen's Decoy (Hasbro 1999 and 2001)   *Saelt-Marae and Saesee Tiin (Kenner 1997 and Hasbro 2001)*

Reissue on *The Empire Strikes Back* header card . 140.00
Reissue on *Return of the Jedi* header card as
   Arfive Defour (R5-D4) 65.00
Reissue on Tri-Logo header card 75.00
Loose, no accessories 10.00

New Power of the Force:
R5-D4 with "Concealed Photon Missile Launcher"
   3" (Collection 2, #69598, Nov. 1996) on red
   header card [535185.00] no small parts warning . 25.00
Reissue on red header card, with small parts
   warning, straight latch [.01] 20.00
Reissue, now with "Concealed Missile
   Launcher" on green header card
   [535185.01], with warning on sticker and
   hooked latch, 1st hook, in original bubble. 20.00
Reissue with holographic picture on green
   header card, with warning, hooked latch or
   straight latch 20.00
Loose, with yellow launching missile 3.00

RUNE HAAKO

As Viceroy of the Neimoidian Trade Federation, he
plots with Darth Sidious to take over Naboo. His plan ulti-
mately fails, while Darth Sidious' plan succeeds.

Episode I:
Rune Haako (#84091) Col. 2 [561175.0000] $6.00
Loose, no accessories 3.00

SABÉ

Queen Amidala's most valuable handmaiden, Sabé, acts
as the queen's decoy in emergencies.

Power of the Jedi:
Sabé, Queen's Decoy (#84137) Col. 2 on Jedi
   Force File header card [571100.0400] $12.00
Loose, ... 3.00

SAELT-MARAE (YAK FACE)

Saelt-Marae, better known to classic series collectors as
Yak Face is an informant working for Jabba the Hutt. He
stands 2.2 meters tall, which helps him keep tabs on people.

The original figure was primarily available overseas,
which has kept its price quite high.

Classic:
Yak Face (#93840, 1985) foreign release
   Original *Power of the Force* header card $1,900.00
   Reissue on Tri-Logo header card 400.00
   Loose, with staff. 275.00

New Power of the Force:
Saelt-Marae (Yak Face) with "Battle Staff" 4½" on
   green holo header card (Collection 2, #69721,
   Oct. 1997) [542923.00] with 2nd hook, in
   stand-up bubble 12.00
Reissue, on Freeze Frame header card [.01] 15.00
Loose, with dark gray battle staff 3.00

SAESEE TIIN

Saesee Tiin is telepathic and a member of the Jedi
Council.

Power of the Jedi:
Saesee Tiin (#84569) Col. 2 on Jedi Force File
   header card [571101.0300] $12.00
   Reissue [.0400] 8.00
   Loose, ... 3.00

SANDTROOPERS

These are human Stormtroopers in desert gear. The original name of the figure, Tatooine Stormtrooper, was changed
almost immediately to Sandtrooper. The weapon was also
changed, but in name only.

New Power of the Force:
Tatooine Stormtrooper with "Concussion Grenade
   Cannon" (Collection 1, #69601, Oct. 1996) on
   red header card [535192.00] $25.00
Reissue as **Sandtrooper**, with "Heavy Blaster
   Rifle" (#69601) on green header card [.01]. . . . 15.00
Reissue with holographic picture on green
   header card. 15.00
Sandtrooper with "Heavy Blaster Rifle" on green
   holo header card (Collection 3, #69808) [.02]
   with 2nd hook, in stand-up bubble 6.00
Reissue on Freeze Frame header card [.03] 125.00

Loose, with black heavy blaster rifle and black
backpack with grey highlights 3.00

Power of the Jedi:
Sandtrooper, Tatooine Patrol (#84579) Col. 1 on
Jedi Force File header card [571090.0400] $8.00
Loose, ... 3.00

See-Threepio: See C-3PO

SEBULBA

Sebulba walks on his hands and steers with his feet, and
is the podracing champion on Tatooine, until Anakin comes
along. Also, he cheats, which may be why he did not get an
action figure in the *Episode I* line, although he was included
in the Watto's Junk Shop Cinema Scenes three-pack and with
his podracer vehicle.

Power of the Jedi:
Sebulba, Bonta Eve Challenge (#84266) Col. 2 on
Jedi Force File header card [.0100] $12.00
Loose, ... 3.00

SENATOR PALPATINE

Senator Palpatine becomes Chancellor after the Senate
votes "no confidence" in Chancellor Valorum. Gee, maybe
that was the plan all along. I wonder if he's any relation to
Emperor Palpatine from the classic movies.

Episode I:
Senator Palpatine with "Senate Cam Droid"
(#84082) Col. 2 [558541.00] $12.00
Reissue [.0100] 6.00
Loose, with cam droid 3.00

SHMI SKYWALKER

Shmi Skywalker was captured by space pirates and sold
into slavery. Currently she belongs to Watto. She is Anakin
Skywalker's mother, but who is his father?

Power of the Jedi:
Shmi Skywalker (#84271) Col. 2 on Jedi Force
File header card [571100.0400] $8.00
Loose, ... 3.00

SIO BIBBLE

Sio Bibble was the governor of Naboo. He stays behind
while Queen Amidala goes to Coruscant.

Episode I:
Sio Bibble with "Blaster Pistol" (#84257, 2000)
Col. 2 [567750.0000] $45.00
Loose, with pistol 15.00

Snaggletooth: See Zutton

SNOWTROOPER

Snowtroopers are human cold assault Stormtroopers.
This new name replaces the original "Imperial Stormtrooper
(Hoth Battle Gear)" They average 1.83 meters in height and
carry an Imperial issue blaster rifle.

The classic figure came with a rifle, but the new figure
carries a backpack and pistol, not a rifle, despite its header
card description.

Classic:
Imperial Stormtrooper (Hoth Battle Gear) (#39740, 1980)
Original *The Empire Strikes Back* header card . . $100.00
Reissue on *Return of the Jedi* header card 50.00
Reissue on Tri-Logo header card 50.00
Loose, with rifle 10.00

New Power of the Force:
Snowtrooper with "Imperial Issue Blaster Rifle" on
green holo header card (Collection 3, #69632,
Sept. 1997) [542915.00] with 2nd hook, in
original or stand-up bubble 8.00
Reissue, on Freeze Frame header card
(#69632) [.02] 20.00
Loose, with black pistol and white backpack 3.00

SPACE TROOPER

"Five years after the Battle of Endor, the Rebel Alliance
has driven the evil Empire into a distant corner of the galaxy.
But a new danger has arisen: The last of the Emperor's warlords has devised a battle plan that could destroy the
Republic. The ability of spacetroopers to operate exclusively

*Sandtrooper, Tatooine Patrol and Senator Palpatine
(Hasbro 2001 and 1999)*

Shmi Skywalker and Snowtrooper (Hasbro 2001 and Kenner 1997)

in space made them a valuable asset to the warlord, Grand Admiral Thrawn. These heavily-armed stormtroopers wear full-body armor and have equipment that enables them to function as personal space-capable assault vehicles." From the *Heir to the Empire* novels.

New: Expanded Universe
Spacetrooper on a 3-D PlayScene header card
    (#69892) Collection 2 [556415.03] $25.00
    Loose, ... 10.00

Squid Head: See Tessek

Star Destroyer Commander: See Death Squad Commander

STORMTROOPER

Stormtroopers are humans used as elite Imperial shock troops by the Galactic Empire. They carry a variety of weapons, including an Imperial issue blaster, blaster rifle and heavy infantry cannon.

Classic:
Stormtrooper (#38240, 1978)
    Original *Star Wars* "12 back" header card $400.00
    Reissue on *Star Wars* "20/21 back" header
       card. 150.00
    Reissue on *The Empire Strikes Back* header card . 125.00
    Reissue on *Return of the Jedi* header card 65.00
    Reissue on *Power of the Force* header card
       as **Imperial Stormtrooper**. 275.00
    Reissue on Tri-Logo header card, new package. . . 65.00
    Loose with weapon 15.00

New Power of the Force:
Stormtrooper with "Blaster Rifle and Heavy Infantry
    Cannon" on red header card (#69575, July
    1995) [521789.00] 12.00
    Reissue, with holo sticker [.00]. 9.00
    Reissue on green holo header card
       (Collection 3, #69803, 1997) [.01] with 2nd
       hook, in stand-up bubble 10.00
    Reissue, on Freeze Frame header card [.02] 15.00
    Loose, with black pistol and blaster rifle 3.00

Stormtrooper (Battle Damage)

Several Stormtroopers were blasted by Han and Luke, as they avoid the pursuit and make good their daring escape from the Death Star. Of course, later it turns out to be a trap.

Stormtrooper with Battle Damage and "Blaster Rifle
    Pack" on CommTech Chip header card
    (#84209) [.0000] $20.00
    Loose, ... 7.00

TC-14

TC-14 greets Qui-Gon and Obi-Wan on the Trade Federation ship at the beginning of *Episode I*. It is serving them refreshments when the Battle Droids attack.

Episode I:
TC-14 Protocol Droid with "Serving Tray" (#84276)
    Col. 3 [566160.0000]. $35.00
    Loose, with tray 15.00

TEEBO

Teebo is an Ewok, one of eight issued in the *Return of the Jedi* series. He had not been issued in any new series at press time.

Classic:
Teebo (#71310, 1984)
    Original *Return of the Jedi* header card $45.00
    Reissue on *Power of the Force* header card. . . . 210.00
    Reissue on Tri-Logo header card 35.00
    Loose, with club, mask and pouch 15.00

TESSEK (SQUID HEAD)

Squid Head from the classic series did not receive much collector interest. He is now called Tessek, and comes from Mon Calamari to serves as Jabba the Hutt's accountant. His plan to kill Jabba and steal his money does not turn out well.

Classic:
Squid Head (#70770, 1983)
    Original *Return of the Jedi* header card $30.00
    Reissue on Tri-Logo header card 25.00
    Loose, with pistol and cloak 10.00

Spacetrooper and Stormtrooper (Kenner 1998 and 1978)

TC-14 and Teebo (Hasbro 1999 and Kenner 1985)

Tessek and TIE Fighter Pilot (Hasbro 2001 and Kenner 1997)

2-1B Medic Droid and Tusken Raider (Kenner 1997)

Power of the Jedi:
Tessek (#84639) Col. 2 on Jedi Force File header
  card [571100.0300] 12.00
  Reissue [.0400] 8.00
  Loose, with pistol and cloak 3.00

TIE FIGHTER PILOT

These elite imperial pilots are human and fly the Twin Ion Engine (TIE) Fighter for the Galactic Empire. They also carry a blaster pistol, but there doesn't seem to be much they could do with it while flying. They average 1.7 meters in height, about 0.1 meters shorter than Stormtroopers.

In the new series, the first TIE Fighter Pilot figures came with a small-parts warning on a sticker. This was quickly changed to a printed warning on the ".01" header card. The original version is scarce and valuable. The first green card issue was in Collection 2, but this was corrected to Collection 3. There is only a small premium for the Collection 2 version.

Classic:
Imperial TIE Fighter Pilot (#70030, 1982)
  Original *The Empire Strikes Back* header card . . $125.00
  Reissue on *Return of the Jedi* header card 60.00
  Reissue on Tri-Logo header card 90.00
  Loose, with pistol 15.00

New Power of the Force:
TIE Fighter Pilot with "Imperial Blaster Pistol and
  Rifle" on red header card (#69584, March
  1996) with small-parts warning printed on
  sticker [527597.00] 25.00
  Warning printed on header card [.01] 12.00
  Reissue on red header card (#69673) [.02] 6.00
  Reissue on green holo header card
    (**Collection 2**, #69673) [.03] with 2nd hook,
    in original bubble 12.00
  Reissue (Collection 3, #69806, 1979) [.04] with
    2nd hook, in stand-up bubble 12.00
  Reissue, on Freeze Frame header card
    (#69806) [.05] 50.00
  Loose, with black pistol and rifle 3.00

2-1B

2-1B is an industrial automaton surgical droid. His new version is supposed to have a medical diagnostic computer, but it looks a lot like a weapon. Classic series figures also came with some of the PDT-8 vehicles.

Classic:
2-1B (#39399, 1981)
  Original *The Empire Strikes Back* header card . $100.00
  Reissue on *Return of the Jedi* header card as
    Too-Onebee (2-1B) (#71600) 50.00
  Reissue on Tri-Logo header card 75.00
  Loose, with grey staff 10.00

New Power of the Force:
2-1B Medic Droid with "Medical Diagnostic Computer" on green holo header card (Collection 2,
  #69618, Feb. 1997) [537994.00] with 1st hook,
  in original bubble 10.00
  Variation, without holo sticker 10.00
  Reissue [.01] with 2nd hook, in original or
    stand-up bubble 5.00
  Loose, with blue-gray gun-shaped medical
    computer 3.00

TUSKEN RAIDER (SAND PEOPLE)

The Tusken Raiders are humanoid nomadic warriors. They average 1.9 meters tall and just about kicked Luke Skywalker's butt in the early stages of the original movie.

The figure comes with a "gaderffii" stick weapon, which seems to have almost as many spellings as *Momar Quadaffi*. It's spelled "gaderffii" some places. The first version of the new figure came with a closed hand. This was replaced with a more open hand. A scarce few of the reissue figures still had the closed hand, making this a valuable variation.

Classic:
Sand People (#38280, 1978)
  Original *Star Wars* "12 back" header card $400.00
  Reissue on *Star Wars* "20/21 back" header
    card 150.00
  Reissue on *The Empire Strikes Back* header
    card as **Sandpeople** (#38280) 125.00

Tusken Raider and Ugnaughts (Hasbro 2001 and Kenner 1998)

Reissue on *Return of the Jedi* header card as
Tusken Raider (Sand People)" (#38280) 75.00
Reissue on Tri-Logo header card 75.00
Loose, with cloak and weapon 15.00

New Power of the Force:
Tusken Raider with "Gaderffi Stick Battle Club"
    on red header card (Collection 2, #69603,
    Nov. 1996) [535179.00] closed hand 25.00
Variation, open hand 75.00
Reissue, now with "Gaderffii Stick" on green
    header card with plain picture [.01] 12.00
Variation, closed hand 45.00
Reissue on green header card with holo-
    graphic picture [.01] open hand 12.00
Loose, with brown-handled silver gaderffi stick:
    Closed hand. 3.00
    Open hand. 3.00

Power of the Jedi:
Tusken Raider, Desert Sniper (#84248) Col. 2 on
    Jedi Force File header card [571101.0000]. 15.00
Reissue [.0100] 15.00
Reissue [.0300] 12.00
Reissue [.0400] 8.00
Loose, ... 3.00

UGNAUGHTS

Ugnaughts work in Cloud City mining Tibanna gas and doing other manual labor. Two versions are available in the classic series, Lavender Smock and Blue Smock, but they generally sell for the same price. In the new series you got two Ugnaughts for the price of one.

Classic:
Ugnaught (#39319, 1981)
    Original *The Empire Strikes Back* header card . . $80.00
    Reissue on *Return of the Jedi* header card 35.00
    Reissue on Tri-Logo header card 45.00
    Loose, in blue smock with white tool case 10.00
    Loose, in lavender smock with white tool case . . . 12.50

New Power of the Force:
Ugnaughts, with "Tool Kit" on green Freeze Frame
    header card (Collection 2, #69837) [551752.00] . 12.00
Loose, with Tool Kit 3.00

Watto and Weequay (Hasbro 1999 and Kenner 1983)

Walrus Man: See Ponda Baba

WAROK

Warok is an Ewok, one of eight issued in the *Return of the Jedi* series. He had not been issued in any new series at press time.

Classic:
Warok (#93810, 1985)
    Original *Power of the Force* header card $75.00
    Reissue on Tri-Logo header card 60.00
    Loose, with bow and pouch 25.00

WATTO

Toydarian junk dealer and the biggest gambler in Mos Espa. He should have bet on Anakin! Rumored to be starting a Mos Espa chapter of Gamblers Anonymous.

Episode I:
Watto with "Datapad" (#84093) Col. 2 [558547.00]. . . $10.00
    Reissue [.0100] 6.00
    Loose, with datapad 3.00

WEEQUAY

Weequays are from the planet Sriluur and several work for Jabba the Hutt as guards.

The new version of Weequay identifies him as a skiff guard and adds a "blaster rifle" to his weaponry. It's more like the size of a large pistol and very similar weapons are frequently just called "Blasters" by Kenner. Initially Weequay came on a Collection 2 header card. This was quickly corrected to Collection 3, making the original ".00" version scarce.

Classic:
Weequay
    Original *Return of the Jedi* header card $35.00
    Reissue on Tri-Logo header card 25.00
    Loose, with spear. 20.00

New Power of the Force:
Weequay Skiff Guard with "Force Pike and Blaster
    Rifle" on green holo header card (**Collection**

Wicket W. Warrick and Wuher (Kenner 1983 and 1998)

Yoda, orange snake and brown snake (Kenner 1980 and 1983)

2, #69707, May 1997) [540901.00] with 1st
hook, in stand-up bubble 30.00
Reissue (Collection 3, #69707, July 1997) [.01]
   with 2nd hook, in stand-up bubble 6.00
Reissue: Freeze Frame header card [.02], scarce 350.00
Loose, with brown force pike and blaster 3.00

WICKET W. WARRICK

Wicket is the first Ewok that Princess Leia meets on Endor, right after she crashes her speeder bike. He was also issued as part of the Ewok pack in the New Power of the Force line-up and, at virtually the same time in early 1998, with Princess Leia in the Princess Leia collection.

Classic:
Wicket W. Warrick (#71230, 1984)
   Original *Return of the Jedi* header card $50.00
   Reissue on *Power of the Force* header card. . . . 210.00
   Reissue on Tri-Logo header card 35.00
   Loose, with spear. 15.00

New: See Ewoks: Wicket & Logray

See also: EWOKS *series*

WUHER

Wuher is the bartender at the Mos Eisley cantina where no droids are allowed. He has a droid detector which facilitates this policy.

New Power of the Force:
Wuher with "Droid Detector Unit" on green Comm-
   Tech header card (#84389) [566864.0100] with
   CommTech Chip $15.00
   Loose, with droid detector 5.00

YODA

Yoda, the diminutive Jedi master, is of an unknown race and lives on the swamp planet, Dagobah. He was one of the 12 members of the Jedi Council, in *Episode I*, when there still was a council, and, for that matter, a republic. He is over 900 years old, so he needs a gimer stick to help him walk. When you are strong in the force, you can speak softly (and with

backward syntax) and carry a small stick.

In the original series, Yoda comes with a snake which fits around his neck as well as a gimer stick. The front photo on the header card was changed during the *Return of the Jedi* figure series. The original photo shows Yoda holding his stick and facing somewhat to the left. The new photo shows him facing significantly to the right. Yoda originally had a brown snake, but some of *The Empire Strikes Back* figures came with an orange snake. The gimer stick is roughly the same color as the snake in each version.

Classic:
Yoda (with **orange snake**) (#38310, 1981)
   Original *The Empire Strikes Back* header card . $225.00
   Loose, with orange snake 20.00
Yoda (with **brown snake**) (#38310, 1981)
   Original *The Empire Strikes Back* header card . . 300.00
   Reissue on *Return of the Jedi* header card. 100.00
   Reissue on *Return of the Jedi* header card as
      Yoda, The Jedi Master 100.00
   Reissue on *Power of the Force* header card. . . . 500.00
   Reissue on Tri-Logo header card 110.00
   Loose, with brown snake 25.00

New Power of the Force:
Yoda with "Jedi Trainer Backpack and Gimer Stick"
   2" on red header card (#69586, March 1996)
   [527603.00] 12.00
   Reissue, red header card (#69672) [.00] or
      [.01] with holo sticker 35.00
   Reissue on green holo header card
      (**Collection 2**, #69672) [.02] with 2nd hook,
      in original bubble 10.00
   Variation, without holo sticker 10.00
   Reissue (Collection 1, #69586) [.03] with 2nd
      hook, in original bubble 12.00
   Loose, with brown gimer stick and blue-gray
      backpack 3.00

Yoda with "Cane and Boiling Pot" on Flashback
   Photo header card (#84039) [557530.00] 15.00
   Loose, ... 4.00

Episode I:
Yoda with "Jedi Council Chair" (#84086) Col. 2

Yoda (Kenner 1998 and Hasbro 1999)

Zuckuss (Kenner 1980 and Zutton (Hasbro 2002)

[.0000]. 7.00
Without "Episode 1" on card. 30.00
Loose, with chair 3.00

Attack of the Clones
Yoda, Jedi Master, Col. 1 . . . . N/A

ZUCKUSS (Classic)

Kenner reversed the names of 4-LOM and Zuckuss in the original figure line-up and corrected it in the new figures.

Classic:
Zuckuss (#70020, 1982)
    Original *The Empire Strikes Back* header card . $125.00
    Reissue on *Return of the Jedi* header card 50.00
    Reissue on Tri-Logo header card 28.00
    Loose, with rifle 10.00

New Power of the Force:
    See 4-LOM

ZUCKUSS (formerly 4-LOM)

The real Zuckuss is from the planet Gand and was one of the bounty hunters who answered Darth Vader's call-up to help in locating the Millennium Falcon and its crew. He worked with 4-LOM, the droid turned bounty hunter.

Classic:
    See 4-LOM

New Power of the Force:
Zuckuss with "Heavy Blaster Rifle" on Freeze
    Frame header card (#69747, 1998) Col. 3
    [550627.00] $30.00
    Loose, ... 10.00

ZUTTON (SNAGGLETOOTH)

"Zutton is a Snivvian artist who turned bounty hunter by chasing down Thalassian slavers. He was given the nickname "Snaggletooth" at the Mos Eisley cantina, because of his pronounced fangs. His exceptional bounty hunter skills have caught the attention of crimelord Jabba the Hutt, who has put his services on retainer."

The classic blue Snaggletooth was only available in the Cantina Adventure Set, which was a Sears exclusive. He is full sized and he wears boots and a blue suit. The figure came polybagged with a Han Solo-style blaster in this set. The only Snaggletooth on a header card is in a red suit and he is the correct smaller size and bare-footed. There is no difficulty in distinguishing between them.

Snaggletooth (blue)
Classic:
Snaggletooth (**blue**) (Sears Exclusive) 3¾" figure
    loose only, from Cantina Adventure Set $350.00

Snaggletooth (red)
Classic:
Snaggletooth (**red**) (#39040, 1978–79) 2¾" figure
    Original *Star Wars* header card 175.00
    Reissue on *The Empire Strikes Back* header card . 150.00
    Reissue on *Return of the Jedi* header card 55.00
    Reissue on Tri-Logo header card 75.00
    Loose, with pistol 10.00

Power of the Jedi:
Zutton, Snaggletooth (#84661) Col. 2 on "Tran-
    sition" header card [6098590400] 8.00
    Loose, ... 3.00

BOOKS

Star Wars mass market Collectible #1, the very first mass market *Star Wars* item produced, was the movie novelization paperback book which appeared in late November 1976, seven months before the movie opened. It can be identified by the line "First Edition: December 1976" at the bottom, on the copyright page. As the movie became a hit, the paperback was reprinted many times, with huge print runs—3.5 million copies in the first year. None of these reprintings is scarce, and none is valuable.

The novel appeared in hardcover in the fall of 1977. The trade hardcover is scarce and valuable. It has a gold dust jacket, and says "Hardbound Ballantine Books Edition: October 1977/First Edition: December 1976" in two lines on the copyright page. While the first paperback edition and the hardcover edition enjoy crossover collector interest from persons who are not primarily *Star Wars* fans, book club editions have no collector following whatever apart from die-hard *Star Wars* fans. Consequently the book club edition of the original *Star Wars* novel, and for that matter, any *Star Wars* novel, is not valuable. The one exception might be the very first printing of the book club edition of *Star Wars*. This can be identified by the printing code "S27" in the gutter on page 183. It appeared before the trade hardcover, making it the first hardcover edition of the book. The book was ghost written by Alan Dean Foster, from the screenplay, a fact now confirmed by Lucas.

Each of the other movies was novelized in turn. Other original novels followed for a few years from Ballantine Del Rey. They were written by Alan Dean Foster, Brian Daley and L. Neil Smith. Then there was a slack period until Bantam got the *Star Wars* novels license. Comics tapered off at this time as well. In mid 1991, *Star Wars* novels returned with Timothy Zahn's *Heir to the Empire*. This book made it to the top of the *New York Times* bestseller lists. Bantam continued a successful publishing program with a number of new novels and juvenile adaptations. Lucas Films licensing has insisted on overall continuity in the storylines for both the books and the comics, so that they constitute a consistent "expanded universe." This makes these novels important in the *Star Wars* universe, because there are only about six hours of actual films. The earlier Del Rey novels were mostly written before the movie series was completed, and thus lack this continuity. The lives of subsidiary characters such as Boba Fett and new

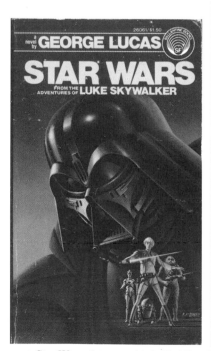
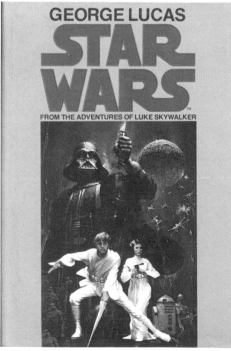

Star Wars, 1st paperback (Del Rey 1976) 1st Hardcover (Del Rey 1977) 1st Book Club Edition (Science Fiction Book Club 1977)

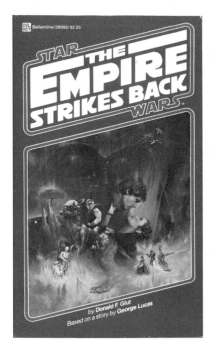 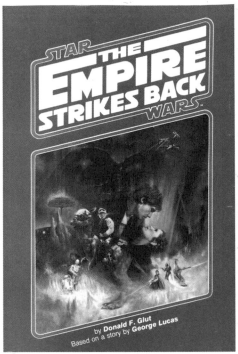 

The Empire Strikes Back, *1st Paperback (Del Rey 1980) and 1st Book Club Edition (Science Fiction Book Club 1980)
and* Return of the Jedi, *1st Book Club Edition (Science Fiction Book Club 1983)*

characters such as Grand Admiral Thrawn are only covered in the novels and the comics. In 1998, Del Rey got the *Star Wars* license back. They have continued to publish *Star Wars* novels aggressively.

FICTION

MOVIE NOVELIZATIONS

Star Wars, by Alan Dean Foster, uncredited ghost writer, from screenplay by George Lucas
1st PB: $1.50, 220pp, Ballantine #26061-9, Dec. 1976, Ralph McQuarrie cover $90.00
2nd PB: $1.95, 220pp, Ballantine-Del Rey #26079-1, Aug. 1977, Movie tie-in, John Berkey cover 10.00
1st SFBC: $2.49, 183pp, Del Rey #2403-4, Aug. 1977, with 16 pages of color photos from the movie, printing code S27, John Berkey cover 20.00
Later SFBC: later printing codes 5.00
1st HC: $6.95, 183pp, Del Rey #27476-8, Oct. 1977, with 16 pages of color photos from the movie, John Berkey cover 100.00
Later PB: 220pp, Ballantine-Del Rey #29368-1 Oct. 1980 . . . . 3.00
Later PB: $2.75, 220pp, Ballantine-Del Rey #30735-6, June 1984 . . . . 3.00
Recent PB: retitled *Star Wars: A New Hope*, $4.99, Ballantine-Del Rey #34146-5. . . . . 5.00
Recent HC: as *Star Wars: A New Hope*, $16.00, 224pp, Ballantine-Del Rey #40077-1, Oct. 1994, new intro by George Lucas, Tom Jung cover 16.00

The Empire Strikes Back, by Donald F. Glut from story by George Lucas and screenplay by Lawrence Kasdan and Leigh Brackett
1st PB: $2.25, 214pp, Ballantine-Del Rey #28392-9, May 1980, Roger Kastel cover 15.00
Later PB: 214pp, Ballantine-Del Rey #29209-X, Aug. 1980, Roger Kastel cover 5.00
1st SFBC: $2.49, Del Rey #3863-8, Aug. 1980, printing code K29, Roger Kastel cover . . 25.00
Later SFBC: later printing codes 5.00
Later PB: $3.50, 214pp, Ballantine-Del Rey #32022-0, 1980s 3.00
Recent PB: Del Rey #32022-0, trilogy logo cover, in silver 5.00
still in print
Recent HC: $16.00, 224pp, Ballantine-Del Rey #40078-X, Oct. 1994, new introduction by George Lucas, Roger Kastel cover 16.00

Return of the Jedi, by James Kahn, from screen play by Lawrence Kasdan and George Lucas
1st PB: $2.95, 181pp, Ballantine-Del Rey #30767-4, June 1983, Movie Tie-in 10.00
Current PB: #30767-4, trilogy logo cover, in gold
SFBC: $3.98, Del Rey #2144-4, Aug. 1983, printing code N31 . . . . 20.00
HC: $16.00, 240pp, Ballantine-Del Rey #40079-8, Oct. 1994, Kazuhiko Sano cover 16.00

Star Wars Trilogy by George Lucas, Donald F. Glut and James Kahn
TPB: $8.95, 471pp, Del Rey #34806-0, May 1987, Sylvain Michaels cover. 10.00
TPB: retitled: *Classic Star Wars: The Star Wars Trilogy*, $10.00, 480pp, Del Rey #34806-0, April 1995, Tom Jung cover 10.00
1st PB: $5.99, 480pp, Del Rey #38438-5, March 1993, John Berkey cover 6.00
still in print

Movie Novelizations: Illustrated Editions
The Empire Strikes Back: The Illustrated Edition,
   by Donald F. Glut, $4.95, 213pp, Del Rey
   #28831-9, Aug. 1980, Ralph McQuarrie
   illustrations and cover 10.00
Return of the Jedi Illustrated Edition, by James
   Kahn, Del Rey #30960-X, June 1983 . . . . 10.00

Episode I:
Star Wars Episode I: The Phantom Menace by Terry Brooks
   1st HC: $25.00 Del Rey # , May 1999 . . . . 25.00
   1st HC: $25.00 Del Rey # , May 1999, Queen
   Amidala cover. 25.00
   1st HC: $25.00 Del Rey # , May 1999, Anakin
   Skywalker cover 25.00
   1st HC: $25.00 Del Rey # , May 1999, Obi-Wan
   Kenobi cover. 25.00
   1st HC: $25.00 Del Rey # , May 1999, Darth
   Maul cover 25.00
   Lim. Ed. signed, slipcase, foil embossed Darth
      Maul cover with Qui-Gon Jinn pin 85.00
   1st PB: $7.50 Del Rey # , Feb. 2000 . . . . 7.50

NOVELS (1978–89)

Splinter of the Mind's Eye, by Alan Dean Foster
   1st HC: $7.95, 216pp, Del Rey #27566-7,
      Feb. 1978, Ralph McQuarrie cover 35.00
   1st PB: $1.95, 199pp, Ballantine-Del Rey
      #26062-7, April 1978, Ralph McQuarrie cover. . 20.00
   SFBC: $1.98, Del Rey #2597-3, May 1978,
      Ralph McQuarrie cover 5.00
   Later PB: $2.50, 199pp, Ballantine-Del Rey
      #32023-9, 1984, Ralph McQuarrie cover 4.00
   Later PB: $5.99, 224pp, Del Rey #32023-9,
      May 1994, Ralph McQuarrie cover,
      different design 5.00

Han Solo Series, by Brian Daley
Han Solo at Stars' End
   HC: $8.95, 198pp, Del Rey #28251-5, April
      1979, Wayne Barlowe cover 30.00
   SFBC: $2.49, Del Rey #3356-3, printing code
      J28, Aug. 1979, Wayne Barlowe cover 5.00
   1st PB: $2.25 Ballantine-Del Rey #29664-8,
      Oct. 1979, Wayne Barlowe cover 5.00
   Recent PB: $5.99, 192pp, Del Rey #29664-8,
      July 1997, Dave Dorman cover 5.00
Han Solo's Revenge
   1st HC: $8.95, 198pp, Del Rey #28475-5,
      Nov. 1979, Dean Ellis cover 35.00
   SFBC: $2.98, Del Rey #3670-7, Feb. 1980,
      Dean Ellis cover 5.00
   1st PB: $2.25, 199pp, Ballantine-Del Rey
      #28840-8, June 1980, Dean Ellis cover. 5.00
   Recent PB: Del Rey #28840-8, Dave Dorman
      cover 5.00
Han Solo and the Lost Legacy
   1st PB: $2.25, 187pp, Ballantine-Del Rey
      #28710-X, Sept. 1980, William Schmidt cover. . 10.00
   SFBC: $3.98, Del Rey #3398-5, printing code
      K42, Dec. 1980, William Schmidt cover 20.00
   Recent PB: Del Rey #34514-2, Dave Dorman
      cover. 5.00
Combined edition: *The Han Solo Adventures*
   1st PB: $5.99, 576pp, Del Rey #37980-2, June
      1992, William Schmidt cover. 6.00
   Recent PB: *Classic Star Wars: The Han Solo
      Adventures*, $10.00, 576pp, Del Rey
      #39442-9, April 1995, William Schmidt cover . . 10.00

Lando Calrissian Series, by L. Neil Smith
Lando Calrissian and the Mindharp of Sharu
   1st PB: $2.50, 182pp, Ballantine-Del Rey
      #31158-2, July 1983, William Schmidt cover. . . 15.00
   1st SFBC: $4.98, Del Rey #3639-2, Jan. 1984 . . . . 5.00

 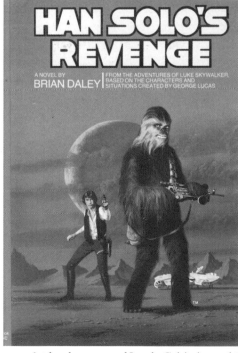 

Splinter of the Mind's Eye *and* Han Solo's Revenge, *1st hardcovers, and* Lando Calrissian and the Flamewind of Oseon, *1st paperback*
(BallantineDel Rey 1978–83)

Lando Calrissian and the Flamewind of Oseon
   1st PB: $2.50, 181pp, Ballantine-Del Rey
      #31163-9, Oct. 1983, William Schmidt cover . . . 15.00
   1st SFBC: $4.98, Del Rey #3588-1, Apr. 1984 . . . . 5.00
Lando Calrissian and the Starcave of ThonBoka
   1st PB: $2.50, 181pp, Ballantine-Del Rey
      #31164-7, Dec. 1983, William Schmidt cover . . 15.00
   SFBC: none
all out of print, but combined as:
Classic Star Wars: The Lando Calrissian Adventures
   1st combined PB: $5.99, Del Rey #39110-1,
      July 1994, William Schmidt cover. 6.00
   Current TPB: $10.00, 416pp, Del Rey
      #39443-7, April 1995, William Schmidt cover. . . 10.00

NOVELS (1990–98)

Timothy Zahn's *Heir to the Empire* launched the current phase of *Star Wars* publishing. It appeared about six months before the first Dark Horse Comic—*Dark Empire* and it reached #1 on the *New York Times* bestseller's list. The story takes place five years after the death of Darth Vader and recounts the efforts of your favorite heroes to bring as many planets as possible into the New Republic and the emergence of Grand Admiral Thrawn as leader of the remnants of the Empire in a counter-revolution.

The novels and story collections are listed below in their approximate order of appearance, based on the first book in the series. Titles first published in hardcover are listed first, followed by paperback series.

It has been common for the Science Fiction Book Club to reprint three-book paperback original series in one omnibus book club edition. For a collector, however, a first edition paperback is more valuable than a hardcover reprint, because it is the true first edition of the work.

In order to be worth collecting, any hardcover book must be in near mint condition, with dust jacket in similar shape. The only defect in a dust jacket that does not significantly reduce value is "price-clipping," where a small portion of the inside front flap of the dust jacket is cut to remove the original price. This was commonly done to books given as gifts and by some used book dealers who wanted to charge more than original price. It is a pointless practice today, because the price is also printed on the bar code box in back.

Now that publication of new *Star Wars* novels is in full swing, print runs are large and price appreciation is unlikely. The best way to collect is to wait until the hardcover book you want is available for about $5.00 on the remainder tables at your favorite book store; and then look through all of them to find a first edition. You can accumulate a handsome hardcover collection this way, at reasonable prices.

NOVELS AND COLLECTIONS (1990–98)

Hardcover originals:
Grand Admiral Thrawn series by Timothy Zahn
Heir to the Empire
   1st HC: $15.00, 361pp, Bantam Spectra
      #07327-3, June 1991, Tom Jung cover $35.00
   Limited Ed. HC $125.00, Bantam June 1991,
      signed, in slipcase. 150.00
   1st SFBC: $5.98, Bantam #18382-2, Summer
      1991, Tom Jung cover 5.00
   1st PB: $4.99, 404pp, Bantam Spectra
      #29612-4, June 1992, Tom Jung cover 6.00
Dark Force Rising
   1st HC: $18.50, 376pp, Bantam Spectra
      #08574-3, June 1992, Tom Jung cover 25.00
   Limited Ed. HC, $125.00, Bantam #08907-2,
      June 1992, signed, in slipcase. 140.00
   1st SFBC: $7.98, Bantam #19949-7, Summer
      1992 . . . . 7.50
   1st PB: $5.99, 439pp, Bantam Spectra
      #56071-9, March 1993, Tom Jung cover 5.00
The Last Command
   1st HC: $21.95, 407pp, Bantam Spectra

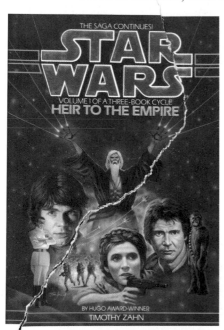
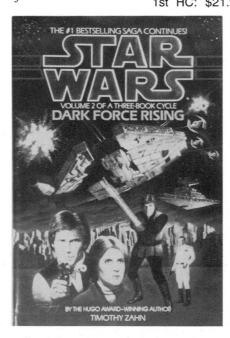

Heir to the Empire, Dark Force Rising, *and* The Last Command, *by Timothy Zahn, 1st Hardcovers (Bantam Spectra 1991–93)*

#09186-7, May 1993, Tom Jung Cover 25.00
SFBC: $8.98, 349pp, Bantam #00913, July
   1993, Tom Jung cover 7.50
1st PB: $5.99, 467pp, Bantam Spectra
   #56492-7, Feb. 1994, Tom Jung cover 5.00

The Truce At Bakura, by Kathleen Tyers
   1st HC: $21.95, 311pp, Bantam Spectra
      #09541-2, Jan. 1994, Drew Struzan cover 25.00
   SFBC: $7.98, 246pp, Bantam #02501, Drew
      Struzan cover 7.50
   1st PB: $5.99, 341pp, Bantam Spectra
      #56872-8, Dec. 1994, Drew Struzan cover 5.00

The Courtship Of Princess Leia, by Dave Wolverton
   1st HC: $21.95, 327pp, Bantam Spectra
      #08928-5, May 1994, Drew Struzan cover 25.00
   SFBC: $7.98, 327pp, Bantam #03409, Drew
      Struzan cover 7.50
   1st PB: $5.99, Bantam Spectra #56937-6,
      May 1995, Drew Struzan cover............. 5.00

The Crystal Star, by Vonda N. McIntyre
   1st HC: $21.95, 309pp, Bantam Spectra
      #08929-3, Dec. 1994, Drew Struzan cover 25.00
   SFBC: $7.98, 260pp, Bantam #06637, Feb.
      1995, Drew Struzan cover 7.50
   1st PB: $5.99, 413pp, Bantam Spectra
      #57174-5, Dec. 1995, Drew Struzan cover 5.00

Children of the Jedi, Barbara Hambly
   1st HC: $21.95, 345pp, Bantam Spectra
      #08930-7, May 1995, Drew Struzan cover 25.00
   SFBC: $8.98, 330pp, Bantam #07692, Aug.
      1995, Drew Struzan cover 8.00
   1st PB: $5.99, 409pp, Bantam Spectra
      #57293-8, July 1996, Drew Struzan cover...... 5.00

Star Wars Darksaber, by Kevin J. Anderson
   1st HC: $22.95, Bantam Spectra #09974-4,
      Nov. 1995, Drew Struzan cover............. 25.00

SFBC: $8.98, Bantam, Drew Struzan cover.......... 8.00
   1st PB: $5.99, Bantam Spectra #56611-9,
      Nov. 1996, Drew Struzan cover. 5.00

Shadows Of The Empire, by Steve Perry
   1st HC: $22.95, Bantam Spectra #10089-0,
      May 1996, Drew Struzan cover. 25.00
   SFBC: $8.98, Bantam, Drew Struzan cover 8.00
   1st PB: $5.99, Bantam Spectra #57413-2,
      April 1997, Drew Struzan cover 5.00

The New Rebellion, by Kristine Kathryn Rusch
   1st HC: $22.95 Bantam Spectra #10093-9,
      Dec. 1996, Drew Struzan cover 25.00
   SFBC: $8.98, 386p, Bantam #14141, Jan.
      1997, Drew Struzan cover 8.00
   1st PB: $5.99, Bantam Spectra #57414-0,
      Oct. 1997, Drew Struzan cover. 5.00

Planet of Twilight, by Barbara Hambly
   1st HC: $22.95, 312pp, Bantam Spectra
      #09540-4, May 1997, Drew Struzan cover 25.00
   SFBC: Bantam 8.00
   1st PB: $5.99, Bantam Spectra #57517-1,
      Apr. 1998, Drew Struzan cover. 6.00

The Hand of Thrawn series by Timothy Zahn
#1: *Specter of the Past*, by Timothy Zahn
   1st HC: $23.95, 344pp, Bantam Spectra
      #09542-0, Nov. 1997, Drew Struzan cover 24.00
   SFBC: Bantam 8.00
   1st PB: $6.99, Bantam #, Sept.1998 .... 7.00
#2 *Vision of the Future*
   1st HC: Bantam Spectra #, Sept. 1998........ 25.00
   1st PB: $6.99, Bantam #, Sept. 1999............ 7.00

I, Jedi, by Michael Stackpole
   1st HC: $23.95, Bantam Spectra #10820-4,
      Feb. 1998. .... 24.00
   1st PB: $5.99, Bantam Spectra #57873-1,
      June 1999. .... 6.00

The Truce at Bakura, *by Kathleen Tyers,* Children of the Jedi, *by Barbara Hambly,* Specter of the Past *by Timothy Zahn*
1st Hardcovers (Bantam Spectra 1994–97)

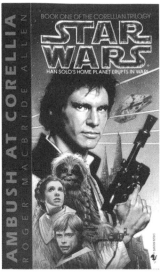 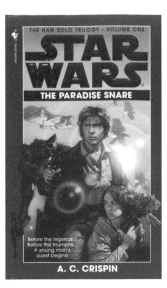

*Ambush at Corellia, by Roger MacBride Allen, and
The Paradise Snare, by A. C. Crispin, 1st Paperbacks
(Bantam Spectra 1995–97)*

Paperback originals:
The Jedi Academy Trilogy by Kevin J. Anderson
#1 *Jedi Search*
    1st PB: $5.99, 354pp, Bantam Spectra
    #29798-8, March 1994, John Alvin cover 6.00
#2: *Dark Apprentice*
    1st PB: $5.99, 354pp, Bantam Spectra
    #29799-6, July 1994, John Alvin cover 5.00
#3: *Champions of the Force*
    1st PB: $5.99, 324pp, Bantam Spectra
    #29802-X, Oct. 1994, John Alvin cover 5.00

The Corellian Trilogy by Roger McBride Allen
#1: *Ambush At Corellia*
    1st PB: $5.99, 308pp, Bantam Spectra
    #29803-8, March 1995, Drew Struzan cover 5.00
#2: *Assault At Selonia*
    1st PB: $5.99, 289pp, Bantam Spectra
    #29805-4, July 1995, Drew Struzan cover 5.00
#3: *Showdown At Centerpoint*
    1st PB: $5.99, 301pp, Bantam Spectra
    #29806-2, Oct. 1995, Drew Struzan cover 5.00

Star Wars Tales edited by Kevin J. Anderson
Star Wars: Tales from the Mos Eisley Cantina
    1st PB: $5.99, Bantam Spectra #56468-4
    Aug. 1995, Anthology of 16 stories, Steve
    Youll cover 5.00
Star Wars Tales From Jabba's Palace
    1st PB: $5.99, Bantam Spectra #56815-9, Jan
    1996, Anthology, Steve Youll cover 5.00
Star Wars: Tales of the Bounty Hunters
    1st PB: $5.99, 339pp, Bantam Spectra
    #56816-7, Dec. 1996, Anthology of 5
    stories, Steve Youll cover 5.00

Black Fleet Crisis by Michael Kube-McDowell
#1: *Before The Storm*
    1st PB: $5.99, 309pp, Bantam Spectra
    #57273-3, April 1996, Drew Struzan cover 6.00
#2: *Shield of Lies*
    1st PB: $5.99, 340pp, Bantam Spectra
    #57277-6, Sept. 1996, Drew Struzan cover 6.00

#3: *Tyrant's Test*
    1st PB: $5.99, 366pp, Bantam Spectra
    #57275-X, Jan. 1997, Drew Struzan cover 6.00
Black Fleet Crisis, combined edition
    SFBC: $14.98, 785pp, Bantam #15119, Drew
    Struzan cover 10.00

X-Wing series, by Michael A. Stackpole
#1: *Rogue Squadron*
    1st PB: $5.99, 388pp, Bantam Spectra
    #56801-9, Feb. 1996, Paul Youll cover 6.00
#2: *Wedge's Gamble*
    1st PB: $5.99, 357pp, Bantam Spectra
    #56802-7, June 1996, Paul Youll cover 6.00
#3: *The Krytos Trap*
    1st PB: $5.99, 355pp, Bantam Spectra
    #56803-5, Oct. 1996, Paul Youll cover. 6.00
#4: *The Bacta War*
    1st PB: $5.99, 349pp, Bantam Spectra
    #56804-3, Feb. 1997, Paul Youll cover 6.00
#5: *Wraith Squadron* by Aaron Allston
    1st PB: $5.99, 403pp, Bantam Spectra
    #57894-4, Feb. 1998 . . . . 6.00
#6: *Iron Fist* by Aaron Allston
    1st PB: $5.99, 310pp, Bantam Spectra
    #57897-9, July 1998, P. Youll cover 6.00
#7: *Solo Command* by Aaron Allston
    1st PB: $5.99, Bantam Spectra, Feb.1999 . . . . 6.00
#8: *Isard's Revenge* by Michael A. Stackpole
    1st PB: $5.99, 336pp, Bantam Spectra
    #57903-7, April 1999, P. Youll cover 6.00
#9 *Starfighters of Adumar* by Aaron Allston
    1st PB: $5.99, Bantam Spectra #57418-3,
    August 1999 . . . . 6.00

Han Solo Trilogy by A.C. Crispin
#1: *Star Wars The Paradise Snare*
    1st PB: $5.99 Bantam Spectra #57415-9,
    June 1997, Drew Struzan cover 6.00
#2: *Star Wars The Hutt Gambit*
    1st PB: $5.99 Bantam Spectra #57416-7,
    Sept. 1997, Drew Struzan cover 6.00

 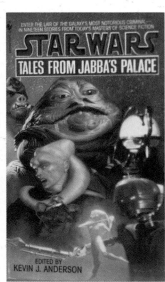

*Rebel Dawn, by A. C. Crispin and
Tales From Jabba's Palace, edited by Kevin J. Anderson,
1st Paperbacks (Bantam Spectra 1996–98)*

#3: *Rebel Dawn*
1st PB: $5.99 Bantam Spectra #57417-5,
Feb. 1998 . . . . 6.00

Bounty Hunter Wars by K. W. Jeter
#1: *The Mandalorian Armor*
1st PB: $5.99, Bantam Spectra #57885-5,
June 1998, Steve Youll cover 6.00
#2: *Slave Ship*
1st PB: $5.99, Bantam Spectra #57888-X, Oct.
1998, Steve Youll cover 6.00
#3: *Hard Merchandise*
1st PB: $5.99, Bantam Spectra #57891-X, July
1999, Steve Youll cover 6.00

Schweighofer, Peter ed.: *Star Wars: Tales from the
Empire*, $5.99 Bantam Spectra #57876-6,
Nov. 1997 . . . . 5.00

THE NEW JEDI ORDER (1999–2002)

Vector Prime was the first book in Ballantine's new fiction program (i.e. they got the rights to do Star Wars novels–not cheaply I'll bet) The story line picks up 25 years after the events in *Star Wars: A New Hope.*

Vector Prime by R. A. Salvatore
1st HC: $24.95, Ballantine Del Rey #42844-7,
October 1999 cover by Cliff Nielsen $25.00
1st PB $7.50 Ballantine Del Rey #42845-5,
July 2000, ... 7.50

The New Jedi Order: Dark Tide
#1: *Onslaught* by Michael A. Stackpole
1st PB: $6.99, Ballantine #, Feb. 2000 . . . . 7.00
#2: *Ruin* by Michael A. Stackpole
1st PB $6.99 Ballantine Del Rey #42856-0,
June 2000, ... 7.00

The New Jedi Order: Edge of Victory
#1: *Edge of Victory: Conquest* by Greg Keyes
1st PB: $6.99, 304pp, Ballantine Del Rey
#42864-1, April 2001, Terese Nielsen cover 7.00
#2: *Rebirth* by Greg Keyes
1st PB: $6.99, 304pp, Ballantine Del Rey
#44610-0, July 2001 . . . . 7.00

The New Jedi Order: Agents of Chaos
#1: *Hero's Trial* by James Luceno
1st PB: $6.99, 304pp, Ballantine Del Rey
#42860-9, August 2000 . . . . 7.00
#2: *Jedi Eclipse* by James Luceno
1st PB: $6.99, Ballantine Del Rey #42859-5,
October 2000 . . . . 7.00

Other New Jedi Order Novels
Star by Star by Troy Denning
1st HC: $26.00, 624pp, Ballantine Del Rey,
42848-X, October 2001, Cliff Nielsen cover 25.00

Dark Journey by Elaine Cunningham
1st PB $7.00 Ballantine Del Rey, #42869-2,
Jan. 2002, Steven D. Anderson cover 7.00

The New Jedi Order: Recovery by Troy Denning
eBook, $2.99, Random House 159061415-1,
Nov. 2001 . . . . 3.00

Balance Point by Kathy Tyers
1st HC $26.00 Ballantine Del Rey 42857-9,

Oct. 2000 . . . . 25.00
1st PB $7.00 Ballantine Del Rey 42858-7,
July 2001 . . . . 7.00

Episode I: Prequel
Star Wars: Cloak of Deception by James Luceno
1st HC $26.00 Ballantine Del Rey June 2001
0-345-44298-9 . . . . 25.00

Episode I:
Rogue Planet by Greg Bear
1st HC $26.00, 341pp, Ballantine Del Rey
#43538-9, May 2000 . . . . 25.00
1st PB $6.99 Ballantine Del Rey #43540-0,
May 2001 . . . . 7.00

Star Wars Darth Maul: Saboteur by James Luceno
eBook $2.00 Random House 3.00
Star Wars Darth Maul: Shadow Hunter by Michael Reaves
1st HC $26.00 Ballantine Del Rey #43539-7,
Jan. 2001 . . . . 25.00
1st PB $6.99 Ballantine Del Rey #43541-9,
Nov. 2002 . . . . 7.00

Attack of the Clones prequel
Star Wars: The Approaching Storm by Alan Dean Foster
1st HC: $26.00 Ballantine Del Rey #44300-4,
Jan. 2002 . . . . 25.00

Rogue Planet *by Greg Bear, 1st Hardcover (DelRey 2000) and*
Young Jedi Knights #5 *by Kevin J. Anderson and Rebecca Moesta,
1st Paperbacks (Boulevard 1997)*

YOUNG ADULT AND JUVENILE NOVELS

Juvenile and Young Adult books do not draw much collector interest, while kiddie books with pictures are fairly collectible. This has little or nothing to do with the quality of the fiction.

YOUNG ADULT

Young Jedi Knights series by Kevin J. Anderson and
Rebecca Moesta, featuring the adventures of Jason
and Jaina at the Luke Skywalker Jedi Academy.
1: *Shadow Academy*
1st PB: $5.99, Boulevard #025-1, 1995 . . . . $8.00
2: *The Lost Ones*
1st PB: $5.99, Boulevard #052-9, 1995 . . . . 7.00

3: *Heirs of the Force*
    1st PB: $5.99, Boulevard #066-9, 1995 . . . . 7.00
Boxed Set: #1–#3 . . . . 15.00
4: *Lightsabers*
    1st PB: $5.99, Boulevard #091-X, 1996 . . . . 7.00
5: *Darkest Knight*
    1st PB: $5.99, Boulevard #129-0, 1996 . . . . 7.00
6: *Jedi Under Seige*
    1st PB: $5.99, Boulevard #163-0, 1996 . . . . 7.00
Combined HC: #1–#6 . . . . 20.00
7: *Shards of Alderaan*
    1st PB: $5.99, Boulevard #207-6, 1997 . . . . 6.00
8: *Diversity Alliance*
    1st PB: $5.99, Boulevard #234-3, April 1997 . . . . . 6.00
9: *Delusions of Grandeur*
    1st PB: $5.99, Boulevard #272-6, June 1997 . . . . . 6.00
10: *Jedi Bounty*
    1st PB: $5.99, Boulevard #297-1, Oct. 1997 . . . . . . 6.00
11: *The Emperor's Plague*
    1st PB: $5.99, Boulevard #331-5, Jan. 1998 . . . . . . 6.00
12: *Return to Ord Mantell*
    1st PB: $5.99, Boulevard #362-8, Mar. 1998 . . . . . . 6.00
13: *Trouble on Cloud City*
    1st PB: $5.99 Boulevard # , July 1998 . . . . 6.00
14: *Crisis at Crystal Reef*
    1st PB: $5.99 Boulevard # , 1998 . . . . 6.00

JUVENILE

Star Wars series by Paul Davids and Hollace Davids
#1: *The Glove of Darth Vader*
    1st PB: $3.99, Bantam Skylark #15887-2, July
    1992 . . . . $3.00
#2: *The Lost City of The Jedi*
    1st PB: $3.99, Bantam Skylark #15888-0, July
    1992 . . . . 3.00
by Paul Davids
#3: *Zorba The Hutt's Revenge*
    1st PB: $3.99, Bantam Skylark #15889-9,
    Aug. 1992 . . . . 3.00
Boxed Set: #1–#3 . . . . 10.00

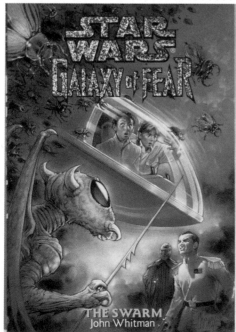

Galaxy of Fear: The Swarm *(Bantam Skylark 1998)*

Combined HC #1–#3 . . . . 10.00
#4: *Mission From Mount Yoda*
    1st PB: $3.99, Bantam Skylark #15890-2,
    Feb. 1993 . . . . 3.00
#5: *Queen Of The Empire*
    1st PB: $3.99, Bantam Skylark #15891-0,
    March 1993 . . . . 3.00
#6: *Prophets Of The Dark Side*
    1st PB: $3.99, Bantam Skylark #15892-9,
    May 1993 . . . . 3.00
Combined HC: #4–#6 . . . . 10.00

Galaxy of Fear series by John Whitman
#1: *Eaten Alive*
    1st TPB: $4.99, Bantam Skylark #48450-8,
    Feb. 1997, 3-D cover 5.00
#2: *City of the Dead*
    1st TPB: $4.99, Bantam Skylark #48451-6,
    Feb. 1997, 3-D cover 5.00
#3: *Planet Plague*
    1st TPB: $4.99, Bantam Skylark #48452-4,
    April 1997, 3-D cover 5.00
#4: *Nightmare Machine*
    1st TPB: $4.99, Bantam Skylark #48453-2,
    June 1997 . . . . 5.00
#5: *Ghost of the Jedi*
    1st TPB: $4.99, Bantam Skylark #48454-0,
    Aug. 1997 . . . . 5.00
#6: *Army of Terror*
    1st TPB: $4.99, Bantam Skylark #, Oct. 1997 . . . . . 5.00
#7: *The Brain Spiders*
    1st TPB: $4.99, Bantam Skylark #, Dec. 1997 . . . . 5.00
#8: *The Swarm*
    1st TPB: $4.99, Bantam Skylark #48638-1,
    Feb. 1998 . . . . 5.00
#9: *Spore*
    1st TPB: $4.99, Bantam Skylark #48639-X,
    Feb. 1998 . . . . 5.00
#10: *The Doomsday Ship*
    1st TPB: $4.50, Bantam Skylark #48640-3,
    Apr. 1998 . . . . 4.50
#11: *Clones*
    1st TPB: Bantam Skylark # , 1998 . . . . 4.00
#12: *The Hunger*
    1st TPB: Bantam Skylark # , Sept. 1998 . . . . 4.00

Jedi Apprentice
#1: *The Rising Force* by Dave Wolverton
    1st PB: $4.99, Scholastic # , May 1999 . . . . 5.00
#2: *The Dark Rival* by Jude Watson
    1st PB: $4.99, Scholastic # , May 1999 . . . . 5.00
#3: *The Hidden Past* by Jude Waston
    1st PB: $4.99, Scholastic # , July 1999 . . . . 5.00
#4: *The Mark of the Crown* by Jude Watson
    PB: $4.99, Scholastic, September 1999 . . . . 5.00
#5: *The Defenders of the Dead* by Jude Watson
    PB: $4.99, Scholastic, Nov. 1999 . . . . 5.00
#6: *The Uncertain Path*, by Jude Watson
    PB: $4.99, Scholastic, Jan. 2000 . . . . 5.00
#7: *The Captive Temple* by Jude Watson
    PB: $4.99, Scholastic, March 2000 . . . . 5.00
#8: *The Day of Reckoning* by Jude Watson
    PB: $4.99, Scholastic, May 2000 . . . . 5.00
#9: *The Fight for Truth* by Jude Watson illustrated
    by Cliff Nielsen PB: $4.99, Scholastic , July 2000 . . 5.00
#10: *The Shattered Peace* by Jude Watson illustrated
    by Cliff Nielsen
    PB: $4.99, Scholastic , August 2000 . . . . 5.00

Star Wars: A New Hope *Shimmer Book (Fun Works 1997)*

#11: *The Deadly Hunter* by Jude Watson,
   illustrated by Cliff Nielsen
   PB: $4.99, Scholastic, October 2000 . . . . 5.00
#12: *Evil Experiment* by Jude Watson,
   illustrated by Cliff Nielsen
   PB: $4.99, Scholastic, Dec. 2000 . . . . 5.00
#13: *The Dangerous Rescue* by Jude Watson
   PB: $4.99, Scholastic, March 2001 . . . . 5.00
#14: *The Ties That Bind* by Jude Watson
   PB: $4.99, Scholastic 043913933-3, July 2001 . . . . 5.00
#15: *The Death of Hope* by Judy Blondell
   PB: $4.99, Scholastic, Sept. 2001 . . . . 5.00
#16: *The Call to Vengeance* by Jude Watson
   PB: $4.99, Scholastic 043913935-X . . . .
#17: *The Only Witness* by Jude Watson
   PB: $4.99, Scholastic, Jan. 2002 . . . . 5.00
Spec. Ed. *Deceptions* by Jude Watson
   PB: $5.99, Scholastic, June 2001 . . . . 6.00

Junior Jedi Knights series by Nancy Richardson
#1: *Golden Globe*
   1st TPB: $4.50, Boulevard #035-9 . . . . 4.00
#2: *Lyric's World*
   1st TPB: $4.50, Boulevard #068-5 . . . . 4.00
#3: *Promises*
   1st TPB: $4.50, Boulevard #097-9 . . . . 4.00

by Rebecca Moesta
#4: *Anakin's Quest*
   1st TPB: $4.50, Boulevard #136-3, Eric Lee cover . 4.00
#5: *Vader's Fortress*
   1st TPB: $4.50, Boulevard #173-8 . . . . 4.00
#6: *Kenobi's Blade*
   1st TPB: $4.50, Boulevard #208-4 . . . . 4.00

Cruise Along Books
Han Solo's Rescue Mission
   TPB: $6.98, 7" x 9", Fun Works #823-7, March
      1998, with Galoob X-Ray vehicle 7.00
Luke Skywalker's Race Against Time
   TPB: $6.98, 7" x 9", Fun Works #824-5, March
      1998, with Galoob X-Ray vehicle 7.00

Other Juvenile Books
Golden, Christpoher: *Shadows of the Empire: A*
   Star Wars Junior Novelization
   TPB: $4.50, Dell Yearling 41303-6, Oct. 1996 . . . . . 4.00
Star Wars: A New Hope Shimmer Book, by Ken Steacy
   HC: $8.98, 24pp, 9" x 9", Fun Works #567-X,
      1997 . . . . 9.00
The Empire Strikes Back Shimmer Book
   HC: $8.98, 24pp, 9" x 9", Fun Works #860-1,
      March 1998 . . . . 9.00

NON-FICTION

Star Wars books come in every conceivable category of non-fiction. There are art books, sketch books, making-of-the-movie books, reference books, humor books, and even "fictional" non-fiction books. Many books include elements of several categories, making organization of the following lists problematic. You may have to search a little for the title you are interested in.

ART OF

The Art of Star Wars, edited by Carol Titelman, plus
   script by George Lucas, includes sketches,
   costume designs, blueprints, production paintings
   and photos.
   1st HC: $17.95, 175pp, Ballantine #28273-6,
      Nov. 1979 . . . . $25.00

The Art of Star Wars, Episode V The Empire Strikes Back
(Ballantine 1994)

1st TPB: $10.95, 175pp, Ballantine #27666-3,
Nov. 1979.................................. 15.00
SFBC: $11.98, Ballantine #3823-2, Summer
1980 .... 15.00
Later TPB: $12.95, Ballantine #29565-X, Nov.
1980 .... 15.00
Reissue TPB: *The Art of Star Wars, Revised
Edition*, Ballantine #30627-9, 1982.......... 15.00
Retitled: *The Art of Star Wars, Episode IV, A New Hope*
TPB: $18.00, 176pp, Del Rey #39202-7, Oct.
1994, 9" x 12", Ralph McQuarrie cover 20.00
TPB: Ballantine #40980-9, 1996, 2nd edition 19.00
Revised as: *Second Edition of The Art of Star Wars:
A New Hope*, by Carol Titelman and George Lucas:
1st TPB: $18.95, 192pp, Del Rey #39202-7,
Feb. 1997, Ralph McQuarrie cover, revised
with material from the special edition 19.00
The Art of the Empire Strikes Back, edited by Deborah
Call, with text by Valerie Hoffman and Vick Bullock
1st HC: Del Rey #29335-5, Oct. 1980.......... 25.00
SFBC: $17.50, Del Rey 5579-8, Feb. 1981...... 15.00
1st TPB: $15.95, 176pp, Ballantine #28833-5,
Oct. 1980, 9" x 12"...................... 15.00
Retitled: *The Art of Star Wars, Episode V, The Empire
Strikes Back*
TPB: $18.00, 160pp, Ballantine/Del Rey
#39203-5, Oct. 1994, repackaged 20.00
TPB: Ballantine #41088-2, 1996, 2nd edition 19.00
Revised as: *Second Edition of The Art of Star Wars
The Empire Strikes Back*, edited by Deborah Call
1st TPB: $18.95, 192pp, Del Rey #39203-5,
Feb. 1997, revised, with material from the
special edition 19.00
The Art of Return of the Jedi, edited by Anonymous,
including the film script by Lawrence Kasdan and
George Lucas
1st HC: $19.95, Del Rey #30957-X, Nov.
1983, 9" x 12" 25.00
SFBC: $19.98, Del Rey 5393-4, Fall 1984 ...... 15.00
Retitled: *The Art of Star Wars, Episode VI, Return
of the Jedi*
TPB: $19.00, 160pp, Del Rey #39204-3, Oct.
1994, repackaged 20.00
TPB: Ballantine #41089-0, 1996, 2nd ed........ 19.00

Revised as: *Second Edition of The Art of Star Wars:
Return of the Jedi*, edited by Anonymous
1st TPB: $18.95, 192pp, Del Rey #39204-3,
Feb. 1997, revised, with material from the
special edition 19.00
*The Art of Star Wars Episode 1, The Phantom
Menace* by Jonathan Bresman
1st HC: $40.00, 215pp, Del Rey #43108-1,
Sept. 1999............................. 40.00
The Art of Star Wars Galaxy edited by Gary Cerani
TPB: 9" x 12", 132pp, Topps #01-5, 1993, Ken
Steacy cover 20.00
HC: $150.00, Underwood Miller March 1994,
limited to 1,000 copies, boxed, signed,
with special card....................... 150.00
2nd TPB: $25.00, 1996 .... 20.00
QVC exclusive.......................... 25.00
The Art of Star Wars Galaxy, Volume Two by C.
Cerani and Gary Cerani
TPB: $19.95, 132pp, Topps #03-1, Nov. 1994,
Boris Valejo cover 20.00
Star Wars: The Art of the Brothers Hildebrandt, by
Bob Woods, TPB: Ballantine #42301-1, Oct. 1997 25.00
Star Wars: The Art of Dave Dorman, edited by
Stephen D. Smith and Lurene Haines, Dave
Dorman illustrations and text
HC: 128pp, Friedlander #38-3, Dec. 1996,
signed, limited to 2,500 copies 75.00
TPB: $24.95, Friedlander #37-5, Dec. 1996 ..... 25.00
Star Wars: The Art of Ralph McQuarrie Artbox
includes 48-page book, 15 postcards, and 6
postage stamps in a box
HC: $18.95, Chronicle #1320-7, 1996.......... 20.00
The Illustrated Star Wars Universe, edited by
Martha Banta, HC: Bantam #03925-4, 1995..... 20.00
The Illustrated Star Wars Universe, by Kevin J.
Anderson, illustrated by Ralph McQuarrie
1st HC, $35.00, 192pp, Bantam Spectra
#09302-9, Dec. 1995, 8½" x 11" 35.00
1st TPB, $17.95 Bantam 37484-2, Oct. 1997 .... 18.00
Industrial Light & Magic: The Art of Special Effects,
by Thomas G. Smith
1st HC:, Del Rey #32263-0, Nov. 1986 .... 25.00

The Art of Star Wars Galaxy Volume 2 *(Topps 1994);* The Art of Dave Dorman *(Friedlander 1996);*
Star Wars Episode I The Phantom Menace Illustrated Screenplay *(Ballantine Del Rey 1999)*

The Essential Guide to Vehicles and Vessels *and* The Essential Guide to Weapons and Technology, *by Bill Smith;*
The Essential Guide to Droids, *by Dan Wallace, Trade Paperbacks (Del Rey 1996–98)*

ILLUSTRATED SCREENPLAYS

Star Wars: A New Hope Illustrated Screenplay
  TPB: Ballantine #42069-7, 1998, 5" x 8". $12.00
Star Wars: The Empire Strikes Back Illustrated Screenplay
  TPB: Ballantine #42070-5, 1998, 5" x 8". 12.00
Star Wars: Return of the Jedi Illustrated Screenplay
  TPB: Ballantine #42079-9, 1998, 5" x 8". 12.00
Star Wars Episode 1, The Phantom Menace Illus-
  trated Screenplay by George Lucas
1st TPB: $14.95, 150pp, Del Rey #43110-3, May 1999. 15.00

GUIDE TO

A Guide to the Star Wars Universe, by Raymond L.
  Velasco
    1st PB, $2.95, Ballantine-Del Rey #31920-6,
    1984 . . . . $7.50
A Guide to the Star Wars Universe, Second Edition,
  Revised & Expanded, by Bill Slavicsek
    1st TPB: $10.00, 448pp, Del Rey #38625-6,
    1996, 5" x 8" Ralph McQuarrie cover 10.00
Star Wars: The Essential Guide To Characters, by
  Andy Mangels
    1st TPB: $18.00, 208pp, Del Rey #39535-2,
    Nov. 1995, Reference 18.00
Star Wars: The Essential Guide To Vehicles and
  Vessels, by Bill Smith
    1st TPB: $18.00, 224pp, Del Rey #39299-X,
    March 1996, Reference 18.00
Star Wars: The Essential Guide to Weapons and
  Technology, by Bill Smith
    1st TPB: $18.00, 200pp, Del Rey #41413-6,
    Oct. 1997. . . . . 18.00
Star Wars: The Essential Guide to Droids, by Dan
  Wallace, drawings by Bill Hughes
    1st TPB: Del Rey 1998. . . . . 18.00
Star Wars: The Essential Guide to Planets and
  Moons, by Daniel Wallace, drawings by
  Brandon McKinney and Scott Kolins
    1st TPB: Del Rey #42068-3, 1999 . . . . 19.00
Star Wars: The Essential Guide to Alien Species,
  by Ann Margaret Lewis, drawings by R. K. Post
    1st TPB: Del Rey #44220-2, 2000 . . . . 19.00

Star Wars: The Essential Chronology, by Kevin
  J. Anderson and Daniel Wallace, drawings by
  Bill Hughes
    1st TPB: Del Rey #43439-0, 2001 . . . . 19.00
Star Wars Technical Journal, by Shane Johnson
    1st HC: $35.00, 192pp, Del Rey #40182-4,
    Oct. 1995, combination of the three Starlog
    technical journals, includes schematics,
    fold-out blueprints, photos, etc. 35.00
    2nd Edition, Del Rey #9127909, 1997 . . . . 35.00
The Secrets of Star Wars: Shadows of the Empire,
  by Mark Cotta Vaz, interviews, guide to
  characters and places, black and white
  illustrations, with 8 pages in color, 7½" x 9¼"
    TPB: $15.00, 320pp, Del Rey #40236-7, May
    1996 . . . . 15.00
Star Wars Episode I Who's Who: A Pocket Guide to
  the Characters in The Phantom Menace, by
  Ryder Windham
    1st HC: Running Press 0-76240519-8, 1999 . . . . . . 6.00
Star Wars Episode I What's What: A Pocket Guide
  to The Phantom Menace, by Daniel Wallace
    1st HC: Running Press 0-76240520-1, 1999 . . . . . . 6.00
Star Wars The Visual Dictionary by David West Reynolds,
    1st HC: $21.00, DK Publishing, March 2001 . . . . . 10.00
Star Wars Episode I The Phantom Menace: The
  Visual Dictionary by David West Reynolds,
  Hans Jenssen & Richard Chasemore
    1st HC: $19.95 DK Publishing, June 1999 . . . . 20.00
Star Wars Episode 1, Incredible Cross-Sections by
  David West Reynolds, oversized
    1st HC: DK Publishing #3962-X, 1999 . . . . 20.00
Star Wars Encyclopedia by Stephen J. Sansweet
    1st HC: Del Rey #40227-8, June 1998 . . . . 50.00

MAKING OF

The Star Wars Album, edited by Anonymous
    1st TPB: Nov. 1977, $5.95, 76pp, Ballantine
    27591-8, 8½" x 11", Bros. Hildebrandt covers . $20.00
Once Upon a Galaxy: A Journal of the Making of
  The Empire Strikes Back, by Alan Arnold
    1st PB: $2.75, Del Rey #29075-5, Sept. 1980,
    photo cover 10.00

The Making of Episode I, The Phantom Menace *(Del Rey 1999);* Star Wars: The Mos Eisley Cantina Pop-up Book*, by Kevin J. Anderson and Rebecca Moesta (Little Brown 1995); and* Star Wars TIE Fighter Pocket Manual *(Running Press 1998)*

The Making of Return of the Jedi, by John Philip Peecher
    1st PB, Del Rey #31235-X, Sept. 1983 . . . . 10.00
Star Wars, The Making of Episode 1, The Phantom Menace by Laurent Bouzereau and Jody Duncan
    1st HC: $39.95, 192pp, Del Rey #43111-1, May 1999 . . . . 40.00
    1st TPB: $19.95, 161pp, Del Rey #43119-7, May 1999 . . . . 15.00

POP-UP BOOKS

Star Wars: The Rebel Alliance, Ships of the Fleet, by Bill Smith, with 6 pop-up paintings by Barbara Gibson, diagrams by Troy Vigil, fold-outs, 10pp, 11¼" x 8¾"
    HC: $15.95, Little Brown #53509-5, 1995 . . . . . . $16.00
Star Wars: The Galactic Empire, Ships of the Fleet, by Bill Smith, with 6 pop-up paintings by Barbara Gibson, diagrams by Troy Vigil, fold-outs, 10pp, 11¼" x 8¾"
    HC: $15.95, Little Brown #53510-9, 1995 . . . . 16.00
Star Wars: The Mos Eisley Cantina Pop-up Book by Kevin J. Anderson and Rebecca Moesta, illustrated by Ralph McQuarrie, 16pp, 8½" x 12¾"
    HC: $19.95, Little Brown #53511-7, 1995 . . . . 20.00
Star Wars: Jabba's Palace Pop-up Book by Kevin J. Anderson and Rebecca Moesta, illustrated by Ralph McQuarrie, 16pp, 8½" x 12¾"
    HC: $19.95, Little Brown #53513-3, 1995 . . . . 20.00
Star Wars: X-Wing Pocket Manual by David West, 3½" x 4" HC: $5.95 Reynolds Running Press #0320-9, 1998 . . . . 6.00
Star Wars: TIE Fighter Pocket Manual by David West, 3½" x 4" HC: $5.95 Reynolds Running Press #0319-5, 1998. . . . . 6.00

SCRIPTS/DRAMATIZATIONS

Star Wars: The National Public Radio Dramatization, by Brian Daley
    TPB: $11.00, 352pp, Del Rey #39109-8, Oct. 1994, Illustrated. $12.00

The Empire Strikes Back: The National Public Radio Dramatization, by Brian Daley
    TPB: $11.00, 352pp, Del Rey #39605-7, June 1995, illustrated. 11.00
Return of the Jedi: The National Public Radio Dramatization, by Brian Daley
    TPB: $11.00, 208pp, Del Rey #40782-2, Dec. 1996, Illustrated. 12.00
Star Wars: The Three-In-One Annotated Scripts, annotated by Laurent Bouzereau
    TPB: $, Del Rey #40981-7, May 1997 . . . . 13.00
Star Wars: A New Hope, facsimile script
    TPB: One Stop Publishing #306-4, 1994 . . . . 20.00
The Empire Strikes Back, facsimile script
    TPB: One Stop Publishing #307-2, 1994 . . . . 20.00
Return of the Jedi, facsimile script
    TPB: One Stop Publishing #304-8, 1994 . . . . 20.00
Star Wars Trilogy, facsimile scripts
    TPB: 1-56693374-9, 1995 . . . . 50.00

SKETCHBOOK

The Star Wars Sketchbook, by Joe Johnston
    1st TPB: $4.95, 65 original sketches, Ballantine #27380, 1977, 8½" x 11" $25.00
The Empire Strikes Back Sketchbook, by Joe Johnston and Rodis Jamero
    1st TPB: $5.95, 95pp, Ballantine #28836-X, July 1980, sketches 35.00
Return of the Jedi Sketchbook, by Joe Johnston
    1st TPB: Ballantine, 1983. . . . . 25.00

SMITHSONIAN

Star Wars: The Magic of Myth: Companion to the Exhibition at the National Air and Space Museum, Smithsonian Institution, by Mary Henderson
    1st HC: $49.95, Bantam Broadway #10206-0, Nov. 1997. . . . . $50.00
    1st TPB: $24.95, Bantam Broadway #37810-4, Nov. 1997 . . . . 25.00

MISCELLANEOUS

The Quotable Star Wars: I'd Just as Soon Kiss a Wookiee!, by Stephen J. Sansweet
TPB: $6.00, 128pp, Del Rey #40760-1, Oct. 1996 .... $6.00

The Ultimate Unauthorized Star Wars Trilogy Trivia Challenge by James Hatfield & George "Doc" Burt
TPB: Kensington #185-3, 1997 .... 15.00

Star Wars Diplomatic Corps Entrance Exam, by Kathryn Rusch
TBP: $12.00, 176pp, Del Rey #41412-8, June 1997 .... 12.00

The Jedi Master's Quiz Book, by Rusty Miller
TPB: Del Rey #30697-X, Nov. 1982 .... 5.00

Star Wars Classic Characters, 1998 edition
TPB: Cedco #55912520-9, 1997 .... 13.00

The Star Wars Diaries
TPB: Cimino 90167422-8, 1997 .... 25.00

The Jedi Academy Entrance Exam: Tantalizing Trivia from the *Star Wars Trilogy*, by Drew Bittner
TPB: Carol #0-80651907-X, Nov. 1997 .... 11.00

Star Wars: Tales from the Empire, ed. by Peter Schweighofer
PB: Bantam #57876-6, 1997 .... 6.00

Star Wars 1996 Datebook, with 36 images from the film, 7" x 5" (Cedco #47995, 1995) 10.00

Star Wars Trilogy Special Edition 1998 Datebook Calendar, 9" x 7" (Cedco #588-8, 1997) 14.00

Star Wars 1996 Book of Days, 80 pages with 15 full-page images from the film, 8" x 8" (Cedco 1995) 12.00

Star Wars Trilogy, 1998, Special Ed., by Abrams
Cedco #55912543-8, 1997 .... 13.00

Classic Star Wars: A New Hope: From the Screenplay by George Lucas, by Cynthia Alvarez
HC: Random #85854-7, 1995 .... 10.00

John Williams Star Wars Suite, edited by Tony Esposito
TPB: Warner 23936-5, 1997 .... 10.00

Star Wars: From Concept to Screen to Collectible by Stephen Sansweet, illustrated by Steven Essig with 150 color photos, George Lucas interview, 10" x 9"
HC: $29.95, 132pp, Chronicle #0101-2, 1992 .... 30.00

TPB: $18.95, 132pp, Chronicle #0096-2, 1992 ... 20.00

Star Wars: Vintage Toys: Postcard Book
TPB: Chronicle #1153-0, 1995, 6" x 5", 3 postcards 13.00

Star Wars: Behind the Scenes: Postcard Book
TPB: Chronicle #1179-4, 1995, 6" x 5", 3 postcards 13.00

Star Wars Cookbook, Wookiee Cookies and other Galactic Recipes by Robin Davis
1st HC: Chronicle Books #2184-6, 1998 .... 10.00

Star Wars Cookbook II: Darth Malt and More Galactic Recipes by Frankeny Frankie and Wesley Martin
1st HC: Chronicle Books #2803-4, 2000 .... 10.00

Star Wars The Magic of Myth
Star Wars Aliens & Creatures: Postcard Book by Stephen J. Sansweet
TPB: Chronicle Books #1386-X, 1996 .... 12.95

Star Wars Scrapbook, by Stephen Sansweet
HC: Chronicle #2062-2, 1998, 11" x 8" 84pg 35.00

Star Wars Chronicles
HC: Chronicle #1498-X, 1996 .... 125.00

Star Wars Series by John Whitman, illustrated by Brandon McKinney:
HC: *Star Wars* Chronicle Books #1480-7, 1996 .. 10.00
HC *The Empire Strikes Back* Chronicle #1482-3, 1997 .... 10.00
HC: Return of the Jedi : Chronicle #1494-7, 1997 . 10.00

COMIC

The Marvel Comics Illustrated Version of Star Wars, by Roy Thomas
1st Comic PB: $1.50, 124pp, Ballantine-Del Rey #27492-X, Nov. 1977, Howard Chaykin art, reprint of 6 comics in black and white $10.00

The Empire Strikes Back, by Archie Goodwin, and Al Williamson
1st Comic PB: $2.50, 224pp, MarvelComics #02114, May 1980 .... 5.00

GAME SECRETS

Star Wars Customizable Card Game: Official Player's Guide by John Fisher
TPB: IFTW Books #1-57280091-7, 1996 ...... $15.00

The Star Wars Cookbook II *(Chronicle 2000)* Star Wars The Magic of Myth *(Bantam 1997)*
The Empire Strikes Back, The Marvel Comics Version, *1st Paperback (Marvel Comics 1980)*

Jar Jar's Coloring Fun; Queen Amidala Royal Coloring Book; *and* Star Wars Posters to Color Mail-in *(Random House 1999–2000)*

Super Empire Strikes Back Official Game Secrets,
   by Rusell DeMaria, Tom Stratton and
   Jeronimo Barrera, for Super NES system
   TPB: Prima #1-55958452-1, 1993 . . . . 13.00
Super Return of the Jedi Official Game Secrets by
   Tim Rooney, for Super NES system
   TPB: $12.95 (1995) 13.00
Dark Forces Official Players Guide by Jeff Hoff for
   LucasArts computer game
   TPB: $18.95 (1995) 15.00

JUVENILE ACTIVITY, COLORING, POP-UP AND STORY BOOKS

ACTIVITY BOOKS

Artoo Detoo's *Activity Book* (Random House 1979). . . $5.00
Chewbacca's *Activity Book* (Random House 1979) 5.00
Darth Vader's *Activity Book* (Random House 1979) 5.00

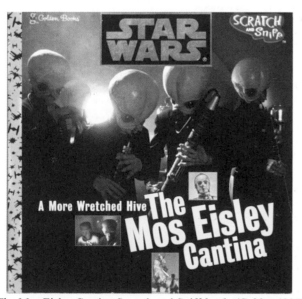

The Mos Eisley Cantina Scratch and Sniff *book (Golden 1997)*

Return of the Jedi Punch-out and Make It book
   (Random House) 10.00
The Rebel Alliance vs. The Imperial Forces,
   Puzzles and Mazes (Golden Book 1997) . . 7.00
Star Wars The Training of a Jedi Knight, Puzzles
   and Mazes (Golden Book #3638, 1997) 7.00
Star Wars Fun Kit (Golden #13592-6, 1997) 10.00
Return of the Jedi Monster Activity Book (Happy
   House 1983) 5.00
Return of the Jedi Picture Puzzle Book (Happy
   House 1983) 5.00
Return of the Jedi Word Puzzle Book (Happy
   House 1983) 5.00
Return of the Jedi Activity Book (Happy House 1983) . . 5.00
Return of the Jedi Maze Book (Happy House 1983) . . . 5.00
The Mos Eisley Cantina Scratch and Sniff Book
   (Golden Book #13552, 1997) 5.00

Episode I: Activity Books (Random House 1999)
Galactic Puzzles and Games, Darth Maul cover
   (#80018-2) 3.00
Lightsaber Marker Activity Book, Jedi & Sith cover
   32p (#80017-4, May 1999) 4.00
Queen Amidala Paper Doll Book, Queen Amidala
   cover (#80020-4) 4.00
Micro-Vehicle Punch-Outs, Naboo Figher cover
   (#80014-X) 4.00
Jar Jar Binks with Punch-Out(s) 10pp (#80011-5) 8.00
Anakin Skywalker with Punch-Out(s) 10pp (#80012-3) . . 8.00
Star Wars Episode I The Phantom Menace: Sticker Book
   TPB: $6.99, DK Publishing #, May 1999 . . . . 7.00
*Star Wars Episode I The Phantom Menace: Classic
   Sticker Book*
   TPB: $6.99, DK Publishing #, May 1999 . . . . 7.00
Podracer Punch-Outs. 4.00
Jedi Punch-Outs, Qui-Gon Jinn and Darth Maul
   battle cover. 4.00
Mask Punch-Out Book, Darth Maul cover. 4.00

COLORING BOOKS

Star Wars: The Empire Strikes Back Coloring Book,
   64 pages (Kenner 1980) cover picture:

Storybooks: Star Wars *and* Return of the Jedi *(Scholastic 1977 &1996); and* Episode I The Phantom Menace *(Random House 1999)*

Cast. $5.00
Darth Vader and Stormtroopers 5.00
Chewbacca and Leia 5.00
Chewbacca, Han, Leia and Lando 5.00
Chewbacca and C-3PO 5.00
Luke Skywalker 5.00
R2 D2 . . . . 5.00
Yoda 5.00
Star Wars: Return of the Jedi Coloring Books
(Kenner 1983) cover picture:
Lando fighting skiff guard. 4.00
Lando in Falcon cockpit 4.00
Luke Skywalker 4.00
Max Rebo 4.00
Ewoks Wicket on vine 3.00
Ewoks Wicket, Kneesa and Logray. 3.00
Ewoks Wicket and Kneesa on hang gliders 3.00
An Ewok Adventure Comics-to-Color book (Golden
Book, 1997) 3.00
Heroes & Villains, My Coloring Book (Golden Book
#8697, 1997) flip-book 3.00
Galactic Adventures Coloring Book (Golden Book,
1997) 3.00
Star Wars Mark and See Magic Book (Golden
Book, 1997) 3.00
Star Wars Posters to Color book (Golden Book,
1997) 3.00
A Star Wars Coloring Book (Golden #05653-8, 1997) . . 2.50

Episode I: Coloring Books (Random House 1999–2000)

Anakin's Adventures to Color, Anakin Skywalker
cover (#80022-0) 3.00
Battles to Color, Qui-Gon Jinn cover (#80016-6). 3.00
Droids and Creatures to Color, C-3PO cover 3.00
Heroes and Villains Coloring Book, Queen Amidala
cover (#80021-2) 3.00
Jar Jar's Coloring Fun, Jar Jar Binks cover
(#80023-9) 3.00
Jedi Missions to Color, Obi-Wan Kenobi cover
(#80024-7) 3.00
Queen Amidala's Royal Coloring Book (#80525-7) 3.00
Star Wars Posters to Color, mail in (Random House) . . . 5.00

POP-UP BOOKS

Star Wars Pop-up Book illustrated by Wayne
Barlowe, HC (Random House 1978). $15.00
The Empire Strikes Back Pop-up Book, (Random
House 1980) 15.00
Return of the Jedi Pop-up Book (Random House
1983) 12.00
Han Solo's Rescue by Kay Carroll (Random House
#86112-4, 1983) 10.00

MOVIE STORY BOOKS

The Star Wars Storybook, by Geraldine Richelson,
with color photos (Random House 1978) $12.50
TPB: Scholastic Book Service TV4466 . . . . 7.50
Star Wars: A Storybook, by J.J. Gardner
(Scholastic #06654-4, 1996) 6.00
Star Wars little chronicles (Chronicle #1480-7, Jan.
1997) 10.00
The Empire Strikes Back Storybook, by Shep
Steneman (Random House 84414-9, Aug. 1980) . 10.00
TPB: (Scholastic Book Service) 5.00
The Empire Strikes Back Storybook by J.J.
Gardner (Scholastic #06656-0, 1996). 5.00
The Empire Strikes Back little chronicles (Chronicle
#4182-3, Jan. 1997) 10.00
Return of the Jedi Storybook, by Joan D. Vinge
(Random House 1983) 12.50
TPB: (Scholastic Book Service) 4.00
Return of the Jedi Storybook by J.J. Gardner
(Scholastic #06659-5, 1996) 6.00
Return of the Jedi little chronicles (Chronicle
#4194-7, Jan. 1997) 10.00
*Star Wars Episode I The Phantom Menace, Movie
Storybook* adapted from the screenplay by
George Lucas
1st TPB: $7.99, #80009-3, 1999, 64 pgs,
Anakin Skywalker cover. 8.00

STORY BOOKS

The Wookiee Storybook, illustrated by Patricia
Wynne (Random House 1979) $7.50
The Mystery of the Rebellious Robot, illustrated by
Mark Corcoran (Random House 1979). 6.00

The Maverick Moon, illustrated by Walter Wright (Random House 1979). 6.00
The Droid Dilemma (Random House 1979). 6.00

Droid Story Books
The Pirates of Tarnoonga, by Ellen Weiss (Random House 1986). 5.00
The Lost Prince, by Ellen Weiss (Random House 1985). 5.00
Escape from the Monster Ship, by Bonnie Bogart (Random House 1986). 5.00
The White Witch, by Emily James (Random House 1986). 5.00
Shiny as a Droid (Random House 1985-6) 5.00

Ewoks Story Books
Wicket Goes Fishing, by Melinda Luke (Random House 1986) 5.00
Wicket and the Dandelion Warriors, by Larry Weinberg (Random House 1985). 5.00
The Ring, the Witch, and the Crystal, by Cathy E. Dubowski (Random House 1986) 5.00
The Shadow Stone, by Cathy E. Dubowski (Random House 1986) 5.00
The Ewoks and the Lost Children, by Amy Ehrlich (Random House 1985). 5.00
Three Cheers for Kneesaa!, by Jane E. Gerver (Random House 1984). 5.00
The Ewoks' Hang Gliding Adventure, by Judy Herbstman (Random House 1984). 5.00
The Adventures of Teebo, by Joe Johnston (RandomHouse 1984) 5.00
The Baby Ewoks' Picnic Surprise, by Melinda Luke (Random House 1984). 5.00
Wicket Finds a Way, by Melinda Luke (Random House 1984) 5.00
The Red Ghost, by Melinda Luke and Paul Dini (Random House 1986). 5.00
How the Ewoks Saved the Trees, by James Howe (Random House 1984). 5.00

Fuzzy as an Ewok (Random House 1985-6) 5.00
Learn-to-Read Activity Book (Random House 1985) . . . 5.00
ABC Fun (Random House 1985–86). 5.00
School Days (Random House 1985–86) 5.00

JUVENILE MOVIE ADAPTATIONS

Star Wars, A New Hope adapted by Larry Weinberg
  1st TPB: $3.99, Random House Bullseye
    #87203-5, 1995 . . . . $4.00
Star Wars, The Empire Strikes Back adapted
  by Larry Weinberg
  1st TPB: $3.99, Random House Bullseye
    #87204-3, 1995. . . . . 4.00
Star Wars, Return of the Jedi adapted by Elizabeth Levy
  1st TPB: $3.99, Random House Bullseye
    #87205-1, 1995. . . . . 4.00

OTHER CHILDREN'S BOOKS

Star Wars: Pilots and Spacecraft Glow-in-the-Dark (Golden Book #13480-6, 1997) $6.00
Star Wars: A New Hope, Golden Book and Tattoos (Golden Book #13067-3, 1997) 6.00
Star Wars: The Empire Strikes Back, Golden Book and Tattoos (Golden Book #13068-1, 1997) 6.00
Star Wars: Return of the Jedi, Golden Book and Tattoos (Golden Book #13069-X, 1997) 6.00
Star Wars: Return of the Jedi by Elizabeth Levy (Random House #87205-1, 1995) 4.00
Star Wars Compendium (Paradise Press) 15.00
The Empire Strikes Back by Larry Weinberg (Random House #87204-3, 1995) 4.00
Star Wars Princess Leia, Rebel Leader, illustrated by Ken Steacy (Golden Book #10105, 1997) 4.00
Return of the Jedi Giant Collector's Compendium (Paradise Press 1983) 10.00
Star Wars: Battling the Empire by Stephen R. Covey (Golden Books #75704-8, 1997) 17.00
The Empire Strikes Back Panorama Book, illus. Gerry Daly (Random House) 15.00
Star Wars Tell-A-Story Sticker Book by Steven Covey (Golden Book #7608, 1997). 3.00

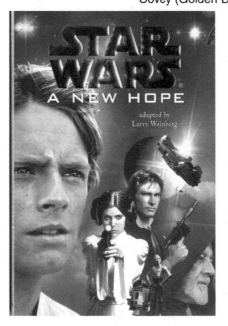

The Star Wars Question and Answer Book About Space; Star Wars A New Hope *and* The Empire Strikes Back
(Random House 1979; 1995)

  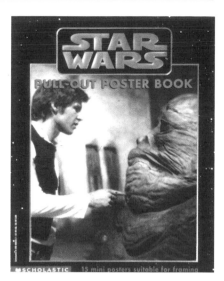

Jar Jar's Mistake, *and* I Am A Pilot *(Random House 1999); and* Star Wars Pull-Out Posterbook *(Scholastic 1996)*

The World of Star Wars (Paradise Press 1981) 10.00
The Jedi Master's Quizbook 8.00
How to Draw Star Wars Heroes, Creatures, Spaceships and other Fantastic Things, by J. Lee Ames 15.00
The Star Wars Question and Answer Book about Space by Ruth A. Sonneborn
    1st HC: Random House #84053-4, 1979 . . . . 15.00
    1st PB: Scholastic Books 1979. . . . . 5.00
The Star Wars Question and Answer Book about Computers, by Fred D'Ignazio, illustrated by Ken Barr
    1st HC: Random House #95686-9, 1983 . . . . 30.00
    1st TPB: Random House #85686-4, 1983 . . . . 7.00

Other *Episode I:* Children's Books
Star Wars Episode I The Phantom Menace: I am a Jedi
    1st PB: $4.00 24pp, Random House #80026-3, May 1999 . . . . 4.00
Star Wars Episode I The Phantom Menace: I am a Droid
    1st PB: $4.00 24pp, Random House #80025-5, May 1999 . . . . 4.00
Star Wars Episode I: I am a Pilot by Anakin Skywalker
    1st PB: $3.25 24pp, Random House #80524-9, 2000 4.00
Star Wars Episode I: I am a Queen by Amidala
    1st PB: $3.25 24pp, Random House #80523-0, 2000 4.00
Watch Out, Jar Jar! by Kerry Milliron, Illustrated by Bob Eggleton
    1st PB: $3.99 Random House # , May 1999 . . . . . . 4.00
Anakin's Race for Freedom by Alice Alfonsi, Illustrated by Jose Miralles
    1st PB: $3.99, Random House #, May 1999 . . . . . . 4.00

Step Into Reading Series (Random House)
Step I
Jar Jar's Mistake by Nancy E. Krulik, Illustrated by Richard Walz
    1st PB: $4.99, Random House #, May 1999 . . . . . . 5.00
    Library Binding 12.00
Step 2
Anakin to the Rescue, by Cecilia Venn, Illustrated by Chris Trevas
    1st PB: $4.99, Random House #, May 1999 . . . . . . 5.00
    Library Binding 12.00

Step 3
Dangers of the Core by Jim K. Thomas, Illustrated by Boris Vallejo
    1st PB: $4.99, Random House #, May 1999 . . . . . . 5.00
    Library Binding 12.00

Step 4
Anakin's Fate by Marc. A Cerasini, Illustrated by John Alvin
    1st PB: $4.99, Random House #, May 1999 . . . . . . 5.00
    Library Binding 12.00

POSTERBOOKS AND SCRAPBOOKS
Star Wars Pull-out Posterbook (Scholastic #06655-2, 1996) $5.00
The Empire Strikes Back Pull-out Posterbook (Scholastic #06657-9, 1996) 5.00
Return of the Jedi Pull-out Posterbook (Scholastic #06663-3, 1996) 5.00
Star Wars Treasy (Scholastic #39635-8) 5.00
The Empire Strikes Back (Scholastic #31791-1) 4.00
The Complete Star Wars Trilogy Scrapbook by Mark Cotta Vaz (Scholastic #06653-6, 1996) 8.00
The Star Wars Trilogy Scrapbook: The Rebel Alliance by Mark Cotta Vaz, $6.99, Scholastic (64pp #12051-4, Nov. 1997) 7.00
The Star Wars Trilogy Scrapbook: The Galactic Empire by Mark Cotta Vaz, $6.99, 64pp (Scholastic #12051-4, Nov. 1997) 7.00

Mouse Works
Rescue Han Solo (Mouse Works #82823-7, 1998) 7.00
Return of the Jedi, A Flip Book (Mouse Works #82579-3,1997) 3.00
The Empire Strikes Back, A Flip Book (Mouse Works #82578-5, 1997) 3.00

Blank Books (1996–99)
Star Wars Journal, Return of the Jedi space battle scene (#78840, 1996) 8.00
Star Wars Journal, Hildebrandt poster art (#78859, 1996). 8.00
Star Wars 20th Anniversary Journal (#79898, 1997) . . . 8.00
Star Wars 20th Anniversary Journal with bookmark (7988X, 1997) 8.00
My Jedi Journal (Ballantine) 6.00
Queen Amidala Diary (1999) 10.00

CERAMICS

BANKS

The Roman Ceramics Company was the first to manufacture ceramic banks. These, like all 1977 collectibles, appeared before the action figures, but many collectors passed them up at the time and they were available at retail for several years. Each bank came in a white box and was hand painted. Sigma made three ceramic banks for the later movies. See also plastic and metal banks under DOLLS AND FIGURES and talking banks under ELECTRONICS.

Ceramic Banks (1977–82):
C-3PO Ceramic Bank, 8" tall, waist up, metallic gold
   (Roman Ceramics 1977) boxed $75.00
Darth Vader Ceramic Bank, 7" tall, head (Roman
   Ceramics 1977) boxed 85.00

Yoda Ceramic Bank (Sigma 1982)

R2-D2 Ceramic Bank, 8" tall, full figure (Roman
   Ceramics 1977) boxed 75.00
Chewbacca Ceramic Bank, 10½" tall, kneeling with
   gun (Sigma 1982) 45.00
Jabba the Hutt Ceramic Bank, 6" tall, figural (Sigma
   1982) 45.00
Yoda Ceramic Bank, 8" tall, figural (Sigma 1982) 45.00

COOKIE JARS

Ceramic cookie jars were another early collectible from Roman Ceramics. R2-D2 is just the right shape to hold a lot of cookies. Cookie jars will be making a comeback in a big way in 1998, with over a dozen scheduled from Star Jars. They also make similar items for *Star Trek* and other licenses. Only 1,000 of each will be produced and they look very attractive in the pictures that they sent me. They can be reached at (561) 622-7693.

Cookie Jars (1977–82):
C-3PO, 10¾" gold metallic glaze (Roman Ceramics
   Corp. 1977) $175.00

R2-D2 Cookie Jar (Roman Ceramics 1977)

Jabba the Hutt Cookie Jar (Star Jars 1998)
Photo courtesy of Star Jars

Darth Vader (Roman Ceramics Corp. 1977) 175.00
R2-D2 13" tall, in white cardboard box with blue
    printing (Roman Ceramics Corp. 1977). 190.00
C-3PO/Darth Vader/R2-D2 Hexagon Cookie Jar
    (Sigma 1982) 130.00

Cookie Jars by Star Jars, limited editions of 1,000 jars
First Batch, First Quarter 1998
Obi-Wan Kenobi (Star Jars #026, 1998) 200.00
Jabba the Hutt (Star Jars #027, 1998) 200.00
Chewbacca (Star Jars #028, 1998) 200.00

Second Batch, Second Quarter 1998
C-3PO (Star Jars #029, Sept. 1998) 200.00
Princess Leia (Star Jars 1998) 200.00
Boba Fett (Star Jars 1998) 200.00

Bookends
Chewbacca/Darth Vader Figural Bookends (Sigma
    1983). 75.00

FIGURES

Sigma produced a dozen 7" ceramic bisque figures in
1983. The faces on the human figures are somewhat juvenile;
the non-humans are better sculpted.

Return of the Jedi, bisque figures
Bib Fortuna (Sigma 1983) $50.00
Boba Fett (Sigma 1983) 65.00
C-3PO and R2-D2 (Sigma 1983). 60.00
Darth Vader (Sigma 1983) 60.00
Galactic Emperor, seated (Sigma 1983) 65.00
Gamorrean Guard (Sigma 1983). 60.00
Han Solo (Sigma 1983). 50.00
Klaatu (Sigma 1983) 50.00
Lando Calrissian (Sigma 1983) 50.00
Luke Skywalker, Jedi Knight (Sigma 1983) 50.00
Princess Leia, Boushh disguise (Sigma 1983) 65.00
Wicket W. Warrick (Sigma 1983) 50.00

HOUSEHOLD AND OFFICE ITEMS

These ceramic items range from bookends to tape dispensers and from toothbrush holders to music boxes.

Ceramic figural items
Chewbacca and Darth Vader bookends (Sigma 1983) $90.00
C-3PO pencil tray (Sigma 1983) 60.00
C-3PO, seated figural tape dispenser (Sigma 1983) . . 60.00
C-3PO, in pieces, "Help" picture frame (Sigma 1983). . 45.00
Darth Vader picture frame (Sigma 1983) 60.00
Darth Vader mirror (Sigma 1983) 60.00
Ewok music box radio (Sigma 1983) 45.00
Gun Turret with C-3PO music box (Sigma 1983) 60.00
Landspeeder soap dish, with C-3PO and Obi-Wan
    (Sigma 1983). 60.00
Luke (Hoth Gear) and Tauntaun teapot set (Sigma
    1983). 150.00
R2-D2 picture frame (Sigma 1983) 75.00
R2-D2 and R5-D4 figural salt and pepper shakers
    (Sigma 1983). 125.00
R2-D2 figural string dispenser, with scissors (Sigma
    1983). 60.00
Rebel Snowspeeder toothbrush holder (Sigma 1983) . 60.00
Sy Snootles & Rebo Band music box (Sigma 1983) . 150.00
Wicket and Kneesa music box (Sigma 1983). 90.00
Yoda pencil cup (Sigma 1983). 50.00
Yoda figural salt and pepper shakers (Sigma 1983) . . . 50.00
Yoda and tree figural vase (Sigma 1983) 50.00
Yoda in backpack box (Sigma 1983) 30.00

MUGS—FIGURAL

Ceramic Drinking Mugs
1st Batch (Sigma 1983) in white corrugated box
C-3PO $40.00
Chewbacca. 40.00
Darth Vader 40.00
Han Solo 40.00
Princess Leia 40.00

Klaatu Mug (Sigma 1983)

Luke Skywalker, X-Wing Pilot 40.00
Yoda 40.00

2nd Batch (Sigma 1983) in *Return of the Jedi* color photo box
Biker Scout 40.00
Gamorrean Guard 40.00
Klaatu 40.00
Lando Calrissian 40.00
Stormtrooper 40.00
Wicket W. Warrick 40.00

Ceramic Mugs (Rawcliffe 1995)
Star Wars 15.00
The Empire Strikes Back 15.00
Return of the Jedi 15.00
Shadows of the Empire 15.00
Rebel Logo 15.00
Darth Vader 15.00
Obi-Wan Kenobi 15.00
Yoda 15.00
AT-AT 15.00
AT-ST 15.00
Shuttle *Tydirium* 15.00
TIE Fighter 15.00

14oz. Figural Mugs, (Applause 1995) boxed, with certificate of authenticity
Darth Vader (#46044) 15.00
Boba Fett (#46045) 15.00
Stormtrooper (#46046) 15.00
C-3PO (gold) (#46047) 15.00

Han Solo and Princess Leia mugs (Applause 1996)

Second Batch (Applause 1996)
Bib Fortuna (#46225) 15.00
Gamorrean Guard (#46226) 15.00
Han Solo (#46227) 15.00
Tusken Raider (#46228) 15.00
Emperor Palpatine (#46235) 15.00

Third Batch (Applause 1997)
Chewbacca (#42679) 15.00
Luke Skywalker (#42680) 15.00
Obi-Wan Kenobi (#42681) 15.00
Princess Leia Organa (#42682) 15.00
Metalized Darth Vader (#42692) 15.00

15" Decal Mugs (Applause 1998)
Darth Vader (#42983) 9.00

Boba Fett (#42984) 9.00
Galactic Empire (#42985) 9.00
Jedi Knights (#42986) 9.00

Episode I: Figural Mugs (Applause 1999)
Darth Maul Ceramic Mug, 15oz (#43067) 18.00
R2-D2 Ceramic Mug, 15oz (#43050) 15.00
Jar Jar Binks Ceramic Mug, 15oz (#43068) 16.00

PLATES

The first *Star Wars* collector plates were made in the late 1980s by the Hamilton Collection. There were eight plates, plus a larger 10th anniversary plate in 1987. The plates originally came in a styrofoam sandwich box.

8¼" Plates, First Series (1985–87)
Han Solo, pictured seated in Mos Eisley Cantina $50.00
Princess Leia, pictured holding blaster 50.00
Luke Skywalker and Darth Vader, pictured fighting
    with lightsabers 60.00
Five heroes, pictured in the *Millennium Falcon* cockpit. 50.00
Luke and Yoda, pictured seated on ground in
    Dagobah swamp 50.00
R2-D2 and Wicket the Ewok 50.00
AT-ATs, pictured shooting 50.00
X-Wings and TIE Fighters pictured in front of Death
    Star 50.00

10th Anniversary commemorative plate
1977–87 Commemorative, picturing Han, Luke,
    Leia and Darth's head in foreground with
    robots, Chewbacca & Obi-Wan in background . . . 60.00

Second Series, Star Wars Trilogy, 8¼" art by
    Morgan Weistling (Hamilton Collection 1993)
Star Wars, featuring Luke Skywalker in X-Wing Pilot
    outfit in foreground 40.00
The Empire Strikes Back, featuring Luke Skywalker
    with Yoda on his back at top, Han Solo and
    Leia kissing underneath 40.00
Return of the Jedi, featuring Luke Skywalker and
    Leia in Jabba's prisoner outfit swinging on rope . . 40.00

Third Series
These plates were originally offered at $40.00, but by 1997 Previews was still distributing them, now for $35.00. The advertisements say they are limited to 28 firing days, but that is not quite the same thing as limiting to a specific quantity. In any event, just about everyone who wants one of them has bought it already, so price appreciation will be slow.

Third Series: Space Vehicles 8¼", art by Sonia Hillios
    (Hamilton Collection 1995–96) 23K gold border
Millennium Falcon (EW1MF, 1995) $35.00
Imperial Shuttle *Tydirium* and landing pad 35.00
TIE Fighters in front of Cloud City 35.00
Red Five X-Wing Fighter pursued by TIE Fighter in
    Death Star trench 35.00
Imperial Star Destroyer orbiting planet (EW5MF, 1996) 35.00
Rebel Snowspeeder circling AT-AT feet (EW6MF,
    1996) 35.00
B-Wing (EW7MF, 1996) 35.00
Slave-1 (1996) 35.00

Fourth Series: Space Vehicles, 9", art by Sonia
    Hillios (Hamilton Collection 1997–98) 24K

Star Wars *(featuring Luke X-Wing Pilot) Plate, Second Series and Snowspeeder Plate, Third Series (Hamilton Collection 1993–95)*

gold border
Medical Frigate (#13609) 35.00
Jabba's Sall Barge (#13602) 35.00
Y-Wing Fighter (#13604) 35.00

Star Wars Heroes and Villains, 8¼" art by Keith
    Birdsong (1997–98) bordered in 24k gold
Luke Skywalker (#, 1997) 35.00
Han Solo (#13661) 35.00
Darth Vader (#13662) 35.00
Princess Leia (#13663) 35.00
Obi Wan Kenobi (#13664) 35.00
Emperor Palpatine (#13665) 35.00
Boba Fett (#13667) 35.00
Yoda (#13666) 35.00

STEINS

Lidded Steins 6" (Metallic Impressions 1995)
    with solid pewter lid
Star Wars: A New Hope $34.00
Star Wars: The Empire Strikes Back 34.00
Star Wars: Return of the Jedi 34.00

Deep Relief Stoneware (Dram Tree 1995) boxed
Star Wars, heroes picture 25.00
Star Wars: The Empire Strikes Back 25.00
Star Wars: Return of the Jedi 25.00

Lidded Steins 9½" (Dram Tree 1997–98)
Unique Darth Vader Stein, solid pewter lid with
    figure, limited to 1977 pieces, with Jason
    Palmer artwork 85.00
Unique Yoda Stein, solid pewter and lid, limited to
    3,000 pieces, with Tsuneo Sanda artwork 80.00
Unique Boba Fett Stein, solid pewter and lid, limited
    to 3,000 pieces, with Dave Dorman artwork 85.00

TANKARDS

Ceramic "Toby" Tankard, sculpted by Jim Rumph
    (California Originals 1977) in white cardboard
    shipping box
Chewbacca, 6¾" tall, 36oz. brown $60.00
Darth Vader 7¼" tall, 52oz. glossy black 60.00
Obi-Wan-Kenobi, 6¾" tall, 36oz, brown 60.00

Star Wars *Stoneware Stein (Dram Tree 1995)*

CLOTHING

You can outfit yourself from head to toe with *Star Wars* clothes, and they are listed here in that order. While many collectors own items of *Star Wars* apparel, few would consider themselves collectors of it. Rather, they own some items that they wear when the occasion arises or the mood hits them. While some accessories, such as belt buckles or watches, have developed a collector following, the general rule can be summed up as "Don't expect to make a killing on your *Star Wars* T-shirts."

CLOTHES

Most of the items listed here are designed for adults, and are priced accordingly. Most of the prices are the original retail price. All this really tells you is that you shouldn't pay $30.00 for a T-shirt if you can get a hundred different styles of T-shirts of the same type for under $20.00 retail at the local shopping mall.

Star Wars Episode I *Logo cap (Fresh Caps 1999)*

Caps and Hats
The Empire Strikes Back logo cap, red/white
    embroidery and black emblem (Thinking
    Cap Co. 1980–81) $15.00
Imperial Guard hat, black with silver medallion on
    front (Thinking Cap Co. 1980–81). 25.00
Rebel Forces Logo cap, tan billed cap with flap in
    back, red/blue/yellow round patch (Thinking
    Cap Co. 1980–81) 20.00
Yoda Ear Cap, red, green cloth ears and artificial
    hair, yellow/black Yoda patch on front
    (Thinking Cap Co. 1980–81). 20.00
Admiral Ackbar cap (Sales Corp. of America 1983) . . . 15.00

Darth Vader and Emperor's Royal Guards cap
    (Sales Corp. of America 1983) 15.00
Gamorrean Guard (Sales Corp. of America 1983) 15.00
Jabba the Hutt (Sales Corp. of America 1983). 15.00
Luke and Darth (Sales Corp. of America 1983) 15.00
Return of the Jedi logo (Sales Corp. of America 1983) 15.00
Jedi Ski cap, white with red and black trim (Sales
    Corp. of America 1983) 20.00
Ewok knit child's hat (Sales Corp. of America 1983) . . 15.00
"Star Tours" baseball caps (Star Tours) 8.00
Star Wars fan club hat (special promo. hat) 15.00
Star Wars embroidered border logo hats (Ralph
    Marlin 1996) 16.00
Most other caps. 12.00

Episode I **Caps:** (Fresh Caps, Hopkins, MN)
Various styles 8.00

Outerwear
Poncho, children's plastic with Jedi logo (Adam
    Joseph 1983). 30.00
Raincoat, plastic children's with Jedi logo (Adam
    Joseph 1983). 30.00
C-3PO and R2-D2 blue rain jacket or poncho 30.00
Darth Vader and Guards poncho. 30.00
Jedi vs. Sith rain poncho (**Pyramid** #94523) rack bag . 6.00
Darth Maul rain poncho (**Pyramid** #94523) rack bag . . 6.00

Jackets
Luke Skywalker Bespin Jacket, tan, resembling one
    worn by Luke in *The Empire Strikes Back*
    (Fan Club promotion) 90.00
Star Tours Jacket, pocket logo on black/blue nylon
    jacket (Star Tours) 50.00
Star Tours Jacket, pocket front logo & full back logo,
    silver satin jacket with blue piping (Star Tours) . . . 90.00
Star Wars X-Wing Rogue Squadron Bomber Jacket,
    black leather with three patches (1997) 300.00
Luke Skywalker Bespin Jacket (1997) 80.00

Sweatshirts
Sweatshirt, Star Tours logo in glitter on black shirt,
    (Star Tours) 35.00
Darth Vader Sweatshirt, black (AME 1995) 28.00
Star Wars Sweatshirt, black with Tom Cantrell
    poster art (AME 1995) 28.00
Boba Fett Sweatshirt, white (AME 1995) 28.00
Yoda Sweatshirt, white (AME 1995) 28.00
Star Wars Galaxy Jawa Wrench Sweatshirt. 28.00

Vest
Han Solo Vest (black vest resembling one worn by
    Han Solo in movies, Fan Club promotion). 100.00
Han Solo Vest (1997) 60.00

T-Shirts

Almost all T-shirts are bought to be worn, not collected. The earliest T-shirts were produced using Iron-on transfers made by Factors, Inc. Enough were still around in 1994 for T-shirts to be available with the original 1977 transfers.

In 1994, American Marketing Enterprises produced a line of T-shirts using the images from the Topps Galaxy trading cards which had appeared in 1993. 1997 T-shirts used the images from the *Star Wars Special Edition* video tape boxes and images of the Kenner action figures. I have also seen images of cards from Decipher's various collectible card games. Maybe someone is interested in using the cover of this book for a T-shirt; who knows? (Contact publisher for rights.)

These days there is a brisk business in this icon of the American popular culture, with several new *Star Wars* T-shirt designs available just about every month. The following list includes primarily ones offered to comic shops through Diamond Previews, and so the items and prices are for teenage and adult sizes. No attempt has been made to list children's and department store items. As with most *Star Wars* items, very few were available in the dark times, from 1985 to 1994, but now the flood has begun and there will be no let-up as the new movies appear.

Light grey T-Shirt with original 1977 Iron-On transfer
Star Wars Han and Chewie (1994) $20.00
Luke and C-3PO (1994) 20.00
C-3PO and R2-D2 (1994) 20.00
Darth Vader (1994) 20.00
Han Solo (1994) 20.00
Hildebrandt Movie Poster (1994) 20.00
Chewbacca (1994) 20.00
Stormtroopers in Battle (1994) 20.00
Space Battle with Darth Vader (1994) 20.00

Star Wars Galaxy card image on T-Shirt, (AME 1994)
At least 16 styles available 20.00

T-Shirts (Changes 1993–1998)
Numerous styles available . . . . 16.00 to 20.00
Star Wars: A New Hope Special Edition Movie
　　Poster (#29331-128, 1997) 16.00
Star Wars: Return of the Jedi Special Edition Movie
　　Poster (#29331-129, 1997) 16.00
Star Wars: The Empire Strikes Back Special Edition
　　Movie Poster (#29331-130, 1997) 16.00

Tie-Dye T-Shirts (Changes 1997)
Various styles available . . . . 25.00 to 30.00

Silkscreened T-Shirts (Liquid Blue 1997)
Various styles available . . . . 25.00 to 30.00

Polo Shirts
Star Tours Polo Shirt, color pocket logo (Star Tours) . . 25.00

Underwear
Nine styles of Underoos (Union Underwear 1983) 20.00
Star Wars: Darth Vader Repeat Silk Boxers (Ralph
　　Marlin #53464, 1998) 17.00
Star Wars ships, cotton boxers 15.00
Star Wars Episode I, several styles, cotton (Briefly
　　Stated 1999) 12.00

Episode I Boys Briefs (Fruit of the Loom 1999)
Various Sizes including 2T/3T, 3, 4T, 6, bagged
　　Anakin Skywalker, any size, each 2.00
　　C-3PO, any size, each 2.00

Sleepwear
Pajamas, *Star Wars*, C-3PO and X-Wing, gold 20.00
Pajamas, *Star Wars*, Darth Vader, C-3PO and
　　R2D2, blue 20.00
Pajamas, "May the Force Be With You, Darth and
　　R2-D2, blue" 20.00
Rebel Alliance Pajamas, 2 piece, kids sizes (1997) . . . 16.50
Galactic Empire Pajamas, 2 piece, kids sizes (1997) . . 16.50
Darth Vader Short Sleeve pajamas with cape, 3-
　　piece, kids sizes (1997) 13.50

Millennium Falcon *and Death Star T-Shirt (Oneita 1997); Yoda T-Shirt (Liquid Blue 1997)*

Sebulba adult underwear (Briefly Stated 1999)

Leg Warmers
Leg Warmers, 22" long, black with red/white stitching, Jedi knit into them (Sales Corp. of America 1983) 20.00

Socks
C-3PO Slipper Socks (Stride Rite 1983) 15.00
Darth Vader Slipper Socks (Stride Rite 1983) 15.00
R2-D2 and Wicket Socks (Charleston Hosiery 1983) . . 10.00
R2-D2 and Darth Vader Socks (Charleston Hosiery 1983). 10.00

OTHER CLOTHING ITEMS

The Ralph Marlin *Star Wars* collection started with one tie in 1992 and has now grown to a whole wardrobe of silk and polyester ties, caps, silk boxer shorts and embroidered T-shirts. Despite the quality, most of these items are still clothing, and thus not very collectible. After all, no one will buy your used boxer shorts, even if they are silk. Ties, belts, belt buckles and the other items listed here at least have some collector potential.

Ties—Silk
Star Wars collectors silk tie in tin litho box (Ralph Marlin #600020, 1995) $40.00
Darth Vader collectors silk tie (Ralph Marlin #306210, 1996) 25.00
Darth Vader Pattern, silk tie (Ralph Marlin 1997) 25.00
Star Wars Fighters collectors silk tie (Ralph Marlin #306220, 1996) 25.00
Star Wars: Cantina Silk tie (Ralph Marlin) 25.00
Star Wars: Vehicles II Black Silk tie (Ralph Marlin) 25.00

Ties — Polyester
Many styles available (Ralph Marlin 1997) 15.00
Star Wars Video tie (Poly Ties #136230, 1996) 16.00
The Empire Strikes Back Video tie (Poly Ties #136240, 1996) 16.00
Return of the Jedi Video tie (Poly Ties #136250, 1996). 16.00

Suspenders
Darth Vader Suspenders, circular plastic badge with raised Empire logo and color pic. of Darth Vader (Lee Co. 1980) 20.00
Yoda Suspenders, circular plastic badge with raised Empire logo and color pic. of Yoda (Lee Co. 1980) 20.00

Belts
May the Force Be With You Elastic Belt (Lee Co. 1983) 25.00
Star Wars Elastic Belt, tan or blue with magnetic enamel *Star Wars* logo buckle (Lee Co. 1983) . . . 25.00
Star Wars/The Empire Strikes Back Elastic Belt, alternating logos on belt, tan or blue (Lee Co. 1983). 25.00
Star Wars/Return of the Jedi Elastic Belt, alternating logos on belt, tan or blue with round character-buckle (Lee Co. 1983) 25.00
Leather Belt, Darth Vader oval buckle (Lee Co. 1983) . 30.00
Leather Belt, Jabba the Hutt rectangular buckle (Lee Co. 1983). 30.00
Leather Belt, Yoda round buckle (Lee Co. 1983) 30.00
Leather Belt, brown child-size with red enamel Empire logo buckle (Lee Co. 1983). 30.00
Star Wars belt, illustrated 12.00
Star Wars stretch belt 8.00
Return of the Jedi belt, illustrated 5.00

Belt Buckles
C-3PO and R2-D2 Belt Buckle (Basic Tool & Supply 1977). 20.00
Darth Vader Belt Buckle (Basic Tool & Supply 1977) . . 20.00
Star Wars logo Belt Buckle (Basic Tool & Supply 1977). 20.00
X-Wing with *Star Wars* logo Belt Buckle (Basic Tool & Supply 1977) 20.00
C-3PO and R2-D2 Belt Buckle (3" rectangular blue enamel background, Lee Co. 1979) 15.00
Star Wars belt buckles (Leather Shop 1977)
    Star Wars logo. 20.00
    R2-D2 . . . . 20.00
    R2-D2 & C-3PO. 20.00
    Darth Vader 20.00

Shoes and Footwear
Darth Vader Sandals, Vader head and *Star Wars* logo (1977) 20.00
Yoda Sandals, "May the Force Be With You" on sides . 20.00
Sneakers, cutouts of characters on sides, assort. colors (Stride Rite) 25.00
Chewbacca booties 25.00
Darth Vader booties 25.00

***Episode I* Slippers** (Kid Nation 1999) Ages 3 to 4
Naboo Fighter (Kid Nation #19475). 8.00

Leather Belt, Yoda round buckle (Lee Co. 1983)

Darth Maul Slippers (Kid Nation 1999)

R2-D2 (Kid Nation #19971). 8.00
Darth Maul (#599775) 8.00

Shoelaces
Star Wars logo/Darth Vader Shoelaces, blister
    packed on card with spaceships and Jedi logo
    (Stride Rite 1983) 5.00
Star Wars logo/R2-D2 and C-3PO Shoelaces blister
    packed on card with spaceships and Jedi logo
    (Stride Rite 1983) 5.00
Return of the Jedi logo Shoelaces, blister packed on
    card with spaceships and Jedi logo (Stride
    Rite 1983) several lengths and styles, each 5.00
Ewoks Shoelaces, blister packed on card with
    spaceships and Jedi logo (Stride Rite 1983). 5.00

Umbrellas
Darth Vader Umbrella (Adam Joseph 1983) 25.00
R2-D2 Umbrella (Adam Joseph 1983). 25.00

ACCESSORIES

PINS—JEWELRY—
WATCHES—WALLETS

Clothes make the man, but accessories make the clothes! Also, it makes a lot more sense to collect accessories than clothes. You can wear them occasionally without damage or reduction in value.

PINS

The market for attractive pins, ones that you might actually wear somewhere other than to a *Star Wars* fan club meeting, has been owned by Hollywood Pins. They also make a very attractive line of *Star Trek* pins. These pins are sold through comic shops and specialty dealers and are available over the Internet. The company has not continued their license for the original movies and, as of this writing, may or may not make pins for the new trilogy. Existing stocks will be available for a while, but when they are gone, prices may start to rise.

Hollywood Pins (1994–97)
Rebel Alliance New Republic Pin (large) (#SW001). . . $7.00
Rebel Alliance New Republic Pin (small) (#SW005) . . . 5.00
Rebel Alliance Logo cut-out pin (large) (#SW030). 9.00
Rebel Alliance Logo cut-out pin (small) (#SW035). 5.00
Rebel Alliance mini-logo (#SW036). 3.50
Star Wars 20th Anniversary (#SW041) 6.00
Star Wars Special Edition (#SW042S). 6.00
Star Wars: A New Hope Theme pin (#SW051). 13.00
The Empire Strikes Back Theme pin (#SW052). 13.00
Return of the Jedi Theme pin (#SW053) 13.00
May The Force Be With You pin (#SW052) 6.00
Star Wars Far Star pin (#SW070) 6.00
Imperial Emblem Pin (#SW160) 7.00
Darth Vader black pin (#SW205) 11.00
Darth Vader 3-D Face cut-out pin (#SW206) 6.00
Luke on Tauntaun cut-out pin (#SW255) 13.00
Yoda cut-out pin (#SW263) 9.00
Chewbacca cut-out pin (#SW275). 11.00
Princess Leia (Jabba's Prisoner) cut-out pin (#SW280) . 9.00
Ben (Obi-Wan) Kenobi cut-out pin (#SW286) 9.00
Lando Calrissian cut-out pin (#SW290) 9.00
Emperor Palpatine cut-out pin (#SW293) 9.00
Rebo Band cut-out pin (#SW320) 11.00
Jabba the Hutt cut-out pin (#SW325) 8.00
Jabba the Hutt tattoo pin (#SW326) 6.00
Boba Fett cut-out pin (#SW330) 11.00
Boba Fett Insignia pin (#SW331). 7.00
Boba Fett Skull pin (#SW332). 7.00
Emperor's Royal Guard cut-out pin (#SW333) 7.00
Stormtrooper cut-out pin (#SW335). 9.00
Gamorrean Guard cut-out pin (#SW340). 6.00
C-3PO cut-out pin (#SW455) 7.00
R2-D2 cut-out pin (#SW456). 7.00
Admiral Ackbar (#SW460). 7.00
Ewok cut-out pin (#SW480) 8.00
AT-AT cut-out pin (#SW520) 9.00

Assortment of Star Wars *pins (Hollywood Pins 1995–97)*

X-Wing Fighter cut-out pin (#SW540) 7.00
X-Wing Fighter antique silver cut-out pin (#SW541). . . . 7.00
Millennium Falcon cut-out pin (#SW552) 9.00
TIE Fighter cut-out pin (#SW561) 9.00
Stormtrooper icon pin (#SW604). 6.00
Boba Fett icon pin (#SW605) 6.00
Millennium Falcon round pin (#SW652) 6.00
Crossed Lightsabers logo cut-out pin (#SW752) 9.00
R2-D2 cut-out pin (#SW840). 7.00
Black Sun logo (#SW901). 6.00

Star Wars Episode I Cloisonne Pins (Applause 1999)
Anakin Skywalker (#43120). 5.00
Battle Droid (#43121) 5.00
Obi-Wan Kenobi (#43131). 5.00
Qui-Gon Jinn (#43133) 5.00
R2-D2 (#43134) 5.00
C-3PO (#43122). 5.00
Jar Jar (Binks) (#43129) 5.00
Naboo Starfighter (#43130). 5.00
Queen Amidala (#43132) 5.00
Darth Maul (#43124). 5.00
Star Wars Episode 1 logo (#43135). 5.00
(Trade Federation) Droid Starfighter (#43136) 5.00
Dark Side Collectible Pin Set with 6" x 6" frame and
    exclusive Darth Sidious Pin (#43123) 5.00
Jar Jar Binks Cloisonne Pin & Keychain (#61583) 7.50

JEWELRY

Star Wars head pendants (Weingeroff Ent. 1977) boxed
    R2-D2 . . . . $25.00
    C-3PO 25.00
    Chewbacca 25.00
    Stormtrooper 25.00
    Darth Vader 25.00
Star Wars earrings
    R2-D2 . . . . 10.00
    C-3PO 10.00
    Darth Vader 10.00
Star Wars stickpins

Wicket the Ewok Jewelry (Adam Joseph 1983)

R2-D2 . . . . 8.00
C-3PO 8.00
Darth Vader 8.00
Charm bracelet. 15.00
The Empire Strikes Back (W. Berrie 1980)
    X-Wing medal 8.00
    Chewbacca medal 8.00
    Darth Vader 8.00
Return of the Jedi pendants (Adam Joseph 1983)
    Darth Vader 8.00
    Yoda 8.00
    R2-D2 . . . . 8.00
    Salacious Crumb 8.00
    Imperial Guard. 8.00
    Wicket stickpin 6.00
    Princess Kneesa stickpin 6.00
R2-D2 Pendant pin and chain, sterling silver, 1fl"
    tall, with chain 100.00
Wicket the Ewok jewelry (Adam Joseph 1983) 7.50

WALLETS

Return of the Jedi Wallets and Coin Holders
Vinyl Wicket the Ewok Wallet, cartoon Ewok artwork
    (Adam Joseph 1983) $15.00
Darth Vader and Imperial Guards Wallet, black
    (Adam Joseph 1983) 15.00
R2-D2 and C-3PO Wallet, blue (Adam Joseph 1983) . 15.00
Yoda Wallet, red (Adam Joseph 1983). 15.00
Star Tours Wallet, black nylon with velcro closure
    ("Star Tours" printed in corner) 8.00
Darth Vader and Imperial Guards Pocket Pal, black
    (Adam Joseph 1983) 10.00
R2-D2 and C-3PO Pocket Pal, blue (Adam Joseph
    1983). 10.00
Yoda Pocket Pal, red (Adam Joseph 1983) 10.00
Darth Vader and Imperial Guards Coin Holder, black
    (Adam Joseph 1983) 10.00

Darth Maul Wallet (Pyramid Handbags 1999)

R2-D2 and C-3PO Coin Holder, blue (Adam Joseph
   1983). 10.00
Yoda "May The Force Be With You" Coin Holder, red
   (Adam Joseph 1983) 10.00
Episode I Wallets (Pyramid Handbags 1999) each 5.00

WATCHES

As with most collectibles, the best way to collect a
watch is in its original packaging. Bradley Time made most of
the *Star Wars* watches in the 1970s and 1980s. There are quite
a number of styles. Digital watches generally sell for a little
less than analog watches and 1980s watches based on the second and third movies sell for a little less than those based on
the first movie from the 1970s.

Recently, plastic figural head watches have been made
by Hope Industries and sold in toy stores. They have not
developed a following among regular watch collectors, but
they are reasonably attractive as *Star Wars* toy items.

Official *Star Wars* Watches (Bradley Time 1977-83)
Analog Watches
C-3PO and R2-D2 drawing, adult size analog
   watch, gold metal case, dark blue vinyl black
   strap, in plastic box $100.00
C-3PO and R2-D2 drawing, child size analog watch,
   silver metal case, light blue vinyl strap in blue
   plastic box with clear plastic lid. 90.00
R2-D2 & C-3PO, black face, black vinyl band 100.00
R2-D2 & C-3PO, black face, silver bezel ring. 120.00
Darth Vader, white face, red logo, black vinyl band . . 100.00
Darth Vader, gray face, white logo, black vinyl band. . 100.00
Darth Vader, stars & planet on face. 120.00
Digital Watches
C-3PO & R2-D2 round digital, red logo, black vinyl
   strap 90.00
C-3PO & R2-D2 oval digital, red logo, black vinyl
   strap 100.00
C-3PO & R2-D2 rectangular digital, X-Wing and TIE
   fighters, musical. 125.00
C-3PO & R2-D2 oval digital, X-Wing fighters. 75.00
Star Wars logo/Darth Vader round digital, blue face,
   black vinyl band 100.00

The Empire Strikes Back and Return of the Jedi
Analog Watches
Yoda, gray face, black vinyl band. 80.00
Yoda, white face, blue logo, black band 90.00
Jabba the Hutt, vinyl band. 75.00
Ewoks, vinyl band. 65.00
Wicket the Ewok, stars & planet on face 65.00
Digital Watches
Yoda round digital. 75.00
Jabba the Hutt, digital. 65.00
Droids, digital 50.00
Ewoks, digital 50.00

Plastic Watches (Hope Industries 1990s)
Imperial Forces Collector Timepiece Gift Set, includ-
   ing 2 watches and Death Star Collector Case
   in window box (Hope Industries #46101)
   Darth Vader and Boba Fett watches. 15.00
   Darth Vader and Stormtrooper watches 15.00
Rebel Alliance Collector Timepiece Gift Set,
   including 2 watches and *Millennium Falcon*
   Collector Case in window box (Hope

C-3PO and R2-D2 child's watch, vinyl band (Bradley Time 1977)

   Industries #46102)
   C-3PO and R2-D2 watches 15.00
   C-3PO and Yoda watches 15.00
Imperial Forces Collector Timepiece 4-piece Gift
   Set, including 3 watches and Death Star
   Collector Case in window box (Hope
   Industries #46103) 20.00
Rebel Alliance Collector Timepiece 4-piece Gift Set,
   including 3 watches and *Millennium Falcon*
   Collector Case in window box (Hope
   Industries #46104) 20.00
Star Wars Collector Timepiece watches in *Mil-
   lennium Falcon* watch case in window box
   (Hope Industries 1996)
   C-3PO (#46212) 10.00
   Darth Vader (#46211). 10.00
   R2-D2 . . . . 10.00
   Boba Fett 10.00
   Stormtrooper. 10.00
   Yoda 10.00

Watches, with face/head cover (Hope Industries 1996)
Darth Vader 7.00
C-3PO 7.00
R2-D2 . . . . 7.00
Boba Fett 7.00
Stormtrooper (#97004) 7.00
Yoda. 7.00

Character head collector watch with Qui-Gon Jinn
   Lightsaber Display Case (Hope Industries 1999)
Darth Maul (#46261) 10.00
Anakin Skywalker (#46262) 10.00
C-3PO (#46263) 10.00
Jar Jar (#46264) 10.00

Die-Cast watches, metal (Hope Industries 1999)
Darth Maul (#46271) 15.00
R2-D2 (#46272). 15.00
Battle Droid (#46273) 15.00
Pit Droid (#46274) 15.00

Character Watches (Nelsonic 1999)
C-3PO Skeletal Character Watch (#27588) 25.00
Darth Maul Sith Probe Droid Pocket Watch with
   Sound & Light Effects (#27591) 25.00
Pod racer Pilot Compass Watch (#27583) 25.00
Queen Amidala Laser-Dial Character Watch (#27614). 15.00
Darth Maul Laser-Dial Character Watch (#27612) 15.00
Qui-Gon Jin Character Watch (#27981). 15.00

Hologram Watches (1990s)
Darth Vader Hologram Watch (A.H. Prismatic
   #8000/SW 1995) 25.00
Darth Vader *Star Wars* Plastic Holographic Watch

C-3PO figural plastic watch with Millennium Falcon case
(Hope Industries 1996)

(Third Dimension 1994) 35.00
Yoda *Star Wars* Plastic Holographic Watch (Third
    Dimension 1994) 45.00
X-Wing *Star Wars* Plastic Holographic Watch (Third
    Dimension 1995) 45.00
Boba Fett *Star Wars* Plastic Holographic Watch
    (Third Dimension 1995) 40.00

Collector Watches (1990s)
Millennium Falcon Watch (Fantasma #90WA-MLF-
    LE, 1993) deluxe analog, brass case with
    flip-up lid, limited to numbered 10,000 pieces 65.00
Darth Vader Watch (Fantasma #90WA-DV-LE,
    1993) deluxe analog, black coin dial, limited
    to 7,500 numbered pieces 65.00
Battle of the Force Collectors Limited Edition Watch
    (Fantasma #90WA-DV-LE, 1993) limited
    to 7,500 numbered pieces 65.00
Star Wars: A New Hope quartz analog watch, gold-
    tone buckle (#46240, 1997) 25.00
Star Wars: *The Empire Strikes Back* quartz analog
    watch, chrome tone buckle (#46240, 1997) 25.00
Star Wars Death Star analog wristwatch, limited to
    10,000 copies (1997) 90.00
Darth Vader Collector's Watch, analog, black
    leather band, silver bezel in Darth Vader
    helmet container, silver edition, limited to
    15,000 copies (Fossil LI-1604) 85.00
Darth Vader Collector's Watch, analog, black
    leather band, silver bezel in Darth Vader
    helmet container, gold edition, limited to 1,000
    copies (Fossil LI-1604) 120.00
Official limited edition Boba Fett watch, limited to
    10,000 pieces, in tin case with litho image and
    with certificate of authenticity (Fossil #LI-1619) . . . 75.00
Official limited edition Boba Fett gold edition watch,
    23k gold plated limited to 1,000 pieces, in tin

case with litho image and with certificate of
    authenticity (Fossil #LI-1620) 120.00

TOTE BAGS

Tote Bags
R2-D2 and C-3PO Duffel Bag, blue (Adam Joseph
    1983) $30.00
Yoda Duffel Bag, red (Adam Joseph 1983) 30.00

Star Tours Fanny Pack, black with blue/silver "Star
    Tours" logo (Star Tours) 15.00
Star Tours Gym Bag, horizontal design with
    blue/silver "Star Tours" logo (Star Tours) 30.00
Star Tours Toilette Case, black with blue/silver "Star
    Tours" logo (Star Tours) 15.00
Darth Vader and Imperial Guards Tote Bag, red
    canvas (Adam Joseph 1983) 25.00
R2-D2 and C-3PO Tote Bag, blue canvas (Adam
    Joseph 1983) 25.00
Star Tours Tote Bag, black design with blue/silver
    "Star Tours" logo (Star Tours) 20.00

OTHER ACCESSORIES

Buttons are popular, but they are easy to make and most
are unlicensed. As such, they can be accumulated, but no
accurate list can be compiled. Just about any such button can
be bought for about $1.00 for regular size and about $2.00 for
large size. Selling later at a profit is another matter. The most
fun way to collect them is to look for free ones, which are
often available at movie openings or shows. A few licensed
items which have developed a collector following are listed
below.

BUTTONS AND BADGES

Buttons, Badges & Tabs
Fan Club membership buttons . . . . $5.00 to 10.00
Fan Club character set, 25 buttons 50.00
Various movie & slogan buttons . . . . 1.00 to 2.00
Revenge of the Jedi logo buttons (1982) 10.00
Star Wars Trilogy Special Edition give-away 1.00

PATCHES

Patches, movies, characters . . . . 3.00 to 10.00
Patches (**Revenge of the Jedi**) 25.00
Star Wars Trilogy Patch Set, reproduction of
    cast/crew movie patches, 5" long, limited to
    1,000 sets (1997) 12.00

PINS

Holographic Pins (A.H. Prismatic 1994)
B-Wing Fighter 2.50
Millennium Falcon and TIE Fighter 2.50
TIE Fighter and X-Wing 2.50
Millennium Falcon and *Star Wars* logo 2.50
Darth Vader 2.50
Imperial Star Destroyer 2.50
X-Wing Fighter 2.50
TIE Fighter 2.50
AT-AT & Snowspeeder 2.50

Star Wars 3-D Square Pins, moving image, 2" x 2"

(A.H. Prismatic #1016SWX 1997)
Darth Vader 3.00
Millennium Falcon 3.00
R2-D2 and C-3PO 3.00
X-Wing Fighter. 3.00

KEY CHAINS

Key chains, die-cast metal (1996)
See-Threepio (Playco 03110) $3.00
Artoo-Deetoo (Playco 03110) 3.00
Darth Vader (Playco 03110) 3.00
Han Solo (Playco 03110) 3.00
Luke Skywalker (Playco 03110) 3.00
Star Wars Key chain four-pack, Artoo-Deetoo, See-
   Threepio, Darth Vader and Luke Skywalker
   (Playco Toys #03120). 10.00

Second Series die-cast gold painted, display box,
   2" x 3" (Playco #3115, 1997)
Luke Skywalker 3.00
C-3PO 3.00
R2-D2 . . . . 3.00
Darth Vader 3.00

Third Series (Asst. #3118, Playco 1998)
Chewbacca, with crossbow. 3.00
Imperial Stormtrooper with blaster. 3.00
Imperial TIE-Fighter pilot 3.00
Greedo with blaster 3.00

Fourth Series (Asst. #3200, Playco 1998)
Emperor Palpatine 3.00
Admiral Ackbar 3.00
Princess Leia 3.00
Luke Skywalker in pilot gear 3.00
Return of the Jedi metal key chains (Adam
   Joseph 1983) 4 different, each. 8.00

Vinyl Key chains (Applause 1996)
Darth Vader (#46221) 3.00
Greedo (#46222) 3.00
Stormtrooper (#46223) 3.00
Boba Fett (#46224). 3.00

Millennium Falcon Keyring (1983, reoffered in 1994) . . 20.00

Pewter Key chains
Rebel Alliance, Blue Card (Rawcliffe Feb. 1998)
Millennium Falcon (#00942, 1998) 7.00
R2-D2 (Rawcliffe #00977, 1998) 7.00
Princess Leia (#00940, 1997) 7.00
Obi-Wan Lightsaber (#00941, 1997) 7.00

Galactic Empire, Red Card (Rawcliffe, Feb. 1998)
Stormtrooper (#00801, 1997) 7.00
Darth Vader Helmet (#00937, 1998). 7.00
Boba Fett Helmet (#00938, 1997) 7.00
Boba Fett with Gun (#00939, 1997) 7.00
Darth Vader Fist (#00943, 1997) 7.00
Boba Fett (#00944, 1997). 7.00
Vader Lightsaber (#00945, 1997) 7.00
TIE Squadron (#00946, 1997). 7.00
Death Star Pewter (#00999, 1998) 7.00

Star Wars Pewter Key chains (Rawcliffe)
20 year anniversary logo (#00947, 1997) 7.00
Trilogy Special Edition (#00948, 1997) 7.00

Star Wars 3-D square key chains, 2" x 2" (A.H.
   Prismatic, 1997)
Darth Vader 5.00
Millennium Falcon 5.00
R2-D2 & C-3PO 5.00
X-Wing Fighter. 5.00

Key chains Hollywood Pins 1994
Star Wars New Republic key chain (#SW801) 7.00
Yoda portrait key chain (#SW805) 7.00
Darth Vader portrait key chain (##SW810) 7.00
Millennium Falcon cut-out key chain (#SW815) 7.00
Episode I Metal Keychains, 2" with moveable,

Episode I *Jar Jar Binks* Pin and Key chain *(Applause 1999)*

arms, legs & neck (Applause 1999)
Pit Droid, 2" (#43048) 5.00
Jar Jar Binks, 2" (#43047) 5.00
Watto, 2" (#43049) 5.00

Episode I Vinyl Key chains, with moveable arms,
   legs & neck (Applause 1999)
Darth Maul, 3" (#43082) 3.00
Jar Jar Binks, 3" (#43083) 3.00

Episode I Cloisonne Key chains (Applause 1999)
Star Wars Episode 1 (#43107) 4.00
Naboo Starfighter (#43101). 4.00
Pod Racing (#43106) 4.00
Jedi vs. Sith (#43100) 4.00

Dog Tags, 2" (Applause 1999)
Trade Federation Droid Fighter (#43128) 5.00
Obi-Wan Kenobi (#43126) 5.00
Darth Maul (#43125) 5.00
Naboo Fighter (#43127). 5.00

COINS AND PREMIUMS

A-Wing Pilot, Amanaman, Anakin Skywalker, AT-AT,
AT-ST Driver, and B-Wing Pilot coins (Kenner 1985)

Barada, Bib Fortuna, Biker Scout, Boba Fett
Chewbacca, and Chief Chirpa coins (Kenner 1985)

COINS AND PREMIUMS

A premium is a secondary collectible issued in a package with a toy, such as an action figure, to enhance its value. Weapons and other items that are on the same scale as the toy are called accessories. When removed from the package, an accessory is included with the toy when sold "loose," while the premium becomes a separate collectible. By far the most valuable premiums are the Power of the Force coins which came with the action figures in the classic series of that name. Some of the newer action figure series also had coins and others came with Freeze Frame slides and with CommTech chips. Some of those action figure series were produced in large numbers, making most of the figures, and their premiums, quite cheap to collect.

POWER OF THE FORCE COINS

There were two ways to get one of the classic Kenner Power of the Force coins—with a figure, or by mailing in a proof of purchase. The figures came with a coin which related to the figure, but when you mailed in a proof of purchase, you got a random coin. Consequently, the coins that came with a figure are a lot more common than the ones that did not. The action figure section in this book lists both the new and reissued figures which came on Power of the Force header cards, with coins. More of the new figures were issued, so their coins are the most common. The exceptions are the Anakin Skywalker and Yak Face coins, since their figures were only available overseas. There are a total of 37 Power of the Force figures, but only 35 coins. The AT-AT Driver and Nikto had Warok coins.

Creatures, C-3PO, Darth Vader, Droids,
Emperor, and Emperor's Royal Guard coins (Kenner 1985)

EV-9D9, FX-7, Gamorrean Guard, Greedo,
Imperial Commander, and Imperial Dignitary coins (Kenner 1985)

Han Solo: Rebel Fighter, Rebel Hero, Carbon Freeze, Hero, Imperial Gunner, and Jawas coins (Kenner 1985)

Lando Calrissian (Cloud City and Millennium Falcon), Logray, Luke Skywalker: Jedi and Jedi Knight coins (Kenner 1985)

Kenner planned to issue Power of the Force figures for Chief Chirpa, Emperor's Royal Guard, Luke, Logray, and TIE Fighter Pilot, but did not. The coins for these figures were probably struck in anticipation of this, because they were commonly used to fulfill the mail-in requests. Interest in the *Star Wars* line was waning in 1985, and thus relatively few people mailed-in, so these coins are still scarce.

The more expensive coins were rarely used to fulfill the mail-in offer. They mostly got on the market from sources within Kenner. There was one other way, however, to get them all. Collectors who pestered Kenner about the missing coins were eventually given the right to buy a whole set, for $29.00! The offer was never made to the public. It turned out to be one of the better purchases of all time, as a complete set is worth more than 100 times that amount today.

All these coins are from the collection of Rob Johnson. Thanks again, Rob!

Star Wars Coins, Silver Color (Kenner 1985) Set . $3,000.00

Amanaman	15.00
Anakin Skywalker, Jedi	125.00
AT-AT, *Star Wars*, mail-in, scarce	100.00
AT-ST Driver, Empire	20.00
A-Wing Pilot, Rebel	10.00
Barada, Skiff Sentry	10.00
Bib Fortuna, Major Domo, mail-in, very scarce	125.00
Biker Scout, Empire	25.00
Boba Fett, Bounty Hunter	250.00

B-Wing Pilot, Rebel	15.00
Chewbacca, Wookiee	25.00
Chief Chirpa, Ewok Leader, mail-in	40.00
Creatures, *Star Wars*, "at local cantinas"	90.00
Variation "at local cafes"	125.00
C-3PO, Protocol Droid	15.00
Darth Vader, Lord of the Sith	25.00
Droids, *Star Wars*, mail-in, scarce	100.00
Emperor, Galactic Ruler	25.00
Emperor's Royal Guard, Empire, mail-in	100.00
EV-9D9, Torture Droid	10.00
FX-7, Medical Droid, mail-in, very scarce	125.00
Gamorrean Guard, Palace Sentry	30.00
Greedo, Bounty Hunter, mail-in, very scarce	125.00
Han Solo, Carbon Freeze	10.00
Han Solo, Rebel	25.00
Variation, "Hans Solo"	75.00
Han Solo, Rebel Fighter	15.00
Han Solo, Rebel Hero (Hoth gear) mail-in, scarce	100.00
Hoth Stormtrooper, Empire, mail-in, very scarce	250.00
Imperial Commander, Empire, mail-in, scarce	75.00
Imperial Dignitary, Empire	10.00
Imperial Gunner, Empire	10.00
Jawas, Desert Scavengers	25.00
Lando Calrissian, Rebel General (with *Millennium Falcon*)	10.00
Lando Calrissian, Rebel General (with Cloud City) mail-in, scarce	90.00
Logray, Ewok, mail-in	40.00
Luke Skywalker, Rebel Leader, mail-in	25.00
Luke Skywalker, Rebel Leader (on Tauntaun)	

Luke Skywalker Rebel Leader (five variations) and Luke Skywalker Jedi Knight (bust) coins (Kenner 1985)

Lumat, Millennium Falcon, Obi-Wan Kenobi, Princess Leia: with R2-D2, Boushh, and Endor outfit coins (Kenner 1985)

*Paploo, R2-D2, Romba, Sail Skiff,
Stormtrooper, and Hoth Stormtrooper coins (Kenner 1985)*

*Star Destroyer Commander, Teebo, TIE Fighter Pilot,
Too-Onebee, Tusken Raider, and Warok coins (Kenner 1985)*

mail-in, scarce	125.00
Luke Skywalker, Rebel Leader (with landspeeder)	50.00
Luke Skywalker, Rebel Leader (on scout bike)	12.00
Luke Skywalker, Jedi (with X-Wing)	25.00
Luke Skywalker, Jedi Knight (head)	25.00
Luke Skywalker, Jedi Knight (bust, on Dagobah)	
mail-in, very scarce	150.00
Lumat, Ewok Warrior	10.00
Millennium Falcon, Star Wars, mail-in, scarce	125.00
Obi-Wan Kenobi, Jedi Master	25.00
Paploo, Ewok	10.00
Princess Leia, Boushh, mail-in, very scarce	125.00
Princess Leia, Rebel Leader (in Endor outfit)	20.00
Princess Leia, Rebel Leader (head, with R2-D2)	125.00
Romba, Ewok	10.00
R2-D2, Rebel Droid	10.00
Sail Skiff, *Star Wars*, mail-in, very scarce	175.00
Variation, Does not say "*Star Wars*"	350.00
Star Destroyer Commander, Empire, mail-in, scarce	100.00
Stormtrooper, Empire	25.00
Teebo, Ewok	25.00
TIE Fighter Pilot, Empire, mail-in	65.00
Too-One Bee, Medical Droid, mail-in, very scarce	150.00
Tusken Raider, Sand People, mail-in, very scarce	150.00
Warok, Ewok	10.00
Wicket The Ewok	25.00
Yak Face, Bounty Hunter	125.00
Yoda, The Jedi Master	30.00
Zuckuss, Bounty Hunter, mail-in, very scarce	150.00

DROIDS COINS

Droids Coins, Gold Color (Kenner 1985)

Kea Moll, Freedom Fighter	10.00
Thall Joben, Speeder Racer	10.00
Jann Tosh, Adventurer	10.00
A-Wing Pilot, Rebel	60.00
C-3PO, Protocol Droid	20.00
Variation, C-3PO, Droids	20.00
Boba Fett, Bounty Hunter	200.00
Tig Fromm, Techno Villain	15.00
Jord Dusat, Thrill Seeker	10.00
Kez-Iban, Lost Prince	10.00
Sise Fromm, Gang Leader	20.00
R2-D2, Droids	20.00
Uncle Gundy, Prospector	10.00

EWOKS COINS

Ewoks Coins, Bronze Color (Kenner 1985)

Dulok, Scout	10.00
King Gorneesh, Dulok	10.00
Dulok Shaman	10.00
Logray, Ewok Shaman	10.00
Wicket, Ewok Scout	15.00
Urgah (Lady Gorneesh) Dulok	10.00

BEND-EM COINS

Bend-Em Coins (JustToys 1994) from 4-packs

Millennium Falcon	5.00
TIE Fighter	5.00

Wicket, Yak Face, Yoda, and Zuckuss coins (Kenner 1985)

Han Solo, Rebel Fighter coin, close-up (Kenner 1985)

X-Wing Fighter 5.00
Star Wars 15th Anniversary Silver Coin (Catch a
   Star 1992) limited to 5,000 . . . . 45.00

MILLENNIUM MINTED
COIN COLLECTION

    Kenner began to reissue Power of the Force coins in 1998. These coins are gold-colored, so they will not be mistaken for the originals, which were silver. The coins come with figures and are mounted in a stand-up display holder. Coin and figure come in a window box, which has a back window as well so you can see the reverse of the coin. The package sells for $10.00, so I have valued the coin at $5.00. Will avid exonumia collectors bid the price up? Who knows. Action figure collectors consider it a shameless gimmick to sell them another copy of a figure that they already own.

Gold-colored Coins (Kenner 1998)
Han Solo Rebel Fighter, with Bespin Han Solo (#84022) $5.00
Hoth Stormtrooper, Empire, with Snowtrooper (#84028) 5.00
Chewbacca Wookiee, with Chewbacca (#84023) 5.00
Emperor Palpatine (#84029) 5.00
Luke Skywalker in Endor Gear (#84026) 5.00
Princess Leia in Endor Gear (#84027) 5.00
C-3PO (#84024) 5.00

OTHER PREMIUMS

FREEZE FRAME SLIDES

    The 56 Freeze Frame Slides include actual movie scenes. The most interesting one(s) came with R2-D2. The text on the slide frame was changed from "Shutting down the Imperial trash compactor" to "Shutting down the Death Star trash compactor." The original slide (and figure it came with) are quite scarce and no one will be eager to remove the slide from the figure in his or her collection. Other slides that came with scarce figures are also scarce.

Freeze Frame Slides
8D8 . . . . $2.00
Admiral Ackbar 2.00
AT-AT Driver 7.00
AT-ST Driver 20.00
Biggs Darklighter 2.00
Boba Fett 15.00
C-3PO, Dismantled protocol droid 4.00
Captain Piett 5.00
Chewbacca, Posing as Boushh's Bounty 2.00
Darth Vader 3.00
Darth Vader (removable helmet) 7.00
Death Star Droid 7.00
Death Star Trooper 5.00
Emperor Palpatine 2.00
Emperor's Royal Guard 5.00
Endor Rebel Soldier 2.00
EV-9D9 . . . . 2.00
Ewoks 3.00
Gamorrean Guard 2.00
Garindan 10.00
Grand Moff Tarkin 2.00
Han Solo, Topping the Empire's most wanted list 3.00
Han Solo in Carbonite 2.00
Bespin Han Solo 2.00
Han Solo in Endor Gear 2.00

Princess Leia Organa (Jabba's Captive) slide (Kenner 1998)

Hoth Rebel Soldier 2.00
Ishi Tib 4.00
Lak Sivrak 4.00
Lando Calrissian, Disguised as a skiff guard 2.00
Lando Calrissian, Lando is appointed general 2.00
Lobot 3.00
Bespin Luke Skywalker 2.00
Luke Skywalker, Celebrating the Rebel victory 2.00
Luke Skywalker, Disguised as a Stormtrooper 2.00
Luke Skywalker, Learning the Ways of the Force 3.00
Malakili 2.00
Mon Mothma 3.00
Nien Nunb 4.00
Obi-Wan (Ben) Kenobi 4.00
Orrimaarko 3.00
Pote Snitkin 7.00
Princess Leia Organa, Caught in the grip of the evil
    Empire 2.00
Princess Leia Organa, Leia is taken captive by
    crime lord Jabba the Hutt 2.00
Princess Leia Organa, Leia is reunited with her
    Rebel companions in the Ewok village 2.00
Princess Leia Organa (Hoth Gear) 7.00
Rebel Fleet Trooper 4.00
Ree-Yees 5.00
R2-D2, Shutting down the Death Star trash compactor . 5.00
R2-D2, Shutting down the Imperial trash compactor . . 15.00
Saelt-Marae 3.00
Sandtrooper 25.00
Snowtrooper 4.00
Stormtrooper 3.00
TIE Fighter Pilot 10.00
Ugnaughts 2.00
Weequay Skiff Guard 40.00
Zuckuss 5.00

Viewers, Holders (Kenner 1998)
Freeze Frame Slide Display Holder, mail-in, with
    two exclusive slides 15.00
Luke Skywalker's Macrobinoculars, slide viewer
    mail-in 20.00

Princess Leia and Aunt Beru Flashback Photos (Kenner 1998)

FLASHBACK PHOTOS

There are only 11 Flashback Photo figures but several variations in the slides exist. Earlier ones have a down-arrow on the back of the pull-tab, while later ones have none. There is no difference in price.

Flashback Photos
Anakin Skywalker	1.00
Aunt Beru	1.00
Obi-Wan Kenobi [556101.00]	1.00
C-3PO [555498.0000]	1.00
Darth Vader (Anakin Skywalker) [556111.00]	1.00
Emperor Palpatine	1.00
Hoth Chewbacca	1.00
Luke Skywalker	1.00
Princess Leia (Queen Amidala) [556103.00]	1.00
R2-D2 [556109.00]	1.00
Yoda [556105.00]	1.00

COMMTECH CHIPS

CommTech Chips came with Episode I figures, CommTech figures, and with the three Cinema Scenes three-figure packs. Those that came with scarce figures are naturally even scarcer loose. They record lines of dialogue or sounds from the movies and play them back with the chip reader. You don't need to remove the chip from the package to play it with the reader. I don't know the number for a few of the figures because I don't want to take my valuable figures off their cards to find out.

From *Episode I* figures
1 Qui-Gon Jinn (Jedi Duel)	$1.00
2 Obi-Wan Kenobi (Jedi Duel)	1.00
3 Anakin Skywalker (Tatooine)	1.00
4 Padme Naberrie	1.00
5 Jar Jar Binks	1.00
6 Queen Amidala	1.00
7 R2-D2	1.00
8 C-3PO	1.00
9 CommTech Chip Reader	1.00
10 Captain Panaka	1.00
11 Ric Olie	1.00
12 Queen Amidala (Coruscant)	2.00
13 Anakin Skywalker (Naboo)	1.00
14 Qui-Gon Jinn (Naboo)	1.00
15 Obi-Wan Kenobi (Naboo)	1.00
16 Naboo Foot Soldier (Royal Security)	1.00
17 Qui-Gon Jinn (Jedi Master)	2.00
18 Senator Palpatine	1.00
19 Obi-Wan Kenobi (Jedi Knight)	2.00
20 Mace Windu	1.00
21 Yoda	1.00
22 Gasgano	1.00
23 Ody Mandrell	2.00
25 Boss Nass	1.00
26 Captain Tarpals	1.00
28 Ki-Adi-Mundi	2.00
29 Adi Gallia	1.00
30 Naboo Royal Guard	2.00
31 Darth Sidious	1.00
32 Darth Maul (Jedi Duel)	1.00
33 Nute Gunray	1.00
34 Rune Haako	1.00
35 Battle Droid	1.00
36 Watto	2.00
37 OOM-9	2.00
38 Destoyer Droid (Battle Damaged)	2.00
41 Chancellor Valorum	1.00
43 Darth Maul Tatooine	1.00
44 R2-B1	1.00
45 Darth Maul (Sith Lord)	2.00
46 Destroyer Droid	1.00
50 Sio Bibble	2.00
51 Pit Droids	2.00
56 Jar Jar Binks (Naboo Swamp)	3.00
71 Queen Amidala (Battle)	2.00
72 Anakin Skywalker (Naboo Pilot)	2.00
73 Darth Sidious Hologram	2.00
74 TC-14	2.00

From Cinema Scenes three-packs
113 Battle with Darth Maul	5.00
114 Viewing the Podrace	5.00
115 Confrontation with Sebulba	4.00

From CommTech figures
C1 Jawa	1.00
C2 R2-D2	4.00
C3 Luke Skywalker	1.00
C4 Greedo	1.00
C5 Han Solo	1.00
C6 Darth Vader	2.00
C7 Stormtrooper	2.00
C8 Princess Leia	3.00
C9 Admiral Motti	4.00
C11 Wuher	2.00

CommTech Reader (Hasbro 1999)
Electronic CommTech Chip Reader (#84151) [.0000]	20.00
Reissue: [.0100]	10.00

JEDI FORCE FILE

Jedi Force File fold-outs from Power of the Jedi figures don't impress me much as an in-pack premium and I doubt that they will be collected. They might be worth $1.00, if you are lucky.

COMICS

Star Wars collectible Number 2 is the comic book adaptation of the movie. It also appeared prior to the movie premiere – just prior. The first six issues of the comic follow the plot of the movie and the adventures continue on their own until issue #39 when the second movie adaptation begins. One interesting feature of the comic version of the movie is the appearance of Biggs Darklighter, Luke's friend. He was originally seen with Luke in the movie, but was edited out to keep the pace of the action as fast as possible. He does appear in the movie, as the last pilot killed by Darth Vader in the final battle against the Death Star, but he is not fully identified. The comic was adapted from a "rough cut" of the movie before the character was eliminated. He is somewhat restored in the 1997 updated version of the movie and now even has an action figure.

Biggs Darklighter from Star Wars #1 (Marvel Comics 1977)

There were two versions of the first issue of the comic book. The more common version has the price of 30¢ in a white box while the rare version has a price of 35¢ in a white diamond.

There were no comics from 1987, when the Marvel series ended, until December 1991 when Dark Horse comics started the current explosion with the publication of *Star Wars Dark Empire*.

It is hard to believe, but there are only eight hours of actual *Star Wars* film footage to date, less than half as many hours as *Star Trek's movies* alone, not counting the over 300 hours of *Star Trek* TV shows (and, yes, completely ignoring the made-for-children *Ewoks* and *Droids* TV shows). Avid fans have made up for this by seeing each of the movies numerous times. Still, comics, and books, supply much needed additional material to the *Star Wars* saga and therefore play a correspondingly greater role than in other series.

The *Shadows of the Empire* book and comic storyline has generated its own supply of action figures. Characters from the books and comics are included as major characters in the *Star Wars* universe in such books as *Star Wars, The Essential Guide to Characters* by Andy Mangels.

CLASSIC STAR WARS
Dark Horse Comics (Aug. 1992 – June 1994)

The events in this series take place between those in the first film *Star Wars: A New Hope* and the second film *The Empire Strikes Back*. The stories were written by Archie Goodwin and the art is primarily by Al Williamson, with occasional help from Allen Nunis. The covers are all new and are mostly by Williamson, with a couple by Nunis, George Evans, Mark Schultz, Tom Yeates, or Bret Blevins. The material was originally published from 1981 to 1984 in newspaper strips, and has been reformatted and newly colored for this series.

Comics

1 Luke and Leia on a scouting mission.	$6.00
2 Afoul of the Imperial fleet.	4.00
3	4.00
4	4.00
5	4.00
6	4.00
7	4.00
8	4.00
8 bagged with *Star Wars* Galaxy promo card.	5.00
9	3.50

*Classic Star Wars #20; Classic Star Wars: Devilworlds #2; Classic Star Wars: The Early Adventures #9
(Dark Horse Comics 1994, 1996, 1995)*

10	3.50
11	3.00
12	3.00
13	3.00
14	3.00
15	3.00
16	3.00
17	3.00
18	3.00
19	3.00
20 final issue	4.00
20 bagged with *Star Wars* Galaxy promo card	10.00

Trade Paperbacks

Vol. 1 In Deadly Pursuit, Al Williamson cover, reprint #1–#7 (1994)	16.00
Vol. 1, rep. 2nd edition (#45043)	16.95
Vol. 2 The Rebel Storm, Al Williamson cover, reprint #8–#14 (#44-422, 1995)	16.95
Vol. 3 Escape to Hoth, Al Williamson cover, reprint #15–#20 (1996)	16.95
Trade Paperbacks, boxed set of 3 (1996)	29.85

CLASSIC STAR WARS: A NEW HOPE
Dark Horse Comics (June and July, 1994)

The classic Marvel Comics adaptation of the first movie from 1977 was newly colored by Pamela Rambo and issued in a two-part prestige-format. The story is written by Roy Thomas and drawn by Howard Chaykin and inked primarily by Steve Leialoha.

Comics

1 Art Adams cover, reprint	$4.25
2 Adam Hughes cover, reprint	3.95

Trade Paperback

Series reprint (1995)	9.95

CLASSIC STAR WARS: DEVILWORLDS
Dark Horse Comics (Aug. and Sept. 1996)

The following two issues are reprints from Marvel U.K. comics from the early 1980s. They feature work by writer Alan Moore and others. Covers are by Christopher Moeller.

Comics

1 Four Stories: "The Flight of the Falcon," "Blind Fury," "Dark Lord's Conscience," "Dark Knight's Devilry"	$2.50
2 Three Stories: "Rust Never Sleeps," "The Pandora Effect," "Tilotny Throws a Shape"	2.50

CLASSIC STAR WARS: THE EARLY ADVENTURES
Dark Horse Comics (Aug. 1994–April 1995)

This is a reprint of the classic 1979–80 newspaper strips written and drawn by Russ Manning and featuring, in the last issue, the first appearance of Boba Fett. The strips were reformatted, colored and expertly retouched by Rick Hoberg, who worked with Manning on the originals.

Comics

1 Gambler's World, Mike Allred cover	$3.00
2 Blackhole, Rick Hoberg & Mike Grell cover	2.50
3 Rebels of Vorzyd-5, Eric Shanower cover	2.50
3 Bagged with trading card DH2	5.00
4 Tatooine, Rick Hoberg cover	2.50
5 A: Lady Tarkin, Rick Hoberg cover	2.50
6 Weather Dominator	2.50
7 Vs. Darth Vader, Rick Hoberg cover	2.50
8 X-Wing Secrets, Kilian Plunkett cover	2.50
9 Boba Fett appears, Killian Plunkett cover	2.50

Trade Paperback

Series reprint, Al Williamson cover (1997)	19.95

CLASSIC STAR WARS:
THE EMPIRE STRIKES BACK
Dark Horse Comics (Aug. and Sept. 1994)

These two issues reprint the 1980 Marvel Comics adaptation (issues #39 to #44) of the second movie and are written by Archie Goodwin with art and covers by Al Williamson. They are newly colored for this series.

Comics
1 Movie Adaptation $4.00
2 . . . . 4.00

Trade Paperback
Series reprint Al Williamson & Carlos Garzon cover . . . 9.95
Special reprint, Bros. Hildebrandt cover 9.95

CLASSIC STAR WARS:
HAN SOLO AT STAR'S END
Dark Horse Comics (March–May 1997)

This series was written by Archie Goodwin and features art by Alfredo Alcala from the original newspaper strips. It's an adaptation of Brian Daley's classic novel and takes place before the adventures in the first movie.

Comics
1 Igor Kordey cover $3.50
2 Stan and Vince cover 3.50
3 Stan and Vince cover 3.50

Trade Paperback
Series reprint, Al Williamson cover (1997) 6.95

Classic Star Wars Han Solo at Stars' End #1 (Dark Horse 1997)

CLASSIC STAR WARS:
A LONG TIME AGO
Dark Horse Comics (B&W) (1999)

This six volume series reprints classic Marvel comics in Black and White.

Comics
1 (of 6) rep. Marvel's King-size Annual #1, Annual #3, etc
. . . . $12.95
2 rep. Marvel #28, #38, #49, #50 . . . . 10.00
3 rep. Marvel #51, #50, #60 . . . . 10.00
4 rep. Marvel #. 10.00
5 rep. Marvel #. 10.00
6 rep. Marvel #. 10.00

CLASSIC STAR WARS:
RETURN OF THE JEDI
Dark Horse Comics (Oct. and Nov. 1994)

The third classic movie adaptation by Archie Goodwin and Al Williamson.

Comics
1 Movie Adaptation, Adam Hughes cover $4.00
1 bagged with trading card DH3 . . . . 5.00
2 Movie Adaptation, Al Williamson cover 3.50

Trade Paperback
Series reprint (1995) 9.95
Special reprint, Bros. Hildebrandt cover 9.95

CLASSIC STAR WARS:
VANDELHELM MISSION
Dark Horse Comics (March 1995)

This takes place after the events in the third movie and was written by Archie Goodwin with art by Al Williamson.

Comics
1 Han Solo, Lando and Nien Nunb $3.95

DARK HORSE CLASSICS:
STAR WARS — DARK EMPIRE
Dark Horse Comics (March–Aug. 1997)

This series reprints the original Dark Horse 1991–92 series written by Tom Veitch with art by Cam Kennedy and covers by Dave Dorman.

Comics
1 Reprint $2.95
2 thru 6 Reprint 2.95

DARK HORSE COMICS
Dark Horse Comics (1993–94)

Dark Horse Comics had two series of *Star Wars* stories. In issues #7 through #9, Tom Veitch scripted a three-part *Tales of the Jedi* story, to introduce readers to the regular comic book series of the same name which debuted in October 1993.

In issues #17 through #19, Dan Thorsland did the same thing as an introduction to the Droids comics which first appeared in Jan. 1994.

 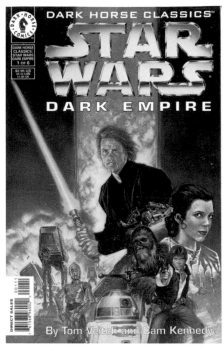 

Classic Star Wars Return of the Jedi #1; Dark Horse Classic Star Wars Dark Empire #1, (Dark Horse Comics 1994 and 1997), and Return of the Jedi #1 (Marvel 1983)

Comics
```
 7 Featuring: Mad Dogs, Robocop, Predator and
   Star Wars. .................................. $12.00
 8 Featuring: X, Robocop, James Bond and Star Wars  14.00
 9 Featuring: X, Robocop, James Bond and Star Wars .  8.00
17 Featuring: Star Wars, Aliens and Predator ........  2.75
18 Featuring: Star Wars, Aliens and Predator ........  2.75
19 Featuring: Alien, X, and Star Wars ..............  2.75
```

A DECADE OF DARK HORSE
Dark Horse Comics (Aug. 1996)

This series was to celebrate 10 whole years of Dark Horse comics with some of the best of their best stories. Issue #2 featured the *Star Wars* story "This Crumb for Hire," which chronicles the first meeting of Jabba the Hutt and his annoying pet, Salacious Crumb.

Comics
```
 2 Allen Nunis cover .......................... $2.95
```

DROIDS
Star/Marvel Comics (April 1986 – June 1987)

The comics were written by Dave Manak and feature art work by John Romita, Al Williamson, Ernie Colon and Jon D'Agostino.

Comics
```
 1 John Romita ............................... $3.00
 2 Al Williamson ...............................  3.00
 3 John Romita/Al Williamson ...................  3.00
 4 Al Williamson ...............................  3.00
 5 Al Williamson ...............................  3.00
 6 Ernie Colon/Al Williamson, A: Luke Skywalker .....  3.00
 7 Ernie Colon/Al Williamson, A: Luke Skywalker .....  3.00
 8 Ernie Colon/Al Williamson, A: Luke Skywalker .....  3.00
```

EWOKS
Star/Marvel Comics (June, 1985 – Sept., 1987)

The comics were written by Dave Manak and feature art work by Warren Kremer, Jacqueline Roettcher and Jon D'Agostino.

Comics
```
 1 Based on TV Series ........................ $18.00
 2 ........................................... 15.00
 3 ........................................... 15.00
 4 A: Foonars ................................. 15.00
 5 Wicket vs. Ice Demon. ...................... 15.00
 6 Mount Sorrow, A: Teebo ..................... 15.00
 7 A: Logray, V: Morag ........................ 15.00
 8 ........................................... 15.00
 9 Lost in Time ............................... 15.00
10 Lost in Time ............................... 18.00
11 Kneesaa Shrunk, A: Fleebogs ............... 15.00
12 ........................................... 15.00
13 ........................................... 15.00
14 Teebo — King for a Day ..................... 15.00
15 ........................................... 15.00
```

MARVEL MOVIE SHOWCASE
FEATURING STAR WARS
Marvel Comics (November, 1982)

Comics
```
 1 Reprint, Stars Wars #1-6 .................... $4.00
 2 December, 1982 ............................  4.00
```

MARVEL SPECIAL EDITION
FEATURING STAR WARS
Marvel Comics (1977 – 78)

Oversized reprints of the original comics.

Star War Marvel Special #1 (Marvel Comics 1977

Comics
1 Reprint of Star Wars #1 thru #3 (1977) $10.00
2 Reprint of Star Wars #4 thru #6 (1978) 8.00
3 Reprint of Star Wars #1 thru #6 (1978) 10.00
Volume 2
2 The Empire Strikes Back (1980) rep. of Marvel
　　Super Special #16 . . . . 7.50

MARVEL SUPER SPECIALS
Marvel Comics (1980 & 1983)

Oversized official movie adaptations.

Comics
16 The Empire Strikes Back $10.00
27 Return of the Jedi 10.00

RETURN OF THE JEDI
Marvel Comics (Oct. 1983–Jan. 1984)

A four part adaptation of the movie, written by Archie
Goodwin, with art by Al Williamson.

Comics
1 Archie Goodwin, Al Williamson $3.00
2 thru 3 Archie Goodwin, Al Williamson 3.00

SERGIO STOMPS STAR WARS
Dark Horse Comics (Feb. 2000)

Comic
1-shot parody by Sergio Aragones 3.00

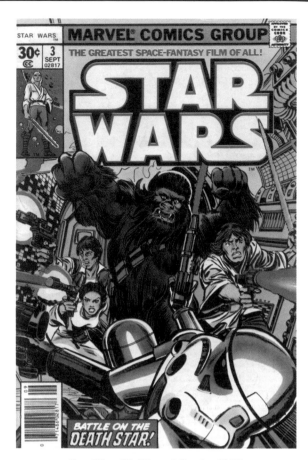

Star Wars #3 (Marvel Comics 1977)

STAR WARS
Marvel Comics (July, 1977)

Although dated July 1977, the first comics actually
appeared before the movie opened. The first six issues adapted the movie based on a "rough cut." This has led to considerable wonder about the "missing scenes" where, at the
beginning of the movie, Luke goes to see his Tatooine pal,
Biggs Darklighter, who tells him that he is going to join the
Rebel forces. This scene was cut from the final version of the
movie. A later reunion scene between Luke and Biggs, just
before they fly off in their X-wing fighters to attack the Death
Star, was also cut. It was restored in the 1997 *Special Edition*.
Biggs is killed by Darth Vader, but Luke's other wing-mate,
Wedge Antilles, survives. In 1998, Biggs was finally immor-
talized in plastic as an action figure.

The most valuable comic in the Marvel series is the 35
cent version of issue Number 1. Only a very few were printed, as a price increase test. The test must have been successful, because the price has increased over 1,000 fold since
then. The second and third movies were adapted in turn and
the series finished out its nine-year run with issue number
107. There was no coordination between the few *Star Wars*
novels being published and the comic book series, and the
comics issued between the movies did not have the benefit of
knowledge of the movie plots. That innovation did not come
until the 1990s, with the many Dark Horse comics series.
Marvel used its better artists on these comics, at least for the
first six years or so, and both comic collectors and *Star Wars*

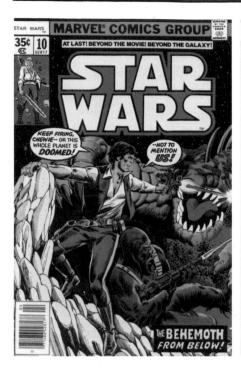  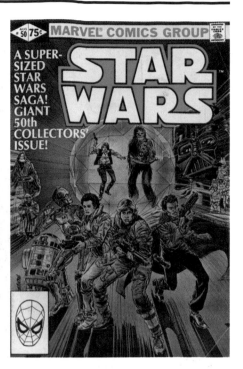

Star Wars #10, #25, #50 (Marvel)

collectors have considered these stories to be worthy additions to their collections.

Comics

1 Howard Chaykin, 30 Cent, begin: movie adaptation. $65.00
1a Howard Chaykin, 35 Cent (square Box). 600.00
1b Reprint 7.50
2 Howard Chaykin, "Six Against the Galaxy". 25.00
2a Reprint 4.00
3 Howard Chaykin, "Death Star" 25.00
3a Reprint 4.00
4 Howard Chaykin, Steve Leialoha, "In Battle With Darth Vader" 22.00
4a Reprint 4.00
5 Howard Chaykin, Steve Leialoha, "Lo, the Moons of Yavin!". 22.00
5a Reprint 3.00
6 Howard Chaykin, Dave Stevens, end: movie adaptation 22.00
6a Reprint 3.00
7 Howard Chaykin, Frank Springer, "New Planets, New Perils!". 20.00
7a Reprint 2.50
8 Howard Chaykin, Tony DeZuniga, "Eight for Aduba-3". 20.00
8a Reprint 2.50
9 Howard Chaykin, Tom Palmer, "Showdown on a Wasteland World!" 20.00
9a Reprint 2.50
10 Howard Chaykin, Tom Palmer, "Behemoth From The World Below" 20.00
11 Carmine Infantino, Tom Palmer, "Star Search" 18.00
12 Terry Austin, Carmine Infantino, "Doomworld". 18.00
13 Terry Austin, John Byrne, Carmine Infantino, "Day of the Dragon Lords!". 18.00
14 Terry Austin, Carmine Infantino, "The Sound of Armageddon!" 18.00
15 Carmine Infantino, "Star Duel!" 18.00

16 Walt Simonson, "The Hunter" 18.00
17 "Crucible!",. 18.00
18 Carmine Infantino, "The Empire Strikes" 18.00
19 Carmine Infantino, "The Ultimate Gamble" 18.00
20 Carmine Infantino, "Death Game" (Scarce) 18.00
21 Terry Austin, Carmine Infantino, "Shadow of a Dark Lord!" (Scarce) 18.00
22 Carmine Infantino, "To the Last Gladiator". 15.00
23 Carmine Infantino, "Flight Into Fury!" 15.00
24 Carmine Infantino, "Silent Drifting" 15.00
25 Carmine Infantino, "Siege at Yavin!" 15.00
26 Carmine Infantino, "Doom Mission". 15.00
27 Carmine Infantino, "Return of the Hunter". 15.00
28 Carmine Infantino, "Cavern of the Crawling Death". . 15.00
29 Carmine Infantino, "Dark Encounter" 15.00
30 Carmine Infantino, "A Princess Alone!". 15.00
31 Carmine Infantino, "Return to Tatooine" 15.00
32 Carmine Infantino, "The Jawa Express" 15.00
33 Carmine Infantino, Gene Day, "Sabre Clash!" 15.00
34 Carmine Infantino, "Thunder in the Stars!" 15.00
35 Carmine Infantino, "Dark Lord's Gambit". 15.00
36 Carmine Infantino, "Red Queen Rising!" 15.00
37 Carmine Infantino, "In Mortal Combat!" 15.00
38 Terry Austin, Mike Gustovich, "Riders in the Void" . . 15.00
39 Al Williamson, Begin: *The Empire Strikes Back*. . . . 25.00
40 Al Williamson, "Battleground Hoth!" 25.00
41 Al Williamson, "Imperial Pursuit!" 25.00
42 Al Williamson, "To Be A Jedi!" 25.00
43 Al Williamson, "Betrayal at Bespin". 25.00
44 Al Williamson, End: *The Empire Strikes Back* 25.00
45 Carmine Infantino, Gene Day, "Death Probe" 20.00
46 Tom Palmer, "The Dreams of Cody Sunn-Childe!". . 20.00
47 Carmine Infantino, Gene Day, "Droid World" 20.00
48 Carmine Infantino, "The Third Law". 20.00
49 Scott Williams, Tom Palmer, "The Last Jedi" 20.00
50 Walt Simonson, Al Williamson, Tom Palmer, "The Crimson Forever!" giant-size issue 20.00
51 Walt Simonson, Tom Palmer, "Resurrection of Evil". 15.00
52 Walt Simonson, Tom Palmer, "To Take the Tarkin" . . 15.00

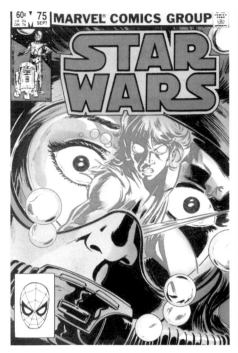  

Star Wars #75; #100; and King Size Annual #2 (Marvel)

STAR WARS
Dark Horse Comics (1998 – 2002)

A continuing series, with four to six-part story arcs.

Comics

PRELUDE TO REBELLION

Written by Jan Strnad, art by Anthony Winn and Robert

Star Wars #4 (Prelude to Rebellion); #24 (Infinity's End); #37 (The Stark Hyperspace War) (Dark Horse 1998–2001)

Jones, covers by Ken Kelly

1 pt. 1 Featuring: Ki-Adi-Mundi	$5.00
2 pt. 2	3.50
3 pt. 3	3.50
4 pt. 4 Sylvn	3.00
5 pt. 5 Ephant Mon	3.00
6 pt. 6 Jabba the Hutt	3.00

OUTLANDER

Written by Tim Truman, art by Tom Raney, Rob Pereira, Rick Leonardi, Al Ri, Mark Heike and Mark Lipka covers by Ken Kelly.

7 pt. 1 Featuring Ki-Adi-Mundi.	2.50
8 pt. 2 A: Jabba the Hutt	2.50
9 pt. 3 A: Tusken Raiders	2.50
10 pt. 4	2.50
11 pt. 5 Aurra Sing.	2.50
12 pt. 6	2.50

EMISSARIES TO MALASTARE

Written by Timothy Truman, art by Tom Lyle and Robert Jones (first four) John Nadeau and Jordi Ensign (last two), covers by Mark Schultz, with last one by Jan Duursema.

13 pt. 1 Featuring the Jedi Council	2.50
14 pt. 2	2.50
15 pt. 3	2.50
16 pt. 4	2.50
17 pt. 5	3.00
18 pt. 6	3.00

TWILIGHT

Written by John Ostrander, art by Jan Duursema and Rick Magyar, covers by Jan Duursema.

19 pt. 1 Featuring Quinlan Vos	3.00
20 pt. 2	3.00
21 pt. 3	3.00
22 pt. 4	3.00

INFINITY'S END

Written by Pat Mills, art by Ramon F. Bachs and Raul Fernandez, covers by Andrew Robinson.

23 pt. 1 Featuring Quinlan Vos	3.00
24 pt. 2	3.00
25 pt. 3	3.00
26 pt. 4	3.00

STAR CRASH

Written by Doug Petrie, art by Randy Green and Andy Owens, covers by Randy Green.

27 Featuring Yoshi Raph-Elan	3.00

THE HUNT FOR AURRA SING

Written by Tim Truman with art by Davide Fabbri and Christian Dalla Vecchia and covers by Jon Foster.

28 pt. 1	3.00
29 pt. 2	3.00
30 pt. 3	3.00
31 pt. 4	3.00

DARKNESS

Written by John Ostrander, art by Jan Duursema and Ray Kryssing, covers by Jon Foster.

32 pt. 1 Featuring Quinlan Vos	3.00
33 pt. 2	3.00
34 pt. 3	3.00
35 pt. 4	3.00

THE STARK HYPERSPACE WAR

Written by John Ostrander, with art by Davide Fabri and Christina Dalla Vecchia, covers by Jan Duursema.

36 pt. 1 Featuring Iaco Stark, Plo Koon	3.00

37 pt. 2	3.00
38 pt. 3	3.00
39 pt. 4	3.00

THE DEVARONIAN VERSION

Written by John Ostrander, art by Davide Fabri and Christina Dalla Vecchia, covers by Killian Plunkett

40 pt. 1 (of 2) Featuring Vilmarh Grahrk	3.00
41	3.00

Trade Paperbacks

Prelude to Rebellion, series rep.	14.95
Emissaries to Malastare, series rep.	15.95
Outlander, series rep.	14.95
Twilight, series rep.	12.95

STAR WARS IN 3-D
Blackthorne Publishing (Dec. 1987 – Fall 1988)

3-D comics have never been all that popular with comics collectors or *Star Wars* collectors.

Comics

1	$3.50
2 through 7, each	2.50

STAR WARS:
A NEW HOPE
Dark Horse Comics (B&W) Manga (1998)

The manga style adaptation of the original classic movie, by Hisao Tamaki with covers by Adam Warren.

Comics

1 (of 4) by Tamaki Hisao, 96pg.	$9.95
2	9.95
3	9.95
4	9.95

STAR WARS:
THE EMPIRE STRIKES BACK
Dark Horse Comics (B&W) Manga (1998)

The manga style adaptation of the second classic movie, by Toshiki Kudo with covers by Adam Warren.

Comics

1 (of 4) by Toshiki Dudo, 96pg.	$9.95
2	9.95
3	9.95
4	9.95

STAR WARS:
THE RETURN OF THE JEDI
Dark Horse Comics (B&W) Manga (1999)

The manga style adaptation of the third classic movie, by Shin-ichi Hiromoto with covers by Adam Warren.

Comics

1 (of 4) by Shin-ichi Hiromoto, 96pg.	$9.95
2	9.95
3	9.95
4	9.95

Star Wars, A New Hope, Special Edition #2
(Dark Horse Comics 1997)

STAR WARS: BATTLE OF
THE BOUNTY HUNTERS
Dark Horse Comics (July 1996)

This is a pop-up comic book featuring Boba Fett battling other bounty hunters for his prize: Han Solo encased in carbonite! It was written by Ryder Windhan, with artwork and cover by Christopher Moeller.

Comics

Pop-up comic	$17.95

STAR WARS: A NEW HOPE
THE SPECIAL EDITION
Dark Horse Comics (Jan.–April 1997)

An all new adaptation of the special edition of the movie. The series was written by Bruce Jones, pencilled by Deuardo Barreto and inked by Al Williamson and others. The four Dave Dorman covers can be placed together to form one large image with the Death Star at the center.

The trade paperback of the first movie was released at the same time as the first comic and sports a cover by the famous Brothers Hildebrandt. In August, they released a special edition boxed set of this trade paperback plus reprints of classic adaptations from the other two movies.

Comics

1	$6.00

 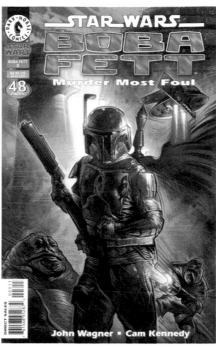 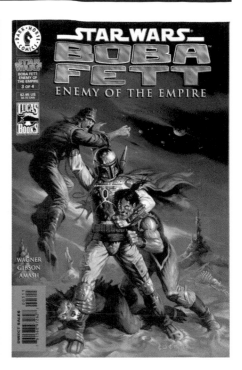

Star Wars: Boba Fett:When the Fat Lady Sings #2; Murder Most Foul #3; and Enemy of the Empire #3 (Dark Horse 1996, 1997 & 1999)

2. . . . . 5.00
3. . . . . 5.00
4. . . . . 5.00

Trade Paperback
A New Hope, Tim and Greg Hildebrandt cover 10.00
Special Edition boxed set 30.00

STAR WARS: BOBA FETT —
AGENT OF DOOM
Dark Horse Comics (Nov. 2000)

Written by John Ostrander, art by Cam Kennedy and cover by Francisco Luis Velasco.

Comics
1-shot $3.00

STAR WARS: BOBA FETT —
BOUNTY ON BAR-KOODA
Dark Horse Comics (Dec. 1995)

First of a series of one-shot comics featuring your favorite bounty hunter, Boba Fett. This one follows the events in Dark Empire II. It was written by John Wagner and contains art and a cover by Cam Kennedy.

Comics
1-shot 48pp $11.00

STAR WARS: BOBA FETT —
WHEN THE FAT LADY SWINGS
Dark Horse Comics (Sept. 1996)

Second in the series of one-shot comics featuring Boba Fett. This one was also written by John Wagner and contains art by Cam Kennedy and a cover by Mathieu Lauffray.

Comics
1-shot $7.00

STAR WARS: BOBA FETT —
MURDER MOST FOUL
Dark Horse Comics (Aug. 1997)

Third in the series of one-shot comics featuring Boba Fett. This one was also written by John Wagner and contains art by Cam Kennedy and a cover by Mathieu Lauffray.

Comics
1-shot. $7.00

STAR WARS: BOBA FETT —
DEATH, LIES & TREACHERY
Dark Horse Comics (Jan. 1998)

Written by John Wagner, art and cover by Cam Kennedy.

Trade Paperback
Death, Lies & Treachery, reprints "Bounty on Bar-Kooda," "When the Fat Lady Swings" and Murder Most Foul" $12.95

STAR WARS: BOBA FETT —
TWIN ENGINES OF DESTRUCTION
Dark Horse Comics (Jan. 1997)

A one-shot comic featuring Boba Fett. This one was written by Andy Mangles with art by John Nadeau and Jordi Ensign and a cover by John Nadeau. It was previously serialized in Topps' *Star Wars Galaxy* magazine.

Comics
1-shot 32pp. $6.00

STAR WARS: BOBA FETT— ENEMY OF THE EMPIRE
Dark Horse Comics (1999)

Written by John Wagner, art by Ian Gibson and covers by Ken Kelly.

Comics

1 (of 4) Vs. The Dark Lord of the Sith	$3.00
2	3.00
3	3.00
4	3.00

Trade Paperback

Enemy of the Empire, series rep.	16.95

STAR WARS: THE BOUNTY HUNTERS
Dark Horse Comics (1999)

A series of one-shots featuring the Galaxy's greatest bounty hunters, by various writers and artists.

Comics

1-shot Aurra Sing, by Timothy Truman	$3.00
1-shot Kenix Kil, by Randy Stradley	3.00
1-shot Scoundrel's Wages, by Mark Schultz	3.00

Trade Paperback

The Bounty Hunters, series rep.	12.95

Star Wars: Crimson Empire II #4 (Dark Horse Comics 1999)

STAR WARS: CHEWBACCA
Dark Horse Comics (2000)

The history of the galaxy's greatest Wookiee, written by Darko Macan with various artists and covers by Sean Phillips.

Comics

1 stories narated Mallatobuck and by Attichitcuk	$4.00
1a gold foil cover	13.00
2 three more stories	3.50
3 Featuring Lando Calrissian	3.50
4 Featuring Luke Skywalker	3.50

Trade Paperback

Chewbacca, series rep.	12.95

STAR WARS: CRIMSON EMPIRE
Dark Horse Comics (Dec. 1997–May 1998)

This story line begins immediately after the events in Empire's End and tells the tale of Kir Kanos, the last remaining member of Emperor Palpatine's Royal Guard. It was written by Mike Richardson and Randy Stradley, with art by Paul Gulacy and P. Craig Russell. Painted covers by Dave Dorman.

Comics

1	$10.00
2	8.00
3	5.00
4	5.00
5	5.00
6 Final battle against Carnor Jax.	5.00

Trade Paperback

Crimson Empire, series rep..	17.95

VOLUME II:

COUNCIL OF BLOOD
Dark Horse Comics (1998–99)

With the death of Carnor Jax, an Interim Council is assembled, but then the assassinations begin and Xandel Carivus takes over. Can Kir Kanos save the day again? Written by Mike Richardson and Randy Stradley, with art by Randy Stradley and Paul Gulacy, with Dave Dorman covers.

Comics

1	$4.00
2	3.00
3	3.00
4 thru 6	3.00

Trade Paperback

Council of Blood, series rep.	17.95

STAR WARS: DARK EMPIRE
Dark Horse Comics (Dec. 1991–Oct. 1992)

This was the first *Star Wars* series done by Dark Horse Comics. The story takes place six years after the Battle of Endor and the death of Darth Vader. The fighting continues and Luke and Lando are shot down over the former Imperial capitol. Naturally Han, Leia, and Chewie try to rescue them. While massive dark side World Devistators ravage entire planets, Leia has to protect her unborn child and Luke is seduced by the dark side. The Emperor wields a mysterious

 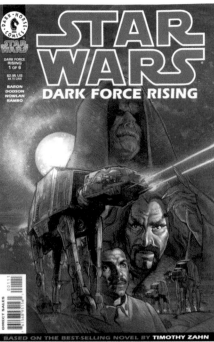 

Star Wars: Dark Empire II #2; Dark Force Rising #1 and #3; (Dark Horse 1995 & 1997)

and intelligent artifact called the Jedi Holocron, which delivers a thousand-year-old prophecy. The Battle of Calimari rages to a climax and everything depends on the data carried by one little robot!

The comics were written by Tom Veitch, with art by Cam Kennedy and covers by Dave Dorman.

Comics
1 Destiny of a Jedi	$15.00
1a 2nd Printing	5.00
1b Gold edition	15.00
2 World Destroyer, very low print run	12.00
2a 2nd Printing	5.00
2b Gold edition	15.00
3 Battle for planet Calamari	8.00
3a 2nd printing	4.00
3b Gold edition	10.00
4 Pursued by a bounty hunter	5.00
4a Gold edition	7.00
5 Captured by the Emperor	5.00
5a Gold edition	10.00
6 The Jedi Holocron	5.00
6a Gold edition	9.00
Gold editions, embossed foil logo, set	50.00
Platinum editions, embossed foil logo, set	100.00

Trade Paperbacks
Preview 32pg.	.99
Dark Empire series reprint, #1–#6 Dave Dorman cover	20.00
Dark Empire 2nd ed. (#44-848)	17.95

Limited Edition Hardcover
Leather bound, foil-stamped, with slipcase	125.00

STAR WARS: DARK EMPIRE II
Dark Horse Comics (Dec. 1994 – May 1995)

In the second Dark Empire series, Luke tries to rebuild the Jedi Knights while the remains of the Empire still hopes to destroy the New Republic with a new super-weapon. In the meantime, Han keeps one step ahead of Boba Fett while he tracks down an old Jedi woman. Luke looks for the Jedi Holocron on the planet Ossus. Lando hides in a shipment of War Droids for an attack on the Empire. Han rejoins Leia as they protect their young twins from the Emperor on New Alderaan.

Written again by Tom Veitch, with art by Cam Kennedy and covers by Dave Dorman.

Comics
1 2nd chapter	$6.00
2 F: Boba Fett	5.00
3 V: Darksiders	5.00
4 Luke Vs. Darksiders	5.00
5 Creatures	5.00
6 Cam Kennedy & Dave Dorman cover, save the twins	5.00
Platinum editions, embossed foil logo, set	50.00

Ashcan
Hero Special Ashcan	5.00

Trade Paperback
Dark Empire II series reprint, plus cover paintings	17.95

Limited Edition Hardcover
Leather bound, foil-stamped, with slipcase	100.00

STAR WARS: DARK FORCE RISING
Dark Horse Comics (May–Oct. 1997)

The ruthless Grand Admiral Thrawn of the dying Empire looks for 200 Dreadnaught heavy cruisers, which were lost to hyperspace in the time of the Old Republic. Luke finds a new Jedi mentor named C'Baoth, and learns new ways to use the force. But are they good ways, or dark ways? Only

Talon Karrde knows where the ships are. When both sides find them, Grand Admiral Thrawn uses a trick not seen since the end of the Clone Wars.

Written by Mike Baron, pencils by Terry Dodson, inked by Kevin Nowlan and covers by Mathieu Lauffray.

Comics
1	$5.00
2	5.00
3	5.00
4	5.00
5	5.00
6	5.00

Trade Paperback
TPB Dark Force Rising, series rep. 17.95

STAR WARS: DARK FORCES —
Dark Horse Comics (1997–99)

A trilogy of graphic novels based on *Star Wars: Dark Forces* interactive games. Written by William C. Dietz, with art by Dean Williams, Ezra Tucker, and Dave Dorman.

SOLDIER FOR THE EMPIRE
The first story features Kyle Katarn, a graduate of the Imperial Military Academy, who becomes a spy for the Rebel Alliance.

Graphic-Story (1997–98)
HC, Soldier for the Empire, cover by Dean Williams. . $25.00
TPB version of the above. 15.00

Star Wars: Darth Maul #4 (Dark Horse Comics 2001)

REBEL AGENT
Second part of the adventures of Kyle Katarn, based on the *Star Wars*: Dark Forces interactive game.

Graphic-Story (1998–99)
HC Rebel Agent, cover by Ezra Tucker $25.00
TPB version of the above. 15.00

JEDI KNIGHT
Third part of the adventures of Kyle Katarn, based on the *Star Wars*: Dark Forces interactive game.

Graphic-Story (1998–99)
HC Jedi Knight, cover by Dave Dorman 25.00
TPB versions of above, each 15.00

STAR WARS: DARTH MAUL
Dark Horse Comics (2000–01)

Darth Maul must deal with the galactic crime organization Black Sun before he can appear on Naboo. Written by Ron Marz, art by Jan Duursema and Rick Magyar, with art covers by Drew Struzan.

Comics
1 The bad guys vs. the really bad guys	$3.00
1 photo cover	5.00
2 The tables are turned	3.00
2 photo cover	3.00
3 Single-handed decimation.	3.00
3 photo cover	3.00
4 Finale	3.00
4 photo cover	3.00

Trade Paperback
TPB Darth Maul, series rep. 12.95

STAR WARS: DROIDS
Dark Horse Comics (April – Sept. 1994)

These whimsical misadventures of Artoo-Detoo and See-Threepio take place years before the events in the *Star Wars: A New Hope* movie. They journey to the Kalarba system where they are acquired by the Pitareeze family. They encounter IG-88 and the notorious Olag Greck plus a variety of pirates, bounty-hunters, and rock monsters.

The adventures actually begin in Dark Horse Comics #17 through #19, and this story is included in the series trade paperback. Most of the stories were written by Dan Thorsland, with one by Ryder Windham. Art was supplied by Bill Hughes, Andy Mushynsky, and Ian Gibson. Covers are by Kilian Plunkett.

The regular series continues these stories, with tales written by Ryder Windham and Jan Strnad. Art is by Ian Gibson, Bill Hughes, Keith Williams, and Rich Perrotta. Covers are again by Kilian Plunkett.

Comics
1 Featuring C-3PO and R2-D2	$5.00
2 Interplanetary thieves steal our droids	3.00
3 A droid battle arena the Hosk moon	3.00
4 Leased to Jace Forno	3.00
5 A meeting with model E droids	2.50
6 A power core rupture	2.50
Spec.#1 Introducing Olag Greck, reprint DHC #17–#19.	2.50

Trade Paperback
The Kalarba Adventures, reprint of #1–#6, the
    Special and an 8-page story from Topps Star
    Wars Galaxy magazine (#44-489) 17.95
Limited Edition Hardcover
Leather bound, foil-stamped, with slipcase 100.00

Regular Series Comics (April 1995 – Dec. 1995)
    1 Deputized Droids 3.00
    2 Marooned on Nar Shaddaa 2.50
    3 C-3PO to the Rescue. 2.50
    4 . . . . 2.50
    5 Caretaker virus 2.50
    6 Revolution 2.50
    7 . . . . 2.50
    8 . . . . 2.50

Trade Paperback
Droids — Rebellion, Reprints #1 through #4 . . . . 14.95

STAR WARS: DROIDS —
THE PROTOCOL OFFENSIVE
Dark Horse Comics (Sept. 1997)

This comic was plotted by Brian Daley, author of *Han Solo at Stars' End* and written by Anthony Daniels (C-3PO in the movies) and Ryder Windham. Art and cover by Igor Kordey. If you guessed that it stars C-3PO, you would be right.

Comics
    1-shot $4.95

STAR WARS: EMPIRE'S END
Dark Horse Comics (Oct.–Nov. 1995)

Following the events in *Dark Empire II*, The Emperor needs a new Jedi clone body to replace his rapidly failing and inferior clone body. Han and Leia's child, Anakin, would do very nicely.

Written by Tom Veitch, art by Jim Baikie and covers by Dave Dorman.

Comics
    1 Return of Emperor Palpatine $3.50
    2 conclusion 3.50

Trade Paperback
Series Reprint 5.95

STAR WARS: EPISODE I
THE PHANTOM MENACE
Dark Horse Comics (1999)

Comics adaptation of the movie of the same name. Written by Henry Gilroy, with art by Rodolfo Damaggio and Al Williamson and art covers by Hugh Fleming.

The Tie-ins contain stories of the major characters that lead up to their appearance in The Phantom Menace. Anakin is written by Tim Truman with art by Steve Crespo and George Freeman. Obi-Wan is written by Henry Gilroy with art by Martin Egeland and Howard Shum. Queen Amidala is written by Mark Schultz with art by Galen Showman and P. Craig Russell. Qui-Gon is written by Ryder Windham with art by Robert Teranishi and Chris Chuckry. All have art covers by Tim Bradstreet.

Comics
    1 . . . . $3.00
    2 . . . . 3.00
    3 . . . . 3.00
    4 . . . . 3.00
    1a thru 4a, newsstand editions, photo cover 3.00
Specials
½ Wizard Special Magazine Comic. 10.00

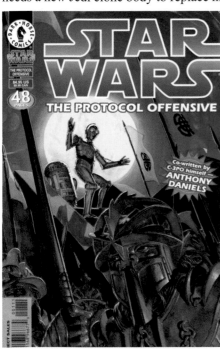

Star Wars: The Protocol Offensive; Episode I The Phantom Menace #4; and Queen Amidala Special (Dark Horse 1997 & 1999)

Graphic Novel The Phantom Menace 12.95
Limited edition hardcover, series reprint, signed 80.00

Comic Tie-ins
Spec. Anakin Skywalker, direct or newsstand 3.00
Spec. Obi-Wan Kenobi, direct or newsstand 3.00
Spec. Queen Amidala, direct or newsstand 3.00
Spec. Qui-Gon Jinn, direct newsstand 3.00

Trade Paperback
The Phantom Menace Adventures, series rep. 12.95

STAR WARS EPISODE I
Dark Horse Comics (B&W) Manga (1999–2000)

Comics
1 . . . . $9.95
2 . . . . 9.95

STAR WARS HANDBOOKS
Dark Horse Comics (1998–2002)

Comics
1 X-Wing Rogue Squadron (1998) John Nadeau cov. . $3.50
2 Crimson Empire (1999) Dave Dorman cover 3.00
3 Dark Empire (2000) Dave Dorman cover 3.00

STAR WARS:
HEIR TO THE EMPIRE
Dark Horse Comics (Oct. 1995 – April 1996)

Five years after the death of Darth Vader, Grand Admiral Thrawn has control of the Imperial Fleet in this

Star Wars: Heir to the Empire #4 (Dark Horse Comics 1996)

adaptation of Timothy Zahn's novel.

Written by Mike Baron, with art by Olivier Vatine and Fred Blanchard and covers by Mathieu Lauffray.

Comics
1 I: Grand Admiral Thrawn $4.00
2 . . . . 3.50
3 . . . . 3.50
4 Luke looses his Jedi powers 3.50
5 Mara Jade captures Luke. 3.50
6 Luke goes to rescue Han. 3.50

Trade Paperback
Heir to the Empire, from novel by Timothy Zahn 19.95

Limited Edition Hardcover
Foil-stamped, 160 pp, tipped-in art plate with
    signatures, in slipcase 100.00

STAR WARS: INFINITIES —
A NEW HOPE
Dark Horse Comics (2001)

Non-continuity Star Wars stories in an alternate reality where Luke's torpedoes miss and the first Death Star is not destroyed. Written by Chris Warner, pencilled by Drew Johnson, covers by Tony Harris.

Comics
1 . . . . $3.00
1a gold foil cover 13.00
2 . . . . 3.00
3 . . . . 3.00
4 . . . . 3.00

Trade Paperback
Infinities a New Hope, series rep. 12.95

STAR WARS: JABBA THE HUTT —
Dark Horse Comics (1995–96)

A series of one-shots written by Jim Woodring, with art by Art Wetherell and Monty Sheldon.

THE GARR SUPPOON HIT

Jabba lives for the art of the deal. Here he barters with Garr Suppoon, an absolute devil at the negotiating table. Which one will live long enough to write his memoirs as the Art of the Comeback? Cover by Steve Bissette and Cam Kennedy.

Comics
1-shot Featuring Garr Suppoon. $2.50

THE HUNGER OF PRINCESS NAMPI

The second Jabba the Hutt one-shot, with cover by Mark Harrison.

Comic
1-shot Wheel and Deal $2.50

THE DYNASTY TRAP

Jabba tries to employ Cabrool Nuum to sell a hot freighter, but he falls into a trap set by Cabrool's offspring. Cover by Mark Harrison.

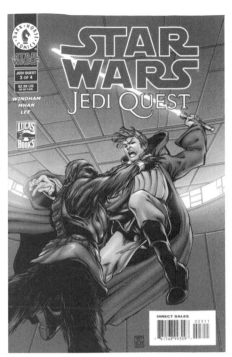

Star Wars: The Jabba Tape; Jedi Academy, Leviathan #1; Jedi Quest #3 (Dark Horse 1998 and 2001)

Comic
1-Shot Featuring: Cabrool Nuum $2.50

BETRAYAL

Bib Fortuna plots a revolt against Jabba. Cover by Mark Harrison.

Comic
1-shot Featuring Bib Fortuna. $2.50

THE ART OF THE DEAL

Jabba trades in the lives of others in this reprint of the four one-shots. Cover by Monty Sheldon.

Trade Paperback
The Art of the Deal, 104-page. 9.95

STAR WARS: JABBA THE HUTT —
THE JABBA TAPE
Dark Horse Comics (1998)

Jabba's dead, and everyone wants a piece of his vast criminal empire. Written by John Wagner, with art and cover by Kilian Plunkett. This was originally serialized in *Star Wars Galaxy Magazine.*

Comics
1-shot The Jabba Tape 3.00

STAR WARS: JANGO FETT
Dark Horse Comics (Feb. 2002)

Mandalorian Warrior Jango Fettis featured in this graphic novel by Ron Marz and Tom Fowler, with cover by Tom Fowler. The graphic novel leads in to a forthcoming series titled "Open Seasons."

Graphic Novel
Jango Fett, 64 pages. 9.95

STAR WARS: JEDI ACADEMY —
LEVIATHAN
Dark Horse Comics (1998)

Luke has trained a new group of Jedi Knights for eight years. Now they have to defend the Republic. Written by Kevin J. Anderson, with pencils by Dario Carrasco, Jr. and covers by Ray Lago and Paul Chadwick.

Comics
1 (of 4) Kyp Durron and Dorsk 82 sent to Corbos $3.00
2 Colony destroyed. What monster did it? 3.00
3 The Leviathan of Corbos. 3.00
4 Its mother wants revenge 3.00

Trade Paperback
Jedi Academy–Leviathan, series rep. 11.95

STAR WARS: JEDI COUNCIL —
ACTS OF WAR
Dark Horse Comics (2000)

It was the duty of the Jedi Knights to keep the peace among the thousand worlds that made up the Republic. Written by Randy Stradley with art by Davide Fabbri and Christian Dalla Vecchia, and covers by Davide Fabbri.

Comics
1 (of 4) Trouble $3.00
1a gold foil cover 10.00
2 Jedi task force to Yinchorri, Jedi temple attacked. . . . 3.00
3 Mace Windu and the Jedi Council. 3.00
4 Against the Yinchorri High Command 3.00

Trade Paperback
Jedi Council–Acts of War, series rep. 12.95

Star Wars: Jedi vs. Sith #6; The Last Command #2; Mara Jade, By the Emperor's Hand #1 (Dark Horse 2001; 1997 and 1998)

STAR WARS: JEDI QUEST
Dark Horse Comics (2001)

This series bridges the gap between *Episode I* and *Episode II* and features the exploits of Obi-Wan Kenobi and his Padawan learner Anakin Skywalker. Written by Ryder Windham, pencilled and covers by Pop Mhan and inked by Norman Lee.

Comics

1 (of 4) An escort mission	$3.00
1a ruby red foil cover	13.00
1b ruby red foil cover, signed	30.00
2 Pirate and slave trader Krayn	3.00
3 Anakin captured	3.00
4 Obi-Wan to the rescue	3.00

Trade Paperback

Jedi Quest, series rep	11.95

STAR WARS: JEDI VS. SITH
Dark Horse Comics (2001)

A thousand years before the movies, the Sith Brotherhood of Darkness, led by Lord Kaan, battled with Lord Hoth and the Jedi Army of Light. Written by Darko Macan, pencilled by Ramon F. Bachs, covers by Andrew Robinson.

Comics

1 (of 6)	$3.00
1a gold foil cover, limited edition	10.00
2 Tomcat, Bug, and Rain	3.00
3 On the planet Ruusan	3.00
4	3.00
5	3.00
6 Final battle	3.00

STAR WARS: THE LAST COMMAND
Dark Horse Comics (Nov. 1997 – May 1998)

Six-part comic adaptation of Timothy Zahn's *The Last Command*. Grand Admiral Thrawn creates an army of clones, while Leia gives birth to twins, Jacen and Jaina Solo. Imperials try to steal the kids, but are confronted by Han and Mara Jade. The last of these comics was just appearing as this book was completed.

Written by Mike Baron, with art by Edvin Biukovic, Eric Shanower and Pamela Rambo. Covers by Mathieu Lauffray.

Comics

1	$3.50
2	3.50
3	3.50
4	3.50
5	3.50
6	3.50

Trade Paperback

The Last Command, series rep	17.95

STAR WARS: MARA JADE— BY THE EMPEROR'S HAND
Dark Horse Comics (1998)

Mara Jade is the Emperor's Hand. After failing to kill Luke Skywalker, she is assigned to take down the crimelord who seeks to reestablish the Black Sun. Written by Timothy Zahn and Michael A. Stackpole, with art by Carlos Ezquerra and covers by Kilian Plunkett.

Comics

1 (of 6) Assigned to destroy Black Sun	$5.00

Star Wars Qui-Gon & Obi-Wan Last Stand on Ord Mantell #3 (Dark Horse 2001) ; Shadows of the Empire #5 (Dark Horse 1996); and Shadows of the Empire, Evolution #4 (Dark Horse 1998)

2 Infiltrates Black Nebula headquarters 4.00
3 Mara Jade captured 4.00
4 Escape from the Imperial Center. 4.00
5 Mara's payback list 4.00
6 Her final mission for the dead Emperor 4.00

Trade Paperback
Mara Jade–By the Emperor's Hand, series rep. 15.95

STAR WARS: QUI-GON AND OBI-WAN — LAST STAND ON ORD MANTELL
Dark Horse Comics (2000–01)

The action takes place five years before the events of *Episode I*. Looking for a missing cargo freighter, Qui-Gon and Obi-Wan end up on the lawless world of Ord Mantell. Written by Ryder Windham with art by Ramon Bachs and Raul Fernandez, and covers by Tony Daniel and Ramon Bachs.

Comics
1 (of 3) Investigation $3.00
1a photo cover 3.00
1b variant Tony Daniel cover 3.00
1c gold foil cover. 15.00
2 Taxer Sundown, ruthless land baron 3.00
2 photo cover 3.00
3 Rescue. 3.00
3 photo cover 3.00

STAR WARS: QUI-GON AND OBI-WAN — THE AURORIENT EXPRESS
Dark Horse Comics (2002)

Qui-Gon and Obi-Wan are on a luxury cruiser about to crash. By Mike Kennedy and Lucas Marangon, with covers by Lucas Marangon.

Comics
1 (of 2) $3.00
2 . . . . 3.00

STAR WARS: RIVER OF CHAOS
Dark Horse Comics (May – Nov. 1995)

Leia is on a spy mission with a small band of rebels, but one of them turns out to be Ranulf, an Imperial counter-spy. Eventually Ranulf must choose between his Imperial allies and the Rebel he has come to love. Written by Louise Simonson with art and covers by June Brigman and Roy Richardson.

Comics
1 LSi, JBr, Emperor sends spies $3.00
2 Imperial in Allies Clothing. 3.00
3 . . . . 3.00
4 F: Ranulf 3.00

STAR WARS: SHADOWS OF THE EMPIRE
Dark Horse Comics (May – Oct. 1996)

This comic, based on the novel by Steve Perry, takes place between the events in *The Empire Strikes Back* and *Return of the Jedi*. It pits the underworld against the Rebel Alliance against the Empire. Prince Xizor controls the largest merchant fleet in the Empire, and also its largest criminal organization. Darth Vader resents the Prince's power, the Prince wants Darth's power, while Dash Rendar just resents the Prince. Our heroes want to rescue Han, but every bounty hunter in the galaxy wants him for Jabba's reward, alive or dead. The Emperor wants Luke, alive, while the Prince wants Luke (and Darth, for that matter) dead. Xizor captures Leia on general principals, leaving almost as many heroes needing rescue as there are in disguise, doing the rescuing.

This story is the only one, so far, which has generated its own group of action figures: Prince Xizor, Dash Rendar, Chewbacca disguised as a bounty hunter, Luke disguised as an Imperial Guard and Leia in Boushh disguise.

The comics were written by John Wagner, with art by Kilian Plunkett and P. Craig Russell and covers by Hugh Fleming.

Comics

1 The Emperor enlists the criminal underworld	$3.50
2 Prince Xizor.	3.50
3 Surprise attack on Luke	3.50
4 Bounty hunters try to steal Han	3.50
5 Bounty hunters seek Luke	3.50
6 Leia a captive	3.50

Trade Paperback
Shadows of the Empire, Christopher Moeller cover . . . 17.95

Limited Edition Hardcover
Deluxe, signed, with original plate 80.00

STAR WARS: SHADOWS OF THE EMPIRE — EVOLUTION
Dark Horse Comics (Feb. – June 1998)

Guri, a human replicant droid was Xizor's personal assassin. Now that her boss has been destroyed, she goes looking for her human side. This series was written by Steve Perry, author of *Shadows of the Empire*. It's adapted by Ron Randall, Tom Simmons, Dave Netelle, with covers by Duncan Fegredo. It's a five issue mini-series and should be concluded by the time this book goes to press.

Comics

1 (of 5)	$3.50
2	3.50
3	3.50
4	3.50
5	3.50

Trade Paperback
Evolution, series reprint 14.95

STAR WARS: SHADOW STALKER
Dark Horse Comics (Nov. 1997)

This one-shot collects a story which was serialized in Topps' *Star Wars Galaxy* magazine. It features Jix, a covert agent whom Darth Vader sends to take care of a defecting Imperial governor. It's written by Ryder Windham, with art and cover by Nick Choles.

Comics
1-shot $3.50

STAR WARS: SPLINTER OF THE MIND'S EYE
Dark Horse Comics (Dec. 1995 – June 1996)

This series is adapted from the Alan Dean Foster novel, which was originally published in 1978. The Kaiburr crystal, "capable of magnifying and clarifying one's perception of the Force," is hidden somewhere on the planet Mimban. Luke and Leia battle massive creatures called yuzzem, wormlike wandrella and a subterranean race of aboriginals to find the crystal before Darth Vader does.

Written and inked by Terry Austin, pencilled by Chris Sprouse, with covers by Hugh Fleming (first two) and Mark Harrison (last two).

Comics

1	$3.50
2	3.50
3	3.50
4	3.50

Trade Paperback
Splinter of the Mind's Eye series reprint, Duncan
    Fegredo cover 14.95

STAR WARS: STARFIGHTER– CROSSBONES
Dark Horse Comics (2001–02)

High-seas adventure on Maramere featuring pirate captain Nym. Written by Haden Blackman and Ramon F. Bachs, with covers by J. H. Williams.

Comics

1	$3.00
2	3.00
3	3.00

Star Wars: Starfighter Crossbones #1 (Dark Horse Comics 2001)

STAR WARS:
TAG AND BINK ARE DEAD
Dark Horse Comics (2001)

Tag Greenly and Bink Otauna are two rebel officers who borrow stormtrooper armor to avoid being killed in the battle where Princess Leia is originally captured. Written by Kevin Rubio, with art by Lucas Marangon and Howard Shum, and covers by Lucas Marangon.

Comics
1 Humorous adventures on the Death Star. $3.00
2 After the Death Star blows up 3.00

STAR WARS TALES
Dark Horse Comics (1999–2002)

Star Wars anthology, each 64 pages, issued quarterly. Several tales in each comic, some beyond the continuity. Various writers and artists contribute to the comics.

Comics
1 "Extinction," pt.1; "A Night on the Town;" "Skippy
  the Jedi Droid". $4.95
2 "Incident at Horn Station;" "Stop that Jawa!" &
  "Extinction," pt.2 . . . . 4.95
3 Featuring Lando Calrissian and Jar Jar Binks 4.95
4 Featuring "Sandblasted;" and Big Gizz and Spiker. . . 4.95
5 Featuring Lando's Commandos. 5.95
5 photo cover 5.95
6 Featuring Boba Fett, Yoda, Luke, C-3PO and Darth. . 5.95
6 photo cover 6.00
7 Featuring Boba Fett, Plo Koon, Yoda, Mace
  Windu and Domo Jones. 6.00
7 photo cover 6.00
8 Featuring C-3PO, Han, Jabba and Luke 6.00
8 photo cover 6.00
9 Featuring Darth Vader vs. Darth Maul 6.00
9 photo cover 6.00

10 "Trooper" 6.00
10 photo cover 6.00
11 Young Han Solo 6.00
11 photo cover 6.00

Trade Paperbacks
Star Wars Tales, Vol. 1, rep. #1 thru #4 . . . . 19.95
Star Wars Tales, Vol. 2, rep. #5 thru #8 . . . . 19.95

STAR WARS:
TALES FROM MOS EISLEY
Dark Horse Comics (March 1996)

Bruce Jones and Brett Blevins bring you these tales of the Mos Eisley Spaceport, infamous as a "wretched hive of scum and villainy."

Comics
1-shot, from *Star Wars* Galaxy Mag. #2–#4 . . . . $3.50

STAR WARS:
TALES OF THE JEDI
Dark Horse Comics (Oct. 1993 – Feb. 1994)

These tales take place 4,000 years in the past, when the Jedi Knights were supreme. The first two comics feature Ulic Qel-Droma, a young Jedi Knight in training, as he battles against the Dark Side to stop a war. The last three focus on Nomi Sunrider, who reluctantly takes up a lightsaber to avenge her husband's death at the hands of Bogga the Hutt.

The comics were written by Tom Veitch, and have covers by Dave Dorman.

Comics
1 Pencils by Chris Grossett, Inks by Mike Barreiro. . . $6.00
  Gold foil edition 15.00
2 Pencils by Chris Grossett, Inks by Mike Barreiro. . . . 5.00
  Gold foil edition 15.00

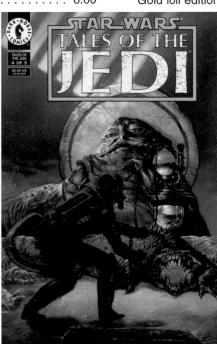

Star Wars: Tag & Bink Are Dead; Tales of the Jedi #4; and Dark Lords of the Sith Trade Paperback (Dark Horse 2001; 1993; and 1996)

3 Art by Janine Johnston 5.00
  Gold foil edition 15.00
4 Art by David Roach 4.00
  Gold foil edition 15.00
5 Art by David Roach 4.00
  Gold foil edition 15.00
Gold foil set 65.00

Trade Paperback
Knights of the Old Republic, series reprint, Hugh
    Fleming cover 16.00
2nd printing (#44-164) 14.95

STAR WARS:
TALES OF THE JEDI:
THE FREEDON NADD UPRISING
Dark Horse Comics (Aug. and Sept. 1994)

This two-part miniseries brings Ulic and Nomi together to battle Freedon Nadd and save the planet Onderon. It's a prequel to the Dark Lords of the Sith.

Written by Tom Veitch, with art by Tony Atkins and Denis Rodier and covers by Dave Dorman.

Comics
1 . . . . $2.75
2 . . . . 2.50

Trade Paperback
Series reprint, ... 5.95

STAR WARS:
TALES OF THE JEDI:
DARK LORDS OF THE SITH
Dark Horse Comics (Oct. 1994 – March 1995)

The adventures of Ulic and Nomi continue, as Exar Kun threatens to use ancient Sith magic to take over the universe, if it doesn't take him over first.

The series was written by Tom Veitch and Kevin J. Anderson, with art by Chris Grossett, Art Wetherell, Mike Barreiro, and Jordi Ensign. Dave Dorman produced the first cover and Hugh Fleming did the rest.

Comics
1 . . . . $3.00
1 Bagged with a trading card DH1 . . . . 5.00
2 . . . . 2.50
3 Krath Attack. 2.50
4 . . . . 2.50
5 . . . . 2.50
6 Final battle. 2.50

Trade Paperback
Series reprint, Hugh Fleming cover. 17.95

STAR WARS:
TALES OF THE JEDI:
THE SITH WAR
Dark Horse Comics (Aug. 1995 – Jan. 1996)

Continuing the Sith saga, Ulic and Exar join up to use their Dark Side power, but they have somewhat different purposes in mind. Its Jedi against Jedi and brother against brother, while Nomi stands firm against Ulic's plan.

The stories were written by Kevin J. Anderson, with art by Jordi Ensign, Dario Carrasco, Jr., Mark Heike, Bill Black ,and David Jacob Beckett. Covers are by Hugh Fleming.

Comics
1 Exar Kun and Ulic Qel-Droma's plans. $3.00
2 The power of the Dark Side 3.00
3 Exar Kun turns novices into assassins 3.00
4 Jedi assassination program 3.00
5 Ulic vs. his brother Cay 3.00
6 Final battle over Yavin Four 3.00

Trade Paperback
The Sith War, Mathieu Lauffray cover 17.95

STAR WARS:
TALES OF THE JEDI —
THE GOLDEN AGE OF THE SITH
Dark Horse Comics (Oct. 1996 – Feb. 1997)

A thousand years before the Sith Empire fell, it had a golden age. This story is told in issue #0. In issue #1, two warring factions hope to fill the void left by the death of Marka Ragnos, Dark Lord of the Sith. Gav and Jori Daragon, two innocent hyperspace explorers, get caught between them, with crucial maps that both sides want.

Written by Kevin J. Anderson, with art by Chris Gossett, Stan Woch, Mark G. Heike, Bill Black, and Jacob Beckett.

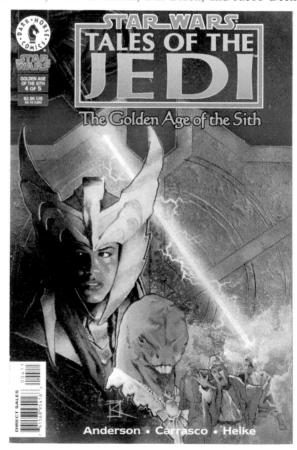

Star Wars Tales of the Jedi, The Golden Age of the Sith #4 (Dark Horse Comics 1997)

Cover #0 is by Christopher Moeller, while the others are by Russell Walks.

Comics

0 The golden age	$2.00
1 Gav and Jori Daragon	3.50
2	3.50
3	3.50
4 Captured by Naga Sadow	3.50
5 Battle for control of the Sith	3.50

Trade Paperback

Series reprint, Duncan Fegredo cover 16.95

STAR WARS: TALES OF THE JEDI — THE FALL OF THE SITH EMPIRE
Dark Horse Comics (June – Oct. 1997)

Naga Sadow, leads the Sith Empire in an all-out assault on the Old Republic. Jori Daragon, an explorer, stumbles on his plans, but as she tries to warn Empress Teta, she ends up on trial instead. This is the story of how the Old Republic wins the battle, but ends up doomed anyway.

Written by Kevin J. Anderson, with art by Dario Carrasco, Jr. Mark G. Heike, Bill Black, and David Jacob Beckett. Covers are by Duncan Fegredo.

Comics

1 Naga Sadow prepares his fleet	$3.50
1 variant cover, signed by Kevin J. Anderson	20.00
2 Jori on trial	3.50
3 First Encounter	3.50
4 The Sith invasion rages on.	3.50
5 The Fall of the Sith.	3.50

Trade paperback

Series reprint, Duncan Fegredo cover 15.95

STAR WARS: TALES OF THE JEDI — REDEMPTION
Dark Horse Comics (1998)

Ulic Qel-Droma killed his brother Cay and was stripped of his powers and is in hiding from the Republic. This is the story of his redemption. Written by Kevin J. Anderson with art by Chris Gossett and covers by Igor Kordey.

Comics

1 (of 5) Ten years after the Sith War	$3.50
2 Nomi Sunrider and the Jedi Knights	3.50
3 Vima Sunrider meets Ulic	3.50
4 Ulic trains Vima. Sylvar plots revenge	3.50
5 Nomi and Sylvar confront Ulic and Vima	3.50

Trade paperback

Redemption, series rep., Alexander McDaniel　　　cover
. . . . 15.95

STAR WARS: UNDERWORLD
Dark Horse Comics (2000–01)

When Han Solo was still a smuggler and charming

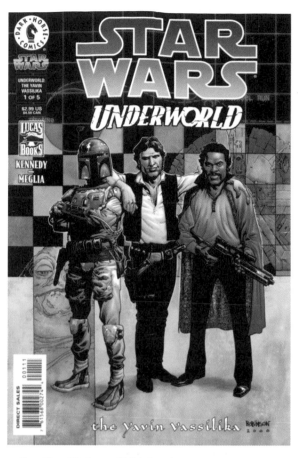

Star Wars Underworld #1 (Dark Horse Comics 2000)

rogue, featuring Chewbacca, Boba Fett, Greedo, Lando Calrissian, and Dengar. Written by Mike Kennedy, art by Carlos Meglia and covers by Andrew Robinson.

Comics

1 (of 5) The Yavin Vassilika	$3.00
1 photo cover	3.00
2 The race is on, on Kalkovak	3.00
2 photo cover	3.00
3 On the oceans of Mon Calamari	3.00
3 photo cover	3.00
4 Beyond the Outer Rim	3.00
4 photo cover	3.00
5 A mad free-for-all.	3.00
5 photo cover	3.00

Trade paperback

Star Wars: Underworld, series rep. 15.95

STAR WARS: UNION
Dark Horse Comics (1999–2000)

The wedding of Luke Skywalker and Mara Jade, written by Mike Stackpole, with art by Robert Teranishi and covers by Duncan Fegredo

Comics

1 The wedding plans.	$3.50
1a gold foil cover	10.00
2 the wedding approaches.	3.00
3 almost there	3.00
4 wedding day, finally.	3.00

Trade Paperback

Star Wars: Union, series reprint 12.95

STAR WARS: VADER'S QUEST
Dark Horse Comics (1999)

Darth Vader's quest to find out who destroyed the death star. Perhaps he can turn the Force-strong young pilot to the dark side. Written by Darko Macan, with art by Dave Gibbons and covers by Dave Gibbons and Angus McKie.

Comics

1 The quest begins	$3.00
2 Darth's network of spys.	3.00
3 Vader sets a trap	3.00
4 Face to face with Luke	3.00

Trade Paperback

Star Wars: Vader's Quest, series reprint 11.95

STAR WARS: X-WING ROGUE SQUADRON
Dark Horse Comics (July 1995 – 1998)

This continuing series stars Wedge Antilles, X-Wing pilot who survived both Death Star missions and now leads the Rogue Squadron. The series is divided into mostly 4-part story arcs, with separate titles, as noted. They are solicited in Diamond Previews as if they were separate 4-issue series, so I have included brief plot descriptions and credits for each arc.

Michael A. Stackpole is the principal writer, with different co-authors and artists on each story arc. He also wrote several of the paperback novelizations.

THE REBEL OPPOSITION

Wedge goes to rescue goes on a rescue mission to the planet Mrlsst, where he joins in an uneasy alliance with the Cilpari natives against the Empire. Tycho Celchu infiltrates the Imperial Forces, but ends up going into battle against his friends. Mike Baron co-authored the series, with art by Allen Nunis and Andy Mushynski and covers by Dave Dorman.

Comics

½ Wizard limited exclusive	$6.00
1 The Rebel Opposition, Pt.1	5.00
2 The Rebel Opposition, Pt.2	3.50
3 The Rebel Opposition, Pt.3	3.50
4 The Rebel Opposition, Pt.4	3.50

THE PHANTOM AFFAIR

Wedge negotiates for a Mrlssti cloaking device with Loka Hask, the pirate chieftain who killed Wedge's parents. Darko Macan co-authored the series, with art by Edvin Biukovic, John Nadeau, Jordi Ensign, and Gary Erskin, and covers by Mathieu Lauffray.

Comics

5 The Phantom Affair, Pt.1	3.50
6 The Phantom Affair, Pt.2	3.50
7 The Phantom Affair, Pt.3	3.50
8 The Phantom Affair, Pt.4	3.50

BATTLEGROUND TATOOINE

Wedge must find Jabba the Hutt's hidden weapons cache on Tatooine. Jan Strnad co-authored the series, with art by John Nadeau and Jordi Ensign, and covers by Mark Harrison.

Comics

9 Battleground Tatooine, Pt.1	3.50
10 Battleground Tatooine, Pt.2	3.50
11 Battleground Tatooine, Pt.3	3.50
12 Battleground Tatooine, Pt.4	3.50

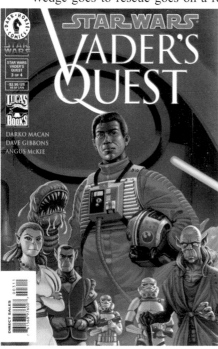  

Star Wars Vader's Quest #3 (Dark Horse 1999); X-Wing Rogue Squadron #11 and #35 (Dark Horse 1996–98)

THE WARRIOR PRINCESS

How did Plourr Ilo, a royal princess of Eiattu, end up in the Rogue Squadron and what will she do with her power now that she's been recalled to the throne? Scott Tolson co-authored, with art by John Nadeau and Jordi Ensign and covers by Mark Harrison.

Comics
13 The Warrior Princess, Pt.1 . . . . 3.50
14 The Warrior Princess, Pt.2 . . . . 3.50
15 The Warrior Princess, Pt.3 . . . . 3.50
16 The Warrior Princess, Pt.4 . . . . 3.50

REQUIEM FOR A ROGUE

Rogue Squadron must rescue a group of Bothan castaways on Malrev 4. It would be a lot easier if they hadn't turned out to be spies instead. Jan Strnad co-authored, with art by Gary Erskin and covers by Kevin Ryan.

Comics
17 Requiem for a Rogue, Pt.1 . . . . 3.50
18 Requiem for a Rogue, Pt.2 . . . . 3.50
19 Requiem for a Rogue, Pt.3 . . . . 3.50
20 Requiem for a Rogue, Pt.4 . . . . 3.50

IN THE EMPIRE'S SERVICE

Its Wedge versus Baron Fel, the Empire's greatest fighter ace. Art by John Nadeau and Jordi Ensign and covers by John Nadeau and Timothy Bradstreet.

Comics
21 In the Empire's Service, Pt.1 . . . . 3.50
22 In the Empire's Service, Pt.2 . . . . 3.50
23 In the Empire's Service, Pt.3 . . . . 3.50
24 In the Empire's Service, Pt.4 . . . . 3.50

MAKING OF BARON FEL

Baron Fel is captured by the Rebel Alliance. One-shot, with art by Steve Crespo and Chip Wallace and cover by Timothy Bradstreet.

Comic
25 The Making of Baron Fel 5.00

FAMILY TIES

Art by Jim Hall, Gary Martin, and Drew Johnson, with covers by John Nadeau.

Comics
26 Family Ties, Pt.1 . . . . 3.50
27 Family Ties, Pt.2 . . . . 3.50

MASQUERADE

Art by Drew Johnson and Gary Martin, with covers by John Nadeau.

Comics
28 Masquerade, Pt.1 . . . . 3.50
29 Masquerade, Pt.2 . . . . 3.50
30 Masquerade, Pt.3 . . . . 3.50
31 Masquerade, Pt.4 . . . . 3.50

MANDATORY RETIREMENT

Art by Steve Crespo and Chip Wallace with covers by John Nadeau.

Comics
32 Mandatory Retirement, Pt. 1 . . . . 3.50
33 Mandatory Retirement, Pt. 2 . . . . 3.50
34 Mandatory Retirement, Pt. 3 . . . . 3.50
35 Mandatory Retirement, Pt. 4 . . . . 3.50

Trade Paperbacks
The Phantom Affair, reprint #5–#8, ... 12.95
Battleground Tatooine, reprint #9–#12, ... 12.95
The Warrior Princess, reprint #13–#16 . . . . 12.95
Requiem for a Rogue, reprint #17–#20 . . . . 12.95
In The Empire's Service, reprint #21–#24 . . . . 12.95
Blood and Honor, reprint #25–#27 . . . . 12.95
Masquerade, reprint #28–#31 . . . . 12.95
Mandatory Retirement, reprint #32–#35 . . . . 12.95

COMIC STRIP REPRINTS

Star Wars, written by Archie Goodwin and drawn by Al Williamson, black and white comic strip reprints, hardcovers, three volumes, (Russ Cochran 1991) boxed set $150.00

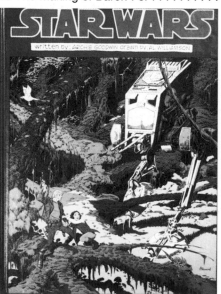  

Star Wars comic strip reprints, 3 volumes (Russ Cochran)

CRAFT AND ACTIVITY TOYS

CRAFT AND ACTIVITY TOYS

In toy industry terminology, Craft and Activity Toys are those that involve painting, coloring, baking, stamping, stickering, etc. MODEL KITS have their own section and coloring books are listed under BOOKS.

CRAFTS

There is some collector interest in the early Kenner items, but whether anybody really collects any other activity toys is questionable. Still, there are some interesting, but generally cartoonish, graphics to be found. Items licensed from Episode I followed the same pattern.

COLORING

Color N' Clean Machine, 50" roll of scenes to color, 4 crayons & wipe cloth (Craft Master 1980) $45.00
Pen and Poster Set, two 17" x 22" posters & 6 pens, (Craft Master 1980) 20.00
Pen and Poster Set, two 11½" x 18" posters & 8 crayons (Craft Master 1982) 20.00
Star Wars Mega-Fuzz Coloring Set, small (Craft House #51473, 1996) 3.00
Star Wars Mega-Fuzz Coloring Set, AT-AT picture (Craft House #51462, 1996) 4.00

Slave 1 Figure Maker (Kenner 1996)

Star Wars Mega-Fuzz Coloring Set, Darth Vader picture (Craft House #51463, 1996) 4.00
Star Wars, A New Hope 3-D Crayon by Number (Rose Art #01629) 4.00
Star Wars Poster Art coloring set (Craft Master 1978) . 20.00

DISPLAY MAKING

Star Wars Wonder World display tank, gel, ships, tweezers (Kenner 09955, 1995) $15.00

DRAWING

Star Wars Trilogy Light-Up Drawing Desk (Rose Art #01671) $10.00
Star Wars Trilogy Deluxe Light-Up Drawing Desk (Rose Art #1630) 15.00
R2-D2 Art Center, includes 17 pieces (Hasbro #63347, 1999) Episode I box. 20.00

FIGURE MAKING

Figure Makers (Kenner 1996) Red Power of the Force box
Millennium Falcon Figure Maker, including 2 cans of air hardening compound & 6 markers (#22161) . $15.00
Droids Kit Figure Maker, including 2 cans of air hardening compound & 6 markers (#22183) 15.00
Slave 1 Figure Maker, including 2 cans of air air hardening compound & 6 markers (#22175) . . 15.00

PAINTING

Playnts Poster Set, 15½" x 23½" posters and paints, 5 different posters, 6 paints, 2 brushes, (Kenner 1977) $35.00
Paint-By-Number, 8" x 10" scene & supplies (Craft Master 1980)
    Darth Vader 20.00
    Han & Leia 20.00
    Luke 20.00
    Yoda 20.00
Paint-By-Number, scenes from Empire 10" x 14" scene plus 12 paints, brush (Craft Master 1980)
    The Battle on Hoth. 25.00
    The Chase Through the Asteroids 25.00
Paint-By-Number, scenes from Jedi (Craft Master 1983)
    C-3PO/R2-D2 . . . . 20.00
    Jabba the Hutt 20.00
    Lando and Boushh. 20.00
    Sy Snootles 20.00
Star Wars Acrylic Paint By Number Set (Craft House #51451, 1996) 4.00
Darth Vader Dimensional Mask poster set 20.00
Battle on Hoth paint set 15.00
The Empire Strikes Back Glow-in-the-Dark paint sets
    Luke 10.00
    Leia & Han Solo. 10.00
    Darth Vader 10.00
    Yoda 10.00

Obi-Wan Kenobi 3-D Figure Painter (Hasbro 1999)

Star Wars Paint-By-number, 16" x 20" b&w image
plus paints (#1411, 1997)................... 12.00

Painting: Figurines
Figurine Painting Set, 5½" plastic figurine, 4 different paints & brush (Craft Master 1980)
    Leia.............................. 40.00
    Luke on Tauntaun 40.00
    Yoda 40.00
    Han Solo.............................. 40.00
Figurine Painting Set, plastic figures, paints, and
brush (Craft Master 1983)
    C-3PO/R2-D2 .... 35.00
    Admiral Ackbar 35.00

***Episode I* Painting: Figurines**
Star Wars Episode I 3-D Figure Painters (Hasbro
Asst. #63356, 1999)
    Darth Maul 3-D Figure Painter (#63357)......... 7.50
    Obi-Wan Kenobi 3-D Figure Painter (#63358)..... 7.50
    Qui-Gon Jinn 3-D Figure Painter (#63359) 7.50

Painting: Water Colors
Dip Dots *Star Wars* Painting Set, 8½" x 11" scenes,
water color (Kenner 1977) 40.00
Water Color Paint Set, 8" x 10" Ewok scene, 8
paints, brush (Fundimensions 1983)
    Ewok.............................. 20.00
    Ewok village 20.00

Ewok flyer 20.00
Star Wars Watercolor by Number (Craft House
#51472, 1996) 3.00

PLAY-DOH

Star Wars Action Play Set (Kenner 1977) $30.00
Star Wars: The Empire Strikes Back Play-Doh Yoda
Playset, with molds for four figures and plastic
X-Wing fighter and 16" x 10" playmat, 3 cans of
Play-Doh and trimmer (Kenner 1980).......... 25.00
Star Wars: The Empire Strikes Back Play-Doh Ice
Planet Playset, with molds for five figures and
plastic Snowspeeder and playmat, 3 cans of
Play-Doh, rolling pin and trimmer 15.00
Star Wars: Return of the Jedi Play-Doh Playset, with
molds for nine figures and plastic vehicle and
playmat depicting Jabba the Hutt, 3 cans of
Play-Doh and roller (Kenner 1983) 15.00
Ewoks Playset (Kenner 1985) 15.00

PRESTO MAGIX

Presto Magix (American Publishing)
Presto Magix, poster from *The Empire Strikes Back*
and six different transfer sheets (1980)
    Asteroid Storm........................ $5.00
    Beneath Cloud City 5.00
    Dagobah Bog Planet 5.00
    Deck of the Star Destroyer................. 5.00
    Ice Planet Hoth 5.00
    Rebel Base 5.00
Presto Magix, poster of *Return of the Jedi* scenes
and transfer sheets (1983)
    Death Star............................ 4.00
    Ewok village 4.00
    Jabba's throne room 4.00
    Sarlaccs Pit 4.00
Presto Magix, 16" x 24" scene & transfer sheets (1983)
    Jabba's throne room 25.00
    Endor 25.00
    Ewok village 25.00
Return of the Jedi Color Transfers (1983) 24" x 5"
background scene plus 30 full color transfers 15.00

RUG MAKING

Latch Hook Rug Kit, 6 different. (Lee Wards 1980)
    C-3PO/R2-D2 .... $40.00
    Chewbacca 40.00
    Darth Vader........................... 40.00
    R2-D2 .... 40.00
    Stormtrooper 40.00
    Yoda 40.00

Figurine Stampers Set (RoseArt 1996)

Space Battle Action Wall Scene, AuraGlow (Illuminations 1999)

STAMP COLLECTING

Stamp Collecting Kit, stamp album, 24 Star War
    seals, 35 stamps (H.E. Harris 1977) $25.00

STAMPING

Stamping (1980s)
1983 rubber stamps, several different. $7.50
Wicket 3-1 stamp set 5.00
Star Tours stamp set. 6.00

Stamping (RoseArt 1990s)
C-3PO Figurine Stamper (#01676, 1996) carded 4.00
Darth Vader Figurine Stamper (#01676,1996) carded . . 4.00
R2-D2 Figurine Stamper (#01676, 1996) carded. 4.00
Stormtrooper Figurine Stamper (#01676,1996) carded . 4.00
Yoda Figurine Stamper (#01676, 1996). 4.00
Star Wars Figurine Stampers Gift Set, including
    Darth Vader, Stormtrooper, Yoda, C-3PO and
    R2-D2 stamps (#01674, 1996) boxed 15.00

STICKING

Wicket the Ewok Transfer Set (Kenner 1985) $12.00
Star Wars Sticker Studio, over 300 stickers (Rose-
    Art#1648, 1997). 6.00
Star Wars Sticker Value Pack, 150 stickers (Rose-
    Art #1664, 1997) 4.00
Star Wars Push Pin assortment, 12 pins per set
    (RoseArt #1666, 1997) 4.00

***Episode I* large Collectible Decals** (Liquid Blue 1999)
Characters
    1. Queen Amidala 1.00
    2. Anakin Skywalker 1.00
    3. Jar Jar Binks 1.00
    4. Darth Maul. 1.00
    5. Oui-Gon Jinn 1.00
    6. Obi-Wan Kenobi. 1.00

Scenes
    1. Jedi vs. Sith 1.00
    2. Obi-Wan & Qui-Gon 1.00
    3. Anakin's Pod racer. 1.00
    4. Battle Droid on STAP 1.00

    5. Space Battle. 1.00
    6. Trade Federation Droid Fighter. 1.00
***Episode I* small Collector Stickers**, three stickers
    on hanging card (Sandylion 1999)
    Series I: Space Battle 0.50
    Series II: Ground Battle. 0.50
    Series III: Podrace 0.50
    Series IV: Jedi 0.50
    Series V: Villains 0.50
    Series VI: Droids. 0.50

"AuraGlow" Glow-in-the-Dark Action Wall Scenes
Bagged (Illuminations 1999)
Jedi vs. Sith (#70040) 6.00
Droids (#70041). 6.00
Land Battle (#70042) 6.00
Space Battle (#70043) 6.00
Boxes (Illuminations 1999)
Battle Zone (#70045) 13.00
Heroes, Villains & Droids (#70046). 13.00
Characters (#70050) 20.00
Space Battle (#70051) 20.00
Hanger Cards (Illuminations 1999)
Anakin Skywalker face (#70000) 5.00
Darth Maul face (#70001) 5.00
Jedi face (#70003). 5.00
Queen Amidala face (#70004) 5.00
Battle Droids face (#70005) 5.00
Droids (#70009). 5.00
Trade Federation Invasion (#70010) 5.00
Gungan Adventure (#70011) 5.00
Jedi vs. Sith (#70012) 5.00
Podrace (#70013) 5.00
Space Battle (#70014) 5.00
Darth Maul (#70020) 5.00
Jar Jar Binks (#70021). 5.00

*Star Wars Episode I sticker (Sandylion 1999) and
Star Wars Episode I sticker (Liquid Blue 1999)*

Star Wars Episode I *Jumbo Stick-Ups (Priss Prints 1999)*

Obi-Wan Kenobi (#70022) 5.00
C-3PO (#70023) 5.00
Large Blister Packs (Illuminations 1999)
Heroes (#70015) 10.00
Queen Amidala (#70016) 10.00

Sticking: Static (Priss Prints 1999)
Star Wars Episode I Jumbo Stick-Ups (#49042) 20.00

Sticking: Magnetic
Star Wars Mix 'N' Match Adventure Playset, magnetic pieces and background (ATA-Boy Inc.) 20.00

SUNCATCHERS

Suncatchers (Lee Wards 1980) *Empire Strikes Back* cards
C-3PO $12.00
Darth Vader head. 12.00
Darth Vader figure 12.00
IG-88 . . . . 12.00
Luke Skywalker 12.00
Luke Skywalker and Tauntaun 12.00
Millennium Falcon 12.00
Princess Leia. 12.00
Snowspeeders. 12.00
Stormtrooper 12.00
X-Wing Fighter. 12.00
Yoda and R2-D2 . . . . 12.00

Suncatchers Makit & Bakit "Stained Glass" (Fun-dimensions
1983) *Return of the Jedi* header cards
R2-D2 . . . . 10.00
Darth Vader 10.00
Gamorrean Guard 10.00
Jabba and Salacious Crumb 10.00

OTHER ACTIVITIES

While skating, kite flying and yo-yoing are not really
like the artistic activities listed previously, these toys have to
be listed somewhere.

BIKING

Riding Speeder Bike (Kenner 1983) $1,000.00
Queen Amidala Bike, 16" Girls (Dynacraft #51794,
1999). 75.00
Darth Maul Bike (Dynacraft #51311, 1999) 80.00
Jar Jar Bike, 12" (Dynacraft #52163, 1999) 75.00

BOPING

Inflatable Bop Bags (Kenner 1977) boxed
Chewbacca, 50" tall (#63050). $60.00
Darth Vader, 50" tall 60.00
Jawa, 36" tall 70.00
Artoo-Detoo, 36" tall. 45.00

KITE FLYING

Darth Vader Parasail Kite (SpectraStar 1997) $15.00

SKATING

Ice Skates (Brookfield Athletic Shoe 1983) Darth
Vader and Imperial Guard $75.00
Wicket 75.00
Darth and Imperial Guard Roller Skates (Brookfield
Athletic Shoe 1983) 75.00
Wicket Roller Skates (Brookfield Athletic Shoe 1983) . 75.00
Star Wars Episode I R2-D2 In-Line Youth Adjust-
able Skates (Seneca Sports #72006) 20.00

Skate Boarding
Star Wars Episode I 8" x 31" Double Sided Decal
Darth Maul & Obi Wan Kenobi skateboard. 20.00
Star Wars Episode I R2-D2 & C-3PO Skateboard. 10.00

Skating & Biking Helmets & Gear
Star Wars Episode I Queen Amidala Multi-Sport
Helmet, Ages 7-14 (Dynacraft #89366) 15.00
Star Wars Episode I Darth Maul Multi-Sport Hel-
met, Ages 7-14 (Dynacraft #89362) 15.00
Star Wars Episode I Darth Maul Glove, Knee and
Elbow Pad set (Dynacraft #89363) 20.00
Queen Amidala Glove, Knee and Elbow Pad Set
(Dynacraft #89370, 1999. . . . . 15.00
Episode I Backpack Protective Combo Set. 10.00

YO-YOING

Star Wars 3D Sculpted Yo Yo (SpectraStar 1995)
Darth Vader (#1624) $5.00
Stormtrooper (#1623). 5.00
Star Wars Episode I Destroyer Droid Yo-Yo
(Tiger Electronics #88-201, 1999) 7.50

Episode I *Destroyer Droid Yo-Yo (Tiger Electronics 1999)*

DIE-CAST FIGURES AND SHIPS

Like ceramics, die-cast figures and ships are their own collecting category. Unlike ceramics, die-cast spaceships are figural. However, they are generally not scaled to fit the characters in the same line nor each other. Typically a die-cast Death Star, Star Destroyer and X-Wing are all about the same size. Die-cast figures and ships which were designed for gaming are listed under "Games." See also "Micro" for Kenner's small die-cast figures designed for plastic playsets.

DIE-CAST SHIPS
Kenner (1978–80)

Kenner issued die-cast ships on header cards and in open boxes. The latter are much more valuable. Several of the boxed ships also came with backgrounds. These say "Special Offer" prominently in red in a yellow oval on the left and right sides of the package.

Ships (Carded)
Darth Vader TIE Fighter (#39160) (removable
    figure of Darth Vader). $50.00
    Loose 25.00
    Variation, small wings, scarce 500.00
Imperial TIE Fighter (#38590) 45.00
    Loose 15.00
Land Speeder (#38570) (Luke and C-3PO in cockpit) . 90.00
    Loose 35.00

TIE Bomber die-cast ship (Kenner 1980)

Slave I die-cast ship (Kenner 1980)

Rebel Armored Snowspeeder (#39680). 125.00
    Loose 45.00
Slave I (#39670) 90.00
    Loose 35.00
Twin-Pod Cloud Car (#39660) 95.00
    Loose 35.00
X-Wing Fighter (#38680) wings and cockpit open 75.00
    Loose 25.00

Ships (Boxed)
Millennium Falcon (#39210) with swiveling cannon
    and antennae dish 150.00
    Loose 50.00
    Reissue, with background 500.00
Imperial Cruiser (#39230) 200.00
    Loose 65.00
    Reissue, with background 500.00
Y-Wing Fighter (#39220) 175.00
    Loose 50.00
    Reissue, with background 500.00
TIE Bomber (#39260) test market figure, scarce 800.00
    Loose 275.00
Metal Figurines (Heritage 1977)

Bantha Set, Bantha with 2 Sand people 45.00
C-3PO 15.00
Chewbacca 20.00
Darth Vader 20.00
Han Solo 15.00
Jawa 15.00
Luke Skywalker. 20.00
Obi-Wan Kenobi 20.00
Leia 20.00
R2-D2 . . . . 20.00
Sand Person, different from Bantha set 15.00
Snitch 15.00
Storm Trooper 20.00

Action Masters Collector 6-Pack (Kenner 1994)

ACTION MASTERS
Kenner (1994–96)

Kenner's Action Masters figures were issued on a header card with an exclusive trading card. A Predator, two Terminators, four Aliens and several DC Superheroes were also available in the Action Masters series. There was a gold C-3PO available as a free mail-in for six proof of purchase points. I mailed-in but I never received the figure, which is one reason you won't find a picture of it here.

Die-Cast Figures
Darth Vader Action Masters figure, with card
  (#62671, 1994) $10.00
Luke Skywalker Action Masters figure, with card
  (#62672, 1994) 10.00
C-3PO Action Masters figure, gold, with card
  (#62673, 1994) 10.00
R2-D2 Action Masters figure, with card (#62674, 1994). 10.00
Stormtrooper Action Masters figure, with card
  (#62675, 1994) 10.00
Chewbacca Action Masters figure, with card (1994) . . 10.00
Snowtrooper Action Masters figure, with card (1994). . 10.00
Special Edition Action Masters "Gold" C-3PO
  mail-in figure 25.00
Star Wars Action Masters Collectors Set (4 Pack):
  C-3PO, Princess Leia Organa, R2-D2, and
  Obi-Wan Kenobi, with four trading cards
  (#62634, 1994) 30.00
Star Wars Action Masters Collectors Set (6 Pack):
  Han Solo, Chewbacca, Stormtrooper, Boba

Luke Skywalker Action Masters figure (Kenner 1994)

  Fett, Darth Vader, and Luke Skywalker, with
  six trading cards (#62640, 1994) 45.00
Star Wars The Power of the Force 6 Pack set: Han
  Solo, Chewbacca, Stormtrooper, Boba Fett,
  Darth Vader, and Luke Skywalker, with six
  trading cards (#69782, 1995) 45.00

MICRO MACHINE DIE-CAST
Galoob (1996–98)

The original packaging for these figures was an oval-shaped header card. The packaging was changed in 1997 to a rectangular card with stripes, similar in design to the action fleet packages (see MicroMachines). The Jawa Sandcrawler was discontinued, however, sufficient stock remained available and in early 1998 I was able to purchase a Sandcrawler at a local Toys "R" Us store for $1.98. Die-cast figures have interested collectors over the years, and these figures, particularly on the original header cards, might turn out to be a good buy at current prices.

First Batch (Asst. #66260, 1996)
X-Wing Starfighter (#66261) $6.00
  Reissue on striped card 5.00
Millennium Falcon (#66262) 6.00
  Reissue on striped card 5.00
Imperial Star Destroyer (#66263) 6.00
  Reissue on striped card 5.00
TIE Fighter (#66264). 6.00
  Reissue on striped card 5.00
Y-Wing Starfighter (#66265) 6.00
  Reissue on striped card 5.00

Trade Federation Droid Fighter (Galoob 1999)

Pod Racer Pack III (Galoob 1999)

Jawa Sandcrawler (#66266) original card only. 9.00
Second Batch (Asst. #66260, 1997)
Death Star 6.00
Executor with Star Destroyer. 6.00
Landspeeder 6.00
Millennium Falcon. 6.00
Slave I 6.00
Snowspeeder 6.00
TIE Bomber 6.00
Y-Wing Starfighter. 6.00
　　　Reissues, on striped card, each. 5.00

Episode I **Die-cast Vehicles** (Galoob Asst. #66520, 1999)
Trade Federation Droid Starfighter with Opening
　　　Wings (#66522). 5.00
Giant Speeder with "Pivoting Blaster Cannons" (#66523) 5.00
Trade Federation Battleship with Retractible
　　　Landing Gear (#66524) 5.00
Royal Starship (#66521) 6.00
Republic Cruiser with "Glowing Engines" (#66526) 5.00
Trade Federation Tanx with "Pivoting Blaster Cannon"
　　　(#66527) 5.00
Sebulba's Pod racer with Hidden "Flame Throwers"
　　　(#66528) 5.00

Episode I **Pod Racers** (Galoob 1999)
Pod Racer Pack I Boles Roor and Neva Kee (#66531) . 5.00
Pod Racer Pack II Dud Bold and Mars Guo (#66532) . . 5.00
Pod Racer Pack III Anakin Skywalker and Ratts
　　　Tyerell (#66533). 5.00
Pod Racer Pack IV Sebulba and Clegg Holdfast(#66534) 5.00

PEWTER FIGURES
Rawcliffe (1993–95)

Star Wars Characters
Admiral Ackbar (#RF969) $15.60
C-3PO 15.60
Chewbacca (#RF963). 22.00
Lando Calrissian 15.60
Princess Leia (#RF958) 14.00
Luke Skywalker (#RF959). 14.00
Obi-Wan Kenobi (#RF961) 22.00

R2-D2 (#RF957) 14.00
Han Solo (#RF960). 14.00
Ewok-Wicket 10.00
Yoda (#RF955) 10.00

Characters, Darkside
Bib Fortuna (#RF970) 15.60
Boba Fett (#RF966) 15.60
Emperor Palpatine (#RF968). 15.60
Gamorrean Guard (#RF971) 15.60
Stormtrooper (#RF965). 15.60
Darth Vader (#RF962). 24.00

PEWTER VEHICLES
Rawcliffe (1993–95)

Star Wars Vehicles
A-Wing (#RF953) $32.00
B-Wing (#RF954) 32.00
Millennium Falcon 30.00
Outrider 36.00
Snow Speeder (#RF972) 30.00
X-Wing, 3" tall (#RF975) 36.00
Y-Wing (#RF973) 36.00

Vehicles Darkside
Sail Barge 34.00
Star Destroyer (#RF964). 60.00
Slave I 28.00
TIE Fighter (#RF974) 32.00
Shuttle *Tydirium* (#RF967) 36.00
TIE Bomber 36.00

Vehicles Special Limited Edition, with base
Death Star 160.00
Millennium Falcon (#RF951, 1993) 140.00
TIE Interceptor 75.00
Vader's Custom TIE Fighter (#RF950, 1993) 108.00
X-Wing (#RF952, 1993) 76.00

DOLLS

Between 1979 and 1980, Kenner produced a dozen Large Size Action Figures, (i.e. dolls) in window boxes with a flap. All the figures were made to the same 12" scale, but R2-D2 and the Jawa were small characters and so their dolls are about 8" tall, while Chewbacca, Darth Vader and IG-88 were about 15" tall. These are highly prized collectibles, both in and out of box (loose). The Radio Control R2-D2, listed under ELECTRONICS, was made to the same scale as the listed figures.

DOLLS (CLASSIC)
Kenner (1979–80)

Dolls, *Star Wars* logo box (1979)
Princess Leia Organa (#38070) 11½" tall $275.00
    Loose, in Alderaanian cape, royal belt, long
        socks and shoes with comb, brush and
        booklet. 125.00
Luke Skywalker (#38080) 11½" tall 425.00
    Loose, in Tattooine desert costume with light
        saber, grappling hook, boots and utility belt . . 200.00

R2-D2 doll, boxed (Kenner 1979)

Chewbacca (#38600) 15" tall 200.00
    Loose, with ammunition belt with removable
        cartridges and crossbow laser rifle 90.00
Darth Vader (#38610) 15" tall 250.00
    Loose, with lightsaber and removable cloth
        cape 100.00
See-Threepio (C-3PO) (#38620) 12" tall 150.00

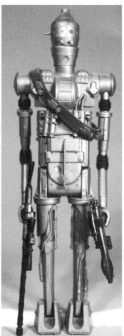

Princess Leia, Luke Skywalker, IG-88, R2-D2, and C-3PO dolls, loose (Kenner 1979–80)

Stormtrooper doll, in box (Kenner 1979)

Loose, issued without equipment 50.00
Artoo-Detoo (R2-D?) (#38630) 7½" tall 275.00
   Loose, with removable Death Star Plans 50.00
Han Solo (#39170) 11¾" tall 650.00
   Loose, with shirts, pants, vest, boots, laser
     pistol, holster and belt, and Rebel Alliance
     Medal of Honor 275.00
Stormtrooper (#39180) 12" tall 325.00
   Loose, with laser rifle 130.00
Ben (Obi-Wan) Kenobi (#39340) 12" tall 425.00
   Loose, in hooded cloak and boots, with

     lightsaber 175.00
Jawa (#39350) 8" tall 300.00
   Loose, with laser rifle, ammunition belt and
     hooded cloak 75.00
Boba Fett (#39140) 13" tall 1,000.00
   In *The Empire Strikes Back* box 1,100.00
   Loose, with cape, Wookiee scalps, utility belts,
     laser pistol, and rocket backpack 200.00

Large Figure, *The Empire Strikes Back* logo (1980)
IG-88 (Bounty Hunter) (#39960) 15" tall 800.00
   Loose, with rifle, pistol, and cartridge belt with
     four cartridges 350.00

STAR WARS: COLLECTOR SERIES
Kenner (1996–98)

Kenner began issuing Collector Series 12" dolls in 1996. The first series of dolls had a dark blue background card inside the package. In December, light blue cards appeared. Obi-Wan Kenobi was scarce and almost impossible to find in stores from the very first. He was just as difficult to locate later with the light blue backing card. Chewbacca is pictured on the back of the boxes, but he was not included in the initial series. He was scheduled for the second series, but again didn't appear and he did not actually arrive until the fourth series. Instead of Chewbacca, the second series had two Tusken Raiders, with different weapons—one with a blaster and one with a more authentic Gaderffii Stick. Lando Calrissian from this batch did not sell out as quickly as the other dolls and could still be found in many stores well into 1998. There is still at least one for sale at a local Kay-Bee store—almost six years after it first appeared.

12" Dolls (Aug. 1996) in window box with flap cover
Luke Skywalker (#27724)
   On original dark blue package card, binoculars

First Collector Series Dolls: Darth Vader, out of box; Han Solo, in box, flap open; and Luke Skywalker, reissue, out of box (Kenner 1996)

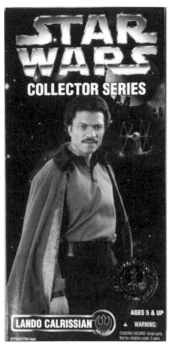

Second Series Dolls: Luke Skywalker, Bespin Fatigues, flap open and Lando Calrissian box (Kenner 1997)

on belt, black lightsaber handle	$60.00
Reissue, binoculars on card	35.00
Reissue, on light blue package card	25.00
Reissue, black and silver lightsaber handle	20.00
Loose, in shirt, pants, boots and utility belt, with lightsaber, blaster and electro binoculars on belt	12.50
Loose figure with loose binoculars	9.00

Han Solo (#27725)

On original dark blue package card	35.00
Reissue, on light blue package card, painted or unpainted belt pouch	20.00
Loose, in shirt, vest, pants, holster and boots with blaster pistol and blaster rifle	12.50

Darth Vader (#27726)

On original dark blue package card, black lightsaber handle	30.00
Reissue, on light blue package card, black lightsaber handle	25.00
Reissue, black and silver lightsaber handle	20.00
Loose, black helmet, outfit, cape, boots, and gloves, with red lightsaber, either handle	10.00

Obi-Wan Kenobi (#27719)

On original dark blue package card, black lightsaber handle and silver belt buckle	60.00
Reissue, on light blue package card, black or black and silver lightsaber handle and silver buckle	45.00
Reissue, gold buckle	55.00
Loose, in hooded robe, shirt, pants, inner robe and boots, with lightsaber, all variations	25.00

Second Batch (Asst. #27754, Jan. 1997)

Lando Calrissian (#27755) 12.00
    Loose, with blaster, cape, shirt, pants, boots
      and comlink communicator 6.00
Luke Skywalker in Bespin Fatigues (#27757) 25.00
    Loose, in Bespin uniform and boots with utility
      belt, blaster and lightsaber 10.00

Tusken Raider (with Rifle) (#27758, March 1997)	35.00
Loose, in robe, wrappings, bandolier, gloves, and boots, with blaster and macrobinoculars	15.00
Tusken Raider (with Gaderffii Stick) (#27758, March 1997)	40.00
Loose, in robe, wrappings, bandolier, gloves, and boots, with Gaderffii Stick and macrobinoculars	15.00

Third Batch (Asst. #27690, 1996 i.e. July 1997)

Stormtrooper (#27689)	40.00
Loose, with Imperial blaster and ammo belt	12.00
Princess Leia (#27691)	45.00
Variation: Packed with hood up	50.00
Loose, in royal white hooded tunic, boots, and belt, with blaster	15.00
Luke Skywalker in X-Wing Gear (#27692)	25.00
Loose, in orange flight suit and boots, with helmet and visor, harness, lightsaber, and galaxy map	12.00
Boba Fett (#27693)	75.00
Loose, in helmet, cape, scalped Wookiee braids, battle-scarred Madalorian armor and boots, with BlasTech EE-3 blaster rifle, wrist lasers and miniature flame projector, and jet pack	25.00

Chewbacca did not appear until the fall 1997, in the fourth batch. The package back depicts the three figures in the earlier assortment (plus Chewbacca) and is unlike the other packages in this assortment, which picture six figures. When Chewbacca did arrive, he was very short-packed in the assortment and only 12" tall, which is not to scale.

Fourth Batch (Asst. #27862, Sept. 1997)

TIE Fighter Pilot (#27864)	35.00
Loose, with blaster, chest respirator and wrist comlink	12.00
C-3PO (#27865)	35.00
Loose, without accessories, as issued	10.00
Admiral Ackbar (#27866)	40.00

Third Series Dolls: Boba Fett out of box, and Princess Leia, box (Kenner 1997)

Collector Series Dolls: Chewbacca (Fourth); Grand Moff Tarkin (Sixth); Chewbacca in Chains (Eighth); and Ponda Baba (Tenth)
(Kenner 1997–98 and Hasbro 1999)

Loose, in jumpsuit, belt and rank badge, no
    weapon 12.00
Chewbacca (#27756) 80.00
    Loose, with bowcaster, pouch and shoulder
    strap packed with ammo.................. 30.00
Chewbacca (#27756) 1996 box 500.00

In 1998, the packaging no longer included a front box flap. Gone, too, is the character bio information. However, the quality of the figures has impressed collectors. This is as it should be. Just about the only reason to pay $25.00 or more for a Collector Series doll, is to get a well made, well sculpted, and highly detailed figure.

The three smaller figures seem to have hung around on store shelves for a little longer than the taller ones. R2-D2 was the easiest to find of the three, Yoda was the hardest.

Fifth Batch, *Star Wars* **Trilogy** (Asst. #27741, Feb. 1998)
    green background window box, no flap
R2-D2, 6" (#27742) with retractable leg........... 15.00
    Loose, without accessories 7.50
Yoda, 6" (#27743)............................. 45.00
    Loose, with Gimmer stick.................. 12.50
Jawa, 6" (#27744) with light-up eyes............. 15.00
    Loose, with gun, cartridge and harness 7.50

Sixth Batch, *A New Hope* (Asst. #27903, April
    1998) in green background window box, no flap
Greedo (#27904) 25.00
    Loose, in jumpsuit, vest and boots with blaster... 12.00
Grand Moff Tarkin with "Interrogation Droid includ-
    ed" (#27905) 30.00
    Loose, with Interrogation Droid, jacket, belt,
    pants, and boots 15.00
Sandtrooper with Imperial Droid (#27906).......... 20.00
    Loose, in Sandtrooper armor with white
    shoulder pauldron, backpack, and blaster rifle .. 9.00
Luke Skywalker in Ceremonial Gear, with Ceremon-
    ial Medal (#27907)......................... 20.00
    Loose, in shirt, pants, jacket and boots, with

lightsaber, blaster and holster.............. 9.00

Seventh Batch, *The Empire Strikes Back* (Asst. #27915,
    April 1998) in green background window box, no flap
Han Solo in Hoth Gear with "Firing Rebel Blaster
    included" (#27916)......................... 20.00
    Loose, with blaster and ammo, pistol, holster,
    helmet and goggles, Hoth jacket, pants,
    and boots.............................. 10.00
Luke Skywalker in Hoth Gear with "Firing Rebel
    Blaster included" (#27917) 20.00
    Loose, with blaster and ammo, pistol, holster,
    helmet and goggles, Hoth jacket, pants,
    and boots.............................. 10.00
AT-AT Driver with "Firing Imperial Blaster included"
    (#27918) 20.00
    Loose, with blaster and ammo, helmet,
    breathing apparatus, armored outfit, and
    boots 10.00
Snowtrooper with "Firing Imperial Blaster included"
    (#27919) 20.00
    Variation: Blue plate, center of chest 150.00
    Loose, with blaster and ammo, helmet, belt,
    armored outfit and boots 10.00
    Loose, blue plate variation 50.00

Eighth Batch, *Return of the Jedi* (Asst. #28025, Nov. 1998)
Barquin D'an (#28026) 20.00
    Loose, with all parts...................... 12.00
Chewbacca in Chains (#28027) 50.00
    Loose, with all parts...................... 20.00
Emperor Palpatine (#28029) 15.00
    Loose, with all parts...................... 9.00
Luke Skywalker in Jedi Gear (#28028) 20.00
    Loose, with all parts...................... 10.00

In 1999, Collector Series Dolls had to compete *Episode I* figures for shelf space and collector dollars. For the first time there were significant numbers available at discount. Emperor Palpatine from the eighth series and especially Chewbacca "over 13" tall" from the tenth series hung around stores much too long. Earlier versions of Chewbacca had something resembling hair or fur but this one is all plastic. There is still a stack of 25 or so at several local Toys "R" Us stores—where it's still priced at original retail.

Ninth Batch, Power of the Force (Asst. #57111, 1999)
Luke Skywalker with "Dianoga Tentacle," in Storm-
    trooper Gear (#57113) 25.00
    Loose, with all parts 12.00
Obi-Wan Kenobi with "Glow-in-the-dark Light-
    saber," Training Droid and Blast Shield Helmet
    (#57112) 25.00
    Loose, with all parts 12.00
Ponda Baba with "Removable Arm," and "Blaster"
    (#57114) 25.00
    Loose, with all parts 12.00

Tenth Batch, Power of the Force (Asst. #57135), 1999)
Chewbacca, "over 13" tall" (#53136) 12.00
    Loose, with all parts 7.00
Han Solo with "Magnetic Detonators" (#57138) 50.00
    Loose, with all parts 25.00
Princess Leia (Jabba's Prisoner) with "Chain" (#57137) 20.00
    Loose, with all parts 10.00

EPISODE I DOLLS

The first batch of *Episode I* dolls was available at one second after midnight, on May 3, 1999, along with all the other figures. I looked for action figures first, then dolls, and all the Darth Maul dolls were gone. I never saw one on the shelf, then or later. The other waves showed up in later months. Most sold well, with the exception of Watto, which can still be found easily at discount. The fifth wave figures are quite scarce at the moment, although there may be a warehouse full somewhere.

12" Dolls (Asst. #57129, Hasbro 1999)
Jar Jar Binks (#57130) $25.00
    Loose, with vest, shirt and pants 10.00
Qui-Gon Jinn with "Lightsaber" (#57131)
    "Trade Fedration" error box 30.00

"Trade Federation" corrected 25.00
    Loose, with lightsaber, boots, cloak, belt and outfit 12.00
Darth Maul with "Lightsaber" (#57132) 35.00
    Loose, with lightsaber 15.00

Second Wave (Asst. #26227) 1999
Anakin Skywalker, "Fully Posable," 6" (#26229) 20.00
    Loose, with all parts 7.00
Pit Droids, "Fully Posable," 6" (#26228) 20.00
    Loose, with all parts 7.00
R2-A6, "Metalized Dome," 6" (#26230) 20.00
    Loose, with all parts 7.00

Third Wave (Asst. #26231) 1999
Obi-Wan Kenobi with "Lightsaber" (#26232) 25.00
    Loose, with Lightsaber with removeable blade,
      boots, belt, cloak, and outfit. 12.00
Watto with "Datapad" (#26233) 15.00
    Loose, with Datapad 5.00
Battle Droid with "Blaster Rifle" (#26234) 20.00
    Loose, with Trade Federation blaster rifle 10.00

Fourth Wave (Asst. #26277) 1999
Battle Droid Commander with "Electrobinoculars"
    (#26284) 20.00
    Loose, with Electrobinoculars, trade federation
      weapon, and communications antenna 10.00
Mace Windu with "Lightsaber" (#26280) 35.00
    Loose, with Lightsaber with removeable blade,
      boots, belt, cloak, and outfit. 20.00
Qui-Gon Jinn with "Tatooine Poncho" (#26465) 20.00
    Loose, with Lightsaber with removeable blade,
      poncho, binoculars, communicator, boots,
      and outfit. 10.00

Fifth Wave (Asst. #) 2000
Anakin Skywalker with Theed Hangar Droid (#28283) . 50.00
    Loose, with all parts 25.00
Boss Nass (#29279) 45.00
    Loose, with all parts 20.00
Sebulba, with Chubas (#28454) 40.00
    Loose, with all parts 20.00

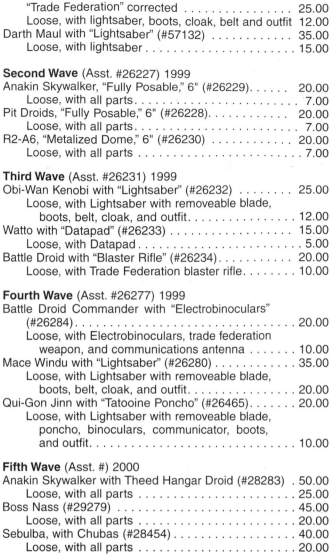

Episode I dolls: Jar Jar Binks; Obi-Wan Kenobi; and Mace Windu; and Power of the Jedi doll: Bossk (Hasbro 1999–2001)

POWER OF THE JEDI
Hasbro (2001–02)

Episode II, Attack of the Clones figures and dolls will out by the time you read this. The Power of the Jedi line of figures and dolls covers the classic movies and, no doubt, *Episode I* eventually. Hasbro has put out 300+ action figures, but only 100+ dolls, so it should have little trouble finding new doll batches in the future. On the other hand, collectors may continue to have trouble finding them as distribution has been uneven, at best.

12" Dolls (Asst. #26470)
Bossk with "Blaster Rifle" (#26472) $40.00
    Loose, with all parts 15.00
IG-88 with "Rifle and Imperial Blaster" (#26471) 40.00
    Loose, with Rifle, Imperial Blaster, and bandoleer . 15.00
4-Lom with "Concussion Rifle" (#26473) 40.00
    Loose, with all parts 15.00

Second Batch (Asst. #32406)
Han Solo in Stormtrooper Disguise (#32489) 30.00
    Loose, with removeable helmet, pole, re-
    moveable blaster, and holster 12.00
Death Star Trooper with "Imperial Blaster" (#32490) . . . 30.00
    Loose, with helmet, officers cap, removeable
    blaster, and holster. 12.00
Death Star Droid with "Mouse Droid" (#32491) 30.00
    Loose, with mouse droid 12.00

ELECTRONIC DOLLS

New Power of the Force Electronic Dolls
Electronic Boba Fett, 14" (#57100) Kaybee Exclusive . $50.00
Darth Vader 14" Electronic Figure, with removable
    helmet that reveals Anakin Skywalker face,
    says four phrases (Kenner #27729, 1998) 35.00
Electronic Power F/X Obi-Wan Kenobi vs. Darth
    Vader with eight authentic recordings for each
    figure, battery powered, J.C. Penney stores,
    Collector Series (#27661, Aug. 1997) 40.00
Electronic Emperor Palpatine and Royal Guard,
    (#) Target stores 50.00
Electronic C-3PO & R2-D2 (#57108, 1998) Toys
    "R" Us stores 50.00
Interactive Yoda with lightsaber, in pentagonal win-
    dow box (Hasbro/Tiger #01248, 2001) 30.00

***Episode I* Electronic Talking Dolls** (Asst. #84075)
Electronic Talking Jar Jar Binks with "Energy Ball
    Throwing Action" (#84166) [562234.0100] 25.00
Electronic Talking Darth Maul with "Lightsaber Com-
    bat Action" (#84162) [562232.0000] 25.00
Electronic Talking Qui-Gon Jinn with "Lightsaber
    Combat Action" (#84163) 25.00
Electronic Talking C-3PO with "Lights, Sounds and
    Removable Parts" (#84197) [565806.0000]. 30.00
Electronic TC-14 doll (#26293) Kay-Bee special 25.00

COLLECTOR SERIES — EXCLUSIVES

While all the collectors were looking for the first Chewbacca, some of them were lucky enough to find one or more of the 1997 store exclusives. Many of these had store shelf-lives of less than one day. The first to appear was the Han and Luke Stormtrooper two-pack at Kay-Bee stores. Target stores got an exclusive Luke Skywalker and Wampa,

Luke Skywalker special 100th figure (Hasbro 2001)

while Toys "R" Us had Han Solo mounted on a Tauntaun. The demand for each figure is different, depending on which stores are nearby. In any given area, exclusive figures from out-of-town stores are usually more in demand, because few, if any, local collectors have one.

Sometimes Hasbro has sent additional shipments of some of the exclusive dolls and re-issued others as part of its regular Collector Series. The dolls in the additional shipments are identical to the originals and the re-issues differ only slightly from the originals. Also, some unsold specials from other stores have been known to show up at Kay-Bee stores the next year. Many collectors are annoyed that Hasbro even considered reissuing the figures that they were lucky enough to acquire, but feel that it's not such a bad idea for Hasbro to produce a few more of the ones they haven't found yet.

12" Special or Exclusive Dolls
Cantina Band (Aug. 1997) in window box with flap
    cover, WalMart stores
    Doikk Na'ts, with Fizzz (#27953) $45.00
    Figrin D'an with Kloo Horn 50.00
    Ickabel with Fanfar 45.00
    Nalan with Bandfill 45.00
    Tech with Ommni Box 45.00
    Tedn with Fanfar 45.00
Greedo (#27976, Aug. 1997) in window box with
    flap cover, J.C. Penney stores 70.00
    Loose 35.00
Sandtrooper (#27928, Aug. 1997) in window box
    with flap cover, Diamond Distribution direct market 60.00
    Loose, with concussion-grenade launcher,
    environmental survival pack and orange
    shoulder pauldron 25.00
AT-AT Driver (#27977, Oct. 1997) in window box
    with flap cover, Service Merchandise stores 60.00
    Loose, with helmet, chest respirator, boots,
    comlink, and Imperial blaster 25.00
R2-D2 with "Detachable Utility Arms" (#27801,

Princess Leia and R2-D2 as Jabba's Prisoners
FAO Schwarz special (Kenner 1998)

1998) WalMart stores 15.00
R5-D4 (#27802, 1998) WalMart stores 15.00
Wicket the Ewok (#27800, 1998) Walmart stores 15.00
Princess Leia in Hoth Gear, with "Firing Rebel Blas-
ter" (#57110, 1998) in window box, Service
Merchandise stores. 30.00
Luke Skywalker (100th Figure) (#32437) 75.00
Loose, with Tatooine Outfit, Poncho, X-Wing
Fighter Uniform, Long Rifle, Imperial Blaster
Rifle with 2 missiles, Blaster, Grenade,
Medal, Lightsaber, Utility Belt, Stormtrooper
Belt, Blastshield Helmet, X-Wing Helmet
with retractable goggles, Floppy Hat, Gog-
gles, Rappel line and Hook, Seeker Ball with
stand, Binoculars, Map of Known Galaxy,
and Checklist of 100 figures 30.00

Special or Exclusive Doll Multi-Packs
Han Solo & Luke Skywalker in Stormtrooper Gear
(KB Limited Edition of 20,000) (#27867, July
1997) in window box with flap cover 175.00
Loose, with helmets, each 15.00
Grand Moff Tarkin & Imperial Gunner with Interrog-
ator Droid (#27923, Aug. 1997) in window box
with flap cover, FAO Schwarz stores. 150.00
Loose, each. 25.00
Jedi Luke Skywalker & Bib Fortuna (#27924, Nov.
1997) in window box with flap cover, FAO
Schwarz stores 140.00
Loose, each. 35.00
Han Solo as Prisoner and Carbonite Block with
Frozen Han Solo (#30018, 1998) Target stores. . . 50.00
Luke Skywalker in Tatooine Gear, Princess Leia in

Boushh Disguise and Han Solo in Bespin Gear
(#57101, 1998) Kay-Bee stores 100.00
Luke Skywalker in Hoth Gear, Han Solo in Hoth
Gear, Snowtrooper, and AT-AT Driver (#57109,
1998) 4-pack in window box, JC Penney stores . . 50.00
Wedge Antilles and Biggs Darklighter (#57106,
1998) in window box with flap cover, FAO Schwarz 75.00
Princess Leia Organa and R2-D2 as Jabba's
Prisoners (#61777, 1998) in window box with
flap cover, FAO Schwarz stores 80.00
Qui-Gon Ginn and Queen Amidala (Defense of
Naboo) Entertainment Earth distribution 100.00
Chancellor Valorum & Coruscant Guard (#26477)
Fan Club, later Kay-Bee stores 75.00
Sith Lords: Darth Vader and Darth Maul (#32438) 40.00
Luke and Yoda (#32486) WalMart stores 30.00

Doll and Beast
Luke Skywalker vs. Wampa (#27947, Aug. 1997)
Target stores 125.00
Loose, pair. 35.00
Han Solo & Tauntaun (#27834, Aug. 1997) Toys "R"
Us stores. 100.00
Loose, pair. 60.00
Dewback and Stormtrooper (#26246) Toys "R" Us
stores 70.00
Captain Tarpals & Kaadu (# 2001) Target stores. 60.00

Doll and Speeder
Darth Maul & Sith Speeder (#26294, 2001)
WalMart stores 90.00
Speeder Bike with Scout Trooper (#26495, 2000)
Target stores. 150.00
Speeder Bike with Luke Skywalker (in Endor Gear
(#26295, 2001) Target stores. 50.00

Book Stores Masterpiece 12" Doll and Book
Anakin Skywalker, Masterpiece doll and book in
traptrapazoidal box with flap (#02158) 75.00
Aurra Sing, Masterpiece doll and book in trapa-
zoidal box with flap (#, 2000). 115.00
C-3PO with Removeable Limbs, Masterpiece doll
and book in trapazoidal box with flap (#) 75.00

FASHION DOLLS
Hasbro (1999–2000)

The "Portrait Edition" dolls are very attractive, in the best Barbie tradition, which may be why they haven't sold all that well to Star Wars collectors. The initial $50.00 price tag may also have had something to do with it. Since way to many were produced, they have all been available at discount for the last few years. Some still are. The quality may be the reason those same collectors change their mind in the future. If so, the discounted price of about $20.00 will be starting price, not the original high price. The "Queen Amidala Collection" dolls are like entry level Barbie dolls. All of them were discounted too.

***Star Wars* Portrait Edition Doll** (Hasbro 1999)
Princess Leia in Ceremonial Gown, 1999 Portrait
Edition (#61772) number 1 in series. $20.00

***Episode I* Portrait Edition Dolls** (Hasbro 1999–2000)
Queen Amidala in Black Travel Gown, 1999 Portrait
Edition (#61773) number 2 in series. 20.00
Queen Amidala in Red Senate Gown, 1999 Portrait

Queen Amidala in Red Senate Gown, close-up (Hasbro 1999)

Edition, in red velvet robe adorned with embossed rosettes and golden, triple-braided soutache (#61774) number 3 in series 20.00
Queen Amidala Return to Naboo, 2000 Portrait
Edition, in deep-purple, full-length gown, velour cloak inscribed with her royal crest, sheer lavender veil and gold-finished crown (#61781) number 4 in series 25.00

Queen Amidala Collection 12" Dolls (Hasbro 1999)
Hidden Majesty Queen Amidala (#61776) 10.00
Ultimate Hair Queen Amidala (#61778). 10.00
Royal Elegance Queen Amidala (#61779) 10.00
Beautiful Braids Padmé (#61780) 15.00

OTHER FIGURES

BEND-EMS — VINYL — PVC

This category includes most of the figural collectibles other than Action Figures, Ceramics, Die-Cast, Dolls, and Model Kits.

BEND-EMS
Just Toys (1993–96)

The Just Toys *Star Wars Galaxy* Bend-Ems were originally shipped in August 1993 and, by early 1994, they were fairly hot items, since the new action figures had not yet been produced. Trading cards were also popular at that time and each figure was accompanied by a Topps *Star Wars Galaxy* variant trading card. The package backs offered a redeemable coupon good for two free trading cards: one checklist card, and a special card not available in the retail packs. The earliest package has eight separate pictures of the original figures

Emperor's Royal Guard Bend-Em (Just Toys 1995)

on the back. Later, as The Emperor, Wicket, Obi-Wan and Han Solo were added, their pictures went on the back as well.

In mid-1994, the Bend-Ems began arriving without any trading card. That was no fun and before 1995 came around, they had the trading cards back and there were more new figures and new packaging. The card back now had one picture of 20 figures around a Darth Vader 20-piece carry case. 1993 and 1994 figures all came on header cards within a plastic bubble which was shaped to fit the figure snugly. In 1995 this was changed to a stand-up box bubble. The trading card was now inside the box and no longer matched the figure, making it difficult to complete the card series.

The popularity of Bend-Ems declined as the action figures appeared and they received little retail rack space. The trading cards are a separate collectible once the package has been opened. They are listed under "Trading Cards."

First Series (1993) with matching *Star Wars Galaxy* card
Darth Vader (#12361) 8-back header card. $10.00
    Reissue, no Trading Card. 9.00
    Reissue, random Trading Card. 9.00
    Loose 2.50
C-3PO (#12362) 8-back header card 8.00
    Reissue, no Trading Card. 7.00
    Reissue, random Trading Card. 7.00
    Loose 2.50
R2-D2 (#12363) 8-back header card. 8.00
    Reissue, no Trading Card. 7.00
    Reissue, random Trading Card. 9.00
    Loose 2.50
Stormtrooper (#12364) 8-back header card. 9.00

Reissue, no Trading Card. 8.00
Reissue, random Trading Card. 8.00
Loose 2.50
Yoda, the Jedi Master (#12415) 8-back header card . . . 9.00
Reissue, no Trading Card. 7.00
Reissue, random Trading Card. 9.00
Loose 2.50
Chewbacca (#12416) 8-back header card. 9.00
Reissue, no Trading Card. 7.00
Reissue, random Trading Card. 9.00
Loose 2.50
Luke Skywalker (#12417) 8-back header card. 9.00
Reissue, no Trading Card. 7.00
Reissue, random Trading Card. 9.00
Loose 2.50
Princess Leia (#12418) 8-back header card 15.00
Reissue, no Trading Card. 9.00
Reissue, random Trading Card. 9.00
Loose 3.00

Second Batch (1994) with matching *Star Wars Galaxy* card
Wicket, the Ewok (#12452) 12.00
Reissue, no Trading Card. 8.00
Reissue, random Trading Card. 8.00
Loose 3.00
Han Solo (#12453) 12.00
Reissue, no Trading Card. 8.00
Reissue, random Trading Card. 8.00
Loose 3.00
Obi Wan Kenobi (#12454) 10.00
Reissue, no Trading Card. 7.00
Reissue, random Trading Card. 7.00
Loose 3.00
The Emperor (#12455) 10.00
Reissue, no Trading Card. 7.00
Reissue, random Trading Card. 7.00
Loose 3.00

Third Batch (1995) with random *Star Wars Galaxy* I or II card
on header card with Stand-up Bubble
Admiral Ackbar (#12549) 11.00
Loose 3.00
Bib Fortuna (#12552) 11.00
Loose 3.00
Boba Fett (scarce) 40.00
Loose 3.00
Emperor's Royal Guard (#12551) (Boba Fett card) . . . 11.00
Loose 3.00
Gamorrean Guard (#12548) 11.00

12 Bend-Ems (Just Toys 1993–95)

Bend-Ems: 4-Piece Gift Set (Just Toys 1993)

Loose 3.00
Lando Calrissian (#12550) 11.00
Loose 3.00
Luke Skywalker in X-Wing gear 20.00
Loose 3.00
Tusken Raider (#12553) 11.00
Loose 3.00

Multi-packs
Kmart exclusive 8-pack includes Leia, Darth
Vader, Wicket, Emperor, R2-D2 C-3PO, Storm-
trooper, and Luke (#12433) 35.00
4 Piece Gift Set: Stormtrooper, R2-D2, C-3PO,
Darth Vader (#12492, 1993) no cards. 25.00
4 Piece Gift Set: The Emperor, R2-D2, Luke
Skywalker, and Darth Vader plus four trading
cards (#12493, 1993). 25.00
4 Piece Gift Set: Ben (Obi-Wan) Kenobi, Princess
Leia, Han Solo, and C-3PO plus four trading
cards (#12494, 1993). 25.00
4 Piece Gift Set: Imperial Stormtrooper, Wicket, an
Ewok, Yoda, and Chewbacca plus four trading
cards (#12498, 1993). 25.00
Darth Vader bust Collector Case (Just Toys
#15018, 1994) 15.00
Deluxe Collector Set, all 20 figures in Darth Vader
bust case (Just Toys #15021, 1995) 70.00
4 Piece Gift Set: Jabba's Palace, with cards and
coin (#12558, 1995) not seen. 12.00
4 Piece Gift Set: Cantina, with cards and coin
(#12557, 1995) not seen 12.00
10 Piece Gift Set (I) R2-D2, Stormtrooper, Darth
Vader, Admiral Ackbar, Chewbacca, Han, Leia,
Luke, Bib Fortuna, and Emperor's Royal
Guard, plus trading cards and brass colored
coin (#12360, 1995) 45.00
10 Piece Gift Set (II) Yoda, Ewok, Tusken Raider,
Emperor Palpatine, C-3PO, Lando, Boba Fett,
Obi-Wan, Luke in X-Wing uniform, and
Gamorrean Guard, plus trading cards and
brass colored coin (#12320, 1995) 45.00
Darth Vader head-shaped Carry Case 20.00

Episode I Figurine Gift Set, PVC Figures (Applause 1999)

PVC FIGURES
Applause (1995–98)

Applause started producing its current series of PVC figures in 1995, with its Classic Collector set of six figures. The figures have been available individually at comic shops and party stores. So far a total of 16 have been produced. The figures all come on a circular molded stand which has a date on the bottom. One cost effective way to acquire figures has been the Read-Along Play Pack. These are from Walt Disney Records and include a 24-page storybook with photos, an audiocassette of the story and three PVC figures. These sold for about $10.00, which is only $1.00 more than the retail cost of the figures alone. There are three of these, one for each movie.

Boxed Set
Star Wars Classic Collectors Series (6 figures):
　　Luke Skywalker, Darth Vader, Han Solo,
　　C-3PO, R2-D2, and Chewbacca with Bespin
　　Display Platform (Applause #46038, 1995) $20.00

3½" figures, First Batch (1995)
Darth Vader (#46104) 5.00
Luke Skywalker (#46105) 3.00
Han Solo (#46106) 4.00
Chewbacca (#46107) 4.00
C-3PO (#46108) 3.00
R2-D2 (#46109) 3.00

Second Batch (1996)
Emperor Palpatine (#46214) 3.00
Princess Leia (#46216) 3.00
Stormtrooper (#46218) 3.00
Boba Fett (#46239) 3.00

Third Batch (1997)
Obi-Wan Kenobi as ghostly Jedi (#42676) 4.00
Lando Calrissian (#42675) 3.00
Greedo (#42677) 3.00
Yoda (#42678) 3.00
Wedge Antilles (#42707) 4.00
TIF-Fighter pilot (#42708) 3.00
Store Assortment Box, 10¾" x 15¼" x 10" listing all

16 figures from 1995–97 (#42674) empty 5.00

Fourth Batch (1998)
Admiral Ackbar (#42946) 3.00
Bossk (#42947) 3.00
Snowtrooper (#42948) 3.00
Tusken Raider (#42949) 3.00
Obi-Wan Kenobi (#42965) 3.00

Gift Boxes
Han Solo, Chewbacca, Boba Fett, Darth Vader, and
　　Luke Skywalker (#42989) 20.00

Episode I PVC Figures (Applause 1999)
Figurine Gift Set, four figures, including exclusive
　　OOM-9 with Theed Hangar Backdrop (#43036) . . . 10.00
Figurine Gift Set, including Anakin Skywalker, Jar Jar Binks,
　　Queen Amidala, and Destroyer Droid (#61580) . . . 10.00
Anakin Skywalker (#43037) 3.00
Darth Maul (#43038) 3.00
Destroyer Droid (#43039) 3.00
Jar Jar Binks (#43040) 3.00
Obi-Wan Kenobi (#43041) 3.00
Queen Amidala (#43042) 3.00
Pit Droid (#43043) 3.00
Qui-Gon Jinn (#43045) 3.00

Jumbo Dioramas (Jan. 1997)
Han Solo and Jabba the Hutt, 4½" x 6¼" x 4" (#42691)　10.00
R2-D2 and C-3PO, 4¼" x 3½" x 2½" (#42690) 10.00

Read-Along Play Packs
Star Wars, A New Hope Cassette and 3 PVCs
　　(Stormtrooper, R2-D2, C-3PO) (Walt Disney
　　Records #02844, 1997) 10.00
Star Wars, The Empire Strikes Back Cassette and
　　3 PVCs (Han Solo, Chewbacca, Boba Fett)
　　(Walt Disney Records #02854, 1997) 10.00
Star Wars, Return of the Jedi Cassette and 3 PVCs
　　(Luke Skywalker, Emperor, Princess Leia)
　　(Walt Disney Records #02834, 1997) 10.00

PVC SHIPS
Applause (1995)

Star Wars Danglers, in clear acetate box, 1¾" x 1¾" x 3¾"
X-Wing Fighter (#46098) $4.00
Millennium Falcon (#46099) 4.00
Rebel Y-Wing Fighter (#46100) 4.00
Death Star (#46101) 4.00
Imperial Star Destroyer (#46102) 4.00
TIE Fighter (#46103) 4.00
Set of six 20.00
Store Display Box (#46037) empty 3.00

Episode I Danglers (Asst. #43034, Applause 1999)
Trade Federation Droid Starfighter 4.00
Sith Infiltrator 4.00
Sebulba's Pod racer 4.00
Trade Federation Tank 4.00
Naboo Starfighter 4.00
Anakin Skywalker's Pod racer 4.00

VINYL FIGURES
Suncoast Vinyl Dolls (1993)

Darth Vader $20.00

Prince Xizor, Dash Rendar, and TIE-Fighter Pilot vinyl figures (Applause 1996–97)

Luke Jedi Knight	20.00
Luke X-Wing Pilot	20.00
Han Solo	20.00
Chewbacca	20.00
R2-D2	20.00
C-3PO	20.00
Leia in white gown	20.00

VINYL FIGURES
Applause (1995–98)

Most of the vinyl figures produced by Applause are sold loose, with only a folded wrist tag or card to identify the figure and contain the UPC code for scanning. The figures are generally available in comic shops and specialty stores like Spencer Gifts, but not in toy stores. They are not articulated, although sometimes the arms or waist allows some motion, but this does not detract from their collectibility. In early 1998, Spencer Gifts was selling much of their stock for about $10.00, making them an attractive purchase. Applause also issued boxed figures of Darth Vader and Luke Skywalker in X-Wing gear, plus a series of boxed resin figurines and dioramas. These are reasonably priced when compared to expensive statues and fine replicas sold by other manufacturers.

9"–11" Figures, First Batch (August 1995)

Darth Vader, limited to 20,000 pieces (#46039)	$20.00
Luke Skywalker with Yoda, 9¼" (#46040)	15.00
Princess Leia with R2-D2, 8½" (#46041)	15.00
Han Solo as Stormtrooper, 10" (#46042)	15.00
Chewbacca, with C-3PO, 11" (#46043)	15.00

Second Batch (1996)

Darth Vader, 2nd edition, removable helmet, 11" (#46234)	17.00
Boba Fett (#46238)	15.00
Princess Leia in poncho with removable helmet	
(#46041)	15.00
Emperor Palpatine (*Star Wars* Classic) 10½" (#46240) with glow-in-the-dark hands	16.00
Tusken Raider, 11" (#46241)	15.00
Dash Rendar (Shadows of the Empire) 10½" (#46243)	17.00
Prince Xizor (Shadows of the Empire) 11" (#46244)	17.00

Third Batch (1997)

TIE Fighter Pilot, 10" (#42688)	15.00
Wedge Antilles, 11" (#42689)	17.00
Greedo, 10" (#42670)	15.00
Lando Calrissian, skiff guard, 10" (#42671)	15.00
Obi-Wan Kenobi, 10" (#42672)	15.00
R2-D2 with sensor scope, 5½" (#42673)	15.00

Fourth Batch (1998)

Luke in Jedi Training, glow-in-the-dark lightsaber and removable helmet, 9" (#42945)	15.00
C-3PO, 9½" (#42955)	15.00
Princess Leia Slave Girl (#42968)	20.00
Emperor's Royal Guard	15.00

Figures in Large Box

Darth Vader, 12" (#61096)	35.00
Luke Skywalker, in X-Wing Pilot Gear, 9" (#61091)	25.00

***Episode I* Mega Collectible Figures** (Applause 1999) 13" with lightsabers that light up, boxed.

Qui-Gon Jinn (#43023)	30.00
Darth Maul (#43021)	30.00
Obi-Wan Kenobi (#43022)	30.00

***Episode I* Character Collectibles** (Applause 1999)

Qui-Gon Jinn, 10½" with Glow-in-the-Dark Lightsabers (#43029)	15.00
Obi-Wan Kenobi, 10½" with Glow-in-the-Dark Lightsabers (#43031)	15.00
Darth Maul, 10½" with Glow-in-the-Dark Light-	

sabers (#43028) 20.00
Queen Amidala, 9" head turns (#43030) 17.00

Episode I Kid's Collectible Figures (Applause 1999)
Anakin Skywalker, 6½" (#43024)................. 10.00
Jar Jar Binks, 7½" (#43026) 10.00
Watto, 7" (#43027)............................ 10.00
Darth Maul, 7" (#43025)....................... 10.00

DIORAMAS AND FIGURINES

Resin Figurines (Applause 1995–97)
Darth Vader Limited Edition Resin Figurine, limited
    to 5,000 pieces (Applause #46048, Aug. 1995)
    light-up base $50.00
Luke Skywalker Limited Edition Resin Figurine,
    limited to 5,000 pieces (Applause #46049,
    Aug. 1995) light-up base 50.00
Bounty Hunters Resin Diorama, includes Boba Fett
    Bossk and Zuckuss, limited to 5,000 pieces
    Fett, (#46196, Sept. 1996) 60.00
Jabba and Leia, with Salacious Crumb, limited to
    5,000 pieces (#46197, Sept. 1996)........... 60.00
Shadows of the Empire, includes Emperor
    Palpatine, Darth Vader and Prince Xizor,
    limited to 5,000 pieces (#46199, Oct. 1996) 60.00
Leia's Rescue Statuette, includes Luke, Leia, Han,
    and Chewbacca (#42669, 1997)............. 40.00
Han Solo Release From Carbonite Statue, with
    built-in light source, limited to 2,500 copies
    (#61064, 1997) Diamond Previews exclusive ... 110.00
Star Wars Rancor Statuette (#42735, 1997) 40.00
Star Wars Sandtrooper on Dewback cold-cast resin
    statuette (#42687, 1997) 75.00
Darth Vader in Mediation Chamber (#42978, 1998) ... 80.00
Wampa Attack Statuette (#42987, 1998) 75.00
Luke Skywalker in Bacta Tank Sculpture (#42988,
    1998) 125.00

Episode I Dioramas & Sculptures (Applause 1999)
Duel of the Fates Diorama, Qui-Gon Jinn, Obi-Wan
    Kenobi vs. Darth Maul Cold Cast Resin, 6" x 7"
    (#43113) with certificate 60.00
The Guardians of Peace Lighted Sculpture, Qui-
    Gon Jinn & Obi-Wan Kenobi, Cold Cast Resin,

Wampa Attack Statuette (Applause 1998)

9" x 7" limited edition of 3,000 (#43119) 75.00
Queen Amidala Miniature Figurine, Cold Cast
    Resin, limited to 7,500 pieces (#43117) 30.00
Qui-Gon Jinn Miniature Figurine, Cold Cast Resin,
    limited to 7,500 pieces (#43118) 30.00
Darth Maul Miniature Figurine, Cold Cast Resin, lim-
    ited to 7,500 pieces (#43115)............. 30.00
Obi-Wan Kenobi Miniature Figurine, Cold Cast
    Resin, limited to 7,500 pieces (#43116) 30.00

FIGURAL BANKS

Plastic (Adam Joseph 1983)
Darth Vader, 9" tall $25.00
Emperor's Royal Guard, 9" tall 25.00
Gamorrean Guard, 9" tall, rare,................ 50.00
R2-D2, 6" tall 30.00
Princess Kneesa, 6" tall, playing tambourine........ 15.00
Wicket, 6" tall, playing drum 15.00

Metal
Darth Vader Bust Metal Bank, 6" high (Leonard
    Silver Mfg. 1981) 65.00
Darth Vader Metal Bank, tin litho box with combin-
    ation dials (Metal Box Co. 1980).............. 50.00
Yoda Metal Bank, tin litho box with combination
    dials (Metal Box Co. 1980) 50.00
The Empire Strikes Back Metal Bank, tin octagonal
    bank with photos of characters (Metal Box Co.
    1980)................................. 40.00

Episode I Figural Banks (Applause 1999)
Darth Maul on Sith Speeder Bank, 7" (#43032)...... 15.00
Jar Jar Binks Bank, 8" (#43033) 15.00

PLUSH FIGURES

Plush
Chewbacca (Regal) $60.00
Chewbacca, 20" tall (Kenner 1977)............... 35.00
R2-D2, 10" tall (Kenner 1977) 50.00
Ewoks (Kenner 1983)
    18" Zephee 40.00
    14" Wicket 30.00
    14" Princess Kneesa 30.00
    14" Paploo 40.00
    14" Latara 40.00
    8" Woklings, six different, each.............. 15.00
Ewok, 12", light brown with green cowl (Disney) 15.00
Ewok, 8", dark brown with pink cowl (Disney) 12.00

Episode I, Small Plush (Applause 1999)
Jar Jar Binks, with bead eyes and removable vest
    and sash, 12" x 3½" plus 5½" ears (#43072)...... 10.00
Watto, with bead eyes and removable vest and
    sash, 10" x 7" (#43073)..................... 10.00

Episode I, Medium Plush (Applause 1999)
R2-D2, 12" (#43071) 15.00
Watto, 14" (#43070) 15.00
Jar Jar Binks, 14" (#43069) 15.00

PUPPETS

Yoda Hand Puppet, plastic, 8½" tall (Kenner 1981)... $40.00
Chewbacca Hand Puppet (Regal)................ 50.00

Episode I Puppets (Applause 1999)

Yoda Latex Latex Puppet, 12" (#42964). 20.00
Jar Jar Binks Latex Puppet, 12" (#43035) 20.00

STAR WARS BUDDIES
Kenner (1997–2000)

Everyone who thinks that Kenner would have made *Star Wars* Buddies even if Beanie Babies were not enjoying their 15 minutes of collecting fame, please raise your hand. For everyone else, these Beanie Baby knock-offs are either cute and imaginative or a curse, depending on your view of the real thing. Most collectors that I have met do not utter the words "Beanie Babies" without adding an "expletive deleted." Sadly, some of these guys have actually gone up in value.

Buddies (Bean Bag)
C-3PO $8.00
Chewbacca, original black bandolier strap. 15.00
Chewbacca, new brown bandolier strap 8.00
Darth Vader 8.00
Figrin D'An 8.00
Gamorrean Guard 8.00
Jabba the Hutt 8.00
Jawa. 10.00
Luke Skywalker 8.00
Max Rebo. 12.00
Princess Leia 8.00
R2-D2 . . . . 8.00
Salacious Crumb 10.00
Stormtrooper 8.00
Wampa. 12.00
Wicket the Ewok. 9.00
Yoda. 20.00

Episode I **Buddies** (Asst. #26242, 1999)
Darth Maul (#26248) 8.00
Jar Jar Binks (#26247). 7.00
Obi-Wan Kenobi (#26245) 6.00
Padme Naberrie (#26244) 7.00
Qui-Gon Jinn (#26243). 5.00
Watto (#26249) 5.00

COMPLETE GALAXY
Kenner (1998)

Each Complete Galaxy figure is a planet or moon which is attached to a base and flips open in the middle to reveal a scene and action figure. I guess they make a nice display, but the only one I like is Endor, with the Ewok and glider. The Ewok makes a neat loose figure. It, and Tatooine with Luke Skywalker, were very scarce, while the first two were quite common.

Complete Galaxy Figures (Asst. #69805, April 1998)
Dagobah with **Yoda** (with flying predator) (#69828)
    [551389.00] $10.00
Death Star with **Darth Vader** (with removable helmet dome) (#69829) [551392.00] 10.00

Second Batch
Endor with **Ewok** (with pop-open glider and rocks) (#69869) [556001.01] 30.00

Complete Galaxy: Endor with Ewok and Death Star with Darth Vader (Kenner 1998)

Tatooine with **Luke Skywalker** (Jedi, with lightsaber) (#69826) [555996.00] 30.00

OTHER FIGURES

Episode I **Battle Bags** (Hasbro Asst. #63349, 1999)
Sea Creatures (#63351) $7.00
Sea Creatures (#63352) 7.00
Swamp Creatures (#63353) 7.00
Swamp Creatures (#63354) 7.00

Episode I (Hasbro 1999)
Jabba Glob, Jabba the Hutt figure with jar of Jabba Glob Play Gel to ooze out of his mouth and six frogs to eat (#63355). 10.00

KOOSH
Hasbro (1999)

Koosh Assortment, all (#09060) on header card
    Sebulba. $5.00
    Jar Jar Binks. 5.00
    Kaadu. 5.00
    Watto 5.00

ELECTRONIC AND COMPUTER

This section covers electronic and computer games and toys, plus related items. Other types of games are covered in the GAMES section. The electronic toys generally produce recorded sound effects, music or short sound bites from the movies. Actual sound tracks, audio performances and *Star Wars* music are listed in the RECORDINGS section. See also the ROLE PLAY section for walkie-talkies and the DOLLS section for electronic, as opposed to radio-controlled, dolls.

ELECTRONIC GAMES AND TOYS

Currently, the predominant manufacturer of *Star Wars* electronic hand-held games and other items is Tiger Electronics, Inc. By 1997, they had produced a large number of such games, but there were no new ones for 1998, and existing stock was discounted. Many Episode I items were heavily discounted by 2000. Tiger's Stormtrooper Laser Target Game contains a 13½" Stormtrooper figure which has drawn some interest from doll and figure collectors. Kenner's classic radio-controlled R2-D2 is often considered a figure for collecting purposes, since it is made to the same scale as

the classic doll series.

Radio-Controlled/Remote Controlled
Radio Controlled R2-D2, 8", *Star Wars* logo
   (Kenner #38430, 1979) $150.00
   Loose 65.00
Radio Controlled Imperial Speeder Bike with figure
   (Kenner #27846, 1997) 25.00
Electronic Remote Control R2-D2 (Kenner #27736,
   Sept. 1997) 25.00
Radio Control Speeder Bike with Luke Skywalker. . . . 125.00

Classic Electronic Games
Electronic Battle Command Game, 9½" x 7" box,
   Star Wars logo (Kenner #40370, 1977) battery
   powered. 75.00
Electronic Laser Battle Game, 20" x 6½" box, *Star
   Wars* logo (Kenner #40090, 1977) 100.00

Radio Controlled R2-D2 (Kenner 1979)

Star Wars *Electronic Game (Micro Games of America 1995)*

Stormtrooper Room Alarm (Tiger Electronics 1997)

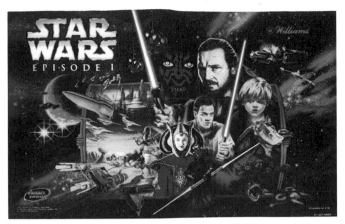

Episode I *Pinball 2000 Game Backpanel (Williams 1999)*

Millennium Falcon Sounds of the Force Electronic
    Memory Game (#88-089, 1997) 30.00
Star Wars Rebel Forces Laser Game (#79-212, 1997) 20.00
Boba Fett Room Alarm with Laser Target Game,
    13½" figure in window box, with Han Solo
    Laser Blaster (#88-080, 1997) 35.00
Stormtrooper Room Alarm with Laser Target Game,
    13½" figure in window box, with Han Solo
    Laser Blaster (#88-081, 1997) 35.00
Star Wars Electronic Galactic Battle game, includes
    10 different vehicles & sound effects (#88-088,
    1997). 25.00
Star Wars Death Star Escape Game (#88-090) 25.00
Star Wars Quiz Whiz (*Star Wars Trilogy* Episode
    IV) Electronic Question & Answer Game
    (#88-091). 25.00

Star Wars Episode I Electronic Games (1999)
Episode 1 Galactic Battle Strategy Game (Tiger
    #88-507). 40.00
Escape From Naboo Skill and Action Game (Tiger
    #88-505) 25.00
Naboo Fighter Game, with **Anakin Skywalker** figure (Hasbro
    #40969) 20.00
Destroyer Droid Game (Hasbro #40967) 20.00
Electronic Naboo Defense Game (Tiger #88-504) 25.00
Lightsaber Duel Game (Tiger #88-502) 25.00
Battle of Naboo Electronic Handheld game (Tiger
    88-003) Captain Tarpals and Battle Droid joy-
    stick figure 20.00
Pinball Games
Star Wars Galactic Laser Pinball (Tiger #88-273) 50.00
Star Wars Episode I Pinball 2000 full-size arcade,
    game (Williams Electronic Games 1999) 5,000.00
    Backpanel, with Episode I art 200.00

Video Board Game
Star Wars Interactive Video Board Game (Parker
    Bros. #40392, 1996). 32.00

COMPUTER GAMES

Computer Games
The Software Toolworks *Star Wars* Chess game
    (Software Toolworks 1992) 15.00

CD-ROM Computer Games and Software (LucasArts)
The Lucas Archives, Vol. I (#80218, 1995) 30.00
The Lucas Archives, Vol. II (#80318, 1996) 30.00
TIE Fighter Wars (#20618, 1995) 25.00
X-Wing vs. TIE Fighter (#20818, 1997) 30.00

X-Wing Aces Target Electronic Game, plug-in, *Star
    Wars* logo (Kenner 1978) very rare, offered in
    mini-catalog 1,000.00
Destroy Death Star Electronic Game, 17" x 25" box
    (Palitoy 1978). 150.00

Electronic Games (Micro Games of America 1995)
Star Wars Shakin' Pinball (MGA 207) (#22623, 1995) . 17.00
Star Wars Electronic Game (MGA 220) (#02033, 1995) 10.00
The Empire Strikes Back Electronic Game
    (MGA 222) (#02034, 1995) 10.00
Return of the Jedi Electronic Game (MGA 224)
    (#02035, 1995) 10.00
Star Wars Intimidator (INT-200) (1995) 10.00

Electronic Games and Toys (Tiger Electronics)
Star Wars Millennium Falcon Challenge R-Zone
    Headgear (#71-196, 1997). 15.00
Star Wars Jedi Adventure R-Zone Xtreme Pocket
    Game (#71-331, 1997). 30.00
R-Zone Cartridges :
    Millennium Falcon Challenge (#71-316) 10.00
    Jedi Adventure (#71-317). 10.00
    Rebel Forces (#71-319) 10.00
    Imperial Assault (#71-321) 10.00
Star Wars Imperial Assault 3-D Figure Hand Held
    Game "Joystick Games" (#88-001, 1997) 20.00
Millennium Falcon Challenge Electronic LCD Game
    (#88-005, 1997). 20.00

Star Wars X-Wing CD-Rom game (LucasArts)

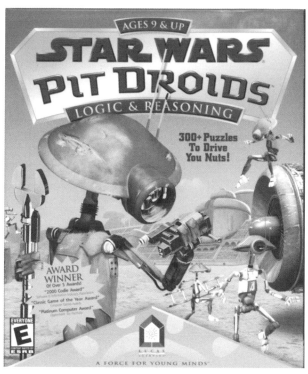

Star Wars Pit Droids (LucasArts 1999)

Shadows of the Empire (#31218, 1997) 30.00
Rebel Assault (#30418, 1993) 30.00
Yoda Stories (#31118, 1997) 20.00
Rebel Assault II (#30918, 1995) 30.00
Star Wars Rebel Assault II, The Hidden Empire
    with Rebel I (#30941) 25.00
Star Wars X-Wing Alliance (#20918) 25.00
Dark Forces (#30618, 1994) 30.00
Dark Forces and Jedi Knight Dark Forces II (#30641) . 25.00
Star Wars X-Wing Collector's with Flight School
    (#20541) 25.00
Behind the Magic (#31418, 1999) 30.00
Episode I: Insiders Guide (1999) 30.00
Star Wars Pit Droids (#35131, 2000) 25.00
Star Wars Math, Jabba's Game Galaxy (#35215) 20.00
Anakin's Speedway (#35180, 1999) 20.00
Gungan Frontier (1999) 20.00
Jar Jar's Journey (1999) 20.00
Episode I Racer (1999) 20.00
Droid Works, Science and Technology (1999) 25.00

Early Electronic Game Cartridges
Star Wars SNES Cartridge (JVC NES 1993) 30.00
Super *Star Wars* SNES Cartridge (JVC NES 1993) . . . 30.00
The Empire Strikes Back Nintendo Cartridge (JVC
    NES #91014, 1992) 30.00
Star Wars Gameboy Cartridge (Capcom #12013,
    1993) 30.00
The Empire Strikes Back Gameboy Cartridge
    (Capcom #12014, 1993) 30.00

CLOCKS

Clocks
R2-D2 and C-3PO Talking Alarm Clock, 9" tall
    (Bradley Time 1980) 90.00
R2-D2 and C-3PO Clock Radio (Bradley Time 1984) . 100.00
R2-D2 and C-3PO 3-D Sceni-Clock, 8" tall (Bradley
    Time) 75.00
Ewok Teaching Clock, shaped like Ewok village

with Wicket on face of clock (Kenner Preschool) . . 75.00
Star Wars Wall Clock, pictures R2-D2 & C-3PO
    (Welby Elgin 1981) 65.00
The Empire Strikes Back Wall Clock, square, Darth,
    Stormtroopers & logo (Welby Elgin 1981) 65.00
Droid wall clock (Bradley) 25.00
The Empire Strikes Back wall clock (Bradley) 25.00

Jar Jar Binks Mini-Clock (1999)

Portable clock/radio (Bradley 1984) 15.00
Star Wars Special Edition Clock, Drew Struzan art,
    9" x 11" battery powered (1997) 40.00
The Empire Strikes Back Special Edition Clock,
    Drew Struzan art, 9" x 11" battery powered (1997). 40.00
Return of the Jedi Special Edition Clock, Drew
    Struzan art, 9" x11" battery powered (1997) 40.00

Episode I Mini Clocks (Nelsonic 1999)
Darth Maul Mini Clock (#27633) 20.00
Jar Jar Binks Mini Clock (#27635) 20.00
Queen Amidala Mini Clock (#27636) 20.00
Qui-Gon Jinn Mini Clock (#27634) 20.00

RADIOS and CASSETTE PLAYERS

Radios and Cassette Players
Luke Skywalker AM Headset Radio, battery
    powered (Kenner #38420, 1979) 40.00
Millennium Falcon Cassette Player (Micro Games
    of America #SW-24M, 1995) 30.00
R2-D2 Data Droid Cassette Player (Tiger
    Electronics #88-083) 10" high 27.00
R2-D2 Personal Cassette Player (Tiger Electronics
    #88-087, 1997) 17.00
Darth Vader AM/FM Clock Radio (Micro Games of
    America #SW-3124, 1995) 32.00
Darth Vader FM Bike Radio (Micro Games of
    America #SW-3180, 1995) 37.00
C-3PO AM/FM Radio (Micro Games of America
    #SW-3190, 1995) 27.00
Darth Vader AM/FM Clock Radio, with molded head
    on top, LCD display (#SW-3124) 25.00

ELECTRONIC TOYS

"Talking" Toys
Star Wars Electronic Talking Bank with 8" C-3PO
    and 5" R2-D2, plus "dialogue, music & effects
    from the movie soundtrack" (Thinkway #13902,
    1995) 22.00
Star Wars Electronic Talking Bank with Darth Vader

R2-D2 Data Droid (Tiger Electronics 1996)

A-Wing Calculator, loose (Tiger Electronics 1997)

    plus "dialogue, music & effects from the movie
    soundtrack" (Thinkway #13903, 1996) 22.00
R2-D2 Repeating Robot (Micro Games of America
    #SW-3194, 1995) 32.00
Darth Vader Power Talker Voice Changing Mask
    #SW-3815 (Micro Games of America #22586,
    1995) 35.00
R2-D2 Ditto Droid game (Tiger Electronics
    #88-031, 1997) 10.00
Darth Vader Voice Changer (Tiger Electronics #88-
    041, 1997) 15.00

Star Wars *Episode I* Wake-Up Systems (Thinkway 1999)
Anakin's Podracer Wake-Up System (#13703) 40.00
Jar Jar Binks Wake-Up System, includes 24"
    talking Jar Jar Binks doll and Pid Droid clock
    (#13704) 40.00
Naboo Starfighter with Anakin Skywalker and R2-
    D2 Wake-Up System (#) 40.00

Star Wars *Episode I* Talking Banks (Thinkway 1999)
Darth Maul Interactive Talking Bank (#13709) 30.00
Obi-Wan Kenobi Interactive Talking Bank (#13708) 30.00
Qui-Gon Jinn Interactive Talking Bank (#13707) 30.00

Electronic Key chains (Tiger Electronics)
Boba Fett Key chain (#88-012, 1997) 7.00
Jabba the Hutt Key chain (#88-014, 1997) 7.00
Chewbacca Key chain (#88-015, 1997) 7.00
Luke Skywalker Key chain (X-Wing) (#88-016, 1997) . . 7.00
R2-D2 Key chain Clock (#88-021, 1997) 7.00
Star Destroyer Key chain (#88-022 1997) 7.00
Lightsaber Key chain (#88-023, 1997) 7.00
C-3PO Flashlight Key chain (#88-025, 1997) 7.00
Millennium Falcon Key chain, with sound effects
    (#88-026, 1997) 7.00
Darth Vader (head) Key chain, with sound effects
    (#88-027, 1997) 7.00
Death Star Key chain with voice record and
    playback (#88-028, 1997) 7.00
Stormtrooper (head) Key chain, with sound effects
    (#88-029, 1997) 7.00
Electronic Pens (Tiger Electronics 1997
Luke Skywalker Way Cool Sounds FX Pen (#88-051) . . 8.00
Darth Vader Way Cool Sounds FX Pen (#88-052) 8.00
C-3PO Way Cool Sounds FX Pen (#88-054) 8.00
Star Wars Lightsaber FX Recording Pen (#88-055) . . . 25.00

Squawk Boxes (Tiger Electronics 1997)
C-3PO Squawk Box (#88-071) includes 3 movie

Destroyer Droid Room Alarm (Tiger Electronics 1999)

sound effects 15.00
Darth Vader Squawk Box (#88-072) includes 3
movie sound effects 15.00
Millennium Falcon Squawk Box (#88-073) includes
3 movie sound effects 15.00

Other Electronic Toys (Tiger Electronics 1997)
A-Wing Calculator (#88-085) 13.00
Star Wars Lightsaber Image Projector (#88-086) 15.00
Star Wars Lazer Tag, Rebel Infantry Deluxe Pack
(#88-094) 45.00

Episode I Electronic Toys (Tiger Electronics 1999)
Queen Amidala Compact Phone (#88-315) 25.00
Darth Maul Compact Phone (#88-316) 25.00
Animated Destroyer Droid Room Alarm (#88-303) 30.00
Darth Maul Binoculars with Listening Device (#88-284) 20.00
Picture Plus Image Camera (#88-304) 25.00

Electronic Toys
Electronic X-Wing Flight Simulator, 30" x 10" x 17",
with "Electronic Lights and Authentic Movie
Sounds" (Kenner #27847, Aug. 1997) green box. . 23.00
Millennium Falcon Flight Simulator (Kenner 1998) 23.00
Millennium Falcon CD-ROM Playset with unique
Han Solo figure (Kenner #99180) 25.00
Dancing Jar Jar Binks (Thinkway #13712, 1999) 30.00

Audioclips
Star Wars Audioclips for IBM-PC 20.00
The Empire Strikes Back Audioclips for IBM-PC 20.00
Return of the Jedi Audioclips for IBM-PC 20.00

Giga Pets (Tiger Electronics 1997)
Yoda Giga Pet, Electronic Virtual Pet (#70-135) 7.50
Rancor Giga Pet, Electronic Virtual Pet (#70-136) 10.00
R2-D2 Giga Pet, Electronic Virtual Pet (#70-137) 7.50

Star Wars Millennium Falcon CD-Rom Playset (Kenner 1998)

Preschool
Ewok Talking Phone, 9" tall (Kenner Preschool 1984) . 70.00
Sit n' Spin (Kenner Preschool 1984) 60.00

Electronic Household Products
Luke Skywalker's Lightsaber Universal (TV) Remote Control (Kash 'N' Gold 2366, 1997) boxed . . 35.00
R2-D2 figural telephone, 12" high, 9¼" wide, 6"
deep, battery powered with handset in leg,
droid movements and sound effects (Kash 'N'
Gold #2363, 1997) boxed 80.00

COMPUTER ACCESSORIES

Computer Mice (Handstands 1998)
Darth Vader 15.00
C-3PO 15.00
Stormtrooper (#40703) 15.00

Mousepads 8½" x 11½" (MousTrak 1995)
Darth Vader Mouse Pad (#SW-1) 12.00
Yoda Mouse Pad (#SW-2) 12.00
Millennium Falcon Mouse Pad (#SW-3) 12.00
Luke & Leia, *Return of the Jedi* Mouse Pad (#SW-4) . . 12.00
Rebel Assault Game Art Mouse Pad (#SW-5) 12.00

Star Wars Mousemats (Handstands 1998)
Darth Vader & Boba Fett (#40106) 8.00
Death Star, circular 8.00
R2-D2 & C-3PO 8.00
Yoda 8.00
3-D Lenticular Motion mat 20.00
PhotoMat 15.00

Star Wars Episode I Mousemats (Handstands 1999)
Jedi/Sith 8.00
Queen Amidala (#40114) 8.00
Star Wars Episode I Logo (#40115) 8.00
Darth Maul 8.00
Naboo Space Battle 8.00
Anakin Skywalker/Pod Race 8.00
Jar Jar Binks, circular 8.00
3-D Lightsaber Battle (#40203) 8.00

Wrist Rests (Handstands 1998)
Star Wars Characters collage 10.00

Star Wars Episode I Wrist Rests
Jedi vs. Sith 10.00
Pod race 10.00

BREAKFAST FOOD, FAST FOOD, JUNK FOOD, AND PIZZA

Over the years, Star Wars has had promotions with each of the four major food groups—Fast, Junk, Breakfast, and Pizza—not to mention a Pet Food promotion in Australia. These promotions generate a variety of collectibles, from food containers, to toys, to mail-in premiums

BREAKFAST FOOD

Every toy collector should start off with a hearty breakfast. General Mills, who owned Kenner at the time, started promotions off with various *Star Wars* Cheerios boxes beginning in 1978. This was probably the high point of *Star Wars* food products, nutrition-wise, until the 1997 Taco Bell promotion. From then on the offers were on cereals like Boo Berry, Count Chocula and Lucky Charms. *Star Wars* moved to Kellogg's in 1984 and C-3PO got his own cereal. Finally, in 1996 Froot Loops had its highly successful Han Solo Stormtrooper action figure offer. Toocan Sam and R2-D2—perfect together. The boxes are just as collectible as the premiums.

Listed prices are for complete and clean boxes. A complete box has all four top flaps, all four sides (no missing coupons) and all four bottom flaps. A box that has the top and bottom flaps opened is a "collapsed" box (but still complete). A "Flat" is a mint (usually a file copy) unused cereal box. A flat commands up to 40% more than the listed price.

If you liked a little toast with your cereal, you should have bought Wonder Bread. They offered a series of *Star Wars* trading cards in 1977. Look for them in the TRADING CARDS section.

General Mills Cereal Boxes

Cheerios, with *Star Wars* tumbler offer	$35.00
Cheerios, 1978, *Star Wars* Poster in Pack, Space Scenes	30.00
Boo Berry, with trading card premium	25.00
Franken Berry, with trading card premium	25.00
Cocoa Puffs, with trading card premium	25.00
Chocolate Crazy Cow, with trading card premium	25.00
Strawberry Crazy Cow, with trading card premium	25.00
Trading Cards, 18 different, see Trading Cards section.	
Frankenberry, with sticker premium	25.00
Count Chocula with sticker premium	25.00
Trix, with sticker premium	25.00
Cocoa Puffs, with sticker premium	25.00
Lucky Charms, with sticker premium	25.00
Stickers, 16 different, each	2.00
Lucky Charms, with spaceship hang glider premium	25.00

Kellogg's Cereal Boxes

C-3PO Cereal (1984) with sticker trading card offer	20.00
C-3PO Cereal (1984) with Mask on Back, six different masks of C-3PO, Chewbacca, Darth Vader, Luke Skywalker Stormtrooper, or Yoda, each	30.00
Set, 8 different C-3PO Mask boxes	200.00
C-3PO Cereal (1984) with Rebel Rocket in pack plus stickers	20.00
Set, 8 different Boxes + Stickers	200.00
Froot Loops (1996) with Han Solo in Stormtrooper outfit mail-in offer	10.00

Froot Loops with Han Solo action figure offer (Kellogg's 1996)

Apple Jacks (1996) with Dark Horse comic book
mail-in offer 2.00
Corn Pops (1996) with *Star Wars* video offer 2.00
Raisin Bran (1996) with *Star Wars* video offer 2.00

FAST FOOD

The 1970s and 1980s promotions of choice with fast food restaurants were glasses and plastic cups. The most famous of these promotions were the Burger King/Coke four-glass sets sold for each of the three movies. Coke also produced a number of collector plastic cups which were distributed in various fast food chains, both national and regional.

Glassware

Star Wars Promotional Glasses (4 diff. glasses:
    Luke, Han Solo, Darth and R2-D2/C-3PO,
    Burger King/Coca-Cola 1977) each $15.00
    set of 4 . . . . 60.00
The Empire Strikes Back Promotional Glasses (4
    diff. glasses: Luke, Lando, R2-D2/C-3PO and
    Darth, Burger King/Coca-Cola 1980) each 12.00
    set of 4 . . . . 50.00
Return of the Jedi Promotional Glasses (4 diff.:
    Sand barge fight scene, Jabba's palace, Ewok
    village, & Luke/Darth fighting, Burger King/
    Coca-Cola 1983) each 10.00
    set of 4 . . . . 40.00
    Plastic cups, Mass. only, each 12.50
    set of 4 . . . . 50.00

Plastic Coca-Cola Cups 1970s–80s

Star Wars numbered 20-cup set, each 10.00
    Set of 20 . . . . 175.00
Star Wars numbered 8-cup set
    Large, "7–11" or "Coke" each 5.00
    Set of 8 Large cups 30.00
    Small, "Coke" each 5.00
    Set of 8 Small cups 25.00
Star Wars unnumbered 1979 8-cup set, each 5.00
    Set of 8 "Coke" cups 30.00
Return of the Jedi 12-cup set, each 5.00
    Set of 12 "7-11" cups, large or small 50.00

Return of the Jedi *glasses (Burger King/Coke 1983)*

The Empire Strikes Back movie theater plastic cup
    (Coke1980) depending on size, each 7.00
Return of the Jedi movie theater plastic cup (Coke
    1983) depending on size, each 6.00
Star Wars Trilogy Special Edition movie theater
    plastic cup, featuring picture of AT-AT (Pepsi 1997) . . 2.00

Taco Bell ran a promotion in late 1996 and early 1997 in conjunction with the release of the *Star Wars Trilogy Special Edition* films. There were a lot of neat toys to collect, along with boxes plus a wrapper and bag. The best part for me is that I get paid to show you pictures of them in this book, enjoy the tacos, and deduct the cost of the meals and toys, all while telling my wife that its not just an excuse to eat at fast food restaurants. This worked for the pizza, Pepsi, and junk food just as well.

The toys each came in a plastic bag, with a two page booklet encouraging you to "collect all seven!" They cost

Star Wars *glasses (Burger King/Coke 1977) and* The Empire Strikes Back *glasses (Burger King/Coke 1980)*

Exploding Death Star toy (Taco Bell 1997)

about a buck each, but the taco wrapper, bag, or box was free.

Fast Food (Taco Bell 1996–97)
Taco Bell taco wrapper picturing C-3PO $1.00
Taco Bell taco bag picturing R2-D2 . . . . 1.00
Taco Bell taco bag picturing C-3PO 1.00

Star Wars Taco Bell food box, with movie scene 2.00
The Empire Strikes Back Taco Bell food box, with
　　movie scene 2.00
Return of the Jedi Taco Bell food box, with movie
　　scene 2.00

Fast Food Toys (Taco Bell 1996–97)
Millennium Falcon Gyro 3.00
R2-D2 Playset 2.50
Magic Cube, Yoda/Darth Vader 2.50
Floating Cloud City 2.50
Puzzle Cube 2.50
Balancing Boba Fett 2.00
Exploding Death Star Spinner 2.50
Under 3 years old
Yoda figure 5.00

EPISODE I FAST FOOD

Star Wars Episode I The Phantom Menace was so big it took three, count them—THREE, restaurant chains to distribute its fast food toys—Pizza Hut, KFC, and Taco Bell. I gained at least 10 pounds just collecting them, and that was before I started in on the potato chips bags and pepsi cans. All of the restaurant's fast food toys were made by Applause and were listed on their Web site, and a poster from *Star Wars Galaxy Collector* magazine. All of the toys came in pictorial boxes which could be put together to form a poster scene. Each restaurant had four figural plastic drink toppers for sale. KFC also had two flying disks, i.e. frisbees, which doubled as chicken bucket toppers. In addition, you could collect paper drink cups with movie pictures and plastic soda cups at the movies.

CORUSCANT (Pizza Hut)

Pizza Hut (Coruscant)
Yoda's Jedi Destiny (#66515) $2.00
Lott Dodd Walking Throne (#66516) 2.00
Planet Coruscant (#66517) 2.00
Sith Holoprojector (#66518) 2.00
Jar Jar Binks Squishy (#66519) under three 2.00
Darth Maul's Sith Infiltrator (#66520) 2.00
Queen Amidala's Royal Starship (#66521) 2.00
R2-D2 (#66522) 2.00
Boxes for above, each 1.00

Drink Toppers with plastic cup and long straw
Jar Jar Binks 4.00
Mace Windu 4.00
Nute Gunray 4.00
Yoda 4.00

NABOO (KFC)

KFC (Naboo)
Queen Amidala's Hidden Identity (#66506) 2.00
Jar Jar Binks Squirter (#66507) 2.00
Swimming Jar Jar Binks (#66508) 2.00
Gungan Sub Squirter (#66509) 2.00
Opee Sea Creature Chaser (#66510) 2.00

Lott Dodd Walking Throne (Pizza Hut 1999); Jar Jar Binks Squirter (KFC 1999); and Anakin's Podracer (Taco Bell 1999)

Yoda Drink Topper (Pizza Hut 1999); Queen Amidala Drink Topper (KFC 1999); and Darth Maul Drink Topper (Taco Bell 1999)

Naboo Ground Battle (#66511) 2.00
Anakin Skywalker's Naboo Fighter (#66512) 2.00
Trade Federation Droid Fighter (#66513) 2.00
Planet Naboo (#66514) 2.00
Boss Nass Squirter (#66535) 2.00
Boxes for above, each 1.00

Drink Toppers with plastic cup and long straw
Boss Nass 4.00
Captain Tarpals 4.00
Queen Amidala 4.00
R2-D2 . . . . 4.00

Flying Disks
Battle Droid 5.00
Jar Jar Binks 5.00

Chicken Buckets
  each 1.50

Cups, paper
Boss Nass, medium 1.00
Boss Nass, large 1.00
Jar Jar Binks, medium 1.00
Jedi Knights, medium 1.00
Jedi Knights, large 1.00
Queen Amidala, medium 1.00

TATOOINE (Taco Bell)

Taco Bell (Tatooine)
Joking Jar Jar Binks (#66488) 2.00
Anakin's Podracer (#66489) 2.00
Sebulba's Podracer (#66490) 2.00
Hovering Watto (#66491) 2.00
Walking Sebulba (#66492) 2.00
Darth Maul's Sith Speeder (#66493) 2.00
Levitating Queen Amidala's Royal Starship (#66494) . . . 2.00

Planet Tatooine (#66495) 2.00
Anakin Bust Viewer (under 3) (#66496) 2.00
Sith Probe Droid Viewer (#66497) 2.00
Anakin Skywalker Transforming Bank (#66498) 2.00
Boxes for above, each 1.00

Drink Toppers with plastic cup and long straw
Anakin Skywalker 4.00
Darth Maul 4.00
Sebulba 4.00
Watto 4.00

Cups
Anakin Skywalker, plastic 2.00
Jar Jar Binks, medium paper 1.00
Queen Amidala, medium paper 1.00
Sebulba, plastic 2.00

Store Signage
Pizza Hut Toy Display containing all eight toys 150.00
KFC Toy Display containing all ten toys 150.00
Taco Bell Toy Display containing all ten toys 150.00

JUNK FOOD

With any food product, the collectible is the container, and any premium, but not the food. The collectible value of the Pepsi cartons, or the Lay's Potato Chip bags listed below are about 90% less if they are not complete. Empty is okay, but cutouts are not, meaning that you can't have a mint bag or box and send away for the mail-in premium too.

STAR WARS TRILOGY SODA

Pepsi had a number of promotional plastic bottles and 12-pack and 24-pack cartons available for the *Star Wars Trilogy Special Edition* movies. The cartons had an offer for three posters for $9.99 plus the order form on the back of the carton. Pepsi also issued various coasters and travel cups related to the trilogy.

Soda (or Pop, if you are a mid-westener)
Diet Pepsi *Star Wars Trilogy Special Edition*
    12-pack box featuring a Stormtrooper, with
    posters offer (1996) $2.00
Mountain Dew *Star Wars Trilogy Special Edition* 12
    pack box picturing X-Wing Fighters, with
    posters offer (1996) 2.00
Diet Pepsi *Star Wars Trilogy Special Edition*
    24-pack box picturing a Stormtrooper, with
    posters offer (1996) 2.00
Pepsi *Star Wars Trilogy Special Edition* 24-pack
    box picturing a C-3PO, with posters offer (1996). . . 2.00
Pepsi *Star Wars Trilogy Special Edition* 24-pack
    box picturing Yoda, with posters offer (1996). 2.00
Pepsi *Star Wars Trilogy Special Edition* 24-pack
    box picturing Darth Vader, with posters offer (1996) . 2.00
Pepsi 20 oz. plastic bottle, picturing Darth Vader 1.00
Pepsi 2-liter plastic bottle, picturing Darth Vader 1.00
Diet Pepsi 20 oz. plastic bottle, picturing C-3PO 1.00
Diet Pepsi 2-liter plastic bottle, picturing C-3PO. 1.00

Other *Star Wars Trilogy* Pepsi Products (1997)
Travel Bottles, four different, each 8.00
Coasters, four different, each 5.00
Cups, four different, each. 6.00

EPISODE I SODA

    Pepsi put out 24 different soda cans in conjunction with *Episode I: The Phantom Menace*. Pepsico generated a lot of initial interest with promo cans, available as internal give-aways. They were sealed, but empty, so they are easy to distinguish from the regular cans. Each came in a white box.

    The regular 24 cans were not randomly distributed. Rather, each 12-pack or 24-pack had only one style of can in it. Collectors should note that cans from different Pepsi Bottlers will have different deposit/recycle information and may list the state, so there are differences between the cans.

Pepsi Promo Can #1 with Box (Pepsi 1999)

The list below, taken from the boxes and confirmed by the cans should be all of them, but isn't. Somewhere I happened on a Seven-Up can with #19 Nute Gunray pictured! Wrong brand and wrong number, so there must be more around.

Star Wars Episode I Soda Boxes (1999)
Anakin Skywalker 12-pack, Pepsi. 2.00
Anakin Skywalker 24-pack, Pepsi. 2.00
Queen Amidala 12-pack, Diet Pepsi 2.00
Queen Amidala 24-pack, Diet Pepsi 2.00
Mountain Dew 12-pack, ... 2.00
Mountain Dew 24-pack, ... 2.00
C-3PO 12-pack, Pepsi One 2.00
C-3PO 24-pack, Pepsi One 2.00

Star Wars Episode I (Can or plastic bottle)
Pepsi: 1. Anakin Skywalker; 2. Sebulba; 3. Qui-   Gon
    Jinn; 4. Watto; 5. Jabba The Hutt;
    6. Senator Palpatine; 7. R2-D2; or 8. Darth
    Sidious, each. 1.00
Mountain Dew: 9. Darth Maul; 10. Jar Jar (Binks);
    11. Mace Windu; 12. Obi-Wan Kenobi; 13. Cap-
    tain Panaka; 14. Rune Haako; 15. Ric Olie; or
    16. Destroyer Droid, each. 1.00
Diet Pepsi: 17. Queen Amidala; 18. Padme;
    19. Shmi Skywalker; 20. Battle Droid, each. 1.00
Pepsi One: 21. Chancellor Valorum; 22. C-3PO;
    23. Nute Gunray; or 24. Boss Nass, each 1.00
Gold Yoda Chase Can 20.00
Seven-Up 19. Nute Gunray 5.00
Episode I Promo cans, sealed in white box, each. . . . 10.00

MOVIE THEATER CUPS

Cups, plastic, large, movie theater
Darth Maul $2.00
Qui-Gon Jinn 2.00
Anakin SKywalker. 2.00
Watto 2.00

POTATO CHIPS

    Lay's Potato Chips had a popular promotion for the *Star Wars Trilogy Special Edition* movies. The UPC symbol from two bags of chips plus $1.99 got you the Spirit of Obi-Wan action figure. It's a 3fl" blue-green semi-translucent plastic figure of Obi-Wan and came in a plastic bag in a plain white mailing box with "SKU #69736" on it. The figure does have the magic "Kenner" name on the bottom, but it has no discernable action. The main reason it gets listed with the action figures in many magazines is that the Froot Loops Han Solo in Stormtrooper Disguise mail-in, which really is an action figure, gets listed and so they think this mail-in should be too. It belongs in this section, with figures like the Taco Bell under three years old Yoda figure listed above.

    Lay's also put out a lot of its 1999 product line in *Episode I* bags. Naturally I forced myself to munch some so I could save the bags – purely in the interest of Collecting Science I assure you. The bags also came with a collectible game card.

Chips
Lay's Potato Chip bag with "Spirit of Obi-Wan"
    figure offer, various sizes . . . . 1.00 to 2.00
Spirit of Obi-Wan translucent non-action figure, with
    mailer box 10.00
Doritos bag with 3-D Motion card premium 1.00

Box of Figural Candy Head Containers (Topps 1997)

Star Wars Episode I Chip bags (1999)
Anakin Skywalker, 5½ oz. Lays Potato Chips 1.50
Obi-Wan Kenobi, 5½ oz. Lays Potato Chips 1.50
Queen Amidala, 5½ oz. Lays Potato Chips 1.50
Jar Jar Binks, 5½ oz. Lays Potato Chips 1.50
Qui-Gon Jinn, 14½ oz. Doritos Chips 1.50
R2-D2, 14½ oz. Doritos Chips 1.50
Game card, each. 1.00

CANDY

Topps Candy Boxes (1980–83)
The Empire Strikes Back figural head candy con-
    tainers (Topps 1980) box with 18 containers. 40.00
    Containers, each 2.50
    Set, including Stormtrooper, Boba Fett, Chew-
        bacca, C-3PO and Darth Vader 12.50
    Box, empty 5.00
The Empire Strikes Back figural head candy con-
    tainers (Topps 1981) box with 18 containers,
    New Yoda series 40.00
    containers, each 2.50
    Set of six, Tauntaun, Bossk, Yoda, 2-1B 12.50
    Box, empty 5.00
Return of the Jedi figural head candy containers
    (Topps 1983) box with 18 containers 50.00
    containers, six different, each. 2.50
    Set of six, Admiral Ackbar, Darth Vader, Ewok,
        Jabba The Hutt, Sy Snootles, and Wicket. 15.00
    Box, empty 5.00

Hersheys Products, 6-pack cartons (1980s) photos on back
Boxes with large C-3PO or Chewbacca photos 15.00
Boxes with smaller Luke on Tauntaun, Boba Fett, or
    Darth Vader photos 10.00

Star Wars Trilogy Candy Heads (Topps)
Star Wars Trilogy Candy Container collection and
    card set, 4 head figural candy containers and
    10-card set, on header card (Topps 1997) 25.00
Star Wars Trilogy Candy Container box (Topps 1997) . . 50.00

Pez Dispensers (Asst #8633, 1997) bagged or carded
Boba Fett. 4.00
C-3PO 3.00
Chewbacca 3.00

Darth Vader 3.00
Luke Skywalker X-Wing Pilot 4.00
Princess Leia. 3.00
Stormtrooper 4.00
Wicket the Ewok 4.00
Yoda. 3.00
Loose, any of the above. 2.00

Episode I Candy Dispensers (Cap Candy 1999)
Jar Jar Binks Pez Handler (Mos Espa Scene) (#4645) . 25.00
R2-D2 Candy Handler, M & M Minis (#46862) 15.00
Naboo Fighter Dispenser, Skittles (#4666) 20.00

Episode I Fruit Snacks (Farley's 1999–2000)
Mega Dual Galactic Berry, double berry flavored,
    Anakin Skywalker box (#73384) 8.8 oz., 8 pouches 2.00
Glitter Roll Galactic Watermellon Lightsaber Fruit
    Roll, Jar Jar Binks box (#) 5 oz., 8 pouches. 2.00
Fruit Snacks Assorted Flavors, Battle Droid box
    (#73383) 9 oz., 10 pouches 2.00

PIZZA

In late 1996 and early 1997, Pizza Hut sold its take-out pizzas in coloring boxes with *Star Wars* pictures promoting the *Star Wars Special Edition* movies. The boxes are 12½" square. Too bad they didn't change their company logo to read "Pizza Hutt" for the promotion and use a picture of their "founder," Jabba the Hutt, on the boxes.

Australian "Pizza Hutters" did a little better. In 1995 they got a series of four PVC figures bagged with interlocking cardboard backdrops. The series was distributed to comic shops in the United States through Diamond's Previews catalog/magazine, which is why it is listed in this book. The figures are a little smaller than the U.S. PVC figures made by Applause, and have jagged yellow bases. Incidentally, there is nothing on any of the figures, bags, or backdrops which says "Australia" and all the text is in English.

Pizza Hut *Star Wars* coloring box, picturing C-3PO
    and *Millennium Falcon* (1996) $1.00
Pizza Hut *Star Wars* coloring box, picturing R2-D2
    and X-Wing fighters (1996) 1.00
Pizza Hut *Star Wars* coloring box, picturing
    Stormtrooper and AT-AT (1996) 1.00
Pizza Hut *Star Wars* coloring box, picturing Darth
    Vader and Star Destroyer (1996) 1.00

Australian Pizza Hut PVC figures with backdrops,
    set of four in original *Star Wars Trilogy*/
    Pizza Hut clear plastic bags (1995) 20.00
Chewbacca, bagged with backdrop. 5.00
C-3PO, bagged with backdrop 5.00
Darth Vader, bagged with backdrop. 5.00
R2-D2, bagged with backdrop. 5.00

Episode I Pizza Hut coloring boxes
Pizza Hut *Star Wars Episode I* boxes (1999)
    Jar Jar Binks. 1.00
    R2-D2 personal pan pizza box 50

GAMES AND PUZZELS

GAMES

Kenner made the first *Star Wars* games, as well as a variety of jigsaw puzzles, bop bags, vans, and of course, action figures. Many of these were advertised in their various mini-catalogs that came in the boxes for the vehicles. Parker Bros. started making the games in about 1983 and continues to do so today. Kenner is now part of Hasbro as is Parker Bros.

Original Kenner Games (1977–82)
Adventures of R2-D2, board game (Kenner 1977)
   Star Wars logo $25.00
Destroy Death Star game (Kenner 1979) *Star Wars*
   logo 30.00
Escape From Death Star board game, 17¾" x 17¾"
   playing board, four sets of playing pieces and
   R2-D2 spinner (Kenner 1979) *Star Wars* logo 25.00
Hoth Ice Planet Adventure Game, with board and
   spinner (Kenner 1980) *The Empire Strikes*
   Back logo 25.00
Yoda, The Jedi Master board game (Kenner 1981)
   The Empire Strikes Back logo 25.00

Parker Brothers Games (1982–98)
Star Wars (Parker Brothers 1982) box pictures
   Luke in X-Wing gear 30.00
Wicket the Ewok (Parker Brothers 1983) *Return of*
   the Jedi logo 25.00
The Ewoks Save the Trees! (Parker Brothers 1983)
   Return of the Jedi logo. 25.00
Battle at Sarlacc's Pit (Parker Brothers 1983)
   Return of the Jedi logo. 30.00
Return of the Jedi Card Game, 3½" x 4½" box,
   (Parker Brothers 1983). 10.00
Star Wars Death Star Assault Game, board, X-Wing
   fighter, 20 TIE fighter pieces (Parker Bros.
   #40390, 1995) 20.00
Star Wars Monopoly Classic Trilogy Edition (Parker

Star Wars Death Star Assault Game (Parker Bros. 1995)

Bros #40809, 1997) including 9 pewter figurine
   playing pieces, plastic spaceships, imperial
   currency, etc. 35.00
Ewok Card Games (several different, Parker
   Brothers 1984). 15.00
Star Wars Escape the Death Star Action Figure
   Game with two exclusive figures: **Luke Sky-**
   walker in Trash Compactor and **Darth Vader**
   with Removable Dome (Parker Bros. #40905) 15.00

Other Games
Star Wars Card Trick (Nick Trost 1978) 10.00
Top Trumps New Spacecraft (Waddington) 15.00
Yoda, the Jedi Master magic answer fortune telling
   toy (Kenner 1981) 50.00
***Star Wars* Episode I Games** (1999)

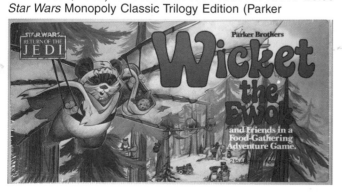

Wicket the Ewok game; and Star Wars *Escape the Death Star Action Figure Game (Parker Bros. 1983 and 1995)*

Battle For Naboo 3-D Action Game (Hasbro 1999)

Naboo Fighter Target Game (Hasbro-Milton Bradley #40971) 20.00
Electronic Lightsaber Duel Game with Qui-Gon Jinn and Darth Maul figures (Hasbro-Milton Bradley #40991) 20.00
Jar Jar Binks 3-D Adventure Game (Hasbro #40997) . . 15.00
Simon Electronic Space Battle Game (Hasbro (#40983)35.00
Star Wars Episode 1 Monopoly (Parker Bros #41018) . . 40.00
Clash of the Lightsaber's Card Game with two pewter figures (Milton Bradley #40993) 13.00
Battle For Naboo 3-D Action Game with 20 Heroes and Villains (Hasbro #40979) 20.00
See also Electronic & Computer

PUZZLES

The earliest puzzles came in blue or purple-bordered boxes. Later they were switched to black borders. Several are advertised in Kenner's mini-catalogs. They are among the earliest Kenner products, since it is fairly easy to put a *Star Wars* picture on an existing jigsaw pattern and add a box. You have to sculpt an action figure before it can go into production. Kenner jigsaw puzzles are not titled. The box contained the movie logo, the puzzle's picture and the number of pieces.

140-Piece Puzzles 14" x 18" (add $5.00 for blue box)

Star Wars Stormtroopers 140-piece puzzle (Kenner 1977–79)

Purchase of the Droids 140-piece puzzle (Kenner 1977–79)

C-3PO and R2-D2 . . . . 10.00
Chewbacca and Han Solo. 10.00
Purchase of the Droids 10.00
Luke and Han in trash compactor 10.00
Tusken Raider. 10.00
Stormtroopers and Landspeeder. 10.00

500-Piece Puzzles 15" x 18" (add $5.00 for blue box)
Ben Kenobi and Darth Vader dueling. 12.00
Cantina Band 12.00
Luke and Leia. 12.00
Luke on Tatooine 12.00
Jawas selling Droids 12.00
Space battle 12.00
Victory celebration 12.00
X-Wing Fighter in hanger 12.00
1,000-Piece Puzzles 21½" x 27½"
Crew aboard the *Millennium Falcon* 15.00
Movie art poster, Hildebrandt Bros. art 15.00

1,500-Piece Puzzles 27" x 33"
Millennium Falcon in space. 20.00
Stormtrooper in corridor 20.00

Craft-Master (1983) *Return of the Jedi* logo
Jig-Saw Puzzles
Battle of Endor, 170 pieces. 12.00
B-Wings, 170 pieces. 12.00
Ewok leaders, 170 pieces. 12.00
Jabba's friends, 70 pieces. 10.00
Jabba's throne room, 70 pieces. 10.00
Death Star, 70 pieces 10.00
Wicket and Friends, 3 different, each 5.00

Frame Tray Puzzles
Darth Vader Frame Tray 5.00
Gamorrean Guard Frame Tray 5.00
Jedi Characters Frame Tray 5.00

Wicket The Ewok Frame Tray Puzzles
Ewoks on hang gliders Frame Tray 5.00
Ewok Village Frame Tray. 5.00
Leia and Wicket Frame Tray 5.00
R2-D2 and Wicket Frame Tray. 5.00
Wicket Frame Tray 5.00
Match Blocks Puzzles

R2-D2 Puzz 3-D (Hasbro 1999)

Ewoks Match Block Puzzle 10.00
Luke and Jabba Match Block Puzzle 10.00

Jigsaw Puzzles (1995–98)
Star Wars Puzz 3D *Millennium Falcon*, 857 pieces
   (Milton Bradley #04678, 1995) 35.00
Star Wars Puzz 3D *Imperial Star Destroyer*, 823
   pieces (Milton Bradley #04617, 1996) 35.00
Star Wars Darth Vader 3-D Sculpture, 144 layers
   (Milton Bradley #04737, 1997) 35.00
Star Wars, A New Hope, 550 piece, 18" x 24"
   (Milton Bradley #4498-1, 1996) 12.50
Star Wars, The Empire Strikes Back, 550 piece,
   18" x 24" (Milton Bradley #4498-2, 1996) 12.50
Star Wars, Return of the Jedi, 550 piece, 18" x 24"
   (Milton Bradley #4498-3) 12.50
The Empire Strikes Back 1,500 piece jigsaw puzzle,
   28¾" x 36" (Springbok/Hallmark PZL9028,
   #45548, 1997) 17.00
Star Wars: A New Hope 500-piece puzzles
   (RoseArt #97033, 1997) 12.00
Star Wars: The Empire Strikes Back 500-piece
   puzzles (RoseArt #97033, 1997) 12.00
Star Wars: Return of the Jedi 500-piece puzzles
   (RoseArt #97033, 1997) 12.00
Star Wars: A New Hope Poster Illustration Puzzle,
   1000 piece (RoseArt #08062, 1997) 7.50

3-D Puzzles (Milton Bradley)
Millennium Falcon Puzz 3D, 857 pieces (#04678) 25.00
R2-D2, *Episode I* Puzz 3D, 708 pieces, battery
   power (#41094) 25.00
Jar Jar Binks *Episode I* 3-D Sculpture, 9" tall,
   133 layers (#41099) 30.00
Darth Vader 3-D Sculpture, 9½" 144 layers (#04737) . . 30.00

Episode I Jigsaw Puzzles (Hasbro 1999)
Yoda Shaped Puzzle, 100-piece (#49035) 4.00
Darth Maul Shaped Puzzle, 100-piece (#49035) 4.00
R2-D2 Shaped Puzzle, 100-piece (#49035) 4.00
Jar Jar Binks Shaped Puzzle, 100-piece (#49035) 4.00
Mos Espa Pod race Puzzle, Glow-in-the-Dark, 200-
   piece (#49034) 12" x 16" 5.00
Jedi vs. Sith, Glow-in-the-Dark, 200-piece 5.00
Movie Teaser Poster Puzzle, 300-piece, (#41229)
   24" x 36" 7.50
Bravo Squadron Assault, 750-piece, two-sided 10.00
Pod race Challenge, 750-piece, two-sided 10.00
Gungan Sub Escape, 750-piece, two-sided 10.00

50-Piece Mini-Puzzles (Asst. #41219)
Queen Amidala 3.00
Pod Race 3.00
Obi-Wan Kenobi, Darth Maul, and Qui-Gon Jinn 3.00
Droids 3.00

Other Puzzles
Darth Maul Rubik's Cube Puzzle (#30020) 15.00
Anakin face Slivers puzzle 10.00

ROLE PLAY GAMES

    West End Games began producing role playing games in the *Star Wars* universe in 1987. This was in the middle of the dark age, when there were no more action figures produced and no new *Star Wars* novels or comics. During this period, they were the only company keeping the *Star Wars* saga alive with anything like new *Star Wars* storylines.

    Role playing games have their own section in most book stores. As such, their books and boxed sets are generally available. They have to compete with CCGs (Customizable Card Games) for the game fanatic's attention. Their fanatics accumulate game modules, rule books, and other items in order to (gasp!) play the games, not collect them. New and revised editions of rule books are much more useful than original editions. The consequences of this are that most of these items, even in near mint condition, are worth little more than their original price!

Boxed Games (West End Games) 9" x 11½" boxes
Star Warriors Role-Playing Board Game, starfighter
   combat, with ship counters, game markers,
   charts, dice, rules booklet, record sheets, and
   map (40201, 1987) $35.00
   Reprint: (1992) 20.00
Assault on Hoth, two person board game, with ter-
   rain map, many stand-up playing pieces,
   cards, dice, and rule book (40203, 1988) 35.00
   Reprint: (1992) 20.00
Battle for Endor, board game, with terrain map,
   many stand-up playing pieces, cards, dice, and
   rule book (40206, 1989) 30.00
   Reprint: (1992) 20.00
Escape From the Death Star, board game, Death
   Star schematic, stand-up cards, score pads,
   dice, and rule book (40207, 1990) 30.00
   Reprint: (1992) 20.00

Basic Game and Sourcebooks (8½" x 11" hardcovers)
Star Wars, The Role-Playing Game, basic rules
   book, 144 pages, 16 pages of color (40001,

Star Warriors; Dark Force Rising Sourcebook; Adventure Journal (West End Games 1990s)

1987) 25.00
2nd Edition (40055, 1993) 25.00
2nd Edition, Revised and Expanded (40120;
   #268-X, 1996) 30.00
Star Wars Sourcebook, background supplement,
   illustrations, descriptions, and statistics, 144
   pages in two-color (40002, #066-0, 1988) 20.00
2nd Edition (40093, 1994) 22.00
Star Wars Movie Trilogy Sourcebook (40076,
   #198-5, 1993) 25.00
Imperial Sourcebook, background supplement
   (40002, #097-0, 1989) 20.00
   TPB reissue (40051, #175-6, 1991) 18.00
   2nd Edition (40092, #210-8,1994) 22.00
Rebel Alliance Sourcebook, background supple-
   ment (40007, #109-8, 1991) 20.00
   TPB reissue (40054, #178-0,1991) 18.00
   2nd Edition (40091, #209-4,1994) 22.00
Heir to the Empire Sourcebook, 144pp, from Timothy
   Zahn's novel (40068, #179-9,1992) 18.00
Dark Force Rising Sourcebook, by Bill Slavicsek,
   142pp, from Timothy Zahn's novel (40074,
   #193-4, 1993) 18.00
Dark Empire Sourcebook (40071, #194-2, 1993) 25.00
The Movie Trilogy Sourcebook (40089, #506-9, 1997) . 28.00
Han Solo and the Corporate Sector Sourcebook
   (40042, #199-3, 1993) 20.00
Shadows of the Empire Sourcebook (40122, 1996) . . . 20.00
The Jedi Academy Sourcebook (40114, #274-4,
   1996) from Kevin Anderson trilogy 22.00
Thrawn Trilogy Sourcebook (40131, #280-9, 1996)
   from Timothy Zahn books. 25.00
Truce at Bakura Sourcebook (40085, #256-6, 1996) . . 22.00
Star Wars Introductory Adventure Game (40602,
   #298-1, 1997) 20.00
Star Wars X-Wing Rogue Squadron Sourcebook,
   based on Michael A. Stackpole novels, 144pg.
   (40148, 1998) TPB. 25.00
Star Wars Hideouts and Strongholds Sourcebook
   (40111, 1998) 22.00

Adventure Modules
Tatooine Manhunt (40005, #069 5, 1988) 10.00
Strike Force: Shantipole (40009, 1988) 10.00

Starfall (40016, #105-5, 1989) hardcover. 10.00
Battle for Golden Sun (40017, #103-9, 1988)
   hardcover 10.00
Otherspace, includes full color map (40018,
   #128-4, 1989) 10.00
Graveyard of Alderaan (40019,#116-0, 1990)
   hardcover 10.00
Scavenger Hunt (40020, 1989) 10.00
Riders of the Maelstrom (40021,1989) 10.00
Crisis on Cloud City (40022, 1989) 10.00
Otherspace II: Invasion (40028, #106-3) hardcover . . . 10.00
Black Ice (40030, #107-1, 1990) hardcover 10.00
The Game Chambers of Questal (40033, #110-1,
   1990) hardcover. 10.00
Domain of Evil (40034, #148-9, 1991) 10.00
Isis Coordinates (40036, #097-0, 1990) hardcover . . . 10.00
Death in the Undercity (40037, 1990) 10.00

Classic Adventures reprints, updated to second edition rules
Classic Adventures, Volume One 40083, #261-2,
   1995) reprints The Abduction of Crying Dawn
   Singer and The Politics of Contraband 20.00
Classic Adventures, Volume Two (#269-8, 1995) 18.00
Classic Adventures, Volume Three (#282-5, 1996) 18.00
Classic Adventures, Volume Four 18.00

Hardcovers
Bounty Hunters (#207-8, 1994) 18.00
Live-Action Roleplaying Game (#283-3, 1996) 20.00

Softcovers 1991-98
The New Republic: Twin Stars of Kira, 96pp (40060,
   #191-8, 1993) 15.00
The New Republic: The Politics of Contraband, 64pp
   (40067, #184-5, 1992) 10.00
Planet of the Mists (40049, #122-5, 1992) 10.00
Mission to Lianna module, 64p (40052, #123-3,
   1992) 10.00
Abduction of Crying Dawn Singer (40053, #177-2,
   1992) 10.00
Heir to the Empire Accessory (#186-1, 1992) 18.00
The Last Command Accessory (40059, #197-7,
   1994) 20.00
Instant Adventures (40137, #293-0, 1996) 15.00

No Disintegrations (#296-5, 1997)................. 15.00
The Black Sands of Socorro Accessory (40154,
    #503-4, 1997) 18.00
Imperial Double-Cross, solo adventure (#502-6,
    1997)...................................... 10.00
Secrets of the Sisar Run, 96pg. (40155, 1997)
    Bros. Hildebrandt cover 12.00
Star Wars Fantastic Technology Personal Gear
    Sourcebook (#40158, 1997)................. 15.00
Star Wars Adventure Journals #1–#14, 6" x 9"
    (41001–14, #400-3–#413-5,1994–97) articles
    and fiction, each 12.00
Best of Star Wars Adventure Journal, Vol. 1, Issue
    #1 to #4, 128p (40129, 1996)............... 20.00
Aliens Compendium (40166, 1998).............. 25.00

Galaxy Guide Books (8½" x 11" Trade Paperbacks)
Galaxy Guide 1: A New Hope (#077-6, 1989) 13.00
    2nd Printing (40038, #125-X, 1991) 12.00
    2nd Edition (40124, #265-5, 1995)............ 12.00
Galaxy Guide 2: Yavin and Bespin (40023, #126-8,
    1989)...................................... 13.00
    2nd Edition: (40119, #262-0, 1995) 12.00
Galaxy Guide 3: The Empire Strikes Back (40039,
    #127-6, 1989) 13.00
    2nd Edition: (40094, 1995).................. 12.00
Galaxy Guide 4: Alien Races (40041, #137-3, 1989).. 13.00
    2nd Edition: 96pp (40094, 1994) 12.00
Galaxy Guide 5: Return of the Jedi (40040, #140-3,
    1990)...................................... 13.00
    2nd Edition (40126, #267-1, 1995) 15.00
Galaxy Guide 6: Tramp Freighters (40027, #146-2,
    1991)...................................... 13.00
    2nd Edition (40095, 1995) 15.00
Galaxy Guide 7: Mos Eisley (40069, 1992) 13.00
Galaxy Guide 8: Scouts (40061,1993)............. 13.00
Galaxy Guide 9: Fragments From The Rim, 96pp
    (40063, 1993) 13.00
Galaxy Guide 10: Bounty Hunters (40073, 1994)..... 13.00
Galaxy Guide 11: Criminal Organizations (40075,
    1995)...................................... 13.00
Galaxy Guide 12: Aliens, Enemies and Allies
    (40087, 1995) 13.00
One Player Games

Scoundrel's Luck, one player game (40102,
    #112-8, 1990) 13.00
Jedi's Honor, one player game (40103, #111-X,
    1990) hardcover........................... 13.00

Other Guide Books (8½" x 11" Trade Paperbacks)
Cracken's Rebel Field Guide (40046, #118-7, 1991) .. 13.00
Death Star Technical Companion (40008, #120-9,
    1991)...................................... 15.00
Planets of the Galaxy, Volume One (40050, 1991).... 13.00
The New Republic: Planets of the Galaxy, Volume
    Two (40057, #180-2, 1992) 13.00
Planets of the Galaxy, Volume Three, 80pp (40072,
    #169-9, 1992) 15.00
Planets Collection (40100, #222-1, 1994) hard-
    cover, collects three above................. 25.00
Shadows of the Empire: Planets Collection (40134,
    1996)...................................... 15.00
The New Republic: Wanted by Cracken (40062,
    #189-6, 1993) hardcover 15.00
Flashpoint! Brak Sector by Sterling Hersey (40077,
    #253-1, 1995) 15.00
Rebel Specforce Handbook (40113, #501-8, 1997) ... 18.00
Galladinium's Fantastic Technology (#215-9, 1995) ... 15.00
Platt's Starport Guide (40107, #224-8, 1995) 25.00
Creatures of the Galaxy (40080,#221-3, 1994)
    hardcover 15.00
Classic Campaigns (#251-5, 1994) 15.00
Operation: Elrood, 96pg. (40132, 1996)........... 15.00
Pirates & Privateers (#294-9, 1996) 18.00
Star Wars Pirates & Privateers Far Orbit Campaign
    (40029, 1998) 25.00
Wretched Hives of Scum & Villainy (#500-X, 1997) ... 18.00
Cracken's Rebel Operatives, 96pg. (40084, #218-3,
    1994)...................................... 15.00
Star Wars Miniatures Battle (40044, #144-6, 1994) ... 18.00
Mos Eisley (#187-8, 1993) 12.00
Droids (40116, #299-X, 1997).................. 15.00
Stock Ships (#244-2, 1995)..................... 18.00
Supernova (#195-0, 1993) 15.00
Goroth: Slave of the Empire (40098, #250-7, 1994)... 15.00
The Kathol Outback (#270-1, 1996) 15.00
The Kathol Rift (The Dark Stryder Campaign)
    (40121, #273-6, 1996) 15.00

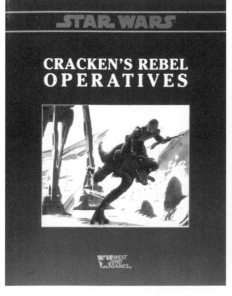

Cracken's Rebel Operatives; Imperial Entanglements; Gamemaster Toolkit (West End Games 1990s)

Heroes & Rogues (40086, #258-2, 1995) 18.00
Cracken's Threat Dossier, 144pg. (40139, #504-2,
    1997). 20.00
Alliance Intelligence Reports (40109, #260-4, 1995) . . 15.00
Shadows Underworld (#290-6,1997) 15.00
Players Guide to Tapani (40155, 1997) 12.00
Live-Action Adventures (#286-8,1996). 15.00
Live-Action Adventures Tool Kit (40152, 1998). 15.00
Starfighter Battle Book (#092-X,1990) 15.00
Imperial Entanglements, 96p (40127, #127-X, 1996). . 15.00

Supplements
Star Wars Rules Companion, 80 pages (40043, 1989) 15.00
Campaign Pack, includes floorplans and screen
    (1988) 15.00
Lightsaber Dueling Pack, includes two flip books
    and score cards (#088-1, 1988) 12.00
Starfighter Battle Pack, includes two flip books and
    score cards (1989) 15.00
Gamemaster Kit (40048, 1991) 12.00
Gamemaster Handbook, 128p (40065, #185-3, 1993) . 18.00
Gamemaster Screen, 2nd edition, with 32-page
    booklet (40064, #183-7, 1992) 10.00
Star Wars Miniatures Battles Companion (40070,
    1994). 15.00
Expanded Gamemaster Screen, revised (40135,
    #288-4, 1996) 10.00
Mos Eisley boxed set (40212, #295-7, 1997)
    hardcover 35.00

GAMING MINIATURES
West End Games (1988–97)

    West End Games produced 25mm lead miniature figures to accompany its games starting in 1988. They are not heavily collected by non-gamers. They were, however, popular with modelers, who paint and display them. There are 14 boxed sets, usually containing 10 figures, which were produced from 1988 to 1991. All of the figures came with statistics for use with West End's role playing games. Bob Charrette and Julie Guthrie were credited as sculptors on the first ten packs, while Jonathan Woods sculpted the last four. In 1993, West End Games began producing three-figure blister packs of figures. They have made over fifty different packs to date, and several sets of ships.

Miniatures: Figures (25mm figures in 4" x 8" boxes)
Heroes of the Rebellion, 10 figures (40301, #074-1,
    1988) $25.00
Imperial Forces, 10 figures (40302, #075-X, 1988) . . . 20.00
Bounty Hunters, 10 figures (40303, #076-8, 1988) . . . 25.00
A New Hope, 10 figures (40304,#077-6, 1988) 20.00
The Empire Strikes Back, 10 figures (40305,
    #130-6, 1989) 20.00
Return of the Jedi, 10 figures (40306, 134-9 1989) . . . 20.00
Stormtroopers, 10 figures (40307,#131-4, 1989) 18.00
Rebel Characters, 10 figures (40308, #132-2, 1989) . . 18.00
Mos Eisley Cantina, 10 figures (40309, #133-0, 1989). 20.00
Jabba's Palace, 8 figures (40310,#138-1, 1989) 20.00
Rancor Pit, beast keeper and Rancor, in 5 pieces
    (Games 40311, #139-X, 1990) 20.00
Rebel Troopers, 10 figures (40312, #141-1, 1990) 18.00
Imperial Troops, 8 figures and one laser cannon
    (Games #40313, #142-X, 1991) 18.00
Zero-G Assault Troopers, 8 figures (40314, #142-X,
    1992). 18.00

25mm pewter, 3-figure blister packs

*Mos Eisley Cantina and Rancor Pit
25mm figure sets (West End Games 1989–90)*

Heroes 1 (40401, 1993) Luke, R2-D2 & C-3PO. 9.00
Heroes 2 (40402, 1993) Han, Chewbacca and Leia . . . 9.00
Stormtroopers 1 (40403, 1993) 5.00
Stormtroopers 2 (40404, 1993) 5.00
Rebel Troopers 1 (40405, 1993) 5.00
Rebel Troopers 2 (40406, 1993) 5.00
Users of the Force (40407, 1993) 5.00
Pilots and Gunners (40408, 1993). 5.00
Stormtroopers 3 (40409, 1993) 5.00
Imperial Crew with Heavy Blaster (40410, 1993) 5.00
Imperial Army Troopers 1 (40411, 1993) 5.00
Imperial Navy Troopers (40412, 1993). 5.00
Rebel Troopers 3 (40413, 1993) 5.00
Rebel Commandos 1 (40414, 1993) 5.00
Imperial Officers (40415, 1993). 5.00
Stormtroopers 4 (40416, 1993) 5.00
Rebel Commandos 2 (40417, 1993) 5.00
Imperial Army Troopers 2 (40418, 1993) 5.00
Imperial Navy Troopers 2 (40419, 1993) 5.00
Bounty Hunters 1 (40420, 1993) 5.00
Rebel Troopers 4 (40421, 1993) 5.00
Bounty Hunters 2 (40422, 1993) 5.00
Droids (40423, 1993) 5.00
Denizens of Cloud City (40424, 1993). 5.00
The Emperor (40425, 1993) 5.00
Bounty Hunters #3 (40426, 1993) 5.00
Denizens of Tatooine (40427, 1993) 6.00
Jedi Knights (40428, 1993) 5.00
Aliens of the Galaxy #1 (40429, 1993) 5.00
Sandtroopers (40430, 1993) 5.00
Snowtroopers (40431, 1993) 5.00
Hoth Rebels (40432, 1993). 5.00
Scout Troopers (40433, 1994). 6.00
Rebel Operatives (40434, 1994) 6.00
Wookiees (40435, 1994) 6.00
Mon Calamari (40436, 1994) 6.00
Heir to the Empire Villains (40437, 1994) 6.00
Ewoks (40438, 1994) 6.00
Noghri (40439, 1994) 6.00
Luke, Leia and Vader (40440, 1995) 6.00
Zero-G Troopers (40441, 1995) 6.00

Stormtroopers 1 and Imperial Speeder Bike 25mm pewter blister packs (West End Games 1993)

Encounter on Hoth (40442, 1995) 6.00
Aliens of the Galaxy 2 (40443, 1995) 6.00
Jabba the Hutt (40444, 1996) 1 figure 6.00
Jabba's Servants: Bib Fortuna, Ooola and Rancor
     Keeper (40445, 1996) 6.00
Dark Stryder 1 (40446, 1996) 6.00
Dark Stryder 2 (40447, 1996) 6.00
Pirates (40448, 1996) 6.00
Mos Eisley (40449, 1996) 6.00
Gamorrean Guards (40450, 1996) 6.00
Mos Eisley Cantina Aliens (40451, 1996) 6.00
Dark Stryder 3 (40452, 1996) 6.00
Aliens of the Galaxy 3 (40453, 1996) 6.00
Mos Eisley Cantina Aliens 2 (40454, 1996) 6.00
Imperial Troop 12-pack (50455, 1997) 20.00
Rebel Troop 12-pack (50456, 1997) 20.00

Ships/Vehicles
Landspeeder (40501, 1994) 6.00
Imperial Speeder Bikes (40502, 1994) 6.00
Rebel Speeder Bikes (40503, 1994) 9.00
Storm Skimmer (40504, 1994) 9.00
AT-PT (40505, 1994) 9.00
Snowspeeder (40506, 1994) 9.00
Bantha with Rider (40507, 1995) 2-pack 9.00
Tauntaun Patrol (40508, 1996) 10.00

Miniatures Battles (Boxed)
Star Wars Miniatures Battle (40044, #264-7, 1995) . . . 35.00
Star Wars Miniatures Rules, 2nd Edition (40090,
     1994) 18.00
Star Wars Miniatures Battle, Starter Set (40210,
     1995) 12 miniatures 35.00
     2nd Edition (1996) 35.00
Vehicles Starter Set, with Rebel Snowspeeder, 2
     speeder bikes and book (40211, #285-X, 1996) . . 35.00
The Darkstryder Campaign, books, cards, poster
     (Games 40209, #254-X, 1995) 30.00
Darkstryder Deluxe Campaign Pack, boxed set,
     includes two 96pg sourcebooks, Timothy Zahn
     story, cards, poster and three supplements
     (Games 40220, 1998) 39.00
Darkstryder: Endgame (40112,#287-6, 1996) 18.00
Lords of the Expanse, books, guides, maps (40215
     #297-3, 1997) 30.00

*Invasion of Theed Adventure Game
(Hasbro/Wizards of the Coast 2000)*

NEW ROLE PLAY GAMES

Hasbro/Wizards of the Coast now produces Star Wars role play games. The Invasion of Theed game has been a popular collectible for non-games because of the exclusive Wookiee action figure. Whether this results in more gaming remains to be seen.

New Role Playing Games (Hasbro/Wizards of the Coast)
Star Wars Invasion of Theed Adventure Game
     Starter Box with exclusive **Wookiee** action
     figure on blister card [601969.0000]
     (0-7869-1792-X, 2000) $30.00
Star Wars Role Playing Game Core Rulebook
     (0-7869-1793) hardcover 35.00
Rebellion Era Sourcebook (0-7869-1837-3,
     2000) hardcover 30.00
The Dark Side Sourcebook (0-7869-1849-7,
     2000) hardcover 30.00
The New Jedi Order Sourcebook . . . .
Star Wars Role Playing Game Character Record
     Sheets (2000) 9.00
Star Wars Creatures of the Galaxy (2000) 13.00
Alien Anthology (0-7869-2663-5, 2000) trade
     paperback 27.00
Starships of the Galaxy (0-7869-1859-4, 2000)
     trade paperback 22.00
Secrets of Tatooine Campaign Pack (0-7869-
     1839-X, 2000) trade paperback 22.00
Secrets of Naboo Campaign Pack (0-7869-
     1794-6, 2000) trade paperback 20.00

CUSTOMIZABLE CARD GAMES

Customizable Card Games (CCGs) are one of the 1990s hottest items. There are many players around and lots of new product. Many of the playing cards are quite valuable. The primary reasons for this are scarcity and play value in the game. Scarcity is always a factor in value, but the other factor is usually some kind of intrinsic desirability or charisma in the item. The simple truth is that game cards are not great art, and even if they were great art, too much of the card is taken up by the game text for one to appreciate the art.

As long as the game is played, scarce cards will be valuable. When the world moves on to the next game, they may not be quite so valuable. But then, as Dennis Miller says, that's just my opinion, I could be wrong.

PREMIERE SET

This initial card set is based on characters and events from the first *Star Wars* movie. It was introduced in December 1995 and was long awaited by Customizable Card Game enthusiasts. It was available in 60-card starter decks, and there are 324 cards in all, divided between light and dark sides. The game is a struggle between the light and dark sides. Each player wields a 60-card deck, either light or dark and the object is to reduce your opponents original force of 60, to zero.

STAR WARS LIMITED

Complete Set: 324 cards	$250.00
Starter Box: 10 starter decks	110.00

Starter Deck: 60 cards	9.00
Booster Box: 36 packs	200.00
Booster Pack: 15 cards	3.00
Common Card	0.15–0.40
Uncommon Card	1.00–2.50

STAR WARS UNLIMITED
Decipher Inc. (1996–98)

Complete Set: 324 cards	$220.00
Starter Box: 5 starter decks	75.00
Starter Deck: 120 cards	10.00
Starter Deck: 90 cards	8.00
Booster Box	75.00
Booster Pack: 15 cards	3.00
Star Wars Unlimited Edition Starter Display, 12 decks and display	125.00
Star Wars Unlimited Edition Booster Display, 36 packs and display	125.00
Rare and Uncommon cards are worth about 75% of the same card in the "Limited Series."	

Enhanced Premiere Expansion Set (Nov. 1998)
Set: 4 unlimited expansion boosters and 6 new premium cards

Booster Box: 20 packs	120.00
Booster Pack: 11 cards	12.00

A NEW HOPE

This initial 162-card limited edition expansion set was introduced in July 1996 and brought Chewbacca and R2-D2 into the game, along with new varieties of cards. The new varieties are creatures, epic events and mobile location cards. Like the original series, it's sold in packs of 15 cards. A revised edition was issued in 1998.

Premiere Set: pack and six cards (Decipher 1995)

A New Hope *Expansion Set, box (Decipher 1996)*

A NEW HOPE

Complete Set: 162 cards. $100.00
Booster Box: 36 pack 90.00
Booster Pack: 15 cards. 2.25
Star Wars: A New Hope Booster Display, 36 packs
    and display 125.00

Revised A New Hope Expansion Set (Sept. 1998)
Set: 162 cards 60.00
Booster Box: 30 packs 25.00
Booster Pack: 9 cards 2.00

STAR WARS SPECIAL EDITION
Decipher (Nov. 1998)

Complete Set: 324 cards. $150.00
Starter Deck: 60 cards 11.00
Starter Box:12 Decks. 75.00
Booster Box: 30 packs 50.00
Booster Pack: 9 cards (inc. One rare) 2.25

EXPANSION SETS

Decipher has released expansion sets frequently since 1996. The first, Hoth, added AT-ATs and Wampa to its CCG environment. It was billed as being part of *The Empire Strikes Back,* but it's all one gaming universe. Revised editions of the earlier series have kept these sets updated.

Limited editon expansion set (Nov. 1996)
Complete Set: 162 cards. $150.00
Booster Box: 36 packs 60.00
Booster Pack: 15 cards. 2.25
The Empire Strikes Back: Hoth Limited CCG
    Booster Display 36 packs and display. 125.00

Revised Hoth Expansion Set (Oct. 1998)
Set: 162 cards 90.00
Booster Box: 40.00
Booster Pack. 5.00

This is the first set to be sold in packs of 9 cards, rather than 15 and boxes of 60 packs, rather than 36. Both ratios yield the same 540 cards per box.

Limited editon expansion set (April 1997)
Complete Set: 180 cards. $30.00
Booster Box: 60 packs 65.00
Booster Pack: 9 cards (inc. 1 rare) 2.25
Star Wars Dagobah Booster Display, 60 packs and
    display 100.00

Revised Dagobah Expansion Set (Dec. 1999)
Booster Box: 30 packs 30.00
Booster Pack: 9 cards 2.00

Limited editon expansion set (Nov. 1997)
Complete Set: 180 cards. $175.00
Booster Box: 60 packs 35.00
Booster Pack: 9 cards (inc. 1 rare) 2.50
Star Wars Cloud City Booster Display, 60 packs and
    display 150.00

Enhanced Cloud City (Dec. 1999)
Set: 12 new cards
Booster Box: 20 packs 25.00
Booster Pack: 11 cards 2.00
Booster Box: 12 packs 25.00
Booster Pack: 39 cards 4.00

Limited edition expansion set (April 1998)
Complete Set: 180 cards. $150.00
Booster Box: 60 packs 75.00
Booster Pack: 9 cards (inc. 1 rare) 2.25
Jabba's Palace Booster Display, 60 packs & display . 150.00

Expansion Sets: The Empire Strikes Back: *Hoth, box and Jabba's Palace, box (Decipher 1996–98)*

Hoth Expansion Set, two cards (Decipher 1996)

Sealed decks, 6 different (Oct. 2000) , featuring
Bib Fortuna; Gamorrean Guard; Han Solo in Carbonite:
Chewbacca; Lando Calrissian disguised; Salacious Crumb
Set: 20 cards 5.00
Set: 74 cards 12.00

Enhanced Jabba's Palace (Jan. 2000)
Set: 12 additional cards cards
Booster Box: 12 packs 65.00
Booster Box: 20 packs 130.00
Booster Pack: 11 cards 15.00

ENDOR

Limited edition expansion set (June 1999)
Complete Set: 180 cards $150.00
Booster Box: 30 packs 75.00
Booster Pack: 9 cards (inc. One rare) 2.25
Foil Set: 18 cards 175.00

DEATH STAR II

Limited edition expansion set (July 2000)
Set: 182 cards 175.00
Boster Box: 36 packs 75.00
Booster Pack: 11 cards 2.25
Preconstructed Starter Deck: 60 cards 7.00

TATOOINE

Limited edition expansion set (2001)
Complete Set: 120 cards 100.00
Booster Box: 30 packs 70.00
Booster Pack: 11 cards 3.00

CORUSCANT

Limited edition expansion set (2001)
Complete Set: 180 cards 250.00
Booster Box: 30 packs 60.00
Booster Pack: 11 cards 3.00

THEED PALACE

Limited edition expansion set (Dec. 2001)
Complete Set: 120 cards 100.00
Booster Box: 30 packs 70.00
Booster Pack: 11 cards 3.00

ANTHOLOGY SETS

The first set includes two white border 60 card starter
decks, two black border 15-card A New Hope expansion
packs, two black border 15-card Hoth expansion packs, a
rules supplement, an 11-card Jedi Pack and six rare white border cards previewing the *Star Wars Special Edition* expansion
set. The second Anthology set featured out of print Dagobah
packs.

First Anthology (May 1997)
First Anthology Set in 15" x 13" x 6" box $20.00
First Anthology preview cards, Set of 6 . . . . 10.00

Second Anthology (July 1998)
Second Anthology preview cards, Set of 6 . . . . 10.00
Second Anthology Set 35.00

Third Anthology (June 2000)
Third Anthology set, 174 cards 20.00
Third Anthology, 6 new cards 10.00

REFLECTIONS
Decipher (2000–2002)

Reflections I, Foil versions of 114 rares from
   previous sets (Jan. 2000)
Set: 114 foils 400.00
Booster Box: 30 packs 100.00
Booster Pack: 18 cards 4.00

Reflections II, complete reissue set (Jan. 2001)
Set: 154 cards 350.00
Booster Box: 30 packs 110.00
Booster Pack: 18 cards 5.00
Darth Vader case card 20.00

Reflections III, complete reissue set (2002)
Booster Box: 30 packs 100.00
Booster Pack: 18 cards 5.00
Six Theed Palace previews 15.00

YOUNG JEDI
Decipher (1999–2001)

Young Jedi is based on *Episode I*. It is a separate game
and does not play with the other cards.

THE MENACE OF DARTH MAUL

Set issued (May 1999)
Set: 140 cards $95.00
Foil Set: 18 cards 100.00
Booster Box: 30 packs 20.00
Booster Pack: 11 cards 2.75
Starter Deck: 60 cards 7.00
Enhanced Set: 6 new cards (Aug. 2000). 5.00
Enhanced Starter Deck 15.00
Enhanced Box: 12 Decks 55.00

THE JEDI COUNCIL

Set issued (Oct. 1999)
Set: 140 cards plus 18 foils $75.00
Booster Box: 30 packs 20.00
Booster Pack: 11 cards 2.75
Starter Deck: 60 cards 7.00

BATTLE OF NABOO

Set issued (April 2000)
Set: 140 cards plus 18 foils $75.00
Booster Box: 30 packs 25.00
Booster Pack: 11 cards 2.75

Young Jedi: The Jedi Council, Star Deck Boxes (Decipher 1999)

Starter Deck: 60 cards 15.00
Enhanced Set: 12 new cards 5.00
Enhanced Booster Box: 12 decks 60.00

DUEL OF THE FATES

Set issued (Nov. 2000)
Set: 60 cards 70.00
Booster Box: 30 packs 20.00
Booster Pack: 11 cards 2.75

BOONTA EVE POD RACE

Set Issued (Sept. 2001)
Set: 60 cards 70.00
Booster Box: 30 packs 50.00
Booster Pack: 11 cards 2.75

JEDI KNIGHTS
Trading Card Game
Decipher (2001)

Jedi Knights is a new trading card game featuring 3-D computer generated images. It will not play with the other games.

Premier Set: 205 cards $125.00
Booster Box: 36 packs 75.00
Starter Box 95.00

SCUM AND VILLANY

Set: 160 cards plus 12 flip move cards $125.00
Booster Box: 36 packs 75.00
Booster Pack: 11 cards 2.75
Booster Box-First Day: 36 packs 100.00
Promo cards, 5 different, each 2.75
Admiral Motti replacement card 2.75

MASTERS OF THE FORCE

Set: 140 cards $125.00
Booster Box: 36 packs 75.00
Booster Pack: 11 cards 2.00

Decipher also offered a variety of additional items for the discriminating player–collector. A few of the cards were corrected, and players could mail in the old card for a replacement. The first of these was the Dagobah Asteroid Sanctuary card, which didn't work properly in game play. You could also get this card in *Scrye* magazine. Decipher intends to continue to produce and distribute the card, so only the error version should become a collectible. Another replaceable card

was the R-3PO card from the Hoth expansion set. It had the wrong image on it (same as the K-3PO card) and you can get a replacement by mail. This is a limited card, so Decipher will destroy the error card when you mail it in and keep the total number in existence at a constant 110,000. The cards have the same play value, but over time there will be more correct cards and less error cards. You can always turn an error card into a correct card for the price of a stamped, self-addressed envelope, but not the other way around.

Decipher distributed Rebel Leader Cards as convention giveaways. There is nothing like a show special freebee to get people to come to your booth. You could also mail-in for one, for $1.00 each, for a short time at the end of 1997 and beginning of 1998. Jedi Packs are available the same way, but without time limit.

Jedi Pack, 11 cards 5.00
Rebel Leader Checklist, 2 cards 2.75

Unfortunately (for Decipher anyway) Wizards of the Coast now has the exclusive license to produce collectible card games. Decipher's license has lapsed and it can't sell any more cards after April 30, 2002. Since all of its existing stock must be sold, prices will be depressed, at least for the moment. My local comic book and gaming shop says the cards are worth squat, or perhaps less than squat, but certainly not more. If so, the prices listed here may be too high. In any event, primary collecting interest is in the black-border limited series cards.

STAR WARS 2-PLAYER
CUSTOMIZABLE CARD GAME
Parker Brothers (Feb. 1996)

The Premiere two-player game was introduced in February 1996 and is distributed by Parker Brothers. That means that it found its way into toy stores. The box includes a Light Side and a Dark Side deck, each comprised of 60 common cards, plus a 15-card expansion pack. It's designed to provide the two players with everything they need to begin play. There are three Luke Skywalker and three Darth Vader cards which are exclusive to this set, although they are common within the set. The first 50,000 games distributed had a limited edition expansion pack, while later boxes had unlimited packs.

Star Wars 2-Players Customizable Card Game,
    licensed from Decipher (#40360, 1996) $20.00

THE EMPIRE STRIKES BACK
INTRODUCTORY TWO-PLAYER GAME

The Empire Strikes Back two-player game was introduced in March 1997 and is also distributed by Parker Brothers. It's the second of a series of three, but I wouldn't bet against others based on the new movies. There are seven unique cards in the set.

Box Set: $20.00

HOUSEHOLD

This household section covers *Star Wars* items for use in the Bathroom, Bedroom, Kitchen, and other rooms in a house, as well as holiday and party items. See also CERAMICS and ELECTRONICS AND COMPUTER.

BATHROOM

Bathroom products include soaps, grooming products, and towels. Some of the combs are designed to be carried in your pocket and some of the towels are designed for the beach, but they are still listed here. Many collectors have one or more of these items in their collections, but they do not seem to be looking for more of them so as to have, for example, every *Star Wars* towel. They just treat what they have as part of their "other *Star Wars* stuff."

Bubble Bath
Bubble Bath Character Containers, 4½" x 9½" tall
    (Omni 1981–83)
        Chewbacca (1981). $15.00

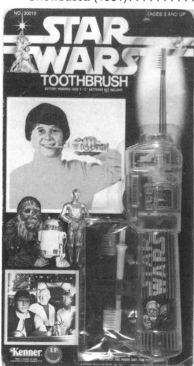

Star Wars Electric Toothbrush (Kenner 1978) and Princess Leia toothbrush (Oral B 1985)

Darth Vader (1981) 15.00
Jabba the Hutt (1981) 15.00
Luke Skywalker in X-Wing Pilot outfit (1981). 15.00
Princess Leia (1981) 15.00
R2-D2 (1981). 15.00
Wicket (1983) 15.00
Yoda (1983) 15.00
Bubble Bath Refueling Station, 6½" tall bottle
    decorated with ships and SW logo (Omni 1981) . . . 5.00
Bubble Bath (Addis 1983)
    Luke 15.00
    Leia 15.00
    R2-D2 . . . . 15.00
    Darth Vader 15.00
    Chewbacca 15.00
    C-3PO. 15.00
    Ben Kenobi 15.00
    Wicket 15.00
R2-D2 and C-3PO Bubble Bath Gift Set, with 2
    soaps (Addis 1985) 30.00
Ewoks Bubble Bath Gift Set, with soap (Addis 1985). . 25.00

***Star Wars Episode I* Bubble Bath** (Minnetonka Brands 1999)
Jar Jar Binks Galactic Bubble Bath bottle, 16oz 3.00
Jar Jar Binks bust figure topper Bubble Bath (#83011) . . 4.00

Personal Grooming
Comb and Keeper (Adam Joseph Industries 1983)
    Cantina Band (*Return of the Jedi* header card). . . 15.00
    Land Speeder (*Return of the Jedi* header card) . . 15.00
    Kneesaa (Wicket the Ewok header card) 10.00
R2-D2 and C-3PO Pop-Up Comb, comb comes with
    flip-up mirror, *Star Wars* logo (Adam Joseph
    1983). 15.00
Darth Vader Pop-Up Comb, comb comes with
    flip-up mirror, *Return of the Jedi* logo (Adam
    Joseph 1983). 15.00
Leia Pop-Up Comb, comb comes with flip-up mirror,
    Return of the Jedi logo (Adam Joseph 1983) 15.00
Ewok Personal Care Kit, picture of Princess
    Kneesaa on front of bag, including comb &
    mirror (Adam Joseph 1983) 25.00

***Return of the Jedi* Toothbrushes**, in box, on header card
Princess Leia Toothbrush (Oral-B 1985) 15.00
Darth Vader Toothbrush (Oral-B 1985) 10.00
Luke Skywalker Toothbrush (Oral-B 1985). 10.00
Ewoks Toothbrush (Oral-B 1985). 12.00
Jedi Master Three-pack, shrink wrapped (Oral-B 1985) 30.00
Electric Toothbrush, battery powered (Kenner 1978) . . 50.00
The Empire Strikes Back Electric Toothbrush, bat-
    tery powered (Kenner 1980). 30.00
Wicket Electric Toothbrush (1984) 25.00

Star Wars & Episode I Toothbrushes (Colgate 1999)
Darth Maul (#68690) soft compact head #77......... 1.00
Queen Amidala, with figural holder (#56007) extra
    soft, ages 5-8 #99.......................... 2.00
Jar Jar Binks, with figural holder (#56007) extra
    soft, ages 5-8 #99.......................... 2.00
Anakin Skywalker, with figural holder (#56007)
    extra soft, ages 5-8 #99.................... 2.00
Darth Maul, with figural holder (#56007) extra soft,
    ages 5-8 #99............................. 2.00

Toothbrushes, Orig. Series (Colgate)
C-3PO & R2-D2 (#56005) extra soft, ages 3-8 #99..... 1.00
Luke Skywalker X-Wing pilot (#56005) extra soft,
    ages 3-8 #99 .... 1.00

Episode I Toothpaste (Colgate 1999)
Anakin Skywalker 5.6 oz tube, Galactic Bubble Mint
    flavor (59604).......................... 3.00
Jar Jar Binks 5.6 oz tube, Galactic Bubble Mint
    flavor (59604) 3.00
Jedi Knights 5.6 oz tube, Galactic Bubble Mint
    flavor (59604).......................... 3.00

Combo Packs: Toothbrush, Toothpaste & Figural Holder
Packages with random combinations of
    Toothbrushes, Toothpaste and holders from
    above (Colgate #78023, 1999) 5.00

Shampoo
Shampoo Character Containers (Omni 1981-83)
    Chewbacca (1981)......................... 15.00
    Darth Vader (1981) 15.00
    Jabba the Hutt (1981) 15.00
    Luke Skywalker in X-Wing Pilot outfit (1981)..... 15.00
    Princess Leia (1981) 15.00
    R2-D2 (1981)............................. 15.00
    Wicket (1983) 15.00
    Yoda (1983).............................. 15.00
Shampoo Refueling Station, 6½" bottle decorated
    with ships & *Star Wars* logo (Omni 1981)........ 5.00
Princess Leia Beauty Bag, 2 oz. shampoo, conditioner
    & cologne in SW logo bottles with Leia
    drawings, soap and comb (Omni 1981) 40.00

Luke Skywalker Belt Kit, 2 oz. shampoo, con-
    ditioner & cologne in SW logo bottles with Luke
    drawings, soap, comb & toothbrush (Omni 1981) . 40.00

Star Wars & Episode I Shampoo, Lotion and Body Wash
    with figure topper (Minnetonka Brands 1999) 11 oz.
    Anakin Skywalker Galactic Shampoo (#83012) 4.00
    C-3PO Galactic Shampoo (#81021) 4.00
    Stormtrooper Galactic Body Wash (#81022) 4.00
    Queen Amidala Galactic Lotion 4.00

Soaps
C-3PO Soap, 4" (Cliro 1977)................... 10.00
R2-D2 Soap, 4" (Cliro 1977) 10.00
Character Soaps, packaged in window boxes with
    Star Wars logo and short description of charac-
    ter on back of box (Omni 1981-83):
    C-3PO..................................... 10.00
    Chewbacca 10.00
    Darth Vader............................... 10.00
    Gamorrean Guard 10.00
    Lando Calrissian 10.00
    Leia...................................... 10.00
    Luke 10.00
    R2-D2 .... 10.00
    Wicket.................................... 10.00
    Yoda 10.00
Star Wars Soap Collection, 4 char. soaps together:
    Leia, Luke, Yoda, & Chewbacca (Omni 1981).... 30.00
Star Wars Soap Collection, 4 char. soaps together:
    R2-D2, C-3PO, Darth, & Lando (Omni 1981) 30.00

Episode I Galactic Glycercin Soap
    3.5 oz. (Minnetonka Brands 1999)
    with Jar Jar Binks head inside (#53050)......... 2.00
    with Anakin Skywalker bust inside (#84060) 2.00
    with Darth Maul bust inside (#84059) 2.00

Towels
R2-D2 & C-3PO beach towel (1980s) 15.00
Darth Vader beach towel (1980s) 15.00
R2-D2 & C-3PO hand towel (1980s)............... 5.00
R2-D2 wash cloth (1980s) 5.00
R2-D2 Bath Towel, 35" x 60" (1997) 15.00

Queen Amidala Lotion; Jar Jar Bubble Bath; Anakin Soap; Queen Amidala Lip Balm; and Jar Jar Bubble Bath (Minnetonka Brands 1999)

Anakin Skywalker Indoor Sleeping Bag (Ero 1999)
"Beware!" Door Hanger (Antioch 1999)

Boba Fett Bath Towel, 35" x 60" (1997) 15.00
Princess Leia Bath Towel, 35" x 60" (1997) 15.00
Darth Vader Bath Towel, 35" x 60" (1997) 15.00
Stormtrooper Bath Towel, 35" x 60" (1997) 15.00
C-3PO Bath Towel, 35" x 60" (1997) 15.00
Darth Vader Beach Towel, 30" x 60" (1997) 20.00
C-3PO and R2-D2 Beach Towel, 30" x 60" (1997) 20.00
Stormtrooper Beach Towel, 30" x 60" (1997) 20.00

***Episode 1* Beach Towels**, 30" x 60" Jumbo
   (Hilasal Company)
Naboo Starfighter (#15210) 10.00
Jar Jar Binks (#15213) 10.00
Pod race (#15215) 10.00

BEDROOM

Star Wars bedding was popular from 1978 to 1984 and
a variety of sheets, pillowcases, blankets, bedspreads and curtains were made. Most collectors are happy if they still have
the ones they slept on as kids, but don't seem to be particularly interested in acquiring the same items in original condition. The problem, I suppose, is that there is little that you can
do with a sheet if you don't sleep on it, and if you do sleep on
it, it would loose its value as a collectible. For this reason,
sheets and similar items, in original packaging are worth, at
most, about the same as a new *Star Wars* sheet in its packaging. Your old sheets may be worth something to you, but
probably not to anyone else.

Star Wars sleep products made a comeback in 1997 and
new ones are available. You can order just about anything you
would want from the Jawa Trader, (i.e. the Official *Star Wars*
Fan Club). Just pick up a copy of *Star Wars Insider* magazine.
More sleep products will undoubtedly come out in time for

the new movies. Your kids, or grandkids or nephews will
probably want to sleep on the new ones, but you still won't
have much you can do with the old designs. If collector interest picks up, today's popular characters such as Boba Fett
would probably be the ones to look for.

Bedding
Star Wars sheets (1978–79) $25.00
Star Wars blanket (1978–79) 35.00
Star Wars pillowcase (1978–79) 7.50
The Empire Strikes Back sheets (1980–82) 20.00
The Empire Strikes Back pillowcase (1980–82) 7.00
The Empire Strikes Back curtains (1980–82) 25.00
The Empire Strikes Back blanket (1980–82) 30.00
Yoda sleeping bag (1980–82) 25.00
Darth Vader pillow (1983–84) 15.00
Return of the Jedi curtains (1983–84) 25.00
Vehicle Diagram Sheets, twin (1997) 35.00
Vehicle Diagram Sheets, full (1997) 45.00
Vehicle Diagram Comforter, twin (1997) 50.00
Vehicle Diagram Comforter, full (1997) 60.00
Character Study sheets, twin (1997) 35.00
Character Study sheets, full (1997) 45.00
Character Study Comforter, twin (1997) 50.00
Character Study Comforter, full (1997) 60.00
Star Wars Dark Side sheets, twin (1998) 30.00
Star Wars Dark Side sheets, full (1998) 50.00
Star Wars Dark Side Comforter, twin (1998) 50.00
Star Wars Dark Side Comforter, full (1998) 60.00
Imperial Forces Blanket, twin (1998) 40.00
Imperial Forces Blanket, full (1998) 50.00
Luke Skywalker/Princess Leia pillowcase (1997) 7.00
Han Solo/Chewbacca pillowcase (1997) 7.00
Yoda/Obi-Wan Kenobi pillowcase (1997) 7.00
Jabba the Hutt/Boba Fett pillowcase (1997) 7.00
C-3PO/R2-D2 pillowcase (1997) 7.00
Symbols of *Star Wars* blanket, twin (1997) 40.00
Symbols of *Star Wars* blanket, full (1997) 50.00

Episode *I* Bedding
Twin Sheets (Westpoint Stevens #80437) 20.00
Pillowcase (Westpoint Stevens #80462) 5.00
Drapes (Westpoint Stevens #80438) 20.00
Valance (Westpoint Stevens #80440) 15.00
Full Set of sheets, pillowcases, etc. (Westpoint
   Stevens #80436) 35.00
Toss Pillow (Liebhardt Inc.) 11.00

Sleeping Bags
Star Wars sleeping bag (1978) 25.00
The Empire Strikes Back sleeping bag (1980) 20.00
Star Wars Indoor Sleeping Bag, child's size, Toys
   "R" Us special (Ero #71924, 1997) 23.00
Star Wars Episode I Indoor Sleeping Bag (Ero
   #72236, 1999) 25.00

Nightlights
Return of the Jedi Night Lights (Adam Joseph 1983)
   R2-D2 . . . . 5.00
   C-3PO 5.00
   Yoda 5.00
   C-3PO head 5.00
   Yoda head 5.00
Wicket the Ewok Night Lights (Adam Joseph 1983)
   Wicket head 5.00
   Kneesaa head 5.00

Darth Maul Head Container (Applause 1999)

Episode I Containers (Applause 1999)
Darth Maul head container, 11" (#43058) 30.00
R2-D2 figural container, 10" (#42967) 25.00

Episode I Treasure Keepers (Applause 1999)
R2-D2, 5" (#43052) 5.00
Queen Amidala head, 3½" (#43051) 5.00
Jar Jar head, 4" (#43050) 5.00
Yoda head, 6" (#43053) 5.00

KITCHEN

Star Wars kitchen items includes the usual plates, bowls, and mugs, plus paper cups and tissues. See also CERAMICS.

Child's Dinnerware
Star Wars china set (Sigma) $25.00
Return of the Jedi dinnerware set (Deka 1983) 20.00
Wicket the Ewok 3 piece set (Deka 1983) 10.00
Bowls (Deka 1980) 10.00
Cups (Deka 1980) 7.00

Cake Baking Items
R2-D2 cake decorating kit (Wilton 1980) 15.00
Darth Vader cake decorating kit (Wilton 1980) 15.00
C-3PO cake pan (Wilton 1980) 10.00
Boba Fett cake pan (Wilton 1980) 25.00
Darth Vader cake pan (Wilton 1980) 15.00
R2-D2 and C-3PO figural CakeTops (Wilton #3607, 1979) 10.00
Darth Vader and Stormtrooper figural CakeTops (Wilton #3643, 1979) 10.00
R2-D2 and C-3PO figural PutOns (Wilton 1980) 8.00
Chewbacca Cake Candle 3½" (Wilton 1980) 5.00
Darth Vader Cake Candle 3½" (Wilton 1980) 5.00
R2-D2 Cake Candle 3½" (Wilton 1980) 5.00

Kids Mugs, 6oz Vinyl (Applause 1997)
C-3PO (#42683) 5.00
Darth Vader (#42684) 5.00
Ewok (#42685) 5.00

Stormtrooper (#42686) 5.00

Episode I Kids Mugs (Applause 1999)
Jar Jar Binks Kids Cup, 6oz (#43060) 5.00
Queen Amidala Kids Cup, 6oz (#43062) 5.00
C-3PO Kids Cup, 6oz (#43059) 5.00
Anakin Skywalker Kids Cup, 6oz (#43061) 5.00

Episode I Kids Straws (Applause 1999)
Jar Jar Binks Curly Straw (#43063) 1.00
R2-D2 Curly Straw (#43065) 1.00
Pit Droid Curly Straw (#43064) 1.00
Watto Action Straw (#43066) 1.00

Paper Cups and Tissues
Puffs facial tissue boxes (Puffs 1981) picturing:
  AT-ATs on Hoth 10.00
  Darth Vader and Luke battle over Bespin 10.00
  R2-D2 in Dagobah swamp 10.00

Star Wars Dixie Cups, 100 5oz. cups in assorted styles (Dixie Cups 1978) in boxes picturing:
  Darth Vader 10.00
  Death Star, X-Wing, and Darth Vader TIE Fighter . 10.00
  Han & Chewbacca 10.00
  Luke Skywalker and X-Wing 10.00
  Obi-Wan Kenobi 10.00
  Princess Leia 15.00
  R2-D2 and C-3PO 9.00
  Stormtrooper and TIE Fighter 10.00

The Empire Strikes Back Film Cup Assortment, 100 5oz. cups in assorted styles (Dixie Cup 1980) in boxes picturing:
  AT-ATs and Snowspeeder 8.00
  Darth Vader 8.00
  Imperial Star Destroyer 8.00
  Luke on Tauntaun 9.00
  Millennium Falcon 8.00
  Twin-Pod Cloud Car and Cloud City 9.00
  X-Wing in Swamp 8.00

Return of the Jedi *Wastepaper Basket (Chein 1983)*

Yoda 8.00

Return of the Jedi 5 oz. Kitchen Cups Dixie
Cups, 100 5oz. cups in assorted styles (Dixie
Cup 1983) in boxes picturing:
Luke Skywalker, B-Wing Fighter, and Yoda 6.00
Princess Leia (prisoner) and Jabba the Hutt 8.00
Two Ewoks 5.00
Emperor Palpatine, Darth Vader, and Royal Guard . 6.00

Star Wars Saga Film Cup Assortment (Dixie Cup
1984) in boxes picturing:
C-3PO and R2-D2 . . . . 10.00
Princess Leia, Han Solo, and Stormtroopers 12.00
Darth Vader 10.00

***Episode I* Commuter Mugs** (Applause 1999)
Darth Maul Commuter Mug, 15 oz (#43097) 10.00
Jar Jar Binks Commuter Mug, 15 oz (#43099) 10.00

OTHER ROOMS

Most *Star Wars* furniture, rugs, and wastebaskets were
initially designed for kids' bedrooms or playrooms, but now
that those kids have grown up, or at least gotten older, and
have their own houses and apartments, *Star Wars* items can be
found all over the house.

Cork Bulletin Boards (Manton Cork)
Star Wars (1979) $15.00
Yoda, 16" x 22" 15.00
AT-ATs, 11" x 17" 12.00
Chewbacca, 11" x 17" 12.00
Darth Vader, 11" x 17" 12.00
Luke on Tauntaun, 11" x 17". 15.00
R2-D2 and C-3PO, 11" x 17" 10.00
Yoda, 11" x 17" 12.00
Max Rebo Band. 15.00

Drapery (1997)
Vehicle Diagram Rod Pocket Drape, 84" x 84" 45.00
Vehicle Diagram Rod Pocket Drape, 84" x 63" 35.00
Vehicle Diagram Rod Valance 84" x 15" 20.00
Character Study Rod Pocket Drape, 84" x 84" 45.00
Character Study Rod Pocket Drape, 84" x 63" 35.00
Character Study Rod Valance 84" x 15" 20.00

Episode I Drapery (1999)
Drapes (Westpoint Stevens #80438) 20.00
Valance (Westpoint Stevens #80440) 15.00

Furniture
Return of the Jedi Bookcase, 20" x 18" x 41", wood
with scenes from Jedi on back panel (Am.
Toy and Furniture Co. 1983) 150.00
Ewok and Droid Toy Chest, 32" x 18" x 41" (Am.
Toy and Furniture Co. 1983) 175.00
Darth Vader Coat Rack, 47" tall, pix of Darth and Jedi
logo on base (Am. Toy and Furniture Co. 1983) . 100.00
Desk and Chair, 32" high, movie scenes on back
and sides (Am. Toy and Furniture Co. 1983) 175.00
Return of the Jedi Nightstand, 20" x 16½" x 25"
(Am. Toy and Furniture Co. 1983) 150.00
Picnic Table, 36" long, movie scenes on table top
(Am. Toy and Furniture Co. 1983) 175.00
Return of the Jedi Table and Chair Set, 25½" round
table with movie scenes on table top (Am. Toy
and Furniture Co. 1983) 175.00
R2-D2 Toy Chest, 28" tall, wooden base on wheels

Jar Jar Chair (Intex 1999)

with plastic lid (Am. Toy and Furniture Co. 1983). 150.00
Inflatable Chairs (Intex 1999)
Queen Amidala, vinyl, 32" x 31½" x 38" (#68524) 13.00
Jar Jar Binks, vinyl, 32" x 31½" x 37" (#68523) 13.00
Darth Mall, vinyl, 42" x 36" x 48" (#685255) 18.00
C-3PO Junior Chair, 22½" x 22" x 30" (#68522) 10.00

Episode I Magnets (Applause 1999)
Naboo Starfighter, 3-D, 4" (#43056) 3.00
Watto, 3-D, 4" (#43057) 3.00
Jar Jar Binks, 3-D, 4" (#43055) 3.00
Battle Droid on STAP, 3-D, 4" (#43054) 3.00
Trade Federation Droid Starfigher, 2-D, 3" (#43085) . . . 2.00
Naboo Starfigther, 2-D, 3" (#43084) 2.00
Jar Jar Binks & Naboo Starfighter 3-D Magnets on
hanging card (#61581) 10.00

Playhouse (Ero 1999)
Star Wars Episode One Playhouse (#11535) 25.00

Switcheroos
The Empire Strikes Back Switcheroos, "light switch
cover for kids rooms" (Kenner 1980)
Darth Vader, head 25.00
R2-D2, figural 25.00
C-3PO, head 25.00

Rugs
Star Wars Wool Hook Rug, 45" x 69" picturing
C-3PO and R2-D2 (1997). 200.00

Tins
Star Wars Special Edition Popcorn Tin (with three
types of popcorn) 8 lbs. (1997). 35.00

Wastepaper Baskets
Return of the Jedi wastepaper basket, multiple
characters pictured, with Luke at top (Chein
Industries 1983) 25.00
Ewoks wastepaper basket (Chein Industries 1983) . . . 20.00

OUTDOORS
Gym Set
Star Wars Gym Set (Gym-Dandy 1983) $1,200.00

Emergencies
***Star Wars* Bandages** (Curad 1998–99)
C-3PO 30-pack. 2.00
Jar Jar Binks 30-pack 2.00

***Star Wars* & *Episode I* Pool Toys** (Intex 1999)
Millennium Falcon Island/River Raft, 66" x 52" (#58283) 15.00
Jar Jar Ride-In, 2-person, 58½" x 27" (#58533). 10.00
Trade Federation Droid Starfighter Pool Ride-On,
    56" x 37" (#58170) 12.00
Naboo Starfighter Pool Ride-On, 74" x 41" (#58525) . . 10.00
Landspeeder Boat/Lounge (#58380) 12.00
Anakin's Podracer Pool Lounge, 82" x 37" (#58810) . . 15.00
Jar Jar's World Aquarium Pool (#58479). 20.00
Trade Federation Droid Control Ship Spray Pool,
    73" diameter x 13" high (#56470) 20.00

HOLIDAY AND PARTY

Hallmark has made collectible Christmas ornaments for many years. In 1991, they discovered *Star Trek*, but they neglected to tell any *Star Trek* fans. Many of them wanted the initial ornament, but none of them had one, so the price went through the roof. Next year Hallmark actually advertised the ornament on "The Next Generation" TV show. They sold lots of ornaments and so they branched out into superheroes. In 1996, Hallmark discovered the marketing hype for the *Star Wars Trilogy Special Edition* movies and produced ... a grand total of one ornament! They have released four or five every year since. The best way to buy them has been to wait until just after Christmas, when they go on sale or 50% or more off.

Christmas Ornaments (Hallmark 1996–2001)
Millennium Falcon ornament (#07474, 1996). $50.00
Darth Vader hanging ornament (#07531, 1997). 25.00
Yoda hanging ornament (#06355, 1997) 30.00
C-3PO and R2-D2 set of ornaments (#04265, 1997). . 20.00
Luke Skywalker hanging ornament (#05484, 1997) . . . 25.00
Vehicles of *Star Wars*, 3 miniatures (#04024, 1997). . . 40.00
X-Wing Starfighter, light-up (#07596, 1998) 30.00
Boba Fett hanging ornament (#04053, 1998) 18.00
Princess Leia hanging ornament (#04026, 1998) 15.00
Ewoks, 3 miniatures (#04223, July 1998) 18.00
Han Solo (#04007, 1999) 15.00
Chewbacca (#04009, 1999) 15.00
Darth Vader's TIE Fighter (#07399, 1999). 30.00
Max Rebo Band, set of three (#04597, 1999) 25.00

Obi-Wan Kenobi (#06704, 2000) 15.00
R2-D2, battery operated (#06875, 2001) 15.00

Episode I Christmas Ornaments (Hallmark 1999–2001)
Queen Amidala (#04187, 1999) 15.00
Naboo Starfighter (#07613, 1999) 19.00
Jedi Council Members, set of three (#06744, 2000) . . . 20.00
Darth Maul (#06885, 2000) 15.00
Gungan Submarine (#07351, 2000) 25.00
Qui-Gon Jinn (#06741, 2000) 15.00
Anakin Skywalker (#06942, 2001) 15.00
Battle of Naboo, set of three (#05212, 2001) 15.00
Jar Jar Binks (#06882, 2001) 15.00
Naboo Royal Starship (#08475, 2001) 19.00

Party Supplies (1980–85)
Napkins 3.00
Invitations. 3.00
Table covers 5.00
Other party supplies 2.50

Party Favors (1997) bagged
8 Blowouts (Party Express #04742) 3.50
8 Small Paper Plates, 7" (Party Express #05187) 2.50
8 Large Paper Plates, 9" (Party Express #05188) 3.00
8 Party Hats (Party Express #05190) 3.50
10 Small Napkins (Party Express #04756) 2.25
10 Large Napkins (Party Express #05186) 2.50
Crepe Paper Streamer 1.75
Party Game/Wall Game 2.00
X-Wing/TIE Fighter/*Millennium Falcon* Decoration
    (#06461) 5.00
Stickers (#04758) 1.50
8 Treat Sacks (#05192). 2.00
Darth Vader Table Centerpiece (#05241). 3.25
C-3PO Thank You Notes (#07320) 2.00

Episode I Party Supplies and Favors (Party Express 1999)
8 Invitations (#08717) 3.50
16 Napkins (#08718) 2.75
8 Small Plates (#08726) 2.75
8 Plates (#08727). 3.00
8 Cups (#08729). 2.75
8 Party Hats (#08732). 3.50

Princess Leia, Han Solo, Anakin Skywalker and Jedi Council Members (Hallmark 1998–2001)

MASKS, HELMETS AND COSTUMES

Mask and Costume collecting extends far beyond *Star Wars*. Just about every famous or infamous person and fictional character has appeared on some type of Halloween costume over the years. Classic monsters, superheroes, and science fiction characters have always been popular and *Star Wars* provides a host of interesting mask and costume possibilities. Both masks and costumes appeared in 1977, months before there were any *Star Wars* action figures.

MASKS AND HELMETS

Don Post Studios has always made the high-end masks — those designed for adults and for display, rather than for a child's Halloween costume. Lately they have added hands and collector helmets to their line-up. They also produce deluxe replica helmets, which are listed under STATUES.

MASKS

Masks (Don Post Studios 1977–98)
C-3PO latex mask (Don Post 1977). $100.00
    reissue (1978) 75.00
    reissue (late 1980s) 50.00
    reissue, 12" gold tone heavy vinyl (#82013, 1994) 45.00
Cantina Band Member rubber mask (Don Post 1980) . 75.00
    reissue (1990s) 60.00
    reissue, 13" latex (#82005, 1994) 45.00
Chewbacca rubber mask (Don Post 1977) 250.00
    reissue (1978) 100.00
    reissue (1990) 75.00
    reissue, 11" multicolored hair (#82003, 1990s) . . . 50.00
Darth Vader Collector Helmet, plastic (1977) 200.00
    reissue (1978–82) 75.00
    reissue (1983) 50.00
    reissue (#82001, 1994) 50.00
Stormtrooper Collector Helmet, plastic (1977) 90.00
    reissue (1978) 75.00
    reissue (#82002, late 1980s) 60.00
Tusken Raider rubber mask (Don Post late 1970s) . . . 90.00
    reissue (late 1980s) 70.00
    reissue, 11" latex (#82016, 1995) 35.00
Ugnaught mask (Don Post 1980s) 75.00
Yoda rubber mask (Don Post 1980s) 60.00
    reissue (1990s) 50.00
    reissue, 10" latex with hair (#82007, 1994) 30.00
Admiral Ackbar rubber mask (Don Post 1983) 75.00
    reissue (1990s) 60.00

    reissue, 13" latex (#82011, 1994) 40.00
Gamorrean Guard rubber mask (Don Post 1983) 75.00
    reissue, 11" (#82017, 1995) 30.00
Klaatu rubber mask (Don Post 1983) 75.00
    reissue (1990s) 60.00
    reissue, 12" latex with hood (#82018, 1995) 35.00
Nien Nunb rubber mask, 11" (#82015, 1996). 30.00
Weequay rubber mask (Don Post 1983) 90.00
Wicket W. Warrick rubber mask (Don Post 1983) 90.00
    reissue (1990) 75.00
    reissue, 10" hair and hood (#82012, 1994) 40.00
Emperor Palpatine rubber mask 80.00
    reissue, 11" latex with cloth hood (#82014, 1994) 45.00
Greedo, 11" latex (#82027, 1997) 35.00
Prince Xizor, 12" latex and hair (#82021, 1994) 35.00
Jawa 40.00

Hands
Prince Xizor's Hands, 9" latex (#82041, 1994) $30.00
Cantina Band Member's Hands, 10" latex (#82043,

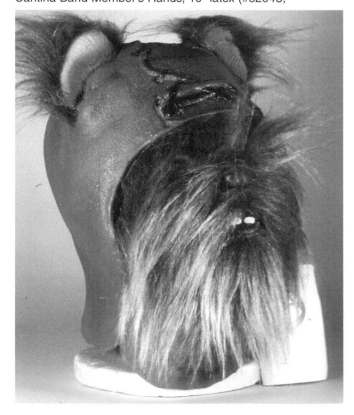

Wicket W. Warrick Mask (Don Post Studios 1994)

1994)................................ 23.00
Greedo Hands (#82045) 30.00
Admiral Ackbar Hands, 15" latex (#82044, 1994)..... 30.00

Episode I Masks (Don Post 1999)
Queen Amidala Theed, throne headdress (#82205) ... 50.00
Jar Jar Binks (#82206)........................ 35.00
Darth Maul (#82208) 35.00
Sebulba (#82212) 40.00
Watto (#82213) 40.00
Ki-Adi-Mundi (#82214) 50.00
Even Piell (#82216) 50.00
Nute Gunray Deluxe (#82219) 75.00
Rune Haako Deluxe (#82220) 70.00
Jar Jar Binks Deluxe (#82302) 120.00
Sebulba Deluxe (#82303)..................... 65.00

HELMETS

Collector Helmets (Don Post 1996–98)
Boba Fett, 10" plastic with smoked viewplate and
    moveable antenna (#82019, 1996)........... $60.00
Darth Vader, 13" plastic faceplate and overhelmet,
    with tinted eyepieces (#82001)............... 50.00
Emperor's Royal Guard, 18" crimson plastic with
    smoked visor (#82020, 1996)................ 85.00
Stormtrooper, 11" white plastic with simulated
    breathing filters and com-link (#82002)........ 60.00
TIE Fighter, 11" (#82025, 1997) 75.00
Scout Trooper Helmet, 11" (#82024, 1997) 75.00
X-Wing Fighter, 13" (#82026, 1997) 80.00

Episode I Collector Helmets (Don Post 1999)
Anakin's Podracer Helmet (#82200) 55.00
Naboo Starfighter Helmet (#82210) 40.00

Classic Action Helmets (Don Post 1997)
Darth Vader Classic Action Helmet, 15" (#82108) ... 180.00
Stormtrooper Classic Action Helmet, 13" (#82107) .. 160.00

TIE Fighter Classic Action Helmet, 15" (#82105) 150.00

RIDDELL MINI-HELMET
Collectible Mini-Helmets, 45% of scale with display base
Darth Vader Mini-Helmet, 3 pieces 95.00
X-Wing (Pilot) Mini-Helmet, moveable pieces 85.00
C-3PO Mini-Helmet, battery powered eyes 80.00
Stormtrooper Mini-Helmet, with die-cast metal parts .. 85.00
Boba Fett Mini-Helmet, die-cast metal parts 85.00

COSTUMES

Ben Cooper was the most famous maker of collectible Halloween costumes in the 1970s and 1980s. All of their product was made for kids. This means that it was made, and sold, inexpensively and was not initially designed as a collectible. Therefore, old costumes in prime condition are hard to find.

Rubies currently makes Halloween costumes for the same market. Their current crop of classic *Star Wars* items may never receive much collector attention, since it must compete with the Ben Cooper originals and with the Don Post Studios higher quality.

Costume and Mask, boxed (Ben Cooper)
Darth Vader (#740, 1977–85)
    Star Wars................................. $35.00
    The Empire Strikes Back 20.00
    Return of the Jedi 20.00
Luke Skywalker (#741, 1977–85)
    Star Wars................................. 35.00
    The Empire Strikes Back 20.00
    Return of the Jedi 20.00
C-3PO (#742, 1977–85)

Stormtrooper and Boba Fett Helmet (Don Post Studios 1996)

Darth Maul Make-up Kit (Rubies 1999)

Star Wars. 35.00
The Empire Strikes Back 20.00
Return of the Jedi 20.00
Luke Skywalker, X-Wing
   Star Wars. 35.00
   The Empire Strikes Back 20.00
   Return of the Jedi 20.00
R2-D2 (#744, 1977–85)
   Star Wars. 35.00
   The Empire Strikes Back 20.00
   Return of the Jedi 20.00
Princess Leia (#745, 1977–85)
   Star Wars. 35.00
   The Empire Strikes Back 20.00
   Return of the Jedi 20.00
Chewbacca (#746, 1977–85)
   Star Wars. 35.00
   The Empire Strikes Back 20.00
   Return of the Jedi 20.00
Stormtrooper (#747, 1977–85)
   Star Wars. 35.00
   The Empire Strikes Back 20.00
   Return of the Jedi 20.00
Boba Fett (#748, 1977–85)
   Star Wars. 35.00
   The Empire Strikes Back 20.00
   Return of the Jedi 20.00
Yoda Costume (#749, 1980–85)
   The Empire Strikes Back 30.00
   Return of the Jedi 30.00
Wicket, *Return of the Jedi* (#735, 1983–85). 25.00
Admiral Ackbar, *Return of the Jedi* (#736, 1983–85) . . 25.00
Gamorrean Guard, *Return of the Jedi* (#737, 1983–85) 25.00
Klaatu, *Return of the Jedi* (#738, 1983–85). 25.00

Costumes and Masks (1995–97)
Darth Vader polyester jumpsuit, bootcovers, cape
   and PVC mask (J.C. Penney 1997) 25.00
Chewbacca costume, includes jumpsuit, mask and
   sash (#15242, 1996) 95.00

Chewbacca rubber mask (#C2867) 20.00
Darth Vader costume, includes jumpsuit, chest-
   piece, cape and mask (#15236, 1996) 75.00
Stormtrooper costume, includes jumpsuit, chest-
   piece and mask (#15243, 1996) 70.00
C-3PO Costume (#15237, 1997) 70.00
Yoda Costume (#15400, 1997) 50.00

Halloween Costumes (1997) Party City Catalog
Darth Vader deluxe child costume, with silk-
   screened jumpsuit, cape, and 3/4 mask (#26)
   small medium or large sizes. 13.00
Super Deluxe Darth Vader child costume, with
   jumpsuit with boot tops, chestpiece, cape, and
   mask (#27) small, medium or large sizes 30.00
Super Deluxe Princess Leia child costume, with
   dress, belt, and wig (#80) small, medium or
   large sizes. 30.00
Stormtrooper deluxe child costume, with silkscreen-
   ed jumpsuit and 3/4 mask (#105) small,
   medium or large sizes 13.00
C-3PO deluxe child costume, with silkscreened
   jumpsuit and 3/4 mask (#14) small medium or
   large sizes. 13.00
Darth Vader adult costume with silkscreened jump
   suit, cape, and 2-piece PVC mask (#231)
   small, medium or large. 40.00

Rubies Costumes
Darth Vader mask (#2865) 25.00
C-3PO hard mask (#2866) 30.00
Chewbacca mask (#2867) 25.00
Stormtrooper latex mask (#2868) 25.00
Yoda mask (#2869). 30.00
Darth Vader Costume Kit, cape, chest armor, mask,
   and lightsaber (#17016, 1996), boxed 15.00
Darth Vader mask (#2993) 25.00
Chewbacca mask (#2994) 30.00
C-3PO mask (#2995) 25.00
Princess Leia wig 20.00

***Episode I* Costumes** (Rubies 1999)
Darth Maul Costume Kit, with Hooded Cloak, Belt,
   PVC Mask & Glo Lightsaber (#17033) on card . . . 18.00
Obi-Wan Kenobi Costume Kit (#17039) on card 18.00
Obi-Wan Kenobi Costume Kit (#17041) boxed 18.00
Qui-Gon Jinn Costume Kit (#17042) boxed 18.00

***Episode I* Adult Masks** (Rubies 1999)
Darth Maul (#2509) 30.00
Jar Jar Binks, and others, each 25.00

***Episode I* Costumes**, sizes 3-4, 5-7 & 8-10
Darth Maul 35.00
Anakin Skywalker 35.00

***Episode I* Costumes**, sizes 4-6, 8-10, 12-14
Jar Jar Binks, one-piece costume & mask 60.00
Anakin Skywalker, costume & helmet. 60.00
Queen Amidala, costume & headpiece. 60.00
Qui-Gon Jinn, one-piece costume 60.00
Obi Wan Kenobi, one-piece costume 60.00

Make-Up Kit
Queen Amidala Makeup Kit (Rubies #19661) 5.00
Darth Maul Deluxe Makeup Kit (Rubies #19658) 10.00
Jedi Hair Braid, 12" 5.00
Anakin Skywalker necklace 7.50

MICRO FIGURES AND VEHICLES

STAR WARS MICRO COLLECTION
Kenner (1982)

Kenner's Micro Collection consists of plastic playsets and plastic vehicles for use with 1" die-cast figures. The nine playsets could be bought individually or grouped into three "Worlds:" Hoth Ice Planet, Bespin Cloud City, and Death Star. With nine playsets and three worlds you might think that there would be three playsets per world, but you would be wrong. There were two Death Star playsets, three Bespin playsets, and four Hoth playsets. The Hoth Generator Attack set was omitted from the Hoth World group.

There were two ships in the original Micro Line: The X-Wing Fighter and the TIE Fighter. Each had a pilot and a crash feature so that it suffered battle damage at the push of a button along with battle damage stickers. Two exclusive ships were offered in 1983—the *Millennium Falcon* was a Sears exclusive, while the Rebel Armored Snowspeeder was a JC Penney exclusive.

There was also two mail-in "Build Your Armies" set of six figures, offered on specially marked boxes with the usual proof of purchase. Certain Kellogg's C-3PO cereal boxes had a mail-in offer for four figures. The offer was good through August 31, 1985, and was fulfilled with existing stock.

All of the die-cast figures have product numbers on the base or body. They are given below to aid in identification of loose figures. Die-cast ships are not listed here. They are in the DIE-CAST section.

Action Playsets

Bespin Control Room (#69920) includes two Luke figures and two Darth Vader figures (#256-001–004)	$36.00
Bespin Freeze Chamber (#69930) includes eight figures (#460-009–017)	75.00
Bespin Gantry (#69910) includes two Luke figures and two Darth Vader figures (#258-001–004)	36.00
Bespin World: Bespin Control Room, Bespin Freeze Chamber and Bespin Gantry sets, includes 16 figures in 12" x 8" x 7" box (#69940, 1982)	150.00
Death Star Compactor (#93300) includes eight figures (#517-014–021)	60.00
Death Star Escape (#69990) includes six figures (#583-018–023)	60.00
Death Star World: Death Star Compactor and Death Star Escape sets (#93310) includes 14 figures	125.00
Hoth Generator Attack (#93420) includes six figures (#668-001–006)	25.00
Hoth Ion Cannon (#69970) includes eight figures (#692-001–008)	35.00
Hoth Turret Defense (#69960) includes six figures (#463-010–015)	25.00
Hoth Wampa Cave (#69950) includes a Wampa and four figures (#269-001–004 & #269-009-A)	25.00
Hoth World: Hoth Generator Attack, Hoth Ion Cannon and Hoth Wampa Cave sets, includes 19 figures	125.00

Bespin Freeze Chamber; Death Star Escape; and Hoth Turret Defense (Kenner 1982)

Vehicles
Imperial TIE Fighter, includes pilot figure (#270-010) . . 75.00
X-Wing Fighter (#69670) includes pilot figure (#270-
014) 65.00
Millennium Falcon (#70140) includes six figures
(#733-001–006) Sears exclusive 400.00
Rebel Armored Snowspeeder, with working
harpoon (#70150) includes pilot and Harpoon-
er figures (#261-015–016) JC Penny exclusive . . 200.00

Mail-In Figures
Build Your Armies, including three Rebel Soldiers
(#088-001–003) and three Snowtroopers
(#088-005–007) 25.00

Return of the Jedi, Micro Machine Vehicles (Galoob 1993)

MICROMACHINES
Galoob (1993–98)
"Think Big, Play Small"

The Galoob *Star Wars* MicroMachines collection debuted in 1994, as part of their "Space" segment. At the time, *Star Wars* was the hottest collectible going, but very few new items had started to appear other than the JustToys *Star Wars* Bend-Ems. The first batch of MicroMachines contained a three ship set for each of the three movies. The earliest ones have a 1993 Lucasfilm Ltd. copyright, an individual movie logo in the front, and only list the first three series on the back (3-back). These were reissued when the next three items were released, with a generic "*Star Wars*" logo on the front, a 1994 copyright, and list all six series on the back (6-back). All were issued on rectangular header cards as part of MicroMachines "Space" series.

By April 1996 they were replaced by the *Star Wars* Vehicle Collection, which also said "Space" on its original packages, but had different figures in the numbered collections and different UPC codes. Packaging was then changed to omit "Space" and just say "*Star Wars*." Packaging was changed again in 1997 to a striped design, similar to the stripes on the Action Fleet packages.

All of the MicroMachines have small parts and small figures, so most of them are destined to an ignominious defeat at the hands of mom's vacuum cleaner. This will make completing any loose set very difficult. The larger X-Ray fleet and the even larger Action Fleet ships are covered below. See also DIE-CAST for Galoob's MicroMachine Die-Cast ships.

"SPACE" VEHICLE SETS (1993–95)

First Batch (Asst. #65860, 1993) on header card
#1 *Star Wars: Millennium Falcon*; Imperial Star-
Destroyer; X-Wing Starfighter (#65886) on
3-back card $15.00
Reissue as *Star Wars: A New Hope*, 1994
copyright, generic logo, 6-back 7.00
#2 *The Empire Strikes Back*: TIE Starfighter;
Imperial AT-AT; Snowspeeder (#65887) on
3-back card 15.00
Reissue, 1994, generic logo, 6-back 7.00
#3 *Return of the Jedi*: Imperial AT-ST (Chicken
Walker); Jabba's Desert Sail Barge; B-wing
Starfighter (#65888) on 3-back card 15.00
Reissue, 1994, generic logo, 6-back 7.00
#4 *Star Wars: A New Hope*: Y-Wing Starfighter;
Jawa Sandcrawler; Rebel Blockade Runner
(#65897) 8.00
#5 *The Empire Strikes Back*: Imperial TIE
Bomber, Boba Fett's *Slave I*; Bespin Twin-Pod
Cloud Car (#65898) 8.00
#6 *Return of the Jedi*: Speeder Bike with Rebel
Pilot; Imperial Shuttle *Tydirium*; A-Wing
Starfighter (#65899) 8.00

VEHICLE COLLECTOR SETS

Special Edition Vehicle Sets (Asst. #65850 1995) boxed
Star Wars: A New Hope, eight ships, pewter finish
(#65851) $20.00
The Empire Strikes Back, eight ships, pewter finish
(#65852) 20.00
Return of the Jedi, eight ships, pewter finish (#65853) 20.00

Gift Sets, boxed
Star Wars Collector's Gift Set, 14 vehicles, 12
figures,bronze finish, with special Death Star
Battle Station 2 (#64624, 1995) 30.00
Master Collector's Edition, 19 *Star Wars* vehicles
inc. exclusive Super Star Destroyer *Executor*
(#64061) 20.00

VEHICLE SETS (1996–98)

First Batch (Asst. #65860, 1996) on header card
I   TIE Interceptor, Imperial Star Destroyer, Rebel
Blockade Runner (#66111) $7.00
II   Landspeeder, *Millennium Falcon*, Jawa Sand-
crawler (#66112) 7.00
III Darth Vader's TIE Fighter, Y-Wing Starfighter,
X-Wing Starfighter (#66113) 7.00
IV   Imperial Probot, Imperial AT-AT, Snowspeeder
(#66114) 7.00
V   Rebel Transport, TIE Bomber, Imperial AT-ST
(#66115) 7.00
VI   Escort Frigate, Boba Fett's *Slave I*, Bespin
Twin-Pod Cloud Car (#66116) 7.00
VII Mon Calamari Star Cruiser, Jabba's Desert
Sail Barge, Speeder Bike with Rebel Pilot (#66117) 7.00
VIII Speeder Bike with Imperial Pilot, Imperial
Shuttle *Tydirium*, TIE Starfighter (#66118) 7.00
IX   Super Star Destroyer *Executor*, B-Wing
Starfighter, A-Wing Starfighter (#66119) 7.00
X   Incom T-16 Skyhopper, Lars Family

Vehicle Set I (Galoob 1996)

    Landspeeder, Death Star II (#66137) 7.00
XI Bespin Cloud City, Mon Calamari Rebel
    Cruiser, Escape Pod (#66138) 7.00

Second Batch (Asst. #65860, 1997)
XII A-Wing Starfighter (Battle-Damaged), TIE
    Starfighter (Battle-Damaged) Y-Wing Star-
    fighter (Battle-Damaged) (#65154) 7.00
XIII Red Squadron X-Wing (Battle-Damaged),
    Green Squadron X-Wing (Battle-Damaged),
    Blue Squadron X-Wing (Battle-Damaged) (#65155) 7.00

Third Batch (1998)
XIV Imperial Landing Craft, S-Swoop, Death Star
    (#65123) 7.00
XV *Outrider*, Tibanna Gas Refinery, V-35
    Landspeeder (#65124) 7.00

SHADOWS OF THE EMPIRE VEHICLES (1996)

First Batch (Asst. #67076) with exclusive Micro Comic
I   Stinger, IG-2000, Guri, Asp, and Darth Vader
    (#66194) $6.00
II Virago, Swoop with Rider, Prince Xizor, and
    Emperor Palpatine (#66195) 6.00
III Outrider, Hound's Tooth, Dash Rendar, LE-
    BO2D9, and Luke Skywalker (#66196) 6.00

MINI-VEHICLES

Single MicroMachine vehicles (Asst. #75290) carded
Snowspeeder $3.00
Death Star II 3.00
A-Wing Starfighter 3.00
Darth Vader TIE Fighter 3.00

EXCLUSIVE SETS

Star Wars Fan Club Star Destroyer vehicle, with
    Darth Vader, boxed $25.00
Star Wars Fan Club *Millennium Falcon* vehicle, with
    Han Solo, boxed 30.00
Star Wars Toy Fair Three-pack, *Millennium Falcon*,
    Slave I, and Death Star, window box 25.00
Rebel Forces Gift Set, four vehicles and four figures
    (#65836, 1994) Target exclusive 12.00
Imperial Forces Gift Set, five vehicles and three

figures #65837, 1994) Target exclusive 12.00
Galaxy Battle Collector's Set, three ships and three
    figures each from the Rebel Alliance and the
    evil Empire (#64602, 1994) K-Mart exclusive 9.00
11 Piece Collector's Gift Set, seven from the Rebel
    Alliance and four from the evil Empire (#65847,
    1994) Kay-Bee exclusive 16.00
Master Collector's Edition 19 vehicle set, six ve-
    hicles from *Star Wars: A New Hope*, seven
    vehicles from *The Empire Strikes Back,* and six
    vehicles from *Return of the Jedi* (#64601,
    1994) Toys "R" Us exclusive 30.00
Star Wars Special Rebel Forces Gift Set, Second
    Edition, four figures and four ships (#65856,
    1995) Target exclusive 12.00
Star Wars Special Imperial Forces Gift Set, Second
    Edition, four figures and four ships (#65857,
    1995) Target exclusive 12.00
Galaxy Battle Collector's Set, Second Edition, six
    figures and six ships (#64598, 1995) 18.00
Collector's Gift Set, 27 piece, bronze color (#64624,
    1995) 40.00
Classic Series I, X-Wing Starfighter and Boba Fett's
    Slave I ships (#67085, 1996) J.C. Penny
    exclusive) 15.00
Classic Series II, Imperial Shuttle and Imperial
    Emblem (#67806, 1996) FAO Schwarz 15.00
Classic Series III, Darth Vader's TIE Fighter and
    Millennium Falcon (#67088, 1996) *Star Wars*
    catalog 15.00
The Balance Of Power, X-Wing Fighter and TIE
    Fighter (#66091, 1996) 15.00
Rebel Forces vs. Imperial Forces Gift Set, eight
    pieces (#68042, 1996) Musicland exclusive 15.00
Master Collector's 40-vehicle set (#68048, 1997)
    Toys "R" Us exclusive 40.00

FIGURES
Galoob (1996–98)

    The first *Star Wars* MicroMachine figure sets appeared
in 1996, at the same time that the "Action Fleet" vehicles
appeared. Each of those vehicles included a couple of small

Star Wars *Imperial Forces Gift Set, Second Edition (Galoob 1995)*

Classic Characters, original poses (Galoob 1997)

figures and the figure sets fleshed-out the line. The first ones came in packaging similar to the small vehicles listed above, and later they were reissued on header cards which featured stripes. At about this time the third batch of figures was produced and this group included a redesigned set of classic characters.

First Batch (Asst. #66080, 1996) on header cards
I   Imperial Stormtroopers, nine figures (#66081) . . . $7.00
II   Ewoks, nine figures (#66082). 7.00
III   Rebel Pilots, nine figures (#66083). 7.00
IV   Imperial Pilots, nine figures (#66084) 7.00
V   Jawas, nine figures (#66096) 7.00
VI   Imperial Officers, nine figures (#66097) 7.00
VII   Echo Base Troops, nine figures (#66098). 7.00

Second Batch (Asst. #66080, 1997)
VIII Tusken Raiders, nine figures (#66109) 7.00
IX   Rebel Fleet Troops, nine figures (#66108) 7.00
X   Imperial Naval Troopers, nine figures (#66099). . . . 7.00
XI   Classic Characters, nine figures (#66158) 7.00
Reissues, on stripe header card, each. 5.00

Third Batch (Asst. #66080, 1998)
XI   Classic Characters, nine figures, new poses (#) . . . 7.00
XII   Endor Rebel Strike Team, nine figures (#67112) . . . 7.00
XIII Imperial Scout Troopers, nine figures (#) 7.00
XIV Bounty Hunters, nine figures (#66114) 7.00

DROIDS COLLECTION (1997)
Droids, 16 articulated droids (#66090) 17.00

EPIC COLLECTIONS (1997)

Figures in a box which looks like a paperback book.
Heir to the Empire, three figures and three vehicles
    (#66281) $3.50
Jedi Search, three figures and three vehicles
    (#66282) 3.50
The Truce at Bakura, three figures and three ve-
    hicles (#66283) 3.50

MINI-ACTION TRANSFORMING PLAYSETS

These are small heads on a header card and each head opens to reveal a micro figure inside the head. They weren't much

of a playset, and only came with one figure, but there were three in each set.

Mini-Action Transforming Playsets (Asst. #68020, 1997)
I   Boba Fett, Admiral Ackbar, and Gamorrean
    Guard (#68021) $6.00
II   Nien Nunb, Greedo, and Tusken Raider
    (#68022) 6.00
III   Jawa, Yoda, Princess Leia (Boushh Disguise)
    (#68023) 6.00
IV   Bib Fortuna, Figrin D'an, Scout Trooper
    (#68024) 6.00

Mini-Action Boxed Set
Mini-Action 7-head set, includes Gamorrean
    Guard, Nien Nunb, Darth Vader, Jawa, Greedo,
    Admiral Ackbar, and Princess Leia (#68038,
    1996) with *Star Wars* Trilogy WideVision promo #4 . 15.00

PLAYSETS
Galoob (1994–98)

The two large playsets are elaborate and excellent collectibles. The small playsets are smaller than the Action Fleet playsets, some of which have similar names. Most of the reissues were available at very reasonable prices during the big Star Wars discount sale.

LARGE PLAYSETS

Millennium Falcon playset, opens into *Star Wars*
    command center, with Y-Wing Starfighter and
    seven figures (#65878, 1995) "Space" on
    package $38.00
    In early box, with 24kt promotion offer 45.00
Death Star, transforms into planet Tatooine and
    Mos Eisley spaceport, includes *Millennium
    Falcon* and four figures plus a pair of rodents
    (#75118, 1997) "Double Takes," stripes package . 40.00

SMALL PLAYSETS

First Batch ("Space" Asst. #65870, 1994) boxed
The Death Star playset, includes X-Wing Starfighter
    and five figures (#65871) $11.00
Ice Planet Hoth playset, includes Imperial AT-AT
    and five figures (#65872) 11.00
Endor playset, includes Imperial AT-ST and five
    figures (#65873) 11.00
Reissues, in stripe design packaging 8.00

Rebel Transport playset (Galoob 1998)

Second Batch
Planet Tatooine playset, includes cargo skiff and
    five figures (#65858) 11.00
Planet Dagobah playset, includes X-Wing Star-
    fighter and five figures (#65859) 11.00
Reissues, in stripe design packaging . . . .

Third Batch (1998)
Cloud City playset, includes Twin-pod Cloud Car
    and four figures (#65995) 11.00
Rebel Transport playset, includes X-Wing Starfighter
    and three figures (#65996) 11.00

TRANSFORMING ACTION PLAYSETS

Originally these were a helmet or head-shape which
transforms into a playset. The reissues were available at very
reasonable prices during the big *Star Wars* discount sale and
make a nice-looking collection in a head-hunter sort of way.
Later a few ships were added. The same concept was used for
some *Episode I* heads.

First Batch (Asst. #65810) Helmet/Head shaped, boxed
C-3PO transforms into Mos Eisley Cantina,
    includes *Millennium Falcon* and six figures
    (#65811) $15.00
Darth Vader transforms into Bespin Imperial out-
    post, includes *Slave I* and six figures (#65812) . . 15.00
R2-D2 transforms into Jabba's Desert Palace,
    includes Jabba Sail Barge and six figures
    (#65813) 15.00
Stormtrooper transforms into Death Star Battle
    Station, includes Darth Vader's TIE fighter and
    six figures (#65814) 15.00
Chewbacca transforms into Endor's forest moon
    (#65815) 15.00
Boba Fett transforms into Bespin's Cloud City,
    includes Twin Pod Cloud Car and six figures
    (#65816) 15.00
Luke Skywalker transforms into Ice Planet Hoth,
    includes Imperial AT-AT and six figures(#65817) . 15.00
Royal Guard transforms into the Death Star II Battle
    Station, includes Imperial Shuttle and six
    figures (#65695) 15.00
TIE Fighter Pilot transforms into Imperial Academy,
    includes two ships and three figures (#65694) . . . 15.00
Reissues, in stripe design packaging 12.00

Second Batch (1998)
Yoda transforms into swamp planet Dagobah (#68063) 15.00

Jabba the Hutt transforms into Mos Eisley Space-
    port, includes Imperial Transport and four
    figures (#68064) 15.00
Slave I transforms into planet Tatooine (#67095) 15.00
Star Destroyer transforms into Space Fortress
    (#67094) 15.00

***Episode 1* Inside Action Sets** (Asst. #66550, 1999)
Battle Droid transforms into Trade Federation Droid
    Control Ship (#66552) 13.00
Jar Jar Binks transforms into Naboo (#66551) 13.00
Gungan Sub transforms into OTOH Gunga (#69554). . 13.00

ADVENTURE GEAR/PLAYSET

Weapon or Gear which opens into a playset, and also
available quite cheaply at red-tag sales. These are similar to
the Transforming Action playsets listed above, but do not
look as nice on display.

First Batch, boxed (Asst. #68030, 1996)
Vader's Lightsaber opens into Death Star Trench,
    includes vehicle and three figures (#68031) 12.00
Luke's Binoculars open into Yavin Rebel Base,
    includes vehicle and three figures (#68031) 12.00
Reissues, in stripe design packaging 10.00

MICROMACHINE X-RAY FLEET
Galoob (1996–97)

X-Ray Fleet vehicles are the same size as Galoob's die-
cast vehicles and considerably bigger than the regular
MicroMachine size, but still a lot smaller than their Action
Fleet ships. For me, it's a very attractive size, because I can
appreciate the details without a magnifying glass.

The outer hull of each X-Ray Fleet ship is clear plastic,
allowing the collector to view the inner portions of each vehicle. This only really works if the inside portions correspond
to the known insides of the ship, as seen in the movies. Some
of the X-Ray Fleet correspond fairly well to the movie version, notably the Imperial AT-AT and AT-ST, but most are not
so successful.

The *Star Wars* Trilogy Gift Set includes only one X-Ray
Fleet ship, the Shuttle *Tydirium*. The other nine ships are the

Boba Fett Transforming Action playset (Galoob 1997)

X-Ray Fleet Collection IV (Galoob 1996)

same size as the X-Ray Fleet (and Die-Cast ships) but are painted. This set was originally a JC Penney exclusive, but left over sets found their way to KayBee Toys and sold for $15.00. That's where I got mine.

First Batch (Asst. #67070, 1996) "Space" packaging
I   Darth Vader's TIE Fighter and A-Wing
    Starfighter (#67071) $7.00
II X-Wing Starfighter and Imperial AT-AT
    (#67072) 7.00
III *Millennium Falcon* and Jawa Sandcrawler
    (#67073) 7.00
IV Boba Fett's *Slave I* and Y-Wing Starfighter
    (#67074) 7.00

Second Batch (1997)
V   TIE Bomber and B-Wing Starfighter 7.00
VI TIE Fighter and Landspeeder 7.00
VII Imperial AT-ST and Snowspeeder 7.00

Large Boxed Set
Star Wars Trilogy Gift Set, 10 larger, X-Ray vehicle-
    sized, ships with display stands (#67079, 1996) . . 35.00

ACTION FLEET
VEHICLES
Galoob (1996–98)

Action Fleet vehicles are larger than Galoob's X-Ray fleet and die-cast vehicles, but still smaller than Kenner's action figure vehicles. It has proven to be a popular size with both kids and collectors.

The first 2,500 pieces, from the production run of each of the first batch vehicles, were numbered with a special blue collector's sticker, The Rebel Snowspeeder was short packed in the assortment.

In 1997, Galoob introduced Series Alpha, which included both an original concept design vehicle and the familiar final design vehicle, along with two figures. This is one of the only ways to collect design prototypes, but some see it as just a gimmick to get them to buy another copy of a vehicle that they already own.

Galoob has also produced a number of battle packs and playsets which include figures and accessories on the same scale as the ships.

First Batch (Spring 1996)
Luke's X-Wing Starfighter, with pilot Luke Sky-
    walker and R2-D2 (#67031) $12.00
    With numbered collector sticker 20.00
Darth Vader's TIE Fighter, with Lord Darth Vader
    and Imperial Pilot (#67032) 12.00
    With numbered collector sticker 20.00
Imperial AT-AT, with Storm Trooper and Imperial
    Driver (#67033) 12.00
    With numbered collector sticker 20.00
A-Wing Starfighter, with C-3PO & Rebel Pilot (#67034) 12.00
    With numbered collector sticker 20.00
Imperial Shuttle *Tydirium*, with Han Solo and
    Chewbacca (#67035) 12.00
    With numbered collector sticker 20.00
Rebel Snow Speeder, with Luke Skywalker and
    Rebel Gunner (#67036) 15.00
    With numbered collector sticker 20.00

*Luke's Landspeeder and Imperial AT-ST two-pack
Kay-Bee exclusive (Galoob 1995)*

Second Batch (Fall 1996)
Jawa Sandcrawler with Scavenger Droid and Jawa
    (#67039) 10.00
Y-Wing Starfighter with Gold Leader and R2 Unit
    (#67040) 10.00
Slave I, with Boba Fett and Han Solo in carbonite
    (#67041) 10.00
TIE Interceptor, with two poseable Imperial Pilots
    (#67058) 10.00

Third Batch (Asst. #67030, Spring 1997)
Rancor, with Luke Skywalker and Gamorrean
    Guard (#66989) 10.00
Virago, with Prince Xizor and Guri (#66990) 10.00
X-Wing Starfighter, with Wedge Antilles and R2
    Unit, X-Wing Squadron colors (#66991) 10.00
Y-Wing Starfighter, with Yellow Leader and R2 Unit,
    Y-Wing Squadron colors (#66992) 10.00
A-Wing Starfighter, with Rebel Pilot and Mon
    Mothma, A-Wing Squadron colors (#66993) 10.00
TIE Fighter, with Imperial Pilot and Grand Moff
    Tarkin (#66995) 10.00
TIE Bomber, with Imperial Pilot and Imperial Naval
    Trooper (#67059) 10.00

Fourth Batch (Asst. #67030, Fall 1997)
Bespin Twin-Pod Cloud Car, with Lobot and Cloud
    Car Pilot (#66996) 10.00

Millennium Falcon *Action Fleet Vehicle (1998)*

B-Wing Starfighter, with Rebel Pilot and Admiral
    Ackbar (#66994) 10.00
X-Wing Starfighter, with Jek Porkins and R2-Unit,
    Red Six colors (#67023) 10.00
Y-Wing Starfighter, with Blue Leader and R2 Unit,
    Y-Wing Squadron colors (#67024) 10.00
Rebel Snowspeeder, with Rebel Pilot and Rebel
    Gunner, Rogue Two colors (#67025) 10.00

Fifth Batch (Spring 1998)
Millennium Falcon, with Han Solo and Chewbacca
    (#67100) 10.00
Rebel Blockade Runner, with Rebel Trooper and
    Princess Leia Organa 10.00
Incom T-16 Skyhopper, with Luke Skywalker and
    Biggs Darklighter 10.00
Imperial Landing Craft, with Imperial Officer and
    Sandtrooper 10.00

Sixth Batch (Fall 1998)
Jabba's Sail Barge with Saelt-Marae (Yak Face)
    and R2-D2 . . . . 10.00
TIE Defender with Imperial Pilot and Moff Jerjerrod . . . 10.00
E-Wing Starfighter with Rebel Pilot and R7 Unit 10.00

Two-Pack, Kay Bee exclusive (1995)
Luke's Landspeeder, with Luke Skywalker and Obi
    Wan Kenobi and Imperial AT-ST with Imperial
    Driver and Stormtrooper (#67077) 20.00

SERIES ALPHA (1997–98)

Concept Design Prototype and Final Design
First Batch (Asst. #73420, Spring 1997)
1. X-Wing Starfighter, with Biggs Darklighter and
    R2 Unit (#73421) $15.00
2. Imperial AT-AT, with Imperial Driver and
    Snowtrooper (#73424) 15.00
3. Imperial Shuttle, with Stormtrooper and TIE
    Fighter Pilot (#73422) 15.00
4. Rebel Snowspeeder, with Luke Skywalker
    Rebel Pilot and Rebel Gunner (#73423) 15.00

Second Batch (Asst. #73420, Spring 1998)
5. Twin-Pod Cloud Car, with Cloud Car Pilot
    and Copilot (#73430) 15.00
6. Y-Wing Starfighter, with R2 Unit and Y-Wing
    Pilot (#73431) 15.00
7. B-Wing Starfighter, with B-wing Pilot and B-
    Wing Gunner (#73432) 15.00

***Episode I* Series Alpha**
Sith Infiltrator 20.00
Royal Starship 18.00
Naboo Fighter 15.00

CLASSIC DUELS (1997–98)

Toys "R" Us special (Asst. #68300, Nov. 1997)
    Millennium Falcon, with Lando Calrissian and
    RebelTrooper vs. TIE Interceptor, with Imperial Pilot and
    Imperial Officer (#68302) $20.00
X-Wing Starfighter, with Luke Skywalker and R2-D2
    vs. TIE Fighter, with Imperial Pilot and
    Stormtrooper (#68301) 20.00

FLIGHT CONTROLLERS (1997–98)

These hold the included fighter, or one of the other flying vehicles in the Action Fleet line, and have lights, sounds

Battle Packs #2 and #10 (Galoob 1996–98)

and spring-loaded missile. Basically its a handle which lets
you mount the ship and use it in simulated battle.

First Batch (Asst. #73416, Spring 1997)
Rebel Flight Controller, with Luke's X-Wing Star-
    fighter, and Luke Skywalker and R2-D2 figures
    (#73417) $20.00
Imperial Flight Controller, Darth Vader's TIE Fighter,
    and Lord Darth Vader and Imperial Pilot figures
    (#73418) 20.00

Second Batch (Spring 1998)
Rebel Flight Controller with Y-Wing Starfighter and 2
    figures 20.00
Imperial Flight Controller with TIE-Interceptor and 2
    figures 20.00

BATTLE PACKS (1996–98)

First Batch (Asst. #68010, 1996)
#1 Rebel Alliance, two Speeder Bikes and five
     figures (#68011) $8.00
#2 Galactic Empire, Imperial AT-ST and four
     figures (#68012) 8.00
#3 Aliens and Creatures, Bantha and four figures
     (#68013) 8.00
#4 Galactic Hunters, Dewback and four figures
     (#68014) 8.00
#5 Shadows of the Empire, two Swoops and five
     figures (#68015) 8.00

Second Batch (Spring 1997)
#6 Dune Sea, Desert Skiff, and five figures (#68016) . 8.00
#7 Droid Escape, Escape Pod, and five figures (#68017) 8.00
#8 Desert Palace, Jabba the Hutt, and five figures
     (#68018) 8.00

Third Batch (Fall 1997)
#9 Endor Adventure, Hang Glider, Speeder Bike,
     and five figures (#68035) 8.00
#10 Mos Eisley Spaceport, Ronto, and five figures
     (#68036) 8.00
#11 Cantina Encounter, Landspeeder, and five fig-
     ures (#68037) 8.00

Fourth Batch (Spring 1998)
#12 Cantina Smugglers and Spies, eight figures
     (#68090) 8.00
#13 Hoth Attack, Tauntaun, Wampa, and four figures
     (#68091) 8.00

#14 Death Star Escape, seven figures (#68092) 8.00
#15 Endor Victory, three glow-in-the-dark figures
   and five hero figures (#68093) . . . . Pod 8.00

Fifth Batch (Fall 1998)
#16 Lars Family Homestead, Landspeeder and five
   figures 8.00
#17 Imperial Troops, Speeder Bike and five figures 8.00
#18 Rebel Troops, eight figures 8.00

PLAYSETS

These playsets are much larger than the MicroMachine playsets, some of which have the same name. They fold open for play and fold closed into a case (with nice side graphics) for storage.

Playsets (Asst. #67090) in box with slant side
Ice Planet Hoth, includes Luke Skywalker on a
   Tauntaun, Wampa Ice Creature, Princess Leia
   Organa, 2-1B, Battle Damaged Snowspeeder
   with Rebel Pilot, plus Ralph McQuarrie
   original box art (#67091) $30.00
The Death Star, includes Battle Damages TIE
   Fighter, Emperor Palpatine, Lord Darth Vader,
   Stormtrooper, Imperial Gunner, and Imperial
   Royal Guard, plus Ralph McQuarrie original
   box art (#69092) 30.00
Yavin Rebel Base, includes six figures, Ralph
   McQuarrie original box art (#69093) 30.00

STAR WARS EPISODE I
MICRO MACHINES
Galoob (1999–2001)

Episode I **Vehicle/Figure Collections**(1999)
Collection I (#66501). $5.00
Collection II (#66502) 5.00
Collection III (#66503) 5.00
Collection IV (#66504) 5.00
Collection V (#66505) Gungans 5.00
Collection VI (#66506) Battle Droids 5.00
Collection VII (#66507) 5.00
Collection VIII (#66508) 5.00
Collection IX (#66509) 5.00
Collection X (#66510). 5.00

Episode I **Platform Action Sets** (Asst. #66540, 1999)
Pod race Arena (#66541). 10.00
Naboo Temple Ruins (#66542). 10.00
Galactic Senate (#66543) 10.00
Galactic Dogfight (#66544). 10.00
Theed Rapids (#66545) 10.00
Tatooine Desert (#66548). 10.00
Deluxe Royal Sarship Repair (#66561) 20.00
Deluxe Theed Palace Assault (#66562) 20.00

ACTION FLEET TURBO POD RACERS

Episode I **Turbo Pod racers** (Asst. #68145, 1999)
Gasgano's Pod racer (#68148). $13.00
Ody Mandrell's Pod racer (#68149) 13.00

ACTION FLEET PLAYSETS

Episode I **Action Fleet Playsets** (Asst. #68155, 1999)
Gian Speeder and Theed Palace with Captain

Panaka, Naboo Foot Soldier, and two Battle
   Droids (#) Sneak Preview $20.00
Pod racer Hanger Bay with Pit Droid and Pit Mech-
   anic (#68156). 15.00
Mos Espa Market with Anakin Skywalker and C-3PO (#68157)
   . . . . 15.00
Trade Federation MTT/Naboo Battlefield (#66566. . . . 20.00
Naboo Hanger–Final Conflict (#68177) 15.00

Episode I **Action Fleet Mini Scenes** (Asst #68120, 1999)
1. STAP Invasion (#68121). 5.00
2. Destroyer Droid Ambush (#68122) 5.00
3. Gungan Assault (#68123) 5.00
4. Sith Pursuit (#68124) 5.00
5. Generator Core Duel (#68128). 5.00

ACTION FLEET VEHICLES

Episode I **Action Fleet Vehicles** (Asst. #68130, 1999)
Naboo Starfighter, featuring Anakin Skywalker
   (#65131) $10.00
Trade Federation MTT, featuring Battle Droid (#68132). 12.00
Sebulba's Pod racer, featuring Sebulba (#68133) 10.00
Republic Cruiser, featuring Qui-Gon Jinn (#68134). . . . 12.00
Trade Federation Droid Fighter, featuring Daultay
   Dofine (#68135) 10.00
Gungan Sub, featuring Qui-Gon Jinn (#68136). 10.00
Flash Speeder, featuring Naboo Royal Guard (#68137) 12.00
Trade Federation Landing Ship, featuring Battle
   Droid (#68138) 15.00
Anakin's Pod racer, featuring Anakin Skywalker
   (#68139). 10.00
Mars Guo's Pod racer, featuring Mars Guo (#68140) . . 15.00

Electronic Fambaa, Episode I Action Fleet (Galoob 1999)

Episode I, Electronic Action Fleet
Electronic Fambaa with Remote-Control Power
   Cord (#68161) 20.00
Electronic Trade Federation Tank with Remote-
   Control Power Cord (#68162) 20.00

POD RACING

Episode I **Pod racing** (Galoob 1999)
Electronic BoontaEve Challenge Track Set (#66570) . $40.00
Pod racer Launchers (#66547) 12.00

MODEL KITS

MPC was Kenner's model kit company. Early kits have their logo. When The Ertl Company bought MPC in about 1990, the logo was changed to MPC/Ertl. Still later, the logo was changed to AMT/Ertl, which is what it is today. The original models have been reissued, and this availability has brought down the collectors' price of the originals. The most notable exception is the original *Millennium Falcon*, with lights, since the reissues are unlighted.

Star Wars Characters

The Authentic C-3PO (See-Threepio) model kit, 10" tall, 1/7 scale (MPC #1913, 1977) 7½" x 10" *Star Wars* box $25.00
Reissue, 6" x 10" box. 20.00
C-3PO model kit (MPC #1935, 1984) *Return of the Jedi* box 15.00
The Authentic R2-D2 (Artoo-Detoo) model kit 6" tall,

1/10 scale (MPC #1912, 1977) *Star Wars* box . . . 25.00
Reissue, 6" x 10" box. 20.00
R2-D2 model kit (MPC #1934, 1984) *Return of the Jedi* box 15.00
Darth Vader model kit, 11½" tall, 1/7 scale, black full figure with glow-in-the-dark lightsaber (MPC #1916, 1979) *Star Wars* box. 45.00
Darth Vader Bust Action model kit, snap-together, 1/2 scale (MPC #1921, 1978) illuminated eyes and raspy breathing sound, *Star Wars* box . . 60.00

Space Ships

The Authentic Darth Vader TIE Fighter model kit, 7½" wide, 1/48 scale, with Darth Vader pilot figure (MPC #1915, 1977) 14" x 10" *Star Wars* box . 35.00
Reissue, 14" x 8" *Star Wars* box. 25.00
The Authentic Luke Skywalker X-Wing Fighter model kit, 12" long, 10" wingspan, 1/48 scale (MPC #1914, 1977) 14" x 10" *Star Wars* box 35.00

C-3PO (narrow box) Model Kit and Darth Vader, Commemorative, glow-in-the-dark lightsaber Model Kit (MPC 1980s)

Star Destroyer, Commemorative Edition and TIE Interceptor Snap model kits (MPC 1980s)

Reissue, 14" x 8" *Star Wars* box 25.00
Han Solo's *Millennium Falcon* model kit, 18" long,
1/72 scale, with lights (MPC #1925, 1979) *Star
Wars* box 120.00

The Empire Strikes Back Ships

Star Destroyer model kit (15" long, MPC #1926,
1980) *The Empire Strikes Back* box 45.00
Luke Skywalker's Snowspeeder model kit, 8" long
(MPC #1917, 1980) *The Empire Strikes Back*
box 40.00
AT-AT model kit (MPC #1918, 1980) *The Empire
Strikes Back* box 40.00
Millennium Falcon model kit, no lights (MPC #1933,
1982) *The Empire Strikes Back* box 40.00
X-Wing Fighter model kit, 12fi" (MPC #1930, 1982)
The Empire Strikes Back box 25.00
Boba Fett's *Slave I* model kit (MPC #1919, 1982)
The Empire Strikes Back box 35.00

Return of the Jedi Ships

AT-AT model kit (MPC #1929, 1983) *Return of the
Jedi* box 25.00
Shuttle *Tydirium* model kit, 20" wingspan (MPC
#1920, 1983) *Return of the Jedi* box 30.00
Speeder Bike Vehicle model kit, 12" long (MPC
#1927, 1983) *Return of the Jedi* box 22.00

Snap Kits

AT-ST model kit, 6" high, Scout Walker (MPC #1976,
1983) *Return of the Jedi* box 30.00
A-Wing Fighter model kit (MPC #1973, 1983)
Return of the Jedi box 15.00
B-Wing Fighter model kit (MPC #1974, 1983)
Return of the Jedi box 15.00
TIE Interceptor model kit (MPC #1972, 1983)
Return of the Jedi box 20.00
X-Wing Fighter model kit (MPC #1971, 1983)
Return of the Jedi box 15.00
Y-Wing model kit (MPC #1975, 1983) *Return of the
Jedi* box 15.00

Dioramas

Rebel Base Diorama Snap model kit (MPC #1924,
1981) *The Empire Strikes Back* box 45.00
Battle on Ice Planet Hoth model diorama, snap
together, 11¾" x 17¾" (MPC #1922, 1981) *The
Empire Strikes Back* box 35.00
Encounter With Yoda on Dagobah model kit, snap
together, 5¾" x 10" (MPC #1923, 1981) *The
Empire Strikes Back* box 35.00
Jabba the Hutt Throne Room model kit, diorama
(MPC #1928, 1983) *Return of the Jedi* box. 40.00

Mirr-A-Kits

AT-ST model kit (MPC #1105, 1984) *Return of the
Jedi* box. 15.00
Shuttle *Tydirium* model kit (MPC #1103, 1984)
Return of the Jedi box 15.00
Speeder Bike (MPC #1106, 1984) *Return of the Jedi*

Slave I and AT-ST Snap model kit (AMT/Ertl 1990s)

box 15.00
TIE Interceptor model kit (MPC #1102, 1984) *Return
    of the Jedi* box 15.00
Y-Wing model kit (MPC #1104, 1984) *Return of the
    Jedi* box 15.00
X-Wing model kit (MPC #1101, 1984) *Return of the
    Jedi* box 15.00

Structors Action Walking models, wind-up motor
AT-AT model kit (MPC/Structors #1902, 1984) 30.00
    AT-AT (AMT/Ertl #6036, 1998) 10.00
AT-ST model kit, 4½" high (MPC/Structors #1903,
    1984) *Return of the Jedi* box 25.00
    Scout AT-ST (AMT/Ertl #6029, 1998) 10.00
C-3PO model kit (MPC/Structors #1901, 1984) 25.00

Vans: Snap together, with glow-in-the-dark decals
Artoo-Detoo Van model kit, 1/32 scale (MPC #3211,
    1979) 30.00
Darth Vader Van model kit, 1/32 scale (MPC #3209,
    1979) 35.00
Luke Skywalker Van model kit, 1/32 scale (MPC
    #3210, 1979) 35.00

MPC/ERTL and AMT/ERTL (1990–98)
Figures
Darth Vader, stands 12" tall, glow in the dark light
    saber (#8154, 1992) 14" x 8¼" *Star Wars* box 15.00
    Reissue: AMT/Ertl 12.50
Darth Vader Model Kit (AMT/Ertl #8784, 1996) 25.00
Luke Skywalker Model Kit (AMT/Ertl #8783, 1995) . . . 25.00
Han Solo Model Kit (AMT/Ertl #8785, 1995) 25.00
Prince Xizor Model Kit (AMT/Ertl #8256, 1996) in
    Shadows of the Empire box 25.00
Emperor Palpatine (AMT/Ertl #8258, 1996) in
    Shadows of the Empire box 25.00

Action Scenes
Rebel Base Action Scene (MPC/Ertl and AMT/Ertl
    #8735, 1993) 18¾" x 12¾" *The Empire Strikes
    Back* box 15.00
Jabba's Throne Room Model (AMT/Ertl #8262, 1996) . 13.50
Encounter with Yoda Model (AMT/Ertl #8263, 1996) . . 13.50
Battle on Hoth Action Scene, with 11½" x 17½"
    vacu-formed base (AMT/Ertl #8743, 1995) 13.50

Flight Displays
TIE Fighter Flight Display (AMT/Ertl #8275, 1996) 20.00
Speeder Bike Flight Display (AMT/Ertl #6352, 1997) . . 20.00

X-Wing Flight Display (AMT/Ertl #8788, 1995) 19.50

Limited Editions
X-Wing Limited Edition (AMT/Ertl #8769, 1995) 31.50
TIE Interceptor Limited Edition (AMT/Ertl #8770, 1995) . 31.50
B-Wing Limited Edition Model (AMT/Ertl #8780, 1995) 25.00

Ships
Shuttle *Tydirium* (MPC/Ertl and AMT/Ertl #8733,
    1992) 18¾" x 12¾" *Return of the Jedi* box 15.00
Speeder Bike (MPC/Ertl and AMT/Ertl #8928, 1990)
    14"x8" *Return of the Jedi* box 10.00
Luke Skywalker's Snowspeeder (MPC/Ertl and
    AMT/Ertl #8914, 1990) 10" x 7" *The Empire
    Strikes Back* box 15.00
Star Destroyer (MPC/Ertl and AMT/Ertl #8915,
    1990) 20" x 10" *The Empire Strikes Back* box 15.00
Darth Vader TIE Fighter (MPC/Ertl and AMT/Ertl
    #8916, 1990) 14" x 10¼" *Star Wars* box 12.00
Millennium Falcon (MPC/Ertl and AMT/Ertl #8917,
    1990) 19¾" x 14½" *Return of the Jedi* box 20.00
X-Wing Fighter (MPC/Ertl and AMT/Ertl #8918,
    1990) 14" x 8" *Return of the Jedi* box 12.00
AT-AT (MPC/Ertl and AMT/Ertl #8919, 1990)
    14" x 8"*Return of the Jedi* box 15.00
Star Wars Shadows of the Empire Virago Model
    (AMT/Ertl #8377, 1997) 15.00
TIE Fighter Plus Pack, with glue, paint, and paint
    brush (AMT/Ertl #8432, 1997) 16.00
Slave I (AMT/Ertl #8768, 1995) 13.50
Fiber Optic Star Destroyer Model (AMT/Ertl #8782,
    1995) *Empire Strikes Back* box 50.00
Millennium Falcon Cutaway Model (AMT/Ertl
    #8789, 1996) 27.00

Snap Kits
AT-ST, Snap together (AMT/Ertl #8734, 1992)
    10" x 7" *Return of the Jedi* box 9.00
TIE Interceptor, snap together (AMT/Ertl #8931,
    1990) 10" x7" *Return of the Jedi* box 10.00
X-Wing Fighter, snap together (AMT/Ertl #8932,
    1990) 10" x 7" *Return of the Jedi* box 11.00
A-Wing Fighter, snap together (AMT/Ertl #8933,
    1990) 10" x 7" *Return of the Jedi* box 10.00
Y-Wing Fighter, snap together (AMT/Ertl #8934,
    1990) *Return of the Jedi* box 10.00
Return of the Jedi 3-piece Gift Set: B-Wing Fighter,
    X-Wing Fighter, TIE Interceptor, (MPC/Ertl and
    AMT/Ertl #8912, 1992) 14¼" x 10" box 20.00

AT-AT Snapfast and Encounter with Yoda on Dagobah (AMT/Ertl 1990s)

Chewbacca and Han Solo Model Kits (Screamin 1994)

VINYL MODEL KITS

Luke Skywalker pre-painted model, 1/6 scale
(Polydata 1995) $35.00
Obi-Wan Kenobi pre-painted model, 1/6 scale
(Polydata 1995) 35.00
Tusken Raider pre-painted model, 1/6 scale
(Polydata 1995) 35.00
Princess Leia pre-painted model, 1/6 scale
(Polydata 1995) 35.00
Chewbacca pre-painted model, 1/6 scale (Polydata
1996) 35.00
Lando Calrissian pre-painted model, 1/6 scale
(Polydata 1997) 35.00
Boba Fett pre-painted vinyl model kit, 13" tall,
9,000 copies, box illo by Nelson DeCastro
(Polydata1997) 35.00

Luke Skywalker Vinyl Model, 1/4 scale (Screamin
#3010, 1996) 65.00
Darth Vader Vinyl Model, 1/4 scale (Screamin
#3200, 1992) 65.00
Yoda Vinyl Model, 1/4 scale (Screamin #3300, 1992) . 60.00
Han Solo Vinyl Model, 1/4 scale (Screamin #3400,
1993) 65.00
C-3PO Vinyl Model, 1/4 scale (Screamin #3500, 1993) 65.00
Stormtrooper, 1/4 scale (Screamin #3600, 1993) 65.00
Chewbacca Vinyl Model, 1/4 scale (Screamin
#3700, 1994) 68.00
Boba Fett Vinyl Model, 1/4 scale (Screamin #3800,
1994) 70.00
Tusken Raider Vinyl Model, 1/4 scale (Screamin
#3900, 1995) 68.00

***Episode 1* Snap Fast** (Ertl)
Naboo Fighter 1:48 (#30117) 10.00
Trade Federation Droid Fighter 1:48 (#30118) 10.00
Anakin's Podracer 1:32 (#30122) 20.00

***Episode 1* Die-Cast Model Kit**
Naboo Starfighter 1:48 (#30130) 18.00

STEEL MODELS

Millennium Falcon Star Wars Steel Tec Kit (Remco
#7140, 1995) $25.00
X-Wing Fighter *Star Wars* Steel Tec Kit (Remco
#7141, 1995) 25.00

FLYING MODELS

Original *Star Wars* Flying Rocket Model Kits
R2-D2 Flying Rocket Kit (Estes #1298, 1979) $25.00
TIE Fighter Flying Model Rocket Kit (Estes #1299,
1979) 30.00
X-Wing Fighter Flying Model Rocket Outfit Kit
(Estes #1302, 1979) 30.00
Proton Torpedo Flying Model Rocketry Outfit with
Launching Kit, Darth Vader picture box (Estes
#1420, 1979) 50.00
X-Wing Fighter Flying Model Rocket with Launching
Kit (Estes #1422, 1979) 50.00

New Flying Model Rocket Starter Sets
X-Wing Flying Model Rocket Starter Set (Estes
#1490, 1996) battery operated 35.00
A-Wing Flying Model Rocket Starter Set (Estes

Luke Skywalker Vinyl Model Kit (Polydata 1995) and Episode I *Naboo Royal Starship flying model (Estes 1999)*

#1491, 1996) battery operated 35.00
Y-Wing Flying Model Rocket Starter Set (Estes
    #1492, 1996) battery operated 35.00
Death Star Flying Model Rocket Starter Set (Estes
    #1493, 1996) battery operated 35.00
Luke Skywalker X-Wing Fighter and Darth Vader TIE Fighter
    Starter Set, with 6 launch engines, con-
    troller and parachutes (Estes #1801, 1998) 50.00

New Flying Model Rockets
R2-D2 Flying Model Rocket (Estes #2142, 1997) 15.00
Death Star Flying Model Rocket (Estes #2143, 1997) . 15.00
Darth Vader's TIE Fighter Flying Model Rocket,
    16½" (Estes #2144, 1997) 15.00
Millennium Falcon Flying Model Rocket (Estes
    #2146, 1997) 15.00
Star Destroyer Flying Model Rocket (Estes #2147,
    1997) 15.00
Shuttle *Tydirium* Flying Model Rocket (Estes
    #2148, 1997) 15.00

Flying Model Rockets with Recovery Parachute
TIE Fighter Flying Model Rocket with Recovery
    Parachute 9" (Estes #2102, 1997) 24.00
X-Wing Flying Model Rocket with Recovery
    Parachute 10¾" (Estes #2103, 1997) 18.00
R2-D2 Flying Model Rocket with Recovery
    Parachute 9" (Estes #2104, 1997) 29.00

Ready-Built Flying Model Rocket
Star Wars Flying Model Rocket, Red Squadron
    X-Wing Starfighter (Estes #01810, 1998) on
    header card 6.00

***Star Wars* Flying Model Rocket Launchers** (Estes)
Darth Vader TIE Fighter (#01820, 1997) 30.00
Y-Wing Starfighter (#01821, 1997) 30.00
Red Squadron X-Wing Fighters, two (#01822, 1997) . . 30.00
R2-D2 (#01823, 1997) 30.00

***Episode I* Flying Models** (Estes 1999)
Naboo Fighter (#01832) 10.00
Trade Federation Droid Fighter (#01833) 10.00
Naboo Royal Spaceship (#01834) 10.00

***Episode I* Flying Model Rocket Starter Sets** (Estes 1999)
Naboo Fighter (#01842) 20.00
R2-D2 (#01844) 20.00

***Episode I* Action Model Rockets** (Estes 1999)
Trade Federation Droid Fighter (#01837) 30.00
Trade Federation Battleship (#01828) 20.00
Sith Infiltrator (#01829) 20.00

Balsa Model Glider Kits (1995–97)
Star Destroyer Flying model kit (Estes #05020) 8.00
A-Wing Fighter Catapult Flying model kit (Estes
    #05021) 8.00
X-Wing Fighter Flying model kit (Estes #05022) 6.00
Y-Wing Fighter Flying model kit (Estes #05023) 6.00

Control Line Aircraft
X-Wing Control Line Fighter kit, with Cox engine
    (Estes Cox #9310) 60.00
Darth Vader's TIE Fighter Control Line Fighter kit,
    with Cox engine (Estes Cox #9330) 60.00
Snowspeeder Control Line Fighter kit, with Cox
    engine (Estes Cox #9320) 60.00
Death Star Battle Station with X-Wing Control Line
    Fighter kit, with Cox engine, Radio Controlled
    (Estes Cox #9420) 150.00
Landspeeder Radio Control Vehicle kit, with Cox
    engine (Estes Cox #9430) 100.00
Star Wars Combat Set, flying 13.6" wingspan
    X-Wing Fighter and 9.5" wingspan TIE fighter
    with motor and control lines (Estes #9410, 1997) 100.00
X-Wing Sterling Model Kit Control Line Fighter, 13"
    wingspan (Estes #6760, 1997) requires Cox
    engine 25.00
Y-Wing Sterling Model Kit Control Line Fighter,
    10¾" wingspan (Estes #6761, 1997) requires
    Cox engine 25.00

Deluxe Rocket Kits
X-Wing Fighter North Coast Rocketry high powered
    model rocket, 20" long, 18" wingspan, with
    recovery parachute (Estes #3540, 1997) 100.00

LEGO SYSTEM
Lego (1999–2002)

Lego has made a lot of *Star Wars* models in the last few years. Unlike the action figures, they have not been available at deep discounts.

***Episode I* Model** (1999–2001)
Lightsaber Duel, 50 pieces (#07101) $8.00
Droid Fighter, 62 pieces (#07111) 8.00

Anakin's Podracer (Lego 1999)

Gungan Patrol, 77 pieces (#07115) 10.00
Naboo Swamp, 81 pieces (#07121) 12.00
Flash Speeder, 105 pieces (#07124) 10.00
Battle Droid Carrier, 133 pieces (#07126) 13.00
Anakin's Pod racer, 134 pieces (#07131) 15.00
Naboo Fighter, 174 pieces (#07141) 20.00
Sith Infiltrator, 243 pieces (#07151) 30.00
Trade Federation AAT, 158 pieces (#07155) 20.00
Gungan Sub, 375 pieces (#07161) 35.00
Mos Espa Pod race, 894 pieces (#07171) 80.00
Trade Federation MTT, 470 pieces (#07184) 45.00
Watto's Junkyard, 446 pieces (#07186) 40.00

Final Duel I, 29 pieces (#07200, 2002) 8.00
Final Duel II, 23 pieces (#07201, 2002) 8.00
Jedi Defense, 58 pieces (#07203, 2002) 8.00
Jedi Defense II, 52 pieces (#07204, 2002) 8.00

Star Wars Model (1999–2001)
Desert Skiff, 53 pieces (#07104) 9.00
Droid Escape, 44 pieces (#07106) 9.00
Land Speeder, 47 pieces (#07110) 9.00
Twin-Pod Cloud Car, 117 pieces (#7119, 2002) 10.00
AT-ST, 107 pieces (#07127) 10.00
Speeder Bikes, 90 pieces (#07128) 10.00
Snowspeeder, 212 pieces (#07130) 25.00
A-Wing Fighter, 123 pieces (#07134) 18.00
Ewok Attack with Biker Scout, 119 pieces (#7139,
   2002) 13.00
X-Wing Fighter, 263 pieces (#07140) 30.00
Slave 1, 165 pieces (#07144) 25.00
TIE Fighter, 169 pieces (#07146) 20.00
TIE Fighter and Y-Wing Fighter (#07150) 45.00
Imperial Shuttle, 234 pieces (#07166) 35.00
B-Wing at Rebel Control Center (#07180) 40.00

Droid Developer Kit (Lego Mindstorms 2000)

Ultimate Collector's Series
TIE Interceptor, 703 pieces (#07181) 80.00
Millennium Falcon, 659 pieces (#07190) 80.00
X-Wing, 1,304 pieces (#07191) 150.00
Yoda, 1,075 pieces (#07194) 100.00

Episode I Lego Technic
Pit Droid, 217 pieces (#08000) 25.00
Battle Droid, 328 pieces (#08001) 30.00
Destroyer Droid, 553 pieces (#08002) 50.00
C-3PO, 339 pieces (#08007) 40.00
Stormtrooper, 361 pieces (#08008) 40.00
R2-D2, 242 pieces (#08009) 20.00
Darth Vader, 397 pieces (#08010) 40.00

Episode I Lego MindStorms
Droid Developer Kit, 657 pieces (#9748) 75.00
Dark Side Developers Kit (#9754) 75.00

Darth Maul Bust (#10018) 17" tall 60.00
Rebel Blockade Runner, 1,748 pieces (#10019) 200.00

Darth Maul, The Emperor, Darth Vader (#3340) 10.00
Luke, Han, Boba Fett (#3341) 10.00
Chewbacca and two Stormtroopers (#3342) 10.00
Pit Droid Leader and two Pit Droids (#3343) 10.00

Lego Web site secials
Darth Vader Key Chain (KC12) (#3913) 7.00
Luke Skywalker Key Chain (KC11) (#3914) 7.00
Darth Maul Key Chain (KC16) (#3922) 7.00

Toy Fair Give-away (1999)
Star Wars Music Box "Building a New Galaxy in
   1999" scarce, market price not established 1,000.00
Star War Logo yellow lego piece 10.00

Episode II (2002) from Lego Web site
Jedi Starfighter (#07143) . . . . N/A
Jango Fett's *Slave I* (#07153) . . . . N/A
Republic Gunship (#07163) . . . . N/A
Super Battle Droid (#08012) . . . . N/A

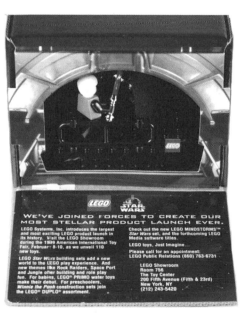

Lego Music Box, Toy Fair give-away (Lego 1999)
(Collection of Marc Patten)

PAPER COLLECTIBLES

CALENDARS — CATALOGS — MAGAZINES — POINT OF PURCHASE AND STORE DISPLAYS — PROOFS

This section includes all kinds of miscellaneous paper collectibles which don't fit in other sections; Books, Comics, Trading Cards, and Wall Art (posters, lithos, etc.) are all covered in their own sections; and Customizable Card Games can be found at the end of the GAMES section.

BOOKMARKS AND BOOKPLATES

Many bookmarks and bookplates contain attractive art work; but as collectibles, they are associated with books, and book collecting is *not* the driving force behind *Star Wars* collecting. This has kept the price of these items at, or near, original retail price.

Bookmarks
Return of the Jedi bookmarks (Random House
    1983) each $4.00
    Set, 16 bookmarks 50.00
Star Wars 20th Anniversary tasseled bookmark
    (Antioch #KBO13986, 1997) 2.00
Return of the Jedi 20th Anniversary tasseled book
    mark (Antioch #KBO13994, 1997) 2.00

Star Wars Bookmarks, full color photographs of
    characters (Antioch 1997)
    Han Solo 2.50
    Lando Calrissian 2.50
    Obi-Wan Kenobi 2.50
    Princess Leia 2.50
Star Wars Bookmarks, Drew Struzan book art plus
    photo, with tassel (Antioch 1997)
    Darth Vader 3.00
    Glove of Darth Vader 3.00
    Truce at Bakura 3.00
    Crystal Star 3.00
    Luke Skywalker 3.00
Star Wars 3-D Bookmarks, 3 piece set (A.H. Pris-
    matic #1006SW, 1997) 6.00

Star Wars Shapemarks: (Antioch 1997)
    Boba Fett 3.00
    C-3PO 2.00
    Tusken Raider 2.00
    Yoda 2.00

Episode I bookmarks (1999) each . . . . 2 to 3.00

Bookplates
Return of the Jedi bookplates (Random House
    1983) each 5.00
    Set, 4 bookplates 20.00
Star Wars bookplates (Antioch 1997)
    C-3PO and R2-D2 photo (#01961) 3.00
    Hildebrandt poster (#02046) 3.00
Episode I bookplates (1999) each 3.00

CALENDARS

Calendars were only made for a few years when the movies first appeared. Since 1995, calendars have been sold every year and you can bet this will continue. Calendars appear in about July of the year before the year printed on the calendar, and by December they are available at discount and by January they are discounted heavily. If you intend to collect them, wait to get them at half price and don't unseal them.

The 1978 *Star Wars* Calendar (Ballantine Books
    #27377, 1977) originally $4.95
    Sealed $30.00
    Open 15.00

Star Wars *1991 Calendar (Cedco 1990)*

1979 *Star Wars* Calendar (Ballantine Books)
 Sealed. 20.00
 Open 10.00
1980 *Star Wars* Calendar (Ballantine Books)
 Sealed. 20.00
 Open 10.00
1981 *The Empire Strikes Back* Calendar (Ballantine Books)
 Sealed. 25.00
 Open 10.00
1984 *Return of the Jedi* Calendar (Ballantine Books)
 Sealed. 15.00
 Open 10.00
Return of the Jedi, The 1984 Ewok Calendar
 (Ballantine Books) with peel-off stickers
 Sealed. 15.00
 Open, complete with all stickers 10.00

Calendars (1990s)
Star Wars 1990 Calendar (Cedco) sealed 10.00
Star Wars 1991 Calendar (Cedco) sealed 10.00
Star Wars 1991 Lucasfilm Calendar (Abrahms) sealed 25.00
Star Wars calendars, 1995–98 (Cedco)
 Sealed. . . . . cover price
 Open . . . . half cover price
Star Wars Vehicles 1997 Calendar (Chronicle
 Books, #1246-4, 1996) with bonus poster. 13.00
Star Wars 20th Anniversary Collector's 1997
 Calendar (Golden Turtle Press #399-1, 1996). . . . 12.00
The Art of *Star Wars* Classic Characters 1998
 Calendar (Cedco #520-9). 13.00
Star Wars Trilogy Special Edition 1998 Calendar
 (Cedco #543-8) 13.00

2000 mini-calendar
Yoda 2000 Calendar (Golden Turtle Press #830) 5.00
C-3PO & R2-D2 2000 Calendar (Golden Turtle
 Press #830). 5.00
Han Solo 2000 Calendar (Golden Turtle Press #830) . . 5.00
Darth Vader 2000 Calendar (Golden Turtle Press #830) 5.00

Episode I Calendars
Star Wars Episode I Flip Animation 366-day
 Calendar (Golden Turtle Press #821) 13.00
Star Wars Episode I 2000 Calendar (Golden Turtle
 Press #822) 13.00
Star Wars 2000 Calendar (Golden Turtle Press #878). . 13.00
Star Wars Episode I 20-Month Collectors Edition
 Calendar (Golden Turtle Press #823) oversized. . . 18.00

Episode I 18-month small calendars
Jar Jar Binks 18-month collectible calendar   (Golden
 Turtle Press #833) 5.00
Darth Maul 18-month collectible calendar (Golden
 Turtle Press #833) 5.00
Obi-Wan Kenobi 18-month collectible calendar
 (Golden Turtle Press #833) 5.00
Queen Amidala 18-month collectible calendar
 (Golden Turtle Press #833) 5.00

CATALOGS

   Kenner issued two kinds of catalogs which covered *Star Wars* toys. The best known are the small pocket or consumer catalogs included in most of the vehicle packages. They were issued for all three movies and contain interesting pictures and early information which is not always accurate to what was actually produced. The larger retailer catalogs were given to the stores to get them to order *Star Wars* toys. Catalogs such as this are issued every year or more frequently by just about every toy company and are often available at Toy Fair, at least to the press and retailers. As you might expect, the earlier catalogs sell for more than the later ones.

   Every toy company with a *Star Wars* license has a catalog, but most of the collector interest focuses on Kenner. The Kenner Fall 1977 *Star Wars* catalog features the Early Bird Certificate Package and naturally pre-dates it, since the retailer must buy the toy before it gets in the toy store for the consumer to purchase. This makes it the very first Kenner collectible, but hardly the first *Star Wars* collectible. After all, the paperback book and the first Marvel comics appeared *before* the movie premiere. Sears Wish Books (Christmas Catalogs) are also interesting because they feature the Sears exclusives, which are some of the most valuable collectibles.

   One of Kenner's more interesting *Star Wars* catalogs is from the 1986 Toy Fair. This is the last one to contain *Star Wars* merchandise until the mid 1990s revival of the line. The 1986 catalog covers the Droids and Ewoks lines and includes pictures of a number of figures which were never actually released.

Consumer Mini Catalogs
Star Wars 1977, logo cover, lists 12 figures $20.00

Star Wars Consumer Mini-Catalog and The Empire Strikes Back Consumer Mini-Catalog (Kenner 1978–80)

Leia and Han valentines, deluxe kit (1997)

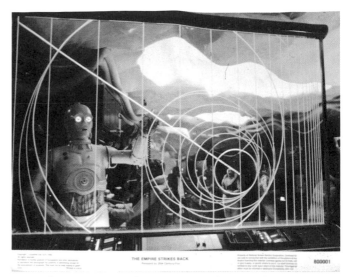

Lobby Card from The Empire Strikes Back *(LucasArts 1980)*

Star Wars, X-Wing cover, lists 8 new figures
(1978–79) 15.00
    Variation, Burger Chef Fun 'N' Games Booklet,
      added puzzle and game pages to 1978 X-
      Wing catalog 10.00
Star Wars, Death Star and X-Wing cover (#428-063,
1979) 10.00
The Empire Strikes Back logo (#359-096, 1980) 10.00
The Empire Strikes Back, Luke and Yoda cover,
    logo back cover (1980) 10.00
The Empire Strikes Back, Luke and Yoda cover
    (#1037-144, 1981) 10.00
Star Wars Collections (#236-068-00, 1982) 10.00
Return of the Jedi, picturing Darth Vader and Royal
    Guards (#175-017-00, 1983) 10.00
Return of the Jedi, picturing Jabba the Hutt
    (#76719000, 1984). 10.00

Retailer Catalogs (Kenner)
"*Star Wars* Toys and Games Available Fall 1977"
    featuring the Early Bird Certificate Package 75.00
Star Wars 1978 Catalog, features the first nine figures   50.00
Star Wars 1979 Catalog, features the Boba Fett
    rocket firing backpack 35.00
Star Wars Collector Series 1984 Catalog 30.00
Kenner 1986 Toy Fair Catalog 25.00

GREETING CARDS

Star Wars Birthday Card (1994) full color multiple
    fold-out $2.00
Star Wars Greeting Cards 12-pack, color (1992) 21.00
Yoda Christmas Cards, art by Tsuneo Sanda, 10
    cards and envelopes (1997) 10.00
Deluxe *Star Wars* Valentine Kit (1997) 3.00

LOBBY CARDS

Lobby cards are large prints containing scenes from a movie, or pictures of the stars which, as the name implies, were designed for display in the lobby of a movie theater. They are 11" x 14" in size and come in sets of eight different cards. Lobby cards are produced for every movie, just like movie posters (covered under "WALL ART") and they are

standard sizes because the theater can't change its display spaces for each movie. Theaters are also sent sets of 8" x 10" photo cards, and frequently star and scene photos in larger sizes.

Star Wars lobby cards, photo cards, and similar items can generally be acquired from dealers who specialize in lobby cards and posters from movies. Since there is ongoing collector interest in movie memorabilia, these items are not thrown away. There is also no great secret to collecting them. Lobby cards from popular movies with famous stars are naturally worth more than ones from movies you refuse to watch on free television, and bigger cards are worth more than smaller ones. However, popular movies like *Star Wars* play for a long time in a lot of theaters and are re-released too, meaning that more lobby cards, photo cards, and similar items are produced, and that more are saved by collectors.

Star Wars
Set of eight lobby cards, 11" x 14" (1977) $125.00
Set of eight photo cards, 8" x 10" (1977) 100.00

The Empire Strikes Back
Set of eight lobby cards, 11" x 14" (1980) 90.00
Set of eight photo cards, 8" x 10" (1980) 75.00

Return of the Jedi
Set of eight lobby cards, 11" x 14" (1983) 75.00
Set of eight photo cards, 8" x 10" (1983) 60.00

MAGAZINES

There have been several magazines devoted exclusively, or almost exclusively, to *Star Wars*—almost as many as Leonardo DiCaprio has today. The only surprising part is that some of these magazines were started more than a decade after the last movie had come and gone. Magazines covering collectibles, general interest, and humor are covered immediately following those which exclusively featured *Star Wars*.

Bantha Tracks #13, inside page (Lucasfilm 1981)

Lucas Film Fan Club #12 (The Fan Club 1990)

BANTHA TRACKS
Lucasfilm

#1 to #4, each.	$15.00
Combined reissue #1–#4	10.00
#5 to #9	6.00
#10 to #19	5.00
#20 to #33	4.00
#34.	7.50
#35 10th Anniversary, last issue	6.00

LUCASFILM FAN CLUB MAGAZINE
The Fan Club (1987–94)

1987
# 1 Anthony Daniels interview, 14pp	$10.00

1988
# 2 Star Tours, 14pp	3.00
# 3 Mark Hamill interview, 14pp	4.00
# 4 14pp	3.00
# 5 14pp	3.00

1989
# 6 George Lucas interview	4.00
# 7 Harrison Ford interview	6.00
# 8 Steven Spielberg interview,	3.00
# 9 Sean Connery interview	9.00

1990
#10	3.00
#11 *The Empire Strikes Back* 10th Anniv.	8.00
#12 Maniac Mansion.	3.00
#13	3.00

1991
#14 Billy Dee Williams interview	6.00

1992
#15	5.00

#16 *Star Wars* comics.	6.00
#17 George Lucas Interview	7.50

1993
#18 Art of Drew Struzan	7.50
#19 *Return of the Jedi* 10th Anniv., 30 pp.	10.00
#20 34 pp.	10.00

1994
#21 36pp	10.00
#22 TIE Fighter video game	5.00

Becomes:

STAR WARS INSIDER
The *Star Wars* Fan Club (1994–98)

1994
#23 56 pages, Obi-Wan photo cover	$9.00

1995
#24 Ralph McQuarrie cover, 60 pages	10.00
#25 James Earl Jones interview, 72 pages	5.00
#26 George Lucas interview, 80 pages	6.00

1996
#27 Luke and Landspeeder cover, 80 pages	8.00
#28 Peter Mayhew interview, 64 pages	5.00
#29 Shadows of the Empire, 64 pages	5.00
#30 Han and Jabba fold out cover, 64 pages.	5.00
#31 Expanded *Star Wars* Universe, 68 pages	4.00

1997
#32 84 pages	5.00
#33 Wampa cover, 76 pages	4.50
#34 Mark Hamill cover, 74 pages	4.50
#35 Tusken Raider cover, 74 pages.	4.50

1998
#36 Jawa cover, Liam Neeson interview	4.50
#37 Senator Palpatine, Ian McDiarmid interview	4.50

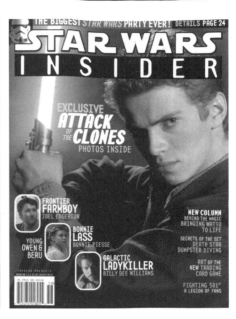

Star Wars Insider #25, #30 and #58 (Star Wars Fan Club 1995–2002)

OFFICIAL POSTER MONTHLY

Star Wars
#1 Stormtrooper cover $10.00
#2 Darth Vader/Luke Skywalker cover 8.00
#3 Han Solo cover 6.00
#4 Chewbacca/Darth Vader cover 5.00
#5 Darth Vader/C-3PO cover 5.00
#6 Droids/Sand People cover 5.00
#7 R2-D2/C-3PO cover 5.00
#8 . . . . 5.00
#9 Luke and Leia circus cover 8.00
#10 Darth Vader cover 5.00
#11 through #18, each 10.00

The Empire Strikes Back
#1 . . . . 6.00
#2 . . . . 5.00
#3 through #5, each 5.00

Return of the Jedi
#1 through #4, each 5.00

Episode I Poster Magazines
Star Wars Episode I The Phantom Menace
   Villains Poster Magazine, Darth Maul cover (Topps) 4.00
Star Wars Episode I The Phantom Menace Heroes
   Poster Magazine, Qui-Gon Jinn cover (Topps) 4.00

STAR WARS GALAXY MAGAZINE
Topps (1994–97)

#1 Fall 1994, *Star Wars* Widevision SWP3 card $7.50
#2 Winter 1995 Luke Skywalker on Tatooine cover
   by Dave Dorman 5.00
#3 Spring 1995 cover by Jae Lee; All Alien issue,
   The Empire Strikes Back Widevision #0, *Star
   Wars* Cap #0, Topps Finest Chromium #3,

Official Poster Monthly #2, #7 and #10 (Paradise Press 1978–79)

Star Wars Galaxy #2, #7 and Star Wars Galaxy Collector #1 (Topps 1994–98)

SWGM3 AT-AT (McQuarrie) chromium 5.00
#4 Summer 1995, collage cover; *Star Wars Galaxy* 3 #000 Princess Leia card; *Star Wars* Galaxy Topps Finest SWGM4 chromium card; *Star Wars Galaxy Magazine* 4-card sheet; Battle of Hoth 4-page poster 5.00
#5 Fall 1995, Luke, Obi-Wan, Darth and Yoda cover, Ralph McQuarrie poster; *Star Wars* Mastervisions P2 large promo card; *Star Wars Galaxy* 3 P6 promo card; *Return of the Jedi* Widevision P1 promo card 5.00
#6 Winter 1996, Bounty Hunter issue, Boba Fett cover by Chris Moeller; *Return of the Jedi* Widevision promo card #0, *Star Wars* Finest #1 promo card 5.00
#7 Spring 1996, Shadows of the Empire cover by Hugh Fleming, Tim & Greg Hildebrandt poster; *Star Wars* Finest #2 promo card; *Star Wars* Shadows of the Empire #1 promo card; Company store catalog 5.00
#8 Summer 1996, The Dark Side cover by Cam Kennedy, Shadows of the Empire #4 promo card, Dark Side cover card. 5.00
#9 Fall 1996, Luke and Xizor cover by the Bros. Hildebrandt, with *Star Wars* 3-D promo card 3Di #1 and *Star Wars* Galaxy Mag. promo C2 . . . . 5.00
#10 Winter 1997, Han Solo vs. a Selonian cover by Joe Jusko, *Star Wars* Galaxy Mag. promo card C3; *Star Wars* Trilogy Widevision promo card P2 . . 5.00
#11 1997, Darth Vader cover by Walt Simonson, with *Star Wars* Trilogy Hologram promo #1 of 2 or #2 of 2; *Star Wars Galaxy* Magazine promo card C4; *Star Wars* Vehicles promo postcard 5.00
#12 Aug. 1997, Princess Leia cover by Dave Devries, with *Star Wars* Trilogy Widevision promo P1 and poster of cover painting 5.00
#13 Nov. 1997, Obi-Wan Kenobi, Yoda and Luke cover by Joe Quesada, Jimmy Palmiotti and Atomic Paintbrush 5.00
Becomes:

STAR WARS GALAXY COLLECTOR
Topps (1998)

#1 Feb. 1998, Drew Struzan poster, SW2 prequel card . 5.00
#2 May 1998, Flying Models poster, SW1 and SW3 prequel cards. 5.00
#3 Expanded Universe. 5.00
#4 . . . . 5.00
#5 Legos 5.00
#6 . . . . 5.00
#7 Mega Toy 5.00
#8 Masks of the Menace. 5.00
Boba Fett one-shot special (April 1998) 5.00

STAR WARS: TECHNICAL JOURNAL
Starlog (1993–94)

#1 *Star Wars*: Technical Journal of the Planet Tatooine, holographic foil logo, 8-page gatefold blueprints, etc. (1993). $9.95
#2 *Star Wars*: Technical Journal of the Imperial Forces (1994) 6.95
#3 *Star Wars*: Technical Journal of the Rebel Forces . . . 6.95

MAGAZINES: COLLECTIBLES

Many collector magazines have run *Star Wars* covers. The prices in the listing below are for newsstand versions—those without promotional giveaways such as trading cards and posters. However, many of these collector magazines came with *Star Wars* promos polybagged with the magazine. Magazines with their original promos can be worth a lot more money, depending on the collectibility of the item, but they can often be found, bagged and complete, at reduced prices in comics shops or at shows. Most promo cards, along with their source, are listed in the TRADING CARDS section. Use this as your guide when bargain hunting.

The following is a sampling of collector and distributor magazines with *Star Wars* covers. There are undoubtedly many others.

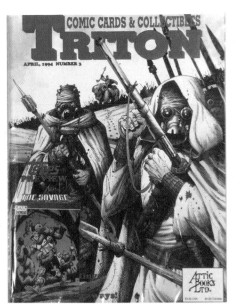
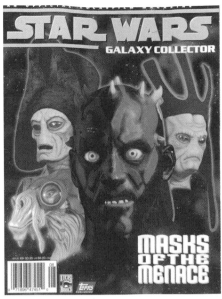

Collect! *June 1999;* Triton *#3; and* Star Wars Galaxy Collector *#8*
(which just proves that a good Star Wars *cover is not always enough to keep a magazine alive!)*

Advance Comics (Capital City Distribution)
Issue #82 Empire's End cover. $10.00

Baby Boomer Collectibles (Antique Trader Publications)
Vol. 3, No. 4 Han, Darth, Luke, Yoda, Chewbacca,
　　C-3PO vinyl figures cover. 3.00

Card Collector's Price Guide (Century Publishing Company)
Vol. 2, No. 5 *Star Wars* Galaxy Yoda cover. 2.00

Cards Illustrated (Warrior Publications)
Issue #20 Star Destroyer and *Millennium Falcon* cover . 3.00
Issue #25 C-3PO and R2-D2 cover. 3.00

Collect! (Tuff Stuff Publications)
Jan. 1995 Issue Darth Vader (McQuarrie art) cover. . . . 7.50
Oct. 1996 Issue Shadows of the Empire, Darth
　　Vader cover (Hildebrandt art) 7.50
March 1997 Issue. 5.00

May 1998 Issue Jabba the Hutt and Leia cover. 5.00

Collectible Toys and Values (Attic Books)
Issue #15 Kenner figures cover. 7.50
Issue #35 Yoda cover 5.00

Combo (Century Publishing Company)
Issue #27, Han and Jabba cover. 3.00

Hero Illustrated (Warrior Publications)
Issue #26 Dave Dorman art cover. 4.00
1994 Science Fiction Annual C-3PO with gun cover . . . 4.00

Lee's Action Figure News & Toy Review (Lee Publications)
Issue #6 Micro Collection cover 7.00
Issue #15 . . . . 10.00
Issue #23 R2-D2 cover. 7.00
Issue #31 *Millennium Falcon* cover 7.00
Issue #32 TIE Fighter cover 7.00

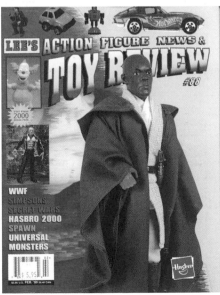

Previews *Feb. 2002;* Lee's Action Figure News and Toy Review #88; Star Wars Gamer *#4*

Issue #43 Galoob AT-ST cover 10.00
Issue #45 Boba Fett cover 9.00
Issue #49 Luke Stormtrooper cover. 9.00
Issue #50 Galoob TIE Fighter Pilot playset cover. 7.00
Issue #56 Kenner Cinema Scenes Han, Luke, and
    Chewbacca cover 8.00
Issue #64 Kenner: Rystall, Greeta, and LynMe cover . . 6.00
Later issues, each 5.00

Non-Sport Update (Roxanne Toser Non-Sport Enterprises)
Volume 4, No. 2 Ken Steacy art cover 5.00

Diamond Previews (Diamond Distribution)
Aug. 95. . . . . 3.00
Nov. 96. . . . . 3.00

Star Wares (Capital City Distribution)
Vol. 1 to Vol. 6, each 3.00

Star Wars Gamer (Wizards of the Coast)
#1 . . . . 7.00
#2 . . . . 7.00
#3 . . . . 7.00
#4 Bongomania in Otoh Gunga. 7.00
#5 . . . . 7.00

Tomart's Action Figure Digest (Tomart Publications)
Issue #27 Chewbacca toys cover 6.00
Issue #32 Darth Vader and Obi Wan Kenobi toys 6.00
Issue #39 Luke Skywalker and Wampa toys cover. 6.00
Issue #40 Han Solo and Tauntaun toys cover 6.00
Issue #45 Mos Eisley toy scene cover. 6.00

ToyFare (Wizard Press)
Issue #1 AT-AT Cover 3.00

Triton (Attic Books)
Issue #3 *Star Wars* Galaxy card art cover 5.00

White's Guide to Collecting Figures (Collecting Concepts)
   "Comic Cover Version"
Issue #1 . . . . 6.00
Issue #8 . . . . 6.00
Issue #13 Boba Fett toy cover. 6.00

Issue #26 Darth Vader vs. Obi Wan Kenobi F/X cover . . 6.00
Issue #30 Boba Fett sculpture cover 6.00
Issue #34 Leia prisoner cover 6.00

Wizard (Wizard Press)
Sci-Fi Invasion 1997 Boba Fett cover 3.00

MAGAZINES: GENERAL

Mass market Collectible #3 is the issue of *Time* magazine (May 30, 1977) which appeared a few days before the movie opened and featured a two-page spread praising the movie as the best picture of the year. The movie opened on a Friday and it wasn't hard to get a ticket for the first evening showing. There was a long line for the second showing and for every showing thereafter for many months.

The value of old magazines generally depends on the cover photo or painting. The *Star Wars* movies have generated hundreds, perhaps thousands, of magazine covers. When something is popular, everybody wants it on their cover. In addition to obvious magazines, like those that cover the movies generally, or science fiction movies, or special effects, magazines like *People* will tell you about the sad love life or happy home life of the stars, while financial magazines will tell you about all the money the movie is making. There is probably some *Bounty Hunter* trade magazine that elected Boba Fett their "Hunter of the Year." There may even be a health food magazine suggesting that Jabba the Hutt could slim down a bit by eating "free range" live creatures, instead of fat domestic ones as seen in the movie.

The list below includes "selections" which I forthrightly admit is merely a euphemism for "the ones that I have photos of" plus the original *Time* magazine issue, which I haven't yet found to photo. I wanted to include some of the photos, so I needed to have a short listing. Generally the covers are photos from the movie, or photos of the stars. Often the photos are promotional releases provided by Lucasfilms, but magazines like to get their own, exclusive, photos if they can.

Starlog *#99;* Time, *May 19, 1980,* Cinescape, *March-April 1997*

 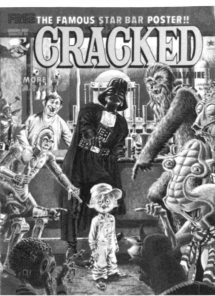 

Mad *Magazine #203,* Cracked *Magazine #148,* Crazy *Magazine #37*

Cinefantastique
Vol. 6 No. 4 The Making of *Star Wars* $20.00
Vol. 7 No. 1 The Making of *Star Wars* 20.00
Feb. 1997 *Star Wars* 20th Anniversary 5.00

Cinescape (MVP Entertainment)
March/April 1997 X-Wing cover. 5.00
Star Wars Special, March 1997. . . . . 5.00

Famous Monsters (Warren)
Issue #148 Darth Vader cover. 5.00

Nickelodeon
March 1997 Luke Skywalker and Princess Leia cover . . 4.00

People Magazine
July 18, 1977 C-3PO cover. 10.00
Aug. 14, 1978 Carrie Fisher cover. 10.00

Reel Fantasy
Issue #1 . . . . 5.00

Science Fiction, Horror & Fantasy
Issue #1 Darth Vader and Stormtroopers cover 7.00

Sci-Fi Entertainment
Feb. 1997 *Star Wars* 20th Anniversary 5.00

Starlog (Starlog Group)
Issue #7, X-Wing and TIE Fighter 35.00
Issue #13 David Prowse 10.00
Issue #14 SF Matte painting cover 10.00
Issue #21 Mark Hammil 10.00
Issue #31 *Empire Strikes Back* 10.00
Issue #35 Billy Dee Williams. 10.00
Issue #99 C-3PO and R2-D2 . . . . 8.00
Issue #236 *Star Wars* 20th Anniversary 6.00
Issue #237 George Lucas. 6.00

Time Magazine (Time Warner)
May 30, 1977 . . . . 20.00
May 19, 1980 Darth Vader cover. 10.00
Feb. 10, 1997 . . . . 3.00

MAGAZINES: HUMOR

Personally, I enjoy humorous take-offs of the movies and TV shows that I like. The quintessential humor magazine (of course I mean *Mad Magazine*) has done quite a few *Star Wars* issues. As with any magazine, it is the appearance of *Star Wars* on the cover that makes it a *Star Wars* collectible.

Mad Magazine
Issue #196, Jan. 1978, Alfred E. Newman as Darth
    Vader cover $10.00
Issue #203, Dec. 1978, The Mad *Star Wars* musical
    cover. 9.00
Issue #220, Jan. 1981, Alfred E. Newman as Yoda
    cover. 7.00
Issue #242, Oct. 1983, Unmasks the *Return of the
    Jedi* cover 7.00
Cracked
Issue #146, Star Warz spoof cover 5.00

Crazy
Issue #37, Darth Vader cover 5.00

Comics
Adolescent Radioactive Black Belt Hampsters in
    3-D issue #2, *Star Wars* spoof cover 3.00
Samurai Cat, issue #3 (of 3) *Star Wars* spoof cover . . . 3.00
Married With Children 2099, issue #3, May the
    Farce Be With You cover 3.00

MISCELLANEOUS PAPER

Doorknob Hangers
Star Wars Doorknob Hangers (Antioch, 1997)
    Darth Vader "Your Destiny Lies with Me"
        (#61085, 1997) $1.50
    C-3PO "Signal Alliance" (#78859, 1997). 1.50

Holograms
Holograms, 2" x 2", mounted on acrylic display
    stand (A.H. Prismatic 1995), 4 different, each. . . . 15.00
Star Wars Hologram stickers, large, 6" x 6" sheets
    (A.H. Prismatic #1019/SW, 1997) 3.00

Return of the Jedi *stamp, First Day Cover (March 19, 1996)*

Star Wars 3-D small stickers 2" x 2" (A.H. Prismatic
    1997) 4 different, each 1.00

Stamps
Star Wars Postage Stamps, issued by St. Vincent
    and the Grenadines
      Metallic Stamp gift pack, folder containing 9-
        stamp sheet, plus a souvenir sheet with
        three triangular stamps printed on metallic foil . 25.00
      First Day Covers stamp set, 3 covers, boxed,
        with certificate of authenticity. 15.00

Wallet Cards
Star Wars Wallet Cards (Antioch, 1997)
    6 different, each 1.00

POINT OF PURCHASE DISPLAYS

Before a *Star Wars* product gets to the consumer, it has to be designed, manufactured, packaged, shipped, and displayed for purchase in your local store. Just about every part of this process produces something that could be, and frequently is, collected.

The design process yields product and packaging prototypes and proofs or samples. Prototypes are internal items, available only to company employees, LucasArts' licensing people (for approval) and possibly advertising agencies. You really have to know somebody to get them initially. Proofs and samples are often more widely available, because they often reach salesmen and store buyers. If you don't have an actual finished sample product to show to the buyers, you may, at least, have a packaging proof to convince them that the item will be a hot seller.

Shipping yields boxes, but they are usually simple light brown corrugated items with black labels, of no real visual interest. Stores throw them away, or give them away if you ask for them. A number of collectors store their *Star Wars* action figures in the original boxes, because they have been designed for this purpose and are just the right size, but they do not consider the boxes to be part of the collection and they have never attracted much of a market for themselves.

Somebody must have boxes from the original shipments of *Star Wars* action figures in 1978, or perhaps a

Star Wars *21-figure store display (Kenner 1979)*

complete set of shipping boxes from the current figures, #69570.01 to #69570.99. Who knows? Maybe they will turn out to be quite valuable someday.

Point of Purchase displays and store signs are much more interesting. They are designed to attract your attention, so they are colorful. They display the product just as nicely in your room as they did in the store. And, best of all, they are items that were never intended to be sold to the general public in the first place, so not everybody has one.

Generally, point of purchase items are not collected so as to acquire an entire set. Rather, a few are acquired to form a backdrop or focal point for the display of one's collection.

STORE DISPLAYS

Kenner, and every other large manufacturer, makes displays to promote their products at the point of purchase. If they have a contest or giveaway promotion, they will want to let you know about it. These come in all sizes and shapes and are frequently made of cardboard. They are hanging or standing or sitting on or over the rack where the toy or other items are selected, or in the store's window. Over the years a lot of them have been produced and many more are to come. Size and artwork are important components of their collectable value, along with the importance of the product they promote. Displays for Kenner's action figures rank at the top.

Since the displays go to stores, it helps to work there if you want to collect them. Undoubtedly many displays are damaged in use or simply thrown away at the end of the promotion; however, there are thousands of stores that sell action figures and each store gets a reasonable supply, so initial print runs have to be 25,000 to 50,000 minimum for ordinary items. This tends to keep the price within reason. Signs and

The Empire Strikes Back, *32-figure store display (Kenner 1981)*

displays that are flat look very nice when framed and make a handsome addition to your collection.

Star Wars Action Figure sign (1978–80) depending
    on size $100–250
The Empire Strikes Back Action Figure sign (1980–
    1982) depending on size. 75–125
Return of the Jedi Action Figure sign (1983–
    1984) depending on size. 40–90

    The most valuable store display is quite recent. In the fall of 1997 many Toys "R" Us stores got a four-foot hanging *Millennium Falcon*, made in plastic and looking just like a scaled up version of the toy. Only 500 were supposed to be made and they were given away in a drawing by Rosie

O'Donnell. You could enter the drawing with a one dollar contribution to her charitable foundation. I entered, but didn't win. You probably entered too. The contest entry forms estimated the value of the item at $500.00, but I would think $2,500.00 would be closer. When you entered, did you think where you would store the item if you won? Of course not, because you just wanted to win one. The store display for the contest is a nice consolation collectible. It shows the *Falcon* in a reversed picture.

PORTFOLIOS AND BLUEPRINTS

The Empire Strikes Back promo art portfolio $40.00
Star Wars Intergalactic Passport & Stickers
    (Ballantine 1983) 10.00
Star Wars Blueprints, includes 15 prints, 13" x 19" in
    vinyl pouch (Ballantine 1977) 15.00
    Reprint: $6.95 (Ballantine 1992). 7.00
Star Wars Portfolio by Ralph McQuarrie, 11" x 14"
    color paintings, originally $7.95 (Ballantine
    Books #27382, 1977). 20.00
The Empire Strikes Back Portfolio by Ralph
    McQuarrie, Ballantine Books (1980). 15.00
Return of the Jedi Portfolio by Ralph McQuarrie,
    Ballantine Books (1983) 15.00
Star Wars Power of the Force Planetary Map, set,
    issued as a mail-in. 20.00
Star Wars/The Empire Strikes Back Portfolio, six
    11" x 14" plates (#875-007, 1994) 12.00
Star Wars Trilogy Print Portfolio set, eight 11" x 14"
    moviecards (Zanart #SW-1 1996). 12.00
Star Wars Post-Art portfolio, 11" x 14" (Classico
    #02762, 1995) 15.00
Star Wars Trilogy Moviecard Portfolio, eight
    11" x 14" movie cards plus 8" x 10" ChromArt
    card of the *Millennium Falcon* (Zanart 1994). 14.00

POSTCARDS

Star Wars Movie Poster Postcards (#110-038,
    1992) pack of 25 . . . . $15.00
The Empire Strikes Back Movie Poster Postcards
    (#110-037, 1992) pack of 25 . . . . 15.00
Return of the Jedi Movie Poster Postcards
    (#110-030, 1992) pack of 25 . . . . 15.00
Stormtroopers Postcards (#110-057, 1992) pack of 25 15.00

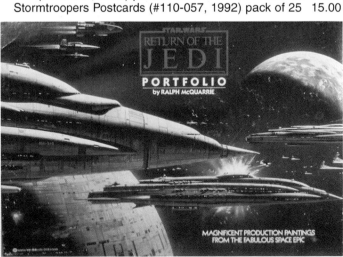

Star Wars Blueprints, *and* Return of the Jedi *Portfolio (Ballantine 1977–1983)*

Luke and Han in the Garbage Chute (#110-058,
    1992) pack of 25 . . . . 15.00
Luke Climbing into X-Wing (#105-059, 1992) pack
    of 25 . . . . 15.00
Artoo-Deetoo (#105-060, 1992) pack of 25 . . . . 15.00
Leia and Darth Vader (#105-061, 1992) pack of 25 . . . 15.00
R2-D2 and C-3PO (#105-062, 1992) pack of 25 . . . . . 15.00
See-Threepio (#105-072, 1992) pack of 25 . . . . 15.00
Han Solo (#105-073, 1992) pack of 25 . . . . 15.00
Luke Skywalker (#105-074, 1992) pack of 25 . . . . 15.00
Luke, Ben and C-3PO (1992) pack of 25. . . . . 15.00
Star Wars Postcard Set, 5 full-color cards (Classico
    1994). 7.50
Star Wars Special Edition postcards, 11" x 14"
    featuring poster art from movies, 4 different, each . 3.50
Star Wars Laser Postcard Set, holographic images
    (A.H. Prismatic 1994). 6.00
    Darth Vader 1.50
    Millennium Falcon in asteroids 1.50
    Millennium Falcon and Death Star 1.50
    X-Wing and Death Star 1.50
The Empire Strikes Back Leia 8" x 10" postcard
    (#422-012, 1994) 2.50
Star Wars Circus Poster 8" x 10" postcard
    (#422-013, 1994) 2.50
Star Wars Movie Poster 8" x 10" postcard
    (#422-014, 1994) 2.50
The Empire Strikes Back Concept 8" x 10" postcard
    (#422-015, 1994) 2.50
Star Wars X-Wing 8" x 10" postcard, Ralph
    McQuarrie art (#422-016, 1994). 2.50
The Empire Strikes Back Romantic 8" x 10" post-
    card (#422-017, 1994) 2.50
Star Wars Character Art Postcards, 12-card set 10.00
Star Wars Complete Postcards, 12-card set 10.00
Star Wars Poster Art Postcards, 18-card set 15.00
The Empire Strikes Back Complete Postcards, 8-cards . 7.00
Return of the Jedi Complete Postcards, 8-card set 7.00
Star Wars Complete Oversize Postcards, 10-card set . 26.00
The Empire Strikes Back Complete Oversize Post-
    cards, 8-card set 21.00
Star Wars Lasergram Postcards (A.H. Prismatic, 1997)
    Deathstar (#2001/SS) 2.00
    Millennium Falcon & TIE Fighters (#2001/FT) 2.00
    Darth Vader (2001/DV, 1997) 2.00
    Millennium Falcon in Asteroids (#2001/FA) 2.00
Luke and Darth Flicker Motion postcard, 1983 Fan
    Club item (offered in previews for Sept. 1997). . . . 10.00

Star Wars *Trilogy* Postcards (1997)
Star Wars Trilogy Postcard Set #1, 8 postcards 6.00
Star Wars Trilogy Postcard Set #2, 8 postcards 6.00
Star Wars Trilogy Postcard Set #3, 8 postcards 6.00
Star Wars Trilogy Postcard Set #4, 10 postcards 8.00

PRESS KITS

Press Kits
    Original *Star Wars* kit (1977) $150.00
    Star Wars kit (1978) 100.00
    Holiday special kit (1978) 175.00
    NPR Presents kit (1979) 35.00
    The Empire Strikes Back kit (1980) 60.00
    Introducing Yoda kit (1980). 35.00
    NPR Playhouse kit (1981) 30.00
    Return of the Jedi kit (1983). 30.00

Lucas Film Media Kit (LucasArts 1996)

PROGRAMS

Star Wars Movie Program (1977) limited quantity
    offered in 1994. . . . . $75.00
The Empire Strikes Back Official Collector's Edition
    (Paradise Press) 15.00
The Return of the Jedi Official Collector's Edition
    (Paradise Press) 10.00

Star Wars Movie program (1977)

Rebel Soldier, Hoth Power of the Force card proof (Kenner 1985)

Yoda Revenge of the Jedi *card proof (Kenner 1982)*

PROOFS

A few header card proofs are made for every action figure, so that design personnel, company executives and others can check the graphics, weigh the sales appeal of the package, and generally bless the product. Everybody wants to get into the act and justify their job, so changes are frequent and often the proof is not quite like the final package. This makes them quite interesting collectibles. The most valuable proofs are those for products that were never made, or where the design was changed in some significant way. After that, the value of proofs varies with the value of the final figure.

ACTION FIGURE CARD PROOFS

The most famous of these changes in the *Star Wars* world was the retitling of the third movie from *Revenge of the Jedi* to *Return of the Jedi*. No product was actually released with a *Revenge of the Jedi* package, but the original name is mentioned on a number of packages and in magazines, and action figure card proofs exist which have the *Revenge of the Jedi* logo. These are the most highly sought of the card proofs, since it is about as close as one can come to an actual *Revenge of the Jedi* product. They sell for about $150, for a minor character, up to $250, for a major character.

COVER PROOFS

Cover Proofs are to books what card proofs are to action figures. They are sent to retailers, along with the publishers monthly catalog, to help solicit orders. You may not be able to "tell" a book by its cover, but you sure can "sell" a book by its cover. I have seen dust jacket proofs for hardcover books, but most cover proofs are from paperback and trade paperback books. All of them have the corner clipped and/or a small hole punched in them to prevent them being returned for credit by the retailer as unsold copies (unsold paperbacks are not returned to the publisher—the retailer rips off the front cover and returns it instead).

I only know of a couple of people who actually collect cover proofs, but they do contain nice cover artwork. The cover proof for the original *Star Wars* paperback book would be the very first thing with the title *Star Wars* which was actually produced. Since I am calling the actual paperback "Collectible #1," I suppose it would be "Collectible #0."

Cover Proofs
Star Wars paperback cover proof $5.00
Star Wars paperback and trade paperback cover proofs:
     From 1977–79. . . . . 3.00
     From the 1980s 2.00
     From the 1990s 1.00

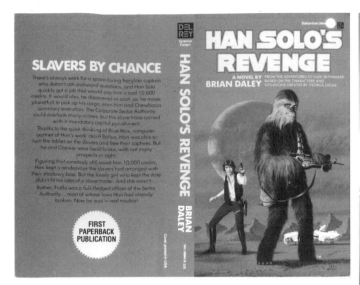

Han Solo's Revenge *paperback cover proof (Ballantine 1980)*

OTHER PROOFS

Just about every *Star Wars* product ever made has generated some kind of printing proof, sample, prototype or similar item. There is also an original piece of artwork or an original photo for every trading card, comic book cover, comic book interior page, paperback cover, hardcover dustjacket, poster, lobby card, video tape box, record jacket, video game box, T-shirt design, or other artistic product or product package. For every original piece of art, there is probably a concept drawing or sketch that went to the art director for approval before the artist did the actual drawing or painting.

The packaging proofs and prototypes for Kenner products, particularly action figures, command high prices today, and will probably always top the list. However, there are a very, very large number of proofs, prototypes, and even originals for other products that were created and someone associated with the company has them. Maybe they even want to throw them away or give them away. Ask around in your area. Don't forget to check the local stores for signs. They won't have much use for it when the promotion is over. The right trash can make a very nice collectible.

STAND-UPS

Standees are near lifesize cardboard figures, designed as store displays and sold by Advanced Graphics. Comic shops and other stores buy them and some dealers get them to highlight their table at shows. Nobody seems to collect them, but if you want one, they are available for their retail price of about $25.00 (maybe a little less for smaller figures, like R2-D2 and Yoda). The same goes for your favorite *Star Trek* figure, movie star or sports hero (maybe a little less for jockeys, girl Olympic acrobats, Danny DeVito, and Mugsy Bogues.)

STANDEES
Advance Graphics (1993–99)

Admiral Ackbar (#247) $25.00

Emperor's Royal Guard Standee (Advance Graphics 1996) and Mace Windu stand up (Pepsi 1999)

Ben Obi-Wan Kenobi (#225)	25.00
Boba Fett (#178)	30.00
C-3PO (#114)	25.00
Chewbacca (#177)	25.00
Darth Vader (#113)	25.00
Darth Vader, with lightsaber (#216)	25.00
Emperor Palpatine, on throne (#232)	30.00
Emperor's Royal Guard (#217)	25.00
Han Solo (#112)	25.00
Han Solo as Stormtrooper	25.00
Han Solo in Carbonite (#214)	30.00
Jawa (#206)	20.00
Luke Skywalker (#110)	25.00
Princes Leia (#111)	25.00
Princess Leia, slave girl (#249)	30.00
R2-D2 (#116)	25.00
Stormtrooper (#115)	25.00
Tusken Raider (#248)	25.00
Yoda (#176)	25.00

Episode I Life Size Characers (Lucas Films 1999)
Darth Maul (#331)	30.00
Queen Amidala (#327)	30.00
Jar Jar Binks (#330)	30.00

RECORDINGS

AUDIO — MUSIC — VIDEO

All of the movies have been adapted as radio plays and many of the new novels and even a few of the comic books have become books on tape. There is collector interest in the former, particularly in the National Public Radio dramatizations. It is not yet clear whether books on tape are collected, in the sense that older tapes will go up in value, or whether *Star Wars* fans buy tapes to play, in which case newer formats with the next generation of sound quality enhancements will always be more desirable than older tapes.

AUDIO

Movie Adaptations

Star Wars: The Original Radio Drama, National Public Radio (Highbridge #005-6, April 1993) 7 CDs $65.00
 Tape: (Highbridge #099-4, 1993) 6 cassettes 35.00
The Empire Strikes Back: The Original Radio Drama, National Public Radio (Highbridge #007-2, Sept. 1993) 5 CDs. 55.00
 Tape: (Highbridge #000-5, 1993) 5 cassettes 30.00
Star Wars/The Empire Strikes Back Limited Edition CD set (Highbridge #006-4, Sept. 1993) 12 CDs 125.00
Complete *Star Wars/Empire* CD set (Lucasfilm #114-1, April 1995) 12 CDs 100.00
Return of the Jedi: The Original Radio Drama, National Public Radio (Highbridge #158-3, Oct. 1996) 3 CDs 35.00
 Tape: (Highbridge #157-5, 1996) 3 cassettes 25.00
Star Wars Complete Trilogy on CD, National Public Radio (Highbridge #164-8, Oct. 1996) 15 CDs . . 125.00
The *Star Wars* Limited Edition Collector's Trilogy CD, National Public Radio (Highbridge #165-6, Oct. 1996) deluxe slipcase, only 7,500 made . . . 175.00
Star Wars Trilogy CD Set (Highbridge #169-2) 9 CDs . 75.00

New Story Adaptations

Children of the Jedi, by Barbara Hambly, BDD Audio Cassette #47195-3, May 1995 . . . . 15.00
The Courtship Of Princess Leia, by Dave Wolverton, BDD Audio Cassette #47193-7, 1994 . 15.00
The Crystal Star, by Vonda N. McIntyre, BDD Audio Cassette #47194-5, Dec. 1994. . . . . 15.00
Dark Empire, The Collector's Edition, by Tom Veitch, Donald I. Fine #347-4, 1995, 5 CDs 60.00
Dark Empire, Donald I. Fine #201-6, 1997. . . . . 15.00
Dark Lords of the Sith, by Kevin J. Anderson and Tom Veitch, Time Warner Audio Books 298-2, 1995, 2 cassettes. 17.00
Dark Lords of the Sith, Donald I. Fine #199-0, 1997 . . 15.00
Darksaber, by Kevin J. Anderson, BDD Audio Cassette #47423-5, Nov. 1995, 180 minutes, 2 cassettes, includes music and sound effects 15.00
I, Jedi, by Michael Stackpole, BDD Audio Cassette #47948-2, Feb. 1998 . . . . 15.00
The New Rebellion, by Kristine Kathryn Rusch, BDD Audio Cassette #47743-9, Dec. 1996. . . . . . 15.00
Nightlily, The Lovers' Tale, by Barbara Hambly, BDD Audio Cassette #45541-9, Nov. 1995 . . . . . . 10.00
Nightlily, The Lover's Tale #2, by Barbara Hambly, BDD Audio Cassette #47413-8, Jan. 1996 . . . . . . 12.00
Planet of Twilight, by Barbara Hambly, BDD Audio Cassette #47196-1, May 1997 . . . . 15.00
Rebel Agent, by William C. Dietz, Highbridge Audio #244-X, Feb. 1998 . . . . 15.00
The Rebel Dawn, by A. C. Crispin, BDD Audio Cassette #47746-3, March 1998 . . . . 15.00
Shadows Of The Empire, by Steve Perry, BDD Audio Cassette #47438-3, May 1996 . . . . 15.00
Soldier for the Empire, abridged ed., by William C. Dietz, Donald I. Fine #202-4, Feb. 1997 . . . . 15.00
Specter of the Past, by Timothy Zahn, BDD Audio

Star Wars, *The Original Radio Drama (Highbridge 1993)*

Cassette #47893-1, Nov. 1997 . . . . 15.00
Tales of the Jedi, by Tom Veitch, Donald I. Fine
    #1982, June 1997 . . . . 15.00
The Truce At Bakura, by Kathleen Tyers, BDD
    Audio Cassette #47197-X, Jan. 1994 . . . . 15.00

Black Fleet Crisis by Michael Kube-McDowell
Before The Storm (Black Fleet Crisis #1) BDD
    Audio Cassette #47422-7, April 1996 . . . . 15.00
Shield Of Lies (Black Fleet Crisis #2) BDD Audio
    Cassette #47424-3, Sept. 1996 . . . . 15.00
The Tyrant's Test (Black Fleet Crisis #3) BDD Audio
    Cassette #47421-9, Jan. 1997 . . . . 15.00

Corellian Trilogy by Roger Allen
Ambush At Corellia (The Corellian Trilogy #1) BDD
    Audio Cassette #47202-X, March 1995 . . . . 15.00
Assault At Selonia (The Corellian Trilogy #2) BDD
    Audio Cassette #47203-8, July 1995 . . . . 15.00
Showdown At Centerpoint (The Corellian Trilogy
    #3) BDD Audio Cassette #47204-6, Oct. 1995 . . . 15.00

Han Solo Trilogy by A.C. Crispin
The Paradise Snare (Han Solo Trilogy #1) BDD
    Audio Cassette #47744-7, June 1997 . . . . 15.00
The Hutt Gambit (Han Solo Trilogy #2) BDD Audio
    Cassette #47745-5, Sept. 1997 . . . . 15.00

Jedi Academy by Kevin J. Anderson
Jedi Search (Jedi Academy Trilogy #1) BDD Audio
    Cassette #47199-6, March 1994 . . . . 15.00
Dark Apprentice (Jedi Academy Trilogy #2) BDD
    Audio Cassette #47200-3, July 1994 . . . . 15.00
Champions Of The Force (Jedi Academy Trilogy
    #3) BDD Audio Cassette #47201-1, Oct. 1994 . . . 15.00
Jedi Academy Omnibus, BDD Audio Cassette
    #47848-6, July 1997, 6 cassettes 35.00

Thrawn Trilogy by Timothy Zahn
Heir To The Empire (*Star Wars* #1) BDD Audio
    Cassette #45296-7, June 1991 . . . . 15.00
Dark Force Rising (*Star Wars* #2) BDD Audio
    Cassette #47055-8, June 1992 . . . . 15.00
The Last Command (*Star Wars* #3) BDD Audio
    Cassette #47157-0, May 1993 . . . . 15.00
Star Wars Audio Boxed Set, BDD Audio Cassette
    #47322-0, Oct. 1994, with exclusive collector's
    cassette in a collector's case featuring a
    molded *Millennium Falcon* 60.00

X-Wing by Michael Stackpole
X-Wing: Rogue Squadron, BDD Audio Cassette
    #47418-9, Feb. 1996 . . . . 15.00
Wedge's Gamble (X-Wing #2) BDD Audio Cassette
    #47419-7, June 1996 . . . . 15.00
The Krytos Trap (X-Wing #3) BDD Audio Cassette
    #47420-0, Oct. 1996 . . . . 15.00
Bacta War (X-Wing #4) BDD Audio Cassette
    #47425-1, Feb. 1997 . . . . 15.00
X-Wing by Aaron Alston
Wraith Squadron (X-Wing #5) BDD Audio Cassette
    #47888-5, Feb. 1998 . . . . 15.00

*Star Wars: We Don't Do Weddings, The Band's
    Tale* by Kathleen Tyers, BDD Audio Cassette
    #47393-X, Aug. 1995, 60 minute adaptation
    of story from *Tales From the Mos Eisley Cantina* . 12.00
Star Wars: We Don't Do Weddings: The Band's

Return of the Jedi *Read-Along Book and Record*
(Buena Vista 1983)

Tale (*Star Wars*) by Kathleen Tyers, BDD
    Audio CD #45540-0, Aug. 1995 . . . . 14.00

Juvenile Adaptations, Read Along Books and Records
Star Wars 24 Page Read-Along Book and Record,
    33 -1/3 RPM record with color photos (Buena
    Vista Records) 15.00
The Empire Strikes Back 24 Page Read-Along
    Book and Record, 33-1/3 RPM record with
    color photos (Buena Vista Records #451) 15.00
Return of the Jedi 24 Page Read-Along Book and
    Record, 33-1/3 RPM record with color photos
    (Buena Vista Records #455, 1983) 15.00
Return of the Jedi 24 Page Read-Along Book and
    Record, 33-1/3 RPM record with color photos:
Ewoks Join the Fight (Buena Vista Records
    #460, 1983) 25.00
Droid World (Buena Vista Records #453, 1983) 30.00
Planet of the Hoojibs (Buena Vista Records
    #454, 1983) 30.00
*Note: The above three items were offered through Diamond
Distribution in 1997 at the prices indicated.*

Other Juvenile Adaptations
Star Wars: A New Hope, Playasound Audio, Feb.
    1997 . . . . 15.00
Star Wars Playpack and book, Walt Disney Audio
    #197-8, Feb. 1996 . . . . 12.00
A New Hope Read-along: with book, Walt Disney
    Audio #195-1, Jan. 1997 . . . . 7.00
The Empire Strikes Back Playpack and book, Walt
    Disney Audio #198-6, Feb. 1996 . . . . 12.00
The Empire Strikes Back Read-along: with book,
    Walt Disney Audio #194-3, Jan. 1997 . . . . 7.00
Return of the Jedi Read-along: with book, Walt
    Disney Audio #193-5, Jan. 1997 . . . . 7.00
Return of the Jedi Playpack and book, Walt Disney
    Audio #196-X, Feb. 1996 . . . . 12.00
Star Wars: The Mixed-Up Droids (#274-5, 1995) 9.00
*See also Read-Along Play Packs, with PVC figures,
    listed under DOLLS AND FIGURES.*

MUSIC SOUNDTRACKS

If you can't hum the *Star Wars* theme by John Williams
you probably bought this book by mistake. While you can get

The Empire Strikes Back soundtrack album back (RSO 1980)

the various movie soundtracks on 8 track tape, on cassettes and in other formats, the collectible items are the original soundtrack LP albums. Obviously you would like to get ones that were never played and are still in their original shrink wrap. Of course, shrinkwraping equipment is not too expensive and so shrinkwrap on a product is not a guarantee of anything. Just about every other format and every other record, whether performed by the Boston Pops, the Utah Symphony Orchestra, the Biola University Symphony Band or the Electric Moog Orchestra can be had for under $20.00. Of course, if it has a colorful insert, its worth a little more.

Albums and CDs

Star Wars LP Soundtrack album, Music composed
  and conducted by John Williams, Performed
  by the London Symphony Orchestra, two
  records, with two sleeves, an insert and a
  poster (20th Century Records #2T-541, 1977) . . $30.00
The Empire Strikes Back LP Soundtrack album,
  Music composed and conducted by John
  Williams, Performed by the London Symphony
  Orchestra, two records with a 12-page color
  insert (RSO Records, RS2-4201, 1980) album
  back features Han and Leia romantic art 40.00
Return of the Jedi LP Soundtrack album, London
  Symphony Orchestra, one record, with 4-page
  color insert (RSO Records, 1983) 25.00
Star Wars Trilogy Special Edition Soundtrack CD

with Bonus Darth Vader shaped single, CDs
set laser engraved with picture, plus 20
pages of liner notes (1997). 110.00

VIDEOTAPES

The three *Star Wars* movies are available in original and special editions and in letterbox and pan and scan formatted for your television set, which, as you should know, has a much different aspect ratio than a widescreen movie. Like all special effects movies, *Star Wars* is much better seen in a movie theater than on TV. Video tapes were released over the years with different box art and they can be collected for the art, but few people do so. Collectors who have videotapes of the movie got them to watch, not collect. Collectors who have Droids and Ewoks video tapes got them for their kids to watch, not themselves. My grandson liked the Ewok tape which I found for a buck. He was four years old. Hey! Start 'em young.

Boxed Videotapes

Star Wars (CBS/Fox Home Video 1991) $20.00
The Empire Strikes Back (CBS/Fox Home Video 1991) 20.00
Return of the Jedi (CBS/Fox Home Video 1991) 20.00
Star Wars Trilogy (CBS/Fox Home Video 1991)
  boxed set. 60.00

From *Star Wars* to Jedi: The Making of a Saga
  (CBS/Fox Home Video #1479, 1992) 10.00
Star Wars Video Trilogy Letterbox Collectors
  Edition, with documentary tape *From Star
  Wars to Jedi*, abridged book *George Lucas:
  The Creative Impulse* (Fox Video #0656,
  1993) in holographic gift box 100.00
Star Wars: A New Hope Special Edition Video
  (#6097, 1997) 20.00
The Empire Strikes Back Special Edition Video
  (#6098, 1997) 20.00
Return of the Jedi Special Edition Video (#6099, 1997) . 20.00
Star Wars Trilogy Special Edition Boxed Set (1997)
  Pan & Scan format (#2930) 50.00
  Widescreen (letterbox) format (#2934) 60.00
Droids: The Pirates and the Prince, featuring
  R2-D2, Jann Tosh and C-3PO plus the voice
  of Anthony Daniels, written by Peter Sauder
  (CBS/Fox Home Video #8467, 1996) 10.00
Ewoks: The Haunted Village (CBS/Fox Home
  Video #8466, 1996) 10.00
Ewoks: Two episode sets (J2 Communications 1990) . . . 7.00
Episode I, The Phantom Menace videotape (2000) . . . 15.00

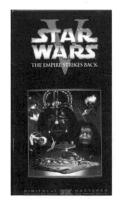

Star Wars Trilogy Widescreen, The Empire Strikes Back; Ewoks *and* Episode I *video tapes*

Empire Strikes Back *Film Frame, Yoda Edition*
(Willitts Designs 1995)

STILLS

FILM FRAMES
Willitts Designs (1995–97)

Film Frames are a full screen, letterbox movie image, with a one-of-a-kind 70mm film frame, in a 7½" x 2¾" acrylic holder. They are sold by Willitts Designs, who also produced the limited edition lithographs by Ralph McQuarrie (listed under WALL ART). The retail price of these strips is $24.95, but dealers have been offering them for as little as $15.00 and they still have some left. They are the only way that a collector can own an actual piece of the film. Each "edition" is numbered and limited to 9,500 sets, but each frame is unique since only a single 70mm print of the film was cut up.

Star Wars: A New Hope (1995)
Luke Skywalker Edition (#50007) $25.00
Darth Vader Edition (#50008) 25.00
Princess Leia Edition (#50009) 25.00
Ben Kenobi Edition (#50010) 25.00
Han Solo Edition (#50011) 25.00
Chewbacca Edition (#50012) 25.00
Creatures Edition (#50013) 25.00
Galactic Empire Edition (#50014) 25.00
Stormtrooper Edition (#50015) 25.00
Rebel Alliance Edition (#50016) 25.00
C-3PO Edition (#50017) 25.00
R2-D2 Edition (#50018) 25.00

The Empire Strikes Back (1996–97)
Luke Skywalker (#50031) 25.00
Rebel Alliance (#50032) 25.00
Imperial Attack (#50033) 25.00
Millennium Falcon (#50034) 25.00
Jedi Training (#50041) 25.00
Luke Skywalker on Cloud City (#50042) 25.00
Jedi Master Yoda (#50043) 25.00
Darth Vader (#50044) 25.00
Lando Calrissian (#50045) 25.00
Rebel Escape (#50046) 25.00
Han Solo and Leia (#50047) 25.00

Return of the Jedi
Jedi Emerges (#50056) 25.00
Final Confrontation (#50057) 25.00

Princess Leia (#50058) 25.00
Han Solo (#50059) 25.00
Droids (#50060) 25.00
Return of the Jedi (#50061) 25.00
Ewoks (#50062) 25.00
Emperor Palpatine (#50063) 25.00
Darth Vader (#50064) 25.00
Rebellion (#50065) 25.00
Imperial Forces (#50066) 25.00
Turning Points (#50067) 25.00
Aliens of Jabba (#50068) 25.00

PHOTOS

The best way to get a signed photograph is to find a show where your favorite star is appearing and go and get the autograph yourself. I can guarantee you that there will be someone at the show selling photos of him or her. This gives you good memories—and a genuine collectible. It won't be free, but then what is? If several stars are available, make the person you dragged to the show wait in the long line for the major stars' autograph, while you get autographs from several of the lesser stars. Their lines will be shorter, and they might even sign multiple items.

Photos of your favorite star from *Star Wars* are also available from a variety of sources. Their value on the market depends more on their movie star status as of today, than on their role in the movie. Consequently, Harrison Ford's autographed photo is expensive, but not the others. The price list below is designed to give you a baseline for evaluating any photo that you wish to purchase, or sell. They are for standard 8" x 10" photos, double matted and ready for framing, with a certificate of authenticity. If the item you are considering buying at a dealer's table, or from and advertisement or cable TV show, is reasonably priced, go ahead and buy it—but don't expect to sell it later at a huge profit.

Signed Photos
Harrison Ford $150.00
Mark Hamill 50.00
Carrie Fisher 40.00
Sir Alec Guiness 50.00
David Prowse 45.00
Peter Cushing 50.00
George Lucas 95.00
Just about anyone else . . . . under $50.00
Return of the Jedi Mark Hamill autographed photo
    plaque (1993) 100.00
The Empire Strikes Back Anthony Daniels auto-
    graphed photo plaque (1993) 80.00
Darth Vader David Prowse autographed photo
    plaque, limited to 2,500 pieces (1997) 70.00
Darth Vader/David Prowse signed photo collage,
    matted (Timeless 1993) 30.00
Star Wars Movie Photos 5.00
The Empire Strikes Back Movie Photos 4.00
Return of the Jedi Movie Photos 3.00

ROLE PLAY TOYS

Role play toys include weapons, communicators, armor, utility belts, and similar items which are full size, or sized for a kid to play with. They are hardly a new idea. Every movie serial and TV Western hero, from the time of Hopalong Cassidy, Roy Rogers, and the Lone Ranger onwards had cap guns, holsters, hats, boots and all manner of full-sized licensed products. It's action figures that are the new idea. Nobody figured out how to sell dolls to boys until the mid 1960s.

With all the different weapons used in the trilogy, it's a miracle there aren't a lot more *Star Wars* role play weapons. There are lightsabers, pistols, and laser rifles. The first Chewbacca Bowcaster arrived in mid 1997, and there are no weapons yet for any of the bounty hunters or Mos Eisley Cantina aliens, except for Boba Fett's armor. Maybe it's just as well. I suppose we'd loose too many little sisters if Kenner made a life-size Carbon-Freezing Chamber.

With so little product, collector interest in the few classic items is quite high. As yet, there has been little collector interest in the 1990s items and they can all be acquired for around their original retail prices. The only exception is the Boba Fett Armor Set which has been scarce, and expensive.

CLASSIC WEAPONS

Classic Lightsabers
Star Wars Lightsaber, inflatable, 35" long, light-up
  (Kenner #38040, 1997) boxed $90.00
    Loose 40.00
Droids Battery Operated Lightsaber (Green)
  (Kenner 1984) 100.00
    Loose 50.00
Droids Battery Operated Lightsaber (Red) (Kenner
  1984) 200.00

3 Position Laser Rifle (Kenner 1978–83)

Empire Strikes Back *Laser Pistol (Kenner 1980–81)*

Loose 80.00

Classic Pistols and Rifles
3 Position Laser Rifle, folding stock, secret on/off button, two-speed laser sound, battery powered (Kenner #69310, 1978) in *Star Wars* package 250.00
  Loose, with *Star Wars* logo. 75.00
  Reissue as Electronic Laser Rifle (1980) in
    The Empire Strikes Back package 250.00
  Loose, with *The Empire Strikes Back* logo 75.00
Laser Pistol replica of Han Solo's laser pistol with secret on/off button, battery powered (Kenner #38110, 1978)
  Original *Star Wars* package 125.00
  Loose, with *Star Wars* logo. 25.00
  Reissue *The Empire Strikes Back* package 100.00
  Loose, with *The Empire Strikes Back* logo 20.00
  Reissue *Return of the Jedi* package. 75.00
  Loose, with *Return of the Jedi* logo . . . . 20 .00
Biker Scout Laser Pistol, battery powered (Kenner #71520, 1983) original *Return of the Jedi* package. 75.00
  Loose 25.00

NEW WEAPONS

New Lightsabers (Asst. #69600, 1995–98)
Electronic Luke Skywalker Lightsaber (Kenner #69795, March 1996) 50.00
  Loose 25.00
Electronic Darth Vader Lightsaber (Kenner #69796, Sept. 1996) red box 60.00

Reissue, green box 50.00
Loose 20.00

Other New Weapons
Chewbacca's Bowcaster (Kenner #27734, June 1997). 18.00
   Loose 6.00
Electronic Heavy Blaster BlasTech DL-44 (Kenner
   #27737, July 1996) in orange box 20.00
   Loose 10.00
Electronic Blaster Rifle BlasTech E-11 (Kenner
   #27738, July 1996) white, in orange box 20.00
    Loose, white. 7.00
   Reissue, striped, in green box 15.00
   Loose, striped. 10.00
Star Wars Electronic Blaster Lazer Rifle, 18½" long,
   battery powered Stormtrooper weapon with
   lights and sounds. 17.00
   Loose 6.00
Star Wars Endor Blaster Pistol (Kenner #27737, 1998) . 14.50
Star Wars Commando Blaster Laser Rifle (Kenner
   #27738, 1998) 20.00

EPISODE I WEAPONS

***Episode I* Lightsabers** (Hasbro 1999)
Electronic Darth Maul Double-Bladed Lightsaber
   (#84103). 30.00
Darth Maul Double-Bladed Lightsaber (#84527)
   [557841.0200]. 20.00
Electronic Qui-Gon-Jinn Lightsaber (#84102) 20.00
Electronic Obi-Wan Kenobi Lightsaber (#) 20.00
Qui-Gon Jinn's Lightsaber (#26264) loose. 10.00

Other *Episode I* Weapons (Hasbro 1999)
Electronic Tatooine Blaster Pistol (#57133) 20.00
Electronic Battle Droid Blaster Rifle (#26237) 20.00
Naboo Foam Firing Blaster (Hasbro #57127) 15.00

COSTUME LIGHTSABERS

New Costume Lightsabers (Rubies #1588, 1995)
Star Wars Lightsaber, battery operated
   White. 7.50
   Blue. 7.50
   Red 7.50
   Loose, any color 3.00

***Episode I* Lightsabers**, battery powered (Rubies 1999)
Darth Maul Lightsaber (#1613). 10.00

Costume Lightsabers (Rubies 1995)

Obi-Wan Kenobi Lightsaber (#1643). 10.00
Qui-Gon Jinn (#1638) 10.00

ACCESSORIES

New Accessories
Luke Skywalker's Utility Belt (Kenner #27735, Aug.
   1997) in green box. 18.00
   Loose 9.00
Boba Fett Armor Set, includes chest shield, blaster,
   two arm gauntlets and face shield (Kenner
   #27796, 1998) 50.00
   Loose 25.00

Electronic Heavy Blaster and Battery Operated Water Blaster (Kenner 1996)

Boba Fett's Armor (Kenner 1998) and Episode I *Jedi Gear (Hasbro 1999)*

Walkie-Talkies & Communicators
Star Wars Imperial Walkie-Talkie (Tiger Electronics #88-061, 1997) reception up to 100 feet 13.00
Darth Vader Voice Changer Walkie Talkies (Tiger Electronics #88-062, 1997) reception up to 200 feet 20.00
Star Wars Rebel Alliance Long Range Walkie Talkies (Tiger Electronics #88-063, 1997) reception over 1,500 feet 35.00
    Loose 12.00
Electronic Com-Link Communicators (Kenner #27791) . 15.00
    Loose 6.00
Darth Vader and Chewbacca Walkie Talkie Masks (Micro Games of America #SW-3980, 1995) 50.00
Darth Vader and Stormtrooper Walkie Talkies (Micro Games of America #SW-WT920M, 1995) 23.00

Episode I Accessories (Hasbro 1999)
Jedi Gear (#57128) 20.00

WATER PISTOLS

Water Pistol
Water Blaster BlasTech DL-44 (Kenner #8402-0) battery operated
    Silver color (March 1997) 15.00
    Black color (Fall 1997) 12.00
    Loose 5.00

Episode I Blaster Water Pistols (Larami 1999)
Battle Droid Rifle Power Soaker (#84030) 4.00
Naboo Pistol Power Soaker (#84030) 4.00
Battle Mauser Power Soaker (#84030) 4.00
Queen Amidala Super Soaker Pistol (#84060) 10.00

ELECTRONIC MINI-PISTOLS

Electronic Pistols, Micro Light & Sound (Larami 1999)
Naboo Pistol (#84010) 5.00
Battle Mauser (#84010) 5.00
Battle Droid Rifle (#84010) 5.00

SPACE SHOOTERS

These are not replica weapons, but disk firing model spaceships. Or maybe they are games, since they come with targets you can knock down. Something tells me the targets are only used when mom is watching or when no friends, siblings, or pets are convenient targets. Anyway, I have listed them here.

Space Shooters
Star Wars Space Shooters
    Millennium Falcon Blaster (Milton Bradley #04622, Feb. 1997) $20.00
    Darth Vader TIE Fighter Blaster (Milton Bradley #04798, Feb. 1997) 20.00
Space Shooter Battle Belt, with 32 Foam Disks (Milton Bradley #04777, Feb. 1997) 10.00

Electronic Blaster Rifle BlasTech E-11 (Kenner 1996)

SCHOOL AND OFFICE SUPPLIES

SCHOOL AND OFFICE SUPPLIES

You awaken from a sound sleep on your *Star Wars* sheets, and outfit yourself from head to toe with *Star Wars* clothing. Are you ready to go forth to do battle with the faceless minions of an evil empire? Are you? Okay, well in that case you will just have to go to school, or to work and pretend that your teacher is Emperor Palpatine or your boss is Darth Vader. Actually, this may not be much of a stretch, in which case you will need to outfit yourself with an array of school and office supplies bearing *Star Wars* pictures and logos.

SCHOOL SUPPLIES

Pencils and Markers
Star Wars pencils & pens, each $5.00
The Empire Strikes Back pencils & pens, each 4.00
Return of the Jedi pencils & pens, each 3.00
Star Wars, 6 Foil Pencils (RoseArt #1653, 1997) 2.50
Star Wars Pen, several styles (Mead 1997) each. 2.00
Pens & Pencils (Pentech 1999)
Eight #2 Pencils (#16200) 3.00
Six-pack of Ball Pens (#16206) 3.00

Two #2 Pencils and Pencil Sharpener (#16202) 3.00
Lightsaber Ball Point Pens (#16207) 3.00
Two-pack, Darth Maul and Jar Jar Binks Pencil
    Toppers (#16203) 2.00
Two-pack, Anakin Skywalker and Queen Amidala
    Pencil Toppers (#16203) 2.00
Eight-pack of Washable Markers (RoseArt 1997) 5.00
Six-pack of Washable Markers with one Darth
    Maul Cap (#16208) 3.50
Six-pack of Washable Markers with on Jar Jar
    Binks Cap (#16208) 3.00
Jumbo Highlighter with Darth Maul Cap (#16211) 2.00

Pencil Sharpeners & Boxes
Star Wars Millennium Falcon Pencil Sharpener
    (RoseArt #1658, 1997) 3.00
Lightsaber Pencil Case (RoseArt #1669, 1997) 4.00
Star Wars Pencil Tins (A.H. Prismatic #1071, 1997). . . . 4.00

***Episode I*, Pencil Box**, metal (Impact 1999)
Darth Maul, Darth Sidious, Qui-Gon Jinn and Obi-
    Wan Kenobi Pencil Box (#70042) 8.00
Watto, Sebulba, Anakin Skywalker and Jar Jar
    Binks Pencil Box (#70042) 8.00
Tin Pencil Box, Darth Maul raised image (#70610) 5.00

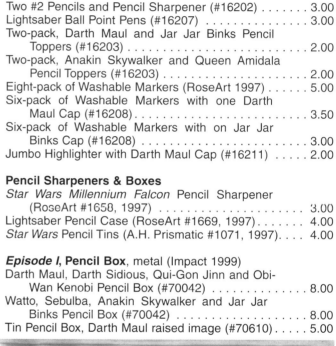

Episode I *Washable Markers (Pentech 1999);* Star Wars *Washable Markers (RoseArt 1997)*

Figurine Erasers 3 Pack (Impact 1999)

Star Wars *Lunch Box (King Seeley-Thermos 1977)*

Star Wars/Return of the Jedi Erasers (Butterfly
   Originals/ Spindex 1983)
Admiral Ackbar Eraser 5.00
Baby Ewoks Eraser 5.00
Bib Fortuna Eraser (#90029). 5.00
Darth Vader Collectible Eraser 5.00
Gamorrean Guard Eraser 5.00
Jabba the Hutt Eraser. 5.00
Max Rebo Eraser 5.00
Wicket the Ewok Collectible Eraser. 5.00
Yoda Collectible Eraser. 5.00
Return of the Jedi Glow In The Dark Erasers,
   Millennium Falcon, Darth Vader, and C-3PO on
   5" x 7" header card (reoffered 1996) 4.00

Episode I Figurine Erasers (Impact 1999)
3-Pack with Anakin Skywalker, R2-D2, and Jar Jar
   Binks (#70043) 5.00
3-Pack with Watto, Darth Maul, and Sebulba (#70043) . 5.00
Single Figurine Erasers, six different, each. 3.00
Starfighter Eraser (#70075) 3.00
Lightsaber Eraser (#70608) 5.00

Episode I Sharpener/Eraser (Impact 1999)
Destroyer Droid Sharpener/Eraser Combo (#70508) . . . 4.00
Federation Tank Sharpener (#70609) 3.00

Notebooks
The Empire Strikes Back notebooks, each 5.00
Return of the Jedi notebooks, each. 4.00
Wookiee doodle pad. 3.00
Pencil tablet 3.00
Darth Vader Duty Roster. 4.00
Star Wars portfolio 5.00
Star Wars Fat Little Neatbook, 180 count (Mead
   #57188, 1997) 10.00
Star Wars Wirebound 60-page Notebook, 6 different
   designs (Mead #05718, 1997). 4.00

Episode I Memo Pads, Notebooks (Impact 1999)
Sith Lord, Darth Maul cover 3" x 5" memo pad (#70053) 1.00
Anakin Skywalker/Pod Race "Fat Book" 180-sheet
   Memo Pad (#70502) 2.00

Darth Maul, Jedi Duel "Fat Book" 180-sheet Memo
   Pad (#70502) 2.00
Jedi, Sith Notebook (#70052). 5.00
Anakin Skywalker and Jar Jar Binks Notebook (#70052) 5.00

Episode I Wire Bound Theme Books, 50 sheets, 8" x 10½"
Anakin's Pod racer notebook (#70036). 2.00
Jar Jar Binks notebook (#70036) 2.00
Queen Amidala notebook (#70036) 2.00
Qui-Gon Jinn notebook (#70036). 2.00
R2-D2 notebook (#70036) 2.00
Sith Lord notebook (#70036) 2.00

Episode I Study Kit (Impact 1999)
Watto, Sebulba, Anakin Skywalker, and Jar Jar
   Binks Pencil Pouch, Sharpener, Eraser, and
   Ruler (#70058) 7.00
Darth Maul, Darth Sidious, Qui-Gon Jinn, and Obi-
   Wan Kenobi Pencil Pouch, Sharpener, Eraser,
   and Ruler (#70058) 7.00

Funkit
Star Wars Funkit, with stickers, pens, scissors
   (RoseArt #1649, 1997) 10.00

Lunch Boxes
    Lunch boxes have their own groups of collectors, mak-
ing these more valuable than other school related items.

Star Wars, space battle on front & Tatooine scene
   on reverse, *Droids* thermos (King Seeley-
   Thermos 1977)
   metal box. 55.00
   thermos 20.00
Star Wars, red with Darth and Droids pictured on
   front, *Droids* thermos (King Seeley-Thermos 1978)
   plastic box 35.00
   thermos 15.00
The Empire Strikes Back, *Millennium Falcon* on
   front & Luke, Yoda and R2-D2 on back, Yoda
   thermos (King Seeley-Thermos 1980)
   metal box. 45.00
   thermos 15.00
The Empire Strikes Back, Dagobah scene on lid,

Episode I *Darth Maul Lunch Bag (Pentech 1999)*

Hoth battle on back, Yoda thermos (King Seeley-Thermos 1980)
metal box 45.00
thermos 15.00
The Empire Strikes Back, red, Chewbacca, Han, Leia and Luke on lid, Yoda thermos (King Seeley-Thermos 1980)
plastic box 30.00
thermos 15.00
The Empire Strikes Back, photo cover with logo and inset pictures, Droids and logo on thermos (King Seeley-Thermos 1980)
plastic box 30.00
thermos 15.00
Return of the Jedi, Luke in Jabba's Palace on lid and space scene on back, Ewok thermos (King Seeley-Thermos 1983)
metal box 40.00
thermos 15.00
Return of the Jedi, red with Wicket and R2-D2 on front, Ewok thermos (King Seeley-Thermos 1983)
plastic box 25.00
thermos 10.00

Episode I Soft-Sided Lunch Bag (1999)
Darth Maul Lunch Bag (Pentech) 10.00

Notebook Binders
Star Wars Zipper Binder (Mead #29254, 1996)
Blue, with Darth Vader 10.00
Black/Gray with *Star Wars* logo 10.00

Portfolios
Star Wars Portfolio, 12 designs (Mead #33384, 1997)
Princess Leia 3.00
Han Solo 3.00
Luke Skywalker 3.00
"A long time ago in a galaxy far, far away" ... 2.00
"Never underestimate the power of the Dark Side" 2.00
R2-D2: "General Kenobi, years ago you served my father" 2.00
C-3PO: "Did you hear that?" 2.00
"May the Force be with you" 2.00

"Freeze, you Rebel scum!" 2.50
Yoda: "A Jedi's strength flows from the Force" 2.00
Darth Vader: Dark Lord of the Sith 2.50
Star Wars spaceships 2.00

Folders (Impact 1999)
Anakin Skywalker folder (#70500) 1.00
Anakin Skywalker/Pod Race folder (#70500) ... 1.00
Darth Maul folder (#70500) 1.00
Jar Jar Binks folder (#70500) 1.00
Jedi folder (#70500) 1.00
Naboo Fighter folder (#70500) 1.00
Queen Amidala folder (#70500) 1.00
R2-D2 folder (#70500) 1.00

Star Wars Zipper Pouch (Mead (50744, 1997)
Star Wars logo, grey and black 5.00
Yoda 5.00
Darth Vader 5.00
"*Star Wars*" in red, in circle 5.00

Calendars, Planners, Telephone Books
Dated Student Planner (DayRunner 1999)
Darth Maul (#93207) 10.00
Jar Jar Binks (#93205) 10.00
Obi-Wan Kenobi (#93206) 10.00
Qui-Gon Jinn (#93198) 10.00

Student Planner, Spiral Bound (DayRunner 1999)
Queen Amidala (#93214) 10.00
Jar Jar Binks 10.00

Monthly Planner (DayRunner 1999)
Anakin Skywalker one-year planner (#93226) ... 5.00
Darth Maul one-year planner (#93226) 5.00
Queen Amidala two-year planner (#93395) ... 5.00

Calendar, Magnetic (DayRunner 1999)
Darth Maul (#93223) 15.00
Jar Jar Binks (#93223) 15.00

Telephone Books (DayRunner 1999)
Jar Jar Binks (#93221) 5.00
Queen Amidala 5.00
Qui-Gon Jinn 5.00

Episode I *Lightsaber Eraser and Glue Stick (Pentech 1999)*

2 Year monthly planners (Dayrunner 1999)

Backpacks
Darth Vader and Imperial Guards Backpack, red
  (Adam Joseph 1983) 30.00
R2-D2 and C-3PO Backpack, blue (Adam Joseph
  1983) 30.00
Yoda Backpack, red (Adam Joseph 1983) 30.00
Return of the Jedi Backpack, blue canvas Darth
  Vader and 2 Stormtroopers on flap, Luke, Leia,
  C-3PO, and R2-D2 on front with Jedi logo 30.00
Star Wars Backpack (Pyramid Handbags #91166,
  1996)
  Black, with Darth Vader pictured. 25.00
  Black, with C-3PO pictured 25.00
  Navy Blue, with Stormtrooper pictured 25.00
Star Wars Backpacks, high tech nylon
  Boba Fett (1997) 25.00
  Darth Vader (1997) 25.00
  Stormtrooper (1997). 25.00
  Yoda (1997) 25.00
Star Wars Backpacks, Interactive, with sounds
  Darth Vader/TIE-Fighter (1997) 18.00
  Luke Skywalker/X-Wing Fighter (1997). 18.00
  Darth Vader breathing (1997) 18.00
Star Wars Backpacks (Pyramid #91066, 1996)
  Black with Darth Vader 13.00
  Black with Stormtrooper. 13.00
  Black, soft side, Dark Lord of the Sith. 13.00

Beltbags
Darth Vader Breathing Beltbag (1997). 11.00
Luke/X-Wing Light Flashing Beltbag (1997). 11.00
Star Wars Beltbags, high tech nylon (1997) picturing:
  Boba Fett 10.00
  Stormtrooper 10.00
  Darth Vader 10.00
  Yoda 10.00

Misc. Supplies (Impact 1999)
R2-D2 figural Glue Stick (#70023) 2.50
Four-pack of rolled book covers (#70013). 5.00

OFFICE SUPPLIES

The only problem with *Star Wars* office supplies is that they favor the rebel alliance, while most offices resemble the galactic empire. To be true to life, they should have faceless Stormtrooper images. Why sell pens one at a time to individual rebels. I bet a carton of Gamorrean Guard pens, with a bonus Jabba the Hutt pen for the boss, would sell better—at least if the boss were doing the buying!

Pens
Star Wars Rebel Fighter Space Pen (Fisher
  #54944,1995). $15.00
Star Wars The Force Titanium Plated Space Pen
  (Fisher #86734, 1996) in plastic box. 75.00
Star Wars Rebel Pen, Fisher Space Pen (#SWR,
  1997) 20.00
Star Wars Stationery Set, 3 designs packaged as a
  paper/ envelope set (#91022, 1997) 5.00

Magnets (Applause 1996)
Imperial TIE Fighter (#42972) 3.00
Rebel Snowspeeder (#42970). 3.00
Rebel X-Wing (#42971) 3.00
Millennium Falcon (#42974) 3.00
Imperial AT-AT (#42969) 3.00

3-D Magnets, 2" x 2" (A.H. Prismatic #1008swx, 1997)
Darth Vader 3.00
Millennium Falcon. 3.00
R2-D2 & C-3PO 3.00
X-Wing Fighter 3.00

Episode I CD Wallet (Pentech 1999)
Star Wars Episode I collage 10.00

Window Decals
Darth Vader (#SW1002, 1994) 3.50
R2-D2 and C-3PO (#SW1003, 1994) 3.50
Yoda (#SW1004, 1994). 3.50
Star Wars Space Fight (#SW1006, 1994) 3.50

Episode I *CD Wallet (Pentech 1999)*

STATUES

STATUES — MAQUETTES — BUSTS — FINE REPLICAS

It would take an impressive bankroll to collect all of the items in this section, and I doubt that very many people do so. However, most collectors could afford to buy, save up for, or convince a relative to buy one (or a few) items, which then forms the centerpiece of their collection.

The prices listed here are either the full list price for the item, or a slightly lower price if I found several dealers selling the items for less. You may be able to find the one you want for even less, particularly if the dealer has had it for a long time. This does not mean that these fine collectibles will never rise in value. The first ones only came out a few years ago, so just about all of them are still available. It takes that long for expensive items to sell through to the ultimate consumer. Prices can't rise until the pieces have finally sold out. When this finally happens, future prices will depend on the statues' intrinsic artistic value.

Don't buy these collectibles to make money. Buy them because you want one to look at and enjoy. Although expensive collectibles hold their value, they are hard to sell quickly. Since almost no one is trying to collect all of them from a series, there is not much extra demand for the first one produced, or any particularly scarce one. A collector with a spare $500 or $1,000 to spend will usually be just as happy to buy the next one produced, and as long as there are collectors willing to buy, the companies will produce new items. This may limit your price speculation, but not your enjoyment. Invite your *Star Wars* buddies to your house to see your fine collectible and go to their house to see their different ones.

Where do I find one of these, you ask? You can't just drive to your local store and look over a large selection in order to make your choice. One place to try is your local comic shop. All these fine items are distributed to comic shops via Diamond Distribution, but most shops would have one or two, at most. If you shop at a comic store regularly, you could buy Diamond Previews and look for your favorite items as they appear. Then you can get your shop to order one for you. They may be able to get older items for you as well. Some stores, like Spencer Gifts or Sharper Image, stock these collectibles, especially around Christmas time. Check their catalogs too, because there will probably be a better selection listed there. Ask the sales staff to check with the other stores in the chain. The Internet is another good place to shop, and it may be the best source price-wise.

MAQUETTES

Yoda Maquette, 26" mounted on black wood base with1" x 4" brass plate, with certificate of authenticity, limited to 9,500 (Illusive Originals #672000, 1995) listed as "sold out" by the manufacturer $950.00

Boba Fett Maquette, sculpted by Mario Chiodo, 15" tall, mounted on black wood base with 1" x 4" brass plate, with certificate of authenticity, limited to 10,000 (Illusive Originals #672001) . . . 300.00

Admiral Ackbar Maquette, sculpted by Mario Chiodo,11" tall, mounted on black wood base with 1" x 4" brass plate, with certificate of authenticity, limited to 10,000 (Illusive Originals #672003) listed as "retired" by the manufacturer. . 150.00

Jabba the Hutt Maquette, sculpted by Mario Chiodo, 27" long, mounted on black wood base with

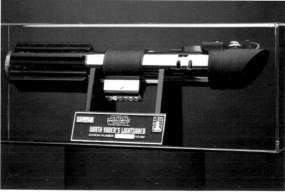

Darth Vader TIE Fighter, Darth Vader Lightsaber Replica, and X-Wing Fighter Replica (Icons 1997) Images courtesy of Icons

Yoda Maquette (Illusive Originals 1995)

1" x 4" brass plate, with certificate of authenticity, limited to 5,000 (Illusive Originals #672004) 300.00

Chewbacca Maquette, sculpted by Mario Chiodo, 17" tall bust, mounted on black wood base with 1" x 4" brass plate, with certificate of authenticity, limited to 7,500 (Illusive Originals #672006). 300.00

Han Solo in Carbonite Prop Replica, 7' tall, cast in fiberglass from the original mold, sculpted by Mario Chiodo, with 2½" x 8" brass plaque, with collector's brochure, limited to 2,500 (Illusive Originals #672008) 2,000.00

Darth Vader Reveals Anakin Skywalker Bust, 26" tall, 40" wide, 17½" deep, 3-piece mask/helmet opens to reveal life-size Anakin Skywalker sculpted head by Mario Chiodo, plus stand, limited to 9,500, with full color collector's brochure and certificate of authenticity (Illusive Originals #672009, 1998) 1,500.00

Rancor Creature Maquette, 21" x 7" x 24", mounted on base, with 2" x 4" silver-plated brass plaque, limited to 9,500 (Illusive Originals #672011) 600.00

STATUES

Cinemacast Darth Vader statue, 15½" cold-cast porcelain, limited to 10,000 (Kenner/Cinemacast 1995) $400.00

Boba Fett Bronze Statue, sculpted by Randy Bowen, 12½" tall, weighs 18 lbs, mounted on black Spanish marble, with certificate of authenticity (Dark Horse Comics, March 1997) 3,000.00

Rancor Bronze Statue, sculpted by Randy Bowen, 15" tall, weighs 25 lbs, mounted on black

Spanish marble, limited edition of 50 numbered copies, with certificate of authenticity (Dark Horse Comics, May 1998) 3,500.00

Darth Vader Bronze Statue, sculpted by Randy Bowen, 14" tall, 1/6 scale, limited edition with certificate of authenticity (Dark Horse Comics, May 1999) 3,500.00

Chewbacca Bronze Statue, sculpted by A. Wasil, 19½" tall, weighs 38 lbs, mounted on polished granite, limited edition of 50 (Dark Horse Comics, Aug. 2000) 3,600.00

Darth Vader Nutcracker, 18" tall, FAO Schwarz exclusive limited to 5,000 pieces (Steinbach) . . . 225.00

Luke and Leia pewter statue, FAO Schwarz exclusive, limited to 1,000 pieces 450.00

REPLICAS

Icons Authentic Replicas

Authentic Darth Vader Lightsaber, die-cast metal and plastic prop replica, with numbered plaque, certificate of authenticity, and plexi-glass display case, limited to 10,000 (Icons 1996) . . . $850.00
James Earl Jones Signature Edition 1,000.00

Authentic Obi Wan Kenobi Lightsaber, die-cast metal and plastic prop replica, with numbered plaque, certificate of authenticity, and plexi-glass display case, limited to 10,000 (Icons) 950.00

Authentic Luke Skywalker Lightsaber, die-cast metal and plastic prop replica, with numbered plaque, certificate of authenticity, and plexi-glass display case, limited to 10,000 (Icons) 750.00
Mark Hammil Signature Edition 900.00

Han Solo Blaster replica with display case and plaque (Icons, 1998) 600.00

TIE Fighter replica miniature, injected polyeurethane with weathered appearances, with numbered plaque, certificate of authenticity, and plexi-glass display case, limited to 1,977 (Icons) 1,500.00

X-Wing Fighter replica miniature, injected polyeurethane with weathered appearances, with numbered plaque, certificate of authenticity, and plexi-glass display case, limited to 1,977 (Icons, 1996) 1,500.00
Mark Hammil Signature Edition, 100 made 1,750.00

Han Solo Blaster (Icons 1997)

Greedo bust (Legends in Three Dimensions 1997)

Rubies Figure
Darth Vader full size Display Figure (Rubies, 1997) . 4,500.00

PORCELAIN BUSTS AND STATUES

Cold Cast Busts (Legends in Three Dimensions)
sculpted by Greg Aronowitz, limited to 3,000,
box art by Drew Struzan
Emperor Palpatine bust sculpture (1997). $100.00
Greedo bust sculpture (1998) 125.00
Boba Fett bust sculpture (1998) 150.00
Cantina Band Member (1999) 125.00
Gamorrean Guard bust sculpture (1999) 200.00
Tusken Raider bust sculpture (1999) 150.00

Attakus Collection Porcelain Statues (Star Wars Fan Club)
Yoda 200.00
Han in Carbonite 235.00
R2-D2 . . . . 215.00
Boba Fett. 300.00
Darth Maul. 270.00
Slave Leia 270.00

OTHER FINE COLLECTIBLES

Star Wars Official Pewter Chess Set, 15" x 15" x 3"
board plus 32 pewter figures on bases, sold
at $19.95 per figure (Danbury Mint, 1995) $650.00
Life-Size Ewok Plush figure, 30" tall in sitting
position, 12 lbs, 3,200 made, PepsiCo promo
(Douglas Toys, 1997) 500.00
Millennium Falcon Hanging Display from Toys "R"
Us stores, large 6 foot ship given away in
charity raffle on the Rosie O'Donnell show, with
shipping box. 2,500.00

Millennium Falcon Toys "R" Us display prop (Kenner 1997)
(photographed at show)

DELUXE REPLICA HELMETS

Don Post Studios, cast from original movie prop
Deluxe Stormtrooper Helmet, 13" fiberglass helmet
with lining (#82102) numbered edition of 1,000. $750.00
Deluxe Scout Trooper Helmet, 13" fiberglass
(#82114) numbered edition of 500 . . . . 950.00
Deluxe X-Wing Fighter Helmet, 13" fiberglass
helmet with lining (#82116) limited edition of 750 950.00
Deluxe TIE-Fighter Helmet, 15" fiberglass helmet
with lining (#82115) limited edition of 500 . . . . 1,200.00
Deluxe Darth Vader Helmet, 15" black fiberglass
(#82100) 1,000.00
Deluxe Boba Fett Helmet, 15" fiberglass (#82101) . . . 950.00

LIFE SIZE REPLICA STATUES

Don Post Studios Statues
Boba Fett Life Size Replica Statue, 6' fiberglass,
cast from original props (#82023) $5,000.00
Stormtrooper Replica Statue, 6' fiberglass, cast
from original props (#82022) limited to 500
pieces. 4,500.00
Deluxe C-3PO Replica (#82031) 15,000.00
Deluxe R2-D2 Replica (#82030) 8,000.00

TRADING CARDS

Star Wars, *Series 1, card #21 (Topps 1977)*

STAR WARS
Topps (1977)

Topps was the major producer of movie tie-in cards in the 1960s, 1970s and 1980s. The standard that they created and followed with just about every movie set was 66 (or 88) cards plus 11 (or 22) stickers. If the cards were successful, a second series of "all new" cards was produced. The cards and stickers came in colorful wax wrappers, and all three came in boxes of 36 packs. In those days there were no holograms, foils, autographed cards, 3-D redemption cards, and not even any promo cards, so collectors had nothing to collect except the cards, stickers, wrappers and boxes.

Star Wars was very successful, so a total of five series of cards and stickers was produced. They are numbered consecutively, so as to form one large set of 330 cards and 55 stickers. Stickers came one to a pack, making a sticker set harder to assemble than a card set. Some stickers were even rumored to have been, (gasp!), peeled off and stuck to something, further reducing the number in circulation. Consequently, stickers are worth about $2.00 each, while the cards go for less.

The "best cards" from all three classic series have now been reissued in chromium as *Star Wars Chromium Archives*. Card series are listed in chronological order, so these cards are listed near the end of this section. Checklists of all the series through early 1998 are included in my previous book, *The Galaxy's Greatest Star Wars Collectibles Price Guide, 1999 Edition*.

Series 1, blue border with stars

Set: 66 cards/11 stickers	$75.00
Pack: 7 cards + 1 sticker	8.00
Box: 36 packs	200.00
Box: Empty	10.00
Wrapper: C-3PO, black background	2.00

Series 2, red border

Set: 66 cards/11 stickers	45.00
Pack:	5.00
Box: 36 packs	110.00
Box: Empty	8.00
Wrapper: Darth Vader, yellow background	2.00

Series 3, yellow border

Set: 66 cards/11 stickers	50.00
Pack:	5.00
Box: 36 packs	120.00
Box: Empty	8.00
Wrapper: R2-D2, purple background	2.00

Card #207 (in Series 4) was originally printed (intentionally or unintentionally, depending on which story you believe) with C-3PO appearing to have a large but very undroid-like male appendage. This would have been appropriate in the movie *Flesh Gordon*, but not in *Star Wars*. The card was reprinted, with the offending item removed. Collectors with warped minds have placed a high value on the card—I'm still looking for it at a better price. Maybe it will be included in some future series of *Star Wars Chromium Archives*, but somehow I doubt it.

Series 4, green border

Set: 66 cards/11 stickers	$45.00

Star Wars, *Series 3 Card 162 & Sticker 26 (Topps 1977)*

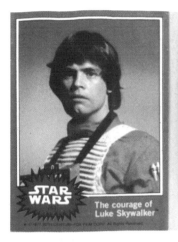

Star Wars, *Series 4, Card #263 and Sticker #43 (Topps 1978)*

Pack: 4.00
Box: 36 packs 100.00
Box: Empty 5.00
Wrapper: Obi-Wan and Luke, green background 2.00

Series 5, brown/orange
Set: 66 cards/11 stickers 40.00
Pack: 4.00
Box: 36 packs 100.00
Box: Empty 5.00
Wrapper: X-Wing Fighter, purple background 2.00

OTHER EARLY STAR WARS CARDS

There were several other types of *Star Wars* cards, stickers, and wrappers which appeared in the late 1970s and early 1980s. The Wonder Bread series of 16 cards came one per loaf of bread. General Mills cereals had two series of stickers and Kellogg's had peel-away sticker cards in its cereal. Meanwhile, Topps produced sugar-free bubble gum with distinctive wrappers and inside photos. Burger King gave out three-card strips, while Hershey's candy bars could be purchased in six-packs with a tray card.

STAR WARS
Wonder Bread (1977)

Set: 16 cards $25.00

Star Wars, *Chewbacca and Jawa cards (Wonder Bread 1977)*

STAR WARS
SUGAR FREE GUM WRAPPERS
Topps (1978)

Set: 56 wrappers $75.00
Wrapper: each 1.25
Box: empty 10.00

STAR WARS
General Mills Cereals (1978–79)

Set: 18 different large cards $50.00
Card: each 3.00

STAR WARS
ALBUM STICKERS
Panini (1977)

Set: 256 stickers with album $35.00
Single sticker 25

STAR WARS AND
THE EMPIRE STRIKES BACK
"Everybody Wins Trading Cards"
Burger King (1980)

Set: 12 different strips $30.00
Set: 36 cards, cut 25.00
Card: cut 75
(Cards are unnumbered)

THE EMPIRE STRIKES BACK
Topps (1980)

While there were only three series of *The Empire Strikes Back* cards from Topps, there were more actual cards and stickers offered than for the previous movie. As before, stickers are more valuable than cards because there was only one sticker per pack. The packs also contained a stick of bubble gum, which is not a collectible and no longer edible. If you open a pack, save the wrapper and throw the gum away.

Series 1, grey and red border
Set: 132 cards/33 stickers $60.00
Pack: 12 cards 4.00
Box: 36 packs 75.00
Box: Empty 4.00

The Empire Strikes Back, *Series 1, two cards (Topps 1980)*

Wrapper: 1.50

Series 2, grey and blue border
Set: 132 cards/33 stickers 50.00
Pack: 4.00
Box: 36 packs 60.00
Box: Empty 5.00
Wrapper: 1.00

Series 3, green and yellow border
Set: 88 cards/22 stickers 25.00
Pack: 4.00
Box: 36 packs 55.00
Box: Empty 5.00
Wrapper: 1.00

THE EMPIRE STRIKES BACK
GIANT PHOTO CARDS
Topps (1980)

Test Issue Set: 60 Giant cards. $70.00
Test Issue, single card 2.00
Regular Set: 30 cards 35.00
Regular Set Box 45.00
Box: empty 3.00

THE EMPIRE STRIKES BACK
Hershey's (1980)

Cards appeared on six-pack candy bar trays
Set: 5 trays (with uncut cards) $8.00
Set: 5 cards cut from trays 5.00

RETURN OF THE JEDI
Topps (1983)

There were only two series of *Return of the Jedi* cards and only about half as many total cards as in the previous two series. Stickers are again more valuable and each comes with two different backgrounds. While modern cards are of much higher quality than these and the previous Topps *Star Wars* cards, hardly anyone collects them! All the collecting action is in the promo cards and chase cards. At least these sets are collected.

Series 1, red border
Set: 132 cards/33 stickers $25.00
Pack: 10 cards, 1 sticker 2.00
Box: 36 packs 40.00

Return of the Jedi, *Series 1, two cards (Topps 1983)*

Return of the Jedi, *Series 2 card (Topps 1983)*

Box: Empty 3.00
Wrapper: 1.00
(Four different wrappers: Luke; Jabba; Ewok; Darth Vader)

Series Two, blue border
Set: 88 cards/22 stickers 20.00
Pack: 10 cards, 1 sticker, ... 2.00
Box: 36 packs 35.00
Box: Empty 3.00
Wrapper: 1.00
(Four different wrappers, Leia; Lando; C-3PO; Young Ewok; all say "New Series")

RETURN OF THE JEDI
ALBUM STICKERS
Topps (1983)

Set: 180 stickers with album $20.00
Single sticker 25
Wax Box 40.00

STAR WARS GALAXY
Topps (1993, Art)

Star Wars Galaxy cards were the first new set of *Star Wars* cards in 10 years and the first to use art rather than pictures from the movies. The first section provides an all new look at the main characters, with art by Joe Smith. Variant

Star Wars Galaxy *(One), promo card (Topps 1993)*

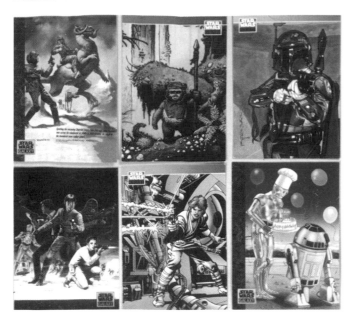

Star Wars Galaxy (One), 6 cards (Topps 1993)

cards with these images were used with the Just Toys Bend-Ems figures as well. A number of them also made their way onto T-shirts. The New Visions 60-card subset features full color illustrations from top comic book artists, including Gil Kane, Sam Keith, Dale Keown, Ken Steacy, Dave Stevens, and Al Williamson. In addition, there are subsets covering the design of *Star Wars* and the art of *Star Wars*.

This first *Star Wars Galaxy* set is also an important element in the *Star Wars* marketing revival. New novels and comics had started in 1991, but very few other collectibles were being produced. This card series was heavily marketed and gave a good boost to the *Star Wars* revival.

It gave a much needed boost to Topps as well. They had fallen behind their competitors in trading card quality and had only begun to catch up the previous year. Superhero trading cards were hot at this time, and Topps was in the process of was loosing their only foothold in this market, the *Batman* movie cards. They were concentrating on promoting their own comic book lines and needed to show that they were still serious about trading cards. They showed everybody, and

have been producing *Star Wars* cards regularly ever since. Their *Star Wars Galaxy* magazine started the following fall.

The *Millennium Falcon* factory set was one of the best publisher/editor freebees Topps ever gave away. Thanks again, Topps, for sending me one.

Set: 140 cards $15.00
Pack: 8 cards 1.50
Box: 36 packs 35.00
Millennium Falcon factory foil stamped set, plus
    holo-foil cards, plus Darth Vader 3-D holo
    gram and #0 card and preview, in plastic ship
    model 75.00
Millennium Falcon factory set, publishers proof,
    "limited to 500 sets" on sticker 100.00
Binder, with card SWB1 . . . . 15.00
Etched-Foil cards, untitled, Walt Simonson art
1 (Darth Vader). 8.00
2 (Lando Calrissian) 8.00
3 (Luke and R2-D2) 8.00
4 (C-3PO and Chewbacca). 8.00
5 (Yoda and Obi-wan) 8.00
6 (Luke) 8.00
Autographed Cards. 30.00
Six-card uncut-sheet (1:case) 30.00
Promo Cards
Boba Fett and Dengar (Cam Kennedy art) from
    Classic Star Wars #8 . . . . 10.00
Jabba the Hutt, Oola and Salacious Crumb (Sam
    Keith art) from *Starlog* #181 and *Wizard* #20 . . . . . 8.00
Princess Leia (Brian Stelfreeze art) from *Non-*
    Sports Update Vol. 4 #2 and shows 8.00
Dewback/Stormtrooper (Al Williamson art) from
    Non-Sports Update Vol. 4 #2 . . . . 8.00
Princess Leia and Dewback promo sheet, from
    Advance Comics #52. . . . . 5.00
Jabba the Hutt/Oola/Salacious Crumb promo sheet,
    from *Previews*, Feb. 1993 and *Comics*
    Scorecard, Feb. 1993, 5½" x 7½" 10.00
SWB1 binder card from *Star Wars* Galaxy Binder 10.00

STAR WARS GALAXY TWO
Topps (1994)

The second *Star Wars Galaxy* card series continued the fine art work and great overall quality of the first series. As

Star Wars Galaxy *Cards*, Millennium Falcon *Factory Set*
(Topps 1993)

Star Wars Galaxy *Two, Biker Scout/Ewok promo card*
and regular series card (Topps 1994)

Star Wars Galaxy Two, Bonus Cards Un-cut Sheet (Topps 1994)

with the first series, most of the collecting has centered around the promo cards and chase cards. Some promo cards, such as those given away at shows, are inevitably difficult to obtain. If you didn't go to the show, you may have to pay a lot for the card. The value of other promo cards, such as those that came with magazines or comic books, can be puzzling. Often they can still be found, bagged with the magazine or comic, for a very reasonable price. I have attempted to list the sources for as many of them as possible. Don't pay a fortune for a promo card without first looking for the original comic, magazine or toy that it came with. You might save money and have another collectible in the bargain.

Set: 135 cards (#141-#275)	$15.00
Pack: 8 cards	1.25
Box: 36 packs	30.00
Factory tin Set, with #00 card, Boris Vallejo hologram card and Galaxy III promo card	50.00

Etched-Foil cards, untitled (1:18) by Walt Simonson
#7 (Grand Moff Tarkin)	7.00
#8 (Imperial Troopers)	7.00
#9 (Emperor Palpatine)	7.00
#10 (Boba Fett)	7.00
#11 (Jabba the Hutt, Bib Fortuna & Salacious Crumb)	7.00
#12 (*Slave 1*)	7.00
Uncut Etched-Foil sheet	70.00
Autographed card (2000)	40.00
Six-card uncut sheet (1:case)	30.00
Album	16.00

Promo cards
P1 Rancor (Jae Lee art) from *Cards Illustrated* #2	10.00
P2 Lightsaber construction (Chris Sprouse art) from *Non-Sports Update*, Vol. 5 #2	10.00
P3 Yoda at Shrine, not released but samples exist	unknown
P4 Jawas and C-3PO (Dave Gibbons art) from *Star Wars* Galaxy I *Millennium Falcon* Factory set	10.00
P5 Chewbacca and droid (Joe Phillips art) from *Cards Illustrated* #5 & Just Toys mail-in	10.00
P6 Boba Fett (Tom Taggart art) from *Hero* #12	10.00
SWG1 promo	8.00
Tusken Raiders (Tim Truman art) from *Classic Star*	

Wars #20 or Just Toys mail in	8.00
Biker Scout/Ewok (Jim Starlin art) from *Triton* #3 variant card #266, Ewok with knife	15.00
Promo sheet with P1 card from *Previews* Feb. 1994, 5¼" x 7"	2.00

STAR WARS GALAXY THREE
Topps (1995)

Set: 90 cards: #276–#365 + #L1–#L12	$15.00
Pack: 5 cards + 1 1st day issue card and 1 insert card	1.00
Box: 36 packs	30.00
First day set: 90 cards	50.00
First day card, each	1.00

Etched Foil Cards untitled (1:12) by Walt Simonson
13 Lando Calrissian	6.00
14 *Millennium Falcon*	6.00
15 Jawas	6.00
16 Jawas	6.00
17 Tusken Raiders	6.00
18 Jedi Spirits	6.00
Uncut Etched Foil panorama sheet	60.00

Agents of the Empire Clearzone (1:18)
E1 Brett Booth	8.00
E2 Jeff Scott Campbell	8.00
E3 Jeff Rebner	8.00
E4 Joe Chiodo	8.00
E5 Tom Rainey	8.00
E6 Brian Denham	8.00

Promo Cards
P1 promo, does not seem to exist	
P2 Snowtroopers, convention give away	10.00

Star Wars Galaxy Three, *four cards (Topps 1995)*

P3 Darth Vader (John Van Fleet art) from *Non-Sports Update*, Vol. 6 #4 . . . . 5.00
P4 Luke Skywalker (Arthur Suydam art) from *Combo #7* . 5.00
P5 Snowspeeder and AT-AT (Steve Reiss art) from . *Advance Comics #83* 5.00
P5 error promo 25.00
P6 cover of *Star Wars Galaxy Magazine #5* (Bros. Hildebrandts art) from *Star Wars* Galaxy Magazine #5 . . . . 5.00
P7 Leia and twins (Russell Walks art) from *Wizard #52* . 5.00
P8 Darth Vader and Boba Fett, from *Cards Illustrated #25* 5.00
No # Boba Fett, from *Star Wars* Galaxy II factory set. . 10.00
#000 Princess Leia promo (Drew Struzan art) from *Star Wars Galaxy Magazine #4* 5.00
One-Card promo sheet, card #000, from *Previews* Sept. 1995 . . . . 5.00

STAR WARS GALAXY—BEND-EMS
Topps (1993–95, Art)

Most of JustToys' Bend-Em figures came with trading cards from 1993 to 1995. The cards are variant *Star Wars Galaxy* cards, which are lettered on the back instead of numbered. Their earliest cards and figures matched, but the later ones were random, making it that much harder to complete a set of cards. Consequently, later cards are worth more than earlier cards. There are 28 cards in the set, plus three mail-in cards. The cards may very well be more collectible (and more valuable) than the figures.

Star Wars Bend-ems, 4 cards (Topps 1993–95

Just Toys Bend-Ems variants (Joe Smith art)
0 Darth Vader mail-in card (Ken Steacy art) $15.00
00 Darth Vader mail-in card (Ralph McQuarrie art) . . . 15.00
Checklist card, variation of checklist card from series, mentions Series Two 15.00
Cards A thru M, each 3.00
Cards M thru X, each 5.00
Star Wars Galaxy Series 2 cards
Cards Y thru BB, each 5.00

STAR WARS
Merlin (1997)

These are a recent set of standard-sized trading cards available to comic shops through Diamond Distribution. The cards cover all three movies, plus character and vehicle profiles. Merlin is owned by Topps, which explains how they have the rights to produce *Star Wars* trading cards.

Set: 125 cards $30.00
Pack: 1.50
Box: 45.00
Chase Cards, oversize, three different, each 20.00

ACTION MASTERS
Kenner (1994–95)

Action Master die-cast figures came with trading cards that were unique to the figures, not promo cards for some card series. Because of this, they are generally overlooked by trading card magazines.

17 different cards from die-cast figures, each $2.00

STAR WARS MASTERVISION
Topps (1995)

Topps Mastervision cards are large enough to be called wall art and come on premium 24-point stock, UV-coated and foil-stamped. The series features full-bleed artwork by Ralph McQuarrie, Dave Dorman, The Hildebrandts, Boris Vallejo, Ken Steacy, Drew Struzan, Hugh Fleming, Michael Whelan and more.

Boxed Set: 36 cards 6¾" x 10¾" $30.00
Card: 1.00
Promos
No # 2.50
P2 promo (*Star Wars Galaxy Mag. #5*) 2.50

STAR WARS FINEST
Topps (1996)

This is an all-chromium set, subtitled "The character guide to the *Star Wars* universe." The cards features text written by Andy Mangels and consist of 10 nine-card subsets by different artists.

Set: 90 Chromium cards $30.00
Pack: 5 cards 2.50
Box: 36 packs 55.00
Topps Matrix Chase Cards (1:12)
Han Solo and Chewbacca (Ray Lago) 10.00
C-3PO and R2-D2 (John Van Fleet) 10.00
Emperor Palpatine (Ray Lago) 10.00
Boba Fett (John Van Fleet) 10.00
Embossed Chase Cards (1:9) Dan Brereton art

Star Wars *Finest, cards #61 and #16 (Topps 1996)*

Star Wars Shadows of the Empire, Cards #32 & #52 (Topps 1996)

6 different, F1 to F6, each 10.00
Topps Matrix six-up chasecard panel (Dan Brereton art)
   one per case ordered by retailer
Topps Finest Refractor (1:12) 90 different, each 55.00
Refractor Set: 90 cards 400.00
Mastervisions Matrix redemption (1:360). 75.00
Mastervision Matrix mail-in 75.00
Album, with card 20.00
Album card 8.00
Promos
SWF1 Boba Fett, from *SW Galaxy Mag.* #6 . . . . 4.00
SWF2 Darth Vader, from *SW Galaxy Mag.* #7 . . . . 4.00
SWF3 Luke on Tauntaun, from *Non-Sports Update*
   Vol. 7 #3 . . . . 4.00
Refractor promo 40.00
Oversize Chromium Promo 15.00

STAR WARS:
SHADOWS OF THE EMPIRE
Painted by Greg and Tim Hildebrandt
Topps (1996)

Shadows of the Empire cards are based on the novel, comic book, and video game "multimedia extravaganza" of the same name.

Set: 90 cards (#1 through #72 and #82 through #100) $15.00
Pack: 9 cards 1.50
Box: 36 packs 45.00
Etched foil, gold gilt (1:9) six different, each 7.00
Foil Embossed (1:18) four different, each 10.00
Redemption card (1:200) 60.00
Autographed Mastervision mail-in redemption 50.00
Promos
One card promo sheet, SOTE#3, 5¼" x 7" 5.00
SOTE1 Prince Xizor (Bros. Hildebrandt art) from
   Star Wars Galaxy Magazine #7 . . . . 3.00
SOTE2 Darth Vader (Bros. Hildebrandt art) from
   Non-Sports Update Vol. 7 #4 . . . . 3.00
SOTE3 Luke and Lightsaber (Bros. Hildebrandt art)
   from *Star Wars* Topps Finest Series One box 3.00
SOTE4 Dash Rendar (Bros. Hildebrandt art) *Star
   Wars Galaxy Magazine* #8 . . . . 3.00
SOTE5 Boba Fett (Bros. Hildebrandt art) from QVC
   and convention giveaway 3.00
SOTE6 Guri (Bros. Hildebrandt art) from *Fan* #19 . . . . . 3.00

SOTE7 R2-D2 and C-3PO (Bros. Hildebrandt art)
   San Diego Con giveaway, *Collect* Vol. 4, #9,
   Combo #24 . . . . 3.00

STAR WARS WIDEVISION
Topps (1995)

With Widevision cards, Topps went back to images from the movies. This time they had high quality and the same aspect ratio as the films (like the letterbox videotape version). The images were transferred directly from the original film master, not a second-generation version. Production was limited to 4,000 cases.

Widevision versions of the other two movies followed and in 1997 the Special Edition was covered in turn.

Set: 120 cards, 4½" $40.00
Pack: 10 cards 5.00
Box: packs 90.00
Topps Finest (1:11) Ralph McQuarrie art
C1 C-3PO and R2-D2 on Tatooine 15.00
C2 Luke watches two suns setting 15.00
C3 Pulled into the Death Star Docking Bay 15.00
C4 On the run within the Death Star 15.00
C5 Darth Vader vs. Luke 15.00
C6 Imperial TIE Fighter chases *Millennium Falcon* . . . 15.00
C7 Rebels approach the Death Star. 15.00
C8 TIE Fighter chases X-Wing 15.00
C9 X-Wing in the Death Star trench 15.00
C10 Award Ceremony on Yavin 15.00
Album, with #00 card 16.00

Star Wars *WideVision, card (Topps 1995)*

Promo Cards

SWP0 Han, Luke and Chewie enter final ceremony, from *Star Wars* Galaxy II factory set 15.00
SWP1 Stormtroopers stop Luke and Ben in landspeeder, from *Non-Sport Update* Vol. 5 #6 and show give-away 5.00
SWP2 Interior of *Millennium Falcon* cockpit, from *Advance Comics* #72 . . . . 10.00
SWP3 TIE Fighters in Death Star trench, from *Star Wars Galaxy Magazine* #1 . . . . 10.00
SWP4 Exterior of Star Destroyer, from *Wizard* #42 . . . . 5.00
SWP5 Darth Vader throttling Rebel, from *Tuff Stuff Collect* Jan. 1995 . . . . 10.00
SWP6 Leia & C-3PO in Yavin IV control room, from *Cards Illustrated* #14. . . . . 10.00
0 Luke outside X-Wing, from *Star Wars* Widevision binder album 8.00
No# promo sheet Han in gunport, from *Previews* Oct. 1994. . . . . 10.00

Promos from Classic Edition 4-Pack action figures

K01 Int. Rebel Blockade Runner—Corridor 8.00
K02 Int. *Millennium Falcon*—Gunport 8.00
K03 Int. *Millennium Falcon*—Cockpit 8.00
K04 Int. Tatooine—Mos Eisley—Cantina 8.00

(STAR WARS WIDEVISION)
THE EMPIRE STRIKES BACK
Topps (1995)

Set: 144 cards $25.00
Pack: 9 cards 2.75
Two different packs
Box: 24 packs 40.00
Chromium cards (1:12)
C1 Imperial Probot 10.00
C2 Luke on his Tauntaun 10.00
C3 AT-ATs and Luke on Tauntaun 10.00
C4 Snowspeeder circles AT-AT 10.00
C5 Yoda and Luke. 10.00
C6 Space Slug 10.00
C7 Cloud City of Bespin 10.00
C8 Carbon-freezing Chamber, Darth vs. Luke 10.00
C9 Luke dangling 10.00
C10 Droids replace Luke's Hand. 10.00
Movie Poster Set (1:24)
1 of 6 Advance One-Sheet. 8.00
2 of 6 Domestic One-Sheet 8.00
3 of 6 Style B Domestic One-Sheet 8.00
4 of 6 Australian One-Sheet. 8.00
5 of 6 German One-Sheet 8.00
6 of 6 Radio Show Poster 8.00

Promos

#0 Darth Vader, from *Star Wars Galaxy Magazine* #3 . . 3.00
P1 Han Solo, from *Advance* #79 . . . . 10.00
P2 AT-AT, from *Non-Sports Update* Vol. 6 #4 . . . . 10.00
P3 Luke, R2-D2 and Yoda, from *Cards Illustrated* #20 . 10.00
P4 Luke hanging by hands, from *Combo* #7 and also *Combo* #12 . . . . 12.00
P5 Stormtroopers and Han Solo in Carbonite, convention giveaway 30.00
P6 Luke, Leia, C-3PO and R2-D2, from *Wizard* #48 . . 10.00
Three-card (P1, P2, P3) promo sheet, from May *Previews* 1995 . . . . 4.00

(STAR WARS WIDEVISION)
RETURN OF THE JEDI
Topps (1996)

Set: 144 cards $20.00
Pack: 9 cards 2.50
Box: 24 packs 60.00
Topps Finest Chromium (R. McQuarrie) (1:12)
C/1 Darth Vader arrives in style. 11.00
C/2 Droids held captive. 11.00
C/3 Jabba's Palace 11.00
C/4 In the Rancor Pit 11.00
C/5 Escape from the Sail Barge 11.00
C/6 Speeder Bikes 11.00
C/7 B-Wings near Death Star 11.00
C/8 Father vs. Son 11.00
C/9 Emperor and Luke 11.00
C/10 Inside Death Star II. 11.00
Mini-Posters (1:box)
1 of 6 Advance One-Sheet. 10.00
2 of 6 One-Sheet Style B 10.00
3 of 6 1985 Re-release One-Sheet. 10.00
4 of 6 Japanese Poster 10.00
5 of 6 Japanese Poster 10.00
6 of 6 Polish Poster 10.00
3-Di (1:case) Admiral Ackbar 50.00
Redemption card 30.00
Promo Cards
#0 Three dead Jedi Warriors at Ewok celebration, from *Star Wars Galaxy Magazine* #6 . . . . 4.00
P1 Han, Luke, and Lando, from *Star Wars Galaxy Magazine* #5 . . . . 4.00
P2 Biker Scout and Luke, from *Advance Comics* #83 . . 4.00
P3 Stormtroopers, Han and Leia, from *Non-Sports Update*, Vol. 7 #1 . . . . 4.00
P4 Emperor Palpatine, from *Cards Illustrated*. #27 . . . . 4.00
P5 Jabba the Hutt and Bib Fortuna, from *Wizard* #54 . . 4.00
P6 Han Solo, Luke, and Chewbacca, from giveaway . . 50.00

The Empire Strikes Back *WideVision, card #67 (Topps 1996)*

Return of the Jedi *WideVision, card #21 (Topps 1996)*

One-card promo sheet (Card #0) from Previews, Nov. 95 . . 5.00

STAR WARS TRILOGY
SPECIAL EDITION WIDEVISION
(Hobby) Topps (1997)

Set: 72 cards $25.00
Pack: cards 2.00
Box: 36 packs 75.00
Lasercut Set (1:9)
1 of 6 A New Customer Enjoys 9.00
2 of 6 "It's Not My Fault" 9.00
3 of 6 The *Tantive IV* Caught. 9.00
4 of 6 Chewbacca Led Away in Chains 9.00
5 of 6 X-Wings Approach Their Target. 9.00
6 of 6 Imperial View: X-Wing Laser Fire 9.00
Holograms (1:18)
1 X-Wings near Yavin 12.00
2 *Millennium Falcon*. 12.00

(Retail) Topps (1997)

Set: 72 cards $15.00
Pack: 9 cards 2.00
Box: 36 packs 40.00
Lasercut Set (1:9)
1 of 6 Luke Skywalker is Entranced 9.00
2 of 6 Han Solo and Co-Pilot Chewbacca 9.00
3 of 6 Admiral Ozzel feels Darth Vader's wrath 9.00
4 of 6 A Hologram of Emperor Palpatine 9.00
5 of 6 A Fate Much Worse 9.00
6 of 6 Emperor Palpatine Unleashes 9.00
Spec. Ed. 3D card (1:Box) X-Wings Departing 15.00
Promos
P0 Lasercut 10.00
P1 Stormtroopers, San Diego Comic Con giveaway . . . 5.00
P2 Jabba the Hutt, *Star Wars Galaxy Magazine* #10 . . . 5.00
P3 X-Wing Fighter Squadron, magazines 5.00
P4 Sandcrawler, from *Star Wars* 3-D I packs. 10.00
P5 Luke in Landspeeder, from *Star Wars* 3-D I packs . 10.00
P6 *Millennium Falcon* and Stormtroopers, from Star
    Wars 3-D I packs 10.00
P7 Landspeeder in Mos Eisley, *Wizard Sci-Fi Spec-*
    ial '97 Star Wars Trilogy Special Edition promo. . . . 5.00
P8 Jabba's Dancing Girls (*Combo*) 5.00
Galoob MicroMachine Promos
G1 R2-D2 on X-Wing 3.00
G2 TIE Fighter and X-Wing. 3.00
G3 Luke in Landspeeder. 3.00
G4 Mos Eisley 3.00
G5 Jawa on Ronto 3.00
Hasbro Vehicles Promos
H1 *Millennium Falcon* 5.00
H2 Massassi outpost 5.00
H3 Han and Jabba 5.00
H4 Droids and Calimari cruiser 5.00

STAR WARS WIDEVISION 3-D
Topps (1997)

This card set contains all new images from the first movie and utilizes an exclusive, multi-level 3-D digital imagery technology. The technology is quite impressive, but also expensive. When Topps (or anybody) uses their best technology for an entire set, then the extraordinary becomes ordinary and anybody can buy some for a couple of bucks. Where's the fun in that? Maybe that's why there were

supposed to be similar sets for the other two movies, but they never appeared.

Set: 63 cards $90.00
Pack: 3 cards 4.00
Box: 36 packs 120.00
Chase Card (1:36)
1m Exploding Death Star 3-D Motion card 30.00
Promos
2m Swoops and Rontos (*Star Wars Trilogy Special*
    Edition promo 10.00
3Di 1 Darth Vader, Stormtroopers and Captain Piett. . . 10.00
3Di 2 Darth and Luke. 25.00
P1 Darth Vader (*Star Wars Galaxy* #9) 10.00
P2 Luke and Darth Vader (2,500 made) 50.00
P1 AT-ATs, *The Empire Strikes Back*! promo 20.00
Dm/o Admiral Ackbar *Return of the Jedi* promo 20.00

STAR WARS VEHICLES
Topps (July 1997)

The *Star Wars* Vehicle cards feature 50 comic art cards by Top Cow Studios, plus 22 cards with movie photos featuring ships. All of the cards come with back blueprints and specs by Bill Smith, author of *The Essential Guide to Star Wars Vehicles and Vessels*. All of the cards are on 20 point Mirror-bond card stock.

Set: 72 cards $20.00
Pack: 5 cards 2.00
Box: 36 packs 45.00
Cutaway cards, (1:18)
C1 AT-ST 8.00
C2 *Slave I* 8.00
C3 X-Wing 8.00
C4 Lamda Shuttle. 8.00
3-D cards (1:36) Chris Moeller art
01 Luke and Shuttle 20.00
02 Leia and Shuttle 20.00
Redemption card (1:360) for uncut pair of 3-D cards . . 50.00
Mail-in card. 40.00
Promos
P1 Speeder Bikes 10.00
P2 Shuttle *Tydirium* 15.00
P1 Speeder Bikes, refractor 50.00
P2 Shuttle *Tydirium,* refractor 85.00
Postcard, 4" x 6" 2.00

Star Wars *Vehicles 3-D chase cards (Topps 1997)*

STAR WARS CHROME ARCHIVES
Topps (1999)

These cards appeared in February, 1999. Topps took cards from the three classic series and reissued them in an all-chrome format. They turned out very well and the set has been popular.

Set: 90 chromium cards $35.00
Pack: 5 cards 4.00
Box: 36 packs 80.00
Double Sided Chrome Insert (1:12) nine diff., each . . . 8.00
Clear Chrome (1:18) four different, each 15.00
Nine-card uncut sheet 50.00
Promos
P1 Darth Vader: "Hate Me Luke! Destroy Me!" 4.00
P2 Yoda: "Welcome, Young Luke!" 4.00

STAR WARS EPISODE I WIDEVISION
Topps (1999)

Series One (Hobby Edition)
Set: 80 cards $12.00
Pack: 8 cards 1.00
Box: 36 packs 30.00
Expansion Cards (1:2)
Expansion Set: 40 cards 30.00
Expansion Card 1.00
Chromium Inserts (1:12) eight different, each 8.00
Promos
0 Strength in Numbers 2.00
00 All Bow to the Boss 2.00
000 The Battle Droids 2.00

Series One (Retail Edition)
Set: 80 cards & 16 stickers 10.00
Pack: 8 cards 2.00
Box: 36 packs 45.00
Stickers (1:2) 16 different, each 1.00
Foil Inserts (1:8) 10 different, each 5.00
Mega Chromes five different, each 10.00
Collectors Tin set: 8 cards 20.00
Hallmark Promos, H1–H3, each 3.00

Series Two (Hobby Edition)
Set: 80 cards 15.00
Pack: 8 cards 1.75
Box: 36 packs 35.00
Embossed Foil Inserts (1:12) six different, each 5.00
Chrome Inserts (1:18) four different, each 10.00
Oversize Promos, 4" x 7½"

Star Wars Episode I *Widevision Oversize Promo card (Topps 1999)*

OS-1 Dueling with Darth Maul 2.00
OS-2 A Time to Rejoice 2.00

STAR WARS EPISODE I 3-D
Topps (2000)

Set: 46 cards $65.00
Pack: 2 cards 3.00
Box: 36 packs 85.00
Multi-Motions Chase Cards
1 of 2 Droideka 10.00
2 of 2 Lightsaber Duel 10.00
P1 Promo, Naboo Hanger 5.00

STAR WARS EVOLUTION
Topps 2001

Set: 90 cards, all foil $15.00
Pack: 8 cards 2.00
Box: 36 packs 60.00
Checklists: C1 to C3 . . . . 5.00
Autographed Card Inserts (1:box) 30.00
Evolution A, 1A to 12A (1:6) 8.00
Evolution B, 1B to 8B (1:12) 12.00
Promos P1, P2 . . . . 1.00
P3 Nien Nunb 20.00
P4 Anakin Skywalker 10.00

STAR WARS ATTACK OF THE CLONES
Topps April 2002

Set: 100 cards . . . . forthcoming
plus 10 Silver foilboard cards; 8 Prismatic foilboard cards; and 5 Panoramic Fold-outs

OTHER STAR WARS CARDS AND STICKERS

Trix *Star Wars* stickers, each $1.00
   set: 4 stickers 5.00
Lucky Charms *Star Wars* stickers, each 1.00
   set: 4 stickers 5.00
Monster Cereals *Star Wars* stickers, each 1.00
   set: 4 stickers 5.00
Cocoa Puffs *Star Wars* stickers, each 1.00
   set: 4 stickers 5.00
Big G trading cards, with *Star Wars* logo
   (General Mills 1978) each 1.00
   set: 18 photos and wallet 30.00

The Empire Strikes Back Sticker set and Album
   (Burger King) 10.00
3-D Ewok Perk-up sticker sets, each 5.00

Star Wars Galaxy Magazine
SWGM1 promo (*Star Wars Galaxy Mag. #1*) 4.00
SWGM2 promo (*Star Wars Galaxy Mag. #2*) 4.00
SWGM3 At-At (McQuarrie) (*Star Wars Galaxy Mag. #3*) chromium 5.00
SWGM4 Dagobah swamp (*Star Wars Galaxy Mag. #4*) chromium 5.00

Dark Horse Comics
DH1 Dark Empire II promo, from Classic *Star Wars*:
   Tales of the Jedi: Dark Lords of the Sith #1 . . . . . . 5.00
DH2 Dark Empire II promo, from Classic *Star Wars*
   The Early Adventures #3 . . . . 5.00

DH3 Dark Empire II promo, from Classic *Star Wars*:
  Return of the Jedi #1 . . . . 5.00

Classic Toys Trading Cards
#37 Darth Vader 12" action figure (doll) 1.00
#56 C-3PO 12" action figure (doll) 1.00

STAR WARS CAPS
Topps (1995)

Now that Milk Caps have come, and gone to their reward, you could buy up a basement full and hope that they come back some day. Just don't hold your breath!

Set: 64 caps + 2 slammers + chase caps $15.00
Pack: 3 regular caps + 1 chase cap 1.00
Box: 48 packs 30.00
Promos
0-A Droids 2.00
0-B Darth Vader 2.00

METAL CARDS

STAR WARS: A NEW HOPE
Metallic Images (1994)

Set: 20 cards in box with certificate (49,900 made) . . $40.00
Promo P1 *Star Wars A New Hope* Poster, Style A 4.00

STAR WARS:
THE EMPIRE STRIKES BACK
Metallic Images (1995)

Set: 20 cards in box with certificate (49,900 made) . . $50.00
Promo P2 Darth Vader Helmet on Starry Background . . 4.00

Series 2
Set: 20 cards in box with certificate (49,900 made) . . . 50.00

STAR WARS:
RETURN OF THE JEDI
Metallic Images (1995)

Set: 20 cards in box with certificate (49,900 made) . . $50.00
Promo P3 *Return of the Jedi* 10th Anniv. Poster 6.00

STAR WARS:
THE ART OF RALPH MCQUARRIE
Metallic Images (1996)

Set: 20 cards in box with certificate (12,000 made) . . $60.00

STAR WARS: DARK EMPIRE
Metallic Impressions (1995–96)

These metal cards reproduce cover art from the Dark Horse Comics series of the same name.

Set : 6 metal cards in tin litho box (72,000 made) . . . $15.00
Card, each 3.00

Series II
Set 2: 6 metal cards in tin litho box (36,000 made) . . $15.00
Card, each 3.00

*Star Wars: Art of Ralph McQuarrie Metal Cards, box
(Metallic Images 1996)*

STAR WARS:
SHADOWS OF THE EMPIRE
Metallic Impressions (1997)

Set: 6 metal cards in tin litho box $15.00
Card, each 3.00

STAR WARS: JEDI KNIGHT
Metallic Impressions (1997)

Set: 6 metal cards in tin litho box $12.00
Card, each 3.00

STAR WARS: BOUNTY HUNTERS
Metallic Impressions (1998)

Set: 6 metal cards in tin litho box $12.00
Card, each 3.00

24K GOLD CARDS
Authentic Images (1997)

Gold *Star Wars* cards, limited to 1,000 units, in acrylic holder, with black vacuum-formed jewel case:
Series One: *A New Hope*
Special Edition Ingot $75.00
Darth Vader 100.00
Other cards, four different, each 75.00
Series Two: *The Empire Strikes Back*
Boba Fett 100.00
Other cards, four different, each 75.00
Series Three: *Return of the Jedi*, five different, each. 75.00

Gold Gallery Series cards, limited to 500 units, in acrylic holder, with black vacuum-formed jewel case:
Gallery Series 1: *A New Hope*
Jabba the Hutt & Han Solo 350.00
Darth Vader & Ben Kenobi 550.00
Gallery Series 2: *The Empire Strikes Back*
Luke and Yoda 325.00
Luke and Darth Vader 400.00
24-karat gold card set, reproduction of three posters, 1,997 sets world-wide, JC Penney exclusive 225.00

Imperial TIE Fighter (Kenner 1978)

VEHICLES, CREATURES, PLAYSETS AND ACCESSORIES

Vehicles are much more important in *Star Wars* than in most other action figure lines. The 3¾" size of the figures allowed the production of vehicles which were large enough to accommodate several figures, and so the larger vehicles became virtual playsets for the figures. Actual playsets, creatures, such as the Tauntaun and Wampa, and accessories, such as the Mini-Rigs, extended this playset environment.

Many collectors have a large supply of loose figures which they display with the appropriate loose vehicles, creatures, playsets, and accessories. This has helped to keep collector prices for these items at a high level. Vehicles, creatures, and accessories from the classic movies are listed first, followed by those from the newer series.

CLASSIC VEHICLES
Kenner (1978–86)

Vehicles were released over the period of all three movies and many which originally came out in *Star Wars* boxes can be found in boxes from one or both of the later movies. As with the figures, vehicles are listed first in their original box, followed by information and values for later

issues. Usually the box logo corresponds to the vintage of the vehicle, but in 1983 Kenner released three of its original vehicles (and one creature) in the *Star Wars* Collector Series, which just meant that an orange sunburst was added to the original box design.

STAR WARS VEHICLES

***Star Wars* Vehicles** (1978–79)
Landspeeder, rolls on spring-loaded wheels, holds
    2 figures plus 2 more on rear deck (#38020, 1978)
      Original *Star Wars* box $75.00
      Star Wars Collector's Series Land Speeder
        (1983) 35.00
      Loose, with all parts 20.00
X-Wing Fighter, 14" long, electronic light and
    sound, cockpit canopy opens, wings open
    and close (#38030, 1978)
      Original *Star Wars* box 125.00
      Reissue in *The Empire Strikes Back* box 200.00
      Loose, with all parts 45.00
Imperial TIE Fighter, 12" wide, battery light and
    sound, red laser cannon, 2 "solar panels"
    can be released to simulate "battle damage,"
    escape hatch (#38040, 1978)
      Original *Star Wars* box 135.00
      Reissue in *The Empire Strikes Back* box 200.00
      Loose, with all parts 45.00
Darth Vader TIE Fighter, grey, 11" across, pop-off
    solar panels, battery light and sound in
    13" x 11½" x 6½" box (#39100, 1979)
      Original *Star Wars* box 125.00
      Loose, with all parts 60.00

Millennium Falcon Spaceship (Kenner 1979)

Landspeeder with added figures (Kenner 1978); Rebel Transport with added figures (Kenner 1982)

Original *Star Wars* box with Battle Scene
　　Setting 500.00
Loose, with all parts, with Battle Scene 150.00
Star Wars Collector's Series (1983) 60.00
Loose, with all parts 40.00
Millennium Falcon Spaceship, 21" long, 18" wide,
　　with "Battle Alert Sound" in 22" x 17" x 6" box
　　(#39110, 1979)
　　Original *Star Wars* box 325.00
　　Reissue in *The Empire Strikes Back* box 225.00
　　Reissue in *Return of the Jedi* box 175.00
　　Star Wars Collector Series *Millennium Falcon*
　　　　(1983) 125.00
　　Loose, with all parts 80.00
Radio-Controlled Jawa Sandcrawler, 17" long, in
　　17½" x 9" x 7" box (#39270, 1979)
　　Original *Star Wars* box 600.00
　　Reissue in *The Empire Strikes Back* box 650.00
　　Loose, with all parts 250.00
Imperial Troop Transporter, compartments for
　　figures, 6 different battery operated sounds
　　(#39290, 1979)
　　Original *Star Wars* box 100.00
　　Reissue in *The Empire Strikes Back* box 115.00
　　Loose, with all parts 45.00

Exclusive Vehicles (1979–80)
Sonic-Controlled Land Speeder, battery operated,
　　with mechanical clicker shaped like R2-D2,
　　JC Penney exclusive (#38540, 1979)
　　Original *Star Wars* box 600.00
　　Loose, with all parts 200.00
Imperial Cruiser, similar to Imperial Troop Trans-
　　porter, Sears exclusive (#93351, 1980)
　　Original *The Empire Strikes Back* box 125.00
　　Loose, with all parts 40.00

THE EMPIRE STRIKES BACK VEHICLES

The Empire Strikes Back Vehicles (1980–82)
Darth Vader's Star Destroyer, 20" long (#39850, 1980)
　　Original *The Empire Strikes Back* box $150.00
　　Loose, with all parts 40.00
Twin-Pod Cloud Car, 10" wide, orange plastic,
　　in 11" x 9½" x 4" box (#39860, 1980)
　　Original *The Empire Strikes Back* box 100.00
　　Reissue in *The Empire Strikes Back* box with
　　　　Bespin Security Guard (white) figure 125.00
　　Loose, with all parts, no figure 40.00
AT-AT All-Terrain Armored Transport, 17½"
　　tall, posable legs, movable control center
　　(#38810, 1981)
　　Original *The Empire Strikes Back* box 300.00
　　Reissue in *Return of the Jedi* box 250.00

Loose, with all parts 110.00
Rebel Armored Snowspeeder, 12" long, 10¾" wide,
　　battery light and sound (#39610, 1982)
　　Original *The Empire Strikes Back* box 110.00
　　Reissue in *The Empire Strikes Back* box with
　　　　Rebel Soldier (Hoth Battle Gear) figure 175.00
　　Loose, with all parts 40.00
Slave I, Boba Fett's Spaceship, 12" long, including
　　Simulated Frozen **Han Solo** (#39690, 1982)
　　Original *The Empire Strikes Back* box 150.00
　　Reissue in *The Empire Strikes Back* box with
　　　　Battle Scene Setting 275.00
　　Loose, with all parts 40.00
Rebel Transport, 20" long, including 5 Hoth Back-
　　packs and 4 Asteroid gas masks (#69740, 1982)
　　Original *The Empire Strikes Back* box 150.00
　　Loose, with all parts 35.00
"Battle Damaged" X-Wing Fighter, battery powered,
　　"Labels Create Battle-Damaged Look" in 14" x

Scout Walker (Kenner 1981)

Twin-Pod Cloud Car and Slave I *(Kenner 1980 and 1982)*

12½" x 4¼" box (#69780, 1981)
Original *The Empire Strikes Back* box 250.00
Reissue in *Return of the Jedi* box. 150.00
Loose, with all parts. 35.00
Scout Walker, 10" tall, hand-operated walking
mechanism (#69800, 1982)
Original *The Empire Strikes Back* box 80.00
Reissue in *Return of the Jedi* box. 60.00
Loose, with all parts. 25.00
Imperial TIE Fighter (Battle Damaged, same mold
as original TIE but in blue with "damage"
decals) (#71490, 1983)
Original *The Empire Strikes Back* box 150.00
Reissue in *Return of the Jedi* box. 125.00
Loose, with all parts. 40.00

RETURN OF THE JEDI VEHICLES

***Return of the Jedi* Vehicles** (1983–84)
Speeder Bike 8" long (#70500, 1983)
Original *Return of the Jedi* box. $30.00
Reissue in *Power of the Force* box 20.00
Loose, with all parts. 15.00
Y-Wing Fighter with Laser Cannon Sound in 21"x
11½" x 3¾" box (#70510, 1983)
Original *Return of the Jedi* box. 120.00

Loose, with all parts. 60.00
B-Wing Fighter, 22" long, battery operated sound
and rotating cockpit (#71370, 1984)
Original *Return of the Jedi* box. 125.00
Loose, with all parts. 60.00
TIE Interceptor, with Battle Sound and Flashing
Laser Light, battery powered, 12" wide
(#71390, 1984)
Original *Return of the Jedi* box. 130.00
Loose, with all parts. 60.00
Imperial Shuttle, 18" tall, wings folded, battery
sound (#93650)
Original *Return of the Jedi* box. 400.00
Loose, with all parts. 200.00

POWER OF THE FORCE VEHICLES

Power of the Force Vehicles (1984–85)
Tatooine Skiff, 12" long (#71540, 1985)
Original *Power of the Force* box $650.00
Loose, with all parts. 325.00

DROIDS VEHICLES

Droids Vehicles (1985)
A-Wing Fighter, 12" long, battery operated sound,
with planetary map (#93700)

Imperial Shuttle with figures and TIE Interceptor Fighter (Kenner 1983)

A-Wing Fighter (Kenner 1984)

Original *Droids* box	$600.00
Loose, with all parts	300.00
ATL Interceptor Vehicle (#93900)	
Original *Droids* box	35.00
Loose, with all parts	15.00
Side Gunner with *Star Wars* Planetary Map (#94010)	
Original *Droids* box	50.00
Loose, with all parts	15.00

NEW VEHICLES
Kenner/Hasbro (1995–2002)

Kenner (now Hasbro) has produced new Power of the Force vehicles right along with all the new action figures, and their boxes have followed the same color sequence—first red, then green, with a few purple boxes for *Shadows of the Empire* vehicles, then a different green design, and currently "Power of the Jedi," with the same green design. There have been box variations as well, and many can be identified by the packaging variation number found near the bar code on most boxes.

Electronic X-Wing Fighter (Kenner 1995)

In February 2000, Toys "R" Us sold Hasbro's excess stock of vehicles for $9.95 each. Many valuable vehicles were included, including expensive AT-ATs and F/X Red-5 X-Wing Fighters. They also sold deluxe creatures such as Rancors and Banthas for the same price. I hope you got the ones you needed, but if you didn't, your friendly neighborhood or Internet dealer may have a few left—but not for $9.95!

(NEW) POWER OF THE FORCE VEHICLES

Power of the Force Vehicles, red boxes (1995–96)

Landspeeder with "Shift-Action Running Gear and Pop-Open Hood" (#69770, July 1995)	$12.00
Loose, with all parts	6.00
TIE Fighter with "Ejecting Solar Panel Wings" (#69775, July 1995)	20.00
Loose, with all parts	10.00
Imperial AT-ST (Scout Walker) (#69776, July 1995)	50.00
Loose, with all parts	15.00
Electronic X-Wing Fighter with "Attack-Action Wings and Authentic Movie Sounds" (#69780, July 1995)	25.00
Loose, with all parts	15.00
Electronic Rebel Snowspeeder with Topps "*Star Wars*" widevision trading card (#69585, July 1996)	35.00
Loose, with all parts	15.00
Electronic *Millennium Falcon* see Playsets	

Power of the Force Vehicles, green boxes (1996–98)

Luke's T-16 Skyhopper with detachable cockpit (#69663, Dec. 1996) [534142.00]	25.00

Imperial AT-ST Scout Walker (Kenner 1995)

Electronic Imperial AT-AT Walker (Kenner 1997) and Boba Fett's Slave I *(Kenner 1996)*

Loose, with all parts 10.00
Cruisemissile Trooper with "Twin Proton Torpedo
Launchers" (#69653, Feb. 1997) 15.00
Loose, with all parts 7.00
Darth Vader's TIE Fighter with "Launcher Laser
Cannons" (#69662, Feb. 1997) 35.00
Loose, with all parts 12.00

Power of the Force Vehicles with figures (1997–98)
A-Wing Fighter with **A-Wing Pilot** figure (#69732,
July 1997) [540039.00] 30.00
Loose, with all parts and figure 15.00
Electronic Imperial AT-AT Walker with exclusive
AT-AT Commander and **AT-AT Driver**
(#69733, Sept 1997) [.00] red graphic covers bottom of
figures' photo 100.00

Darth Vader's TIE Fighter (Kenner 1997)

Variation [.00] decal over graphic. 100.00
Variation [.01] full photo shown. 90.00
Loose, with all parts and figures 40.00

Second Batch, new green box (Hasbro 1999–2000)
Tatooine Skiff with **Jedi Knight Luke Skywalker**
with "Lightsaber" (#26458) Target exclusive 50.00
Loose, with all parts and figure 25.00
Y-Wing Fighter with **Rebel Alliance Pilot**. 30.00
Loose, with all parts and figure 15.00

SHADOWS OF THE EMPIRE VEHICLES

Shadows of the Empire Vehicles, purple boxes (1996)
Boba Fett's *Slave I*, including **Han Solo in Carbon-
ite** (#69565, July 1996) $30.00
Reissue in Power of the Force green box 25.00
Loose, with all parts and figure 15.00
Dash Rendar's Outrider, with Topps "*Star Wars*"
widevision trading card (#69593, July 1996) 45.00
Reissue (#69814) in Power of the Force green
box 30.00
Loose, with all parts 10.00
Swoop vehicle with **Swoop Trooper** figure

Power Racing Speeder Bike (Kenner 1998)

Imperial Speeder Bike (Kenner 1996) and Cloud Car (Expanded Universe) (Kenner 1998)

(#69591, July 1996) in a purple *Shadows of
the Empire* window box [none] 15.00
Loose, with all parts and figure 9.00

SPEEDER BIKES

Speeder Bike Vehicles with figures (Asst. #69760)
Imperial Speeder Bike with **Biker Scout Storm-
trooper** figure (#69765, Feb. 1996) in a red
Power of the Force window box [none] $25.00
Loose, with all parts and figure 9.00
Speeder Bike with **Luke Skywalker** in Endor Gear,
figure with "Lightsaber and Blaster" (#69651,
Feb. 1997) in a green Power of the Force
window box [538126.00] two white gloves in
front photo 20.00
Variation [.01] wearing one black glove. 15.00
Loose, with all parts and figure 9.00
Speeder Bike with **Princess Leia Organa** in Endor
Gear (#69727, July 1997) in a green Power of
the Force window box [541948.00] with rocks
in side photos 25.00
Variation [.01] moss airbrushed over rocks 15.00
Loose, with all parts and figure 9.00
Power Racing Speeder Bike with **Scout Trooper**
(#60588, 1998) in a green Power of the Force
box 15.00
Loose, with all parts and figure 9.00

EXPANDED UNIVERSE VEHICLES

Expanded Universe Vehicles (Asst. #69620, 1998)
Cloud Car with Exclusive **Cloud Car Pilot** figure,
from *The Art of Star Wars* (#69786, Feb. 1998) . $15.00
Loose, with all parts and figure 9.00
Airspeeder with "Firing Proton Torpedo and
Exclusive **Airspeeder Pilot**" figure, from *The
Art of Star Wars* (#69774, Feb 1998) [547323.00]. 15.00
Loose, with all parts and figure 9.00
Speeder Bike with **Rebel Speeder Bike Pilot**
figure (#69772, June 1998) 15.00
Loose, with all parts and figure 9.00

ELECTRONIC POWER F/X VEHICLE

Electronic Power F/X Vehicle, green box
Electronic Power F/X Luke Skywalker Red Five
X-Wing Fighter, battery operated, with 12 real
movie sounds and phrases, plus non-remov-
able lever activated Luke Skywalker and
R2-D2 (#69784, 1998) [.00] $75.00

Reissue [.01] 75.00
Loose, with all parts. 35.00

EPISODE I VEHICLES

Large Vehicles
Royal Starship, see Playsets
Electronic Naboo Fighter (#84099, 1999) [556975.]
    [.02] "with Lights and Sounds" $25.00
    [.03] "with Real Movie Lights and Sounds" 20.00
    Loose, with all parts. 10.00
Trade Federation Tank with "Blow-Up Battle
Damage" (#84101) [567066.0100] 30.00
Loose, with all parts. 15.00

Mid Size Vehicles (Asst. #84025)
Trade Federation Droid Fighters, including three
Droid fighters (#84171, 1999) [559868.0100] 20.00
Loose, with all parts. 10.00

Pod Racer Vehicles with figure (Asst. #84020, 1999)
Anakin Skywalker's Pod Racer with "Blast-Open
Directional Vanes" and **Anakin Skywalker**
(#84097) [558747.0200]. 20.00
Loose, with all parts and figure. 10.00
Sebulba's Pod Racer with "Spring-Out Spinning
Blade" and **Sebulba** (#84098) [558750.0200]. . . . 25.00

Electronic Power F/X Luke Skywalker X-Wing (Kenner 1998)

Ammo Wagon and Falumpaset (Hasbro 2000)and Fambaa and Shield Generator, with Gungan Warrior (Hasbro 1999)

Loose, with all parts and figure. 10.00

"Transport" Vehicle (Asst #84165)
Flash Speeder with "Launching Laser Cannon"
   (#84191) 15.00
   Loose, with all parts. 7.00

"Small Vehicle" and figure (Asst. #84135)
Stap and **Battle Droid** (#84139) [559519.00] 15.00
   Loose, with all parts and figure 7.00
Sith Speeder and **Darth Maul** with "Launching Sith
   Probe Droid" (#84141) [559522.0100] 20.00
   Loose, with all parts and figure. 10.00

Episode I **"Invasion Force" small vehicles** (Asst. #84205)
Armored Scout Tank with **Battle Droid** (#84367)
   [565940.0000] 25.00
   Reissue: [.0100]. 15.00
   Loose, with all parts and figure. 10.00
Gungan Assaault Cannon with **Jar Jar Binks**
   (#84368) [565943.0000] 15.00
   Loose, with all parts and figure 7.00
Gungan Scout Sub with **Obi-Wan Kenobi** (#84397)
   [567700.0000] 25.00
   Loose, with all parts and figure 7.00
Sith Attack Speeder with **Darth Maul** (84399#) [.0000] 25.00
   Loose, with all parts and figure. 10.00

Episode I **Exclusive Vehicles**
Famba with Shield Generator and **Gungan Warrior**

(#84369) [566702.00] FAO Schwarz exclusive . . 100.00
   Loose, with all parts and figure. 60.00
Ammo Wagon and Falumpaset with "Launching
   Energy Balls" and non-removable Gungan
   Warrior (#84358) [566166.0000] WalMart exclusive 25.00
   Loose, with all parts. 15.00

POWER OF THE JEDI VEHICLES

Power of the Jedi Exclusive Vehicles (Hasbro 2001–02)
B-Wing Fighter with **Sullustan Pilot** (#26481)
   Target exclusive $25.00
   Loose, with all parts and figure. 15.00
Imperial AT-ST and Speederbike with **Paploo** (#)
   Toys "R" Us exclusive 30.00
   Loose, with all parts and figure 15.00
TIE Interceptor with **Imperial Pilot** figure (#32457)
   Toys "R" Us exclusive. 30.00
   Loose, with all parts and figure. 15.00

SHIPS
Kenner (1997–98)

Ships differ from "vehicles" because ships are not scaled to fit action figures, but vehicles are. Obviously Kenner can't make a Star Destroyer that is the same scale as its other vehicles—it would be over 100 feet long!

Collector Fleet in try-me box (Kenner 1997–98)
Electronic Rebel Blockade Runner (Kenner
   #27844, 1997) $25.00

TIE Interceptor (Hasbro 2001) and Electronic Star Destroyer ship (Kenner 1997)

Tauntaun (Kenner 1980)

Electronic Star Destroyer (Kenner #27835, 1997) 25.00
Electronic Super Star Destroyer *Executor* (Kenner
   #27914, 1998) 30.00

CLASSIC CREATURES
Kenner (1979–84)

Classic Creatures
Patrol Dewback, 10¼" long, with reins and saddle
   in 11" x 6" x 4½" box (#39240, 1979)
   Original *Star Wars* box $75.00
   Reissue in *The Empire Strikes Back* box 250.00
   Star Wars Collector Series Patrol Dewback
      (1983) 50.00
   Loose, with all parts 25.00
Tauntaun, 8" tall, with saddle and reins in
   9" x 7" x 4" box (#39820, 1980)
   Original *The Empire Strikes Back* box 75.00
   Loose, with all parts 25.00
Tauntaun, with Open Belly Rescue Feature
   (#93340, 1982)
   Original *The Empire Strikes Back* box 75.00
   Loose, with all parts 25.00
Wampa, Snow Creature from Hoth, 6¼" tall, mov-
   able arms and legs (#69560, 1982)
   Original *The Empire Strikes Back* box pictur-
      ing Rebel Commander 60.00
   Reissue as **Hoth Wampa** in *The Empire
      Strikes Back* box picturing Luke Skywalker
      in Hoth Gear 35.00
   Reissue in *Return of the Jedi* box. 40.00
   Loose, with all parts. 20.00
Jabba the Hutt Action Playset, including **Jabba** and
   Salacious Crumb molded figure (#70490, 1983)
   Original *Return of the Jedi* box. 60.00
   Reissue in *Return of the Jedi* box (Sears) 40.00
   Loose, with all parts. 30.00
Rancor Monster, 10" high (1984)
   Original *Return of the Jedi* box. 75.00
   Reissue in *Power of the Force* box. 60.00
   Loose, with all parts. 30.00

NEW CREATURES
Kenner (1997–2002)

The first three creature and figure combination boxes

arrived in August 1997. The figures are all based on the new footage from the first movie. A lot of them were produced, and Hasbro's overstock was available in early 2000 at Toys "R" Us at $4.95 each. Distribution of the 1998 figures was poor, and local stores rarely had them available, but a few showed up in 2000 along with more of the original three. The Han Solo and Tauntaun is notoriously scarce. Deluxe creatures came out in 1998 and distribution was good, so only a few were left over for red tag sales. Only action figure (3¾") scale creatures are listed here. All doll (12") scale creatures are listed in the "Dolls" section.

"Special Edition" Creature and Figure Combos (Asst.
   #69645, Aug. 1997)
Ronto and Jawa in green *Power of the Force*
   window box with exclusive **Jawa** figure
   (#69728) [541088.00]. $18.00
   Loose, with all parts and figure 8.00
Dewback and **Sandtrooper** in green *Power of the
   Force* window box (#69743) [541085.00]
   Galactic Empire and Unaffiliated logos on front . . 18.00
   Variation, [.01] Galactic Empire logo only 15.00
   Loose, with all parts and figure 8.00
Jabba the Hutt and **Han Solo** in green *Power of the
   Force* window box (#69742) [541082.00]
   Galactic Empire and Rebel Alliance logos,
      Han pictured to Jabba's right 35.00
   Variation [.01] Han pictured to Jabba's left in
      data file 18.00
   Variation [.02] Unaffiliated and Rebel Alliance
      logos, Han pictured on left 18.00
   Loose, with all parts and figure 8.00

Second Batch (May 1998)
Tauntaun with **Han Solo in Hoth Gear** (#84107)
   [554184.00] 85.00
   Loose, with all parts and figure. 30.00
Luke Skywalker and Tauntaun (#69729) [545238.00]. 25.00
   Loose, with all parts and figure. 10.00
Wampa and **Luke Skywalker (in Hoth Gear)**
   (#69768) [551530.00]. 45.00
   Loose, with all parts and figure. 10.00

Deluxe Creatures and Figure (Asst. #69655, May 1998)
Rancor and Luke Skywalker, with "Exclusive Battle-

Bantha and Tusken Raider (Kenner 1998)

Wampa and Luke Skywalker (Kenner 1998)

worn **Jedi Luke**" (#69771) [552624.00] 40.00
Loose, with all parts and figure. 15.00
Bantha and Tusken Raider, "includes exclusive
Tusken Raider with Gaderffii Stick" (#69769)
[552621.00] 40.00
Loose, with all parts and figure. 15.00

EPISODE I CREATURES

The first two *Episode I* creatures were over-produced like all of the early *Episode I* action figures. Jabba with the 2-headed announcer, and Eopie with Qui-Gon Jinn came out later and are very scarce. On the other hand, Jabba the Hutt was available in quantity, on a header card with a can of slim and some frogs to eat, as "Jabba Glob." This is listed in the "Figures" section.

***Episode I* Creature & Figure** (Asst. #84125, 1999–2001)
Kaadu and **Jar Jar Binks** with "Energy Ball Atlatl"
and "Realistic Running Action" (Kaadu)
(#84094) [558588.00]. $15.00
Loose, with all parts and figure 8.00
Opee and **Qui-Gon Jinn**, with "Snapping Jaws"
(Opee) and "Articulated Ankles for Swimming"
(Qui-Gon Jinn) (#84096) [559135.0000] warn-
ing on sticker 15.00
Loose, with all parts and figure 7.00
Jabba the Hutt with **2-Headed Announcer** with
"Spitting Action and Real Feel Skin," (Jabba)
(#84167) [.0000] 30.00
Loose, with all parts and figure. 15.00
Eopie and **Qui-Gon Jinn** with "Lightsaber Slashing
Action" (#84354) 75.00
Loose, with all parts and figure. 35.00
Femba with Gungan Warrior, see "Exclusive Vehicles"

CLASSIC PLAYSETS
Kenner (1979–85)

With all the classic playsets that Kenner produced in the 1980s, you would think that they would have reissued some of them in 1990s. So far they have not done so.

STAR WARS PLAYSETS

***Star Wars* Playsets** (1979)
Death Star Space Station, 23" high, three-story
playset, manual elevator, exploding laser
cannon, light bridge, trash compactor with
garbage, and Trash Monster (#38050, 1979)
Original *Star Wars* box $225.00
Loose, with all parts. 60.00

Creature Cantina Action Playset, with lever-
activated functions, no figures in 14" x 8" x 3½"
box (#39120, 1979)
Original *Star Wars* box 125.00
Loose, with all parts. 40.00
Land of the Jawas Action Playset (#39130, 1979)
Original *Star Wars* box 160.00
Reissue in *The Empire Strikes Back* box 225.00
Loose, with all parts. 60.00
Droid Factory with 31 plastic robot parts, plastic
base and movable crane, in 13" x 11" x 3" box
(#39150, 1979)
Original *Star Wars* box 125.00
Reissue in *The Empire Strikes Back* box 175.00
Loose, with all parts. 50.00

THE EMPIRE STRIKES BACK PLAYSETS

***The Empire Strikes Back* Playsets** (1980–82)
Imperial Attack Base, Hoth scene, in 18" x 10¼"
x 3¾" box (#39830, 1980)
Original *The Empire Strikes Back* box $125.00
Loose, with all parts. 30.00
Hoth Ice Planet Adventure Set (1980, 1980)
Original *The Empire Strikes Back* box 150.00
Reissue in *The Empire Strikes Back* box, with
**Imperial Stormtrooper (Hoth Battle
Gear)** figure. 225.00
Loose, with all parts, no figure 50.00
Dagobah Action Playset, lever-operated functions
(#38820, 1981)
Original *The Empire Strikes Back* box 100.00
Loose, with all parts. 40.00
Turret & Probot Playset, with **Probot** figure
(#38330, 1981)
Original *The Empire Strikes Back* box 150.00
Loose, with all parts. 60.00
Rebel Command Center Adventure Set, including
R2-D2, **Luke Skywalker**, and **AT-AT Com-
mander** figures (#69481, 1981)
Original *The Empire Strikes Back* box 275.00

Death Star Playset (Kenner 1979)

Ewok Village playset (Kenner 1984); Electronic Naboo Royal Starship playset (Hasbro 1999)

Loose, with all parts 120.00

RETURN OF THE JEDI PLAYSET

***Return of the Jedi* Playset** (1983)
Ewok Village Action Playset, 12" high, 2-story
   playset (#70520, 1983)
   Original *Return of the Jedi* box $125.00
   Loose, with all parts 50.00

EWOK PLAYSET

Ewok Playset (1984)
Ewok Family Hut, 12" high, Hut plus 15 accessories
   and 4 non-poseable figures (Kenner Pre-
   school, 1984)
   Original *Ewoks* box $50.00
   Loose, with all parts 15.00

Exclusive Playsets
Cantina Adventure Set (Sears' promotional set) 4
   figures, including: Greedo, Hammerhead,
   blue Snaggletooth, and Walrus man (#38861, 1979)
   Original *Star Wars* box 700.00
   Loose, with all parts 300.00
Cloud City Playset (Sears' exclusive) including
   4 figures: Han Solo in Bespin outfit, Ugnaught,
   Lobot, and Dengar, (#38781, 1981)
   Original *The Empire Strikes Back* box 450.00
   Loose, with all parts 175.00
The Jabba the Hutt Dungeon Action Playset
   Variation #1, including Klaatu, Nikto, and 8D8
      action figures, red box, Sears exclusive
      (#71381, 1983)
      Original *Return of the Jedi* box 130.00
      Loose, with all parts 60.00
   Variation #2, including EV-9D9, Amanaman,
      and Barada figures, green box, Sears
      exclusive (#59262, 1984)
      Original *Return of the Jedi* box 350.00
      Loose, with all parts 250.00

NEW PLAYSETS
Kenner/Hasbro (1995–2001)

The Electronic *Millennium Falcon* is pretty much the

same as the Classic vehicle of the same name. This was the
only new playset for the first few years. If this had come out
a few years later, Kenner would have included an exclusive
action figure. An "Imperial Scanning Crew" figure was
included with the reissued *Millennium Falcon* carrycase, but
the only secret compartments to scan are in this playset/vehi-
cle. See also "Accessories" for some mini-playsets.

Power of the Force Playset, red box
Electronic *Millennium Falcon* playset/vehicle, with
   "4 Real Movie Sounds" (#69785, July 1995) $65.00
   Loose, with all parts 25.00

EPISODE I PLAYSETS

The premiere *Episode I* playset is the Naboo Royal
Starship. Like so many other *Episode I* items, it was eventually available at deep discount. It has a number of interesting
features, but the one that intrigued me the most was the
Queen's throne. There is no Queen Amidala figure that bends
at the knees so even if you could get the queen to sit in it, in
one of her fancy dresses, her legs would stick straight out!

***Episode I* Starship Playset**
Electronic Naboo Royal Starship Blockade Cruiser/
   Playset with "15 Distinct Movie Sounds"
   (#84146) [565146.0000] with **red R2 unit** $100.00
   Loose, with all parts and figure 60.00

***Episode I* Playset** (Asst. #26220)
Theed Generator Complex with **Battle Droid**
   (#26222) 20.00
   Loose, with all parts and figure 10.00

***Episode I* Power F/X Playset**
Motorized Theed Hangar Playset with **Qui-Gon
   Jinn (Power Spin)** and **Battle Droid (cut in
   half)** (#84173) 30.00
   Loose, with all parts and figure 15.00

POWER OF THE JEDI PLAYSET

Power of the Jedi Playset (2001–02))
Carbon-Freezing Chamber with **Bespin Security
   Guard** (#) $40.00

Loose, with all parts and figure. 20.00

CLASSIC ACCESSORIES
Kenner (1981–84)

Some of the accessories listed in this section were called "playsets" or "one-figure vehicles" on their boxes. What places them in this category is their small size.

Accessories

Vehicle Maintenance Energizer in 6" x 4½" x 3¾" box (#93430, 1983)
  Original *The Empire Strikes Back* box $20.00
  Reissue in *Return of the Jedi* box. 15.00
  Loose, with all parts. 9.00
Radar Laser Cannon (#93440, 1983)
  Original *The Empire Strikes Back* box 20.00
  Reissue in *Return of the Jedi* box. 15.00
  Loose, with all parts. 9.00
Tri-Pod Laser Cannon, 4½" x 6" box (#93450, 1983)
  Original *The Empire Strikes Back* box 20.00
  Reissue in *Return of the Jedi* box. 15.00
  Loose, with all parts. 9.00
Ewok Assault Catapult, 4½" x 6" box (#71070, 1984)
  Original *Return of the Jedi* box. 18.00
  Loose, with all parts. 8.00
Ewok Combat Glider, 4½" x 6" box (#93510, 1984)
  Original *Return of the Jedi* box. 18.00
  Loose, with all parts. 8.00
Ewok Battle Wagon, 12" long with *Star Wars* Planetary Map (#93690, 1984)
  Original *Power of the Force* box 300.00
  Loose, with all parts. 125.00
Imperial Sniper Vehicle, 1-figure vehicle with overhead wings (Asst. #93920, 1984)
  Original *Power of the Force* box 100.00
  Loose, with all parts. 40.00
Security Scout, camouflage colored, 1-figure vehicle (Asst. #93920, 1984)
  Original *Power of the Force* box 150.00
  Loose, with all parts. 60.00
One-Man Sand Skimmer, small 1-figure vehicle (Asst. #93920, 1984)
  Original *Power of the Force* box 80.00
  Loose, with all parts. 30.00
Ewok Fire Cart, accessories plus 2 non-poseable figures (Kenner Preschool, 1984)

Original *Ewoks* box 40.00
Loose, with all parts. 15.00
Ewok Woodland Wagon, covered wheel cart, horse and accessories (Kenner Preschool, 1985)
  Original *Ewoks* box 75.00
  Loose, with all parts. 20.00

MINI-RIGS

Mini-Rigs were one-man "crawling, climbing, flying" accessories for the action figures, that were too small to be part of the regular vehicle line-up. They came in a box with a hanging flap and the best graphics are on the back of the package.

None of these mini-rigs ever appeared in the three movies, but a few showed up in the animated *Droids* series. These days Hasbro packages such items with a figure and sells them as a "Deluxe" figure.

Mini Rig 1-Figure Vehicles, 6" x 4½" boxes (1981-83)
MTV-7 Multi-Terrain Vehicle (#40010, 1981)
  Original *The Empire Strikes Back* box $35.00
  Reissue in *The Empire Strikes Back* box with
    AT-AT Driver figure 60.00
  Reissue in *Return of the Jedi* box. 25.00
  Loose, with all parts, without figure 9.00
MLC-3 Mobile Laser Cannon, 6" x 4½" x 1" box with flap (#40020, 1981)
  Original *The Empire Strikes Back* box 35.00
  Reissue in *The Empire Strikes Back* box with
    Rebel Commander figure 60.00
  Reissue in *Return of the Jedi* box. 25.00
  Loose, with all parts, without figure 9.00
PDT-8 Personnel Deployment Transport (#40070, 1981)
  Original *The Empire Strikes Back* box 30.00
  Reissue in *The Empire Strikes Back* box with
    2-1B figure 60.00
  Reissue in *Return of the Jedi* box. 15.00
  Loose, with all parts, without figure 9.00
INT-4 Interceptor (#69750, 1982)
  Original *The Empire Strikes Back* box 30.00
  Reissue in *The Empire Strikes Back* box with
    AT-AT Commander figure 60.00
  Reissue in *Return of the Jedi* box. 15.00
  Loose, with all parts, without figure 9.00
CAP-2 Captivator (#69760, 1982)
  Original *The Empire Strikes Back* box 25.00

PDT-8 Mobile Laser Cannon (Kenner 1981) and ISP-6 Imperial Shuttle Pod (Kenner 1983)

Endor Attack Accessory (Kenner 1997); Tatooine Accessory Set; and Electronic Flash Cannon Accessory Set (Hasbro 1999)

Reissue in *The Empire Strikes Back* box with
   Bossk figure 60.00
Reissue in *Return of the Jedi* box 20.00
Loose, with all parts 9.00
AST-5 Armored Sentinel Transport (#70880, 1983)
   Original *Return of the Jedi* box 15.00
   Loose, with all parts 7.00
ISP-6 (Imperial Shuttle Pod) (#70890, 1983)
   Original *Return of the Jedi* box 25.00
   Loose, with all parts 9.00
Desert Sail Skiff (#93520, 1984) mini rig
   Original *Return of the Jedi* box 15.00
   Loose, with all parts 10.00
Endor Forest Ranger (#93610, 1984) mini rig
   Original *Return of the Jedi* box 15.00
   Loose, with all parts 10.00

NEW ACCESSORIES
Kenner (1996–2002)

New Power of the Force Accessories are more like mini-playsets than anything else. Some of the larger weapons, that might have been issued as accessories, were instead sold with figures on header cards as "Deluxe Figures." In *Episode I*, Hasbro changed tactics and issued packages of small weapons and equipment as accessory sets, along with larger light-up weapons.

NEW POWER OF THE FORCE ACCESSORIES

First Batch (Asst. #27597, Oct. 1996) red box
Detention Block Rescue with "Opening Escape
   Hatch and Shooting Launcher" (#27598) $15.00
   Loose, with all parts 7.00
Death Star Escape with "Firing Cannon and Remov-
   able Bridge" (#27599) 15.00
   Loose, with all parts 7.00

Second Batch (Asst. #27857, Aug. 1997) green box
Hoth Battle with "Rotating Gun Turret and Shooting
   Laser" (#27858, Aug. 1997) 20.00
   Loose, with all parts 10.00
Endor Attack with "Swinging Tree Branch and Rock
   Launcher" (#27859, Aug. 1997) 20.00
   Loose, with all parts 10.00

EPISODE I ACCESSORY SETS

Episode I Accessory Sets (1999–2001)
Naboo Accessory Set with "Retracting Grappling
   Hook Backpack" (#26208) $6.00
Tatooine Accessory Set with Pull-Back Droid
   (#26209) 6.00
Underwater Accessory Set with Bubbling Backpack
   (#26211) 6.00
Sith Accessory Set with "Firing Backpack and
   2 Droid Missiles" (#26210) 6.00
Tatooine Disguise with "Spring-Activated, Attack
   Backpack" (#26215) 10.00
Rappel Line Attack with "Rolling Rappel Line"
   (#26212) 10.00
Pod racer Fuel Station with "Fuel Dispenser
   Shoots Water" (#26214) 10.00
Hyperdrive Repair Kit includes "5 Removeable
   Panels and 4 Tools" (#26213) 10.00

Electronic *Episode I* Accessories
Electronic Flash Cannon Accessory Set (#26217) . . . 15.00
Electronic Gungan Catapult Accessory Set (#26218) . 15.00

VANS AND RACERS
Various (1978–80)

A less authentic toy than a *Star Wars* van would be hard to design. Not only are there no cars or vans in the movies, there aren't even any roads. Anyway, I suppose it could have been a lot worse. Kenner might have made a Superman and Darth Vader motorcycle set? After all, they both wear capes! I guess we were lucky.

Star Wars Van Set, 2 toy vans, 7" in length, black
   van with Darth Vader picture; white van with
   good guys, plus 12 barrels, 4 pylons and
   2 T-Sticks (Kenner #90170, 1978) $150.00
Darth Vader SSP (Super Sonic Power) Van, black,
   with Blazin' Action, gyro powered (Kenner
   #90160, 1978) 50.00
Star Wars Heroes SSP (Super Sonic Power) Van,
   white, with Blazin' Action, gyro powered
   (Kenner #90160, 1978) 50.00
Star Wars Duel at Death Star Racing Set, 19" x 20"
   box (Fundimensions 1978) 200.00

WALL ART

Wall art includes just about every kind of picture, poster, or other item that is designed to be framed and/or hung on a wall. Calendars are covered under PAPER.

ANIMATION CELS
Royal Animation (1995–97)

Royal Animation makes sericels from the *Droids* and *Ewoks* animated TV series. Sericels are silk-screened from the original cel, with an added lithograph background. Each comes with a certificate of authenticity and a Lucas Films seal. The sericels are double-matted and 14" x 18" in size.

Droids Sericels
R2-D2 & C-3PO, Best Friends (DR-1) $90.00
Battle Cruiser (DR-2) 90.00
R2-D2 & C-3PO Stranded (DR-3) 90.00
Bounty Hunter, Boba Fett and Stormtroopers (DR-4) . . 90.00

Ewoks Sericels
The Big Hug (EW-1) 90.00
Celebration (EW-2) 90.00

CHROMART

ChromArt prints are 8" x 10" in an 11" x 14" matte. They are made with acrylic, foil and etching to give an illusion of depth. The images come from CD-ROM game boxes and Video Tape Boxes, but the enhancements make them quite striking.

ChromArt Prints (Zanart Entertainment)
SW-C *Return of the Jedi*. $12.00
SW-C2 Darth Vader (1994) 12.00
SW-C3 C-3PO and R2-D2 (1994) 12.00
SW-C4 Star Destroyer 12.00
SW-C5 AT-ATs 12.00
SW-C6 Darth Vader Gold, artistic head 12.00
SW-C7 B-Wing Fight (1995) 12.00
SW-C8 Bounty Hunters (1995) 12.00
SW-C9 Asteroid Chase (1995) 12.00
SW-C10 *Star Wars* One-Sheet poster 12.00
SW-C11 *The Empire Strikes Back* One-Sheet poster . 12.00
SW-C12 *Return of the Jedi* One-Sheet poster 12.00
SW-C13 Rebel Assault (CD-ROM game cover) 12.00
SW-C14 Dark Forces (CD-ROM game cover) 12.00
SW-C15 TIE Fighter (CD-ROM game cover) 12.00
SW-C16 TIE Fighter: Defender of the Empire (CD-ROM game cover) 12.00
SW-C17 X-Wing (CD-ROM game cover) 12.00

Dark Forces *Chromart Print (Zanart 1995)*

SW-C18 *Star Wars* (video box cover) 12.00
SW-C19 *The Empire Strikes Back* (video box cover) . . 12.00
SW-C20 *Return of the Jedi* (video box cover) 12.00

Second Series
Bounty Hunters. 13.00
AT-ATs 13.00
Darth Vader 13.00
Darth Vader 13.00
R2-D2. . . . . 13.00
Space Battle. 13.00
Star Destroyer 13.00
Millennium Falcon. 13.00
B-Wings 13.00
Star Wars Trilogy Movie Cards 14.00

Third Series
X-Wing Starfighter Blueprint Chromium Print (#SWPB-C1) 12.00

Star Wars *One-Sheet Poster Chromart (Zanart)*

Imperial TIE Fighter Blueprint Chromium Print
(#SWPB-C2) 12.00
B-Wing Starfighter Blueprint Chromium Print
(#SWPB-C3) 12.00
Imperial Star Destroyer Blueprint Chromium Print . . . 12.00
AT-AT Walker Blueprint Chromium Print 12.00
Y-Wing Blueprint Chromium Print 12.00
A-Wing Blueprint Chromium Print 12.00
AT-ST Walker Blueprint Chromium Print 12.00

Fourth Series

Star Wars Bounty Hunters Framed Chromart,
11" x 14" (44-113, 1997) 20.00
Star Wars Droids Framed Chromart, 11" x 14"
(44-114, 1997). 20.00
Star Wars Heir to the Empire Framed Chromart,
11" x 14" (44-127, 1997) 20.00
Star Wars Splinter of the Mind's Eye Framed
Chromart, 12" x 15" (44-128, 1997) 20.00
Star Wars Shadows of the Empire Framed Chrom-
art, 12" x 15" (44-125, 1997) 20.00
Star Wars Xizor Framed Chromart, 12" x 15"
(44-126, 1997). 20.00

Star Wars Trilogy International Release ChromArt
print, John Alvin art, three prints, matted in
wood frame (SWI-3W, 1996) limited to 2,500
copies 250.00

Star Wars International Video Chromium Print
(#SWI-C1) 12.00

The Empire Strikes Back International Video
Chromium Print (#SWI-C2) 12.00
Return of the Jedi International Video Chromium
Print (#SWI-C3) 12.00

LITHOGRAPHS

Many *Star Wars* limited edition lithographs were created by well-known science fiction and *Star Wars* artist Ralph
McQuarrie. They are 18" x 12" in size, framed and matted,
and each comes with an Illuminated 70mm Film Frame. They
were issued by Willitts Designs, which is not surprising, since
they also produced the many series of 70mm Film Frames
covered under STILLS.

Many other prominent *Star Wars* artists have also produced lithographs, including Boris Valejo, Drew Struzan, the
Bros. Hildebrandt, and Dave Dorman. Lithographs fall in the
realm of fine art and the high prices that they command are
based on this, rather than being driven up by collector
demand. They make excellent gifts.

Star Wars, A New Hope (Ralph McQuarrie art)
The Cantina on Mos Eisley (Willitts Designs
#50002) limited to 2,500 copies, framed $150.00
Signed by Mark Hammil. 200.00
Millennium Falcon (Willitts Designs #50004) limited
to 2,500 copies, framed 180.00
Rebel Attack on the Death Star (Willitts Designs
#50005) limited to 2,500 copies, framed 200.00
Rebel Ceremony (Willitts Designs #50006) limited
to 2,500 copies, framed 150.00

The Empire Strikes Back (Ralph McQuarrie art)
Rebel Patrol of Echo Base (Willitts Designs
#50036) limited to 2,500 copies, framed 150.00
Luke Skywalker and Darth Vader Duel (Willitts
Designs #50037) limited to 2,500 copies,
framed 150.00
Battle of Hoth (Willitts Designs #50038) limited to
2,500 copies, framed 150.00
Cloud City of Bespin (Willitts Designs #50039)
limited to 2,500 copies, framed. 150.00

Return of the Jedi (Ralph McQuarrie art)
Jabba the Hutt (Willitts Designs #50050) limited to
2,500 copies, framed 175.00
The Rancor Pit (Willitts Designs #50051) limited to
2,500 copies, framed 175.00
Speeder Bike Chase (Willitts Designs #50052)
limited to 2,500 copies, framed. 175.00
Death Star Main Reactor (Willitts Designs #50053)
limited to 2,500 copies, framed. 175.00

Other Lithographs (Various artists)
Star Wars 15th Anniversary Serigraph, by Melanie
Taylor Kent, 20¼" x 30½" limited to 1,100
copies (1992) 1,750.00
Star Wars Lithograph by Ken Steacy, 17" x 24"
signed and numbered, limited to 500 copies,
Darth Vader image from *The Art of Star Wars
Galaxy Cards* (Gifted Images 1994) 600.00
In a Galaxy Far, Far Away, limited, signed litho-
graph by Michael David Ward, 20" x 30", sign-
ed by Anthony Daniels and Kenny Baker,
limited to 1,000 copies 175.00

Luke Skywalker Limited Edition Lithograph by Al
   Williamson, limited to 500 copies, 22½" x 23"
   in 29" x 29" frame (1996) 300.00
Darth Vader Limited Edition Lithograph by Al
   Williamson, limited to 500 copies, 24" x 24" in
   30½" x 30½" frame (1996) 300.00
Star Wars R2-D2 Remarked Lithograph by the
   Bros. Hildebrandt, signed, 24" x 18" 175.00
Star Wars Luke and Yoda Lithograph by Boris
   Vallejo, signed and numbered, 30" x 36" limited
   to 500 copies 600.00

Star Wars, Special Edition Lithographs by Dave Dorman

Star Wars Dewback Patrol Lithograph by Dave
   Dorman, 34" x 16", limited to 1,500 copies (1997) 75.00
Star Wars Battle of Hoth Lithograph by Dave Dor-
   man, 34" x 16", limited to 1,500 copies (1997) . . . 75.00
Star Wars Tales of the Jedi, Freedon Nadd Uprising
   Lithograph by Dave Dorman, 18" x 22", limited
   to 1,500 copies (1997) 75.00
Star Wars Star's End Lithograph by Dave Dorman,
   18" x 22", limited to 1,500 copies (1997) 75.00
Star Wars Princess Leia (Boushh outfit) Lithograph
   by Dave Dorman, 16" x 22", limited to 1,500
   copies (1997) 75.00
Star Wars Throne Room of Jabba Lithograph by
   Dave Dorman, 32" x 14", limited to 1,500
   copies (1997) 75.00

Gallery Pieces

Star Wars: A New Hope 24k gold Gallery Pieces
   (1997) limited to 500 pieces, engraved with
   limited edition number, with certificate of
   authenticity:
Han Solo & Jabba the Hutt 10" x 5" . . . . unknown
Darth Vader and Obi-Wan Kenobi 10" x 9" . . . . unknown

POSTERS

There are many types of posters, from those sold in toy
stores to those that come in magazines and as fast food giveaways, but the most valuable by far are the theatrical posters
that were issued to promote the movie. These had no initial
price—they were sent to movie theaters or given away at
shows. Their value is entirely collector driven. There are a
considerable number of general movie poster collectors who
compete with *Star Wars* collectors for these posters, keeping
the prices high. Posters are most valuable when they are
rolled, not folded, and should never be put on your wall using
thumb tacks. As a practical matter, this will make it hard to
show it to your friends in order to impress them. If your
poster is worth $150 or more, you should probably have it
professionally framed, which will cost you close to $100, but
at least you can then hang it on your wall and show it off.

Unfortunately, valuable posters can be reproduced and
sold as if they were the original. These bootlegs are worth a
lot less money—and less than nothing to a collector. It's not
easy to tell a fake unless you have a real one for comparison
and if you have a real one, why are you looking for another
one? Naturally the most expensive and most popular posters
were the first ones to be counterfeited. Collectors are advised
to buy with care, from reputable dealers.

POSTERS — THEATRICAL

Star Wars

Advance A One-sheet, "A long time ago in a galaxy
   far far away..." $275.00
Star Wars advance, 2nd version 175.00
Style A One-sheet, Tommy Jung art 175.00
Star Wars, style A, with record promo 175.00
Star Wars advance, style B 150.00
Star Wars, style C 150.00
Style D One-sheet (Circus poster) Drew Struzan
   and Charles White III art 350.00
Anniversary One-sheet (1978) theater give-away. . . . 600.00
'79 Re-release One-sheet, "It's Back!" 100.00
'81 Re-release One-sheet. 60.00
'82 Re-release One-Sheet 50.00

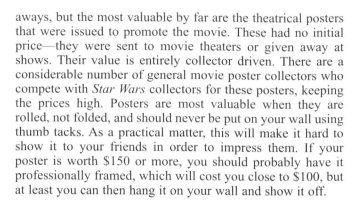

One-Sheet Posters: Star Wars, *Style A;* Empire Strikes Back, *Style A;* The Return of the Jedi, *Style A (Lucasfilm 1977–83)*

One Sheet Posters: Revenge of the Jedi *Advance, version I;* Star Wars *Concert;* Star Wars Trilogy, *Special Edition (Lucasfilm 1983–97)*

The Empire Strikes Back
Advance One-sheet 200.00
Style 'A' One-sheet (Love Story) Rodger Kastel art . . 200.00
Style 'B' One-sheet Tommy Jung art 75.00
'81 Re-release One-sheet, Tommy Jung art. 50.00
'82 Re-release One-sheet, Tommy Jung art. 40.00

Revenge of the Jedi
Advance Revenge of the Jedi One-sheet, 41" x 27"
     with release date 400.00
Variation, no release date 450.00

Return of the Jedi
Style 'A' One-sheet 35.00
Style 'B' One-sheet 50.00
Return of the Jedi, 1985 reissue 30.00

Star Wars Trilogy Special Edition, One-sheets (1997)
Advance One-sheet 50.00
Version 'B' *Star Wars: A New Hope* Drew Struzan art . 40.00
Version 'C' *The Empire Strikes Back* Drew Struzan art   40.00
Version 'D' *Return of the Jedi* Drew Struzan art. 40.00

Episode I The Phantom Menace, One-sheets (1999)
Advance One-sheet 75.00
The Phantom Menace 50.00

POSTERS–SPECIAL EVENTS
The Art of *Star Wars*, Center for the Arts. $50.00
Caravan of Courage 60.00
Immunization Poster 10.00
Star Tours Poster 5.00
Public Radio Drama poster 150.00
Vintage Action Figures Photo poster 15.00

POSTERS–COMMERCIAL
Star Wars 10th Anniversary Poster, 27" x 41"
     (1987) by Drew Struzan $10.00
Star Wars 10th Anniversary Poster, 27" x 41"
     (1987) signed by Drew Struzan, limited to 200
     copies (1992). 100.00

Star Wars 15th Anniversary poster by Melanie Tay-
     lor Kent, 20" x 30" (1992). 25.00
Star Wars 15th Anniversary Movie Poster, by Greg
     and Tim Hildebrandt, limited to 5,000 copies,
     27" x 41" (Collector's Warehouse 1992) 15.00
     Deluxe, signed edition of 1,000 . . . . 50.00
     Star Wars "A New Hope" variation 15.00
Style D One-sheet (Circus poster) Drew Struzan
     and Charles White III art, reprint, 27" x 41"
     (Collector's Warehouse 1993) 15.00
Star Wars Space Battle Poster (1995). 5.00
Star Wars Movie poster reproduction, 24" x 36". 5.00
The Empire Strikes Back 10th Anniversary Poster,
     by Larry Noble, 27" x 41" (1990) 15.00
The Empire Strikes Back Movie poster repro-
     duction, 24" x 36". 5.00
Return of the Jedi 10th Anniversary Advance
     Poster, 27" x 40" (1993) 15.00
     Deluxe version, gold foil border 50.00
Return of the Jedi 10th Anniversary Style A poster,
     27" x 40" by Kazo Sano (1994) 15.00
Star Wars Checklist Poster, 27" x 40" (Killian Enter-
     prises 1995) full color reproductions of all
     movie one-sheet posters and variants 20.00
Star Wars: A New Hope movie poster, 27" x 40" 15.00
Heir to the Empire poster, from book cover,
     22" x 28" (1992) Tom Jung art 12.00
Jabba's Palace Poster, 24" x 36". 6.00
Darth Vader Photomosaic Poster 24" x 36" (PHL
     #568, 1998) 10.50
Yoda Photomosaic Poster 24" x 36" (PHL #567, 1998) 10.50
Wisdom of Yoda Poster 24" x 36" 6.00

Star Wars Radio Poster, advertising that the shows
     are "Now Available on Cassettes and Com-
     pact Discs" (1993) 15.00
Return of the Jedi Collector's Poster (#2909) 5.00
Star Wars: A New Hope Collector's Poster (#2910) 5.00
The Empire Strikes Back Collector's Poster (#2911) . . . 5.00
Return of the Jedi Collector's Poster (#2909) 5.00

Ewok Adventure *TV Show poster;* Episode I *Movie Teaser poster; Jar Jar Binks commercial poster (Lucasfilm 1990–99)*

Star Wars Space Battle Poster (PTW #651) 5.00
Star Wars Movie Poster, 24" x 36" (PTW #531) 5.00
The Empire Strikes Back Movie Poster, 24" x 36"
    (PTW #532) 5.00
Star Wars: A New Hope Video Poster, 24" x 36"
    (PTW #740) 5.00
The Empire Strikes Back Video Poster, 24" x 36"
    (PTW #741) 5.00
Return of the Jedi Video Poster, 24" x 36" (PTW #742) . 5.00
Star Wars: "All I Need to Know About Life I Learned
    From *Star Wars*" Poster, 24" x 36" (PTW #743) . . . 5.00
Star Wars: X-Wing Fighters Poster, 24" x 36" (PTW
    #744) 5.00
Return of the Jedi–Rancor Poster, 24" x 36" (PTW
    #745) 5.00
Star Wars: Star Destroyer Poster, 24" x 36" (PTW #748) 5.00
The Art of *Star Wars*: Luke Battles Darth Vader
    poster, Ralph McQuarrie art, 24" x 36" (PTW #767) 5.00
Star Wars Special Edition Gold Ingot poster,
    24" x 36" (#789) 5.50
Star Wars Special Edition Movie Poster, 24" x 36"
    (#795) 5.50
Star Wars Special Edition *The Empire Strikes Back*
    Movie Poster, 24" x 36" (#796) 5.50
Star Wars Special Edition *Return of the Jedi* Movie
    Poster, 24" x 36" (#797) 5.50
Death Star Trench Poster, 24" x 36" (#3166, 1997) 5.00
Star Wars Cantina Poster, 23" x 35" (#3173, 1997) 5.00
Star Wars Darth Vader Poster (#2905, 1997) 5.00
Star Wars Cutaway *Millennium Falcon* Poster (1997) . . 20.00
Star Wars Cutaway *Millennium Falcon* deluxe
    poster, signed and numbered, certificate of
    authenticity (1997) 40.00
Star Wars Cutaway X-Wing/TIE Fighter poster (1997) . 20.00
Star Wars Cutaway X-Wing/TIE Fighter deluxe
    poster, signed and numbered, certificate of
    authenticity (1997) 40.00
AT-AT and Snowspeeder Cutaway Poster,
    36" x 24" black and white 20.00
    Deluxe, signed and numbered 40.00
Boba Fett Poster, smoking gun, 24" x 36" (1997) 10.00

Star Wars Cantina denizens poster print
    17" x 36" by Tsuneo Sanda (1997) 15.00
Yoda, 24" x 36" by Tsuneo Sanda (1997) 15.00
George Lucas: The Creative Impulse by Drew
    Struzan, 24" x 36" (1997) 15.00
Slave I by Tsuneo Sands, 24" x 36" (1997) 15.00
Millennium Falcon pursued by the Empire,
    24" x 36" (1997) 15.00
Star Wars: A New Hope Special Edition One-
    Sheets by Drew Struzan, 27" x 40" (1997) 20.00
The Empire Strikes Back Special Edition One-
    Sheets by Drew Struzan, 27" x 40" (1997) 20.00
The *Return of the Jedi* Special Edition One-
    Sheets by Drew Struzan, 27" x 40" (1997) 20.00

Episode I Commercial Posters (At-A-Glance, 1999)
    Darth Maul, 24" x 36" (#1800) 5.00
    Queen Amidala, 24" x 36" (#1801) 5.00
    Jar Jar Binks, 24" x 36" (#1802) 5.00
    Jabba The Hutt Presents Pod racing, 24" x 36"
        (#1809) 5.00
    Jedi Battle, 24" x 36" (#1811) 5.00
Episode I Movie Teaser 10.00
Almost all other commercial posters, each 5.00
A few larger or fancier commercial posters, each up to 15.00

Food Premiums
Burger Chef Premium posters (1978)
    Luke Skywalker 10.00
    R2-D2 . . . . 10.00
    Chewbacca 10.00
    Darth Vader 10.00
General Mills Premium posters (1978)
    Star Wars montage 10.00
    TIE Fighter & X-Wing 10.00
    Star Destroyer 10.00
    R2-D2 & C-3PO 10.00
Proctor and Gamble Premium posters (1978)
    Ben Kenobi & Darth Vader 10.00
    R2-D2 & C-3PO 10.00
    Death Star 10.00

Nestea Premium poster (1980)
 Luke Skywalker 8.00
 Darth Vader 8.00
Burger King Premium poster (1980)
 Hoth 5.00
 Dagobah 5.00
 Bespin 5.00
The Empire Strikes Back montage by Boris Vallejo
 (Coca Cola 1980) 20.00
Proctor and Gamble Premium Poster (1980)
 Luke Skywalker 5.00
 R2-D2 & C-3PO 5.00
 Darth Vader 5.00
 Bespin Scenes 5.00
Dixie Cups Story card poster (1981) 15.00
Hi-C *Return of the Jedi* poster (1983) 8.00
Oral-B *Return of the Jedi* poster (1983) 8.00

Star Wars Trilogy Special Edition Pepsi mail-in
 posters, 24" x 36" originally sold as a set for
 $9.99 and proof of purchase, set 15.00
 Star Wars, picturing Darth Vader 8.00
 The Empire Strikes Back, picturing C-3PO 8.00
 Return of the Jedi, picturing Yoda 8.00

Retail Posters
Star Wars
 Sword montage 20.00
 R2-D2 & C-3PO 15.00
 Luke Skywalker 20.00
 Princess Leia 25.00
Star Wars concert 30.00
Star Wars radio program 30.00
The Empire Strikes Back
 The Empire Strikes Back 5.00
 Boba Fett 10.00
 Darth Vader & Stormtroopers 5.00
The Empire Strikes Back Fan club montage poster 5.00
Vehicle scene 7.00
Darth Vader montage 5.00
Read and the Force is With You (Yoda) 10.00
The Empire Strikes Back radio program 15.00
Darth Vader, life size 10.00
Return of the Jedi Space Battle (fan club) 10.00
Return of the Jedi poster album 10.00
The Ewok Adventure 5.00
Caravan of Courage, style A 5.00
Caravan of Courage, style B 5.00
Star Tours posters, 8 different, each 3.00
First Ten Years poster 7.00
First Ten Years mural poster 10.00
Star Wars Movie one-sheet poster, 24" x 36" (Portal
 PTW #531, 1992) 5.00
The Empire Strikes Back Movie one-sheet poster,
 24" x 36" (Portal PTW#532, 1992) 5.00
Return of the Jedi Movie one-sheet poster,
 24" x 36" (Portal PTW#533, 1992) 5.00
Star Wars: Space Battle Poster one-sheet poster,
 24" x 36" (Portal PTW#651, 1991) 5.00

PRINTS

Shadows of the Empire signed print, 24" x 36" by
 Dave Dorman (1996) $40.00
Boba Fett: Bounty Hunter Print, by Dave Dorman,
 15" x 20" on 19" x 24" paper, limited to 1,500
 copies, signed and numbered (Rolling

 Thunder Graphics 1995) 65.00

Star Wars: Smuggler's Moon Print, by Dave
 Dorman 15" x 21" on 19" x 24" paper, limited to
 1,500 copies, signed and numbered (Rolling
 Thunder Graphics 1995) 65.00
Star Wars: Dark Empire II Print, by Dave Dorman
 16" x 21" on 19" x 24" paper, limited to 1,500
 copies, signed and numbered (Rolling
 Thunder Graphics 1995) 65.00
Obi-Wan Kenobi Art Print, by Dave Dorman 12" x
 15½" on 16" x 20" paper, limited to 1,500
 copies, signed and numbered (Rolling
 Thunder Graphics 1996) 65.00

TIN SIGNS
Tin Signs International

Embossed Movie Posters
Star Wars, tin litho, 15" x 24" $25.00
The Empire Strikes Back, tin litho, 15" x 24" 25.00
Return of the Jedi, tin litho, 15" x 24" 25.00

1997 Batch
Star Wars: A New Hope, tin litho, 12" x 17" 13.00
Star Wars: A New Hope, tin litho, horizontal poster
 17" x 12" 13.00
The Empire Strikes Back, tin litho, 12" x 17" 13.00
Return of the Jedi, tin litho, 12" x 17" 13.00

HOLOGRAMS

Darth Vader Hologram Picture, 5" x 3" in 8" x 10"
 matte (A.H. Prismatic #1021/99, 1994) 30.00
Millennium Falcon Hologram Picture, 3" x 2" in
 5" x 7" matt (A.H. Prismatic #1020/33, 1994) 15.00
 Mounted on Acrylic display stand (A.H.
 Prismatic #1020/33AS, 1994) 15.00
Star Wars Deluxe Fight Scene Limited Edition 3-D
 Hologram (Fantasma 90MT-MLF, 1993) in
 deluxe 8" x 10" Black Matte 30.00
Millennium Falcon Deluxe Hologram Picture
 3½" x 5" in a 8" x 10" matte (90MT-MLF, 1994) . . . 25.00

Star Wars Holograms (A.H. Prismatic, 1997)
 Darth Vader matted (#1021-99PM, 1997) 30.00
 Millennium Falcon on Acrylic Stand
 (#1020-33AS, 1997) 17.00
 Millennium Falcon matted (#1020-33PM, 1997) . . 17.00

LIGHTED POSTERS

Star Wars Neon Movie Poster (Neonetics 1993)
 framed $200.00
Darth Vader Neon Framed Picture (Neonetics 1995) . 225.00
Star Wars Millennium Falcon Neon Framed Picture
 (Neonetics 1994) 225.00
Star Wars Millennium Falcon LED Framed Picture
 (Neonetics 1994) 140.00

Power of the Jedi TIE Bomber (Hasbro 2002)

**Power of the Jedi Imperial AT-ST &
Speeder Bike (Hasbro 2002)**

Episode II The Reek

Episode II Sneak Preview Clone Trooper

Episode II Sneak Preview Jango Fett

Episode II Sneak Preview R3-T7

Episode II Sneak Preview Zam Wesell

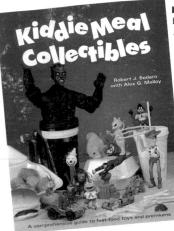
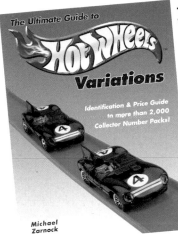

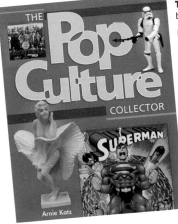